Bruno Bettelheim

Bruno Bettelheim

The Other Side of Madness

Nina Sutton

Translated from the French by
David Sharp in collaboration
with the author

Duckworth

First published in English in 1995 by
Gerald Duckworth & Co. Ltd.
The Old Piano Factory
48 Hoxton Square, London N1 6PB
Tel: 0171 729 5986
Fax: 0171 729 0015

A catalogue record for this book is available
from the British Library

ISBN 0 7156 2687 6

Nina Sutton asserts her moral
right to be identified as the
author of this work.

Picture credits
Plate pages 1 and 16 (centre): Ian Berry/Magnum;
plate page 14 (bottom): Laurent Jurgensen.

Typeset by Ray Davies
Printed in Great Britain by
Redwood Books Ltd, Trowbridge

Contents

Acknowledgements   vii
Foreword   xi

PROLOGUE   1

'The Affair'   2

PART ONE. THE FORMATIVE YEARS   15

    I. Vienna: Once Upon a Time   17
   II. One Big Family   34
  III. Gina   60
  IV. Patsy   80
   V. The Anschluss   103
 VI. Dachau: The Making of a Survivor   120
VII. Buchenwald: The Price of Freedom   141
VIII. A Short-Lived Reunion   165

PART TWO. 'DR B'   181

  IX. From Chicago to Rockford, and Back   183
   X. A New Man for the New World   202
  XI. Orthogenic School: The Magical Years   231
 XII. Dr B the Enchanter   268
XIII. The Ultimate Limit   292
XIV. The Big Bad Wolf   329
 XV. Israel: Understanding is Not Enough   354
XVI. The Bad Guy   371

EPILOGUE   415

XVII. Trude and the Children   417

Notes   465
Bibliography   508
Index   518

Plates between pp. 272 & 273

To Emilie,
to Louise.

Acknowledgements

Researching and writing this book has brought me a great deal. But, over five years, it has also weighed heavily on those closest to me. Someone very dear to Bettelheim once told me: 'It was a real meeting of minds between you. It's impossible to understand Bruno if one hasn't suffered.' Maybe ... I only wish I could have spared my family the experience. Thanks to all of them for having held strong, even when there seemed to be no light at the end of the tunnel.

Friendship also played a major role in this endeavour. Without my friends' support, I certainly could not have completed it. Some offered me shelter, in the United States, Israel or Austria. Others saw me through tight spots. Some generously put their knowledge at my disposal, letting me decide how to use it. Several listened patiently, as I struggled with doubts and over-simplistic judgements. Some read and reread, helping me find the right words to express often difficult ideas. In short, they were there whenever I needed them. My warmest thanks to Helga Abraham, Marie-Ange d'Adler, Anne Albertson, Gordon Anderson, Thérèse Binchet, Danièle Braunschweig, Jean-Michel Braunschweig, Frank Browning, Faye and Charles Carey, Marie-Pierre Carretier, Shalom Cohen, Simone Conrad-Eybesfeld, Marie-Odile Fargier, Micheline Faure, Anita Frankel, Danièle Granet, Jean-Guy Gourson, Mark and Carol Hosenball, Rony Koven, Catherine Lamour, Martine Ledieu, Marie-José Lepicard, Danièle Lévy, Charles Lutz, Katia Lutz, Denise Mairey, René Major, Marie-Charlotte Maupas, Andrée Mazzolini, Jean-Michel Normand, Nora Pouillon, Pierre Pouillon, Renée Shiponi, Mary Sills, Michèle Slung, Noreen Taylor, Christiane Tenenhaus, Bénédicte Thiéfine, Micheline Weinstein and Paul Zimmerman.

My deep gratitude also goes to all those who, having known Bettelheim, believed in my capacity to bring to life some of his true spirit. To Naomi and Eric Bettelheim, first of all, who acquiesced to most of my requests without ever demanding anything in return. Their generous and non-interfering attitude helped me recover the respect for their father that, at one point, I had started to lose. And to all the others: Etti Andreani, Ronald Angres and his parents, Hans Bandler, Bill Blau, Heda Bolgar, Heidi Braham, Stuart Brent, Heidi and Willy Brown, Jean Brown, Steve Cahodes, Madeleine Chapsal, Leslie Cleaver, Bert Cohler, Mary-Ellen

Cowan, Lee Cronbach, Preston Cutler, Gayle Donovan, Ronnie Dryovage, Nechama Edelman, Eliott Eisner, Kurt Eissler, Rudi Ekstein, Alex Elsen, Ernst Federn, Seymour Feshback, David Fisher, Maurie Formigoni, Ugo Formigoni, Charlotte Fowler, Seymour Fox, Ljuba Frankenstein, Elio Fratteroli, Marylin Garner, Desy Gerard, Jakob Getzel, Gilo Goetzl, Myles Gordon, Sue Gotschall, Joelle de Gravelaine, Richard Grossman, Leah Hadoumi, Nina Helstein, Candace Hilldrup, Emmi Hornton, Roland Humery, Katherine Isenstadt, Gayle Shulenberger Janowitz, Geneviève Jurgensen, Diana Grossman Kahn, George and Cathy Kaiser, Jeremiah Kaplan, Linda Kaplan, Daniel Karlin, Connie Katzenstein, Jerry Kavka, Moshe Kerem, Oliver Kerner, Shelton Key, Charles Kligerman, Don Kofall, Robert Koff, Maria Kramer, Adrian Kuypers, Gretel Lowinski, Kathy and Mark Lubin, Patsy Lyne, Augusta Wallace Lyons, Tom Lyons, Jacky and Alan Manne, Ruth Marquis, Rahel Messinger, Leo and Ruth Nedelsky, Bernice Neugarten, Eva Neurath, Tom Neurath, Joseph Noshpits, Julie Newman, Heather Ogilvie, Nell Pekarski, Charles Pekow, Patty Pickett McKnight, Eleonor and Gerard Piel, Maria Piers, George Pollack, Emmi Radanowicz-Vischer, Betty-Lou Pingree Rellahan, Albert Reiss Jr., Jacquelyn Sanders, Edwin Shneidman, Louis Shapiro, Edward Shils, Judy and Lee Shulman, Ada Skyles, Johanna Tabin, Ralph Tyler, Fae and Bob Tyroler, Jane Ullman, Annie Urbach, Charles Walton, Saul Wasserman, Gina Weinmann, Clifford Wilk, Miriam Williams, Wanda Willig, Josette Wingo, Ben Wright, Luitgard Wundheiler, Richard Younker and Karen Zelan. Some were more enthusiastic than others in talking to me. Some trusted me immediately, others were more wary. Some even became real friends. But all contributed to shaping in my mind the image of a complex man I had never met. That is no less true of those who do not appear in the following pages than of those who do.

Many thanks also to those who, without having known Bettelheim well, helped me to understand some aspects of his life. First of all to Laurence Dahan-Gaida, whose knowledge of Vienna – and reading of Bettelheim's dissertation – proved invaluable. And to Elisabeth Badinter, Ralph Bettelheim, Werner Bettelheim, Howard Buten, Marie Cardinal, René Diatkine, Alan Dundes, Ellen Fine, André Green, Russell Jacoby, Betty Looram, Paul Marcus, Jeffrey M. Masson, Léon Poliakov, Michael Pollak, Jean-Bertrand Pontalis, Jean Pouillon, Paul Roazen, Alan Rosenberg, Elisabeth Roudinesco, Claudine Vegh, Annette Wieviorka. Thanks to Herbert Belch, Edith Buxbaum's executor, who let me read a few pages of her unpublished memoirs. Thanks also to the many archivists and librarians who helped me, many of them well beyond the call of duty, notably at the Regenstein Library, the Centre de Documentation Juive Contemporaine, the Dachau Memorial, the Vienna Freud Haus, the Albertgasse Realgymnasium, the Israelitische Kultusgemeinde, the Ford Foundation, the Rockefeller Archives, the Franklin D. Roosevelt Library, Columbia

University's Lehmann Library, the Chicago Psychoanalytical Institute and many others, including the Singer Company archives.

This English-language edition owes a great deal to David Sharp, who translated the French version as I was writing it – no easy task.

I am grateful to Tom Neurath and Thames & Hudson for permission to quote from Bettelheim's works.

And many thanks to my publishers, Claude Durand, Jo Ann Miller and Robin Baird-Smith, for having been so patient.

Paris, July 17 1995

Foreword

In July 1990, when I undertook to write this biography, Bruno Bettelheim was for me the brilliant inventor of a unique method of treating autism in children, the first educator to have practised total milieu therapy based on the teachings of Sigmund Freud, and as such a pioneer of psychoanalysis.

I was aware that, after growing up in Freud's Vienna, Bettelheim had also witnessed the takeover of the city by Adolf Hitler, and that before emigrating to the United States he had been interned in the Nazi camps of Dachau and Buchenwald.

I was intrigued by this Jew who seemed to reject the inevitability of the Holocaust, daring to criticize, for example, Anne Frank's father. I was touched by the enlightened lover of fairy tales. A man who despite his forbidding exterior had remained close enough to the little boy he had once been to delve into and explain the true roles played by those weird and wonderful characters that populate our childhood.

But most of all this noble old gentleman had always impressed me, in his TV appearances or press articles, by the loftiness, rigour and yet the simplicity of his ideas.

What he was saying – or at least what I was hearing him say – was that insanity does not exist as such. The unorthodox forms of behaviour which we view as insane in fact make up a language, the best one available for those whose suffering is too great. It is up to us to decipher that language. In order to break through the walls of such people's 'empty fortresses', what is needed is intuition, total availability, ceaseless vigilance concerning one's own motives and a great deal of time. Last but not least Bettelheim said that, whether 'crazy' or not, children must always be respected.

I feel it necessary to recall the above because, in the four and a half years I spent tracking Bruno Bettelheim's footsteps from Vienna to Los Angeles, via Chicago, Basel and Jerusalem, I heard so many terrible things that at times I forgot what my starting-point had been. The question 'What made you decide to write this book?' was asked so many times – not least by myself – that I felt it should be answered one last time for the reader who has chosen to seek with me that unruly bundle of truths that makes up the life of a man. In this case, a man of rare complexity.

Here, an observation is in order. In France, the country in which I live, Bruno Bettelheim has a particularly strong image. In 1974 French TV viewers had the rare privilege of discovering the Sonia Shankman Orthogenic School of the University of Chicago from the inside, thanks to a documentary which, because French television staff happened to be on strike that evening, was broadcast simultaneously in prime time on all the three channels then in existence. It made a big impression.

Filmed just before Bettelheim retired from his post as director, Daniel Karlin's stunning four-hour documentary has the feel of a testament. And yet it has never been shown in the United States. The French director had to accept that limitation – imposed by the need to protect the privacy of Bettelheim's young charges – before being allowed to take a movie camera into the school.[1]

A year earlier, Bettelheim's reputation in France had already been shaped by the publication of *La Folie des Autres* (Other People's Madness), in which the writer Geneviève Jurgensen tells of the two years she worked as a counsellor at the Orthogenic School.[2] It is a very lively book which also provides a glimpse into daily life in the institution, even though its author never claims to do more than describing her experiences as a young Frenchwoman thrown into an unknown world. Yet, for the same reasons as for Karlin's documentary, it remains unknown to the American public.

Finally, and without getting prematurely involved in a debate to which we will return below,[3] it should be noted that since psychoanalysis was hounded out of Vienna by the Nazis in 1938, it has evolved differently in France and in the United States. To sum it up roughly, in the US the notion of therapeutic efficiency rapidly took precedence over all other aspects of psychoanalysis. Whereas in France the view of psychoanalysis as an investigatory process, always very precious to Sigmund Freud, has retained its importance. This may explain why Bettelheim's message has been interpreted by the French in a more dispassionate, less result-oriented way.

A life spanning eighty-six and a half years, sixteen published books, a considerable number of essays and articles on weighty subjects (insanity, anti-Semitism, parent-child relations, mass society, totalitarianism, etc.); thirty years spent trying to save young people. And an almost magical idea: that from an absolute evil – Nazism – could be drawn the salvation of insane children. When I started out on this investigation, my subject had all the trappings of a saint.

Very rapidly however, the flesh-and-blood man, with his little lies and major bouts of rage, began to emerge from behind the idealized image. As is no doubt the lot of most biographers, I started to feel a measure of disappointment, of irritation at the way reality was failing to live up to the idea I had built around it. And I was just beginning to get acquainted with my subject when what might be called 'the Bettelheim Affair' broke out, disrupting the getting-to-know-you process with a vengeance.

I use the word 'affair' advisedly, since the scandal that erupted in the six months following Bettelheim's death, at least in the United States, was unprecedented in its violence, suddenness and excess, particularly in the worlds of academe and psychoanalysis. Not that hatred is foreign to those worlds; but rarely had it burst out so instantaneously and publicly. One has to hark back to the arrest and imprisonment of Wilhelm Reich in 1956 to find a precedent for such an outpouring of insult and repudiation. For wrecking on such a grand scale.

By December 1990, I no longer had any idea who Bruno Bettelheim was. I was by no means alone: most of the people I had interviewed over the two previous months, people who had known him well, had betrayed their own confusion by asking me more questions about him than they gave me answers. One of them, although quite close to him at the end of his life, asked for time to think before seeing me, because, he confessed, 'I no longer know what to think of him.'

This was hardly surprising: in the space of six months, not a single stone of the Bettelheim monument had been left standing. The man had always had his detractors, and even enemies. He was provocative, he had set opinions on a whole range of controversial subjects, he could easily be curt or condescending, and did not suffer fools gladly. He was, all told, not the kind of person who generates a calm consensus about himself.

But this was something else. In just a few months, as if by magic, every facet of his reputation had come under attack. The psychoanalyst was nothing more than a charlatan, the benevolent pedagogue who understood children so well had turned into a sadistic brute, and even the writer, author of several international best-sellers, was no more than a common plagiarist.

Fortunately, Paris is a long way from Chicago, and after an initial trip to the United States, a spell at home allowed me to get things back in perspective. Far from the sound and fury of the scandal, I reread my notes, played back the taped interviews, compared different accounts of the same incidents. And I began to hear what was being said alongside the actual words. This allowed me to go back to the States and listen to the stories I was told with the necessary distance.

I was then struck by how each person who had known, loved or even hated Bettelheim was eager to learn more, to finally understand the man as a whole. He had always remained very discreet about himself, despite the handful of anecdotes about his past that he would readily trot out to illustrate an idea, set people thinking or make a point. He could simultaneously carry on parallel relationships, equally intense but very different, with a wide range of people, many of whom did not even suspect the others' existence.

There were those in whose eyes he sought a reflection of the admirable man he would have liked to have been. There were those – more often than not women – to whom he served as father-figure, teacher or guru. Those whom he treated with condescension, since he always knew what made them tick better than they did themselves. There were rivals, peers against whom he liked to score points. There were those, usually men, to whom he turned for the few robust certainties that helped him fight the depression that pursued him throughout his life. Others, women usually very dear to him, in whose gaze he sought confirmation of what he believed to be his ugliness. There were some rare people to whom he confessed his weaknesses. And then there were his own children; to exist alongside a man like Bettelheim they had no choice but to focus their lives elsewhere.

In almost all of these people I felt that same curiosity, that same desire at last to get a grip on the truth of the man, be it to hate or love him all the better. And after spending four years listening to them, I am now convinced of one thing: even if he had remained for the rest of his life the lumber merchant that the death of his father condemned him to be for a good dozen years in Vienna – a plausible if unlikely proposition – the true Bruno Bettelheim would still be difficult to apprehend. Because, as his younger daughter Naomi remarked: 'When my father said things, there were always at least two, and sometimes three levels. So, people who read Level One reacted one way; people who heard Levels One and Two reacted another way. They saw the same things, but read them differently.'

To muddy the waters even more, or perhaps simply because the life of a complicated man is only fully satisfying when it involves situations and people who are also complex, Bettelheim had to choose the field of mental disorders for his life's work – a world of distorting mirrors in which every gesture and word has meaning only in relation to the understanding of the other person.

I hesitated for a long time over the best way to approach the scandal. Several people, particularly in Paris, recommended mere disdain. All this hubbub, they said in essence, is much ado about nothing; it was whipped up by the media in the first place and will just as soon be forgotten. It is but a parasite feeding on Bettelheim's teachings. Others, mostly in the United States, clamoured for me to take sides. 'So you're writing Bettelheim's biography,' they would say. 'But will it be for or against?'

Rather than seeking to answer that question, I tried to imagine what Bettelheim himself would have thought of it all. It was the least I owed him after having gone through his mail, checked his public statements against various records, pried into his every reaction and quizzed those who had worked for him about his slightest idiosyncrasies – after having violated the intimacy of a man whose privacy was so jealously guarded during his lifetime.

Taking a leaf from Freud's book, Bruno Bettelheim was no great believer in biographies. Even if he read a few with obvious relish, he most
definitely did not want anyone to write his own. He said this time and time
again, publicly in the case of Ernest Jones's biography of Sigmund Freud,[4]
and privately in a number of letters to which I was granted access.[5]
Toward the end of his life, he finally yielded to the entreaties of an old
friend and admirer with whom he had worked for many years, and agreed to
answer a few questions into a tape recorder. But even that effort weighed
heavily on him, as he was to remark gloomily on the day before his death.

This is without a doubt the reason why he took advantage of the three
house moves that punctuated the last years of his life to destroy so many
papers, depriving his future biographers of much precious material. But
that was something that Freud also had done to some extent[6] – and yet he
allowed Jones to get on with his work as official biographer. As for
Bettelheim, while ostensibly covering up his tracks,[7] he kept on dropping
little white pebbles along his path, just like the Hansel of his favourite
fairy tale. So that whoever is really determined to do so can follow the signs
to almost every aspect of his life – including his lies. This, I feel, was his
ultimate way of expressing himself on 'at least two and sometimes three
levels' at once.

Having chosen to defy the prohibition of Level One ('Thou shalt not
write my biography') it seemed to me that I at least owed it to Bettelheim
to respect the commandment of rigour which is the ideal of Level Three. It
is a rigour which allows for no soft-heartedness, which is often brutal, as
was Bettelheim himself. Beyond appearances, it constantly seeks out, if
not the truth, at least the reality of each person. It is stern, obstinate and
uncompromising, utterly devoid of any of the Viennese frills and flourishes
which Level Two handles so adroitly.

I realized quite early on that it would be impossible to take on a study
of Bettelheim's life with the required objectivity as long as I had not dealt
with 'the Affair'. It was there, standing in the way of my research,
colouring everything I learned. I needed not to cover it up, but to put it
aside for a while. I therefore decided, three years ago, to write it all down
in a kind of introduction, knowing that I could always place it elsewhere
in the book if at some later date I considered, as did another publisher,
that it gave too sensationalist a tone to the whole work.

Today, it is quite intentionally that I have left the description here. Not
because I don't know where else to put it, but because it is its rightful place.
'The Affair' is not part of the chronological story of Bettelheim's life,
because he was no longer around to reply to his critics when it began. But
it is not just a postscript either. For I am now convinced that behind the
blows that then rained down on his memory, some of them well below the
belt, one can discern not only Bruno Bettelheim's weaknesses, but also
what made him a truly great therapist.

This is why, at the risk of shocking some readers (particularly French ones) I have tried not to ignore any of the accusations levelled against Bettelheim after his death. Since the most serious of these accusations were made not by outsiders but by some of the children who were once in his care, they form an integral part of his life. Whether true or false, they have a place in his story because they express suffering born of the relationships that he had developed with those children, and because, as their educator and therapist, he only had the power to terminate those relationships unilaterally. Which is what he did when, during the night of March 12, 1990, he took his own life. And that, alas, is something he is not yet through paying for.

PROLOGUE

Not even the most tempting probability is a protection against error;
even if all the parts of a problem seem to fit together like the pieces of
a jigsaw puzzle, one must reflect that what is probable is not necessarily the truth, and that the truth is not always probable.

Sigmund Freud, *Moses and Monotheism*

'The Affair'

March 13, 1990: 'The well-known child psychoanalyst Bruno Bettelheim was found dead this morning at his home in Silver Spring,
Maryland. According to the medical examiner, his death was the result
of suicide by asphyxiation. The body of Bruno Bettelheim was found by
the janitor of the retirement home he had recently moved into. His
head was covered with a plastic bag ....'

Voice One

Bruno Bettelheim dead?
... No! I don't believe it.
It's not true ... It's an-
other of his tricks ...

... Besides, he doesn't
even live around here;
he's in California.
I know it; I read it
in the paper ...

... So, he killed himself,
the son of a bitch. Good
riddance! That's the best
thing he ever did.
No more lectures,
no more lies, no more
torture ...

... And there's no way
anyone can blame it on
me; I haven't spoken to
him in years. Sure, he
drove me mad. And for
good reasons: he damaged
me for life ... But that's
the past. I've got my own
life to lead now! ...

... There wasn't anything
wrong with me when I
first went to that school.
Not a thing! He did it all.
He wrecked me. And now
he's done it to himself. So,
you see ... He's responsible. I had nothing to do
with it ...

Voice Two

*S.U.I.C.I.D.E. ... He killed
himself ...Him! ... Dr B
has killed himself ...
He's abandoned us ....*

*How could he have done that to
me? ... I trusted him. I really
believed him when he said there
was always a chance for a new
beginning. When he said that
harm could be undone, that
life would always have
something to offer.
When he insisted that I never
give up ...*

*... I believed him when
he said he loved me,
when he said I was
worthy of love ...*

*Lies, that's what it was.
All lies. He was doing
his job, that's all ...
Just proving his theories
... Love is not enough?
That's for sure! When you
really love people, you don't
leave them ... Not like that!*

*True, he was old, and he'd been
sick ... After all, it was his own
life ... What he gave me,
I can keep ... That's mine. ...
yes, mine; I can do whatever
I want with it. And if he's
not here to see it, it's his
problem! ... Still, I'll
miss him.*

Voice Three

**A plastic bag?
A nursing
home? That's ...
that's crazy! ...**

**... That's right, it's
crazy! I tell you,
it's crazy ...**
He **was crazy.
Sure, he was crazy
... I knew it,
I knew it
all along! ...**

**I should have known!
He was a paranoiac ...
Of course ... That lousy
temper! All those crazy
threats ... God!
When I think how
much he hurt me ...**

**The great Dr B was
nuts! That's too
funny for words! ...
And to think that
my mother thought
of him as a genius!
What will she
say now?**

**A plastic bag, you've
got to be kidding! ...
I have to talk to the
others. He was mad! ...
When I think of all he
said to me! And all that
time,** ***he*** **was the crazy
one ... Do you hear?
He was mad,** ***not me.***

The first letter appeared in *The Reader*, a free Chicago weekly, on April 6, less than three weeks after Bettelheim's death. It was unsigned. It described an unpredictable Bettelheim, prone to periods of rage during which he beat and cruelly insulted the children. In particular, it told how the author, then aged fifteen, had been taking her shower when 'Dr B', as everyone called Bettelheim at the Orthogenic School, suddenly burst into the bathroom, grabbed her by the hair and dragged her naked and dripping out into a bedroom full of people, where he proceeded to beat her in front of them all. Far worse than the physical pain, the writer stressed, was the terrible humiliation she had felt. To this day, she added, she had not the slightest idea what she had done to deserve such abuse.

Two weeks earlier, a unanimous press had been paying tribute to Bruno Bettelheim as a 'pioneer in treating childhood mental disturbances',[1] known for his 'warmth and wisdom'.[2] That letter threw open the flood-gates. Soon the letters-to-the-editor page of *The Reader* became the arena for an animated debate between former patients and counsellors of the Orthogenic School, with Bettelheim being depicted as a monster. The debate was further enlivened by contributions from a number of outsiders, all too eager to point out the contradictions between the man's high-sounding pronouncements and the allegations now levelled against him.

Numerically, the 'antis' deployed more firepower than the 'pros'. They congratulated one another on their courage, often referring to each others' texts as if they had never met, much less been brought up together. In the trenches on the other side, most of Bettelheim's defenders were fighting with one arm tied behind their backs, being unable for reasons of professional ethics to reveal what they knew, as former counsellors or therapists, about their patients. Their replies to the barrage of criticism more often than not fell wide of the mark, appearing at best beside the point, at worst a cover-up.

Soon the ranks of the protagonists were swelled by the enemies of psychoanalysis in general, and in particular those who had always combatted Bettelheim, arguing that mental illnesses had nothing to do with either family environment or upbringing, but were attributable only to physical, even chemical factors.

Chicago soon became the arena for an all-out, no-holds-barred battle.

The hostility, incomprehension and bitterness involved were commensurate with the role that Bettelheim had played in the city for more than three decades. People who had known each other for years took to avoiding one another. Some sank into a despairing silence, while others poured out their feelings for all the world to hear.

On August 26 the controversy finally brimmed over into a wider arena. Charles Pekow, a freelance journalist who had spent eleven years at the Orthogenic School, finally managed to get a piece into the Sunday edition of the *Washington Post*. It appeared under the headline 'The Other Dr Bettelheim; The Revered Psychologist Had a Dark, Violent Side.'

After briefly recalling the glowing tributes paid to Bettelheim by the press, Pekow proceeded to list the charges against him. Not only had Bruno Bettelheim been a sadistic brute, he asserted, but he had also been a racist, since there had been no black kids at the Orthogenic School. Bettelheim had above all been a charlatan, whose fame enabled him to cover up his mistaken diagnoses and abuses of power; in short, his most noteworthy talent had been for self-promotion.

To back up his indictment, Charles cited Alida Jatitch, by now revealed as the anonymous writer of that first letter to *The Reader*: 'Those who were going through normal adolescent pains were labeled psychotic .... What bothered me the most, more than the beating, insults, whatever, [was that] throughout my adolescence I was basically treated like I was a two-year-old.' On this point, Charles Pekow noted that students at the school were not allowed to engage in music lessons or other such activities on the pretext that they needed all their available time for 'personality rebuilding'.

Pekow also quoted Bill Blau, a former counsellor: 'I would characterize the atmosphere at the Orthogenic School, at that time [1949-50], as the beginnings of a cult, with "Dr B" as the cult leader.'

That statement was echoed by a quote from Jacquelyn Sanders, who had run the Orthogenic School since Bruno Bettelheim's departure in 1973, after having worked under him for thirteen years as a counsellor. 'I believed blindly in him, and I don't like to think of myself as the type of person who would believe blindly in anything,' she admitted.

Some may find it surprising to see Dr Sanders being quoted in an article so hostile to Bettelheim. Her reply would be that she never refused to talk to a former student, be it Charles Pekow or anyone else. One might however have expected a more spirited defence of the man who had been her teacher for so long, and who later picked her to step into his shoes. Yet this was not to be the last occasion on which Jacquelyn Sanders's statements betrayed the ambivalence of her feelings towards Bruno Bettelheim.

In September 1990, for example, she wrote a letter to the editor of the *Chicago Sun-Times* in which, while ostensibly protesting about a hostile article, she conceded: 'I have long felt that Bettelheim did a disservice to the field by not discussing more thoroughly the issue of discipline.' The letter also stressed that as director of the Orthogenic School Mrs Sanders had expressly forbidden any use of corporal punishment whatsoever. It also noted that she had long since stopped admitting autistic children. Finally, Bettelheim's successor asked the paper's readers not to hold it against him that 'a powerful and brilliant man made some powerful and brilliant mistakes'.

The scandal was now spreading far beyond the confines of Chicago, as Pekow's article was reprinted by the *International Herald Tribune* and other non-US publications.[3] It was received with amazement, and often with a measure of scepticism, throughout the world.

In France, in particular, most observers dismissed the allegations out of hand as yet another example of transatlantic hyperbole, of how Americans were forever tearing down yesterday's idols, as undiscerning in their debunking as they had formerly been in their adulation.

The secrecy in which Bruno Bettelheim had shrouded the Orthogenic School contributed powerfully to the attention attracted by the scandal in the United States. For everyone except those who had lived and worked there, the institution had always remained a mystery. Insisting that the children had to be protected from all intrusions, and that the slightest change in their daily routine could prove traumatic, Bettelheim had allowed hardly a single visitor to pass the famous fire doors that separated the reception area from the residential quarters.

In later years, even when professionals such as psychiatrists, doctors or psychoanalysts had come to visit, they had seldom been invited to go any further than the staff room. There was thus no way to contradict even the most fantastic allegations; those who had known the school from the inside could say what they liked about it without fear of being challenged, except by others whose information was every bit as subjective – not to say defensive, in the case of counsellors who were accused of ill-treatment. Previously the secrecy surrounding the school had allowed people to see it as a paradise; now that same secrecy let them project on to it the image of a living hell.

The wider it spread, the more the debate became reduced to almost comic-strip simplicity. Pretty soon it boiled down to one 'yes-no' question: Did Bruno Bettelheim, who had so often condemned corporal punishment, beat the children placed in his care? Just as quickly the answer became obvious to all but the most uncritical: Yes, he did on occasion hit them. Sometimes, it seemed, Bettelheim was trying to force a reaction from a child who was completely shut off from the outside world, but more often the gesture appeared to be simply one of ill-controlled anger. He had in fact practically answered the question himself back in 1984, when a reporter had put it to him bluntly. 'That's between me and the children,' Bettelheim had replied.[4]

But that half-admission, published long before in a small New England paper, was hardly enough to satisfy the morbid curiosity that had now been aroused by the controversy. On the contrary, the accusations of brutality were only amplified by the whiff of hypocrisy. Things quickly became all black and white, and the wall between Bettelheim's detractors and his apologists grew even higher. One was either for or against, there was no middle ground.

'Beno Brutalheim?' The heights to which the scandal had risen could be gauged by the headline of the article published by *Newsweek*[5] less than six months after the same magazine ran a glowing obituary. The article, below an ostensibly balanced appraisal of Bettelheim's work, concluded that 'Bettelheim's experiences in the concentration camps probably affected his methods.' The argument was all the more damning in that it was backed up by a quote from one of the dead man's most faithful friends: 'He had seen a dictator who destroys people, and he became a dictator who wanted to rescue people.'

In October it was Ronald Angres's turn to go public, in the conservative Jewish monthly *Commentary*. His account, entitled 'Who, Really, Was Bruno Bettelheim?' had a livelier, less acrimonious tone than Charles Pekow's, showing both more distance and more personal feeling. It was even more damaging.

Angres, described in the magazine as a graduate student in international affairs at George Washington University, started by inverting one of Bettelheim's pet quotes, speaking of the 'shock of non-recognition' that he, like Charles Pekow, had experienced on reading the newspaper obituaries.[6]

Ronald Angres had been close on seven when he entered the school and nineteen when he left it. Running through his text, the careful reader once again detects agonizing yet unasked questions: 'Why was I sent there? Was I really sick the way they said I was?' ('They' in his case being his psychoanalyst father, his mother, Bruno Bettelheim and others.) And, 'Am I still sick today?' The questions were all the more haunting for Ronald in that he had been one of the 'autistic' children whose treatment had brought fame to Bruno Bettelheim. At least, he had been presented as such by his counsellor of seven years, Jacquelyn Sanders, in the master's dissertation she had devoted to his case in 1964.[7]

Initially at least, even a lay reader was sure to conclude that if the young man really had been autistic, and if he was now capable of writing the article published in *Commentary*, there could be no better tribute to the work of Bettelheim – even if Ronald Angres had nothing good to say about him. No parent or counsellor of an autistic child could wish for a more spectacular result. And this was precisely the argument put forward by many readers of the review to counter Angres's damning testimony. The problem with that line of defence was the apparent ease with which Ronald contested the original diagnosis, reached in 1959 when the definition of infantile autism was vaguer than it is today. As the article unfolded, the open-minded reader found the natural suspicions aroused by a patient's assessment of his own illness gradually dissolving. And as the original diagnosis began to appear questionable, so did all the rest.

Angres gave a host of examples of the 'tyranny' exercised by Bettelheim, who, he wrote, made him live for twelve years 'in terror of his beatings, in terror of his footsteps in the dorms – abject, animal terror'. He recounted how his comic books were confiscated, how the little toy train that he had brought from home, and which for that reason was dear to him, was dismissed as a 'stupid toy'. He also recalled how Bettelheim had on one occasion accused him of being a 'megalomaniac' simply because he had chosen to sit apart in an armchair while waiting for a meal, rather than join the other children on an overcrowded bench, how Bettelheim slapped him during a game for hitting the ball too hard so it landed on a fellow student's head, etc.

It was a long list of miseries, and it was all the more shocking for those readers who were aware of the descriptions of the Orthogenic School that Bettelheim had given in his books. The latter portrayed a world in which the golden rule was to leave the children free to do as they pleased, within the limits of physical safety, in order to allow the language of their 'madness' to be deciphered, with each symptom being seen as part of a puzzle.

Some of Angres's less serious accusations could however be seen in perspective by the informed reader. An example: having read in Bettelheim that it was essential to accept a child's bedwetting to make him realize that one loved him for himself, and that a counsellor should put a higher priority on the child's treatment than on the school's hygiene, the reader was not unduly surprised to find Ronald Angres complaining about the smell of urine that permeated the junior dormitories.

There were also incidents that such a reader could easily see from both the therapist's and the child's point of view. Example: writing of his first encounter with Bettelheim, Angres told how:

> I drew for him a picture of a man. I don't remember now if he asked me to, but all psychologists seemed to crave such pictures, and I may have tried in this fashion to break the ice.
>
> 'What a stupid and ugly picture,' he snapped. (I did not yet know that he fancied himself as an art connoisseur.) 'You did not draw his hands!'
>
> 'They're behind his back,' I explained.
>
> 'You just did that because you can't draw hands! Do you know what it means when a boy can't draw hands?'
>
> 'I did not. I still don't. To appease him, I redrew the picture and added some hands, carefully showing all five fingers.
>
> 'Preposterous! You drew the hands entirely out of proportion! They're bigger than his head!'

Once more he scowled darkly, as if I were expected to know the sinister significance of such a reversal of normal proportions.[8]

Ronald was articulate and obviously highly intelligent,[9] and his indictment of Bettelheim was devastatingly effective, whatever comments could be made about it by a psychiatrist. Indeed, even though in the article he stressed the beatings, his main complaint was the constant 'analytical' scrutiny to which his every act had been subjected while he was at the Orthogenic School.

As an example, Angres told how he had given up playing baseball after a few years – even though his physical awkwardness was one of his major problems: 'They kept us from forming teams, from deciding with whom we would play, from keeping score,' he explained.[10] But, above all, 'every ball that hit a child was regarded as an intentional assault, requiring punishment. Needless to say, the intent did not have to be "conscious".' 'Most of us were clumsy, if not "spastic",' he wrote, quoting the adjective which he said Bettelheim often used to deride his physical performances. However, 'our "unconscious" was credited with superhuman skill and with the single determination to bean other kids with tennis balls'.

The account may have been tinged with paranoia; it was nevertheless disturbing. Ronald, whose father was a psychoanalyst, was able to quote Freud, draw parallels between Bettelheim and Wilhelm Reich, and in general come across as an insider. Faced with his description of how he had suffered as a little boy and an adolescent from having his every gesture, drawing or utterance minutely observed and analysed, the professional psychiatrist might react by slapping a label on Ronald's symptoms. But the lay reader would find the overall picture a far cry from the 'Home for the Heart' so often described in Bettelheim's writings.

It was also easy to see how Ronald Angres's testimony would become grist for the mills of the foes of psychoanalysis. His article already betrayed signs of the phone conversations he had had with Jeffrey Moussaiev Masson, professor of Sanskrit and fallen angel of psychoanalysis who was then the figurehead of the anti-Freudian forces in the United States. Masson, a trained analyst, had risen spectacularly in the psychoanalytic community to become deputy director of the Freud Archives with the blessing of Kurt Eissler, the director, and to a lesser extent of Anna Freud herself. He had been cast out in disgrace just as suddenly as he had risen to fame.[11]

For a time, Masson was to find himself becoming the rallying point for some of Bruno Bettelheim's lost children, in search of someone who would listen to their stories. For Masson, a complex individual who is at once exasperating and endearing, the attention must have been intellectually pleasing, although somewhat difficult to handle in practice. Soon Jeffrey Masson was writing to the director of the Orthogenic School to ask for biographical data about Bruno Bettelheim, to amend the article he had devoted to him in his anthology of psychoanalysis!

In the meantime a group of fourteen former counsellors and teachers from the Orthogenic School had replied to Charles Pekow's attacks in the *Washington Post*. Their letter[12] was signed by two of Bettelheim's most trusted colleagues, notably Karen Zelan, with whom he had co-authored a book on reading.[13] Zelan had been the counsellor of 'Marcia', one of the three cases of autism described in *The Empty Fortress*. The other signatory, Fae Tyroler, had acted as counsellor to 'Joey the Mechanical Boy', the most famous case in the same work.

This was heavy artillery, and could have been expected to strike a major blow for the Bettelheim camp. Strangely, however, the text seemed almost to miss the point, as though it were replying to other accusers than Pekow and Angres. This was all the more obvious since the *Washington Post* chose to publish it beneath a second letter from Pekow – a reply to yet another former counsellor who had sought to defend Bettelheim. The correspondence had become such a regular feature of the *Post* that it ran under the heading 'The Bettelheim We Knew (Cont'd)'.

Karen Zelan and her associates failed to score any points because they remained too aloof to counter the arguments of Bettelheim's critics, either directly or implicitly. Their text appeared awkward, even clumsy, in contrast with the anger, suffering and anxiety expressed by the latter. The letter did not even try to address the specifics of the accusations, and it also failed to score on the broader level of principles. It simply did not mesh with Bettelheim's own oft-published view that warmth and personal commitment were the most essential traits of a good counsellor or educator. Such traits were conspicuous by their absence from the letter, and that could only reinforce the reader's suspicion that there had been a yawning gulf between theory and practice in Bettelheim's institution. Rather than lifting the debate on to a higher plane, the text seemed merely defensive.

The first argument used by the school's defenders rested on the world-wide reputation of the University of Chicago. 'Is the public to believe that [Bettelheim] concealed the existence of this "concentration camp" environment within one of the world's great research universities?' they asked. And without stooping to discuss a single one of the everyday details which had made the accusations so effective, the writers simply vouched for 'Bettelheim's contribution to the understanding and treatment of children who otherwise would have been considered untreatable'.

Finally, in an all-too-brief paragraph, they evoked some of the emotions that filled their daily lives at the school: 'Bettelheim was deeply moved by the inner chaos, rage, misery and terror of the children, which was often manifest in extreme behavior, ranging from endangering themselves or others, to the ludicrous or puzzling. Of course, he responded with a range of feeling and action. There was a great deal to be upset about, and sufficient to enjoy with good humor.' Nevertheless, they added: 'Bettelheim exhorted us never to give up in our efforts, because even the most hateful or bizarre behavior could be understood and perhaps remediated.'

Meanwhile Pekow continued to pull no punches in his campaign, even seizing on the looming war in the Persian Gulf to compare the Orthogenic School to Saddam Hussein's Iraq. Neither side in the debate appeared to be making any impact on the other, but to the lay reader, seeking an immediate and therefore simplified view of events, the score was clearly not running in favour of the defence.

By late fall of 1990 the anti-Bettelheim wave had wreaked its havoc. It had become impossible even to mention the man's name without sparking off a loaded, impassioned debate, fraught with humiliation for all its participants. Humiliation for the memory of Bruno Bettelheim and for his defenders, of course. But humiliation also for his former students/patients, whose every word and action was being subjected to the full glare of public scrutiny.

'Why wait until Bettelheim was dead to say all this?'

'Because up until then nobody would believe us.' The answer was as painful and bitter as the question was obvious. Charles Pekow, for example, had tried to persuade another journalist to write an article about the Orthogenic School. Although fascinated by his story, the reporter had dropped it after talking to his editor. What does the testimony of a former mental patient count for against that of a man respected throughout the world?

'Because an estate can't sue.' Bettelheim's defenders of course had a very different answer, which was summed up in this rather naïve, or perhaps overly frank, admission made by one of the reporters covering the story. Dead men tell no tales. And, in the United States at least, only their financial interests can give rise to court cases. But the most obvious reason for the media's post-mortem interest in Bruno Bettelheim was best summed up by former counsellor Bill Blau: 'No doubt the fact that Bettelheim committed suicide, and the way he did it, played right into our hands,' he commented.[14]

These then are the basic elements of 'the Bettelheim Affair'. Subsequent events were to add a few more sub-plots, but not to change the overall drama that was being played out between Bettelheim's ghost and some of his former charges.

Some investigators, their curiosity aroused by the revelations, started rummaging around in what had up until then been virgin territory: Bettelheim's childhood, education and eventual deportation by the Nazis. On November 11, the *Chicago Tribune* set off new ripples by revealing that not even those who had worked most closely with Bruno Bettelheim were able to say exactly what diplomas he had. One witness was even quoted as saying that in Vienna Bettelheim had mainly been known as an ambitious businessman, and not at all as a psychologist.

The writer of the article, Ron Grossman, was himself a former college teacher, and Ronald Angres had been one of his students. The *Commentary* article had come as no surprise to him; indeed, he had already read a portion of it, in a longer and less structured version, several years earlier. As a student, Ronald Angres had at first been incapable of producing the slightest essay. Grossman had spent weeks trying to get through to this obviously gifted young man. Then one day, out of the blue, Angres had dumped his report on the Orthogenic School on his teacher's desk. From that day on, he had been able to complete his assignments like any other student.

The incident had so intrigued Grossman that he became fascinated by Bettelheim. His *Chicago Tribune* article was the best documented so far, with a real attempt having been made to sound out the views of all sides. Grossman had talked to nineteen former students of the Orthogenic School and at least as many of Bettelheim's former collaborators. He had also interviewed psychoanalysts and even Ralph Tyler, the former head of the University of Chicago's Education Department, who back in the 1940s had given Bettelheim his first job in the United States. The Bruno Bettelheim that emerged from all these contradictory statements was a strange man indeed, part genius, part Svengali. A remarkably intelligent but also an extremely ambitious person, not very scrupulous and something of a dandy.

By then Bruno Bettelheim's writings were the only part of his life's work that had not yet come under attack – or at least not directly. It was only a matter of time; in February 1991 he was accused of plagiarism. Writing in the *Journal of American Folklore*, a Berkeley University professor of anthropology charged Bettelheim with having purely and simply lifted some of the ideas in his best-selling book *The Uses of Enchantment* from the thesis of a little-known teacher of psychiatry, Dr Julius Heuscher.[15]

The only consolation for Bettelheim's supporters in the spate of articles that ensued was the response of Heuscher himself. Questioned by reporters, he stated that when he had read *The Uses of Enchantment* – upon its publication fifteen years previously – he had not at all felt that he was being plagiarized. Specifying that he had not known Bettelheim personally, he added: 'We all plagiarize. I plagiarize. Many times, I am not sure whether it came out of my own brain or if it came from somewhere else .... Poor Bruno Bettelheim! I did not always agree with him. But I would not want to disturb his eternal sleep for this. I'm only happy that I would have influenced [him].'[16] Thanks to this simple and eminently sensible statement, which concluded many of the articles on this latest 'scandal', the fuss died down almost as quickly as it had flared up, leaving only a slight whiff of fraud to blend in with the earlier allegations.

And this leads to a final question: Why had the most effective defenders of Bettelheim in this posthumous scandal been people who did not know him well? Why did those who had known and admired him, those who had worked with him and who therefore suffered most from the distorted image created after his death, defend him so feebly?

They too could have found simple and sensible arguments, words that would have been convincing for most people. Without violating their former patients' privacy, they could for instance have pointed out that Charles Pekow, Ronald Angres, Alida Jatitch and most of the others who publicly attacked Bettelheim after his death all knew each other, since they all belonged to the same generation of Orthogenic School kids. It was the last that Bettelheim was to know, and undoubtedly one that he had somewhat neglected, absorbed as he then had been with engineering his own tricky succession. Above all, it was the generation that he had abandoned by retiring.

It would not have needed much more, no doubt, to get across the message that nothing occurring in the Orthogenic School, not even the slapping, should be viewed out of context. That nothing in the relationship between therapist and patient is ever clear cut. And that interested outsiders should therefore avoid rushing to judgement. It seemed however that the Bettelheim faithful were simply unable, even twenty years later, to strike the right tone when talking about him, to treat him just as a man, with human strengths and weaknesses.

They had been the privileged witnesses of his powerful clinical intuition; they had seen him find just the right words to pacify a terrified child after everyone else had tried and failed. They had also experienced the illuminating effect of some of his analyses, and all of them could remember the relief they had felt when Bettelheim had got them out of a tight spot with a child by helping them identify the painful memory that it evoked in them.

However they had also seen him lose his self-control, and knew how hurtful some of his interpretations could be. Most of them had been very young when they had met him. They owed him a great deal, but they were often unable to say exactly what. The Orthogenic School had been such a strange place; its atmosphere was so difficult to describe. They had not just worked there, they had lived there twenty-four hours a day. Elsewhere, psychotics are parked in hospitals, and the staff leave at the end of the day. Or else patients return to their families in the evenings. There, in Chicago, they had shared the everyday life of their young patients, often for many years. It had not always been clear to them exactly what differentiated them from their charges, since Bettelheim was continually encouraging them to examine their own motives in their relationships with the latter. Interminable working days, and for many of them practically no life outside the school – how could one get all that across to outsiders?

And how to communicate one's experience of a man who was at once learned, generous, attentive and caring, but also unpredictable, temperamental and intellectually dominating? The years spent at the school were buried inside each of them like a rare secret, something almost impossible to talk about. During those years they had shared in the dream of an extraordinary man. Extraordinary for his ambition – to cure those said to be incurable – but also for his excessive personality. A man from another age, another world, one which they as Americans had never completely understood.

PART ONE

The Formative Years

Chapter I

Vienna: Once Upon a Time

Vienna, occupied by the Nazis in 1938, then successively shattered by Allied bombing and beseiged by the Soviets, is not the ideal place to search for someone's roots. Particularly not if that person is a Jew. A few documents can be retrieved, almost by chance, amid mounds of dusty archives. The visitor will locate a few addresses, but in general only to be told 'Oh, it's changed a great deal, you know,' or even worse, 'You can't get much of an idea from this place; it was rebuilt after the war.' There is a handful of memories, passed on to the next generation. And there are Bruno Bettelheim's writings.

His roots do not seem to have loomed very large among his concerns. He mentions them only briefly, in *Freud's Vienna and Other Essays*. Along with practically all the other Bettelheims whose opinions I was able to sound, he apparently subscribed to the belief that the whole family could be traced back to a single origin in the city formerly known as Pressburg. Now Bratislava, the capital of Slovakia, it was practically Vienna's back yard, being only some 30 miles distant.

The Bettelheims are less unanimous, however, on the etymology of their name. Many of them believe it to be simply a corruption of 'Bethlehem', But Bruno advanced another theory when discussing his paternal grandfather, Jakob Morris Bettelheim. 'He never talked about his parents, either because he was orphaned at such an early age that he knew nothing about them or because he was born out of wedlock and deserted by his mother to cover her shame,' Bettelheim wrote.[1] The implication was that young Jakob Morris had been assigned his surname by the orphanage, which was run by a prominent Jewish family. At the turn of the nineteenth century, when the empire's Jews were granted the right to a civil identity, the family was said to have quite naturally recorded the name under which it had been known until then – a contraction of the words *Bettler* (beggar) and *Heim* (home).

In support of the theory, Bruno Bettelheim cited the many efforts made later by his uncles, the brothers of his by-then dead father, to establish their kinship with the said Jewish family, which had died out leaving no known heir. Their quest had been in vain, however, because according to family legend Jakob Morris Bettelheim had destroyed all documents pertaining to his birth. The reason for that, it was whispered, was that he was in fact the bastard child of an aristocrat, and did not wish to bring down opprobium on his real father's head.

A fine tale indeed, and one which would certainly have appealed to the art historian and psychoanalyst Ernst Kris. In the 1930s, at the time when Sigmund Freud was examining the possibility that Moses could have been an Egyptian prince,[2] Kris was showing how in most great artists' biographies, the origins of at least one ancestor are always shrouded in mystery, thus allowing a myth of noble, or even royal, extraction to spring up behind the real-life situation of misery.[3]

Nevertheless, the records of the Vienna Jewish Community are clear: Jakob Morris Bettelheim was born not in Pressburg but in the Hungarian city of Pest, on March 21, 1825. His father Markus and mother Lewia must even have been fairly well known there, since Markus exercised the respectable profession of notary, to a Jewish community so large and flourishing that the Hungarian capital[4] was soon to be nicknamed 'Judapest', from the word *Jude*, or Jew. As for Pressburg, it is true that the family name can be traced back there to at least the start of the eighteenth century, first as Betlehem, then Bethlehem and finally as Bettelheim.[5] But although the city was then under Hungarian administration, I was unable to find any indications as to when, or why, Jakob Morris would have been placed in an orphanage there.

Among the various hypotheses put forward by Bettelheim, only two are consistent with existing records. The first was that one or both of Jakob Morris's parents died when he was very young, and that the other members of his family had then refused to take care of him. The second was that Jakob Morris was the fruit of an adulterous union on the part of his mother, who abandoned him out of shame. Bruno Bettelheim obviously tended to give more credence to the second version (it was the only one which left his origins shrouded in mystery), even though it implied not only that his great-grandmother had sinned, but also that the surname he bore was in fact usurped.

Bruno Bettelheim probably never tried very hard to ascertain whether the received version of his family history was the true story. Indeed, his brief account of how both his grandfathers 'went up' to Vienna and made their fortunes has all the ingredients of the fairy tales he was so fond of. In both cases, the story starts out in misery and misfortune and finds a happy ending in the good city of Emperor Franz-Joseph. Bettelheim himself stressed the fairy-tale character of the story by including it in a chapter called 'The Child's Perception of the City'. For his aim was precisely to underline the rose-tinted image of Vienna that his mother had handed down to him, and in which he long believed.

'Happy as a Jew under Franz-Joseph,' was the stock phrase at the time. Once the new ruler was on the throne, it was only a short time before Vienna became a glittering magnet for all Jews who aspired to emerge from their *shtetls*, or ghettos,[6] across the Austro-Hungarian empire. Up until then, even though their lives had been incomparably less harsh than those of the Russian Jews, who were still subject to regular pogroms, the Austro-Hungarian Jews had not been allowed to buy property in the imperial capital without a special permit.[7] Faced with an upsurge in nationalist movements which threatened to tear apart the frail patchwork of the Hapsburg empire, Franz-Joseph, who had taken over from his uncle during the heat of the 1848 revolution, was soon to realize how useful it would be to have the Jews on his side.

Austria, a feudal, baroque and deeply Catholic country, had until then managed to remain untouched by the ideas and reforms inspired by the Enlightenment. The young sovereign decided to give reform a chance by effectively putting the liberals, who belonged to the German-speaking, city-dwelling élite, in the driving seat. The Jews were scattered across the length and breadth of the empire, forming a group united primarily by common traditions rather than by geographical origins. They also spoke German or, in the ghettos that were furthest from Vienna, Yiddish, which after all is a dialect of German with some Hebrew and a few local Slav expressions thrown in. Treating them well to gain their allegiance therefore made sense for Franz-Joseph, whose central concern was to hold together what remained of the Germanic Holy Roman Empire.

In 1868, after having tried to head off revolt in Hungary by having himself crowned king in Budapest, Franz-Joseph therefore granted the Jews full citizenship rights, allowing them to practise any profession they wished and abolishing the special tax they had previously been subjected to. As the new constitution also proclaimed freedom of movement for all citizens of the empire, the reforms sparked off a huge tide of emigration towards the capital. Between 1857 and 1890 the percentage of Jews in the Viennese population thus rose from less than two to more than twelve. They in fact made up quite a heterogeneous group. To simplify things a little, the further away from the capital they originated, the less likely they were to be assimilated. But, once they had made Vienna their home, it took no more than two or three generations for even the most traditionalist among them to cast off the long black kaftans, round hats and sidelocks which made them stand out so much on the city streets. Although some resisted assimilation, there have been few periods in Jewish history when the desire for integration, and the opportunities for accomplishing it, have been as great as they were in Vienna during the second half of the nineteenth century.

The trend was in complete harmony with the general sea-change in European attitudes. Everywhere religion had lost ground and faith was being supplanted by rationalism. The Napoleonic armies had carried the ideals of the French Revolution, and in general had emancipated the Jews, wherever they had passed.[8] At the same time the ideas of the Enlightenment had made inroads amongst the Jews themselves, discrediting the

purely religious content of Judaism and inciting the most adventurous
souls to leave their *shtetls* and become fully-fledged citizens.

The social geography of assimilation can be easily traced on maps of the
period; the 'ghetto', the neighbourhood in which Jews made up around a
third of the population at the beginning of this century,[9] is Leopoldstadt,
the second district. It forms a long strip between two branches of the
Danube, to the east of the old town. To the north is the twentieth district,
into which many of the families from Galicia or Bukovina (today Polish
and Russian provinces respectively) moved. It was home to the most
orthodox Jews, and although some of its streets were very poor, others
were very fashionable, in particular the ones bordering the Augarten and
Prater parks. The latter were royal lands that Emperor Joseph II had
opened to the public, and they were favourite haunts of the aristocratic
horse-and-carriage set.

The Prater park was Vienna in a nutshell: there was a part for the
aristocracy with avenues for horses, a working-class area with a large
funfair, and above all a range of middle-class attractions, such as cafés and
bandstands, where Strauss and his waltzes were all the rage. The park
was a favourite place for Sunday walks *en famille*, a tryst for lovers and a
talking shop for intellectuals. Even vagrants were allowed to sleep in it as
long as their behaviour remained 'decent' – a favourite Viennese concept.
It was a courteous, tolerant city, in which one greeted one's equals and left
room for everyone else. Its residents were prone to hypocrisy, and felt
secure in the belief that they inhabited one of the world's two most civilized
cities; the other being of course Paris.

From Leopoldstadt one only had to cross the canal to be in the first
district, the heart of the city with the old town, the imperial palace, the
opera house and St Stephen's Cathedral. It was also the home of the main
Jewish institutions, including the grand synagogue. The existence of a
'Jews' street', just behind the cathedral, was a reminder of the fact that
before Vienna grew to its modern dimensions, the 'ghetto' used to be right
in the city centre. At the end of the nineteenth century the percentage of
Jews living in the first district was still relatively high, between ten and
twenty-four. The same was true in the ninth, just to the north, where
many doctors lived. But as one moved outwards from the Ringstrasse, the
majestic loop boulevard which was being built around the old town at that
time, the proportion of Jews fell, to less than five per cent in the city's outer
areas.

It is interesting to compare the above structure with the social geography of Vienna mapped out by Stefan Zweig in his book *The World of
Yesterday*, which describes the city into which Bruno Bettelheim was born
in 1903. The centre of this universe was the imperial palace, around which
'The palaces of the Austrian, the Polish, the Czech, and the Hungarian
nobility formed as it were a second enclosure .... Then came "good society",
consisting of the lesser nobility, the higher officials, industry, and the "old

families", then the petty bourgeoisie and the proletariat. Each of these social strata lived in its own circle, and even in its own district, the nobility in their palaces in the heart of the city, the diplomats in the third district, industry and the merchants in the vicinity of the Ringstrasse, the petty bourgeoisie in the inner districts – the second to the ninth – and the proletariat in the outer circle.'[10] It is clear that at the dawn of the twentieth century, Jews were represented in every 'stratum' of Vienna society. Whether true or not, the beguiling stories Bettelheim told about his forebears are totally in keeping with the spirit of the age. They are stories that are worth studying, if only because, as their author was to point out on many occasions, the psychological life of a child begins with its grandparents.

The first one Bettelheim mentions is Adolf Seidler, his maternal grandfather. He was born in 1847 in Redschkau, Bohemia, and lost his mother at a tender age. He then found himself in a Hansel-and-Gretel-like situation, with a stepmother who was determined that her own natural children should get the lion's share of the household's meagre resources. His father was a pedlar who spent the weekdays doing the rounds of local villages, returning home only on the eve of the Sabbath and then, being a devout Jew, spending most of the latter at the synagogue. The stepmother was eventually able to persuade the well-meaning but weak father to throw the boy out. At the age of thirteen, Adolf Seidler thus found himself on the road, with nothing more than the clothes on his back – his bar mitzvah suit – and a five-guilder coin which his father had been able to slip him as he left (worth, says Bettelheim, around two dollars and fifty cents). 'To protect his only pair of shoes, the boy walked barefoot the hundred miles from his village to the big city, Vienna. There, in a very hard struggle, he eventually managed to make a great fortune,' Bettelheim concludes.

In private, Bruno Bettelheim was somewhat more forthcoming about exactly how his maternal grandfather had made that fortune. Again, the story has a fairy-tale quality to it, but in this case, not a very moral one. On arriving in Vienna, the young Seidler was taken in and given a job as an apprentice by a distant relative, who was a mechanic. The family was so poor that the boy had to sleep in the workshop, but he learned fast and had a sharp mind. When the first Singer sewing machines appeared in Vienna, Adolf was quick to grasp their potential, and he resolved to try to become the company's distributor in the city. From the distant United States, the reply came back that he would need to prove that he had a workshop and capital of around 10,000 florins.

Neither Adolf nor anyone in his circle possessed such a large sum, but he did not let this deter him. He managed to persuade not only his cousin but also a large number of other people, impressed by his talent, and also no doubt by his *chutzpah*, to show up at the bank and deposit their savings on an account in his name for just the time it took Adolf Seidler to get certification of the deposit. After which, added Bettelheim, the contributors all rushed to take their money out again, not trusting either each other or their enterprising friend. It was thanks to that stratagem – Bruno Bettelheim was on occasion to call it a 'fraud' – that Adolf Seidler was able to open the first Singer sewing machine store in Vienna.

That was only the beginning, however, for Adolf soon hit upon a technique which was to make the business a runaway success. As he could not at first afford to import more than a few machines at a time, he tried to choose clients who looked as though they would be incapable of keeping up the monthly payments. As soon as they defaulted, he would recover the merchandise, keeping the deposit and the instalments and then refurbishing the machine to sell it again as new. This could happen with the same sewing machine two or three times in a row; Bruno Bettelheim's mother could even remember, when she was a little girl, hearing her father raging when too many of his customers managed to keep up with their payments!

The received family version of events is only contradicted by official records on one point. Although it is true that Adolf Seidler started out by selling American sewing machines, they were labelled not Singer but Neuest. He is indeed found opening a shop – in 1875, at the age of twenty-eight – but in partnership with a certain Adolf Gizidi. The latter, probably his cousin with the workshop, disappears from the commercial records three years later. It is however indisputable that Adolf Seidler possessed considerable business acumen, and that he quickly became very rich. Ten years after setting up in business, he had added jewellery and silverware to his sewing machine business and three years after that he became head of a construction company. He subsequently became a registered real estate dealer and even invested some money in a locksmith's firm. His home was on Lerchenfeldstrasse, a quiet bourgeois street in the city's seventh district.

In the same year that he founded his business, Adolf Seidler entered into an arranged marriage with a young woman from the Bohemian city of Luk. She first had a son, and then in December 1877 she gave birth to Pauline, soon known as Paula, who would be Bruno Bettelheim's mother.

The story of how Jakob Morris Bettelheim, the other grandfather, made his money is more uplifting. Bruno Bettelheim's version[11] is as follows. Jakob Morris soon impressed his teachers with his great intelligence, and they decided that he should become a rabbi. At the same time Baron Anselm von Rothschild – 'the richest man of the realm', writes Bettelheim – was looking for a tutor for his three sons. Jakob Morris was brought to his attention, and in the twinkling of an eye the young man was projected 'from living in desperate poverty into the grand palace of the Rothschilds in Vienna'. Bettelheim continues: 'There he educated his charges, who grew so fond of him and were so impressed by his brilliance that when they became leaders of the Rothschild bank, they put him in charge of many of its operations. In consequence, he not only became very rich but exercised great influence over the social life of the Jewish community of Vienna.'[12]

The gratitude of the Rothschild sons even extended to the whole family, Bettelheim told his children, since after Jakob Morris, they promised always to have at least one of his descendants among their inner circle of employees.

Anselm von Rothschild was to die in 1874, leaving his position as chairman of the family firm to his youngest son Albert, then aged thirty. The records show that Jakob Morris Bettelheim, who was then forty-nine, did become his *Gütterdirektor*, or estate manager. Which is logical given that in the meantime he had already been in business as a lumber merchant, and that the Rothschilds owned vast forests.[13] As regards the Rothschild bank itself, it was not Jakob Morris but one of his sons, Richard, who was later to hold the post of *Prokurist*, or officer with power of attorney.[14]

At about the same time Jakob Morris was elected to the honorary title of *Kommerzialrat*, and thus became a member of the Chamber of Commerce. His residence was one of the fine buildings on Glockengasse, a street in the well-off part of the second district. In 1859 he married one Eleonor Frankl, who was twelve years his junior and who came, as he did, from Pest. Bruno Bettelheim often expressed admiration for his grandmother, who underwent no fewer than sixteen pregnancies to produce eleven children, all but one of them boys. Morris, the eldest child, was fifteen when the old Baron Rothschild died and Anton, Bruno's future father, was five. Born on April 4, 1869, at a time when Jakob Morris was still a lumber merchant, Anton was apparently the Bettelheims' fifth child.

He too was to go into the lumber trade. For when Anton was fourteen tragedy struck the family with the death of his eldest brother Morris in a duel.[15] Morris had been a law student, and duels were common at the university. 'I did not bring up my sons for them to be killed by *goyim*,'[16] Jakob Morris exclaimed, according to his grandson. As a result, he decreed that no more of his children would attend university, thus crushing Anton's hopes of an education.

The story does not tell whether or not Morris Bettelheim knew Theodor Herzl, who some twelve years later was to found the Zionist movement, but it is quite probable. The two were the same age, they had the same roots – the Jewish bourgeoisie of Budapest – and both were studying law at Vienna University. At that time, the early 1880s, the city's students were particularly affected by the rising tide of anti-Semitism which accompanied the influx of Jews into Vienna. It was not long before Jewish students found themselves banned from taking part in duels and from membership in the main student clubs. Theodor Herzl's first awareness of his own Jewishness is generally believed to have been sparked by these developments.[17]

In this *fin-de-siècle* period, anti-Semitism was on the rise all over Europe. Berlin saw a long series of anti-Jewish riots, and in 1880, when

Nietzsche's brother-in-law called for a special census of Jews and their eviction from all teaching and civil service jobs, he was able to collect 250,000 signatures in a matter of weeks. In the same year the first mass anti-Semitic parties were born in Vienna. They were the Pan-German party, whose leader Georg von Schönerer, a small landowner from the Tyrol, was both anti-monarchist and anti-Catholic, and, more importantly, the Christian Social Union of the wildly popular and very populist Karl Lueger, known to his supporters as 'handsome Karl'. In 1897, the latter was to be triumphantly elected mayor of Vienna, after Emperor Franz-Joseph had tried twice to veto his appointment.[18] In the meantime, the Dreyfus scandal in Paris had served as a reminder that, even in the country which had once promoted the emancipation of the Jews, they had not yet become ordinary citizens.

While both Morris Bettelheim and Theodor Herzl were busy pursuing law degrees, the future playwright and novelist Arthur Schnitzler was studying medicine, the other discipline open to Jews at Vienna University. His autobiographical notes show very clearly what kind of impact the rising tide of hatred must have had on the first generations of post-assimilation Jews, who had been raised in a world as far removed as possible from *shtetl* traditions. To have their ethnic origins suddenly and brutally thrown in their faces was a shattering experience for young people who had grown up Viennese through and through, bourgeois, liberal, progressive and in most cases atheist. In an opening commentary on his diaries,[19] made some years later, Schnitzler was to write:

> In these pages a lot will be said about Judaism and anti-Semitism, more than may at times seem in good taste, or necessary, or just. But when these pages may be read, it will perhaps no longer be possible to gain a correct impression (at least I hope so), of the importance, spiritually almost more than politically and socially, that was assigned to the so-called Jewish question when these lines were written. It was not possible, especially not for a Jew in public life, to ignore the fact that he was a Jew; nobody else was doing so, not the Gentiles and even less the Jews. You had the choice of being counted as insensitive, obtrusive and fresh; or of being oversensitive, shy and suffering from feelings of persecution. And, even if you managed somehow to conduct yourself so that nothing showed, it was impossible to remain completely untouched; as for instance a person may not remain unconcerned whose skin has been anaesthetized but who has to watch, with his eyes open, how it is scratched by an unclean knife, even cut into until the blood flows.

Although the metaphor is clearly drawn from Schnitzler's medical studies, the statement is all the more striking when one considers that it was penned some two decades after the university diaries themselves. Obviously, the distinguished man of letters that Schnitzler had by then become, fêted in all the best salons and enormously fashionable, had been marked for life by these experiences of youth.[20]

The Vienna into which Bruno Bettelheim was born, twenty years after the death of his uncle, had made ambiguity towards the Jews into a fine art, although unlike Schnitzler, many of them preferred not to notice the fact. It was indeed the Vienna of legend, described by the pamphleteer Karl Kraus as the 'weather station of the world's end', a plurinational ferment of thought in which all the great ideas that were to haunt the twentieth century were being tried out and refined, under the benevolent yet autocratic rule of an ageing monarch. But if Jews, half-Jews and converted Jews were preponderant among the prime movers in this 'Joyful Apocalypse',[21] that fact was due much more to their own desire for assimilation than to any acceptance of that process on the part of those around them.

Some, like Arthur Schnitzler, Sigmund Freud and Theodor Herzl, accepted their own Jewishness while rejecting Judaic ritual as something from another age, while the likes of Gustav Mahler, Hugo von Hofmannsthal or Karl Kraus considered that they had put their origins behind them by converting to, or marrying into, Christianity. All may have believed that their science or their art transcended the contingency of their origins. Yet in the eyes of their compatriots they were still seen first and foremost as Jews, whatever was said openly. And at the end of the nineteenth century, it was being spelled out more and more often.

This phenomenon is studied in a considerable body of remarkable works, not least Carl E. Schorske's *Fin de Siècle Vienna*, or William Johnston's *The Austrian Mind*,[22] and a detailed examination would be beyond the scope of this biography. But Jewishness, anti-Semitism and 'ghetto thinking' all loom too large in Bruno Bettelheim's life and work for us to ignore what life was like for an assimiliated Jew growing up in Vienna in those days.

There is no doubt that Bettelheim's feelings about the city of his birth were shot through with a deep ambivalence, for which anti-Semitism was the main reason. The idealized image of the city projected in *Freud's Vienna*[23] contrasts harshly with the many disillusioned and even cruel remarks he made to friends and also, when on visits there, in interviews and lectures.[24] In a review of Ernest Jones's biography of Freud, written in the 1950s, Bettelheim states that 'Freud's supposed "hatred" of Vienna was probably the expression of a deep early love that became frustrated by anti-Semitism in the early twentieth century, a frustration the more keenly felt as the earlier love was never given up'.[25] It is not difficult to see how much of his own feelings the writer is putting into this passage, especially if one compares it to the rags-to-riches stories of his two grandfathers, which Bettelheim chose to include in the same book.

As Arthur Schnitzler notes, the specific type of anti-Semitism experienced in turn-of-the-century Vienna was neither social nor economic in nature. In spite of the huge wave of immigration sparked off by the constitutional reform, the fundamental issue was not a question of population thresholds, of Jews suddenly becoming too visible in the imperial capital. It is true that some politicians exploited such fears, which no doubt played a role in the election of the explicitly anti-Semitic Karl Lueger, much supported by small shopkeepers. But for Jews born and bred in Vienna during this period, that was not the main problem. However unpleasant it may be, such 'economic' racism is not sufficient to explain why their self-image became so distorted as to turn many of them, in the eyes of many writers, into typical sufferers from 'Jewish self-hatred'.

Much more important, it seems to me, was the interaction during that period (from around 1880 to 1920) between the types of questions that artists, writers and philosophers were asking in Vienna and the content of anti-Semitic discourse itself. The latter was not yet purely race-based, as it was to become later in the twentieth century: 'I decide who's a Jew,' Mayor Lueger was fond of saying. Nor was anti-Semitism founded purely on religion, in that strongly rationalistic and positivist era – even though the charge that Jews had murdered Christ was used to express it.

The main accusation levelled against the Jews did not so much relate to who they were or what they believed in as to the way they thought, and even the way they felt. Against a backdrop of rampant nationalism, they stood accused of being a rootless, 'cosmopolitan' group.[26] But above all the anti-Semitism of the period, co-opting an ill-digested version of Nietzsche's ideas, painted a picture of the 'Jewish mind' as the great corrupter of the valorous Germanic soul.

Many anti-Semites of the period found inspiration in the way Richard Wagner, towards the end of his life, took to decrying the influence of 'Judaism in Music'.[27] The composer ascribed what he saw as 'the sterility of the age in musical art' to 'the Jewish mind', for which he stated his 'invincible antipathy'.[28] *Fin-de-siècle* anti-Semites attacked Jews both for being over-sensitive and for harbouring negative ideas. Their principal defect in their eyes was not the shape of their noses but their habit of always asking questions. That was what anti-Semites saw as the corrupting feature, depriving the German people of its natural vigour, of the strength that only a direct relationship to the earth could foster. The charge concealed a measure of admiration, and in the case of Wagner one could even say of jealousy. Anti-Semites imagined that Jews possessed superior powers of handling abstract concepts, which when added to their supposed gift with money, made them all the more 'dangerous'. Their influence was seen as insidious, and their intelligence as aimed only at undermining what others had built – as befitted a people with no fixed roots, living in a state of perpetual exile.[29]

The period was one of great upheaval in all fields of thought, with philosophers and scientists questioning the blithe certainties that had provided the very foundations of nineteenth-century thought. Belief in progress, reason and science was under attack. Vienna was not the only city in which this process was taking place, but it was one of its main centres, with artists and scientists joining in a quest which found its most complete expression in Robert Musil's book *The Man without Qualities*.[30]

Most of all, in Vienna, this effervescence in the world of ideas took place against the backdrop of the break-up of Europe's oldest empire. By contrast, Berlin was at the same time the capital of a rapidly expanding state, while France had weathered the disasters of the Napoleonic wars without losing its national identity. The Viennese, however, looked on helplessly as the various peoples of Austria-Hungary drifted apart. Only now did they realize to what an extent those peoples had served to define their own identity. Changes which elsewhere were giving birth to *La Belle Epoque* or *Art Nouveau* in Vienna took on the appearance of an 'apocalypse'.[31]

Nothing seemed certain any more. The philosopher-physicist Ernst Mach, whose lectures were attended not only by fellow scientists[32] but also by writers and even artists, had undermined the very foundations of what passed for objective knowledge by questioning the distinction between subject and object. Some two decades later, others would question language itself. In the meantime Sigmund Freud had further shaken the foundations of rationalism by showing how, behind Descartes' 'I think therefore I am', the ego was no more than a lid keeping down a seething mass of impulses and repressions.

The empire was coming apart at the seams, and so was the individual. Light itself broke up into a mass of dots on canvases, and the human soul had been exposed as an explosive cocktail of contradictory forces. What is inside and what is outside? Where are the limits between me and the world? How does one know about reality? Can I trust my senses? Is there any truth except in words? Human identity seemed less and less sharply defined; even the frontier between the sexes was being thrown into doubt. Man or woman, who am I? And what exactly is an Austrian – a German, a Moldavian, a Moravian, a Ruthenian?

For anti-Semites, one thing at least was clear: the fact that such questions were being asked was the surest sign that the culture had fallen under the baleful influence of the Jews. That idea is quoted as the reason why the American racist Stewart Houston Chamberlain chose Vienna as his home in 1889 while completing his *Foundations of the Twentieth Century*. Jews certainly made up a high proportion of the actors in this intellectual revolution,[33] and the reasons for that have been studied elsewhere.[34] Our concern here is to understand how all this could affect a young Jew born and raised in the city at that time. To see how a world that was apparently filled with excitement and stimulation, teeming with potential role models in all avenues of intellectual and artistic life, could at the same time appear to confirm the expressions of contempt and even hatred that were part of his everyday life.

Bruno Bettelheim came into the world on Friday August 28, 1903. At that time the autocratic director of the Vienna Opera was one Gustav Mahler, who as everyone knew was a converted Jew. Emil Steinbach, another convert, was shortly to be appointed president of the Supreme Court, while at the Burgtheater the talk of the town was Arthur Schnitzler's play *Reigen*. The star literary commentator in the *Neue Freie Presse*, the city's great liberal newspaper, was Theodor Herzl. Ernst Mach was not Jewish. But the origins of Sigmund Freud were well known, as were those of the other great agitator of the period, Karl Marx, although he did not live in Vienna. Last but not least, there was the talented essayist Karl Kraus, who bitingly satirized all of the above. He also was Jewish, although he devoted much of the space in his wildly popular newspaper to attacking his fellow Jews.

It was by no means uncommon to find Jews themselves joining in the chorus of anti-Semitism. A key reason for this was the mind-set that went along with assimilation, which by definition involved rejecting all outward signs of religious identity as being backward and anti-progressive. To which can be added psychological reactions, of fear, shame or anxiety, sparked by reminders of ancestral traditions which, long since rejected by one's parents, were only heard mentioned in negative terms. Although they are rare, traces of such suffering can clearly be detected in the writings of Bruno Bettelheim.

In an article dated 1963 on the subject of race relations in the United States he wrote: 'In Vienna there was a "Carl" with whom I walked to school every day, who was my friend, and who nevertheless suddenly hit me one day, announcing that we were quits from now on because my people had killed Jesus. There were the boys who extorted money: who beat us if we handed it over because we were dirty cowards, and who beat us if we didn't, because we were miserly Jews ... It was the natural fate of the Jew.'[35]

This incident appears to have taken place around 1910, a time when, according to most historians, the wave of anti-Semitism in Vienna had subsided somewhat (it was to reach new heights in the closing years of World War I). For those of us whose only experience of anti-Semitism is the watered-down form in which it has been forced to express itself since the discovery of Hitler's extermination camps, an effort of imagination is required to understand the powerful effect it could have on a child at that time. Particularly one who had hardly emerged from the protective cocoon of his family, and who had been all the less prepared for the shock because his parents had invested heavily in trying to put their Jewishness behind them and become assimilated. It was a shock that each individual had to deal with as best as he or she could, and the process of adaptation could easily lead to what, since Theodor Lessing, has been widely referred to as 'Jewish self-hatred'.[36] It should also be noted that the discovery of the anti-Semitism that pervaded the world outside the family was likely to affect the image a child had of his father.

Self-hatred can take many forms, but all result from the young Jew's attempts to dissociate himself from the negative image projected by the anti-Semites. The paradox being that by so doing he to some degree makes that negative image his own.[37] As a result he finds himself, consciously or unconsciously, mounting an attack on everything inside himself which seems 'Jewish', everything that serves to remind him of his forebears' past existence in the *shtetl*. Some young people's way of dealing with the problem led them to affect elaborate dress, and even become dandies, as was the case for both Herzl and Schnitzler. Others would adopt a superior, condescending tone when speaking of their orthodox brethren. But almost all were especially concerned to achieve perfect mastery of German. For 'Jewish patter' had indeed come to symbolize all the imagined defects associated with Jewishness, as can be seen in the following passage from *The Man without Qualities*, in which Count Leinsdorf says:

I have a banker, of the Mosaic faith of course, whom I've been seeing regularly for years. And at first his intonation always used to bother me a bit, so that I couldn't quite keep my mind on the business in hand. The fact is, the way he talks is exactly as if he were trying to convince me he's my uncle. I mean it's just as if he'd only got out of the saddle a moment earlier or had just come in from a day's grouse-shooting, exactly the way our own sort of people talk, if I may put it that way. Well, to cut a long story short, now and then when he's carried away he can't keep it up, and then, to make no bones about it, he falls into a very marked Jewish sing song. It used to bother me a great deal, as I think I said before, because, the point is, it always happened at the most important moments from the business point of view, so that I couldn't help waiting for it, and finally I became quite incapable of paying attention to what he was saying or else simply believed I was listening to something important the whole time. But then I found the way to get round it. Every time he began to talk like that, I simply said to myself: Now, he's talking Hebrew. And I only wish you could have heard how attractive it sounded! Positively enchanting. The point is, it's a liturgical language. Such a melodious chanting – I'm very musical, you know – in a word, from then on he had me lapping up complicated calculations in compound interest or discount positively as if he were at the piano singing it to me.[38]

This passage sums up perfectly the 'benign' anti-Semitism of the enlightened aristocracy of the period. Jewishness here is a question of accent, of music, money and complicated interest-rate calculations. The subtext being that Jews, while talented people, should above all refrain from

trying to ape their betters. Count Leinsdorf has just been railing against
civil servants, whom he blames for 'a piece of impertinence' aimed at the
old nobility in having assigned aristocratic names, such as Rosenberg,
Rosenthal, Löw, Glelb, Blau or Rot, to Jews once emancipation made such
registrations possible. He adds that 'The whole so-called Jewish question
would disappear in a twinkling if the Jews would only make up their
minds to speak Hebrew, go back to their old Hebrew names, and wear
Oriental garb.'[39]

This was of course the exact opposite of what many Jews desired, just
as the majority of aristocrats had no longer any intention of confining their
daughters to convents. Indeed, when Franz-Joseph had granted Jews
their civil rights he had made it clear that they were perfectly justified in
striving to blend in with the mass of their fellow Austrians. Half a century
later, however, it had become obvious that this was not going to happen,
even though many Jews had achieved positions of great prominence.

In some cases 'Jewish self-hatred' could lead to extreme reactions, as
was shown by the case of the young writer-philosopher Otto Weininger.
His suicide in August 1903, a week after Bruno Bettelheim's birth, was to
send a shock-wave through Vienna's intelligentsia.[40] Weininger, a pure
product of Vienna's Jewish bourgeoisie, was to achieve spectacular yet
posthumous success with his *Sex and Character*, an adaptation of his
doctoral thesis which was to run through no fewer than twenty printings
between 1904 and 1920. He had for a while frequented the 'Young Vienna'
school of writers, before rejecting their ideal of 'art for art's sake' as
evidence of a decadent culture. Then, aged only twenty-three but already
fêted as an up-and-coming writer, Weininger abruptly underwent a mystical conversion. He opted not for the Catholicism of Austria and the
Hapsburgs, however, but for Protestantism, the creed of Kant and the
all-conquering Prussians. A few weeks later, the tortured young man
rented the house in which Beethoven had died, located in the Schwarz-
panierstrasse (a few hundred yards from where it changes its name to
become Berggasse, the street Freud lived in) and went there to put a bullet
through his head.

Sex and Character is a work that sums up many of the anxieties of the
age. For Weininger, the decadence and instability that he detected all
about him had two causes: the predominance of what he called the
feminine principle in Viennese society, and the influence of Jewish ways
of thinking. Weininger saw bisexuality as being the basic nature of all
individuals, and argued that human existence on both the individual and
the social levels was governed alternately by the masculine or the feminine principle.[41] The latter, characterised by sensuality and what Freud
was to call the pleasure principle, was the common fate of mankind. To
transcend it required renunciation, mental power and even genius, the
masculine qualities which alone could save society from decadence. As for
the Jews, they basically had the same effect as the feminine principle,

sapping the foundations of society with their mercantile and hedonistic ethos. The main difference between the Jews and women being, as Poliakov notes, that for Weininger women at least believed in something, i.e. in men, whereas the Jew was totally devoid of any beliefs whatsoever.[42]

Otto Weininger is cited by many authors as the epitome of 'Jewish self-hatred'. It is however too extreme a case to provide a clear understanding of the overall phenomenon which affected practically all the assimilated Jews of the period, even those who were apparently the most well integrated.[43] Nevertheless *Sex and Character*, a work which drew grudging admiration even from some, such as Sigmund Freud, who were most shocked by it, at least had the merit of clearly defining the terms of the problem: mind-body, man-woman, Jew-Gentile (the term 'Aryan' was not yet in use in this context). With, in the background, the idea of a redeeming nature characterized by authentic roots and virile regenerative power, as opposed to the 'bestial' nature of the woman and the Jew. Such ways of defining humanity were to leave their mark on all the Viennese Jews of the period. Bruno Bettelheim was no exception.

Like Schnitzler, Bettelheim was fully aware of the prevailing anti-Semitism, and made no attempt to play it down. He nevertheless displayed a tendency to choose his anti-Semites. In his above-mentioned review of Ernest Jones's biography of Freud, for example, he in particular criticizes the author for having failed to point out that 'the leading aristocracy was strongly opposed to the lower-middle-class anti-Semitism of Lueger'.[44] While it was true that the Viennese nobility tended in general to be more open to the upward mobility of Jews than the petty bourgeoisie, this was no doubt because they felt much surer of their status and privileges. As is shown by Musil's character, their anti-Semitism would reappear whenever they perceived that some Jew, however rich, talented and intelligent he might be, was trying to be like them. Even in the world of the arts, where the great Jewish families had gradually taken over the role of patron formerly played by the aristocracy, admiration expressed by non-Jews for Jews was rarely devoid of undertones. This can be clearly seen in the diary of Alma Mahler,[45] the daughter of the then-famous painter Emil Schindler, who moved in the very best circles. Even though she was twice married to a Jew, and could not in any way be suspected of 'active' anti-Semitism, she at several points lets slip expressions of irritation at what she calls 'the Jewish mind', or 'Jewish music'. Such comments are reminiscent of those made by her idol, Richard Wagner. It is also significant that her husband Gustav, when writing his application to become head of the City Opera, considered it necessary to state: 'Given the current situation in Vienna, I feel it is worth pointing out that, in line with a long-standing plan, I converted to Catholicism a long time ago.'

Several critics have detected traces of self-hatred *(selbsthaß)* in the tone used by Bettelheim to criticize 'ghetto thinking', the lack of initiative shown by Anne Frank's father, or more generally the passivity shown by traditionalist Jews in the face of the Nazi threat. Others have noted that when Bettelheim decided to begin a psychoanalysis, he chose Richard Sterba, one of the very few non-Jews among the analysts then practising in Vienna. And yet others have expressed indignation at the fact that, even though many of the students at the Orthogenic School were Jews, the institution celebrated Christmas but not the Jewish religious holidays.

All these signs certainly show that Bruno Bettelheim felt a degree of ambivalence about his Jewishness. Depending on one's point of view, they can be read as indications of liberal thinking or as evidence of an implicit rejection of his origins. At no point during his life, however, did he ever deny his Jewishness. He accepted that he had been born Jewish, and continued to do so very explicitly until the end of his life, when it was unfashionable, and even when it was dangerous. In 1987, in an interview published at the time when Kurt Waldheim was elected president of Austria, Bettelheim was quite candid about it: 'I think that, if it hadn't been for Hitler, Austrian and German Jews would have been assimilated within three or four generations ... Freud, in his optimism, believed that religion, that illusion, would eventually disappear completely. But on the other hand he wrote *Moses and Monotheism*. Here you have all the ambivalence of the assimilated Jew. You can't get out of it; you are Jewish.' 'What about you, did you ever want to get out of it?' 'No ... in fact, no. That's what I am, that's my history, my evolution. As a psychoanalyst, I know very well that one can never free oneself from one's parents.'[46]

Bruno Bettelheim's parents showed little or no interest in Judaism and according to him they never set foot inside a synagogue. In the Jewish section of Vienna's main cemetery, the tombs of both Anton and Jakob Morris are extremely simple, and bear no inscriptions in Hebrew. However both do feature a small, elongated jug, which is the symbol of the Levys, the second tribe of Israel and the servants of the temple. Although Bruno Bettelheim can hardly have had any influence over the tombstone chosen for his grandfather, who died before he was born, he must have had some over that selected for his father, of whom he was the only son. That small symbol is therefore also to be taken into account when assessing the complex relationship Bettelheim had to his own Jewishness.

There is another significant clue, even though it relates to a memory evoked by Bettelheim towards the end of his life, and then almost in passing. In an article written in 1987, and then included in *Freud's Vienna*, he confirms how the pain and injustice felt by young Viennese Jews as a result of the regular irruption of anti-Semitism in their lives were aggravated by the fact that they knew so little about Judaism. Brought up to be 'just like anyone else', they had but a dim understanding of the reasons behind the attacks made on them.

Discussing the books that had most influenced his life, Bettelheim relates how in late adolescence he discovered the works of Martin Buber, a Zionist writer who was both agnostic and mystical, and who favoured

Jewish-Christian dialogue. Buber had been raised in an ultra-orthodox family of Hassidic Jews, and while he rejected all the dogmatic aspects of their faith, he strongly believed that it was necessary to preserve Jewish culture in the form of its myths, i.e. the stories that circulated in the *shtetls*. A large part of Buber's work consisted of recording those stories. This is what Bettelheim wrote about him:

> As I tried to fight free of the world of my parents, more haphazardly than by design, I encountered books by Martin Buber which told about the world of the Hasidim, a world as strange and exotic as those in the utopian novels I read during my efforts to escape reality. But this was a world of my ancestors, and yet not even a glimmer of it was left in the life of my parents, although they were barely two genera-tions away from the world about which Buber was writing. Because of the assimilated life of my entire family, all I knew about being a Jew was that I and my closest friends, most of whom were also Jewish, had to suffer from the taunts, the rejection, and occasionally the open aggression of some of our gentile schoolmates and even some of our teachers. Now suddenly, my Jewishness had a positive content.[47]

Chapter II

One Big Family

Those who, like Korczak, single-mindedly devote themselves to making this a better world for children are usually motivated by their own
unhappy childhoods. What they suffer then makes such a lasting
impression that all their lives they try to come to terms with it by
working to change things so that other children will not have to suffer
a similar fate.

Bruno Bettelheim, lecture on Janusz Korczak, published in
Freud's Vienna and Other Essays

Anton Bettelheim was nearly twenty-nine years old when, in February
1898, he wed Pauline Seidler, who had just turned twenty. It was an
arranged marriage. He was then employed in a sawmill, where he was
completing his training as a wholesale lumber merchant.[1] Whatever the
truth about Jakob Morris's fortune, it is clear that he saw to it that his
sons were not spoiled. It is difficult however to gain any very clear idea of
the surroundings in which Bruno Bettelheim spent his early childhood,
since unlike most middle-class Viennese at the time, who were resolutely
sedentary, his parents seem to have moved house a great deal in those
early years.

At both the time of their marriage and that of Bruno's birth, Pauline
and Anton Bettelheim are listed as living at number 3 Rampengasse, in
the nineteenth district. But when their daughter Margarethe was born –
between those two events – the Jewish community records a different
address, in the more elegant third district. There follow another two
locations, one in the fifth and the other in the seventh, with the family only
settling down in 1911, by which time Bruno was almost eight. One possible
explanation for this multiplicity of abodes could be the severe financial
setback that Anton suffered at the start of the marriage, when he lost his
wife's dowry in an ill-inspired lumber trade investment. Another explanation could have been the real estate activities in which Adolf Seidler was
getting involved at the time of his daughter's marriage.

Rampengasse, the street in which Bettelheim was born, is a tiny alley
giving on to a small footbridge over the Danube Canal just above Leopoldstadt. The street's location between the river and a railroad line suggests
a possible link to the lumber trade practised by both Anton and his father

before him, but this could not be confirmed. The neighbourhood was razed during the war, and is now home to warehouses.

As an illustration of just how stable and influential a place Vienna was at the time of his birth, Bettelheim harks back to the sixteenth century and the reign of the Hapsburg emperor Charles V.[2] The imperial city which he describes, with its serenity, comfort and warmth, irresistibly conjures up the opening passages of Stefan Zweig's *The World of Yesterday*: 'When I attempt to find a simple formula for the period in which I grew up, prior to the First World War, I hope that I convey its fullness by calling it the Golden Age of Security. Everything in our almost thousand-year-old Austrian monarchy seemed based on permanency, and the State itself was the chief guarantor of this stability.'[3]

Paula, as Bettelheim's mother was known to everyone in the family, brought Bruno into the world on August 28, 1903. The birth occurred at home, as had been the case four years earlier for Bruno's sister. The young mother was 'comforted and helped in her labour by a midwife', as her son was later to write.[4] Bettelheim added regretfully that to his knowledge, he was the last member of the entire family to have been born in such surroundings, far from the antiseptic atmosphere of a medical institution. As was common in bourgeois families at the time, the baby was handed over to a wet nurse. She was a German peasant girl who had abandoned her own infant to the care of her mother. According to Bettelheim she was very inexperienced, but the care she gave him was all the more affectionate in that she was often somewhat drunk. She had heard that beer helped keep the milk flowing, he explained.

He would no doubt have preferred to have been nursed by his own mother. Bettelheim was, after all, a strong proponent of breast-feeding, and he was aware of the contradiction. But although he described his wet nurse in one interview as 'a strong-smelling woman, who staggered', and in another as 'a young sexual delinquent', who had abandoned her own child, the overall picture he gives of her in *A Good Enough Parent* is that of an attentive and gentle young woman. He explains that he was her only charge, and that she had a strong incentive to look after him well, as a successful wet nurse would traditionally be rewarded with a generous gift. 'The respect my nurse had for my parents and her happiness at being part of our home (it was very important to my parents that she should be healthy and happy, so that she would have plenty of good milk, and enjoy taking care of me, so she received excellent care) were important elements in convincing me how lucky I was that it was my home.'[5] His mother's social obligations would have prevented her from giving him as much attention as did his nurse, who as Bettelheim notes was 'entirely devoted to my care'.

The overall picture which Bettelheim gives of his first years of life is a happy one, and it is difficult to find, in 400 pages of a book scattered with

personal anecdotes illustrating the upbringing of children, a single incident to show that Bettelheim's own parents were not 'good enough'.[6]

The nurse was to be succeeded by a nanny, and then by maids. But each
time young Bruno fell ill it was Paula herself who took care of him. 'She
spent many hours caring for me and entertaining me, and she fed me all
my meals,'[7] he writes. It was also his mother who told him fairy tales at
bedtime. And if sleep would not come, there would always be one or the
other of his parents to hold him in their arms until he finally dropped off.
If a nightmare woke the little boy up, Paula did not appear worried or
strained; she would go and sit on the side of his bed, talking calmly to him,
playing or telling him stories until he fell asleep again.

Bruno's parents appear to have known instinctively what their son
would later devote so much energy to trying to drill into the minds of his
American audience: that it was their own anxiety, rather than any external event, that was likely to spark anxiety in their children. Bettelheim
recalls, for example, how one night when he was six years old the house
opposite theirs burned down. As the street was narrow, the firefighters
sprayed not only the burning house but all the nearby ones as well to stop
the blaze spreading. Bruno was sleeping in a room at the other end of the
house and his parents, far from panicking, 'woke me up and took me to the
window to watch the unusual and exciting spectacle. Since they were calm
and talked with me about the varying colors and forms of the flames, it did
not occur to me to be afraid.'

Once the fire was over, Bruno went quietly back to sleep, and never felt
worried by what he had seen: 'During the following months, whenever I
left our house I was confronted by the ruins across the street. I never felt
anxious; it never occurred to me that I might have been in danger, or that
our house might go up in flames. All I thought was that it had been a most
unusual experience, and that I had been fortunate to witness it.'[8]

Apparent in Bruno Bettelheim's writings about his infancy, maybe
more than the gentleness and understanding of his parents, is the happiness he felt at belonging to a large family. Later in life one of the main
charges he would level at the American way of life was the way it split
families up. 'I grew up in a big family. My father had ten living brothers
and sisters and my mother had four. And even if everything was not
perfect all of the time, even if there were fights and jealousy, we were a
family. Here, we are very alone, and so are our children,' he wrote in 1980.[9]

Each year, on the occasion of Eleonor Bettelheim's birthday, all her
grandchildren gathered at her house to put on a show they had rehearsed
in secret. Bruno's pride at taking part in the collective effort was to remain
one of his strongest, and earliest, memories.[10] Other favourite moments
came on Sundays, when the Bettelheim family gathered. 'Among the
happiest memories of my childhood are the times when I and the cousins
near my age – we were called "the little ones" – played under the huge table
around which a dozen or more adult members of the family had gathered,

often forgetting that we were literally underfoot. We would play together in the cozy darkness, hidden by the huge tablecloth that hung down nearly to the floor; as we played we listened to the talk and arguments of those we called "the big ones". We and they, each group on its own level, thus had a grand time every Sunday.'[11]

Among Bruno's many cousins was a boy who suffered from schizophrenia. Although he was not dangerous, he spoke and acted strangely. One day Bruno, who saw the boy frequently and was puzzled by his behaviour, asked his aunt what she thought of it. 'Listen, my boy, I have ten children. One out of ten, that's not a bad average,' she replied. Bettelheim saw this answer as a good example of the wisdom often found in the parents of large families, in contrast to the anxieties and obsessions with perfection found in parents with only one or two children.[12]

A large family also offers mutual support. As an example of the latter, Bettelheim cites another of his cousins who 'went astray' when Bruno was a child. 'Naturally this was viewed as a terrible misfortune but, in those times, nobody blamed his parents.' On the contrary, the two dozen or so families that made up the clan got together to provide comfort, and decide what could be done to help the wayward boy. Money was found to send him to the United States, where he could start a new life. The result was that 'encouraged by the unexpected support he had received from so many relatives, my cousin took heart, and soon succeeded where he had failed before. Because his parents had also received emotional support from the wider family when they needed it most, it was easier for them to send their son away with blessings rather than recriminations.'[13]

Twenty years later, things had already changed. When a similar situation arose, the rescue operation no longer involved the entire family, but only those relatives closest to the black sheep (who in this case had not even been guilty of acts of delinquency, but only of an inability to hold down a job, and excessive spending). The relatives involved could not help harbouring resentment against the trouble-maker, who was packed off to South America. In this case, Bettelheim writes, 'This boy's low opinion of himself was not allayed ... [and] he did not manage to do better in the new world than he had in the old.'[14]

Jakob Morris Bettelheim was to die two months after Anton's marriage. His grandson, who therefore never knew him, noted that 'My paternal grandparents were the last members of my family who died at home in their beds, surrounded by all their children. My other relatives died either in hospitals or at home, but neither their children nor their grandchildren were present; the family assembled after they had died for their funerals. Thus the emphasis has shifted from the rite of passage in which the death of a loved one is actually witnessed to the comforting of survivors.'[15]

This nostalgia for old rites and customs, with its idealized vision of large families as clans within which people worked hard and helped one another, in which characters were formed and respect was forged as sons learned their crafts by watching their fathers or uncles at work, can be detected all through Bruno Bettelheim's work. Even at those times when his approach to mental illness appeared at its most revolutionary, and even when, pointing a finger at the negative role played by parents, he would recommend that a child be cut off from all contact with its family for a year or more. As Bettelheim got older the nostalgia came more and more to the surface, and *A Good Enough Parent*, a book which he found very difficult to write precisely because he saw it as a kind of summing-up of his life and work, can be read as a veritable ode to the past. To a time when parents, without needing to ask why, reared their children in line with all the strictures of modern psychology.

This contradiction between a stern and censorious Bettelheim, scourge of possessive and ill-loving mothers, and a man haunted by nostalgia for a time when father and son worked shoulder-to-shoulder, is of course symptomatic of the wounds of exile, which never completely healed. But it also betrays other scars, even deeper and better hidden.

'When I was four years old I nearly died of dysentery at the same time as my father contracted a deadly disease of which he knew that he would die. This projected him and my mother into a state of deep anxiety which was not lost on my sister and me – only she had at least eight good years before it all happened. From this moment on the life of my parents was a nightmare for them which they kept hidden from everybody, even their parents and siblings. But they suffered quietly.'[16]

Bruno Bettelheim spoke and wrote very little about the wounds he suffered in early childhood, referring to them only briefly in private correspondence late on in life, when he could no longer get the better of his depression. He also confided on a few occasions in his children. In two years of research, I unearthed only one letter that refers explicitly to the question, and even that, from which the above quote is taken, omits a key detail. It dates from November 1986, precisely when Bettelheim was busy reading the proofs of *A Good Enough Parent*. He was finding the work rough going, in particular because his publisher was demanding that he make deep cuts. The book, into which Bettelheim had poured a lot of himself, was considered too stern in its prescriptions for an American public.

Dr Carl Frankenstein, to whom the letter was addressed, was a German-born Israeli psychoanalyst and educationalist who late in Bettelheim's life had become a close friend. By the standards of Bettelheim's correspondence the letter is extraordinarily intimate. What is said in it, as well as what is not said, provides a number of clues to the fear, anxiety and suffering that lay behind the idyllic picture of a model Viennese family. Suffering that was no doubt also at the root of the remarkable insight Bettelheim would later bring to bear as a healer of sick children.

First of all, there were all the illnesses. Bruno Bettelheim must have been a sickly child indeed, to judge from the catalogue of maladies he reels off: 'scarlet fever, diphtheria, measles, mumps, and other ailments, not to mention several bouts of influenza and tonsillitis, which kept me in bed for many weeks at a time.'[17] And then there was the above-mentioned attack of dysentery, which was clearly no ordinary illness. 'I remember that as a child of four I was very sick and was rushed to [the doctor's] office where he instantly bedded me down on the couch of his living room, adjacent to his office. In his own home he cared for me for four days and nights, going back and forth between me and his consulting room till the danger was past.'[18]

It is impossible to know for sure whether the young Bettelheim's life-and-death struggle against dysentery really did coincide with his father's discovery that he was suffering from an incurable illness. The essential fact remains that the two incidents were linked in his mind.

'Depressive' is the word most commonly used to describe the Bettelheim household by the very few witnesses still living, all of whom frequented it at a somewhat later date. The sources have very little to say about Paula, other than that she was a warm and caring woman, very protective of her 'menfolk', above all when they were ill. Indeed, Bruno Bettelheim confirms that his mother would on occasion spend the entire night at his bedside, sponging his burning forehead and applying cold compresses.

Bettelheim, frequently sick and afflicted with severe myopia, was certainly a coddled child. His first wife recalled with some irony how, when she spent a summer with the family in the Italian Alps, Bruno's mother would, after eating her own breakfast with her daughter-in-law while her son still slept, carefully lay out his place setting, even putting a cushion on his chair.

Paula Bettelheim appears to have been a courageous woman. She was not yet thirty when she learned that she could at any time find herself widowed with two young children to care for. She nevertheless kept her household going, caring for her sick husband and shielding the children from his ailment. Indeed she faced up to the disaster on her own, refraining from seeking help from her parents. When she visited the latter, which she did almost every day, she acted as if everything was all right, avoiding any mention of Anton's illness. All of which prompted one of Bettelheim's cousins to comment: 'I remember her husband's death was kept secret from my grandparents, because they were old and sick. I don't know who imposed this secrecy on her, but to imagine the cruelty! These types of secrets and hypocrisies were the rule in our families, all in the name of protecting somebody's feelings.'[19]

The atmosphere in the Seidler household was indeed bad enough not to need aggravating by the news of Anton Bettelheim's illness. Adolf Seidler, who remained very rich at least up until World War I, had a truly awful temper. His marriage was an unhappy one, and he bullied everyone in the family so much that, with the exception of Paula, they all fled from him. Although he seems to have been one of their favourites, the young Bruno hated visits to his grandparents' home. Even when the couple were not fighting, the tension between them made him uneasy. His grandmother had gradually taken refuge in violent attacks of asthma, which gave her an excuse, once her children were grown, to flee Vienna and her despotic husband for health reasons for several months each year. The family's younger daughter, Jenny, followed suit, Bettelheim recounted, adding that his aunt's chronic and supposedly serious heart trouble vanished as if by magic once she set foot in the United States!

Adolf Seidler's abiding chagrin was that none of his three sons had a head for business. As Bruno Bettelheim pointed out, if he had not terrorized them so much they might have fulfilled themselves in their chosen fields, which were artistic. Instead of which, Seidler was continually spending large sums to set them up in one business or another, with invariably disastrous results. Thus, in 1908, did he agree to give Anton Bettelheim another sum equal to Paula's ill-fated dowry, on condition that he take his youngest son Rudolf on board as a partner.

Bruno got on well with his uncle Rudolf, who was a great connoisseur of Wagner and the only Seidler son to have made a happy marriage. But he proved to be such a bad businessman that Anton soon began to resent him, the more so in that he was unable to break the partnership. Anton would pour out his bitterness about the situation to his wife; Bettelheim later told his children that although his parents were not very happy together, the only open fights he ever witnessed were those over Rudolf. The partnership was to disappear along with the company, which vanished from the business records at the start of World War I. Later, Bruno Bettelheim would say that his uncles had tried to wrest his father's company away from him after the latter's death.

Information on Paula Bettelheim is scarce. People who knew her in Vienna do not have much to say; in general they portray her as a kind-hearted, discreet and brave woman, but basically as someone who did not count for very much. One recalls that she was a good cook, another that she took to learning Italian late in life. But there is nothing substantial to go on, and no way of distinguishing between what could have been her true personality and the clichés which tended to define women at that time. Housewives and mothers were by definition not very interesting. And yet one would like to know more about the woman behind a man who was later to prove such a stern judge of the maternal function.

At first glance, everything Bettelheim wrote about her appears extremely positive. But a closer examination reveals hints of criticism. One example is the explanation he gives for the fact that he was cared for by a wet nurse. It would appear that no mother anywhere could entirely free herself from her 'social obligations' to 'devote herself entirely' to her baby. But then if Paula had been right to hand him over to a nurse, how could

Bettelheim later so firmly recommend maternal breast-feeding for other children? Then there was a light-hearted anecdote that Bettelheim passed on to his children. 'When I was a child,' he said, 'I was very impressed because, unlike all the other women, who had only a feather or two on their hats, my mother had a whole bird on hers.'

In comparison with the rather colourless picture of Paula Bettelheim one gets from Bettelheim's writings and from the memories of his friends, the image he handed down to his children was one of a woman of character. Paula, who was born sixteen months after Adolf's first son, is shown as very much her father's daughter. A brilliant student, she would have liked to have gone into business, which at the time was the only career avenue open to an ambitious young woman, Bettelheim stressed. For Adolf Seidler, however, the scholastic successes of his daughters (Jenny also was a good student) served only to underline the failings of his sons. He forbade them to carry on with their studies, and married them off as soon as he could. Being a devoted daughter, Paula knuckled under, marrying the man her father had chosen for her and later, when Seidler himself fell ill, going religiously to her parents' home five afternoons a week to care for them. The only breaks in that routine were on Fridays, when she had coffee with her circle of friends, and on Sundays, when the Bettelheims gathered.

The few people who ran into Paula Bettelheim in Chicago, when she went there to visit her son, have memories of a rather imposing, stern-faced lady, with a very strong accent. 'She looked like the queen of Rumania,' says one. To complement a sketchy picture, I have only two other clues. One is the last letter that Paula sent to her son, and the only one he still had in his possession at the time of his death. While its contents are relatively uninteresting, its style is quite remarkable. Written in Old German in a long, spare handwriting that is not unlike Bruno's, it is couched in language of great purity and concision. Paula Bettelheim, behind the role that life thrust upon her, must have been a cultured and intellectually rigorous woman.

The other clue is somewhat at odds with the image projected by Bruno Bettelheim and his friends of a mother concerned above all with the well-being of her children. It was provided by Joan Little, an early counsellor at the Chicago Orthogenic School. Towards the end of the 1940s she had been spending a long holiday weekend in New York, and decided to go with a colleague to hear one of Bettelheim's first public lectures. When he stood up to speak, the two young women, who knew him well from working alongside him every day in Chicago, noticed his nervousness, and his evident embarrassment at his faltering, accented English. An elderly lady entered the lecture hall as he was speaking, and rather than taking the first available seat she walked right across the hall to take up a place in the front row, which irritated Joan somewhat. When her companion whispered to her that the lady was in fact 'Dr B's mother', it occurred to Joan that Bettelheim's relations with her could not have been simple.

As a child, Bettelheim resented the fact that his mother did not care for him more in person. He refers explicitly to this in a letter to the editor of the *New York Times Magazine*, published in 1970 and written in denial of a widely circulated rumour about him. According to the story, Bettelheim, who had gained a reputation as an autocratic professor, had sharply rebuked a student in the front row who was knitting while listening to him. 'Miss, don't you know that knitting is a substitute for masturbation?' he purportedly said. And the young woman shot back: 'Dr Bettelheim, when I masturbate I masturbate, but when I knit, I knit.' In his letter, Bettelheim not only denied the story but also explained the origins of the supposed link between knitting and sexuality,[20] noting that similar anecdotes had frequently been cited about psychoanalysts.[21] He went on: 'But something did indeed happen in one of my classes, when I had just started teaching at the University of Chicago. One young lady was sitting in a front row knitting, which distracted my attention. I pondered whether to say anything about it, but decided that if I wanted my students to acquire self-knowledge, I certainly had to be the first to apply this principle to myself. So I asked her whether she would be so kind as to refrain from knitting in my class, because it distracted my attention from my teaching, due to a childhood experience which I obviously had not yet fully mastered. When [I was] a little boy, my mother often concentrated on her embroideries, knitting, etc., when I wanted her to play with me, or otherwise give me her full attention.'[22]

Bruno's sister, Margarethe, was four years older than him. Sources who knew her then describe her as independent, ambitious, rather spoilt, and subject to mood swings; likely, for instance, to throw a tantrum on receiving a birthday present she did not like. There was strong rivalry between the two children, and their relationship was fraught with conflict. Bruno's best childhood friends were his two cousins, Kitty and Edith. The former, who was the same age as Bruno, was the daughter of his uncle Adolf Bettelheim and the latter, a year older, that of his aunt, Jenny Buxbaum. 'We grew up together like brother and sister,' Edith was to explain shortly before her death.[23] 'His older sister Margarethe did not get along with him at all and wrote me only when she needed me as an ally against him .... But Bruno and I were very close.'

There is now nobody alive to testify to that period in Bettelheim's life, the only available sources being two of his close friends, who visited his parents' home much later on. But the picture revealed is always the same: of an inward-looking, rather mournful household, where the guest would be well received, but where one had to be careful where one trod.

There was also, apparently, some shouting and door-slamming, mostly by Margarethe, but also by Bruno. Although generally calm and reserved, he was prone to sudden bursts of temper which always left him feeling upset. On one occasion, when he was around ten, he found a few coins lying around on a piece of furniture, forgotten there by someone he does not identify. On a sudden whim, he pocketed the money. As he tells the story, Bettelheim spent the remainder of that day 'fearing that the theft would be discovered, and that it would be apparent that I was the culprit, but also hoping it would, so that the matter would be settled'. Twenty-four hours later, however, he put the money back where he had found it. 'I was greatly relieved, but now I wondered more and more why I had stolen it in the first place, since I had had no intention of spending it. I became angry that I had been led into temptation by someone who, moreover, was so careless that he didn't even realize the money was missing. And then, young as I was, I realized that I had wanted to punish him for tempting me, that this had been my motive.'[24]

Another childhood memory reported by Bettelheim in *A Good Enough Parent* throws some light on his relations with his parents. 'I forget what I was annoyed about, but I said something offensive to my mother,' Bettelheim writes. 'She was shocked and hurt, but she said and did nothing. When she told my father about it, he was visibly upset. He asked me in a very firm voice, "Do I really have to punish you for you to watch the way you speak to your mother?" This was all, but it made a deep impression on me, a much greater one, I believe, than any punishment could have made. The idea that he might have to punish me obviously distressed my gentle father. And so I worried, not that I might be punished – I never was – but that I had upset and worried my father to such a degree.'[25]

What is striking about this anecdote is that the only regrets expressed by Bettelheim relate to his father. Although he says himself that his mother was 'shocked and hurt', he does not express any remorse at his 'offensive' outburst. It is almost as if his mother's feelings were of no importance, as if it were assumed that she was strong enough to take it. Whereas Anton has to be protected in his role as the family's moral authority. The same imbalance in Bettelheim's treatment of his parents can be found in practically everything he says about them. Any reference to his mother usually relates to services that she provided him, rather than to their relationship. With Anton, however, the few comments Bettelheim makes give the impression of a cosy and affectionate complicity between father and son. Many of the personal memories that Bettelheim used to illustrate his educational precepts related to his father.

Anton was fond of playing cards. Bruno was often allowed to watch, on condition that he kept quiet, and when his father won, he would share his winnings with his son. On rainy days Anton would occasionally entertain his children by playing card games with them too. On such occasions, even though the games involved were the same ones he played with his adult friends, his attitude would be completely different. It would be 'that of a parent who enjoys what he is doing because it is enjoyable to his children .... When parent and child, each for his very own reasons, are engrossed in the same play, this can form a bond between them that is truly *sui generis*,'[26] Bettelheim comments, in a chapter devoted to the role of play in personality development.

Furthermore, when Bettelheim mentions a mistake his father made, he does not identify him. Of his early interest in carpentry, no doubt to be expected in the son of a lumber merchant, he writes: 'Before I was permitted to build anything ... I had to learn to make perfect joints. It took me a few months to be able to make those joints well. By then I had lost all interest in carpentry, due to the drudgery involved in learning to make joints .... Fortunately, we no longer make such mistakes in teaching carpentry.' The passage is drawn from an article on teaching children to read.[27]

On the rare occasions when Bettelheim refers to his mother, however, the image is flat, inert and frozen. He never quotes her directly, only in indirect speech. In four years, I found only one exception to that rule. It comes in an anecdote which he cited, among other occasions, in 1986, when being interviewed by Geneviève Jurgensen. Although clearly at ease with the former Orthogenic School counsellor, Bettelheim suddenly turned to the photographer, who had been snapping away at him from all angles. 'You are very talented, young man, but that's enough pictures. Don't waste any more film; I'm an impossible subject. When I was born, my mother exclaimed: "Thank God it's a boy!" '

This surprising statement was uttered in the self-mocking tone of one who has resolved to make the best of a bad job, and treats his misfortune as a joke. But the pain Bettelheim was also expressing in the anecdote, which he told consistently although not very frequently throughout his life, stands out behind the humour.

At first sight, for a mother at the start of this century, having already produced one girl, to exclaim, 'Thank God it's a boy!' may not seem remarkable. Particularly coming from the granddaughter of a religious Jew, whose required daily prayers contained the phrase 'Blessed art thou, o Lord our God, who hast not made me a woman.' For Bruno Bettelheim, however, it was clear that the utterance could have only one meaning: a reaction to his ugliness. However he came to know of his mother's sup- posed exclamation, the wound was a deep one, which remained with him until the very end of his life. Eighty-five years after the event, a depressed and suicidal Bettelheim would still be ruminating on what he saw as his unredeemable ugliness when confiding in a fellow psychoanalyst in Los Angeles.

The anecdote also surfaced on happier occasions, however, as in the short speech Bettelheim delivered in 1977, on accepting the National Book Award's prize for Contemporary Thought, awarded for *The Uses of En- chantment*. He said: 'Once upon a time, in a faraway land across the big sea, there was a very old city. Some thought of it as a fairy-tale city .... It bordered on some woods and there, in a little house close to them, many many years ago, a boy was born. His mother had wanted another child, and was very glad .... She was a woman who loved poetry, but she also had a healthy, down-to-earth sense of reality. So when ... her son was shown to her, she took in his appearance carefully and then breathed a deep sigh of relief. "Thank God," she said, "it is a boy."

'This mother told her children many fairy tales. And since they lived at the most remote edge of the German land, she told the tales of the Brothers Grimm, not those of Hans Christian Andersen. Thus the boy never got the idea that an Ugly Duckling could turn into a beautiful Swan. This was fortunate, and saved him from disappointment, because his looks remained very much the same as they had been when his mother first beheld him.'

In 1911, the Bettelheims moved into a spacious and comfortable apartment in Neubaugasse, in Vienna's seventh district. Paula was to remain there until after the Anschluss in 1938. The move came two years after Bruno had started at primary school, at the age of six. 'The first day of school for the child is not just another new experience along the lines of many, often startling ones he has met in the past. Instead, it adds a new dimension to his life, which will never again be the same.'[28]

It was around the same time that Bruno was roughed up by his non-Jewish pal on his way to school.[29] As he stresses in those opening lines of *On Learning to Read*, starting school was above all the discovery of a new world, outside the family. Which in his case meant discovering anti-Semitism. In spite of the fact that his parents were confirmed atheists, Bruno had to follow compulsory religious education classes. Even much later, when he was preparing for his *Matura*, or school-leaving exam, he still had two semesters of religious instruction. Half a century later, on discovering Israel, he found it very difficult to accept that Hebrew could have become a living language.

Bruno Bettelheim was a short, puny, sensitive and day-dreaming child; the exact opposite of a schoolyard toughie. He enjoyed kicking a ball around with his friends, but was no good at sport. Not only did he feel handicapped by his glasses, but they were not much use to him. Being both very myopic and astigmatic, he often did not see the ball until it was too late. He was to find out ten years later that he had not had the right type of lenses; in the meantime he suffered from a permanent feeling of clumsiness. The transition from the cosy world of home to the cold, impersonal classroom environment was a shock. Each evening, he insisted on sitting next to his mother at the kitchen table to do his homework. He was serious and hard-working, a good pupil.

'When I went to school I was taught penmanship in all the primary grades. Now I'd say that my handwriting is, by and large, a little more legible, maybe even a little prettier, than the children we educate nowadays. On the other hand, I didn't get any social studies, and very little natural history. And, you know, I'm so terribly deficient in some of the natural sciences, because the time was spent on penmanship ... the point is that everything has a price.'[30]

Bettelheim was later to come out very strongly against bad ways of teaching children to read and write, centred exclusively on technical skills such as calligraphy rather than on awakening the child's interest in the subject-matter. He himself had suffered considerably from poor and boring instruction as a child. But he had also learned early on how to use his head: 'In former times, when learning to read was much more exclusively the central issue in early education, the main way – often the only way – to gain the pleasure of receiving the teacher's attention and praise was to learn to read well. It was this reward that made learning to read a sensible reason ... to be in school.'[31]

In September 1914, Bruno Bettelheim entered high school, in the form of the Albertgasse *Bundesrealgymnasium* in Vienna's eighth district. It was a mere ten minutes' walk from his home, and next door to the school his cousin Edith Buxbaum was attending. Bruno's new school, opened in 1905, was the most modern in the whole city. Unlike the five 'noble schools', as the most exclusive Vienna institutions were called, the *Bundesrealgymnasium* stressed forward-looking subjects such as mathematics and foreign languages. There were so many Jews among its students that after World War II, when the school principal tried to round up information on former alumni, he found that entire classes had been wiped out.[32]

There were no fewer than fifty-four pupils in Bruno's class, among them Hans Willig and Walter Neurath, who in spite of Hitler and exile were to remain among his closest friends until the end of their lives. But he hated the *gymnasium*. German-style education, with its overcrowded classes, its harsh discipline and its authoritarian and needlessly boring teaching methods, would become for Bettelheim the symbol of how not to teach children. He was also to come out strongly against the tendency of many parents to push their children at school, turning them into exam-passing machines to the detriment of their overall maturity and the development of their critical faculties.[33]

Plans for educational reform were indeed being aired at the time Bettelheim was at school. The general cultural upheaval underway in Vienna, including advances in psychology and psychoanalysis, had led many intellectuals to start looking at education from a point of view which nobody had previously considered: that of the child itself. The process was to lead in 1918, when the Socialists took control of the city council, to a vast reform aimed at making schools more accessible to all layers of the population, banning religion in all its forms and catering to the child's personal development as well as to its intellectual performance.

That was still some time in the future, however; but already the reform movement was causing ferment in circles close to the Social Democrats, and particularly in youth movements, of which there were many in Austria at that time. Bruno Bettelheim was in his early to mid teens[34] when he joined one such organization, the *Jung Wandervogel*, literally, 'young migratory bird', at the suggestion of Hans Willig and Edith Buxbaum. The main activity was hiking and picnicking in the forests and mountains around Vienna on Sundays. This above all provided an excuse for the young people to talk, and much of the talk was about what kind of world lay in wait for them. Although the *Jung Wandervogel* had been born in Germany as a conservative and nationalist group at the turn of the century, in Austria it was very close to the Social Democratic Party. This meant, as Bettelheim himself stresses,[35] that it was pacifist (World War I was by then in full swing), socialist and anti-monarchist. He adds that the group was relatively small, with membership varying between fifty and a hundred.

Why did Bettelheim and most of his friends plump for the *Wandervogel*, a group which on its foundation in 1901 had explicitly declared itself to be *Judenrein*, or 'cleansed of Jews'? No doubt because the only alternative for young socialistically inclined atheists like them were the Zionist movements, and they were assimilationist. Sundays with the *Jung Wandervogel* played an important role in the lives of Bettelheim and his friends. The long outings were an opportunity for intense discussion, and also for the first contacts between young men and women outside the family setting. They saw their love of the great outdoors and the simplicity of their clothes as a form of rebellion. 'Our locus for emancipating ourselves from our parents,' Edith Buxbaum would write later. The jolly element in Bruno's group was Walter Neurath. 'Hans and Bruno were the serious types,' recalls the woman who would later become Hans Willig's wife. 'They spent all their time talking.'[36]

While Sundays were spent discussing how to change things, notably through Socratic ideas of teaching based on respect for the individual, weekdays at the *gymnasium* were given over to dealing with the all-too-real world. In the first year Bruno came top of his class, while the next year he was outdistanced by his friend Neurath. The only really serious act of insubordination committed by Bettelheim during his school years – one that produced 'such a deep impression on me that it has stayed vividly in my mind for the more than sixty-five years which have passed since'[37] – occurred around his fourth year at the *Bundesrealgymnasium*. 'I was a very good student, a quiet, introspective, even subdued youngster. But one day the behavior of one of our schoolmasters, which I had found annoying all along – as had most of my fellow students because it was so unlike that of all our other masters, past or present – provoked me so much that suddenly, without forethought. I laid hands on him and, with a couple of other boys, whom my example enticed to help me, pushed him out of the classroom. As soon as we had accomplished it, I was shocked by what I had done; it was so unlike my usual behavior in school and out. I only knew that I had felt so outraged that I had had to do something; but of what triggered my action, what motives other than rage had been at work in me, I had not the slightest idea; nor did I know what had caused my rage.'

The chapter in which Bettelheim relates the above anecdote is entitled 'The Question "Why?" ' In it, he stresses that parents are often wrong in insisting that their child should explain a shocking attitude or action. The reason for this is that 'there is always the possibility that the child doesn't know his reasons, as I didn't (in this case).'[38] However strange it may seem, any action on the part of a child always has a meaning, and it is always the best response that the child is capable of giving at that particular time and in those particular circumstances. That idea was indeed to become the cornerstone of his teaching and work as a therapist.

Fortunately for the errant schoolboy, the principal did not demand that he explain his extraordinary act, nor, to his great surprise, did he expel him. Neither did Bruno's parents ask the reasons for his attack on the teacher, at least as far as Bettelheim could remember when he wrote about the incident. Instead, on the evening after the event, and before he knew that he was off the hook, they had a calm talk with him on where he could go if he had to select another school.

The following morning the principal showed up in the classroom, which was a rare occurrence. The whole class was made to stand to attention while the principal gave a short, sharp speech, singling out Bettelheim, but also the companions who had failed to hold him back, for harsh criticism. Bruno was particularly wounded at hearing himself described as a hypocrite, on the grounds that he had always behaved like such a good boy. Indeed, up until the incident with the teacher his behaviour record had been exemplary. But then, instead of the expected punishment, he was astounded to hear the principal acknowledging that the teacher in question was simply not up to the job. 'Tomorrow you will stay for two hours, after school, working on your own on studies which Dr X should have made so interesting that there would have been no place for such behavior,' he concluded.

Bettelheim was understandably relieved, and also impressed by the principal's ability to admit to having made a mistake. He nevertheless spent most of the following night wondering what he would have said if he had been asked to explain his act. He simply could not comprehend what had got into him. It was to be a quarter-century before understanding would finally come – on a psychoanalyst's couch.

To return to Bettelheim's letter to Carl Frankenstein, after referring to his own dysentery and to his father's illness, as well as the oppressive silence that had descended on the household, the writer comments: '... Part of the trouble was that our parents were good parents and tried to shield us from the family tragedy, which meant that we could not be angry at them.... When I was thirteen, my father had, as a consequence of his illness, a severe stroke. He could not move or talk for nearly two weeks. Another trauma for me who at this age did not understand what went on. He recovered to some degree, but lived the next ten years as a wreck till he died when I was 23, much too early for me ....' Even in this unusually intimate letter to a close friend, written as late as November 1986, Bettelheim could still not bring himself actually to name his father's illness. Two years later, however, depression had won out over discretion.

The scene takes place on November 24, 1988 in Los Angeles, a city which epitomized everything Bettelheim hated about America. He saw it as the capital of superficial glitter, of show business and psychoanalysts for movie stars, of egotism and slavery to the sole god of money. He was now living there alone; he felt physically diminished and was obsessed by thoughts of suicide. Connie Katzenstein, one of his former Chicago students who had since become a therapist, was fully aware of Bettelheim's condition, as she regularly accompanied him on outings, to the doctor or sometimes to concerts.

Worried at seeing the old man so miserable, she tried to cheer him up by inviting him to her Thanksgiving dinner. This well-meaning gesture was to be a disaster from the outset. Bettelheim proved unable to clamber up the steep wooden stairs leading to her house and had to be half carried up by Connie's husband, which enraged him. He found himself wondering what on earth he, who normally loved meaningful celebrations, was doing at this party, far from his own children and surrounded by people who knew practically nothing about him, except that he was an ageing celebrity. Bettelheim, seated in front of the huge turkey of which he was unable to partake due to an ailing oesophagus, glowered and remained obstinately mute. Connie Katzenstein, seeing her star guest casting a pall over the proceedings, was at her wits' end.

After a while, when he had repulsed a number of attempts to get him involved in the conversation, the other guests carried on talking without paying him much attention. Almost inevitably, the conversation drifted towards the number-one fear of the moment: Aids, and how to protect oneself from it. It was then that Bettelheim's gruff voice suddenly boomed out. 'I was four years old when my father found out that he had syphilis. For the next twenty years, he never touched my mother again. Aids patients can do the same thing!'

Leaving the old man aside for a time, let us imagine the thirteen-year-old, just out of bed and set to leave for school, running as usual to say goodbye to his parents and finding his father silent and inert, unable to understand or even recognize him. Then fighting back his fear and leaving for the *gymnasium*, to spend the day acting as if nothing had happened, telling no one. How much pain was tied up in that dinner-table growl!

Anton's condition remained stable for a week after that attack, and then it began to improve. The family doctor, the same one who had treated Bruno for his dysentery and for whom the boy had the greatest respect,

then told him that if his father recovered, he would be able to lead a
more-or-less normal life for a further ten years.

At thirteen,[39] Bruno Bettelheim had obviously not been told that his
father's illness was the most terrifying affliction of the age. As he would
later explain to others, however, a child always understands whatever his
parents think they are hiding from him, particularly when it causes them
anxiety. Thirteen is an age when one does not know much, but when one
can guess a lot. A time when ignorance only amplifies the fears generating
from a budding sexuality. It is an age at which the reproachful silence of
a mother and the ill-disguised guilt of a father can lead one to imagine the
worst.

This was especially true for a boy brought up in bourgeois Vienna at the
start of the twentieth century. One need only flip through a few pages of
Stefan Zweig's memoirs – his generation was half-way between that of
Anton and that of Bruno – to realize to what extent the blanket censorship
of all things sexual served only to sharpen young people's curiosity and
fantasies. In the Middle Ages, sexuality had been seen as 'the sting of the
devil', Zweig wrote, noting that this was at least a form of recognition of
sensual desire. But the enlightened bourgeoisie of late nineteenth-century
Vienna no longer believed in the devil. 'A silent pact was reached, by which
the entire bothersome affair was not mentioned in school, in the family, or
in public, and everything which brought its existence to mind was sup-
pressed.' Nothing could be more effective in stirring a young man's
curiosity than this clumsy attempt at suppressing human nature. 'There
was scarcely a fence or a privy that was not besmeared with obscene words
and drawings, hardly a bathing pool in which the wooden wall of the
women's quarters was not bored full of peepholes …. "Art" and nude
photographs in particular were offered to half-grown boys for sale under
the table by peddlers in every café ….'[40] Not to mention the dimly-lit
backstreets just behind the glittering Ring, where, if one bumped into an
acquaintance, one pretended not to recognize him.

In such an atmosphere, the fear of syphilis was never far from anyone's
mind. The disease was widely seen as a form of divine punishment visited
upon sinners. Vienna's suburbs were dotted with small clinics in which
middle-class families hid their afflicted members. The shame was all the
greater in that in its terminal phases syphilis causes disfigurement and
madness, brought on by paralysis of the brain. Is it really conceivable that
Bruno Bettelheim, a sensitive and observant child who was clearly imbued
with the moral values professed by his family, could not have suspected
what was the matter with his father? Particularly given that Anton often
had to return to hospital, since his treatment was not proving effective.[41]

In a syphilitic's home, the fear of contagion meant obsessive concern
about such things as 'a badly-washed towel, toilet seats, razor-blades, cups
and cutlery … coins that one holds in the mouth, and all the daily gestures
of household and working life, such as using spittle to clean a small child's

face, or simply kissing. Scientific treatises were dotted with warnings about such things,' notes one historical work on the subject.[42] Worse, experts were at that time wondering very seriously whether syphilis, which was known to cause progressive degeneration of the central nervous system, was not hereditary. This idea had already found its way into popular songs and literature, which depicted mentally retarded and malformed children on whom had been visited, in a literal sense, the sins of the fathers. Indeed in 1914, two years before Anton suffered his first major stroke, the Ministry of War had decreed that the French play *Les Avariés* (literally, The Damaged Ones) by Eugène Brieux should be performed in all the empire's military academies. The play's theme was transmission of the disease from parents to their offspring.[43] It should also be borne in mind that as a child, Bruno Bettelheim was frequently sick.

For how long did he know the truth without being sure of it, hope against hope that he was mistaken, without daring to confide in anyone? There can be no definitive answer to that question, although some impressions may be gleaned from the texts he was later to write about adolescence. For example: 'Like adolescents, we must all learn to live in a continuous state of insecurity.'[44] When discussing the awakening of sexuality that accompanies puberty, Bettelheim saw it as a mistake to believe that the adolescent was simply frustrated at not being able to fulfil his or her desires immediately. 'The truth is that most adolescents are terrified by anything grossly sexual,' he wrote, adding that what the adolescent needs above all is reliable information. Because what the young person does not know, he will seek to find out. And 'the starting point for this sex exploration is unfortunate; since he was not told, he is not supposed to know. Therefore he feels guilty about his attempts to learn.'

Bettelheim cites two types of pathological reaction to the anxieties generated by puberty, exemplified by the 'rigid' and the 'explosive' adolescent. The former strives to deny the existence of his inner struggle, while the second, refusing to grow up, chooses to let his tensions burst out. He recommends that such adolescents be encouraged to dominate their problems intellectually. This, he writes, will avoid them being 'immediately overwhelmed by [their] conflicts'. At the same time, 'intellectualization ... gives [the adolescent] the prestige and strength of ego that he badly needs'. He adds that the required intellectual effort can take several forms, which may include day-dreaming. But whatever the form, it is better than trying to act out the problems. 'Thinking strengthens the adolescent's ego, while action usually weakens it by defeat because he cannot yet act successfully with regard to his most pressing problems.'

Bettelheim made no mention of his father's syphilis in any of his books and articles.[45] He told his son that his father had been infected by a prostitute one summer while his wife and children were vacationing in the Alps: certainly the least unacceptable type of explanation he could have given the young man. Prostitution, to quote Stefan Zweig, was indeed the 'dark underground vault over which rose the gorgeous structure of middle-class society with its faultless, radiant facade'.[46]

As for the effect the uncertainty and suspicions about his father's ailment must have had on Bettelheim, one can note the vehemence with which he was later to denounce the hypocrisy of Vienna and its bourgeoisie. It was a city in which, he once wrote, it was common to see little mirrors suspended outside the windows of middle-class houses, allowing their occupants to observe what was going on in the street without themselves being seen![47] Or the following anecdote: 'When I was a young man of good intentions, I objected to legalized prostitution. But my Victorian father told me: "It is these girls who protect nice women like your mother from the danger of being raped." ' '– But not from the worst of all venereal diseases!' one could imagine the young Bettelheim thinking. As he gives no date for the conversation, his actual response remains unknown. It is certainly no coincidence, however, that this anecdote should be cited in an article entitled 'Children should Learn about Violence',[48] aimed at warning parents against giving their children an over-idealized, sugar-sweet view of the world.

Bruno Bettelheim was clearly deeply attached to his father, a man who was described by all those who knew him as very charming, kind and gentle. How could this love cohabit with the perception of the syphilitic man as 'a web of desire, shame, confusion and even of despair'?[49] Without being able to document it, I suspect that Bruno Bettelheim derived much of his own intellectual ambition from Anton. The latter had no doubt regretted never having received a university education (why otherwise would he have handed down Jakob Morris's stated reasons for depriving his younger sons of such an education?). But even on the intellectual plane, the father-son relationship must have been undermined by fearful doubts. Syphilis, which was very widespread in literary and artistic circles at the end of the nineteenth century, was often presented as a mark of genius by those who suffered from it.[50] This myth gained currency from the symptoms of the disease itself, which in its later stages could include 'intellectual exaltation, ideas of grandeur and hyper-activity'.[51]

In the light of the above elements one cannot but wonder how much of himself Bettelheim put into his portrait[52] of the great Polish educator Janusz (Henryk[53]) Korczak. Below the passage reproduced at the start of this chapter, he writes: 'In all external respects, little Henryk's early life was spent in very comfortable circumstances in the well-to-do upper-middle-class home of his parents. Yet he was familiar with emotional difficulties from an early age on – his father held often grandiose and unrealistic notions of the world, and had a poorly-developed ability to relate to reality.' '... When Henryk was only eleven years old, his father began to suffer from serious mental disturbances, which eventually required his placement in a mental institution. He died there when Henryk was eighteen years old .... From then on, Henryk had first to contribute to the family's livelihood and later to provide for it.'[54] The two men's early lives had enough in common for Bettelheim to have been tempted to identify with the admirable Korczak, who had passed up the opportunity to escape from the Warsaw Ghetto in order to stay with the little orphans he looked after there, and thus died with them at the Nazi death camp of Treblinka. According to Korczak's American biographer, the educator suspected that his father may have been suffering from syphilis.[55]

Bettelheim's first bout of serious depression came shortly after he had witnessed the sudden and dramatic aggravation of Anton's condition. But being his mother's son, the young Bruno knew how to keep up appearances and go through the motions of normal life. He kept on going to school and seeing a few friends; he even got good grades. He 'functioned', as he was later to tell his children, but mechanically and joylessly. On returning home from school he would shut himself up in his room and spend hours sitting in darkness doing nothing. As he recalled, he was not suicidal but simply depressed, convinced that life had nothing to offer him. He was to remain in that state for between eighteen months to two years.

It could well have been around the age of fifteen, i.e. at the time he situated his apparently inexplicable outburst of rage at the incompetent schoolteacher, that Bettelheim began consciously to formulate his suspicions about his father's illness. This is the explanation he was later to give for the classroom incident, based on his analysis. 'Dr X had been a simpering fool who spoke with the voice of a eunuch,' Bettelheim writes. 'We boys were at an age when we had anxious doubts about our budding masculinity and needed suitable masculine figures with which to identify. Dr X, far from offering a suitable image for identification, increased our anxieties that we might not make it as male adults; he presented us with our worst fears about ourselves.' The anxiety was aggravated for the young Bettelheim by the recent attack of paralysis suffered by his father. He was therefore 'confronted with the possibility – as the only other male in the family – that I might have to step into my father's shoes. This was a terrifying prospect to an insecure teenager already wracked by doubts about his masculinity and afraid he lacked male assertiveness .... My father's severe illness ... made me fear that I might turn into someone like Dr X. This was an intolerable thought.'[56]

A father who did not touch his wife for twenty years (one wonders how Bettelheim came across that piece of information!), a teacher whose castrato voice made his lessons unbearable, and a young man whose mother had not only told him on numerous occasions that he would soon be called upon to shoulder his father's responsibilities, but who treated him as though this was already the case.[57] To anyone schooled in Freud's ideas, this is probably enough to explain the depression into which Bettelheim plunged, and his anger. But there is no need to delve into the Oedipus complex to understand what Bettelheim is trying to say when he refers to the 'personal bent' that lay behind his interest in autistic children: 'What first disturbed me and aroused my interest in these children was how deliberately they seemed to turn their backs on humanity and society.'[58]

That oppressive society, laden with hypocrisy and prejudices, was deeply mistrusted by its young people. 'A single untruthfulness on the part of teachers and parents inevitably leads a young person to regard his entire surroundings with a suspicious and therefore a sharper eye,' noted Stefan Zweig. And such adolescent crises 'brought about an awakening in another sense: for the first time it taught us to observe more critically the social world in which we had grown up, and its conventions,' he added.[59]

Trapped between a family tragedy made worse by its shameful secret and the rigours of an authoritarian teaching system that stressed intellectual abstraction above all, Bruno found solace in books, becoming an insatiable reader. It so happened that one of his best friends, Walter Neurath, also entertained doubts about his own father. His mother lived openly with her lover in the family apartment, while Neurath's father slept in a separate room on the same premises. Amid such contradictions the younger generation dreamed of a better, more just and joyful world, in which people's actions would be at one with the principles they professed. Neurath was soon to become a militant Marxist. Bettelheim was more of a sceptic. Along with adventure stories, he devoured history and philosophy books.

'Personal experiences within my family and my adolescent turmoil combined with a terrible war to make me feel deeply pessimistic about life and myself.' In the light of what we know of Bettelheim's childhood, his essay entitled 'Essential Books of One's Life' is a moving document.[60] 'The belief in progress which my parents had instilled in me, and which the teachings of history in school had solidified could not be maintained in view of what was now happening in the world,' he adds, going on to explain the influence that the works of Theodor Lessing, F.A. Lange and Hans Vaihinger had on him. From Lessing[61] he learned that 'history is not an account of man's progress over time, but that this progress and the meaning of historical events are only projections of man's wishful thinking.'

In Vaihinger's *The Philosophy of 'As If'*, however, Bettelheim discovered that his own pessimism, far from being only destructive, could in fact give him the moral strength to go on living. Lessing, Bettelheim writes, had taught him to see fiction as a means of making life bearable, and to bet on the hypothesis that the cosmos did have some kind of order. Vaihinger showed him how to use hypotheses that he knew to be false to help him act.[62] 'Together these two authors provided the guidance I needed most of all: how one may manage to live a meaningful life despite one's inner doubts,' he writes.

To defeat the causes of suffering by the sheer force of intellect; to literally make sense of whatever happened to him and his environment, through the greatest joys or the sharpest pain: such was to be Bruno

Bettelheim's main mental activity from that point on. As he writes in the opening pages of *Surviving*: 'In times of trouble, ... it seems that if we could just grasp life's deeper significance, then we would also comprehend the true meaning of our agony – and incidentally that of others – and this would answer the burning question of why we have to bear it, why it was inflicted on us.' Each time his 'inner doubts' would get the better of him, suggesting a gloomy, pessimistic view of events, he would call on his moral sense, or if that failed him on his imagination, to nevertheless find a positive interpretation and pass it on to others. He would go on doing so until age and solitude overwhelmed him, and he could no longer keep up the effort.

It was at about this time that he first discovered Martin Buber and his Hassidic tales. This was probably no coincidence: Buber's tales must have both awakened his interest in the Jewish traditions that his parents had rejected and helped him interpret some of the harsh realities of his everyday life. Not only did they provide him with a sense of belonging that had eluded him up until then, but they also echoed, in a more realistic tone, the beautiful and reassuring fairy tales that his mother used to tell him. Indeed, the gap between fairy tales and Jewish stories is not all that great. Simply remove the princesses' crinolines and replace the princes' castles with the narrow streets of the *shtetl* and you will find the same cast of characters: wise old men and foolish youngsters, witches bent over their cauldrons and pretentious young girls. Take out some of the miracles and replace them with a good measure of humour, and you will find that the moral is often the same.[63]

The Bettelheim drama was being played out against the backdrop of a much larger, worldwide, disaster. Bruno was not yet fourteen when, in June 1914, Archduke Franz Ferdinand was assassinated in Sarajevo. A month later the aged emperor, his uncle, was obstinately and arrogantly to strike the first blow in a World War of which his own empire was to be the first victim. The loyalty of the empire's Jews to Franz Joseph was such that, along with most other Austrians, they blindly supported his foolish obstinacy. They subscribed massively to his war loans and gladly accepted mass mobilization.[64]

A mere two years later, when the emperor breathed his last in the same Schönbrunn Castle in which he had been born eighty-six years earlier, the atmosphere was very different. The empire's industrial backwardness had proved a terrible handicap right from the first months of war. Military defeats were piling up, while production was sagging dangerously for lack of manpower. The unresolved national questions sapped the morale of the imperial troops, while galloping inflation undermined that of the civilians. While there were still many Jews to turn out for the emperor – in this case to attend his burial at St Stephen's Cathedral on November 21, 1916 –

many of them, including both Anton Bettelheim and Adolf Seidler, had by then been ruined by the collapse of the Austrian war loans.

'That my father lost a great fortune at the beginning of World War I did not improve matters, because up to then he was convinced that even if he died soon, his family would be well off. 1914 changed all that,' Bettelheim wrote in the 1986 letter to his friend Carl Frankenstein.

The empire began to break up well before the end of the war, and the death of the emperor, who had been the last symbol holding the disparate entity together, hastened the process. One by one the Czechs, Slovaks, Serbs, Croats, Poles and Italians were to break away, either to found new states of their own or to seek incorporation into other existing states. By 1919 Austria had become a huge head with no body left to keep it alive. Here is how a French encyclopaedic periodical described it: 'What is now referred to as "Austria", since the secession of the Czecho-Slovaks and the Yugo-Slavs, since the Hungarian Revolution, is a modest entity of six million inhabitants, too small for a too-large capital, submerged in central Europe and left to its own devices. [Austria is thus] almost unable to survive. Ruined, with no trade or industry, threatened with Bolshevism, it will only survive if it is given a status which provides it with outlets and reliable protection.'[65]

Starting in the autumn of 1918, Vienna suffered full-scale famine. Its citizens had consumed 900,000 litres of milk daily in 1913; in 1919 the figure was a mere 100,000. In October 1918, rations for each Viennese amounted to a mere 40 grams of fat and 1 kilogram of potatoes per week, and a few months later even that meagre hand-out had been cut back by half. Bread was so adulterated as to be practically uneatable, and a loaf cost fifteen times more than before the war. There was no coal at all, and only half a litre of kerosene weekly per household.

Like other Viennese families, the Bettelheims shivered with cold throughout the winter, and had to spend hours waiting in line to buy even a tiny loaf of bread. In the early days of the war Anton had been able to get food from the countryside via his business connections, but with the advance of the Russian troops, who burned down sawmills and cut the roads to Vienna, the supplies ended. The family now inhabited a hungry world of anarchy and *sauve-qui-peut*, in which the legend of Vienna as a beacon of civilization was but a distant and absurd memory. The following incident, reported in the *Reichpost* newspaper on April 19, 1919 during a period of social unrest, gives a good idea of the deprivation suffered by the city's inhabitants: 'During a wave of shooting, a policeman's horse was hit, bringing the animal down and wounding the policeman in the process. In the wink of an eye, the crowd rushed at the fallen horse, and a sailor finished it off with his knife, encouraging his fellows to help themselves to a cheap roast. The horse was instantly torn to pieces by the crowd, with men and women fighting over the remains. A few minutes later people could be seen running away, clutching still-fuming chunks of meat.'

For Bettelheim, the chaos in the world outside could not but amplify the conflicts he felt inside himself. 'It is hard to revolt against a parent whose whole world has suddenly fallen shattered to pieces. Revolt is the less avoidable because the adolescent feels even more betrayed at suddenly realizing that the parent he thought an oppressive but protective hero is just a clay god. He can no longer test his new values against those of his parents ... All of a sudden, he feels deprived of the firm support, not of his parents but of the values they instilled in him; and this happens just when he needs them most as a safe harbor from which to venture on his new and anxious moves into semi-adult independence.'[66] Bettelheim was often to write that his father never recovered from the ruin into which the First World War plunged him. And, even worse, that he had never been able to grasp the fact that a page of Austria's history had been turned, and that the world in which he had grown up was gone for ever.

Up until the end of his life, Anton Bettelheim was to seek compensation for the losses he had suffered during the war. But the provinces conquered by the Russians had in the meantime become Communist, and he was never to recover a single cent. He did not however throw in the sponge. In January 1919, with famine still raging in Vienna and strikes paralysing all of southern Austria, Anton Bettelheim registered a new wholesale timber company, with himself as director and a new partner in place of his brother-in-law: a certain Hans Schnitzer, aged twenty. Their offices and warehouses were located at number 3A Gaudenzdorfergürtel in the twelfth district, on the main road leading to Graz. It was there, at the age of twenty-three, that Bruno would later step into his father's shoes.

Meanwhile, Bruno's outings with the *Jung Wandervogel* did him a lot of good and helped him over his depression. Led on by his cousin Edith Buxbaum, who had now become his constant companion, he started taking a keen interest in the social and political situation. He lost his fear of public speaking, and was even to head one of the discussion groups to which the *Wandervogel* gave rise towards the end of the war. The young people, fired by concern for the new world that would necessarily emerge from the ruins of the old, discussed everything: politics, art, literature and even sex. Unsurprisingly, they saw peace as the number one precondition for accomplishing their aims. Bruno Bettelheim would later tell his son how in his early teens he and his socialist friends had gone out to greet soldiers returning from the front with pacifist slogans, asking them to hand over their guns. I was not able to ascertain whether this story was true, or whether Bettelheim was attributing to himself a role played by one of his friends. In spite of what he said later, however, my impression is that Bettelheim was never really a political activist.

The monarchy was not to survive the war. On October 17, 1918, Emperor Charles I, grand-nephew and heir to Franz Joseph, signed a document transforming Austria into a federation of national states. On October 21, the German members of the *Reichrat*, or parliament, declared a 'Provisional National Assembly of the autonomous State of Austrian Germans' *(Deutschösterreich)*, considering themselves to have the same right to self-determination as the Poles, Czechs, Slovaks and other nationalities. On November 11 the emperor abdicated, and the next day the Provisional National Assembly declared an Austrian German Republic. Executive power passed to a twenty-three-member Council of State.

For Bettelheim and his peers, the fate of that other great pre-war European empire, Czarist Russia, at the hands of the Bolsheviks served to underline all the more starkly the dramatic collapse of the old world. Soon, with shortages spreading, the situation in Vienna was explosive. In general, however, Austrians were not much given to violence, and their strain of socialism remained a moderate one. Having chosen democracy rather than revolution, the Austrian Social Democrats agreed to take part in the new coalition government, and it was even one of their number, Karl Renner, who was to head it. Social reform was to get under way even before the holding of the first republican elections. Legislation was passed to create an eight-hour working day and a system of unemployment benefit, and to ban child labour.[67] And then in December 1918, the government embarked on the major plan for educational reform that Bruno Bettelheim and his friends had been dreaming of.

But prejudices still ran deep, and since 1916 anti-Semitism had been on the rise again. During the war, Jews were accused of avoiding combat;[68] after it they were held to be profiteering.[69] Eternal scapegoats for society's ills, they found their situation made even more difficult by the sudden arrival in Vienna of some 100,000 dispossessed *Öst Juden*, Jews who had fled the empire's eastern provinces before the advancing Russian troops. Unlike preceding generations of immigrants, these new arrivals had come against their will, seeking not assimilation into Viennese society, but simply a safe haven.

Providing an easily identifiable target for the anti-Semites, the new arrivals could not have come at a worse time from the point of view of the Viennese Jews, whose contradictions and fears were thus heightened even more. They often counted among the most pro-German of the 'Austrian Germans', and indeed some of them firmly believed that only by uniting with Germany could Austria become a modern state.[70] Most of them felt nothing whatsoever in common with the new arrivals. The latter were religious, while most of the Viennese Jews were free-thinkers, and they observed customs which the Viennese considered medieval. Not even their language united them: most Viennese Jews considered German their natural tongue, and even Theodor Herzl had never imagined the inhabitants of his planned Zion speaking anything else. Nevertheless, when in 1919 *Landeshauptmann* (regional governor) Sever, caving in to pressure, ordered the expulsion of the *Öst Juden* immigrants from Vienna,[71] the young Bruno Bettelheim, who had only recently discovered the world of the Hassidim in the works of Martin Buber, could not but have felt concerned.

Outside, a world bursting apart like a rotten fruit, shedding seeds that could promise a better future, but still reeking with the stench of old prejudices. In the family home, an unmentionable disaster, with a father who fought courageously against irreversible physical decay to go on supporting his family. Such was the environment in which Bruno Bettelheim completed his secondary schooling, not before plunging once again into depression, although only for a short time, at the age of seventeen. The spring of 1921 found him revising for his final high school exams in the company of his cousin Edith and her best friend, Annie Pink. He helped the two girls with their mathematics; the following year, at university, Edith was to repay the debt by helping him with his Latin. On July 12, 1921 Bruno Bettelheim received his high school diploma, the *Matura*, with good grades. He had done very well, receiving 'honourable mentions' in German, mathematics, geography, English and French.

When asked the inevitable question – 'What do you want to do later?' – he replied, 'Philosophy.' As if he was leading an affluent, trouble-free life, and expected to have all the time in the world to read, study and become a distinguished man of letters.

Sixty-five years later, however, he was to sum up the story of his childhood as follows, in his letter to Carl Frankenstein: 'My parents obviously suffered, and tried their very best to be very good parents, tried even to make up for it all to us. So we could not blame them, and if we occasionally questioned their depressive way of life, we had to feel guilty because they were good parents, tried to be, beyond their ability caused by conditions.

'... So there you have the story of my life, and also the explanation why I could devote it so single-mindedly to work strenuously to help children overcome the damages their childhood experiences did to them.'[72]

Chapter III

Gina

Gina Weinmann, née Altstadt, cannot remember exactly where she first met Bruno Bettelheim. At an exhibition, a concert maybe. ... What she knows for sure, however, is that she was never at any time in love with him. 'He was always homely, you know,' she says, almost apologetically, 'but I liked his voice, his manners ....'[1]

He was maybe nineteen, and she two and a half years younger. They shared a passion for beautiful things, art and theatre. She was impressed by his culture, intelligence and lordly manner; he was fascinated by this slight young woman with exquisite legs, and could sense an independent mind and sharp judgement behind her apparent frailty. Petite, coquettish and always impeccable, Gina was more than pretty, she had class. She was also proud, neurotic, demanding and something of a tease. Totally under her spell, he showered her with gifts, took her everywhere, introduced her to all his friends and thought only of winning her heart.

It was not the first time Bruno had been in love. In *Freud's Vienna and Other Essays*,[2] he refers to a girlfriend he saw on outings with the *Jung Wandervogel*. As he would later confide to his friend Wanda (who was to marry his friend Hans Willig), her name was Lisl Lazarsfeld,[3] whose elder brother Paul was at the time a rising star in the Social Democratic youth movement.[4]

One Sunday towards the end of the war a former *Wandervogel* member named Otto Fenichel joined the group. Five years older than Bruno, he had just been demobbed in order to complete his medical studies and was still wearing his uniform. Fenichel, who was to become a star of the psycho-analytic left, quickly attracted a circle of admirers within the group by explaining Sigmund Freud's lectures, which he was attending at the university. One attraction was his readiness to analyse his listeners' dreams.

Bettelheim was dismayed to see that Otto Fenichel appeared to hold a particular fascination for Lisl Lazarsfeld. At the same time, he could not but be intrigued by the dream interpretations offered by the young man, which were mostly sexual. The subject made him feel ill at ease. Yet the issue of sex education was central to the debate on education. 'Only the transformation of sexuality can remedy our contemporary and crippled situation,' Fenichel wrote at about that time. 'Affirmation of oneself means affirmation of one's sexuality.'⁵ For Bruno and his friends, these principles remained somewhat abstract: although 'committed to sexual freedom in theory', Bettelheim acknowledged, they practised a good deal of self-repression, justifying it by 'the principles of a superior morality'. No doubt this was particularly true of a young adolescent convinced of his own ugliness.

That night Bettelheim went to bed deeply troubled, filled with jealous hatred for his rival and contempt for psychoanalysis. The next day, however, he recalled adopting a more positive attitude. No sooner were his morning classes over than he rushed out into the maze of streets behind the Vienna Opera House to the Deuticke bookshop, which published the works of the Psychoanalytic Society. He emerged weighed down with as many of Freud's books as his pocket-money would buy, notably *The Psychopathology of Everyday Life* and *Jokes and their Relationship to the Unconscious*. Plus, as he was interested in art, Freud's studies of Leonardo da Vinci and Michelangelo's Moses.

That first contact with psychoanalysis had a sinful feeling to it: 'I soon realized that my Victorian family, although personally acquainted with members of the Freud family, would be utterly shocked to find me perusing such obscene literature. My solution was to hide it from them by taking it to school and reading it there surreptitiously while I was supposed to be attending to studies which, by comparison, were utterly boring.'⁶

Within the week, Bettelheim writes, he had devoured the lot, and thus felt armed the following Sunday to face up to Fenichel for the attentions of his beloved Lisl. Only to hear the latter brusquely declare that one weekend of psychoanalytic chat had been enough, and that now she felt like talking about something else. Bettelheim does not tell us the rest of the story, simply noting that 'The young lady and I lost our romantic interest in each other a while later, but remained good lifelong friends.'

Unsurprisingly, the purpose of this anecdote was not to illustrate Bettelheim's early romantic life but to explain how he first came to Freudian theory. 'One week of complete concentration on psychoanalysis and I was hooked for life,' he concluded.⁷ Of this, more later. To return to his emotional life, it should be noted that although he freely discussed sexuality, he rarely mentioned his own experiences. Such coyness was not restricted to his writings: his two daughters were only to learn in the late 1950s, by which time both were adolescents, that Gina Weinmann, that old family friend who was married to one of their father's colleagues and who regularly spent Christmas and Thanksgiving and on occasion even vacations with them, had been the first Mrs Bettelheim, married to their father for ten years!⁸

When the two met, Gina Altstadt was living on Burggasse, not far from the Ringstrasse and just behind the former imperial stables. She lived with her mother and her brother Leopold, who was three years her senior. Her father, a good-looking man who enjoyed life and doted on his daughter, had only recently died of tuberculosis. Gina had then been a little over fourteen.

The following summer, her mother had taken her on vacation to the Dolomite mountains. There she had met and fallen madly in love with a young would-be painter named Dolf. Art, breathtaking landscapes, long walks in the woods, and a first love affair: all the ingredients needed to help a wounded young girl overcome the pain and anguish of losing her father. She spent hours lying in the grass, watching Dolf paint and dreaming of a world of beauty.

But the return to Vienna was to bring her down to earth with a bump. At the Fine Arts Academy, to which Dolf had just been admitted, his teachers recommended that he devote himself entirely to painting. At least that was the reason he had given her for his decision to break off the relationship. There could have been other considerations, such as social differences, or her Jewishness; Gina can't remember. Like many Viennese Jews, she does not much like to discuss such things.

She remembers meeting Bruno shortly after the end of that unhappy love affair, which had come so soon after her father's death. Gina was depressed; she was living in what she describes as 'a fantasy world'. She whiled away the hours day-dreaming and embroidering on the balcony, incapable of taking an interest in real life. But she had a true love of music. Her brother, whom she much admired ('he was very handsome, you know'), played the violin. So she was elated when the father of her friend Lotte, an infant prodigy who had been giving piano recitals since the age of thirteen, offered to let her follow the same music lessons. Gina was only too happy to drop out of the Langegasse high school she had attended until then to follow this new path. She had no thought for her future, or rather she had only dreams.

Life was anything but easy for the Altstadt family. Unlike the Bettelheims, who by this time had been settled in Vienna for two generations, they were relatively recent arrivals. Gina herself had been born on Christmas Eve 1905, in what was then known as Lemberg and which is now Lvov, one of the main cities in Ukraine. Lemberg was Austrian up until 1918, and as such was the capital of Galicia, a region in the farther reaches of the empire which the Austrians, Russians and Poles had always fought over. It was a garrison town, so prized by Austrian officers for its elegant social life that they had dubbed it 'Little Vienna'. It was also one of the main centres for the religious, ghetto-dwelling *Öst Juden*, who were looked down on by most of the Viennese Jews.[9]

Gina's parents, however, were assimilated Jews, who spoke Polish and German and lived in the Austrian part of the city. She never heard her parents speak Yiddish, a tongue she viewed with some disdain as a corruption of German.[10] Later in Vienna, when she was to visit her grandparents in the Leopoldstadt neighbourhood, she was to have the same irritated reaction on hearing her grandmother refer to non-Jews as 'others' and even 'enemies'. 'Some of my classmates weren't Jewish, but that didn't make them "enemies",' she comments.

Max Altstadt, Gina's father, was the eldest brother in a large family. She was only two when he left for Vienna, at the request of his youngest brother Moritz, who was considered the financial genius of the family. She recalls waiting for Max's return in the courtyard of their home, all dressed up with a blue ribbon in her hair. She above all remembers her mother's sadness. Mina Alstadt was a former seamstress, very pretty and sensitive but from a much poorer background than her husband. She probably attributed his departure to her own lack of formal education, Gina believes. She does not know whether her father had a mistress in Vienna, but she does have a vague memory of certain photographs of him displayed on her grandparents' sideboard which showed signs of having been carefully cropped – as if the image of somebody else had been cut out.

When she was five, however, her father sent for the family – herself, her brother and her mother – to join him in Vienna. She was not to see much more of him than before, however, since Moritz, who had become a rich shoe manufacturer, had asked Max to go and manage a factory in Bohemia. This was around the beginning of World War I. Gina could recall marvellous moments spent with her father, but they were few and far between. She had no doubt that he loved her mother, but she could also understand his need for something different, to go out, have fun and meet friends in cafés to play cards. All of which he did, while his wife stayed in to run the home and keep open house for her many brothers-in-law. Then one day Max Altstadt came home with a bad cough. The doctor diagnosed pleurisy, and Gina remembers the damp towels her mother applied to help him breathe. Later he was in hospital, where she visited him. One day Max announced that to really get better, he would have to go to Italy. Shortly afterwards her mother too left, to attend him on his death-bed, but Gina stayed behind in Vienna. She never saw her father again.

When Bruno Bettelheim met Gina, he was more worried than ever about the condition of his own father, though he hid his fears even from his closest friends. In September 1921 he had fulfilled his desire to become a university student. But at the same time, only a few days after receiving his *Matura* (high school diploma), he had also enrolled in the *Hochschule für Welthandel in Wien*, or international trade school, to study management. For it was becoming more and more obvious that he would soon have to take Anton's place as the family breadwinner.

In *Freud's Vienna and Other Essays*, Bettelheim recounts a strange memory concerning Freud's apartment building on Berggasse. The latter, he writes, 'is a dull and undistinguished street in a nondescript part of the ninth district of Vienna. And what goes for the street also holds true of number 19 ... As a young man I used to walk by the building, more often than not choosing to use this hilly, unattractive street to where I was going only because Freud lived there. Upon looking up at his quarters, I always wondered why this great man chose to live there, when Vienna had so many other streets that were either more attractive in themselves, had more beautiful buildings, or at least offered charming or historically interesting vistas.'[11] Bettelheim goes on to explain how he eventually realized that the location of Freud's residence in a certain way reflected the latter's life story. It was half-way up the Berggasse, a long street which runs from the banks of the Danube up to the university and some of the city's best neighbourhoods, on the hill. The lower end, Bettelheim explains, started in a flea market area mainly inhabited by poor Jewish pedlars, not far from Leopoldstadt, where Freud's parents had lived. The top half represented Freud's career: the university and the affluent homes of many of his patients.

A clever explanation, but what struck me most about the passage was the condescending tone used by Bettelheim when referring to Freud's residence. For although Berggasse 19 is indeed a clearly middle-class building[12] – the previous tenant of Freud's apartment had been the socialist leader Victor Adler – it does not seem much different in terms of social standing from the one which the Bettelheim family then inhabited in the eighth district. On discovering that the *Hochschule für Welthandel* was situated almost straight across the street from Freud's home, I better understood the ambivalence of Bettelheim's tone. This probably had much less to do with Freud's social standing than with the frustration of a young man who after nurturing great academic ambitions found himself obliged to study accountancy and management. And what Bettelheim presents as a voluntary detour was simply the route he had to take every day to get to his classes. But in one way it must have felt like a detour; one that he had been forced to take in his career due to his father's illness.

Bettelheim, however, would certainly never have admitted that. In his 1986 letter to Carl Frankenstein, he writes: 'You mention Kafka: his father probably was also a pretty good father but Kafka could afford not to see it. So he could be angry at him ….'[13] Note the envy. For little Bruno could not allow himself to harbour resentment against his father. Not only was the latter soon going to die, that was certain, but he was also worrying ceaselessly about his children's future. Having been painfully aware of his father's anxiety, Bruno Bettelheim later bitterly regretted that he had died too early to know of his own successes. As regards his mother, he sadly noted in the same letter that although she had seen his early breakthroughs, having died only in 1953, 'her long life of sorrows did not permit her to really enjoy it'.

There is one quality of Bettelheim's that no one, not even his enemies, ever denied: he was not afraid of hard work. He now resolved to try and reconcile the fulfilment of his own dreams with the rigours of the life that had been thrust upon him. He probably did so with a feeling of interior rage, as is shown by his correspondence. Without having any other clues than the character traits he was to show later on in life, one can imagine him being extremely intolerant of any interruption to his study-time, and making heavy demands on those around him. 'When I studied as a youngster, the door to my room had to be closed, and everything had to be quiet. Only then could I concentrate on myself and my work to the exclusion of everything else,' he writes, in an article on the right to privacy.[14] Which no doubt accounts at least in part for Bruno Bettelheim's habit of doing much of his work at night.

Faced with his parents' unhappiness and the obligation to take over from his father, Bettelheim thus began leading a double life. At the *Hochschule* he attended classes in international and commercial accountancy, trading law, economics, what today would be called marketing, statistics, geography, foreign exchange dealings, letter-writing in French and even shorthand and typing. At the university, meanwhile, he continued to pursue a higher path of learning.

His choice of classes was indeed indicative of an aspiration towards 'noble' disciplines. There were, for example, five hours per week of Latin, a subject without which no young Viennese could consider himself truly cultured. This was to involve, in July 1923, an extra exam, since the subject was not on the curriculum of the modern-minded Albertgasse *gymnasium*. He also took three hours a week of seventeenth-century German literature, one of contemporary literature, one devoted to 'readings of dramatic works' and a course on *Vor Sonnenaufgang*, a novel of the realist school by Gerhard Hauptmann.[15]

In *Freud's Vienna and Other Essays*,[16] Bettelheim writes that he only became interested in art history at a later date. Nevertheless, the courses he followed as a freshman already show a clear penchant for the fine arts. He had a two-hour weekly course entitled 'Description of a Trip to Italy' with Julius von Schlosser, then the head of the sculpture department at the *Kunsthistorisches Museum* and a prominent specialist on the history of art literature,[17] one hour of 'Reflections on Art' with Josef Strzygowski, famed for being the first historian to have devoted a comprehensive work to the art of the period, and the proponent of a 'genealogy' of art which traced the roots of European, Asian and Arabian art-forms back to common Greek and Roman origins,[18] and an hour on 'Buddhist Art in Eastern Asia'. Bettelheim also followed a two-hour course on 'Richard Wagner's Musical Dramaturgy'. And he read philosophy, with a once-weekly class on 'Great Conceptions of the World', 'History and Critique of Socialism' and 'General Studies of Races'.

By the start of the second semester, the young man had narrowed down his choices. His taste for theatre, German literature and the history of both art and ideas came through more clearly. In particular, he enrolled in a four-hour-per-week course on 'The Religions of the Enlightenment', and a two-hour one on Indian philosophical systems. He attended some of the same classes as his cousin Edith Buxbaum, who had started her freshman year at the same time as him, but was less interested in art and more in

history. At that time the two cousins were practically inseparable, and
Bruno spent more time at her home than he did at his own. When she was
not being ill, his Aunt Jenny, Edith's mother, was a good pianist, and it
was at her home that Bettelheim discovered music. At the Buxbaums'
house he also met the brilliant and turbulent Wilhelm Reich, who was to
be first the psychoanalyst and then the husband of Edith's best friend,
Annie Pink.

With the exception of Edith and her friends, however, Bruno Bettelheim
did not spend much time with his fellow students. He was to be seen on
occasion at the Landtmann, a famous café just opposite the university,
which was co-owned by Walter Neurath's mother. But while most other
students spent hours there, reading newspapers, playing cards or talking,
he was forever in a hurry, rushing from one place of learning to another.

At the end of that first year at university, Bettelheim's results were
uniformly excellent. At the *Hochschule* the only field in which his teachers
considered him to have attained no more than the basic pass level was
'accountancy and practical office work'. In all the other subjects his grades
were either 'very good' or 'excellent'. At the end of the school year, by way
of a reward, his parents paid for a trip to Italy. It was not his first time
abroad; after obtaining his *Matura* he had visited Berlin. But it was his
first journey to the birthplace of the Renaissance, the cultural and artistic
movement which was to loom larger than any other in Bettelheim's life for
the following ten years.

On returning from that vacation, in August 1922, he immediately
started working at the Riunione Adriatica de Sicurta insurance company,
where he was to spend a year as part of the requirements for his
Hochschule diploma. At the end of the period, having gained the passport
that would allow him to run the family firm, he was able to resume, for a
few months, the life of a college student. At the same time, though, his
father probably trained him to take over the lumber business.

In his relations with Gina, Bruno took care not to show just how tough
his life was. She never knew, for example, about his courses at the
Hochschule or his insurance job. On the contrary, he liked to act the
gentleman of leisure. He may not have understood all of her problems, but
there was one at least that he could easily sympathize with: her feeling of
impotence and guilt as regards her mother's deep sadness. For a long time
he told her nothing of his father's illness, or of his other worries. He liked
to play a protective, Pygmalion role. No doubt he hoped that with time, he
would be able to replace both of the men she had just lost, not only
boyfriend Dolf but also her father. But deeper down, he may also have
recognized in her more diffuse needs, which he hoped one day to be able to
satisfy.

Although head-over-heels in love, Bruno Bettelheim could not but
realize that while Gina enjoyed being with him, she did not feel any real
physical attraction to him. She did not admit this to herself at the time,

but her strong need for beauty was frustrated by her suitor. In those days, she liked his personality, intellect and even his moral qualities, but to really win her over he should also have been handsome, like her brother, her father, or Dolf.

Far from discouraging him, the young lady's hesitations probably only served to strengthen Bruno's attraction. As he was to admit to his children towards the end of his life, he was very frightened of sex at that time. That had been the reason he had broken off with his second girlfriend, Lilly Krugh. He had still not been officially told that his father's illness was syphilis, but he sensed that sex had something to do with his parents' unhappiness and the depressive atmosphere in his household. Lilly had been a classmate of his cousin Edith, who had introduced her to Bruno when they were celebrating their *Matura*. They rapidly became very close, and were to spend a lot of time together over the following two years. However, Lilly was a political revolutionary. She had discovered Communism with a previous boyfriend, a Trotskyite, but Bruno Bettelheim refused to be indoctrinated. Above all, however, she believed in sexual liberation, and could not understand why Bruno refused to plunge into such a fulfilling experience. Although he was very fond of Lilly, his inhibitions proved too strong, as he would later admit. He therefore decided to introduce her to his friend Walter Neurath, who he reckoned was readier than him for the experience. His hunch that the two would be a good match turned out to be right, and sixty years later he was still priding himself on having been the catalyst for their marriage.

Bruno had nothing of the sort to fear with Gina, whom he appears to have met shortly after the break-up with Lilly. His new girlfriend was no man-eating Amazon, just a very depressed young woman who put on a lady-like facade. He did everything he could to entertain her. They lived only a few streets apart, and the walk between their respective houses on Burggasse and Neubaugasse provided the opportunity for interminable discussions, during which Bruno was able to deploy his knowledge of art, history and literature. For her it was by no means the total communion she felt she had experienced with Dolf, but it was at least a door opened on to a world of culture and intelligence. He took her to the movies, then a very new form of entertainment, to concerts, which she adored, and to the theatre, which was his favourite. Although they spent very little time together with their respective families, Gina was well received at Bruno's home, where Anton was clearly responsive to her charm.

Bruno also provided Gina with an entrée to an idealistic new world, that of the *Jung Wandervogel*. When I interviewed her, Wanda Willig still remembered the spotlessly white percale gloves Gina was wearing the evening he introduced them to each other. Gina herself needed no prompting to recall the event: 'I was dressed up to the nines, with an elegant outfit and, of course, white gloves ....' Then, laughing as if with retrospective embarrassment, 'They were in the *Wandervogel*. They would never have dressed that way!'[19]

Although not greatly interested in politics, Gina had a thirst for new ideas. She had already been wounded by life, having had to learn at an even earlier age than had Bruno to grit her teeth and hide her pain so as not to deepen her mother's suffering. Both of them found solace in the contemplation of beauty and greatness, but while Bruno had gained an escape route from his inner conflicts via books and studying, she was still feeling her way. The art world attracted her, but being too much of a perfectionist, she could not believe there would ever be a place in it for her. The intellectual ferment of the socialist youth group opened up new vistas for her.

The world of yesterday was gone, its conventions and inequalities were dead, and everything was going to change, or so it appeared to these young people. They had nothing but contempt for the established order, which had led humanity through years of conformism to unprecedented butchery and ruin. They dreamed of a future based on justice and a deeper understanding of humanity. And it seemed that in front of their eyes a new world was indeed being born.

In Moscow, Budapest and even in Munich, the Communists had seized power. In Vienna, the oversized capital of an empire that no longer existed, the upheavals of 1918 and 1919 had given birth to a compromise. The ruling Social Democrats, who favoured a legalistic revolution, had combated the workers' uprisings that had broken out here and there in the aftermath of the war. They had managed to defuse the crisis without excessive repression, through an ambitious social reform programme. They had since left the ruling coalition but still ran Vienna's City Hall, from which they continued to pursue their dream of creating a socialist society by peaceful means. In the early twenties the city was beginning to emerge from the worst of its suffering. Times were still hard, but every month brought a new round of social reforms, which earned the former imperial capital the nickname of 'Red Vienna'.

The first-ever municipal low-cost housing projects were going up, strict labour regulations – on the employment of women and children, night work, paid vacations, etc. – were being enacted. The city was beginning to live again, with outsiders attracted both by the social experiments of 'Austro-Marxism', seen as an alternative to the Bolshevik Revolution, and by the work of Sigmund Freud, which was starting to gain world-wide attention. The young intellectuals of Bettelheim's generation were convinced they had the tools to create a new world, inhabited by a new type of man. There was much debate as to whether the latter had to be created first, so he could then build the new world, or whether it was the other way round, but they had no doubt that they were on the way to something completely new, arising from the ashes of the old, unjust world that their parents had seen as unchangeable.

Bruno Bettelheim, however, was more sceptical than most of his friends as to the meaning of history in general, and of socialist ideas in particular. One of the books in fashion at the time was Oswald Spengler's *Decline of the West*, a vast messianic history of civilization which Bettelheim was later to cite as one of the 'essential books' of his life.[20] Spengler's pessimistic vision was coherent with that of another of Bettelheim's favourite authors of the day, the art historian Jacob Burckhardt.

According to Spengler, the history of humanity has in itself no meaning and no final purpose. While he saw German culture as being socialistic by nature (in comparison, for example, with the individualistic British culture), he saw the rise and fall of civilizations as a cyclical but not a continuous process. Spengler posited a cycle of around a thousand years, and in a brilliant analysis which must have appealed to the young Bettelheim, he found points of comparison between different civilizations. Parallels between Pythagoras and Descartes, Alexander the Great and Napoleon, and Greek art and contemporary Western painting and music, for example.

Spengler's analysis was based on a double opposition. First, he divided civilizations into those with an 'Apollonian' or 'antique' soul, characterized by an accent on the finite and the present (*hic* and *nunc*), and those with a 'Western' or 'Faustian' persona, which were dynamic and strove towards infinity. Secondly, he distinguished between the rise and fall of cultures: the creative build-up, which gave birth to great ideas, religions and art, and the decadent decline, characterized by materialism and a stress on science and technique. The conclusion was all too clear; for Spengler, Germany (of which the 'Republic of Austro-Germans' was but a part) was clearly in the decadent stage, characterized by morbid sterility masked by an external reliance on force. Its decline and fall, like that of the West as a whole, was ineluctable. But just as the decadent Roman Empire had followed the high point of Greek civilization, so the twilight of the West would be preceded by *imperium germanicum*.

This is one of the works which Bettelheim later identified as 'essential' to his intellectual development.[21] In explaining his selection, he admitted that 'I knew not all of them were great books while I was reading them, powerfully impressed by them as I was,' but noted that in each case he had experienced a 'shock of recognition'. They were books which 'enlightened me about what were (at the time) my most pressing problems in finding my way in life'. He went on to compare that 'shock of recognition'[22] to the experience he was to have later on a psychoanalyst's couch: ' "This is it!" – the "it" being something with which I had been struggling, perhaps even to the point of obsession, without knowing that this was going on in my mind.' Even later, with some of his patients, Bettelheim was to notice the moment 'when suddenly things fell into place for them and confusion was replaced by clarity'. Continuing his demonstration, Bettelheim noted that while he had been unable to put down Dostoevsky's works, and while

Sinclair Lewis's *Arrowsmith* had given him a fleeting desire to drop everything else and go into medical research, none of those books touched closely enough on his own experience to influence his life. Whereas, alongside Goethe and Freud, he quotes writers such as Theodore Lessing, Friedrich-Albert Lange, Hans Vaihinger and then Oswald Spengler as having played key roles in his life. So much so that the influence of the latter four was behind his decision to concentrate on philosophy at the end of his second year at university.

This reading list is more revealing about Bettelheim than might appear at first sight. Although, like most of his contemporaries, he was deeply affected by the horrors of World War I and thus a convinced pacifist, he appears to have been unable to follow his friends into the whirling torrent of hope that was to occupy most of Vienna's intelligentsia for at least the next decade. At that time Walter Neurath and Lilly Krugh, along with two other couples, were founding one of a series of forward-looking communes based on equality and sexual freedom. Many of those closest to Bettelheim had answered the siren call of psychoanalysis, which was in the process of becoming a fully fledged movement and appeared to offer a path to a new, juster type of society by helping people rid themselves of their unconscious conflicts. One was Wanda Willig, who was studying medicine; another was Edith Buxbaum, who remained deeply involved in left-wing politics[23] while starting an analysis with Herman Nunberg. Meanwhile Edith's friend Annie Pink was about to marry her own analyst, Wilhelm Reich, who along with Otto Fenichel and a few others was trying to build bridges between psychoanalysis and Marxism. Gina too was attracted by psychoanalysis.

While all this was going on, Bruno Bettelheim, according to his own account, was finding an answer to his deepest doubts and questions not in Freud or Marx but in the apocalyptic vision of Oswald Spengler. He could not but be aware of the social changes going on all around him: just across the street from the offices and warehouses of the Bettelheim & Schnitzer company, the 'Red' town council was erecting a huge low-cost housing project dedicated to the principle that the poor too had the right to decent living conditions. Even Karl Kraus, another of Bettelheim's favourite writers, had temporarily curbed his acerbic wit enough to throw in his lot with the socialists. Despite all this, something in Bettelheim clearly prevented him from becoming a true believer; behind the vision of a better world, he could not help foreseeing a catastrophic future.

By around 1925 Anton Bettelheim's condition had deteriorated so much that he had to be admitted to a clinic, at Tulln in the Vienna suburbs. I was not able to establish the exact circumstances, since the institution's records have since been destroyed, and neither Gina nor Wanda Willig has any recollection of the episode. In the case of Wanda, this is not surprising, given that although both she and her husband were very close to Bruno Bettelheim, he never once spoke to her of his father's illness. Wanda thinks Hans might have known about it, but if he did, he too did not betray the secret. As for Gina, she has but vague memories of Anton Bettelheim's end; of a final painful decline which lasted only for a few months. 'It's true that Paula was very protective of her husband,' she adds. It is also possible that the demise of a man that she liked, and who died away from home, reminded her of a past that she preferred to forget. Or perhaps, more simply, Bruno managed to protect her from the whole process. This would not have been very difficult, since the two were not yet living together, and in any case they spent as little time as possible at their parents' homes.

Edith Buxbaum was later to confess, somewhat remorsefully, that although she was vaguely aware of Bruno's father's illness, she had pushed the thought into the back of her mind. The two cousins had been seeing much less of one another since Bruno had started dating Gina. They no longer moved in the same circles of friends, or had exactly the same interests. So Edith had no particular reason to dwell on the subject, which is certainly one reason why Anton's funeral, the first such ceremony she ever attended, shook her very deeply.

Much later, Bruno would admit to her that he had resented his cousin's absence from his life, which he saw as a betrayal. He had suffered greatly during his father's final period which, according to what he told his children, lasted around two years. His sister Margarethe had left home early to study acting, notably in Germany, and even when she was in Vienna she went out a great deal. Which meant that for much of the time Bruno was alone in the house with his mother. He probably often remembered the prediction made so long before by the family doctor: the ten-year reprieve he had foreseen for Anton after that terrible attack had by then almost run out. What is certain is that the drawn-out agony of a terminal syphilitic patient is a terrible experience for those around him. Bettelheim was to remain marked for the rest of his life by the slow process of deterioration, both physical and mental, suffered by his father. Anton Bettelheim died on April 13, 1926; the family doctor had been only a few months wide of the mark.

On June 11 of the same year, Bruno Bettelheim's name officially replaced that of his father in the statutes of the Bettelheim & Schnitzer company. That autumn he re-enrolled at the university, but his new schedule left him with little time to spare. The following spring, in early 1927, his name disappears from the faculty records. That February Bettelheim's maternal grandfather, Adolf Seidler, also died, leaving him the only man in his mother's life.

Bruno Bettelheim, not yet turned twenty-four, was thus being called upon to make a great sacrifice. He had dreamed, as he often said, of a university career, but he was now convinced that it was out of his reach forever. Just as, at sixteen, his poor eyesight had forced him to drop an early ambition to become an architect. He now had to face up to reality, shoulder responsibilities and let his dreams take second place to his sense of duty. To be sure, there were some compensations. As Gina points out, he at that time wanted very much to get married, and to do so he needed money. Dropping out of school was thus also a way of asserting himself, of becoming independent of his family and carving out his own world. It is also true that a university career remained off-limits for Jews, especially in the fields that particularly interested him.[24] That was indeed the reason he would later give for dropping out of university.[25]

Nevertheless, the documents clearly show that Bettelheim's switch from being a student to a wholesale lumber merchant took place only a few months after his father's death. I was not able to glean much information about his partner, Hans Schnitzer, other than the fact that he had joined the firm seven years earlier at the age of twenty-one. It can be assumed that Schnitzer's influence had grown as Anton Bettelheim's condition had deteriorated; he was therefore probably not especially happy to see Bruno arrive, particularly as the latter was the majority shareholder and five years his junior. Bruno was certainly better educated than his partner, and furthermore had a business school diploma; it is probable that he did not show too much tact as he levered himself into his new job. What is established is that there was no love lost between the two men. Right up until his departure from Vienna, Bruno Bettelheim consistently complained about his partner, whom he suspected of trying to cheat him.

In the meantime, the relationship with Gina was blossoming; the two had finally become lovers. In 1927 they went on a trip with the recently married Willigs. One day, on bursting into Gina's room, Wanda was astonished to find her in bed with Bruno. 'He's so homely – how can she sleep with him?' is the first thought that came into her mind, even though she is now reluctant to admit it.[26] Bruno Bettelheim's obsessive fears about his physical appearance were clearly not without foundation. 'The difference between him and Hans, who was not much of an athlete either, was that at least Hans had a handsome face,' says Gina.

The young woman's feelings towards her lover remained as ambivalent as ever. She got on well with him, and he was both generous and full of good advice whenever she was worried about her future. When she dreamed of starting a psychoanalysis, for example, but did not dare mention it to her mother, he volunteered to pay the fees. A little later he even gave her a beautiful leather-bound edition of Freud's complete works. But she would have preferred their relationship to have remained platonic. It was not that she did not enjoy playing the emancipated young woman; indeed she was proud to belong to a circle of intellectuals who thumbed their noses at bourgeois conventions. No, the real problem was that she just could not find Bruno physically attractive. One of her ways of expressing it was to be forever chiding him for his poor posture. Above all, their sexual relationship was not very satisfying, at least not for her. Both of them were novices.

Although Gina does not make any explicit connection between the couple's sexual problems and her desire to start a psychoanalysis, it is very likely that there was one. For although Freud's theories were beginning to be seen, particularly outside Austria, as a major discovery, at home they were still considered highly controversial and even scandalous, as is shown by Bettelheim's comments on his early reading. For most people, psychoanalysis remained synonymous with sex. Medical students taking the discipline, those who would become known as the 'second generation' of analysts, knew this to their cost as they had to run the gamut of daily sniggers and sneers; foremost among the mockers was Wagner von Jauregg, head of Vienna University's Psychiatry Department.[27]

The group then known as the 'young analysts', in which some observers would much later tend to place Bruno Bettelheim, were markedly different from their pioneering predecessors. They were the first to have chosen psychoanalysis as a career, and the first to undergo real training in the Institute, which had been founded in 1925. Even more importantly, unlike their predecessors they had personal experience of a real psychoanalysis. On the couch, they had spent time exploring the intricacies of their own psyches, reaching beyond the mind-games and the promptings of their conscious insights, sometimes against those very insights, to understand their previously inexplicable joys and fears and thus grasp the links that made up the geography of their unconscious minds. And precisely because that process had not taken place only in their intellects, but through the relationship to their analyst, the experience had changed them deeply. Which is why most of them were fired by a passionate desire to go even further, to improve psychoanalytic techniques and to push back the frontiers of their chosen science.

The slim volume that Richard Sterba, soon to be the analyst of Gina and then Bruno Bettelheim, published towards the end of his life is very revealing of that generation's state of mind. 'The tireless enthusiasm with which we devoted ourselves to the "cause", our shared pride at playing a role in propagating Freud's theories and discoveries, all gave us the exhilarating feeling that we were directly participating in Freud's monumental work. Even if we had only indirect contacts with him personally, we were close to his creative genius and his powerful mind,' he wrote.[28] And again, writing after the 1924 International Psychoanalytical Congress in Salzburg: '... The atmosphere of the congress made me feel I was witness to and participant in a cause that would be of tremendous consequences for the whole of mankind once it was generally recognized and became influential in all fields of human studies.'[29]

Gina's first inquiry about treatment was to Grete Lehner Bibring, one of the first analysts to work at the Vienna psychoanalytic clinic. She agreed to take the young woman on as a patient, but only if she broke off her relationship with Bruno for at least the time it took to see where the cure would lead. In spite of her mixed feelings about her lover, Gina refused.

It was then that she turned to Richard Sterba. Slightly older than Bruno, he was a medical doctor by training, a former patient of Edward Hitschmann's, and he held another of the clinic's first three salaried consultancy posts. Although he was close to Wilhelm Reich and shared some of his socialist ideals, he was not involved in politics. As Gina remembers him, he had an engaging, charming personality (half a century later, she cannot help smiling as she recalls their first encounter), and was all the more attractive to her in that he was also a good musician. She thus began visiting him in the Mariahilferstrasse five times a week, hoping to uncover the hidden wellsprings of her psyche.

Gina did not really know what to do with her life. She had stopped studying the piano as she was convinced that she would never be good enough to make a career of it. For a while she had taken dance classes with a student of Isadora Duncan's. She enjoyed that a great deal, as it went well beyond the basics of ballet; she even remembers a summer during which the educator August Aichorn came to lecture on psychoanalysis. But she finally dropped her dance classes too, once again convinced that others were much more gifted.

It was either just before or just after she started her analysis – Gina's memory for dates is rather hazy – that she decided to enrol for a course in Montessori teaching methods. Among its many reforms, the Vienna city council was then promoting a wide variety of educational experiments. One of these was the much-talked-about *Haus der Kinder* (children's house), which had just opened on Rudolfplaz square. It had been designed and built in accordance with the principles of the Italian paediatrician and educator Maria Montessori, by then world-famous. Her revolutionary teaching method relied not on getting the child to use his memory to imitate adults, as others did, but instead focused primarily on his feelings and his appetite for learning, leaving him to make discoveries for himself. Everything in the nursery was built to the scale of the children; the rigid classroom structure of blackboards, wooden benches and desks had been replaced by a flexible, child-centred approach. Montessori teachers let their charges express their creativity, make choices and move around freely. They took games seriously, always making the child's way of approaching the world the starting point for their teaching.

Although Maria Montessori had not been directly influenced by psychoanalysis, her methods could not fail to interest Freud and his students. If, as many of them hoped, the unravelling of the secrets of the unconscious was to lead to the creation of a new type of human being, capable of changing the world more effectively than a whole army of Bolsheviks, then it was clear that education would have to be a top priority. Another reason for psychoanalysts to take an interest in the Montessori method was the new light it shed on the development of children's minds. Although Freud himself was not much involved in that area of study, it attracted many of his younger students. The teacher-training seminars held at the Montessori school drew a large audience, and a wide variety of lecturers, including Anna Freud who taught there once a week.[30]

Whether or not Bruno Bettelheim realized that Gina was less than wholehearted in her feelings for him, he succeeded in concealing the pain this caused him. More in love than ever, and determined to finally be his own man, he had but one thing on his mind: getting married. He pressed her, and she continually found new excuses. The more she said no, the more insistent he became. She fell ill. So he visited her daily, laden down with flowers and gifts. Finally, she said yes.

Leopold Altstadt, who had for several years been working as an agent for his uncle's shoe business in New York, visited Vienna for a few weeks. Gina adored her brother, the one man in her life who had never failed her. He embodied everything that was important to her: music, beauty and intelligence. During our interviews, the memories of that visit come back only with difficulty. She remembers one evening at her mother's house, looking up and seeing reflected in a mirror the elegant silhouette of her brother, talking to her fiancé. The contrast was too much for her to take; how could she possibly spend her life with a man who was so gauche, so lacking in nature's graces? When Leopold was due to return to New York, Gina resolved to go with him. She too would find a life for herself in the New World, under the wing of her beloved brother.

Her lovely dream was to fall apart in Paris. Gina has difficulty remembering the details; she starts out by citing Leopold's sudden death, getting her dates mixed up. Then, confronted with the contradictions in her first version, she slowly begins to get the story straight. She remembers sitting at a sidewalk café in Paris with a friend of Leopold's, an older man. She does not recall exactly what it was he told her about her brother; but it was then that she decided to return to Vienna and Bruno. Had the man told her that her brother was a homosexual? No, says Gina. At least not in so many words. But the basic message was crystal-clear: after Dolf and her father, Leopold too was now abandoning her; he could not take care of his sister in New York. The only man she could count on to be faithful and reliable, in spite of all his defects, was Bruno Bettelheim. Two years later Leopold Altstadt was to commit suicide in a New York hotel room. According to the *New York Times* he had suffered from depression and had taken an overdose of morphine. Gina does not remember that. In the meantime, on March 30, 1930, she had become Mrs Bruno Bettelheim. At the registrar's office, Hans and Wanda Willig, who were the two witnesses, had to lend their rings to the couple, as theirs were not yet ready.

Far from smoothing out the differences between them, marriage increased them. In Taormina, Sicily, where they ended their long honeymoon, Gina fell ill again. They seemed to have different views on everything. She was attracted to mountains, he swore only by the sea. She wanted to walk, climb, scramble up the rocks to discover Mount Etna, he preferred to spend his time reading, or on occasion going swimming. And when they finally managed to agree on visiting the medieval castle or the Greek amphitheatre together, she could not help ribbing him about his need to plan his every move, and take along his Baedeker guide wherever they went. She loved improvising, and trusted her own intuition.

In the article he devoted to his favourite books,[31] Bruno Bettelheim implicitly gave his own version of the same events: 'At the end of my first year at university, I travelled to Italy, motivated largely by my reading of Burckhardt's writings. His *Der Cicerone* was my vademecum; it is no exaggeration to say that for more than a decade it became my bible. I tried to make every year at least one and sometimes two prolonged trips to Italy, the *Cicerone* at all times in my hand.'[32] It indeed appears that the two newly-weds had not gone to Sicily looking for the same things.

Other aspects of Bettelheim's personality began to grate on Gina once they started living together. She who was so demanding in all things intellectual was upset by what she saw as his flippant attitude towards books. Earlier she had been impressed by his learning; now that she knew him better she realized that in many cases he only had to read the first and last fifteen pages or so of a book, plus a few pages in the middle, to talk about it as though he had read the whole thing. Rather than perceiving this as a useful gift, she saw it as intellectual dishonesty.

Even the qualities that they had in common, such as their intuition, could be a source of discord. One day Gina made a comment to Bruno on D.H. Lawrence's *Sons and Lovers* which she had been reading with great pleasure. 'You should write a book,' he replied. Far from flattering her, the comment irritated her. 'What arrogance,' she thought, 'to think that one can write a book simply because one has a good grasp of the characters in a novel!'

After their marriage, Gina and Bruno moved into a truly beautiful apartment. All their friends have retained vivid memories of its opulence and style. It was Gina who had found it on her return from Paris, in Glorietgasse, a pretty, tree-lined street in the thirteenth district's Hietzing neighbourhood. Calm and full of greenery, the area had been open country only half a century before, and it attracted the type of people who prided themselves on their good taste. Only a hundred metres or so from the Bettelheims' building were the ramparts of Schönbrunn Castle, the Hapsburg family's former summer residence, with its French-style formal gardens now open to the public. The cypress-lined alleyways were ideal for quiet contemplative walks or long philosophical discussions. The gardens also contained a small zoo and a very rococo but nevertheless beautiful little theatre, in which the Vienna Chamber Opera gave summer performances.

The inside of the Bettelheims' apartment was almost as grand as the neighbourhood outside, albeit in more modern style. On Gina's prompting, Bruno had had its rooms completely remodelled during the couple's six-week honeymoon. Out had gone all the wainscoting, friezes and woodwork;

everything which gave the place an old-fashioned, nineteenth-century bourgeois look. In had come oriental carpets and simple but elegant furniture, which Bettelheim had had designed and installed during their honeymoon. The fixtures included a gigantic set of bookshelves, of which he was especially proud. The two art-lovers had adorned the walls with a number of contemporary works, in particular lithographs by Käthe Koll-witz and Egon Schiele (the latter a former Hietzing resident). Later, they were also to acquire a painting by Schiele. Huge mirrors reflected the light throughout the large rooms from the garden outside. Whatever their political ideas, Gina and Bruno enjoyed the refined, bourgeois Vienna lifestyle of the period; they lived well.

Indeed, Bruno Bettelheim was the first person in his entourage to possess an automobile, a grey Steyr Baby 50 convertible.[33] It was his pride and joy: cars at that time were still extremely rare, and thus a major status symbol. Although Bettelheim certainly still dreamed of academic glory and the life of the mind, he was clearly also more than happy with the things that money could buy. And he knew how to use his wealth, showing both taste and generosity. Money was no object whenever he wanted to please his loved ones – or to impress the outside world.

The thing Gina Bettelheim disliked most about her husband, in fact, was his taste for ostentation. And she was not the only one to feel that way, as is shown by the following (no doubt apocryphal) anecdote told by the Austrian writer Friedrich Torberg. In a light-hearted little book of Vien-nese recollections written much later on his return from exile in the United States, Torberg tells of a tea-party that was supposed to have taken place in the 1930s. The essayist Egon Friedell is described in conversation with a certain 'Dr B, a soul doctor who was destined for great fame,' on the subject of sexual symbols in everyday life. According to Torberg, the said Dr B pointed to a basket filled with small round Viennese buns, with their characteristic furrow across the middle, and declared with authority that they were female sexual symbols. To which Friedell shot back: 'To he who is pure, everything is pure. To me, they look like babies' bottoms!'[34]

Torberg's description leads me to suspect that if he ever met Bettelheim it was not in Vienna but much later, and that the only authentic part of his story is the feelings it expresses on his part about 'Dr B'. The latter is described as someone who 'having recently achieved analytical notoriety, was anxious to seize any opportunity to show off his knowledge.' Through-out his life, Bruno Bettelheim indeed had a knack for exasperating certain people by his pushiness, his too-obvious desire to make an impression. Others, more aware of the underlying fragility that this attitude belied, were able to get beyond the surface level to the real man underneath, often using humour as the key. For many people, however, and firstly for Gina, the effort required was just too great.

Bruno Bettelheim's own references to his first marriage are few and far between. In *Freud's Vienna and Other Essays*, he refers in passing to a 'crisis in my married life' which finally pushed him to go into psychoanalysis. Elsewhere, he refers to a 'bad marriage'. People who knew them together usually remember them as a pleasant but not very easygoing couple. The impossibly high standards that Gina set for herself became even more impossible when applied to Bruno. One witness notes that he went to a great deal of trouble to try and please her, through the apartment, furniture, pictures, etc., but nothing ever seemed to be good enough. It was as though he was not sufficiently handsome or noble to pass muster. And even if she never told him of them in so many words, he was clearly aware of his perceived shortcomings.

But an unhappy marriage is always two-sided, as Bettelheim himself was to point out in a letter to an old friend, written some fifteen years after his divorce: 'My relationship with Gina, as you know, was very difficult, and we were both really to blame for that.'[35] Although Bruno was starved of the admiring, positive feelings which would have brought out the best in him, he was also very demanding of his wife, while refusing to give her what she wanted most of all: a child. That issue was the cause of the only real quarrel between the two that Wanda Willig recalls witnessing.

Again, the crucial events took place when the friends were travelling together. One day, emerging from her room to enjoy the morning air, Wanda found Gina and Bruno in the middle of a blazing fight. Later, Gina told her about it. The argument put forward by Bruno for his refusal was rather strange: 'You'll leave me if we have a child.' Naturally Gina denied that this was the case, but she had already sufficiently lost interest in Bruno to wonder about his real motives. On that question, it is again worth looking at what Bettelheim wrote about the Polish educator Janusz Korczak:[36] 'As far as we know, he never specifically said why he did not want to marry or have children, but it seems probable that he was afraid he might have inherited his father's tendency to insanity and feared to pass it on, or have a child suffer from such predicaments as he had experienced because of his father's mental instability.'

The truth is that up until the war, Bruno Bettelheim lived with the constant fear that he had inherited his father's illness. As Edith Buxbaum's memoirs confirmed: 'Bruno told me he was afraid to be syphilis infected, not knowing whether he was conceived before or after the infection. What a punishment for forbidden wishes.'

With the benefit of many years of hindsight, and based mainly on the recollections of Gina, Bruno Bettelheim's first marriage thus appears to have been a mistake. They were clearly ill fitted to live together, with each partner's anxieties sparking the behaviour most likely to exacerbate the other's fears. Bettelheim was to write: 'I can hardly understand now why we were once so important for each other and even less why we made things so difficult for one another.'[37] It would nevertheless be going too far to call the marriage a total fiasco. Practically all I know about their relationship comes from Gina Weinmann,[38] and she still shows herself to be a very demanding lady, who will not make do with second-best. Asked to recall a marriage which ended up on the rocks, she certainly has a tendency to stress only the bad and painful things about it. Particularly since, as she is the first to admit, she harboured long-standing resentment against her ex-husband for his subsequent behaviour (of which more below). But when, in speaking of Vienna, she chances on memories unrelated to her domestic woes, she on occasion shows that she shared many intellectual pleasures, and even friendship, with her first husband. And when this is pointed out to her, she ends up admitting, almost coyly, 'It's true that we got on well together, that we had a lot of things in common, and that we had a good life in Vienna.' When it is further pointed out that after being husband and wife for ten years, she and Bettelheim remained friends until the end, she adds, with a charming smile: 'Sure. If it hadn't been for Hitler we would not have divorced.'

Bruno Bettelheim later wondered exactly what role psychoanalysis had played in the break-up of his first marriage.[39] Which is indeed a good question, although one which cannot be answered. When Grete Bibring asked Gina to suspend her relationship with Bruno during the time it would take to see where her analysis was headed, she was simply applying the golden rule laid down by Freud himself: there should be no major upheavals, no great commitments, in a patient's life during an analysis. It was a precautionary rule: whatever happened on the analyst's couch, the experience had to remain a symbolic one, with no direct repercussions on real life. But there is often a large gap between theory and practice, a gap into which human emotions all too easily stream, especially when the powerful mechanisms of transference come into play, and before the patient has been able to identify them.

Whatever may have been the case, when Gina had returned from Paris to marry Bruno, she had carried on as if nothing at all had happened. With one difference: she had changed psychoanalysts.

Chapter IV

Patsy

Bruno Bettelheim was aware of the changes his wife was going through, but from a distance. It is a period about which he did not write, and on which very few documents still exist. Those that do indicate that he managed his business well. Under his direction the Bettelheim & Schnitzer company branched out, adding furniture-making to its lumber activities. A business career had not been what Bettelheim had wanted for himself, but he took to it with ease, displaying obvious managerial abilities. Some members of the family may well have commented that he took after his grandfather Seidler, a comparison which would certainly not have been to his liking. Nevertheless he enjoyed bringing in comfortable amounts of money and used it to good effect, leading a busy social life and often playing host in the couple's beautiful apartment, which thanks to Gina was always impeccably elegant.

Bruno kept up with his two closest friends, Hans and Walter, but with the exception of his mother he did not see much of his family any more. In particular, he lost touch with his cousin Edith Buxbaum. She did not much like Gina, and though she did not admit it to herself until later,[1] she was jealous of her for having taken Bruno away. He was also seeing much less of his friends from the *Jung Wandervogel*, both the politically committed ones and the students of psychoanalysis. His forced transformation into a businessman had not killed off all the idealistic impulses of his youth, and he continued to read a lot, but it had confirmed his basic pessimism as to the prospects of humanity changing for the better.

Events in the wider world served only to confirm his pessimistic views. In Austria itself, after an easier period in the mid-1920s, social tensions were building under the new Social Christian government, which was losing its grip. In 1927 the national guard opened fire on a workers' protest held in the most famous of the housing complexes built in the days of 'Red Vienna', sparking off an unprecedented wave of rioting. Two years later with the aftermath of the Wall Street crash, things got even worse. Although many Viennese continued to sympathize with the left, in the country as a whole more and more voices were being heard clamouring for a strong leader who could set back the clock to the stable days of the Hapsburg dynasty.

Farseeing though he may have been, Bruno Bettelheim was not endowed with powers of prophecy. Not even the election to the chancellorship in 1932 of Engelbert Dollfuss, soon nicknamed 'Milli Metternich' because he responded to the prevailing mood by setting up a clerical dictatorship, could give him an inkling of what was in store just a few years ahead. On occasion, he did toy with the idea of emigrating, particularly on weekends, when he and Gina went to visit her Uncle Moritz in his beautiful villa in Hietzing, not far from Glorietgasse. Then he would talk of starting a new life in the United States, but as it became clear that Uncle Moritz had no intention of providing the required funds, nothing came of it. Bettelheim had to make the best of what he had.

His private relationship with Gina, meanwhile, showed no signs of improving. After her fruitless effort to leave for New York, he may have hoped for a while that he could finally win her love. But during their six-week honeymoon in Italy, he had had ample time to measure the gulf that separated them. In Vienna, they slept in separate bedrooms, but they never had open fights, and had enough interests and tastes in common for their differences to remain hidden from the outside world.

One thing at least must have pleased Bruno: his wife's decision to change psychoanalysts, switching from Richard Sterba to his wife Editha. And yet Gina is quick to point out that she always felt closer to him than to her, even though she could see the results of her analysis with Editha much more quickly. She was very sensitive to Richard Sterba's charm (and he maybe to hers, she feels). She found him more sensitive and artistic than his wife, and even though Editha had a degree in music and was a good pianist, she remembers above all how well Richard played the violin![2]

Editha Sterba, née von Radanowicz-Harttmann, was three years older than her husband. Gina thought her 'a little masculine', but at the same time found her strong personality reassuring. Editha's father and grandfather were high-ranking military officers and she had travelled a lot during her childhood, but nevertheless got a solid education. At university, she studied musicology and psychology, and worked for a time as secretary to Otto Rank, then Freud's favourite student, later to be rejected by him. Editha Sterba began her own training in 1925; she was thirty-seven when Gina Bettelheim became her patient.

Meanwhile Gina continued to frequent the Montessori school after her training was over. She worked for a time as an unpaid teacher at the *Haus der Kinder*, and she also went there regularly to attend Anna Freud's seminars. Thanks in part to what she was learning about infant development, Gina was becoming more and more drawn to psychoanalysis. She loved her work, and was excited by the possibilities it was opening up for her. She also attended seminars at the Institute, where she met Fritz Redl, a young high-school teacher who was equally fascinated by psychoanalysis, and who had also been a patient of Richard Sterba's. Redl was a flirt, and showed great interest in Gina. She found him charming, enjoying his intellectual company as well as his jolly disposition.

One day Annie Hatchek, a friend and fellow teacher from one of the city's progressive training schools, suggested that she and Gina pool their experience to set up their own kindergarten. Vienna was then full of foreigners, many of them Americans who had come over to go into psychoanalysis, either for personal reasons or in order to learn the new discipline. A lot of them had brought their children, and there was thus a demand for educational facilities. Dorothy Burlingham, a friend and supporter of Anna Freud, had just set up a primary school for such children, with the young psychoanalyst Peter Blos. Annie Hatchek's idea was to have the new kindergarten take in both American infants and Austrian children from poor backgrounds, with the former subsidizing the latter. It was to be a small institution, designed and run along Montessori lines. The aim was not only to stimulate the children's imagination and creativity, but also to promote social integration. Gina was enthusiastic about the project. Inspired by what psychoanalysts were discovering about children, she suggested also taking in a few disturbed infants.

When asked to provide funds for the new venture, Bruno readily agreed. He was curious about the circles in which his wife was now moving. In particular, he quickly became friends with Fritz Redl. Although the two men came from very different backgrounds they had shared interests, and personalities that were complementary in many ways. Fritz Redl came from a Catholic family, he was a year older than Bettelheim and like the latter had studied philosophy. He had been a brilliant student, obtaining his PhD at the age of twenty-three on an austere subject: 'The Epistemological Foundations of Kantian Ethics'. Hans Vaihinger, the same philosopher whose writings had helped the young Bettelheim get out of his depression, had been so impressed by Redl that he had invited him to spend a vacation with him in Germany.

Fritz Redl's childhood had been even more tragic than Bruno Bettelheim's. At the age of five, he had seen his mother burned alive in a fire that had also destroyed the family home. But he was no depressive; on the contrary, he was a great socializer, the life and soul of the many parties he went to. After his doctorate he obtained a secondary-school teaching degree at university and started work as a literature and philosophy teacher at the *Realgymnasium*. He had also written a few textbooks, including one on psychology. Redl later explained that he had been drawn to the study of the mind by observing the behaviour of his pupils. He had undertaken a psychoanalysis at the same time as he was attending the university courses of Professor Karl Bühler, who along with his wife Charlotte ran the Institute of Psychology and was at the time considered the supreme authority on the subject. But Fritz Redl was interested in much more than pure theory. He had immediately applied his new-found knowledge to his students, and had gradually moved from simply observing them to proffering advice, devoting more and more time to adolescents with problems. This work had started to win him a reputation, and he was being consulted as an expert by several schools.

One summer, probably in 1932, Fritz Redl suggested to Gina Bettelheim and Annie Hatchek that the three of them jointly organize a summer camp for a group of difficult and deprived children. The two women liked the idea, but none of them had either funds or a place to take their charges. Once again, Bruno was asked to help, and once again he came up with a solution. Through business contacts, he obtained permission for the three to camp with the children in the disused imperial castle of Shalaburg. The place was falling apart, and they spent the month surrounded by piles of crumbling masonry, but it was nevertheless a magnificent setting. The experiment was a total success, as the abilities of the three adults complemented one another perfectly. Gina was very impressed by Fritz Redl's ability to handle group activities, while she got her best results in one-to-one relations with the children. While they were away, Bruno passed his driver's licence, and was thus able to surprise them one weekend by visiting in his flashy new convertible.

Gina was becoming thoroughly absorbed in her new existence when one day, probably in the autumn of that same year 1932,[3] Editha Sterba told her about a little American patient for whom she was trying to find a school. Patricia ('Patsy') was seven years old, but she behaved like a child two or three years younger. She was very introverted, and hardly spoke. Her mother Agnes came from the Piel family of Connecticut, second-generation German immigrants who had become a force in the brewing industry. Being very concerned about Patsy's development, she had consulted a host of American specialists in vain, before bringing the child to Vienna, attracted by what she had heard about the Freuds, both father and daughter. But Anna Freud had found Patsy either too disturbed or too old for the nursery that she was in the process of setting up, and she had referred her to Editha Sterba, who at the time was running the Psychoanalytic Society's clinic for children.

Gina immediately accepted Editha's suggestion that she admit Patsy to her school as a boarder. Some six decades later, she still has a vivid memory of her first meeting with the frail little girl, whose terrified eyes peered out from under brown hair cut short in a pageboy style. As the child sat there, twisting her fingers apparently without realizing it and wearing an absent look on her face, Gina felt deeply touched. Her mother, meanwhile, was explaining Patsy's symptoms. But Gina was much more interested in the child than in the label. She gave Patsy some crayons and she drew some animal pictures, in which Gina detected a clear artistic disposition. Then she held out her arms, and after a few moments' hesitation, Patsy let herself be hugged. Gina's instincts told her that a bath would reassure the child. Patsy did not resist, and Gina sat nearby, talking gently to her as she bathed.

Patsy was a very quiet child, probably too quiet. But apart from occasional jerky movements, and the absent expression she frequently wore, she showed few outward symptoms of being 'disturbed'. Gina decided to seek the opinion of August Aichorn, whose skill with disturbed children was admired by all at the Psychoanalytic Institute. Aichorn, then aged fifty-four, had trained as a schoolteacher, but his understanding of delinquents and other difficult children was such that the city authorities very quickly put him in charge of two correctional facilities for adolescents. The results he achieved so impressed Anna Freud that she invited him to the Institute to discover psychoanalysis. It was ten years after that, when Aichorn had just been put in charge of the Psychoanalytic Society's guidance clinic for adolescents, that Gina came to him for advice about Patsy. 'When you cannot decide whether a child is disturbed or not, just turn to other children for an opinion,' he told her. 'They will know for sure.' The test, applied to Patsy, was conclusive: her peers treated her as someone apart. She kept herself to herself, and they quickly gave up trying to reach out to her.

Patsy's first week at the school went off reasonably well. At the weekend, however, she was clearly miserable at being left alone with so many other children she didn't know, in a totally foreign environment. On arriving at the school on Monday morning, Gina found the little girl in a state of complete distress. 'We didn't have much money, and living conditions at the school were very primitive compared to what Patsy had been used to,' she explains.

For that reason, or perhaps simply because she was becoming involved with the American girl, Gina suggested to Agnes Piel that she take Patsy to her home for the following weekend. After a few such experiences, it also became clear that the child hated spending even week-nights at the school, and soon she was living full time at the Bettelheims' home at number 15 Glorietgasse. This was a great relief to Agnes Piel, who had been in Vienna for several months and was becoming impatient to return to her home and friends in Greenwich Village.

Thus, not long after her attempt to leave for a completely new life, Gina had found herself the child that Bruno was refusing to give her. She became totally devoted to Patsy, caring for and playing with her as if she was her own daughter.[4] Everyone around her was amazed at the patience she displayed with the little girl. Gina, who could often be irritable and make provocative or biting comments, softened as if by magic whenever she was with Patsy. Which was not to say that she was indulgent. She insisted that the girl be obedient, that she hold herself well in public, and like most Viennese mothers at that time, she would give her a slap on occasion. But Gina's affection for Patsy was obvious to all. She spent countless hours trying to get through to the girl, and work out what was terrorizing her.

After a year or so at the kindergarten, Patsy started attending classes at the Montessori primary school on Grünetorgasse, in the city's ninth district. Some months later, Gina even let her go alone on the bus. But it was a long ride, and fearing that the little girl, lost in her inner world, might miss her stop, Gina for a long time sat discreetly at the back, unbeknown to her charge, who never once noticed her presence. Over the years, Patsy learned to read and write, and above all to relate a little to other people.

Patsy herself has kept good memories of her stay in Vienna. With one big reservation, however: 'I wanted to be with my mother. I never understood why she couldn't keep me with her,' she says. A complaint which was to be echoed almost word-for-word by some of the children who, twenty or thirty years later, would attend the Orthogenic School in Chicago. To hear the protest expressed so spontaneously by a woman whose experience dates back some sixty years is troubling indeed.[5] It is difficult not to take it as a reflection on the concept of 'milieu therapy' that Bruno Bettelheim was later to develop, even if one allows that it may simply reflect the difficulty a vulnerable child could have in admitting that she had found happiness with someone other than her mother.

For Agnes Piel was not unlike many of the mothers who in the 1950s and '60s would bring their children to the then-famous Dr Bettelheim. Raised as the only girl among seven children, she was demanding and ambitious, dreaming of becoming a successful writer but managing only to publish a handful of articles, which failed to satisfy her desire for intellectual fame. Agnes was not the only eccentric in her family, but she was probably the one who best managed to live out her fantasies in her private life. She was restless, intellectual, emancipated and sexually free, given to smoking, drinking and partying. At that time, in the early 1930s, she was between her first and second husbands, and had come to view Patsy's erratic behaviour, her refusal to utter more than a few sentences, as living proof of her own failings, perhaps even of her evil influence. Like many parents, Agnes was prepared to do almost anything to assuage the feelings of guilt that her child's unorthodox behaviour stirred in her. It is worth noting that Agnes's articles were usually on the subject of education.

In handing over her daughter to Gina, who was not only a schoolteacher versed in psychoanalysis but also an intelligent, sensitive and elegant lady, Agnes must have felt a huge sense of relief. And the presence of Bruno at Gina's side must also have been reassuring: it meant not only that Patsy would be living in material comfort, but also, and perhaps more importantly, that she would be growing up in a 'normal' family, with a strong father-figure. I doubt that Agnes was aware of the conflict between Bruno and Gina over having a child, but it is easy to imagine how the American woman, who had an eccentric love-life, could have felt reassured by Bruno Bettelheim's obvious sense of responsibility.

It is also probable that Bruno Bettelheim was happy to turn on his intellectual charm in the presence of the strange American lady who had showed up in his life, out of the blue. Agnes Piel, so different from any of the women he had known until then, probably inspired in him a feeling of fascination. Her wealth and her authoritarian manner, contrasted with the obvious distress she was experiencing as a result of Patsy's problems, must have both confirmed and moulded the image he had of America, the distant land to which so many of his friends dreamed of emigrating, and to which he had so nearly lost Gina. Although Bettelheim had no idea what the future held in store for him, such an opportunity to obtain insights into the United States and its people can only have aroused his interest.

What, indeed, was his image of America at that time? He knew of course that it was rich and powerful, as it had saved many Viennese from dying of hunger during the war and had finally tipped the balance of the conflict through its intervention. But his images came from the first movie serials, such as the smash hit *The Perils of Pauline*, or the popular writings of the German novelist Karl May, whose Westerns were dreamed up long before he had even set foot in America. All of which must have added up to a familiar image: the America of wide-open spaces, cowboys and self-made men, a country which was rich and generous, but also brutal and uncouth. His father-in-law Adolf Seidler must have told him about the fabulous fortune amassed by their fellow Austrian Jew, sewing-machine tycoon Isaac Merritt Singer, and Bettelheim surely knew about the rags-to-riches stories of other European immigrants, such as John Davidson Rockefeller. There was also Agnes Piel's grandfather, Godfried, who had left a small German village in 1883 and rapidly become one of the richest brewers in the United States.

But Agnes showed the Bettelheims another facet of American life: New York-Greenwich Village chic, with its intellectual and musical sophistication, including no doubt jazz. Their fascination was however tempered with the usual condescension of educated Europeans towards Americans, whose naïve aspirations to nobility and a sense of history were more often than not a source of mirth. Gina still remembers how much she and Bruno laughed at the Anglo-French film *The Ghost Goes West*, which satirizes an American millionaire seeking to transport an entire castle, complete with its resident phantom, to the United States.

During part of her spell in Vienna, Agnes Piel even stayed in the Bettelheim apartment, Gina sleeping on the sofa and giving her her room. Agnes went out a great deal. She too had started an analysis with Richard Sterba. And she socialized a lot, leaving the care of Patsy entirely in Gina's hands. When she was in the house she would talk to her hosts and their friends rather than look after her daughter. Such discussions took place in German, even though Bruno spoke a little English. Agnes liked Gina a great deal, and appeared impressed by the couple's standard of living. She would often complain about how difficult it was back home to find good domestic servants, like the Bettelheims' Hedwig, who would still be up to serve dinner for them after an evening out at the theatre. None of which deterred her from returning to New York after a few months, once she felt confident that her daughter was being well looked after.

In June 1936, Gina took Patsy to the US to visit her mother. For the first month of the stay, Agnes packed the two off to a summer camp run by one of her friends at Wellfleet, Cape Cod. Gina was given the status of a camp counsellor, but she took care only of Patsy. The young Viennese woman was avid to learn all about this strange new country. She remembers only one occasion on which she balked at the local customs. One Sunday, for reasons which she cannot recall, her hosts wanted her to dress up in a strange green outfit with puffy pants and a sailor's collar to go to church. 'Going to church in itself is not easy for me,' she told them. 'Don't ask me to also don a disguise!'

After the month at the camp, Gina and Patsy stayed with Agnes, who proved a marvellous hostess. Gina was enchanted by the New England landscape; she was reading Henry James's *What Maisie Knew*. But she also greatly appreciated a very different type of outing, with Agnes's younger brother Paul, a painter and the other eccentric of the family. He showed her the poor neighbourhoods of Harlem and the Bronx, saying, 'You must get acquainted with all sides of America.' The initiative infuriated Agnes, who was already laying schemes to have the Viennese couple come and settle in the United States. She spoke of buying a large house in which they could all live together; Bruno would carry on his business affairs while Gina looked after Patsy. Gina was not interested, but her hostess persisted. 'Be realistic,' Agnes told her. 'Look what's happening in Germany. How long do you think it will be before Hitler gets his hands on Austria?'

Gina stood firm however, being unable to imagine ever living anywhere else than in Vienna, except maybe at a pinch in Paris. In October, therefore, she and Patsy took the boat back to Europe. On returning to Vienna, she felt that Bruno had changed, although she was unable to figure out exactly how. He seemed calmer, more at peace with himself. One obvious change was that he had decided to re-enrol at the university, and had therefore handed over the day-to-day running of the company to Hans Schnitzer.

Before seeing what Bruno Bettelheim had been up to during the summer of 1936, let us for a moment examine his relationship with the little American girl, who was to play a key role in his future life. For the story which he tells differs significantly from the account I have tried to piece together here, based mainly on Gina's recollections but also on those of half a dozen other people, including Patsy herself. The account given above corresponds to the verifiable facts as regards the actual sequence of events, and the relations between Agnes, Patsy and Gina. What remains to be elucidated is the relationship between Bruno and Patsy during the six years that the two lived under the same roof. Here we are on much more slippery ground, as there are no completely reliable witnesses.

After he arrived in the United States, Bruno Bettelheim was gradually to appropriate the story of Patsy, as if the little girl had in fact been put in his care, and not in that of his wife. We will examine his motives for doing this later. He was even at one point to paint a picture from which it could be inferred that he, and not Editha Sterba, was the little girl's psychoanalyst. Neither woman was ever to publicly contradict his statements. But while Dr Sterba's reaction can only be surmised from a discreet footnote in her husband's brief autobiography,[6] Gina was never able to forgive him. She saw his appropriation of her story not only as a lie, but as a total denial of herself. And the issue is all the more hurtful in that she never once dared to confront Bettelheim over it in the fifty or so remaining years of his life.

Her view of the issue is categorical. 'Relations between Bruno and Patsy? They were practically non-existent. Like those of any European man with his children in those days: he saw her a little at the dinner table. The rest of the time, he was reading a lot and she didn't bother him. She was very quiet.' Gina even denies that Bruno showed any particular interest in Patsy's strange behaviour, even from a distance.

In that, she is no doubt unfair. For if Bettelheim was able to spin such an elaborate yarn about what would soon be diagnosed as Patsy's autism, he must have at least observed her behaviour while she was living in his home. It was a time when he was plagued by self-doubt, and he must have been intrigued by this child who differed from him in almost every way, but who had so deliberately 'turned its back on humanity and society',[7] just as he himself had tried to do, intermittently, around twelve years earlier. The sight of this little girl who spent whole days lost in her own fantasy world could not but have reminded him of the hours he himself had spent lying in darkness, his mind a blank.

The tapestry Bettelheim wove around the story of Patsy became richer and more elaborate over time, almost as if the very silence of the people who could have torn it to shreds served as an encouragement. The most elaborate version of the story is to be found in his penultimate book, *A Good Enough Parent*, although Bettelheim was to add further touches during interviews after the book's publication.[8] Because Bruno Bettelheim loved telling stories, and was unable to resist the temptation whenever he had an appreciative audience.

After having described Patsy as 'virtually mute' on her arrival in Vienna, Bettelheim writes: 'It took more than a year during which we carefully respected her wish to be left alone, while still trying to take tender, loving care of her, before she moderated her total isolation and permitted occasional approaches, although she did not respond to these in any discernible way.'[9] Finally, writes Bettelheim, Patsy took to just one of the games that her surrogate parents tried to engage her in, a variant of 'peek-a-boo'. In the course of describing the game Bettelheim starts out in the first-person plural, but soon switches to the first-person singular. 'Eventually she actually hid behind a curtain, even peeked out from behind it, mimicking what I had done innumerable times in my play of finding her.' After that incident, Bettelheim writes, the little girl allowed him to cuddle her for the first time, spontaneously and without recoiling. Enchanted, he repeated the game on several subsequent days. It was during one such session, according to Bettelheim, that Patsy uttered the first complete sentence of her life. Not only the first, but a sentence in perfect English, even though she was immersed in a German-speaking environment. This sentence, Bettelheim writes, was 'Give me the skeleton of George Washington.'

Bettelheim is not the only writer to have noted that when autistic children emerge from their silence, it is often by uttering complete sentences. And that since such utterances usually relate to the central reason for their withdrawal from the world, they should be carefully analysed. Happily, explains Bettelheim, he was able to comprehend the hidden meaning of Patsy's statement. 'The tragedy of her life had originated in the fact that her father was completely unknown, not just to her but also to her mother, because of the strangest of circumstances.'[10] Bettelheim was later to explain those circumstances, although they are not specified in *A Good Enough Parent*. In a discussion with Daniel Karlin, for example, he explained that Agnes had conceived Patsy with a stranger after a party at which she had had too much to drink. To avoid a scandal, her family had rushed her into a marriage, while she tried on several occasions to abort. When Patsy reached the age of five Agnes, racked with guilt at the idea that her daughter's problems must have resulted from her own desire to get rid of her, started looking for a therapist for the child. However the mother's wish to be rid of her daughter could not be concealed from the latter, Bettelheim went on. The interpretation of her strange sentence was thus that 'what she needed was a father, and as an American girl with no known father, she could think only of the father of her country as a solution to her problem. Since her unknown father was the "skeleton in the closet" of her life, she asked for his skeleton.'[11]

A pretty story indeed, and one that is full of lessons for both the psychotherapist and the educator! The only problem is that it does not fit in with a single one of the statements I was able to obtain from other people. Everyone who frequented the Bettelheims in Vienna confirms that it was indeed Gina who took care of Patsy, and Gina alone. Patsy herself concurs: 'All the nurturing and all the discipline were Gina's.'[12] Gina goes even further: 'When I was taking care of Patsy, Bruno took no interest at all in her psychological development,' she states categorically. 'He didn't ask me any questions, and we hardly talked about it at all. It was my work, and he had his own business to take care of.' As for the story about Patsy's purported 'first words', it makes her burst out laughing. 'I never saw Bruno play with Patsy. And Patsy was never mute. She would never have said anything like that.' Indeed, according to other witnesses, when Patsy arrived in Vienna she spoke but little, and poorly, but she did speak. In today's terms, her condition would probably not be diagnosed as autistic. But it was, as the Piel family confirmed, the term used by Agnes herself, after having taken her daughter to see the most eminent psychiatrists of the age.[13]

As regards the source of Patsy's problem, the facts, and the recollections of Agnes's cousins, appear to contradict Bettelheim's version of events. At the time of Patsy's birth, they say, her mother was living with her first husband and, officially at least, the birth was perfectly legitimate.[14] It is true however that Agnes Piel could have confided certain things to Bruno Bettelheim that were unknown to anyone else in her entourage, and notably to younger members of her own family. Certain chronological inconsistencies in official records do leave open the possibility that things were not what they seemed. But if there was a secret, is it conceivable that Agnes would not have mentioned it to Gina, who was most directly concerned by Patsy's welfare? Did Agnes have closer relations with Bruno than people in their entourage realized? Or did he guess that she could be hiding something, and ask a few questions? It is impossible to be categorical on any of these points, now that the two parties most directly concerned are dead.

As for Bettelheim's relationship with Patsy, things may also have been a little more complex than they seemed. While not being involved in the day-to-day care of the little girl, he may have had contacts with her that were all the more significant for being rare, as was indeed the case for many European fathers in that period. He gave her presents, and occasionally took her on an outing when Gina was busy. It is also established that Bettelheim attended a birthday party held for Patsy at her school. And the familiar way in which Patsy refers to 'Bruno' to this day implies that he was once very much part of her life. Not to mention the letters that she would occasionally send him later when he was living in Chicago.[15]

That having been said, it is true that Patsy's stay in Vienna provided Bettelheim with his first 'fine tale', all the easier to tell because, in accordance with Agnes's wishes, neither he nor Gina ever revealed the little girl's true identity.

Gina has no recollection of Patsy's birthday party at the Montessori school, which probably took place in April 1936. She was no doubt otherwise occupied on that day, which would explain why Bruno stood in for her. The Montessori primary school on Grünetorgasse was located on the first floor of a former boys' school, and the premises, owned by the city, were small. There were only two classes, and Patsy was in the senior one, taught by the school's principal, Emma ('Nuci') Plank, a pioneer of the movement. The other class, which also included one of Editha Sterba's patients, a severely disturbed little boy,[16] had been taught until the previous year by Emmi Vischer, a young Swiss woman. A trained teacher, Emmi Vischer had come to Vienna to undertake a psychoanalysis and to study the various educational experiments then under way in the city.

Her curiosity had first been aroused by the stories she had heard from Richard Sterba, when he had stayed at her family home in Switzerland. For during the terrible Vienna famine, the young medical student had periodically found refuge in the Vischers' welcoming household. Not long after their marriage, Richard had taken Editha to meet his Swiss friends, and invited Emmi to come to Vienna whenever she wanted. She had done so in 1931, and before long the competent young woman had achieved everything she had set out to do in the city. As soon as she had completed her Montessori training, Nuci Plank put her in charge of the junior class in the school; meanwhile Emmi had also been deepening her knowledge of psychoanalysis by following Anna Freud's seminars at the *Haus der Kinder* and at the Psychoanalytic Institute. There she had got to know August Aichorn, and among others Fritz Redl and Gina Bettelheim.

Although shy, and by her own account very naïve, Emmi was an attractive young woman, and her presence in Vienna did not go unnoticed.[17] During a conference in Rome, where they had all met Maria Montessori in person and visited her *Casa dei Bambini*, Fritz Redl even proposed to Emmi. But although she liked him, he was not her type, and in any case she had already met the man who was to become her husband: Editha Sterba's brother Hubert von Radanowicz. An engineer, he was at the time the Madrid representative of the German electrical company Siemens. In the spring of 1935, Emmi Vischer had married him and left for Spain, handing over her class to Gertrude Weinfeld, the young woman who had been her deputy for the previous two years.

Trude Weinfeld, who was then aged twenty-four, a year younger than Emmi, had been sad to see the latter go. In the years they had worked together the two women had become firm friends. From her contact with Emmi, Trude had not only gained a lot of insights into her work at the school, but she had also been introduced to psychoanalysis. On Emmi's recommendation, she too had become a patient of Editha Sterba. The experience had spelled the end of her first love affair, since the young man involved could not stand the idea of her discussing their relationship with a perfect stranger. She, meanwhile, had gradually realized that she could not go on loving someone who did not see the point of exploring his own unconscious. For Trude, who had up until then suffered greatly from her shyness, psychoanalysis had indeed been a revelation. But she had never told her family about it, knowing that they would not have understood.

Trude's father was an accountant, and although the family had experienced financial problems during World War I and the Depression, she had had a relatively comfortable childhood in Vienna's eighteenth district. Her parents, who were liberal assimilated Jews, got on well together. Even though her mother manifested a preference for Trude's younger brother, born while the father was a prisoner in Siberia, Trude had not suffered too much from it, as she was nevertheless well cared for. For example, when the generally well-behaved Trude was publicly humiliated and unjustly made to stand in the corner at her primary school for talking out of turn, her mother immediately found another establishment for her. Above all Trude had a wonderful relationship with her father. He was always kindly and attentive, and she could not bear to disappoint him. She was generally successful in her studies, but her ambitions were more in the social than the purely intellectual field. After obtaining her *Matura*, she had attended a few classes at university but then decided it was not the place for her. Inspired by her readings of Schiller and Goethe, she enrolled instead in the new social work training school.

Trude had discovered the Montessori school during fieldwork for her social studies. She was so fascinated that she decided to sign up for courses at the *Haus der Kinder* at the same time as she was completing her training. This turned out to have been a good move, since after graduating in 1933 she was to realize how difficult it had become for a Jew to find work in Dollfüss's Austria. Thanks to the *Haus der Kinder* training she was able to get a job at the school on Grünetorgasse, as Emmi's deputy.

Exactly how Bruno Bettelheim and Trude Weinfeld met at Patsy's birthday party we shall never know. Maybe in the course of a conversation about Emmi, whom Bruno had met a few times with Gina and Fritz Redl. Much later, he would confess that he had been attracted to the young woman, without ever daring to tell her. Or perhaps Trude and Bruno were introduced to one another by Bruno's old girlfriend, Lilly Krugh, who also worked at the school. Whatever the case, Bruno Bettelheim drove Trude home that evening. And from then on he started going out with her occasionally, when Gina was otherwise engaged. On one such occasion, he invited her to go with him and Patsy to the Prater funfair. During that outing, for the first time, Trude felt a real friendship being born, as she was to tell her children not long before her death, in a brief account of her youth that she recorded on tape at their request.

What Bettelheim may have thought of the young woman, so very different from his wife, is difficult to surmise. It is certain however that he never for one moment envisaged that she could become his new life-companion. Divorce was simply not an option. Would he have considered it, if social mores had been different? Probably not, for to do so would have been a terrible admission of failure.

Nevertheless, Bruno Bettelheim was not happy. He was later to use an expression coined by Erik Erikson, 'psycho-social moratorium', to describe this period of his life.[18] Of course, he led a comfortable existence and no doubt derived satisfaction, as Gina noted, from being the only person in his entourage to own a car. But such material advantages only served to underline how much in his life was unsatisfying and meretricious. For even if no one else was aware of what lay behind the facade, Bettelheim himself was. What was the use of having a desirable wife if she did not desire you, or of having lots of money if you had had to sacrifice all your youthful ambitions to obtain it? The depth of Bettelheim's malaise can be gauged from the fact that he had slowly but surely drifted away from most of his friends, particularly those who had continued to pursue their ideals, be it through psychoanalysis or politics.

The one exception was Hans Willig, who had also turned his passion – in his case, music – into a hobby in order to devote himself to the all-too-real world of business. He was practically the only personal friend Bruno Bettelheim still had (as opposed to friends met through Gina) at the time he met Trude. And in 1935, Hans had left town, to move to Prague. The intellectuals Bettelheim frequented were now those introduced to him by his wife. Meanwhile, even though the couple never talked about it, the arrival of Patsy in the household had also affected the balance of power between them. From that point on Gina was able to make a financial contribution, which boosted her self-confidence. Her nursery school had closed down after a while, but she then started taking patients at home, notably a deeply depressed Chinese lady with whom she spent several hours each afternoon. And then, after having remained faithful to Bruno during the first years of their marriage, Gina started feeling more and more restless and flirtatious. Her need to play and feel desired began to get the upper hand.

'My relationship with Gina was very difficult. I can hardly understand now why we were once so important for each other and even less why we made things so difficult for one another ....'[19] These words, written much later, were those of a man who had already built himself a new life, and was happy in it. But when one is in the middle of a relationship, when the expression in one's partner's eye only serves to accentuate the poor image one has of oneself, it is difficult to take such a detached view, simply to imagine that things could be any different.

Trude Weinfeld was the opposite of Gina. She was tall, brown-haired and sturdy, and concealed considerable shyness beneath a sporty, out-going exterior. Although attractive she was in no way coquettish, and while intelligent she had no great intellectual pretensions. She liked being able to help people, but her generosity often manifested itself as practical good sense and efficiency. And though her dynamic exterior could some-times give way to a discreet, almost reserved mien, she had an iron will, and a certain type of self-assurance. People who knew her often refer to her very upright posture, and some even admit to having been slightly intimidated by her.

What Bruno Bettelheim found first in Trude, I think, was a friend, with whom relations were reassuringly straightforward. She felt no rivalry with him, but simply listened to him and shared his thoughts and con-cerns. Thanks to her, psychoanalysis and the education of children were suddenly no longer Gina's prerogatives, but subjects of conversation which fascinated him, and on which he too could make a contribution. Not only did Trude listen, she also expressed admiration for what he had to say. Where Gina's critical and impatient ear detected only bluster and second-hand ideas, Trude saw new concepts and ideas being born. And because she was intelligent, she made him feel that his ideas were credible, thereby encouraging him to actually make them so. Indeed it was she, during the summer that Gina spent with Patsy in the United States, who persuaded Bruno to return to his studies and take his PhD.

The relationship between Bruno and Trude deepened gradually. After a few outings to concerts or the theatre, they got into the habit of going swimming together. One day, Bruno took her out into the woods and let her drive his car, a memorable experience for a young woman who did not know anyone else who even possessed an automobile. Little by little they grew very close. After the summer Gina had spent in the United States, Trude would rush out from from work whenever she could to telephone him at his office. She felt guilty at carrying on a relationship with a married man, but at the same time this made the affair even more exciting.

It was after a Shrove Tuesday ball that Trude realized just how much Bruno meant to her. She and Gina had dressed up as young maidens with long braids, and had helped each other make up. During the evening, a young dentist by the name of Peter Weinmann had shown great interest in Trude, who had a great time. As it was too late for her to get back to her home on the other side of town, Gina offered to put her up in a spare room. There, she lay awake all night, unable to sleep from being so close to the man she loved, and who was married to another woman.

Psychoanalysis, while having a disastrous effect on Trude's first love affair, had freed her of a lot of sexual inhibitions. As she was to tell her children, self-mockingly, it was Editha Sterba who showed her the first pictures of naked bodies she had ever seen ('And I was over twenty-five!' she added). She was not, however, a virgin: Trude was very much in tune with the times, convinced of the need to break with Victorian traditions, and her relationship with her first boyfriend had been going on since their schooldays. But it was only around the time that she met Bruno that she began to really understand and acknowledge her desires as an adult woman. I do not know at what point her relationship with Bruno Bettel-heim ceased being a platonic one. However, if only because of the fear of syphilis that still haunted him, I suspect that it would have been she who made the decisive move.

The fact that the outwardly reserved Trude already had some sexual experience was probably reassuring for Bruno. On that level too, things were very different than with his wife. Although externally much more sophisticated and worldly than Trude, Gina had been as inexperienced as Bruno when they became lovers, and that no doubt had played a part in their failure to develop a good sexual relationship. By 1936, however, at about the same time when the affair between Bruno and Trude was becoming more serious, Gina was herself about to meet the love of her life.

Patsy had a toothache and Gina took her to see Peter Weinmann on a recommendation by the Sterbas. Although only forty, Weinmann had already quite a reputation in medical circles; he had just finished rebuilding Sigmund Freud's dental prosthesis, a very tricky job since cancer and several previous operations had destroyed half of his jaw. He was also very charming. But above all Weinmann, for whom the University of Illinois would later create a chair of 'oral pathology', was a true man of science, more interested in research itself than in any honours it could bring. In Gina's eyes he was the just the opposite of Bettelheim.

Gina and Peter Weinmann were immediately attracted to one another. But both were married, and the relationship developed slowly. Peter Weinmann and Richard Sterba were great friends, and as the rules of psychoanalytic etiquette, governing social mixing by doctors and patients, were not as strict as they are today, they often ended up having coffee together in the restaurant where the Weinmanns ate all their meals. Or at social events such as the Shrove Tuesday ball, where Peter had flirted with Trude, perhaps in order to lead Bruno off the scent. And Gina still has vivid memories of a trip to the south of France with the Weinmanns, a few months before the arrival of the Nazis in Vienna. That was when she realized how deeply she loved Peter, who like her was fond of music, nature and beauty, and preferred his own discoveries to those listed in guidebooks. Even at that point, however, neither of them envisaged divorce.

'Although some of my closest friends had become psychoanalysts, I had hesitated to follow their example, partly because I did not wish to be a copycat, and partly because I was not impressed by what becoming psychoanalysts had done for them personally .... It was finally a crisis in my married life which convinced me to give psychoanalysis a try.'[20] The Bruno Bettelheim who made an appointment to see Dr Richard Sterba with a view to starting an analysis was a grown man and a prosperous merchant. But one who did not like his career, and had problems with his wife. As shown by these lines, from his last book, he went to that appointment with reservations, 'to give it a try', knowing that he was not committing himself to anything, and that he was free to change his mind at any point. Sterba was barely five years older than Bettelheim. But as the latter himself recounts, the young analyst soon got the measure of this patient-to-be.

Once they had discussed the practical details of fees and appointments, Bettelheim asked him whether he thought he needed a psychoanalysis. To which Sterba replied that he did not have the faintest idea. It would take at least a year or even two to find out, by which time Bettelheim would know himself, he explained. The future patient's next question, according to Bettelheim's account, was 'whether psychoanalysis could help me'. The analyst's reply was equally neutral.

Up to this point, the conversation had followed a classic pattern. Then Bettelheim thought of a new angle. 'With some desperation, I finally asked him what reason there could be for me to go into psychoanalysis.' Sterba said he had gathered that for many years Bettelheim had been interested in the subject. For that reason 'the only promise he felt able to give me was that I would find the experience very interesting because I would discover things about myself that I had not known before. This would permit me to understand myself better and would make many aspects of my life and my behavior more comprehensible to me.'[21]

With this reply, Sterba clearly made an impression on Bettelheim, showing incidentally that he understood Gina's husband much better than he himself would have admitted. While apparently promising nothing, he was in fact offering Bettelheim the one thing he could not resist: the opportunity to extract meaning from apparent chaos. Deciding that Sterba was a man who could be trusted, Bettelheim resolved to 'give it a try'.

It appears impossible to determine precisely when this conversation took place, and exactly how long Bettelheim spent in analysis afterwards. In his own statements he was always vague, generally speaking of 'several years'. But this is one of the fields in which Bettelheim's assertions are not very reliable, in which he later tended to exaggerate to suit his professional requirements. Gina Weinmann, on the other hand, tends to minimize things. 'Less than a year, I'm sure,' she says. But her statements cannot be considered fully reliable on this point either, although for different reasons. None of the other people who were in contact with Bettelheim at this stage of his life could provide an authoritative answer: the events had occurred half a century earlier, and did not concern them directly. A few of the surviving witnesses to Bettelheim's early life are also reluctant to contradict him on what they see as an essential point.

Wanda Willig, who seems to be the most reliable of those witnesses – because her affection for Bettelheim is so devoid of ambivalence that it would apparently not occur to her to protect him with a lie – cannot be of much help on this point. She knows that his psychoanalysis was not very long but she cannot say anything about it because she and her husband had left Vienna in 1935. Which only tells us that Bruno Bettelheim had not yet started his analysis at that time.

When talking about it to his children, Bettelheim noted that it would have been 'logical' for him to have started an analysis at about the same time as his cousin Edith Buxbaum and so many of his friends (around 1925), particularly given his already strong interest in Freudian ideas. However he cited two basic reasons for not having done so. First, his fear of reawakening the depression that he was just getting over at the time. And secondly, he saw little point in trying to analyse the events of his early life as long as he had not elucidated the dark secret that hung over his and his parents' lives.

Conversely, Bettelheim gave two main motives for undertaking an analysis: a 'crisis' in his married life, and dissatisfaction with his job. All of which leads me to surmise that his treatment must have started in late 1936 or early 1937. For it was then that he must have begun to suspect that Gina was no longer simply flirting with some of her friends, but that she was beginning to fall in love with somebody else. Would he have known who? Gina feels certain that he did not. However, during that trip to the south of France of which she retained such strong memories, the Wein-manns and the Bettelheims travelled as two couples, and I find it hard to believe that Bruno, who was so good at tuning in to other people's feelings, did not realize what was going on.

Another reason to believe that Bettelheim's psychoanalysis began in either late '36 or early '37 is Trude's influence. In the same way that she convinced him to return to university to get a PhD, it seems obvious that she would have wanted to share her enthusiasm for psychoanalysis with the man she loved and admired so much. In telling him of her own experience she must not only have excited his curiosity but also soothed some of his fears about the analytical process. His own lack of self-confidence is indeed another of the reasons Bettelheim advanced to explain his early reticence about analysis.

If I am right about the starting-point of Bruno Bettelheim's analysis, it cannot have lasted for much more than a year, as it was to be abruptly ended by the German annexation of Austria in the spring of 1938. This would however have been a year of intensive Viennese-style analysis, i.e. of five or six sessions per week. (Gina says five, and Bettelheim gave the figure as six.)

The second key question raised by Bettelheim's psychoanalysis is his choice of a doctor. 'Being good friends with so many of the small group of younger Viennese analysts proved to be a problem, because I had to find one with whom I was not well acquainted,' Bettelheim wrote.[22] 'But there was at least one among them – Dr Richard Sterba – who was well recommended to me by an analyst friend whom I trusted. So with some hesitation I made an appointment with him to discuss matters.'

A strange statement indeed. Even if he was not personally acquainted with the analyst, Bettelheim can hardly have been unaware of his existence, for both his wife Gina and Agnes Piel had been Sterba's patients. At the same time, Bettelheim must have known that Gina had subsequently been a patient of Richard's wife Editha, as had both Patsy and Trude.[23] The way Bettelheim tells it, one could be forgiven for thinking that at the end of the 1930s there were only a mere half-dozen analysts practising in Vienna!

Richard Sterba's decision to accept this new patient was no less strange. Rules of professional ethics in psychoanalysis were still being developed;

nevertheless to take on a former patient's husband must already have been a questionable practice. While Bettelheim may have been seeking, perhaps unconsciously, to avoid washing his family's dirty linen in public by choosing a doctor who obviously knew of his marital problems, it is more difficult to understand how an analyst of Sterba's calibre did not regard this as suspicious, and therefore as fraught with risks for the would-be patient. He could hardly have been unaware of Gina's ambivalent feelings towards Bruno, and he was best placed to appreciate the powerful mechanism of transference[24] that her analysis had sparked towards himself. Did Sterba not realize that Bettelheim may have seen him as a rival? Unfortunately, I was unable to find out his side of the story, since people who were close to him refused point-blank to talk to me. Which of course proves nothing, except maybe that they felt uneasy about discussing Bettelheim.

One of the latter's motives for going to Sterba may have been the desire, conscious or otherwise, to find the magic spell that would rekindle his wife's affection for him. But even if that was the case initially, and whatever the exact duration of Bettelheim's analysis, there is no doubt that it helped him lay bare some of the hidden recesses of his psyche. Gina recalls noting quite a change in him during that period. And Bettelheim himself was later to write: 'I cannot blame my analysis for not having done a good enough job, because it made me ready for Trude, and she and our relation was my salvation.'[25]

Nevertheless Bruno Bettelheim was to remark on many occasions, and particularly towards the end of his life, after Trude's death, that although his analysis had helped him to uncover the causes of his depression (which he usually described as 'legitimate' ones), it had not given him the means to overcome it.

He alluded to what he had discovered on Richard Sterba's couch to his friend Carl Frankenstein, and also outlined it a little for his children. His explanations were sketchy, but candid and given in a spirit of authenticity. His analysis, it seems, allowed him to uncover the role played by what he described as a 'shameful secret' in his psyche. In his childhood, his father's hidden illness appears to have become mixed up in his unconscious with the mystery surrounding his grandfather's origins, fostering the idea of an indelible blemish on his paternal origins. The burden was all the more difficult to bear in that during his boyhood an oppressive silence had prevented him from ever finding out what exactly was wrong with his family. Echoing this ignorance was the fact that he knew practically nothing about his Jewishness, except that it laid him open to humiliating remarks. Hence his lack of self-confidence.

This is the only aspect of his psychoanalysis that Bettelheim alluded to. It is however worth noting that the young Bettelheim, who was continually being reminded by his mother that he would soon have to step into his father's shoes, singularly lacked positive masculine role models. At least if we follow his version of events, which from the psychoanalytic point of view is the only one that counts. The only male in his immediate family who had achieved real success without having had anything to hide was his maternal grandfather, Adolf Seidler. But he was a man who had ridden roughshod over everyone, both inside and outside his family. He had been a domestic tyrant who had literally turned his wife into a lifelong invalid, and who had so terrorized and cowed his sons that none of them had dared face up to him and follow the profession he wanted. Even his daughters had been denied the right to choose their own destinies, as Bruno could see from his own mother. Moreover, Adolf Seidler's success had been based on business methods that were shady, if not downright 'fraudulent' (selling the same sewing machines as new several times over). The way Bettelheim talked about him provides ample evidence of his ambivalent feelings. While he was proud at having such a successful and clever grandfather, he obviously found the man's character and methods hateful and took pains to distance himself from them.

On his father's side of the family the picture was not much happier, and from Bettelheim's point of view it was even harder to come to terms with. Jakob Morris Bettelheim's success had been achieved honourably. But as he had died by the time his grandson was born, taking the secret of his origins with him to the grave, Bruno inherited an image of him that was marred by resentment, and a feeling of injustice. For whatever the reasons for Jakob Morris having been abandoned as an infant, that rejection was clearly not his fault. In analytical terms, the deep-seated feeling that a wrong had to be righted probably explains the considerable lengths to which his sons, Bruno's uncles, went in trying to establish their kinship with the influential Bettelheims of Pressburg. Whenever Bruno Bettelheim told that story, however, he never failed to point out that those efforts had been in vain. The wrong had never been righted.

As for Bruno's own father, far from removing the stain from his family's reputation, he appeared to have paid for it with his life. Although Anton Bettelheim was an honourable, caring man, concerned about his children's future, he emerges from his son's descriptions as above all a weak character, a victim. First of all he loses his wife's dowry in a foolhardy lumber deal, and is thus reduced to begging for further aid from the tyrannical Adolf Seidler. As a result he is forced into an unwanted partnership with his brother-in-law. Then he contracts a mysterious and shameful ailment that destroys him and plunges his family into misery and despair. Even when Bruno Bettelheim told his own son that his father's illness had been contracted through treating some business acquaintances to an evening out in a brothel – in other words that he had been the 'the unhappy victim of a bad encounter', as Stefan Zweig put it[26] – this explanation only serves to reinforce the image of the father as a weak, luckless character, doomed to pay off the curse afflicting the family. To return to the classroom incident, does not Bettelheim's violent reaction to a 'simpering eunuch' become clearer when set against the background of the deep doubts he probably entertained as to the virility of his own father? A man who had 'not touched his wife for twenty years'.[27]

It is of course impossible to find out exactly what happened during those sessions on Dr Sterba's couch. This is particularly unfortunate, given the complexity of Bettelheim's relationship to psychoanalysis. However some clues can be gleaned about Sterba's technique from some of his other patients, and also from the slim volume he himself published.[28] Bettelheim's analyst was a strict Freudian in the sense that he intervened very little during sessions. Indeed, that was one of the complaints made by Gina, who found the long silences oppressive. But Sterba was also prepared to take liberties with orthodox procedures when he considered it necessary, such as when he allowed a young trainee psychoanalyst two sessions a day rather than one for a few months so that she could finish her training before emigrating to the United States. 'It wouldn't have worked with everybody, but no doubt he knew that it would work with me,' the former patient told me.[29] Later, when he too was in the United States, Richard Sterba had a problem with the Detroit Psychoanalytic Society concerning his fees. But overall nobody contests the fact that he was a very good analyst.

Similarly, one can only guess what type of patient Bruno Bettelheim was, by gleaning a few clues from remarks he made on analysis at various times. Later, when there was no longer any risk of anyone challenging the title of psychoanalyst that exile had helped him to acquire, his learned comments on the subject would gradually evolve from a critique of one aspect of Freudian thought (as seen in *Symbolic Wounds*, 1954) to a vigorous defence of the latter against the distortions it had undergone in the United States (*Freud and Man's Soul*, 1982). Along the way he had made some cutting comments on the effectiveness of psychoanalysis (in the introduction to *The Informed Heart*, for example) which on the contrary show a markedly 'American' perspective on the subject. On reflection, the most remarkable aspect of his evolution would be the way he seemed to have rediscovered the 'mystery' that lay at the heart of the analytical process, in spite of the fact that he had never resumed his own analysis, brutally cut short by the arrival of the Nazis in Vienna.

Two passages from Bettelheim's writings provide food for thought on the subject. The first is to be found in *The Empty Fortress*, a book which was to mark a key stage in Bettelheim's career, and which appeared around half-way between *Symbolic Wounds* and *Freud and Man's Soul*. In the first part of the book, when discussing the defective development of the ego that characterizes an autistic child, Bettelheim explains the 'secret of psychoanalytic technique'[30] as follows. In order to communicate his or her fantasies to the analyst in words, the analysand[31] is obliged to sort through them and order them into sentences. 'Hence,' he writes, 'as we tell our free associations they are no longer free, but ordered.' A little further on

Bettelheim explains that only sentences constitute material for the analysis, as they reflect the way in which ideas follow on from one another.

Without entering into theoretical debates, I would read such a definition as an indication that during his own analysis, Bettelheim did not get to the stage of letting his own fantasies express themselves freely. For while the words that an analysand utters on the couch do provide a mirror reflecting the landscape of his unconscious, which he learns to look at over time, the organization of those words into sentences involves control by the conscious mind, which is thereby acting as a screen. However this only becomes apparent to the patient once he has broken through the screen by letting himself listen to the words *per se*. And this would be particularly true, it seems to me, in the case of a man who devoted so much of his mental energy to extracting meaning from (and thereby imposing order on) his life and surroundings.

If we put together the various early memories cited by Bettelheim, it becomes obvious that although he was pampered in many ways, he was never allowed to simply be a child. At the age of four, fate in the form of his father's illness had already singled him out as the future mainstay of his family's well-being. But by that age, according to Freud, a boy is embroiled in the Oedipus complex, which leads him to fantasize about the death of his father. Little wonder that Bettelheim should thereafter have struggled to control his unconscious life by imposing order on things. When one has such dangerous fantasies (or rather when life has played the dirty trick of making them come true), one can no longer afford to give them free rein. And when one has spent more than thirty years learning to live with them, it takes time, patience and a great deal of trust in one's analyst to succeed in letting them come to the surface and facing up to them.[32] However, time was one commodity which was fast running out for Bettelheim in Vienna. As for his trust in Richard Sterba, given the existing links between the two men, I find it difficult to believe that it could have been total.

The second remark which I consider revealing about Bettelheim's analysis is to be found in *Freud and Man's Soul*, a long essay he wrote towards the end of his life and in which he accused the English translators of Freud's works of having emasculated their meaning. Although somewhat repetitive in places, this pamphlet (of which more later) vibrates with passionate anger, and has the ring of truth about it. Above all, it shows an understanding of Freud which goes well beyond what can be found in books alone.

In one passage, Bettelheim roundly condemns what he sees as the hijacking of Freud's thinking by those who, like Dr Spock, sought to justify an 'anything goes' attitude. He accuses such advocates of permissiveness of failing to understand Freud's 'tragic belief that man's destructive tendencies spring from a dark side of the soul.'[33] This beautiful though sombre remark refers to a concept put forward by Freud on the way to his discovery of the death instinct, a part of psychoanalytic theory which was not well received in America. And Bettelheim's remark seems to me to reflect, more than just an opinion about psychoanalysis, inside knowledge of the process itself. But wherever Bettelheim acquired such under-standing, I doubt that it was on Richard Sterba's couch in 1937.

On a less conjectural note, let us return to what Bruno Bettelheim said himself about his psychoanalysis. Another thing he admitted to having discovered during his sessions with Sterba was his fear of sex, made worse by all the years in which he was kept in the dark about the nature of his father's illness. That was why Lilly's amorous advances terrified him so. The admission[34] certainly sheds light on Bettelheim's remark that his psychoanalysis allowed him to form a good relationship with Trude. It is worth setting against his account of his first encounters with Freud's writings, considered too obscene to be read in the family home. Indeed, Bettelheim concludes the latter account by underlining the mixed feelings of repulsion and fascination he then experienced. 'Now I believe that coming to psychoanalysis in such a personal way, becoming so deeply involved emotionally and yet so ambivalently, was a most auspicious beginning,' he writes.[35] A promising start, perhaps, but also a remarkably 'family-oriented', and even a somewhat incestuous one, one is tempted to add.

Chapter V

The Anschluss

When Bruno Bettelheim went to sign up for his second semester at Vienna University in the spring of 1937, he had to notice how much the political climate had changed. A new box had appeared on the enrolment form, beneath the one asking the potential student to state his religion; now he had also to state the 'people' he belonged to. Bettelheim thus had to enter not only 'Mosaic', under religion, but also 'Jewish'. This at a date when Nazism was still confined to Germany, and when Hitler had promised Austrians not to seek fulfilment of the 'most ardent and heartfelt wish' he had expressed in *Mein Kampf*: to wit 'the union of my beloved homeland with the common fatherland'.[1]

Bettelheim had considerably narrowed the focus of his studies. Apart from two hours weekly devoted to art history,[2] he was concentrating on only two disciplines, philosophy and psychology. All his courses were taught by Professors Reininger and Bühler, the two men who then headed the philosophy faculty. Both had taken part in the great teaching reform programme of the 1920s.

Reininger, who directed Bruno Bettelheim's doctoral dissertation, was first and foremost a philosopher, although he had done some work in the Psychology Institute, run by Karl and Charlotte Bühler, on the social organization of school classes (at the time both sociology and psychology were merely branches of philosophy). Reininger's best-known work was a study of love, entitled *The Problem of the Psycho-Physics*, which placed him in the school of thought founded by Ernst Mach with his *Analysis of Sensations*. During his first semester with Reininger (autumn 1936), Bettelheim had studied Renaissance thought, rationalism and the philosophy of Nietzsche. The following semester he focused on Aristotle and empiricism.

But Karl Bühler's teaching figured more prominently in the schedule of the re-enrolled student. Ten years earlier, Bettelheim had already signed up for four hours per week of classes with Bühler. That coincided with his father's confinement in a clinic, however, and Bettelheim appears not to have attended very regularly, since in 1936 the university was only willing to credit him with four of the nine semesters he had supposedly completed during his first period as a student. This time Bettelheim signed up with Bühler for four hours a week of general psychology and two hours of language theory (*Sprachtheorie*) in the first semester, and for four hours of the theory of knowledge (logic and epistemology) in the second (spring 1937).

Karl Bühler, whose work was to strongly influence Roman Jakobson and the other Prague Circle linguists, was a major figure in the university. Unlike the idealist German tradition, the Austrian strain of philosophy was analytical, owing more to Leibnitz than to Kant.[3] It was a tradition which accorded considerable importance to experimental psychology. Bühler's *Sprachtheorie* was the core of his teaching. For him, all living creatures had to be seen from the point of view of the creativity principle, i.e. as a function of their ability to perceive and create new forms. In that sense, he may be seen as one of the pioneers of Gestalt psychology, believing the perception of forms to be governed by precise laws.

Bühler was also the proponent of a biological view of the psyche that could not easily be reconciled with psychoanalysis. In spite of that fact, a large number of Freud's students frequented his institute and followed his classes. In those days the distinction between psychology and psychoanalysis, both emerging fields of study, was much less clear-cut than it is today. Psychoanalysis was in fact a branch of psychology; a research orientation, and a somewhat offbeat one at that. In a society that remained in the grip of the Church and bourgeois mores, the new discipline suffered from the stigma engendered by Freud's emphasis on sexuality as the primary source of human energy.

There was thus considerable ambivalence about psychoanalysis in university circles. Although many of the best professors already sensed the scope of its potential, as guardians of academic orthodoxy they were often all too ready to encourage the popular view of it as somehow disreputable. This placed would-be students of psychoanalysis in a difficult position. It was easier for medical school students, as they could take psychoanalysis as a separate topic, either concurrently with their main studies or afterwards. But the idea of lay analysis was also gaining ground; as Freud's work moved forward it was becoming less and less attached to its roots in medicine, and several of his most brilliant students were not doctors at all. Indeed, a glance at the minutes of the Psychoanalytic Society in the 1930s reveals that a solid grounding in the classics was much more relevant than a medical background for those taking part in its discussions.

As psychoanalysis began to turn the spotlight on children and adolescents, many followed the lead given by Anna Freud and August Aichorn, and trained as primary- or secondary-school teachers. Such was the case, for example, for Bettelheim's cousin Edith Buxbaum or his friend Fritz Redl. Others, more drawn to the theoretical side, opted to read psychology at university. This led to a seeming paradox: in spite of the apparent incompatibility between the two views, Freudians flocked to Bühler's courses. In such numbers that many joked about the door of the Psychology Institute giving directly on to the Psychoanalytic Institute.

This does not necessarily imply that, foreseeing world events, Bettelheim had planned on becoming a psychoanalyst when he re-enrolled at university at the age of thirty-three. But neither can such a possibility be completely ruled out. If it were to be the case, many of the later statements he made on the subject, seen today as lies, would turn out to have been merely half-truths, since Bettelheim would only have been prevented from changing his career orientation by the sudden arrival of Hitler. However, if he did not have some radical change of lifestyle in mind, one is left to wonder why, when already a successful businessman, he should have returned to university, and at a time when the situation in Austria meant he could not possibly have hoped to ever teach there. Bettelheim's immediate aim, however, was clear: to get his PhD. Eight months after his enrolment, on May 19, 1937, he registered his dissertation[4] under the title 'The Problem of the Beautiful in Nature and Modern Aesthetics' (*Das Problem des Naturschönen und die moderne Aesthetik*).

His central idea was that the aesthetic experience causes the boundaries between subject and object to dissolve, and that the viewing of real-life landscapes was the original form of that experience. Having examined from a historical standpoint how nature gradually became an object of aesthetic enjoyment, Bettelheim deplores the fact that idealism and formalism, the two main schools in aesthetics at the time, reduce it to a second-rank experience. He analyses how this happened, then seeks to show that the enjoyment of nature is an aesthetic experience in the full sense of the word. An authentic one – because unlike art, it is not mediated by a third party – and one which provides the subject with an opportunity to transcend the dualistic oppositions of rationalist thought, and to achieve a fusion between the subject and the world. Thus does the observer of a landscape become the artist, constructing a work of which he himself is a part.[5]

It was thus a rather academic piece of work, very much in keeping with the spirit of the times, in which Bettelheim demonstrated his familiarity with the main aesthetic theories of the age as well as his knowledge of the history of art and the prevailing tendencies in the humanities, notably psychology. But it was also a well-turned-out work, displaying intellectual agility and, already, a number of highly effective short cuts. However Bettelheim's dissertation showed no trace of any psychoanalytic influence, with the exception of one name in the bibliography: that of Ernst Kris, for his book *Die Legende vom Kunstler*,[6] published three years earlier.

Bettelheim's dissertation was rewarded with a 'very good' evaluation from Reininger and an 'excellent' from Bühler and the other two examiners called upon to assess it.

Another reflection comes to mind, one which has no bearing on the strictly academic nature of the work. As anyone who knew Bettelheim can testify, he was fond of nature, but not excessively so. He enjoyed hiking a little, but was not the kind of person who spends hours gazing at a beautiful landscape. Which suggests to me that Trude Weinfeld must have played some role in his thinking on the subject. She was less interested in art than he was, but she was fascinated by the natural world. Perhaps it was through observing her on the long forest walks they took in the summer of 1936, or listening to her hold forth on her love of nature, that Bettelheim decided on his subject. What is certain is that he did not discuss these ideas with Gina.

So this is another of those periods in which Bruno Bettelheim managed to carry on two almost completely separate existences. For although he had plunged into his studies with determination, he continued to go to his office every day. He was no longer running Bettelheim & Schnitzer, but he was still doing the books, as shown by the audit carried out by the Nazis a year later. Once again, having set his heart on a goal, Bettelheim managed to make miraculously efficient use of his time. Alongside his work and studies, he was carrying on his psychoanalysis, leading a married life and seeing Trude Weinfeld.

All in all, 1937 seems to have been a happy year for Bruno Bettelheim. The changes in him that Gina attributed to his analysis no doubt also had something to do with his growing involvement with a woman who believed in him – an affair of which, too caught up in her own love-life, Gina was unaware – plus an ambition he was determined to fulfil and a grinding daily schedule that left no time for doubts or depression. It may be a simple coincidence that in February of that year he took out a life insurance policy, with the same Riunione company in which he had once worked for a year. It was a twenty-five-year contract with yearly premiums of 200 Austrian shillings, which was no mean sum. Bettelheim's future may have been uncertain, but he clearly felt that it was worth insuring.

Bettelheim still had to take two oral examinations, in philosophy and art history. The former took place on July 17, 1937 and the latter on January 16, 1938; his results in both were 'excellent', and on February 2, 1938 he graduated *summa cum laude* as a doctor of philosophy. The diploma was grandly drawn up in Latin, to one *Brunonem Bettelheim*. On the cards he had printed up the very next day, however, Bettelheim dropped the accusative to announce the news to his friends and relations. Given the atmosphere in Vienna at the time, they probably had other things on their minds. But for the same reason his diploma, among the very last to be granted to a Jew in Vienna before the war, was the passport that would get him out of collapsing Austria and into a new life elsewhere. Without it, wherever he landed up he would have been nothing more than a ruined lumber merchant. With it, he could use his past to create a future.

Six months previously his cousin Edith Buxbaum, faced with the threat of arrest for her political activities, had fled to the United States. In the space of a few months she had not only got set up with a teaching job but was in the process of starting a psychoanalytic practice in New York, even though she was not a medical doctor. A few months before her, Fritz Redl had also left for the New World. He had not fled, he had simply been head-hunted by the Rockefeller Foundation, then actively recruiting European intellectuals. Neither he nor Edith would have got where they were without their diplomas.

On Friday March 11, 1938, less than a month after Bruno finally obtained his PhD, Peter Weinmann and his wife came to the Bettelheim home for a farewell dinner. With a Nazi invasion looming, the Weinmanns had decided to leave immediately for London, with a stop in Paris, where Emmi and Bertel von Radanowicz were then living. It was an icily cold evening, but the weather was not what they, or most other people in the city, were worrying about.

Right up until the start of that fateful evening, the most optimistic Viennese had hoped that the last-ditch referendum on Austria's future, planned by Chancellor Kurt von Schuschnigg, Dollfuss's successor, would succeed in its aim of heading off annexation by Germany. A massive 'yes' vote would have undermined Hitler's stated pretext for unifying the two countries: the safety of Austrian Germans. And viewed from Vienna at least, the 'yesses' appeared set to carry the day by a huge majority.

What Hitler had in mind for the Viennese they all knew; in *Mein Kampf* he described his own last days in the city, in 1913, as follows: 'My inner aversion to the Hapsburg state was increasing daily .... This motley of Czechs, Poles, Hungarians, Ruthenians, Serbs and Croats, and always the bacillus which is the solvent of human society, the Jew, here, there and everywhere – the whole spectacle was repugnant to me .... The longer I lived in that city the stronger became my hatred for the promiscuous swarm of foreign peoples which had begun to batten on that old nursery ground of German culture.'[7]

Precisely one month before that farewell dinner at the Bettelheim home, Schuschnigg had been summoned to Hitler's eyrie at Berchtesgaden to hear the dictator's conditions. After having kept the Austrian leader waiting for several hours, and then showering him with insults, Hitler demanded that the Austrian head of the Nazi party (NSDAP, or *Nationalsozialistische Deutsche Arbeiterpartei*), the Viennese lawyer Arthur Seyss-Inquart, be made interior minister with untrammelled powers over the police, that all jailed Nazis be freed, including those who had plotted against Dollfuss, that the NSDAP be legalized and that Austria enter into a customs union with Germany. Hitler stated that the demands were non-negotiable, and gave the hapless Schuschnigg three days in which to comply or face immediate annexation. Schuschnigg had complied.

Along with the jailed Nazis, however, the government had also freed the Social Democrats and the Communists. After having vainly sought help from other European governments, and after Mussolini had made it clear that he would not honour the Italian-Austrian defence treaty if Hitler made a move, Schuschnigg had turned in desperation to his former enemies, the very trade unionists and left-wing activists that his predecessor had outlawed in 1934, to try and create a broad Fatherland Front against the external threat. In exchange for the restitution of their civil rights, the Communists and Social Democrats had accepted the offer. Schuschnigg had then announced that a referendum on the future of Austria would be held the following Sunday.

For the past two days, therefore, anti-Nazis of all hues had been rallying behind Schuschnigg in a motley alliance, and an atmosphere of sacred union was spreading throughout the country. Or at least, throughout Vienna, as told by the writer George Clare, then aged seventeen: 'On 10 March Vienna woke to a fever of patriotic fervour. The painting columns of the 'Fatherland Front' had been at work all night stencilling Schuschnigg's portrait, huge "yesses", crutched crosses and slogans on walls and streets. Everything with a large enough surface had been covered with "Fatherland Front" symbols and with exhortations to vote for the Government. Aeroplanes showered leaflets over the city. Lorries draped in the national colours, packed with men and women yelling "Red-White-Red unto Death!" cruised through the streets distributing more leaflets .... Vienna had last witnessed comparable scenes in August 1914, when its crowds acclaimed the outbreak of war.'[8] An idea of just how broad the coalition was can be gained from the fact that on the following day, Friday March 11, the leader of the Revolutionary Socialists, Karl Hans Sailer, was due to go on the radio to call for a 'yes' vote.

Sailer never made his speech. From the middle of the afternoon, a rumour began to circulate that the referendum was being cancelled. Early in the evening, it became official. The radio switched to playing nothing but slow and mournful music instead of the news bulletins and martial tunes that had made up its programmes for the past two days. In homes all over Austria, people kept their sets on.

At 8 p.m. Kurt von Schuschnigg went on the air. His voice breaking with emotion, he announced that Hitler had threatened to invade Austria if the post of chancellor was not immediately handed over to the man of his choice. Schuschnigg, who had again spent the afternoon in a fruitless quest for foreign help, informed his compatriots that he had decided to resign. It was a poignant speech, one that nobody who heard it was ever to forget. In it Schuschnigg also held the foreign governments responsible for refusing to come to his country's aid.[9] 'President Miklos has asked me to tell the Austrian people that we have yielded to force, since we are not prepared even in this terrible hour to shed blood. We have decided to order the troops to offer no resistance.'[10]

For the past two hours, gangs of hoodlums wearing Nazi insignia, many of them drunk, had been marauding in the city centre, insulting passers-by. Their leaders were beginning to move into government offices, where they indeed met no resistance. And as Schuschnigg spoke, Marshal Goering in Berlin was on the telephone to Arthur Seyss-Inquart, giving him the go-ahead. Less than an hour after that call, Hitler signed the order for German troops to cross the border at dawn, 'to help prevent bloodshed' in Austrian cities.[11]

The Glorietgasse was some distance away from the main outbursts of hatred, but neither the Bettelheims nor their guests could have been unaware of what was going on in the city centre. They were no doubt still listening to the radio when Schuschnigg's speech was followed by the national anthem, and then by Seyss-Inquart announcing that he was taking over. The Nazi leader also stressed that the Austrian army would not resist the arrival of the German forces, thereby confirming that Hitler's ultimatum to Schuschnigg had been nothing more than a lie, and that the invasion had been intended all along, whatever the Austrian government did.

'Gina, why don't you and Patsy leave with the Weinmanns, in a couple of days?'

'No, I'll wait for you. I won't leave without you.'

'That's impossible. I've still got lots of things to deal with, and I'll be able to cope much better on my own.'

That is essentially how Gina remembers the exchange she had with her husband at that point. She comments: 'Bruno would never have left Vienna leaving his mother behind.'

The account of that evening given by Bruno and Trude was somewhat different, however. In her memoirs, the latter reported that 'the first ones to leave were Gina and Patsy, because Patsy's mother called from America .... Although Bruno wanted to go with them, I learned quite recently that his sister became hysterical when he tried to tell her and their mother what he was going to do. So he stayed behind ....'

Trude's version is of course hearsay, since she was not present that night, but her account is consistent with a remark made by Bettelheim to a counsellor at the Orthogenic School in the mid-1970s: 'My mother almost caused my death on two occasions. The first was the day after the Anschluss. I was all ready to leave with my wife and the little American girl we were looking after, when I made the mistake of calling her to say goodbye. After that, I no longer had the courage to leave.'[12]

What documentary evidence exists, however, seems to back up Gina's version; she obtained her visa for the United States the next day, on March 12, 1938, whereas Bruno apparently did not apply for his until some weeks later. As for Patsy, over fifty years later she has only one memory of the evening in question: her mother's telephone call. Agnes Piel, having heard the news on the radio, was beside herself, and during her long conversation with Gina she on occasion shouted so loudly that everyone in the room could hear her. She did not want her daughter to stay a single day longer in Austria. Gina tried to reason with her, explaining how difficult it was to obtain the necessary papers, to get packed for such a major trip. To no avail, Agnes insisted that Patsy be brought home without further delay. And she pointedly reminded Gina of the warnings she had proffered during the summer of 1936: 'If you'd listened to me, you'd have been in New York by now.'

After dinner the Bettelheims accompanied the Weinmanns back to their home near the city centre. The situation had already deteriorated considerably; hardly had Schuschnigg finished speaking than trucks carrying SS and SA men had converged on the Ring, with shouts of '*Heil Hitler*,' soon followed by '*Ju-da-ver-recke*' (Die, Jews!), filling the air. Among those chanting could be seen people who only that morning had been handing out leaflets calling for a 'yes' vote in the expected referendum. Others had triumphantly pinned on to the front of their lapels the Nazi insignia that they had up until then kept hidden behind them.

Vienna had gone crazy. It seemed that even those who the previous day had been ready to line up behind Schuschnigg in favour of Austrian independence now had only one desire: to see Hitler arrive as soon as possible. The young George Clare observed the scene with his parents from the window of their ninth-district apartment, with the lights out so that nobody could see them. He watched the neighbourhood policeman, whose friendly 'good morning' had for years reassured him every day on the way to school, furiously clubbing a man who had dared to complain about the marauding Nazi mobs.

At around 2 a.m., the *Wehrmacht* crossed Austria's southern border. In Vienna, persecution of the Jews started immediately. Shops were vandalized and passers-by were seized by gangs of thugs and forced to kneel on the pavement, scrubbing off Patriotic Front slogans with a caustic solution that burned their hands.[13] 'Work for the Jews! At last the Jews are working! We thank our Führer – he's created work for the Jews!' the gangs chanted, as Austrian policemen looked on, in some cases impassively and in others approvingly.

Of all the characters involved in this account, it appears that only Trude's mother was subjected to the humiliation of the scrubbing-brush treatment. But Bruno Bettelheim was soon to gain first-hand experience of the new methods, for right on that first day, March 12, he was to lose his car. As the correspondent for the British *Daily Telegraph* reported, every single vehicle belonging to a Jew was indeed expropriated, with the gangs often demanding money to buy gasoline as well.[14] The car of which Bettelheim had been so proud, as well, apparently as the one owned by his partner Hans Schnitzer, had been confiscated even before the German troops arrived in Vienna, by the number III *Kreisleitung*, or local Nazi cell, in the twelfth district, where his company was located. In a letter he would send to his mother from Dachau, listing his possessions, he wrote that the car had been confiscated 'by the police'. He may have written that to avoid the letter being censored, or it could be that the men who seized his car were in fact wearing police uniforms. Whatever the case, it was Bettelheim's status as a businessman that attracted the attention of the Nazis during those early hours.

That Saturday morning the violence continued with increasing intensity throughout the city, while the sky was filled with the roar of the *Wehrmacht's* bombers, flying over at very low altitude to drop leaflets. The radio, meanwhile, brought more and more bad news. In the early hours of dawn, SS chief Heinrich Himmler arrived in the city, with his deputy Reinhard Heydrich. Midday brought a message from Nazi propaganda chief Goebbels, announcing that a 'real' referendum would be held, under the protection of the Nazi troops, which he said had been 'called in' by the Austrian government to ensure the country's independence. Then at 7.30 p.m., Hitler himself arrived in the town of Linz, after a detour via his birthplace of Braunau. At his side, Goebbels launched the slogan that was to become the battle-cry of the Austrian Nazis: *'Ein Volk, Ein Reich, ein Führer.'*[15] It was a motto that, beyond the lies of propaganda, perfectly summed up the situation: the remains of the once-proud Hapsburg empire had in fact become nothing more than an ordinary province of Germany.

During those hours Gina was furiously busy, getting ready to leave with Patsy for a period which seemed certain to be very long, if not indefinite. She gave final instructions to the faithful Hedwig, who had offered to watch over the Bettelheims' valuables and see if they could be forwarded later, and she scrambled to get together the required papers for her trip. At the US embassy, besieged by a frantic crowd of would-be emigrants,[16] she appears to have been given priority treatment, as she got her visa on the same day. But the US authorities were already becoming reticent about helping the fast-growing number of people trying to escape Nazi persecution. In spite of the affidavit that Agnes Piel had given her, promising to support her until she found a job in the United States, Gina was granted only a tourist visa. This was to have unexpected consequences, but it nevertheless allowed her and Patsy to leave, either the next day or the following one, on the 9.45 p.m. express for Paris, passing through Innsbruck and Zurich.

In the pandemonium at the railroad station, Gina and Patsy said goodbye to Bruno and also to Richard Sterba, who had come to see the Weinmanns off on the same train. As the two parties were not in the same car, they resolved to meet up in Paris. But Gina was heavy-hearted, knowing that the reprieve for her relationship with Peter Weinmann was to be a short one; he had decided to make his home in London. Patsy, convinced that Gina's sadness was due to her separation from Bruno, was even quieter than usual. She recalls that when some Nazi officers got on to the train, just before the Swiss border, Gina started to panic somewhat. Knowing that she was not allowed to take a large sum of money out of the Reich, and preferring not to take any risks on her way to freedom, she according to Patsy threw an envelope full of dollar bills that Bruno had given her out of the train window. However Gina denies that any such incident ever took place.

It indeed seems that Bruno Bettelheim was not caught as unawares by the Anschluss as were some other Viennese Jews. According to a Nazi audit of his company carried out at the time of its 'Aryanization', from 1937, a small number of transactions were no longer recorded in his ledgers. He had also mortgaged off his life insurance policy. Bettelheim himself claimed that he had been able to smuggle 10,000 dollars out of Austria, with the help of an American journalist friend. Although the sum seems improbably large – it would be worth over 200,000 of today's dollars[17] – it is no doubt impossible to verify this, Gina having no recollection of any such transaction.

The situation was less clear-cut at the time than it appears with hindsight. Nothing that had happened in Germany since Hitler had come to power could have prepared the Austrian Jews for the firestorm that was to descend on them the minute Germany annexed their country. The repression was so ferocious in the weeks after the Anschluss that it drew favourable comments in the SS newspaper *Schwarze Korps*, which wrote that the Austrian Nazis 'have done in one night what we haven't yet managed to do here in the heavy, slow-moving north. In Austria there was no need to organize a boycott of the Jews – the people themselves did the job, with honest joy.'[18]

Some anti-Nazis had indeed started to send savings out of the country whenever they could, especially after the Austrian-German treaty of 1936. Richard Sterba, although not Jewish, had for example had the foresight, three years earlier, to start asking the father of a young Canadian patient to send his fees to a Swiss bank account.[19] George Clare tells how his father had started preparing for exile long in advance[20] – but then he was a banker. Many other people did not have the means to take such precautions, or else did not see the point, believing that no harm would befall them as long as they did not stand out from the crowd. The Zionist historian and journalist Josef Kastein, in a famous article entitled '*Was Nun?*' (What Now?), published in 1935 on his return to Vienna from Berlin, was quoted as saying that 'once the Nazis got into power the worst that could happen to the Jews would be to be shut up in ghettos as they were in the Middle Ages, and obliged to wear a yellow star'. However, he added, these passing problems would not be such as to warrant emigration. Which was why Kastein recommended that only younger Jews go to settle in Palestine, while their elders waited for the storm to pass. That opinion had been very widely shared.[21]

Given the opinions Bruno Bettelheim was to express later, and notably the severity with which he was to judge the unpreparedness of many of the victims of Nazism, it is legitimate to ask just how far-seeing he proved to be as the Anschluss loomed. Disappointingly, the few scraps of information available do not provide a clear answer, especially since the statements Bettelheim himself made on the subject are often at odds with the recollections of other witnesses. An example is Bettelheim's account of the hours following the Anschluss announcement, given in testimony for the Nuremberg Tribunal: 'Immediately following the occupation of Austria on or about March 12, 1938, it became apparent to me that I would not be permitted to live in peace in Austria. Therefore I resolved to leave the country. My wife and I left Vienna on about 12 or 13 of March and were stopped at the Czechoslovakian-Hungarian border that night. The next day we undertook to leave Vienna by train, and while my wife was permitted to proceed, I was detained by the police, ordered to remain in Vienna and my passport was taken away from me. Within the next day or two the police searched my home. I was extensively questioned but not taken into custody, the police stating that it did not appear that I had violated any of the laws of Austria. Three or four weeks later I was taken into custody by the Austrian police and for three days questioned about my political activities. At the conclusion of the questioning the police officer who was in charge of the investigation dictated a statement to the effect that there appeared to be no basis whatever for any legal action against me. Thereupon I was released. Two weeks later I was taken into custody and imprisoned. It was stated to me that my confinement was the result of orders issued by the Gestapo in Berlin. I spent three days in jail in Vienna after which I was transferred to the concentration camp at Dachau ....'[22]

Gina however, was categorical when interviewed on the subject: at no point did the couple attempt to cross over into Czechoslovakia, either by train or car. As we have already seen, Bettelheim's automobile had been confiscated on March 12. Gina no longer remembers whether she and Patsy had left Vienna on the 13th or the 14th.[23] What is certain, however, is that the pair were aboard the US ship *President Roosevelt* when it weighed anchor in the French port of Le Havre on March 17. The night before that had been spent with the Radanowiczes in Paris; there was thus no room in Gina's and Patsy's tight travel schedule to have fitted in a trip towards Bratislava.

It is conceivable that Bettelheim made the reported trip with Trude, after Gina had left. But if that were the case Trude would most certainly have alluded to it in the memoirs that she left for her children, which are extremely detailed on the period. The contradiction is all the more puzzling in that if Bettelheim simply invented the Bratislava story, it is difficult to understand why. It would indeed be the only example I came across of a story being made up by Bettelheim for which no obvious external motive – be it the need to obtain a job, or the desire to pass himself off as being cleverer or more important than he really was – could be found. For although some Austrians did opt to flee from the German invasion towards the east, Czechoslovakia then being a democratic state with an apparently robust army, they were of course soon to regret it. So that by inventing such a tale for an American audience, Bettelheim would not even have been likely to impress anyone with his foresight.

This is unfortunately another mystery which cannot be conclusively resolved. As Vienna's police archives for 1938 remain to this day closed to the public, it is impossible to check the facts, just as it is impossible to determine in what circumstances Bettelheim was arrested and then freed on two occasions before his final deportation, as he also told the US prosecutor.

What is indisputable, however, is that on May 28, acting on orders from Berlin, the Gestapo arrested Bruno Bettelheim at his home as part of the *Juden-Aktion*.[24] This was a full-scale official pogrom carried out in the three months following the Anschluss and involving the arrests of some 70,000 Austrian Jews in all, most of them in Vienna.[25] Many were to be released after two or three days of detention and interrogation, but attacks and 'home visits', during which neighbours and doorkeepers in apartment blocks often helped the Nazi gangs to single out Jews, continued, intensifying during the Passover period. In May the order came from Berlin for the arrest of some 2,000 intellectuals whose names were on a list drawn up long in advance by the Austrian Nazis. Those arrests were to result in the sending of three trainloads of prisoners to Dachau between May and June 1938; Bruno Bettelheim was in the one which left on June 2. A previous deportation exercise on April 1, calculated to make a strong impression in the first days after the annexation, had taken all the leaders of Vienna's Jewish community, as well as a large number of leading political, media and business figures, not all of them Jewish, to the same concentration camp. They were accused by the Nazis of having supported the ill-fated Patriotic Front.

Bettelheim was later to hint that he had aided the underground Social Democratic movement prior to his arrest, but I was unable to find confirmation of that. Such political activity by definition does not often leave records. None of the witnesses who could have shed light on the subject were still alive, and Bettelheim's only documented political affiliation was his membership of the Fatherland Front. Since anti-Nazis of all tendencies had joined the Front *en masse* in the months prior to the Anschluss, that is not a particularly significant piece of evidence. To judge from his Red Cross certificate of incarceration, however, the truth appears both simpler and more tragic. Bruno Bettelheim, the refined intellectual who loved German literature and Expressionist painting, had been arrested solely because he was a Jew, and a prosperous businessman to boot.

The fate reserved for the Bettelheim & Schnitzer company only serves to confirm that impression. The firm was officially closed down on Thursday July 7, 1938, only to reopen a week later. The new owner was a certain Nikolaus Lackner, a Nazi activist who had been born in the Croatian city of Zagreb in 1902. At the time of the annexation he had been an accountant with the Frid & Thiemann bank. This institution, specializing in finance for the lumber trade, was Bettelheim & Schnitzer's own bank.

The take-over process was carried out with rapid efficiency. On April 26 1938, the new authorities enacted a law obliging all Jews to register their assets by the end of July. On May 19, Bettelheim and his partner were told that a provisional administrator had been appointed for their company, a fellow lumber merchant by the name of Paul Hudl. Was he responsible for finding the so-called 'buyer', or did the firm simply fall into the lap of someone who knew about and coveted it? A person in a position to assess its value, as he had worked in the same bank for the past fourteen years? The latter explanation seems the more plausible. Nikolaus Lackner appeared ideally suited to carry through the company's 'Aryanization'. He had joined the Austrian NSDAP in 1933, and as shown in a letter of reference from the party dated September 1938, he was considered a model activist, and authorized to carry a weapon. He was also described as being married to an Aryan, having a sixteen-month-old child and living in the fifth district. Lackner had always served the party well, even during its time underground, the letter stated. Its purpose was to recommend that Lackner, who had been given a provisional lease on the Bettelheim & Schnitzer company in June, be allowed to purchase the firm outright. He was to get what he wanted, becoming the owner on September 22, 1938. He was even to go on running the company right up until December 1955!

The first contract with Nikolaus Lackner is dated June 9, 1938, which was less than a week after Bettelheim had been shipped off to Dachau. The documents for the so-called sale were drawn up by his partner Hans Schnitzer, who being married to an Aryan had apparently not been arrested. They stated that the company employed four workers, who were not Jews (in 1937, one of them had been), and set its value at 28,055 Reichmarks, equivalent to around 250,000 dollars today. The documents also gave the name of the official buyer (Lackner's brother-in-law, who was apparently his financial backer). In another document, issued in June 1938, the Austrian timber industry trade association asserted that an agreement in principle to sell the Jewish firm Bettelheim & Schnitzer to Nikolaus Lackner had in fact been reached some time previously, but that Bruno Bettelheim had been arrested just before it was formally concluded. Finally another document, dated 1942, records four payments made by Lackner over a period of just over two years for the total amount of RM 28,055. The payments were indeed made into an account in the names of Bettelheim & Schnitzer, in the bank at which Lackner worked. But an accompanying letter stated that the two purported beneficiaries were forbidden from drawing on the account!

On August 20, 1940, the Gestapo wrote to the *Vermögensverkehrsstelle*, or merchandise transit office, the body in charge of the 'Aryanization' of Jewish assets in Vienna, confirming that the Jews Bettelheim, Bruno and Gina née Altstadt had been stripped of their civil rights and asking how much their possessions were worth so that the confiscation process could go ahead. Finally, a letter from the bank dated November 25, 1943 confirmed that the assets of Mr Bettelheim and Mr Schnitzer had been confiscated by the Moabit-West tax office in Berlin.

It was thus a classic case of 'Aryanization', i.e. outright theft dressed up to look like a legitimate sale thanks to an outwardly convincing mass of paperwork. Thousands of similar expropriations took place all over Austria at this time, once again bringing expressions of jealous admiration from the German Nazis.[26] It is generally reckoned that in the months following the Anschluss, seized Jewish assets were valued at around fifty per cent of their true market value (later on, the percentage fell steadily), but in spite of the existence of a very thorough audit of Bettelheim's company, it is impossible to assess the relative value of the sum decided upon. It is also difficult to determine what role Bruno Bettelheim himself played in the process. Once he had realized that the expropriation could not be prevented, it is likely that he opted to play the game in order to settle things as quickly as possible. After all, it had clearly become impossible for him to stay on in Vienna. His wife was already settled in the United States, where he was lucky enough to have a few good friends and, thanks to Patsy, to be able to count on having a roof over his head. Two years earlier, Agnes Piel had even offered to buy a large house in which all of them could live together. What was more, Bettelheim had never wanted to be a lumber merchant in the first place; the job had been thrust on him by circumstances, and had prevented him from fulfilling his own ambitions. He must therefore have seen a lot to be gained from getting rid of it. What clearly never occurred to him, however, as is shown by his letters from Dachau, was that he would not receive a single cent from the proceeds of the 'sale'.

Before his hoped-for departure, Bruno Bettelheim had wanted all his affairs to be settled. One example: he could not bear the idea of losing all the beautiful fitted furniture he had had made for the apartment. Even from Dachau, he continued trying to get it taken care of, asking his mother to have it put into storage, and stressing that it belonged to Gina. (The latter detail presumably being intended to show that the items could not be seized, as their owner was a US resident.)

While struggling to preserve what remained of the good life he had enjoyed with his wife, Bettelheim was also trying to ensure that his remaining loved ones could leave the country. As a US citizen could only sign a limited number of immigration affidavits, depending on his or her financial means, and as the Prohibition era had eaten into the Piel family fortune, Agnes was not in a position to provide such documents for all the people Bettelheim wanted to help.

On May 5, Jenny Buxbaum, Paula Bettelheim's sister, managed to leave for New York, where her daughter Edith awaited her. That meant that Paula would have a place to go to if Bruno was unable to vouch for her upkeep in America. Meanwhile Bruno's sister Margarethe had contacts that could allow her to go to Britain. But there was also Gina's mother, Mina. And there was Trude. 'It is almost impossible to describe the turmoil, fear and anxiety that permeated the lives of the Jews,' she was later to tell her children, in the memoirs she recorded for them. Trude Weinfeld also was caught up in a whirl of activity. On the day of the Anschluss, her father had been in Switzerland on business. On hearing the news he wanted to return at once, but she persuaded him not to. She had a more difficult time convincing her mother to leave immediately and join him. Fortunately, her horrible experience of scrubbing the pavement made her change her mind. Shortly afterwards, Trude learned that one of her father's sisters, unable to bear life after his departure, had committed suicide.

She was also laying plans to leave, of course, but was not sure where to go. She knew nobody who could vouch for her in the United States. She had considered Switzerland, but as her parents were finding out to their cost, that country had no intention whatsoever of becoming a refuge for all the people made homeless by the Third Reich. (The Swiss Justice Minister in person had suggested to the Nazis that they mark Jews' passports with a large red 'J' to make them more easily recognizable.) And then Trude was in no hurry to leave Vienna as long as Bruno was still there.

She also had other worries. The Montessori school had straight away attracted the Nazis' attention as a hotbed of Jews and leftists. Although expelled from their Grünetorgasse premises, which belonged to the city, the teachers had managed to complete the school year. Nuci Plank had persuaded a Christian friend, a museum curator, to provide a cover for the school by becoming its official director. He was apparently a good-hearted and cultivated man, no doubt representative of that fraction of the non-Jewish Viennese population who were appalled at what was happening. Such people did exist, although there were not as many of them as was to be claimed after the collapse of the Third Reich.

The referendum on reunification organized by the occupying power on Sunday April 10 resulted in a 99.75 per cent 'yes' vote. As eyewitness William Shirer pointed out, it would indeed have taken a lot of courage to vote 'no' given that in voting centres, 'wide slits in the corner of the polling booths gave the Nazi election committee sitting a few feet away a good view of how one voted'.[27] Meanwhile the membership of the Austrian Nazi party, 43,000 before the Anschluss, shot up to 127,000 in just six months.

Amid the torment, Bruno Bettelheim had also lost his psychoanalyst. Richard Sterba had been present in November 1936 when the German analyst Felix Boehm came to Vienna to try to convince Sigmund Freud that he had 'saved' psychoanalysis in his own country by agreeing to purge the Berlin Psychoanalytic Society of all its Jewish members. This made Sterba afraid that the Nazis would try and force him to become a traitor in his turn, as he was then the only non-Jew on the bureau of the

Psychoanalytic Society.[28] On March 16, Richard Sterba left Vienna for Switzerland, after informing his patients of his departure by telephone.

Bettelheim's main problem, however, was that his application for a US visa was being held up by unexpected red tape. As soon as Gina and Patsy had arrived in the United States, on March 26, Agnes Piel (who in the meantime had become Mrs Crane) had asked the US consul in Vienna to speed up proceedings for Bruno. She meant well, but would probably have done better to go straight to the State Department's visa section. Accusations of anti-Semitism have since been made against certain members of the US mission there; whether they are true or not, it is clear that when faced with the sudden stampede of desperate people clamouring for visas, the first reaction of the diplomats in Vienna had been to say 'no'. Although Bruno Bettelheim had all the required backing, and the profile of a 'good' immigrant, his application was not treated any better than any of the others, at least not at first.

Having acknowledged receipt, on April 8, of the affidavit that Agnes Crane had sent for Bruno, Consul General George Wiley appears to have mislaid the document. At least that was what Bettelheim was told when he responded to an invitation for an interview on April 20. A Mr Medeley even told him not to return until the Labor Department in Washington had provided clarification of his wife's status.

Tipped off immediately by Bruno, Agnes Crane then launched into a furious exchange of letters with both Vienna and Washington. In early May she suggested that the affidavit originally intended for Gina be instead assigned to Bruno. But that was quite impossible, she was told, since the US authorities could not give immigrant status to a man whose wife had entered the country as a simple tourist! Although Agnes Crane managed to keep the tone of all her letters within the bounds of courtesy, she was clearly boiling inside. It would appear, if my calculations are correct, that it was around the time this 'technical hitch' came up that Bruno Bettelheim was arrested and held for three days.

Agnes stepped up her campaign, firing off letters and bombarding Washington with telephone calls. She pointed out that Gina had used a tourist visa only so that she could bring her daughter back home as quickly as possible. She rounded up all the help she could get, including the National Coordinating Committee for Aid to Refugees and Emigrants Coming from Germany and, through Edith Buxbaum, the New York Psychoanalytic Society. She even offered to pay for all the telegrams needed to settle the case, an offer that the State Department was only too happy to accept.

In spite of all her efforts, things had not moved much by May 28, when the police knocked on Bruno Bettelheim's door at number 15 Glorietgasse. In the most recent of his letters on the matter, the head of the State Department visa section had courteously explained to Agnes Crane that for Bruno to be accepted as an immigrant, his wife would have to leave the

US and herself file a new application for an immigration visa from a foreign country. He helpfully pointed out that this did not have to be done from Vienna!

Chapter VI

Dachau: The Making of a Survivor

'Now that all that has fortunately been behind me for fifteen years, I can admit it: the year I spent in concentration camps did me good,' wrote Bruno Bettelheim in 1954. The ten months and eleven days he had spent in the concentration camps of Dachau and Buchenwald had indeed played, and would continue to play, a key role in his life. Like all the survivors of the Nazi camps, he remained marked for life by the experience. And the imprint stamped on his psyche may explain, for example, his obsessive desire to control his own death. But in his case there was an additional, more material effect. To put it crudely, as he expressed it himself on occasion, it also opened the door to the 'second life' that he described in that letter to a long-lost friend.

Long before the publication of *Love is Not Enough*, of *The Empty Fortress* or any of his essays on psychotic children, and well before he had even set foot in the Orthogenic School, Bettelheim had made a name for himself through his writings on the Nazi camps, and on the related subject of anti-Semitism. It was thanks to those texts that he achieved recognition in the United States as a specialist on human behaviour. The observations he had recorded in the camps played a role in awakening Americans to the reality of Nazism, and they also gave a powerful illustration of the depth of Bettelheim's own insights into the human soul. They invested him with moral authority.

In other words, it was in Dachau and Buchenwald that the lumber-merchant-cum-philosophy-student, whose psychoanalysis had been so abruptly cut short by the Anschluss, gave birth, through a process of fear, pain and permanent humiliation, to Bettelheim-the-psychoanalyst. It was there that his reading of Freud, his time on Richard Sterba's couch, his talks with Gina and the experience of living with Patsy all came together to light up the way ahead, both in the short and the long term.

Which is why I consider it essential to try to retrace, as faithfully and precisely as possible, the circumstances in which the experience took place. Fifty years on, this is no easy task. First, for practical reasons: both documents and witnesses are rare, and although Bettelheim wrote a great deal about the camps, he went into very little detail regarding his daily life there, always preferring a more distant, analytical standpoint.

But another more subtle difficulty arises when trying to reconstitute the atmosphere of Dachau and Buchenwald in 1938-39. It results from the pictures etched on all our minds since Soviet troops entered Auschwitz in January 1945. As Bettelheim himself stressed, the logic of the death camps was different from that of the concentration camps. Even though, at least as far as the Jews were concerned, the former were but the diabolical extrapolation of the latter; even though Dachau served as the laboratory for Auschwitz.

Three types of source were used in this research. First, Bettelheim's own writings and statements, the testimony he gave in July 1945 to the Washington office of Judge Jackson, the US Chief Counsel at the Nuremberg War Crimes Tribunal, the nineteen letters he sent to his mother while he was in the camps and the few snippets of information he revealed later to those close to him. Secondly, books and other publicly available documents on the camps.[1] And finally, the testimony of two of Bettelheim's fellow inmates at Dachau and Buchenwald. One was Ernst Federn, the youngest son of one of Sigmund Freud's closest collaborators,[2] who was twenty-eight when he met Bettelheim in Buchenwald and remained an inmate right up to the liberation of the camp in 1945.[3] The other was Hans Bandler, an engineer ten years younger than Bettelheim who arrived at Dachau in the same train as he did and was to go through more or less the same stages. Bandler, however, was released three months before Bettelheim.[4]

Three types of source, providing data of three different types, which unfortunately do not always fit perfectly together. After several attempts to arrange them into some kind of hierarchy and thus create a seamless picture, I slowly came to the conclusion that they simply had to be allowed to coexist, without seeking at all cost to make them perfectly coherent. The reality of the camps is to be apprehended via these testimonies taken as a whole. Bettelheim's testimony, first of all, because even when it does not completely tally with objectively known facts, it nevertheless reflects what went on in his head. And then the stories of his two companions in misfortune, men who were as different from him as they were from one another. From all of this there emerges a world, an experience, which it is often more enlightening to feel before trying to analyse it.

Before many others, Bruno Bettelheim used the expression 'dreamlike' to describe what went on in the camps. 'Dream' as in 'nightmare', of course, but above all a world that was dreamlike in its unreality, offering its inhabitants no way whatsoever of linking their previous existences to the one into which they had been plunged. A world from which, as Hermann Langbein put it, all the normal laws of human society had been banished.[5] A world in which everyday words such as 'good', 'evil', 'work', 'honour', 'justice', 'merit', 'man' or 'Jew', did not have the same meanings, and in some cases had precisely the opposite meanings, as they did elsewhere. A world, therefore, which was quite literally unspeakable to all those who had not known it at first hand.

Those who never experienced the Nazi camps must resign themselves to the fact that whatever knowledge they can obtain about them will never be either completely real or totally rational (indeed, it is for precisely that reason that some people can dare to claim that the genocide never occurred). The only objective truths that can be acquired about the camps concern factual data such as the number of beds, the times of the trains, and even they are only partial. For the rest, i.e. for the essentials, we have only the testimony of men and women, the deportees and their warders, who were deliberately put in the situation of being unable objectively to grasp what was happening to them. And Bettelheim was indeed one of the first people to understand, or at least to explain, that crucial aspect of life in a concentration camp.

When Bruno Bettelheim arrived in Dachau, the 'model' camp on which all the later ones were to be based,[6] it was as yet inhabited only by Germans. The Dachau *Konzentrationslager*, opened in 1933 in a former explosives plant a few miles from Munich in upper Bavaria, was originally designed to house 5,000 prisoners, essentially Communists. Soon, however, it was also taking in Social Democrats, and all those categories of the population that the régime defined as 'asocial', such as the handicapped, priests, Jehovah's Witnesses, homosexuals, people labelled 'work-shy' and criminals. As yet, however, there were not many Jews.

The Austrians who were shipped to Dachau from Vienna between April and June 1938, immediately after the Anschluss, were in fact the first major groups of Jews to be detained in concentration camps for no other reason than their Jewishness.[7] Bettelheim mentioned this fact in passing, but did not elaborate on it.[8] Twenty years later, however, when he was to lash out at the 'ghetto thinking' which he considered to have facilitated the extermination of many Jews by preventing them from taking timely measures to survive and above all to flee,[9] those who accused him of arrogance and even of anti-Semitism, or who retorted with a 'What about you, then?', tended to overlook the fact that, even if he had been able to get out of the camps relatively quickly, Bruno Bettelheim had been among the first to be detained as a result of the Nazis' racial policy.

Even though Germany's Jews had been subjected to persecution, insults and plunder ever since Hitler had come to power in 1933, the only ones actually interned in concentration camps before the spring of 1938 were there either as a result of their activities, political or criminal, or because they had, from the fall of 1935 on, contravened the Nuremberg Laws which forbade sexual relations between Jews and non-Jews.[10] And, although those laws did indeed single out Jews as such, there is a genuine difference in the way a man experiences ill-treatment resulting from a risk taken consciously through breaking a law, even an iniquitous one, and ill-treatment meted out solely on the basis of who he is.

The Viennese were also the first foreigners to be interned, even though their jailers refused to label them as such. The detainees were drawn from a wide variety of age groups, social classes and professions – including politicians, shopkeepers, workers, artists and intellectuals – and yet they were all treated alike, which in itself was a shock for the Viennese, who had in general little experience of social mixing.

Bruno Bettelheim arrived at Dachau on Friday June 3, 1938,[11] and was registered as prisoner number 15029. On the signing-in book, he is recorded as 'Sch. D. J.' The 'J' of course stands for *Jude* (Jew), and the 'D' for *Deutsch* (German), a label which simply reflected the annexation of Austria.[12] The 'Sch.' is short for *Schutzhaft*, which literally means 'protective detention'. The term had been enshrined in law by the Nazi state in order to justify the indefinite detention of anyone who happened to get in its way, and thus the existence of the new camps.[13] It was a catch-all category that could include not only avowed anti-Nazi activists such as Ernst Federn, but also vague sympathizers, whose only crime may have been to have signed a petition or donated a bit of cash to movements supporting the underground struggle. According to Federn, Bettelheim fell into the latter category. And that is why his striped deportee's jacket, like those worn by Federn and Bandler, carried a two-coloured Star of David. The upper triangle, in red, announced that he was a political prisoner, while the lower one, in yellow, symbolized his Jewishness.

As is well known, the Nazis were sticklers for administrative formalities. New arrivals had to wait for hours, watched over by SS guards and with their bundled possessions at their feet, to fill out the camp admission forms. Surname, first names, religion, race, full address, name of closest relative, parents' address, membership of the Communist party or other dissident groups, previous convictions, etc. And little mercy could be expected by anyone found guilty of 'intellectual falsification of documents'.

Outside, the vast camp with its identical blocks lay spread out on each side of the *Lagerstrasse*, or central alley. On June 3, 1938, the weather was hot at Dachau. For the new arrivals the long wait, although frustrating, was a welcome respite after the tough journey they had just been subjected to, which had lasted around twenty hours. As David Rousset put it,[14] it was a period of 'soothing indifference'. And although the new detainees feared what lay ahead, they as yet could not be sure of anything.

Most of these men were educated, and many of them had already had access to information about the concentration camps. However, as Bettelheim himself admitted,[15] they were still at the stage of wondering whether the reports were really true. How many of them, for example, were likely to be taken in by the slogan displayed in wrought iron above the camp gate: *Arbeit Macht Frei* (Work makes men free)? A sign which Himmler, who had insisted on being the one to announce the opening of the Dachau camp in March 1933,[16] was to have reproduced seven years later over the gates of Auschwitz.

In different circumstances, Bruno Bettelheim would probably have been the first to point out the sick humour of the slogan. He would no doubt have found even more ironic the statement painted in huge white letters on the roof of the camp's administrative section. 'There is a path to freedom,' it read. 'The stages along it are obedience, zeal, honesty, order, cleanliness, sobriety, sincerity, the spirit of self-sacrifice and love of the fatherland.' At the time of his arrival, however, Bettelheim was in no state to appreciate such absurdities. In the train which had brought him from Vienna he had been brutally beaten about the head and he had even been stabbed with a bayonet.

His practical initiation into Nazi dehumanization techniques had begun the previous evening at Vienna's main station, the Westbahnhof, not far from the company premises which were to go on bearing his name for a few days more. Gina and Patsy had departed from the same station for Paris two and a half months earlier, and if Bettelheim's train had left just twenty hours later than it did he might have crossed paths with Sigmund Freud, headed regretfully for exile along with his wife and daughter Anna.[17]

Up until that point the prisoners had certainly not been handled with kid gloves, but they had not been subjected to excessive cruelty. After their arrests they had been herded together in a school building and had suffered the anxiety of not knowing what was to become of them. But many of them, including Bettelheim, had already been detained since the Anschluss, and they had usually been allowed to go home a few hours or days later. They had been ill treated, but they were still in their own city, close to friends and relatives.

'I thought they'd send us home any time,' Hans Bandler told me. 'I had belonged to the socialist youth group before Dolfuss. And when the Nazis marched in the streets, I looked out of the window and I could see some of my former comrades from the movement! The whole thing seemed absurd .... I felt they were essentially kids claiming to be in command of things. I kept asking myself: "When will they come to their senses?" '

The real nightmare had started in the late afternoon on June 2, when the Nazis had suddenly packed their charges into their notorious *Schwarze Marias* (black marias, or police vans), their windows blacked out to prevent the prisoners from seeing where they were being taken.

Bruno Bettelheim's account of his journey to Dachau, which took him across two-thirds of Austria and southern Germany, opens with a few lines of footnotes at the beginning of *Surviving*: 'On the train ride from Vienna to Dachau, which had lasted a night and the better part of a day, all the prisoners were severely mistreated. Of the approximately 700 to 800 prisoners who were part of this particular transport, at least twenty were killed during the night. Hardly anybody escaped unharmed, and many were wounded severely.'[18]

That rather laconic statement was confirmed by everyone who survived the journey. There may have been discrepancies as to the figures,[19] but all agreed that the SS guards were extremely brutal during the trip.[20] As the deportees were hustled into the carriages amid shouts, insults and barked orders, blows from rifle-butts rained down on them. Whatever the age or status of the victims, the tone was always the same: 'You, the Jew! Get a move on, get back, keep your eyes up,' etc.

Once in the train, the prisoners were ordered to sit down and keep their eyes fixed on the lights that hung from the ceilings of the rattling railway carriages. According to Bettelheim, the Nazis had deliberately had more powerful bulbs put in, to make the lights more blinding. Machine-guns were trained on the prisoners, and anyone who let himself slump down or appear to fall asleep was rewarded with a hail of blows. In some cases, this led to death. Hans Bandler, who was in the same train, could not tell me how many people died. As he kept his eyes glued to the ceiling during the whole trip he saw practically nothing. He did witness an execution, however: that of a young man who had tried to escape by jumping out of a window during the night. The guards stopped the train and shot him dead. Some time later, Bandler discovered that the victim had been one of his classmates.

Further on in Bettelheim's account,[21] he describes the ill-treatment the prisoners were subjected to during the interminable journey, which was punctuated by long, inexplicable halts. It included kicks, beatings with sticks and whips, slaps, and also shootings and blows from bayonets, one of them landing on him. All of this was in addition to the slow torture of having to keep one's eyes fixed on the lights, and on occasion of being ordered to remain kneeling for hours.

Bettelheim soon detected method in the apparent madness of the SS guards. The periods of physical torture alternated with mental ill-treatment, which included obliging the prisoners to blaspheme their God or call their wives or mothers whores. On some occasions the guards also got the prisoners to fight amongst themselves. Bettelheim noted that the ill-treatment tended to decrease in intensity the longer it lasted, only to return to full strength each time the guards were rotated. He saw this as proof that the torture was part of a deliberate strategy. Around twelve hours into the journey, he heard an order go round among the guards: 'Stop mistreating the prisoners.' The ill-treatment stopped immediately, and did not resume until after their arrival at Dachau.[22]

It seemed to Bettelheim that the torture served two purposes: to break any resistance on the part of the prisoners themselves, and to train the young SS guards, many of whom had been only recently recruited from rural regions. They obviously had to be taught that their charges, who came from very different backgrounds than they did, and could all too easily have intimidated them, were in fact the inferior beings that the official ideology said they were.

Bettelheim's wound was apparently inflicted at the beginning of the train ride. He does not describe the incident itself, but says he suspected that the attack was inspired by his horn-rimmed spectacles, which 'marked me as an intellectual'. He reports that the glasses were shattered by the first blow. He lost a lot of blood, and became gradually weaker and groggier as the journey dragged on. He was also in a state of psychological shock; like Hans Bandler, he had simply not believed such things to be possible. But at the same time, he felt himself becoming curiously detached from what was going on, and began asking himself questions such as 'whether [a] man can endure so much without committing suicide or going insane'.[23]

Although Bettelheim felt very much like fainting in order to escape the physical pain, he resisted the temptation, realizing, as apparently most other prisoners did, that to do so would be suicidal. 'Anyone unable to follow orders was killed.'[24] He also felt it was essential for him to observe what was going on.

At the same time he found himself fighting a growing sense of unreality, telling himself that no, it was not a nightmare, it was really happening. He wondered whether the guards were stupid, or simply sadistic. After a while, he even took grim comfort from their obvious lack of imagination. He almost smiled to himself on hearing them repeat how they preferred to beat the prisoners to death rather than shoot them, since a bullet cost six pfennigs, and they were not worth that much.

But his overriding concern was 'to safeguard his ego in such a way that, if by any good luck he should regain liberty, he would be approximately the same person he was when deprived of liberty'.[25] That, at least, was the way he remembered it when he came, three years later, to describe the journey in his first article on the camps. The passage was emphasized by italics.

Later, when he began 'interviewing' his fellow inmates, Bettelheim found that all the new arrivals expressed the same will to get through the nightmare so as to find both themselves and the outside world unchanged when they came out, to the extent that they sometimes went into a rage when they learned from a letter or other message that one of their possessions had been sold, even though the sale was often aimed precisely at purchasing their freedom. Later still, when Bettelheim tried to put his thoughts in order so as to write about the camps, he made this desire to maintain both oneself and the outside world in the same state one of the defining characteristics of what he called the 'new prisoners', meaning those who had been inside for less than a year.

Once checked in to the camp, the new arrivals were taken to the clothing block, where each was issued with underwear, a shirt, a pair of trousers, a jacket, cap and shoes, without the slightest attention being paid to sizes. They were then ordered to strip naked, and subjected to a humiliating and intimate body search. All the clothing they had arrived in, and all other possessions, had to be handed over to the inmates who were in charge of the stores; all valuables such as watches and jewellery were put into a cloth bag with their name on it.[26] These formalities completed, the new prisoners could finally go to their block.

Bettelheim had lost so much blood during the train-ride that the morning after his arrival the prisoner in charge of Block 22, to which he had been assigned, sent him, along with a few others, to the *Revier*, or camp infirmary. There, a doctor prescribed three days of complete rest, followed by three days of *Schonung*, or 'preferred treatment'. As Bettelheim later observed, this probably saved his life, giving him time to marshal his strength before facing the life of the camp. And, 'what may have been more beneficial in the long run, it was also an opportunity to attempt taking stock of my experience, to sort out first impressions of what being in this horrible predicament was doing to my comrades and to me .... Had I been projected immediately into the dreadfully destructive grind of deadly mistreatments and utterly exhausting labor, as were my comrades, I do not know whether I would have succeeded equally well in reestablishing some parts of my psychological protective system,' he wrote.[27]

The Dachau day started at 4 a.m., with the cleaning out of the block. The SS guards insisted that beds had to be perfectly made up, which was no easy job given that they consisted of shapeless straw mattresses laid three abreast on three-level bunks. It was 'such a difficult task that prisoners sometimes preferred to sleep on the floor sooner than risk destroying their well-built beds,' writes Bettelheim.[28] The morning ablutions were also a rush: not enough washbasins to go round. Screams, pushing and constant anxiety were the norm. Then came two roll-calls, the first outside the block and the second, the main one, on the camp parade ground at 5.15 a.m. In theory, the work teams were formed at 6 a.m., but in practice the roll-calls always went on later than that. The SS guards made so many mistakes in their count that the prisoners began to wonder if they were not doing it on purpose. Each time a discrepancy was found, the whole process would begin again.

After the roll-call, the prisoners were given their daily ration of around half a pound of bread. They then formed up into lines, three abreast, to begin the long day's work. There was a one-hour break at lunchtime, during which they had to resist the temptation to wolf down all of their bread in one go. Work would then continue until 6 p.m., when they returned to their blocks pending the evening roll-call, an hour later. Dinner was a bowl of soup, which on good days might contain a scrap of sausage or fish. It was lights out at 9 p.m.

The Nazi régime was not yet concerned with getting as much free labour as possible out of its prisoners. Its aim was above all to break them, to strip them of absolutely all pride in themselves and their abilities. Which is why plumbers found themselves pressed into activity as hairdressers (each prisoner's head was shaved on arrival) and tailors were made to do carpentry. As for the middle class people and intellectuals rounded up in

Vienna, they were forced, at least for a time, to spend the day carrying enormous rocks from one end of the camp to the other, only to take them back again the next day.

Columns of men being driven to their tasks like beasts of burden with mechanical movements and lowered eyes, always at the mercy of an accident, or worse still, of some whim on the part of an SS guard or a *Kapo*.[29] Men who appeared to be devoting all their remaining energy to merging into their surroundings, avoiding being noticed. 'The most dangerous was when you needed to go to the toilet – and, given what we ate, we often had diarrhoea. You had to ask for permission. Then, you never knew if a bullet wasn't going to hit you as you turned your back. "Shot while trying to escape," was the way they called those deaths,' Hans Bandler recalled.[30]

It was not yet Treblinka or Auschwitz, not yet systematic extermination, but death was nevertheless omnipresent. Death that could be caused just by some SS guard's need to let off steam, as mentioned by Bandler; death from exhaustion, or, and above all, the death that comes from simply giving up. Some prisoners, in a last desperate act of revolt, threw themselves on to the electrified barbed wire that surrounded the camp; others, a larger group, simply grew weary of fighting for survival. Because, as Bruno Bettelheim immediately noticed, the first of many inversions that took place in the concentration camps, even at that early stage, was between life and death. In the world the prisoners had been removed from, life was the norm and death something accidental or unusual. Here in the camps, it was the other way round.

Survival could no longer be taken for granted; it required unremitting vigilance. Maybe Bettelheim recalled, with bitter irony, the long drawn-out agony of his father, those two endless years during which he had had to watch helplessly as Anton, in spite of the terrible illness, the pain, the horrible deterioration of both his body and his mind, had clung on stubbornly to life. Perhaps it was that memory which gave Bruno Bettelheim the determination and strength to hold out against a despicable enemy, whether it be called syphilis or Nazism. Maybe he told himself, once again: 'Not me! That won't happen to me.'

One evening, shortly after his arrival in Dachau and at a time when he was still recovering from his injuries, Bettelheim was staring at his soup, unable to touch it. A German Communist worker who had already been inside for four years told him: 'Listen, you, make up your mind: do you want to live or do you want to die? If you don't care, don't eat the stuff. But if you want to live, there's only one way: make up your mind to eat whenever and whatever you can, never mind how disgusting. Whenever you have a chance, defecate, so you'll be sure your body works. And whenever you have a minute, don't blabber, read by yourself, or flop down and sleep.'[31] Bettelheim says he did not fully understand all the implications of that lesson in survival until several years later. But from that moment on, swallowing the awful soup became for him an act of freedom, simply because it was no longer something imposed on him by the Nazis, but the result of his conscious decision to remain alive.

Bettelheim's small stature, his extreme short-sightedness and his frail constitution, in other words all the characteristics which had made him vulnerable in the school yard, now became doubly dangerous. Furthermore his short-temperedness and his well-known physical clumsiness marked him out from the start as a high-risk prisoner, of the type who often did not make it through the first few weeks of life in a concentration camp. The same inmate told him: 'If you survive the first three months, you will survive the next three years.'[32] Bettelheim immediately started working out how he could avoid being assigned work that would rapidly prove too much for him. After spending several days pushing heavy wagons loaded with rocks alongside Bettelheim, Hans Bandler has a recollection of his friend being put for at least a while on latrine duty. The inmates who were given that foul-smelling job were derisively referred to as '*Kolonne 4711*', after the well-known brand of eau de Cologne. However the task, which consisted of hauling buckets laden with excrement, had two genuine advantages. First, the SS guards kept their distance due to the nauseating odour, and secondly, the inmates had the right to a warm shower every evening.[33] Although Bettelheim himself never explained what type of work he had done during his detention, Bandler's recollection is supported by Austrian psychiatrist Eugen Kogon's book on the camps.[34] Kogon states that although for a certain time latrine duty at Dachau was reserved for the Jews, the task was also at one point assigned to Max and Ernst Hohenburg, the two sons of Archduke Franz Ferdinand. This could explain why Bettelheim later wrote that he had rubbed shoulders with 'two Austrian dukes, closely related to the former Emperor'.[35] And in *The Informed Heart*, published much later, he was to describe an incident during which 'a duke of Hohenburg, grandnephew of the Austrian Emperor, was cruelly mistreated and humiliated'. The preceding sentence states that 'at one time, I worked alongside of a count'. The relative lack of surveillance of the latrine squad made it easier for the inmates to communicate with one another. Later, when analysing the behaviour of his fellow inmates, Bettelheim would put the three members of the high aristocracy he had met in the camps in a category all of their own, stressing how their innate feeling of superiority helped protect them against the general degradation, even though some SS guards singled them out for especially brutal treatment. Kogon also notes that the two Hohenburg dukes showed great courage during their incarceration.

'My year in the concentration camps … was to teach me much, so much, that I am not at all sure I have even now exhausted what was implied in that learning experience,' wrote Bettelheim in 1960,[36] as he sought to define the role played by the experience in his life as a whole. The reaction is typical: while others simply suffered, Bettelheim felt right from the outset the need to be in control of what was happening to him. And in the state of powerlessness which was the prisoner's lot, the only available option was to try and make mind rule over matter. To try and once again understand, and give meaning to, the events around him.

This type of defensive reaction had been triggered as soon as Bettelheim had been arrested. Even before he had fully realized what was in store for him, he had felt the need to observe, assess and analyse the behaviour of the men who had got him in their grip. It was his way of holding his head up, of refusing to admit defeat. Although he credited his persecutors with both intelligence and power, as his writings clearly show, he quickly saw that they were already seriously affected by the very process of dehumanization to which they were submitting their victims.

Very soon, however, Bettelheim's attention was drawn to something even more important to him than the Nazis' behaviour: his own. 'Almost from the moment I was imprisoned, and particularly during the transport to Dachau and my first days inside it, I was aware that I not only acted, but often felt differently than I used to.' Observing his own moods, scrutinizing his own behaviour to check whether it was 'normal', was an exercise Bettelheim was used to. His long-running fight against depression had taught him to be on the alert for danger signs.

'At first I made myself believe this was only on the surface, changes that did not touch my personality. But soon I realized that what had happened to me – for instance the split within me into one who observed and one to whom things happened – was a typical schizophrenic phenomenon. So I began to ask myself: "Am I going insane, or am I already insane?" '[37]

When the Nazis had marched into Vienna, Bettelheim had been in the middle of a psychoanalysis. Such a process cannot be terminated from one day to the next; the ever-fickle doors of the unconscious, which often require so much effort to push ajar, cannot be simply slammed shut again. The perception that the analysand has sought to attain, over a period of months or years, of his or her most secret wounds, those which are the most painful and therefore the best-protected, cannot suddenly be made to go away. The habit of questioning every daily gesture, dream or thought does not come to a halt simply because he or she puts a stop to the treatment, with or without the analyst's agreement. Why therefore should the process end any more easily after a shock like the one Bettelheim had experienced: the Anschluss, followed by separation, the expropriation of all his property and internment in a concentration camp?

This concern about his mental health was what led Bettelheim to undertake the study that, several years later, would make his reputation in the United States. The idea occurred to him towards the end of his first month in Dachau: 'Early one morning ... I was deep in the middle of what was the favorite free-time activity: exchanging tales of woe and swapping

rumors about changes in the camp conditions or possible liberation.'
Although they did not last very long, the conversations got the prisoners
very worked up. 'As before on such occasions, I went through many severe
mood swings, from fervent hope to deepest despair, with the result that I
was emotionally drained before the day even began, a day of seventeen
long hours that would take all my energy to survive it. While swapping
tales that morning, I suddenly realized: "this is driving me crazy," and I
felt that if I were to go on that way I would in fact end up "crazy." That
was when I decided that rather than be taken in by such rumors, I would
try to understand what was psychologically behind them.'[38]

At the same time, Bettelheim began to notice the strange behaviour of
many of his fellow inmates. Even though nothing indicated that they had
been anything but normal before their arrests, in Dachau Bettelheim saw
them behave like pathological liars, incapable of controlling their emotions and having seemingly lost all ability to assess situations objectively.
He wondered if he was not headed down the same path. After all, perhaps
what was happening to him was not the onset of insanity, but simply a
process of adapting to the particular circumstances of camp life. But if that
were so, another serious question arose: how could one protect oneself
against such a process?[39]

When faced with his father's illness, the young Bruno Bettelheim had
finally drawn on the strength of his own will to fight a totally unjust,
oppressive and deadly situation. Now, behind the Nazis' barbed wire, he
found the same type of strength. He could count neither on his physical
stamina nor on his charm, and he lacked any practical know-how. He had
only his mental powers to rely on.

'All my thoughts, all my energies went into the desperate struggle to
survive the day, to fight off depressive moods, to keep up the will to resist,
to gain some small advantages that might make seemingly impossibly
difficult efforts to survive just a bit more likely to succeed, and to frustrate
as much as possible the SS's unrelenting efforts to break the spirit of the
prisoners. When I was not too exhausted or downhearted to do so, I tried
to understand what went on in me and in others because this was of
interest to me.'[40]

That was how Bettelheim found a way of answering both his questions
at once, by undertaking the study of his own and his fellow inmates'
behaviour. To turn what came naturally to him into a conscious project,
he started talking to the prisoners around him whenever he got the
chance. He would quiz them about their lives, their families and their
hopes. He would make them talk about their work. And then he would
spend the long working hours trying to commit every detail to memory,
since he did not have any way of keeping notes. Bettelheim soon realized
that he had resolved another problem along the way: 'By talking with my
fellow-prisoners with a particular purpose in mind, by pondering my
feelings for the hours without end during which I was forced to perform

exhausting labor which did not ask for any mental concentration, I succeeded in killing the time in a way which seemed constructive.'[41] On occasion, he even found himself forgetting that he was in a concentration camp.

Even more important, Bettelheim realized a short time later that his undertaking had given him back his pride. After all, 'it was one of the rare satisfactions that the SS could not deprive me of'.[42] It was a purely private victory over the enemy, but it nevertheless pulled him out of a slide into depression which in the circumstances would almost certainly have proved fatal. He had found his own way of adapting to an environment which, in the full meaning of the word, was insane.

On Sundays, the prisoners did not work. They could talk to each other more or less freely, read some newspapers and write to their families. They were allowed two letters a month. These had to be written on small-sized ruled paper, twelve lines a page with the camp regulations stamped on the first sheet. Bettelheim's letters to his mother were impeccable, his long hand usually filling all the available space on the authorized lines. The writing is very legible (obviously for reasons of censorship), and most of the time quite firm. Their tone is also firm; the letters discuss almost exclusively practical matters: forms to be filled out, debts to his tailor or shirtmaker to be paid off, requests to be filed for the various documents needed for his release, etc.

Whether it was due to the censorship, or to avoid worry for his family, Bruno Bettelheim made no mention whatsoever of what he was going through, either physically or emotionally. If it were not for their format, his letters could at first sight be taken for those of an executive on a business trip, giving instructions to his secretary. A second reading, however, shows up rare passages in which a hint of pain or anxiety seeps through.

On July 3, for example, he wrote: 'Don't worry about me, there's no point as it would serve no purpose.' Or on July 17: 'As regards myself, I haven't got very much to tell you. My life is filled with work, and the nostalgia I feel for you …. Think of yourselves, not of me, for over time that would be too heavy a burden.' Or again, on July 31: 'I am torn by feelings of nostalgia …. Tell Gina that all my hopes rest on the future she is building for us.'

As one reads on, the image of the strong businessman in control of everything, displaying irritation when his orders are not carried out in double quick time, gradually gives way to a very different one: that of a man struggling desperately to remain in touch with the outside world. A man determined to repress the pain and nostalgia that threaten to overwhelm him. A man who has set himself a single goal: to make sure that no stone is left unturned to try and get him out, and should he be set free, that no red tape will prevent him from going into exile as soon as possible.

He had placed his business affairs in the hands of his cousin Norbert Bettelheim, a lawyer, to whom he had formally given power of attorney on the morning of his arrest. Norbert took care of the so-called sale of Bettelheim's company, made an official inventory of his assets and oversaw the efforts of a variety of people to obtain his release. He was well connected, and as he was married to an Aryan and had converted to Protestantism, he appeared to have a good chance of being left alone by the Nazis, at least in the period immediately after the Anschluss. But Bruno Bettelheim became impatient; as he saw it, his cousin was not acting speedily enough. At the end of July, for example, he was expressing surprise that the business inventory had still not been completed, in spite of the fact that he had sent Paula a second proxy statement, along with a list of all of his assets and liabilities, as soon as he had arrived at Dachau.[43] He was also bursting for news of his US visa application, his Internal Revenue receipt of taxes and his *Unbedenklichkeitserklärung*, the 'certificate of innocence' without which nobody was allowed to leave Austria. Attending to every possible detail, he shot off a stream of instructions to his mother and sister. And in spite of what he was going through himself, he clearly did not imagine how appalling life had become for the Jews still in Vienna. Just as he did not mention his sufferings in his letters to Paula, she also refrained from mentioning her lot: how she had been obliged to seek refuge with her neighbours, and how she was surviving by selling off her jewellery, having not received a cent from the sale of his company.

At the same time, Bettelheim took an interest in the fate of all his near and dear, including Trude. Why had she not yet left Austria? And his aunt, Grete Bettelheim – if she had an opportunity to emigrate to Honduras, let her take it! What about Gina's mother, Mina, was she being taken care of? In spite his forced absence, he remained very much a *paterfamilias*, even down to remembering everyone's birthday. And above all, having quickly learned how to get his message across in spite of the camp censors, he succeeded in communicating the idea that henceforth, exile was the only possible option for everyone.

On September 23, after the morning roll-call, the inmates were told to get their possessions together. Then, in what Hans Bandler remembers as a bolt from the blue, the guards ordered them to pile into military trucks. '*Schnell, schnell!*' Each man was given a chunk of bread, a small piece of sausage and a minute ration of margarine. Then, in great haste, all the camp's inmates were hauled off northwards, with no idea of where they were being taken.

On the eve of his meeting at Munich with Messrs Daladier and Chamberlain, and with his invasion of Czechoslovakia already planned, Hitler had decided to empty the Bavarian concentration camp, considering it too exposed in the event of a Franco-British reaction. So the Dachau prisoners were being taken further into the German heartland, to the Prussian camps of Sachsenhausen and, for the Jews, Buchenwald.

When Bettelheim arrived at Buchenwald, it was already known through-out the Reich as one of the toughest of the concentration camps.[44] Opened in 1937, it was in the process of being enlarged when the 'Dachau Jews' arrived, and of course the job was being carried out by the inmates themselves.

One day, Ernst Federn's labour team was ordered to form a human chain to supply bricklayers working on new blocks. The men were spaced just far enough apart so that they had to throw the bricks, rather than passing them from hand to hand. Federn quickly became irritated at his immediate neighbour, who managed to drop every single brick he threw to him. He didn't know the man, but did know that he was playing a dangerous game. He ran the risk of hurting his foot, or worse still of getting himself noticed by a guard. Federn made a remark.

'Is that your brick?' came the reply.

After a few similarly curt exchanges, Federn finally blurted out: 'You nobody!'[45]

'Who is a nobody for you – are you an anybody? I am Bettelheim.'

'And I am Federn.'

'Are you a relative of Paul Federn?'

'I am his son.'

Thereupon the two men 'shook hands and remained friends from that hour,' as Federn concludes in his book *Witnessing Psychoanalysis*.[46] 'I think even friends of a very special kind, because as far as I can remember, Bettelheim has never raised his voice against me,' he added. The manner of their meeting was to set the tone for their whole relationship, a tone which, to judge from the correspondence that Ernst Federn showed me, consisted of affectionate camaraderie spiced with a fair measure of rivalry.

There were considerable differences between Dachau and Buchenwald. The Prussian camp was much larger, the size of a small town. Above all, it was filthy, the lack of paving, the endless rain and the construction work having all conspired to turn it into a giant mudbath. The sticky dirt was practically impossible to get rid of and made the inmates' lives a misery; in wintertime they were often up to their knees in the slimy mess. After a few days, some of them even ended up laughing at fellow sufferers who collapsed into it, too weak to lift their legs out of the slime, which seemed like a metaphor for all their sufferings.[47] Inside the blocks, they were forced to spend their time sweeping, mopping and boot-cleaning if they wanted to avoid yet more blows and insults from the SS and their surrogates. The latter were all the more fearsome in that it was the 'Greens', or common-law prisoners, who were in charge of the camp at that time.[48]

The Nazi system was based on having the concentration camps run by the inmates themselves, following a well-defined hierarchy that included the *Kapo* (work-team leader), the *Blockältester* (block leader), etc., right up to the *Lagerältester*, who was a kind of shadow camp commander. (It was a hierarchy that resembled that within the SS itself.[49]) In exchange for appreciable material privileges (better food, more freedom of movement, including in some cases access to the camp brothel) the SS were thus able to offload much of their daily drudgery on to certain of their victims. Needless to say, the latter could be stripped of their role and privileges just as arbitrarily as they had been elevated to them in the first place. For the Germans, it was a system which shielded them from the everyday hatred of the inmates,[50] but also no doubt from their own feelings of disgust. Above all, it served to break the prisoners even more radically, by compromising them and undermining any trust between them.

But the effectiveness of the system depended on the type of men chosen to be so elevated above their fellows. On arriving in Buchenwald, in the same convoy as Bettelheim, Benedikt Kautsky, another Viennese arrested after the Anschluss, immediately noticed the difference between a camp run by political detainees, as Dachau had been, and one in the hands of common-law prisoners: being ruled by the 'Greens', he wrote, meant 'corruption, torture, hunger, and ill-treatment inflicted on inmates by other inmates'.[51]

Bruno Bettelheim did not write about his arrival at Buchenwald. However another first-hand account, that of the German journalist Walter Poller, is worth citing. A socialist, he had been sentenced in 1934 to four years' imprisonment for his anti-Nazi activities, and after having served his term in various ordinary jails he was sent to Buchenwald two months after the 'Dachau Jews'. His account of his arrival at the camp is very similar to that given by the Viennese detainees of their first transfer: the terrible rush, being made to run an SS gauntlet of gunshots and blows from rifle-butts along what was known as the 'Karacho way',[52] the long narrow alley that ran between the camp's administrative buildings. And woe betide anyone who stopped to worry about those of his fellows who had not made it. Once at the other end, the prisoners would be greeted with the phrase that was to become a *leitmotif* of the concentration camps: 'You are not in a sanatorium here! Those of you who haven't realized that will be made to understand, you can count on that!'

After comparing his experiences with those of many other inmates, Bettelheim came to the conclusion that the terrible initiation rite was systematically inflicted on all new prisoners, whatever their origins. On his arrival at Dachau, he had noticed that when longstanding prisoners mingled with his group, the guards did not subject them to the same violence as the others. It is thus likely that, on their arrival in Buchenwald, the 'Dachau Jews' avoided the worst treatment. But they certainly did not escape the long speech detailing the camp rules, as described by Poller. Political discussion was forbidden, as were gatherings of any kind. Whoever witnessed an act of disobedience was immediately to report it.

Any prisoner who failed to work to the limits of his strength would be punished, and as they soon found out, the standard punishment at Buchenwald was twenty-five strokes of the whip, or blows from a club, delivered on the back with the victim stretched out on the *Bock*, a crude wooden whipping-block that stood in a corner of the huge parade ground. Those who had money on arrival were allowed to keep ten marks, the rest had to be handed over to the camp purser on pain of a beating. Inmates were held in Buchenwald indefinitely, with release depending on their behaviour. They were allowed to write fifteen-line letters to their families, on condition that they contained no information on life in the camp and no politics. The lecture concluded: 'You are not convicts here, you are only "under detention",[53] and what that means you will soon learn, if you have not done so already! You are dishonourable and defenceless! You are outlawed! Yours is a serf's lot! ...That's all!'[54]

In addition to the down-to-earth details it provides, Poller's account is interesting in that he viewed the Jewish blocks in Buchenwald from the outside. As a non-Jewish German who from his arrival in the camp had received discreet protection from a network of political friends already there, Walter Poller was somewhat privileged. In particular, he had the opportunity of visiting various sections of the camp. His account gives an idea of the gulf between the living conditions of the 'yellow triangles' and those of the others.

At the time of Poller's arrival, some 10,000[55] Jews were crammed into five crudely-built wooden blocks, designated 'Ia' to 'Va', in conditions of extreme overcrowding and squalor (Dachau, by comparison, was almost the lap of luxury). The special barracks, which gave on to the vast *Appelplatz*, or parade ground, were separated from the rest of the camp by a ten-foot high barbed-wire fence. They housed the Jews arrested during the *Kristallnacht* pogrom.[56]

On November 7, 1938, a young exiled Polish Jew, shattered at receiving news of his family's persecution at the hands of the Nazis, went to the German embassy in Paris and shot a diplomat, third secretary Ernst vom Rath. The latter's death in hospital two days later was the excuse the Nazis had been waiting for to launch a major operation – the SS called it simply an *Aktion* – against Germany's Jewish population. On the night of November 9, Nazi gangs in towns and cities across the country torched synagogues and wrecked Jewish shops and stores in what became known as the 'night of crystal' (*Kristallnacht*), due to the huge number of windows that were smashed. The gangs seized some 30,000 Jews, who were held in ordinary prisons for a few days before being dispatched to Dachau, Buchenwald and Sachsenhausen.

Living conditions for the 'Dachau Jews', who had arrived in the camp six weeks earlier, were not as appalling as those inflicted on the *Kristallnacht* detainees. However as Poller, who was able to visit one of their barracks, noted, their lives were in every respect more difficult than those of the non-Jewish inmates. They had less food, even less space, and were subjected to extra deprivation on the slightest pretext. They were housed in wooden structures in the centre of the camp; Bruno Bettelheim and Hans Bandler were in Block 17.

Even in *The Informed Heart*, by far the most detailed of his writings on the subject, Bettelheim sticks to relatively abstract terms when discussing the difference between Dachau and Buchenwald. He notes for instance that in the latter camp, which 'reflected a later phase of National-Socialism',[57] inmates were no longer treated as individuals. In particular, punishments were almost always collective, so that the group's resentment would be directed towards the person whose behaviour had provoked them, and neither heroes nor martyrs could emerge. But Bettelheim never really discusses everyday life in Buchenwald in any detail; indeed he opens most of his texts by stressing that his aim is not to give yet another account of the horrors of the Nazi camps. And the rare personal anecdotes he indulges in are almost always relegated to the status of footnotes. Once again, he shows his determination to rise above the material, flesh-and-blood level of events.

Nevertheless, on reading the accounts of other inmates of Buchenwald – the camp on which both archives and personal accounts are more numerous and more comprehensive than those relating to any other – it is difficult to imagine how Bruno Bettelheim could so completely put to one side the purely material details of his life in such a place, where he spent more than six months without ever knowing whether he would come out of it alive. In his letters, which are shorter than those he sent from Dachau, his determination to go on settling his affairs with a view to a purely hypothetical release shines through, all the more so in that his handwriting has become disorderly. The reasoned content of the letters is belied by their spiky, frantic form, which suggests that the writer was at the very least physically exhausted.

Of course, Bettelheim the survivor had learned a lot during his four months of internment in Dachau. In Buchenwald, taking advantage of the extraordinary level of corruption presided over by *Lagerkommandant* Karl Koch,[58] he was able relatively quickly to manoeuvre himself into a somewhat 'cushy' position. At least that was how Ernst Federn viewed Bettelheim's assignment to the camp's sock-darning workshop. The job allowed Bettelheim to work indoors during the bitter winter cold, and above all, it meant he was under the orders of a political rather than a common-law *Kapo*, and one who was relatively easy-going. As a result, he was spared the continual insults that were the lot of other camp inmates, at least during daytime. Bettelheim himself does not clearly state that he was assigned to the darning shop, but in *The Informed Heart*, he refers to conversations that took place in 'very safe commands, such as that of the sock menders, where prisoners were seated rather comfortably at tables and worked quietly at very easy tasks'.[59]

Nevertheless, throughout the six months he was to spend in Buchen-wald, Bettelheim shared his fellow inmates' lot of overcrowded living-quarters, in which they had to stand even while they swallowed their evening soup. He had to sleep on the awful straw mattresses, on which the prisoners were so tightly packed together that if one turned over he awoke several others. He was forced to take part on occasion in the terrible 'sports sessions', during which the SS guards enjoyed themselves by forcing a few prisoners to exercise until they died of physical exhaus-tion. He also had to use the horrendous latrines, which consisted of huge pits over which were placed two parallel tree trunks. The prisoners, having quickly had to lose all sense of shame, sat crammed side by side, being pressured to get a move on by those awaiting their turn and terrified of losing their balance or being pushed to a horrible death. (That fear has continued to haunt Hans Bandler to this day. It also seems to have been one of the factors that triggered Bettelheim's long essay 'Surviving',[60] written after he had seen Lina Wertmuller's film *Seven Beauties*, in which such a scene is dealt with in a comical vein.)

During the winter he spent in the camp with the deceptively pretty name (Buchenwald means 'beech forest'), located on Ettersberg hill, best known up until then to music- and poetry-lovers, as a place where Bach, Goethe and Schiller all loved to stroll,[61] Bettelheim also experienced the interminable roll-calls in the freezing cold. On at least two occasions that year these ordeals, during which weaker prisoners would collapse and die under the eyes of comrades who could not do anything to help them without themselves risking death, lasted all night. He must also have witnessed, equally powerless, a few suicides, and certainly saw some prisoners perish during punishment on the *Bock*. He saw others shot down like dogs, or rather as 'sub-humans', and he witnessed the disastrous effects of the typhus epidemic that broke out shortly after the arrival of the 'November Jews'.

That is not to mention the impact that the bloodbath staged by the SS guards to mark the latter's arrival must have had on the 'Dachau Jews', only recently transferred themselves. In their book on the *Kristallnacht* pogroms,[62] Rita Thalmann and Emmanuel Feinermann give an idea of what it was like: 'How could anyone forget the sight of Captain Wolf, the Jewish officer who had commanded the World War I flotilla in which Goering had served, and who had thought he could invoke his Medal of Merit, the highest German distinction for acts of bravery, but who instead was rewarded by being crucified alive over the camp entrance, where he perished?' An entrance over which was written: 'My Fatherland, Right or Wrong.'

Bettelheim's remarkable detachment had at least two explanations: his determination to retain control by an effort of mind over matter during his incarceration, and the distance which he very deliberately put between his personal experience and the account he wrote of it once he was in the United States.

But a third possible explanation is betrayed by a remark he made about his first hours as a prisoner. In *Surviving*, after describing that traumatic trip to Dachau, Bettelheim goes on to write, using the third person singular which is so disconcerting when discussing such personal experiences: 'The author has no doubt that he was able to endure the transportation and all that followed because right from the beginning he became convinced that these horrible and degrading experiences were somehow not happening to him as a subject, but only to him as an object.'[63]

There is one dimension which Bettelheim hardly touches on at all when writing about the camps: the way the Nazis spoke to the Jews. In spite of the fact that he spent every minute of those endless days striving to memorize everything that had happened to him, for the want of pencil and paper with which to jot it all down, Bettelheim's writings contain no hint of the insults to which he was subjected day and night on account of his Jewishness. Those of us who are lucky enough to have grown up in societies where racist insults are considered inadmissible therefore have to turn to other sources to get an inkling of what it was like. 'Jewish swine', 'hook-nose', 'Jewish shit', 'synagogue nag', 'Jewish scum', etc. All of this from men who although despicable, and amply despised by Bettelheim, nonetheless had considerable, indeed absolute, power over his body. 'Get a move on, dirty yid!' 'Get back!' 'Run!' 'Jump!' 'Down on your knees, down on your belly, you son of a Jewish sow!'

What effect could such a continual outpouring of racist obscenities have on this assimilated Jew, who for all his life had felt much closer intellectually to the German poets than to the bearded talmudists from Leopoldstadt? In *Freud's Vienna*, Bettelheim writes that the positive sense of his Jewish identity which he had found in Martin Buber's books became especially important to him, and even life-preserving, in Buchenwald. But that remark made at the beginning of *Surviving* may provide an additional answer to the question.

It is only a guess, but might it not be that the conviction he acquired from the very start that he was only the 'object' and not the 'subject', of his experiences under Nazi domination reflected in some way the feeling that 'these horrible and degrading experiences were somehow not happening to "him",' to Bruno Bettelheim, but instead to that 'other', a person similar to him yet not the same, whose reflection he kept seeing in the eyes of every SS soldier he encountered – to Bettelheim-the-Jew?

One of the most basic aims of that steely determination to observe, analyse and understand may have been simply to escape from the bounds of identity within which his torturers sought to enclose him, to keep sight of the fact that even though his birth had made him Jewish, it was not his only destiny. Hence the need to rise above the merely physical, the flesh-and-blood level; to rise above a body enslaved by the enemy. A body upon which his Jewishness had been indelibly marked at birth, for better or worse and above all for worse, by the rabbi's scalpel.

Chapter VII

Buchenwald: The Price of Freedom

After the evening roll-call on December 14, 1938, the inmates waited in vain for the usual order to return to their quarters. In the early afternoon the SS guards had found out about an attempted escape by two 'Green' prisoners,[1] and had decided to inflict harsh punishment on the entire camp. In the midst of a driving blizzard, without hats, coats or gloves and with empty stomachs after a twelve-hour work-day, the prisoners were kept standing to attention for nineteen hours under the camp spotlights.

One after the other the oldest and weakest collapsed; if any of their neighbours made a move to try and help them, the SS guards opened fire. After a day spent hunting for escapees, they were like mad dogs, beating and killing the inmates at the slightest excuse. Bettelheim noted that after a while, what was clearly an attempt to destroy all solidarity between the inmates began to have the opposite effect. Having seen around twenty of their fellows collapse and die of cold, the inmates began to feel supremely indifferent to their own fate. Once again, it was as if they had split into two parts, one of which was observing what was happening to the other. The guards' threats lost their potency; each individual's chance of survival was so slim that the fear of death receded, and he felt himself becoming more courageous, readier to help his fellows. Paradoxically, they were almost happy. When the order finally came for them to return to their blocks, the survivors were of course relieved. But at the same time they felt the fear, which the overdose of torture had freed them from, welling back, while the feeling of mutual support they had briefly experienced on the *Appelplatz* receded. The following day, the total number of deaths from the ordeal stood at eighty,[2] while several hundred other men had suffered such serious frostbite that they had to have limbs amputated.

A week later, Bettelheim wrote to his mother to ask her to have a new pair of glasses made for him; solid ones with a strong case. He did not explain how his existing pair had been broken. He still remembered to wish Paula a happy birthday, and sent Christmas greetings to everyone. He also asked for 30 marks.

On Christmas Eve the prisoners were to get a surprise. On marching on to the parade ground for the evening roll-call, five abreast as usual, they saw that a gibbet had been erected, close to the *Bock* used for beatings. The SS commanding officer had decided to stage a hanging. Hans Bandler still has vivid memories of the event; it was not the first of its kind and would not be the last, but it appears to have impressed the prisoners more than others. The entire SS hierarchy was present, including Koch and his wife. The victim was an officer who had escaped from the camp in May and fled to Czechoslovakia; he had been handed over to the Nazis after they invaded that country. When there were no executions to stage, the SS diverted themselves by forcing a group of Jews to fight a group of Jehovah's Witnesses in front of the assembled prisoners. On other occasions, they would order the prisoners to form a circle, and then choose a few of them at random to inflict some form of cruelty on them, or even shoot them down like rabbits, depending on their mood. It was also at this time that the SS commander, Rödl, decided that Buchenwald should have its own anthem. On some evenings, the prisoners were kept behind for hours after the roll-call in order to rehearse this ditty.[3] All the while, back in their living quarters, their thin soup of whalemeat or 'sausage', complete with fishbones, would be cooling down to room temperature, several degrees below zero.

Two weeks after Christmas, Bettelheim wrote to his mother to explain how to get his passport photographs certified, stressing every detail of the procedure. He gave instructions for the purchase of his transatlantic boat ticket, and asked Paula to mail 150 marks to a certain Frieda Goldstein in Berlin ('it is a debt of honour,' he wrote, 'and therefore very important'). He also asked for Gina's address in New York, and expressed concern for the fate of Trude, who had by then left Vienna. A week later he was able to send another letter, with ever more demands, couched in even more imperious tones. Among his new requests was one for an English phrasebook. It was as if the worse his living conditions became the more he struggled to give himself the impression that he was mentally in control of things. Only his handwriting betrayed him: in spite of the new glasses he had received, it had become chaotic and straggly. He had a hard time staying on the lines, and the letters were badly co-ordinated.

The mud which invaded every nook and cranny at Buchenwald constituted a major health hazard, as the slightest cut became infected. Given the extreme living conditions, this often led to gangrene, in effect a death warrant. Hence the anxiety that the Jewish prisoners felt when, after the *Kristallnacht* pogrom, they were abruptly forbidden to seek treatment at the *Revier* for anything other than injuries sustained during labour, as Bettelheim reported.[4]

With the onset of the tough 1938 winter, almost all the inmates suffered from terrible frostbite, brought on by working without adequate protection in the stone quarries close to the camp, or during evening roll-calls. If untreated, the ensuing inflammation could become infected, which is what happened to Bettelheim. In spite of the ban, he decided to take his chance at the infirmary. He was by no means the only one; the line of prisoners outside the *Revier* was every bit as long as usual.

The decision on whether or not to admit a prisoner to the *Revier* was made by an SS corporal posted at the entrance. As they shuffled and tried to keep warm in the long line stretching ahead of Bettelheim, the Jewish prisoners had only one subject of conversation: the careful stratagem each had worked out to try and get round the ban. Some planned to cite their service in the German army during World War I, mentioning medals won or injuries sustained. Others preferred to simply make something up, for example to say that an SS officer had ordered them to report to the infirmary.

When one of his neighbours asked him what his intentions were, Bettelheim said he didn't have a precise plan. He preferred to observe the guard's attitude towards the persons in front before making up his mind what to say. He added that in his opinion, as it was difficult to predict the reactions of a man one didn't know, it was not a good idea to have a cut-and-dried plan worked out in advance. This remark, according to Bettelheim, earned him jeering comments on the lines of 'Gestapomen are all the same.'[5] Other prisoners insulted him, accusing him of not wanting to share his plan with them, or even of wanting to steal theirs.

In the queue ahead of him, prisoners wearing the yellow triangle were being systematically denied access to the infirmary. Bettelheim noticed that the more an inmate tried to convince the guard, the more the latter became violent. The expressions of suffering appeared even to amuse him. When a prisoner tried to invoke his past military service in the German army the guard became indignant, accusing the man of lying and saying proudly that he was not the kind of guy to be taken in by a Jew. The time when a Jew could get anything he wanted just by whining was over, and a good thing too. Bettelheim went on:

When my turn came the Gestapoman asked me whether I knew that work accidents were the only reason for admitting Jews to the clinic, and whether I came because of such an accident. I replied that I knew the rules, but that I could not work unless my hands were freed of the dead flesh. Since prisoners were not permitted to possess knives, I asked to have the dead flesh cut away. I made these statements in a matter-of-fact way, avoiding pleading, deference or arrogance.

The Gestapoman replied: 'If this is really all you want, I am going to tear the flesh off.' He started to pull with force at the festering skin. Because it did not come off as easily as he might have expected, or for some other reason, the Gestapo soldier ordered me to enter the clinic.

Once I was inside the clinic, he gave me a malevolent look and pushed me into the treatment room. There he told the orderly to attend to the wound. While this was being done, the Gestapoman again watched me closely. I succeeded in suppressing signs of pain.

As soon as the cutting was accomplished, I started to leave. The Gestapoman seemed surprised and questioned me as to why I did not ask for further treatment. I replied that I had received the service which I had requested. At this he told the orderly to make an exception and to treat my hand. After I had left the room, the Gestapoman called me back and gave me a card entitling me to further treatment and to admittance to the clinic without inspection at its entrance.[6]

Before continuing our account, it is worth examining this anecdote, first published in April 1947. It was to spark controversy, with some critics saying that any exchange between a Jew and an SS man would have been impossible in the camps, some flatly accusing Bettelheim of lying and others reproaching him for failing to show support for his fellow inmates.

Bettelheim's aim in telling the story was to illustrate the idea that in reacting to the Nazis' ideological stereotyping of Jews by developing counter-stereotypes ('the Nazis are all the same, they are stupid brutes, they can be easily hoodwinked,' etc.), the victims in fact made their own situation worse, as they deprived themselves of the ability to react to real-life situations in which their lives were at stake. The article in which he outlined his thesis, rather brilliantly, was provocatively entitled 'The Dynamism of Anti-Semitism in Gentile and Jew'.

Ten months later Bettelheim published another piece on the same subject, in the Jewish monthly *Commentary*. This time he went straight to the point, as the title, 'The Victim's Image of the Anti-Semite: the Danger of Stereotyping the Adversary', suggests. The article, aimed at a less specialized audience, is much shorter than the previous one. The writer's ideas have had time to mature; the style is even more effective, and details have been pared to the bone. He uses the same incident to support his argument, but devotes only half the space to it, and ends his account at the point where the SS guard reluctantly lets the prisoner into the infirmary. More surprisingly, the hero is this time presented as another person, identified only as 'N... a trained psychologist, capable of observing the mental processes at work with substantial objectivity'. Bettelheim was to rework the account a last time some twelve years later, for inclusion in *The Informed Heart*. There, he reverted to the initial version.

Is it absolutely essential to determine whether 'N' and 'BB' were one and the same person, whether the incident really happened to Bettelheim himself, whether it was told to him by a fellow inmate, or whether he simply made the whole thing up? Essential, certainly not. Psychoanalysts who have worked with former camp inmates are familiar with the process that sometimes leads them to confuse the stories of their fellow sufferers with their own. Not so much because they want to appropriate another person's experience as because, being but one of a mass of Jews deprived of any identity other than a number, a man can easily end up not being very clear about where his own suffering ends and that of his neighbour begins, and not even considering it important.

The ambiguity is interesting, however, because it touches on one of the most controversial aspects of Bettelheim's personality. Amid the storm of recrimination and accusations that broke out immediately after his death, one of the charges was that he had lied. And as there were indeed points on which he did touch up his biography, the accusation lent weight to other, less easily verifiable, charges. In my opinion, however, when he did lie it was in a very specific context, over a short period of time and in relation to a very narrow set of facts.[7] Indeed Gina Weinmann, who is one of his sternest critics as regards his honesty, says that in Vienna, Bettelheim had not yet started lying.

That is why the Buchenwald infirmary anecdote stands out as one of the little white pebbles that Bettelheim dropped along his path in the course of a life whose details he otherwise tried to obscure. Because his concentration-camp experience was to play a crucial role both in the public figure he would become in the United States and in the way his thinking would develop. Because the closed, barbaric world of the camps was the ideal breeding ground for those larger-than-life stories which can help one stay alive. But also because all of Bruno Bettelheim's work on the camps consisted precisely of trying to retrieve the reality of this world which drove people mad.

Whether or not the story itself is authentic, Bettelheim's conclusion has the ring of truth about it. As is often the case with him, when one has finished reading through the argument (and even if along the way there were specific points one did not agree with), it all seems so crystal-clear that one emerges feeling somewhat disconcerted, wondering how one could not have worked out such an obvious chain of ideas for oneself.

Sceptical readers are nevertheless assailed by contradictory thoughts. It would seem that somebody assigned to working in the sock-mending shop would be less vulnerable to frostbite than most other prisoners. Indeed, Ernst Federn has no recollection of Bettelheim suffering from such an ailment; but then he did not sleep in the same block. It is also true that during the *Kristallnacht*, the roll-call for Jews had also lasted until dawn, and that Bettelheim did not spend all of his time in Buchenwald protected from the cold in the sock workshop; Federn thinks it was probably his last work assignment.

As for Hans Bandler, he has no memory either of the frostbite episode or of the sock-darning workshop. However he finds it difficult to believe that an inmate could have carried on such a lengthy conversation with an SS guard. As he remembers it, communication with the guards was purely one-way, consisting of a series of barked insults and orders. But then again, what may have applied to the young Hans Bandler, an idealistic and somewhat naïve socialist engineering student, was not necessarily true of Bruno Bettelheim, a man in the prime of life; perceptive, cultivated and used to holding his own in the world of business. It is clearly impossible to establish the truth with any certainty.

What is incontrovertible is that it was horribly cold in Buchenwald in November 1938, that many of the inmates suffered from frostbite and some died as a result, and that a ban on visits to the infirmary was a major source of anxiety to men who were famished and exhausted. And above all that resorting to preconceived ideas is never the best way to get out of a dangerous situation. That is after all the only point that matters and it is also, I believe, the key to the problem. Bruno Bettelheim was a quick reader, of people as well as of books. He caught on fast, and although he let no details escape him, was interested only in the essentials. In his constant search for meaning, he would only consider an incident to be of relevance if it helped him towards his goal of reaching a conclusion, or as some would put it, of identifying the moral of the story. To that end he was willing to ride roughshod over details if they did not fit in. This I believe was the basis of Bettelheim's overall attitude to truth, after his experiences in the camps.

The story of his broken glasses is another case in point. Contrary to what he was to write later, his letters seem to indicate that it was not during the train ride to Dachau that they were smashed, but six months later, in Buchenwald.[8] I was not able to ascertain in what circumstances, but what is certain is that the letter in which he asked his mother for new ones was sent a week after the December ordeal on the parade ground. Judging from his handwriting, that was clearly the worst period of his entire spell in the camps. Bettelheim had weighed 150 pounds when he arrived at Dachau; by April 1939 he weighed a mere 86. He had lost most of his hair (although as mirrors were not an everyday luxury in the camps, he was not aware of the fact), and his teeth were in a terrible state. He was also suffering from a stomach ulcer.

Two months prior to the letter mentioning his glasses, in mid-October, his mother had received a brief form letter bearing her son's signature. The printed message said: 'I am currently subjected to a mail ban. I therefore cannot receive either letters or parcels. Representations to the camp *Kommandantur* are forbidden, and their only effect would be to cause the punishment to be extended.'

On November 22 he was allowed to send a short eight-line card, after which his letters resumed their normal twice-monthly flow. It was in the ensuing missives that his handwriting became the most erratic and disorderly. The terrible events in the camp following the *Kristallnacht* pogrom may be sufficient to explain that change, but the ban on Bettelheim's mail predates them by three weeks. Clearly, something had happened in the meantime. It could have been then that he had received the blows to the head which he said had smashed his glasses, which would imply that he had to wait two months before getting permission to write to his family for a replacement pair.

By the time he made that request, he writes, he knew that a prisoner should above all never complain of having been ill-treated. When asked about it, he said simply that his glasses had been broken. The SS man on duty then started beating him, shouting, '*What* did you say happened?' Realizing his mistake, Bettelheim explained that he had broken his glasses himself, by accident. The blows ceased, and, before sitting down to write out the permit, the SS man said: 'Okay. Just remember that for the future.' The change in the guard's attitude had been too sudden, Bettelheim concluded, to have been spontaneous. 'No sadist bent on satisfying his desires will instantly stop mistreatment on getting a correct formula reply. Only a person simply after a specific goal will behave in that way.'[9]

Bettelheim used the episode of the glasses to make three important observations about camp life. First, that it was dangerous to attract attention to oneself. 'Having learned my lesson, I requested – and a while later received – glasses of the simplest and cheapest kind. Even so, I found it best to hide my glasses and do without them whenever the SS went on a rampage; I was much safer that way. This was but one of the many precautions a prisoner had to take if he wanted to increase his chances for survival.'[10]

Secondly, he realized that it was even more dangerous to see than to be seen. Indeed, in many situations 'not to see or not to know was not enough; in order to survive one had to actively pretend not to observe, not to know what the SS required one not to know.' And thirdly, Bettelheim realized that the troops of the SS *Totenkopf* (death's-head) unit in charge of the camp were not simply cruel brutes: they were clearly obeying precise orders. The violence, torture and insults they meted out were not in general the expression of ill-controlled tempers, but rather the application of a coldly thought-out plan.

Bettelheim thus used the glasses incident to illustrate the message that was hardest of all to get across to his American readers at the time he published it, two years before the discovery of the death camps: that the Nazis' behaviour could not be simply dismissed as the stuff of all wars, part of the inevitable catalogue of atrocities and excesses, but that it was the specific product of a very specific system. Later, when the defeat of the Third Reich and the accounts of thousands of other survivors had corroborated his own writings, he was to present that system as the prototype of the modern mass state, which brings to bear the full panoply of science and technology in order to subjugate the individual.

'I saw prisoners come back to life on hearing Bruno tell stories about his own life,' Hans Bandler told Trude Weinfeld when, a few months after his release on January 19, 1939, he met her in Australia. In the light of that, who would dare blame Bettelheim for having on occasion embroidered around the truth? Primo Levi, referring to his retrospective relief at having one day given a few words of advice to an eighteen-year-old Italian boy who had just arrived in Auschwitz, wrote: 'I forget what I told him, certainly words of hope, perhaps a few lies, acceptable to a "new arrival", expressed with the authority of my twenty-five years and my three months of seniority; at any rate, I made him the gift of a momentary attention. But I also remember, with disquiet, that much more often I shrugged my shoulders impatiently at other requests.' In the camp, Levi noted, 'the demand for solidarity, for a human word, advice, even only a listening ear, was permanent and universal'.[11] Of course Buchenwald was not Auschwitz, and at the time when Bettelheim was there, all the prisoners at least spoke the same language, which made communication easier. Even at that early stage, however, the golden rule of survival was to first and foremost take care of one's own needs. Bettelheim's willingness to simply listen to some of his companions in misfortune was therefore a priceless gift, even if, as he himself stressed, it was one given mostly out of a desire to preserve his own sanity.

'They can say what they like about Bruno, but I will always have the greatest admiration for him because, in the camps, he got us to talk about our previous lives,' says Hans Bandler. 'He was the only one to do that. And for me, being able to talk about things I knew, to see someone who was not at all involved taking an interest in my profession as an engineer, being able to teach him something, was an extraordinary aid to survival. It gave me back my self-esteem in a situation in which everything was designed to demean us, both in our own eyes and in those of others. For that, I will be eternally grateful to him.'

Hans Bandler was clearly one of Bruno Bettelheim's 'interviewees'. Their conversations often took place after the evening roll-call. Thanks to the Nazis' passion for alphabetical order, Bandler and Bettelheim were in the same block. Other conversations took place when the two men found themselves side by side pushing heavy wagons full of stones in Dachau. Hans recalled his engineering classes, and explained to Bruno how to build a bridge, what precautions had to be taken to make sure it didn't collapse, etc. Bruno listened, and asked questions. When it was his turn to talk he discussed psychoanalysis, mentioning Freud, Wilhelm Reich, etc. Bandler, for whom this was all completely new, was fascinated.

One of the very first things Bettelheim noticed on questioning his fellow inmates was that they did not talk in the same way about everyday ill-treatment and the particularly horrible ordeals, such as the December 14 roll-call, the 'initiation ceremony' during the trip to the camp, or the reception they got on arrival. They preferred not to talk about the daily insults, blows, kicks and other humiliations, and would in some cases deny they even took place, as if they were ashamed of them.

Whenever the ill-treatment went beyond the 'normal' level, on the other hand, they were ready to launch into detailed descriptions. And yet it was almost impossible to get them to discuss their feelings during such ordeals. The few who would do so spoke only in vague terms, as if trying to justify the fact that they had done nothing to defend themselves. In their accounts, Bettelheim detected the same feeling of unreality that had invaded him at such times, but he could not persuade them to discuss that either. He concluded that this was a natural defence mechanism, thrown up by the ego against unbearable attacks. He also noted that during the ordeals, which he was to call 'extreme situations', many prisoners behaved as though their life bore no relation whatsoever to what it had been in the outside world; their way of viewing both themselves and others had changed. It was as if they were thinking: 'What I am doing here, and what is happening to me, does not count. Here, anything is permissible inasmuch as it helps me to survive.' Some inmates indeed asserted that this was the only way to behave.

Bettelheim also noticed a clear difference between the behaviour of new prisoners and that of camp veterans. The former would spend all their energy – and money – on trying to get in touch with their families and friends; all their thoughts were directed towards the outside world. Whereas the 'old prisoners' were concerned first and foremost by internal camp affairs. The appointment of a new *Kapo* was far more interesting to them than the results of the Munich conference. They appeared to have lost their ability to assess external events, as if the latter no longer concerned them.

At Buchenwald such an introverted attitude was easier to maintain, as the prisoners were not allowed to receive newspapers. At Dachau, Bettelheim had at least been able to read, each Sunday, the daily newspaper to which Paula had got him a subscription,[12] and the *Frankfürter Zeitung*, which he had requested, obviously to keep abreast of what was happening in Germany itself. There was no such privilege in Buchenwald, where prisoners often spent at least half of each Sunday working. Bettelheim was by no means the only inmate to notice the contrast between new and old prisoners. Everyone was aware of it, and so much so that some inmates decided to die before they turned into concentration camp types, as Eugen Kogon described them. Bettelheim thus witnessed the suicide of a man who had resolved that six years was his limit. On the day, despite all attempts to dissuade him, he threw himself on to the electrified barbed wire fence surrounding the camp.

'Old prisoners' did not like to talk about either their previous lives or their families. And when they did so it was often with bitterness, accusing their relations of having abandoned or even betrayed them. Having made that observation, Bettelheim was shocked by his own reaction to a passage in a letter from his mother. In it, she told how 'one of my colleagues had presented a paper, using some of my ideas, and that it was very well received,' he wrote.[13] On one level, he explained, he knew perfectly well that Paula only wanted to please him. 'Nevertheless, on a much more important level it sent me into a cold fury to think that my colleague was enjoying success with my ideas while I lived in such misery.' The end result was that, rather than bolstering his courage, the letter filled him with anger, an emotion all the more destructive in that he could only turn it against himself (i.e. by plunging into depression, as he had learned to do since his childhood. But he did not write that). This incident, about which I have no other details,[14] was to remain in Bettelheim's memory as the second occasion on which his mother had almost caused his death (the first being her exhortations for him not to leave Vienna at the time of the *Anschluss*).[15]

One thing surprised Bettelheim. After having often relived in dreams a car crash that had deeply shaken him a few years earlier, he had been expecting to suffer from recurring nightmares at the start of his imprisonment. Far from it; none of the incidents, not even the train ride to Dachau or other such trials, ever troubled his sleep. When he did dream about the camp, it was always to relive some minor incident, which generally provided an opportunity for vengeance against an SS guard. On questioning his fellow inmates, he found they all had a similar story to tell.

For a long time Bettelheim kept his observations to himself. Then, apparently in Buchenwald, he started trying to compare notes with other prisoners. 'Unfortunately,' he writes, '[the author] found only two others who were trained and interested enough to participate in his investigation. Although they seemed less interested in the problem than the author, these two each spoke to several hundred prisoners. Every day during the morning count of the prisoners, and while waiting for the assignment to labor groups, reports were exchanged and theories discussed. These discussions proved very helpful in clarifying mistakes that were due to taking a one-sided viewpoint.'[16]

One of Bettelheim's two confidants was Ernst Federn. But in his first article on the camps, in October 1943, he refrained from citing his name, as Federn was then still in Buchenwald. Details on the second man, a certain Dr Alfred Fischer, are hard to come by. Bettelheim wrote, in 1943, that Fischer was at that time working in a military hospital in England. He was not a psychoanalyst but a general practitioner. According to the Buchenwald archives he was also a Viennese Jew, the same age as Bettelheim, and he was released from the camp on May 10, 1939. In *The Informed Heart*, published in 1960, Bettelheim added that he had lost touch with him.

Only two direct eyewitness accounts of this joint research project are therefore available: Bettelheim's and Federn's. When they met at Buchenwald, neither of them was as yet a psychoanalyst. But while the former had become gradually fascinated by the 'new science' during his studies and the unfolding of his life in Vienna, the latter had been born into it. When he was a child, Sigmund Freud had bounced him on his knees, and in 1936 he had become his father's secretary. Today, he still describes himself smilingly as 'a psychoanalyst by birth'. But the humour conceals a deeply committed stance; Ernst Federn takes his role as an intellectual heir very seriously, and has defended Paul Federn's work throughout his whole life.

He is also an idealist, as is shown by the second paragraph of his book *Witnessing Psychoanalysis*: 'From early youth – in fact, from the age of fourteen – I had decided to devote my life to the betterment of mankind, having taken this romantic idea from my father.'[17] Federn became politically active very early on, his aim being to reconcile the ideas of Marx and Freud. He was fully engaged in the underground struggle against the Nazis when they invaded Austria and he was among the first arrested in Vienna. As his father was Jewish, the Germans had also made him wear the yellow triangle, but for him things were clear: he was in Dachau because his side had lost. And as Bettelheim pointed out, 'Those prisoners ... who had expected to be arrested because of their political activities resented their fate, but somehow accepted it as something which happened in accordance with their expectations ... [they] found support for their self-esteem in the fact that the Gestapo had singled them out as important enough to take revenge on.'[18]

That was not Bruno Bettelheim's own situation. Whatever his ideas, his arrest could not be attributed to any political action on his part. Although he despised the Nazis every bit as much as Federn did, he had done nothing outwardly to express those feelings, beyond becoming a card-carrying member of the Fatherland Front party. When he defines the category of political prisoner in his writings, however, he remains just vague enough to be able to count himself among their number. That is technically correct, as he wore the red political prisoners' triangle, and above all as he was clearly in the politically aware category. But when he writes of the stronger self-esteem which helped 'Red' prisoners to endure the initial trauma of their arrest and imprisonment, he can only be referring to the politically active.

The two men were thus in very different situations when they met, even according to Bettelheim's own definition. With the exception of a certain sense of humour they had mainly one thing in common, their interest in psychoanalysis. The fact that Federn was the son of the most loyal of Sigmund Freud's followers instantly attracted Bettelheim to him. For his part, Federn could not but be impressed by Bettelheim's astonishing intuitive power, and his determination to find meaning in everything going on around him.

No doubt the political activist in Federn was a little contemptuous of the accommodations his friend was prepared to make with the camp system, although he recognizes that without them a man 'so ill-prepared to face the practical aspects of life', as he describes Bettelheim in *Witnessing Psychoanalysis*, would probably not have survived the rigours of

Buchenwald. That attitude can still be detected today, when Federn discusses Bettelheim's labour detail in the sock-darning workshop, or the armband for the blind, which he saw him wear on a few occasions in Buchenwald. 'It cost him too much,' is his comment.

That armband, of which Hans Bandler has no recollection, appears to have played a certain role in the Federn-Bettelheim relationship. I do not know at what point the latter procured it, but it must have been when he was deprived of his glasses. There is no doubt at all that he would have paid to obtain it, as in Buchenwald at that time there was a price on everything. From the top echelons of the SS right down to the lowly *Kapos*, the word was to 'make the Jews cough up' for everything and anything. Indeed, in *The Informed Heart*, Bettelheim makes no secret of the fact that he used his money to purchase a few advantages that helped him to survive the camps, but he does not mention the armband. Without glasses, however, he was practically blind; his driver's licence, issued in 1932, specifies that he could only take the wheel when wearing nine-diopter lenses on both eyes. And the six months of concentration camp life could not have done anything to improve his eyesight. Nevertheless, Bettelheim was ashamed of having worn that armband.

He was to admit as much in a letter he wrote to Ernst Federn in January 1969. Federn must have raised the issue, as Bettelheim says: 'Your point about hiding is well taken, but for me hiding was not the opposite of courage. It was a temporary defense, which often was absolutely indispensable, but, when it became habitual, it led to destruction. And I have seen that happen.' Then he writes: 'Twice, during my time in the camps, I hid, which I could do very well, because I had the arm sleeve that declared me as blind .... In both cases, after less than two weeks, I took it off and stopped hiding, because I found it too self-destructive, and had seen the destruction it wreaked in others. So much for that.'[19]

Vintage Bettelheim, that willingness to confront an unpleasant memory, followed by a short, expeditious discussion of the subject. But those few words, repetitive and awkwardly put together, speak volumes about the struggle he must have waged in Buchenwald to avoid slipping into a state of mind that he knew would have been fatal, to marshal the strength to go on living. As he would write later, he envied the Jehovah's Witnesses, whose unshakeable faith allowed them invariably to rise above the surrounding degradation of the camp. But his atheism was too deeply rooted; he could not bring himself to believe even to save his own life. In the absence of religious faith, he could have benefited from political convictions, which also helped some of his fellow inmates to remain themselves in this dangerous and above all degrading world. But there too, his scepticism was too strong.

What he means by 'destructive', a word to which he clearly attaches considerable weight, since he uses it three times in nine lines, is spelled out clearly in *The Informed Heart*, in a chapter section entitled 'The Last

Human Freedom'. After referring to the category of prisoners known as 'moslems', those who gave up all hope and simply let themselves die, he writes: 'To survive as a man not a walking corpse, as a debased and degraded but still human being, one had first and foremost to remain informed and aware of what made up one's personal point of no return, the point beyond which one would never, under any circumstances, give in to the oppressor, even if it meant risking and losing one's life. It meant being aware that if one survived at the price of overreaching this point one would be holding on to a life that had lost all its meaning. It would mean surviving – not with a lowered self respect, but without any.'[20] That point of no return, Bettelheim went on, varies from person to person, and with the different stages of incarceration. Over time, as material considerations gradually give way to interior demands and basic convictions, it shifts. The key thing is to always be aware of just where it is – to keep one's heart 'informed', to quote the title that so aptly sums up the type of introspection involved.

This is central to the issue of the blind man's armband, and the relationship between Bettelheim and Federn. As the French *Résistance* fighter and former camp inmate Germaine Tillon has written, 'One day, someone will bring together all the testimony about the concentration camps, and on that day it will have to be remembered that there were a thousand camps within each camp, and that for some beings anything that was not of immediate concern to them did not exist.'[21] Although they shared an interest when they were imprisoned together, it would be difficult to imagine two men more different from one another than Ernst Federn and Bruno Bettelheim. In Buchenwald, a place in which one was constantly obliged to face up to one's own inner demons, their experiences were certainly very different.

Nothing better illustrates the gulf between them than the exchange of letters in which, thirty years after Bettelheim had left Buchenwald, that famous armband came up again. It was sparked by an article of his to which Federn had raised an objection: 'The Ultimate Limit', which deals with the fate of survivors of Hiroshima. In it, Bettelheim compared the effects of two extreme situations, the atom bomb and the Nazi camps.[22] He also for the first time gave a theoretical definition of an 'extreme situation', an expression he had coined over twenty-five years earlier, and used ever since. 'We find ourselves in an extreme situation when we are suddenly catapulted into a set of conditions where our old adaptive mechanisms and values do not apply any more and when some of them may even endanger the life they were meant to protect.'[23]

Bettelheim prefaced the article with a quotation from Horace, explaining his title: 'Death is the ultimate limit of all things,'[24] and continued: 'It is the certainty of death which gives human life its meaning.'[25] In his letter, Federn had objected, saying that in his opinion it was love that gave life its meaning. 'I fully agree with you,' replied the author of *Love is Not*

Enough.[26] However, he went on, 'I am equally convinced that without the awareness of death, what we call "love" would be a very different thing. If there would be no end to it, and if there would be unlimited time for it, it might very well become so different that we would not recognize it.'[27] The two men simply did not function on the same wavelength, and the subjects of their anxiety in Buchenwald were of a different nature. They were nevertheless friends, and in spite of the slight irritation that certain of Bettelheim's eccentricities inspired in him, Federn would be among those who were the most indignant at the scandal that blew up after his death.

The word 'destruction' also recurs in 'The Ultimate Limit'. There, what is being destroyed is the ego, which disintegrates when a man is suddenly subjected to an 'extreme' experience of death. For example, the prisoner who sees the bodies of his former companions piled ever higher, and wonders why his is not among them. Or the Hiroshima survivor, who on looking about him discovers the potential deadliness of the very scientific progress with which modern men had replaced God as the key to salvation – a 'defense against death anxiety', as Bettelheim puts it.

Bettelheim first notes that the sight of a single corpse is in fact more shattering than the sight of thousands. If a person survives such gigantic massacres, he writes, 'then the fact of survival is the problem – not the corpses piled all around one ...', and '... the only way one could go about doing what was absolutely necessary for survival was not to be swallowed up by one's feelings,' he added, referring here to Hiroshima..

Thus it was with the camp inmate made to carry corpses, and to whom his burdens seemed like nothing more than logs. Bettelheim interprets this emotional numbing as man's reaction to the destruction of his ego. 'One jettisons one's normal personality because its reactions now endanger one's life ... the old ego, the old self which did respond, proved to be of no help in meeting the radically new experience.' Faced with an extreme situation, Bettelheim goes on, 'what is required is an equally radically new ego', even if it is only a temporary one.

In Bettelheim's thinking at that time, and in this essay,[28] the ego is akin to a conductor, in charge of orchestrating the contradictory demands of the unconscious drives and the prohibitions and ambitions that result from the individual's upbringing. Sometimes the desires and fears generated by the unconscious gain the upper hand, and the individual's behaviour appears irrational. At other times, the demands of his ideal are stronger, and he represses his drives, at the risk of drying up the very sources of life and creativity. Psychological health, or 'integration of the ego', as Bettelheim calls it, lies somewhere between those two extremes, in a delicate and balanced regulation of the gates of the unconscious.

In the concentration camps, there was indeed no place for the prisoner's ego, or at least the Nazis did everything they could to ensure that that was the case. What indeed was an *Unterman* ('sub-human', or 'under-man') – as they called Jews – if not a person who has been stripped of his freedom to manage his passions in the light of what he believes to be right and wrong, a man reduced to being governed by his most basic instincts – to being *Das Es*, an 'it'?[29] It was hardly surprising that the people who stood up best to the experience were those whose ideals were the strongest, or even the most unbending, as Bettelheim noticed. And it did not matter whether the ideals in question were political, religious or simply moral; they could even, in the case of aristocrats, consist of a grandiose idea of their own family heritage.

And it was also unsurprising that a man who was as hard on himself as Bettelheim was should have felt himself in mortal danger every time that he reacted to the flagging of his hopes by donning the mask of somebody weaker than himself. Taking refuge behind the armband for the blind was certainly no crime. Considering the state of his eyesight, some people would simply have called it a measure of self-preservation, but for Bettelheim, whose lucidity had up until then served mainly to bolster a deep feeling of pessimism, it amounted to reducing even more the ego's room for manoeuvre. As he was to write later of his young patients, referring to the effect that traumatic events in the outside world could have on them, 'with each such experience the child becomes ... more withdrawn from reality, more beholden to his unconscious alone, and consequently less master of it'.[30] Instead of getting on with creating the 'radically new ego' needed for survival, he thus gave free rein to his fear and shame, his eyes filled with a devalued image of himself, the very image to which the Nazis wanted to reduce him.

It was during free time on Sundays, and also in the evenings between soup and the 'lights-out' siren, that Bettelheim and Federn would try to analyse their experiences. Ernst Federn recalls, for example, how the two of them discussed an incident which seemed to them typical of the behaviour of 'old' prisoners. This is how Bettelheim later reported it:

Often an SS man would for a while enforce some nonsensical rule, originating in a whim of the moment. Usually it was quickly forgotten, but there were always some old prisoners who continued to observe it and tried to enforce it on others long after the SS had lost interest. Once, for example, an SS man was inspecting the prisoners' apparel and found that some of their shoes were dirty on the inside. He ordered all prisoners to wash their shoes inside and out with soap and water. Treated this way, the heavy shoes became hard as stone. The order was never repeated, and many prisoners did not even carry it out the first time, since the SS, as was often the case, gave the order, stood around for a few minutes and then left. Until he was gone, every prisoner busied himself with carrying out the order, after which they promptly quit. Nevertheless, there were some old prison-

ers who not only continued to wash the insides of their shoes every
day, but cursed all who failed to do so as being negligent and dirty.[31]

The two men had seen the funny side of such behaviour, as when certain
other prisoners tried to obtain bits and pieces of old uniforms in order to
ape their tormentors. At the same time, they tried to make sense of it.
Today, Federn says lightheartedly: 'Oh, I don't remember which of us first
noticed how some prisoners tried to copy the behaviour of the SS. In any
case, it was nothing new; Anna Freud and Sandor Ferenczi had already
mentioned it ....' In *The Ego and the Mechanisms of Defence*,[32] published
just two years before the two men's arrests, Anna Freud had indeed put
forward the new theory of 'identification with the aggressor'. She saw it as
a stage in a child's normal development during which, having internalized
the strictures of its parents and adopted their values, it begins to project
the aggressivity that it nevertheless feels when reprimanded on to somebody else, such as a sibling, or a friend who is smaller or weaker.

More generally, the two men had been struck by the process of infantilization which seemed to have set in for so many of their fellow inmates.
By the obsession with food and excretion to which camp life condemned
them. The masturbation, which soon became the sole means (homosexual
relations being relatively rare) for the prisoners to prove to themselves
that, despite their state of deprivation, they had so far escaped the
castration with which the guards were constantly threatening them. The
obligatory use of the familiar 'du' form of address, the insults, the need to
lie continually (as they could never do everything asked of them) and to
hide (getting noticed was the surest way to come in for an extra beating).
The continual threats, the fear. And above all, the impotent, dangerous
rage, which they could only either repress or turn against themselves or
their fellow inmates. All conditions which were obviously calculated to
make them regress to childhood. For the two apprentice psychoanalysts,
measuring these symptoms against the arguments of Anna Freud was an
exciting exercise. It not only allowed them to spend their time usefully, but
it helped make them aware of the camp's pitfalls, and provided the feeling
of superiority which Bettelheim cites on several occasions as being essential for survival in such degrading conditions.

The two men promised to one another that the first of them to be freed,
should they be so lucky, would write down their observations so that the
whole world would know what was going on behind the barbed wire fences
on the Ettersberg hill.

In mid-January, Bettelheim's instructions to his mother became even
more precise: he wanted Gina's address in New York and worried about
his passport, emigration card, tax release, boat ticket, etc. He also wanted
to be sure the debt to Frieda Goldstein had been paid, and asked that his

sister go to Berlin 'to wrap things up over there'. Concluding this catalogue of demands, he wrote: 'Only when you have answered all these points, talk to me about other things.' It was in the same letter that he asked for an English phrase-book, and thanked his mother for his new glasses.

The recovery of his sight appears to have provided a huge boost to his morale; he had to make it out of the camp. He knew that degradation threatened him. He was weak, not only physically but because of his own doubts about himself, and the meaning of life. In the camp, everything was calculated to reinforce such doubts. Rather than the memory of his father, who had died in complete physical and mental dereliction, ought he to prefer that of grandfather Seidler, whose cunning had helped him make good in all circumstances, even the worst? And what about the political prisoners, those who had noble ideals to uphold; were they doing any better? Some of them were, indeed, but others were taking advantage of their power in the camp to obtain privileges for their friends, to the detriment of the weaker, the less organized, or the Jews. No, he could rely only on his own resources: he wanted to keep his self-respect, to still be able to look at himself in the mirror without shame. He did not want to sink, he did not want to die.

As he needed an outlet for the mental self-lashing that he required to keep him going, he used the only safe one available to him: his family, those who loved him – or at least those he knew would feel guilty if they failed to do all they could to save his life. 'Follow my instructions to the letter,' he wrote in one missive, one which contained not the slightest trace of either emotion or kindness. Poor Paula and Margarethe! Knowing what living conditions were like for Jews in Vienna at that time, one can easily imagine the mixed feelings that such a letter must have inspired in them. Thank God, he was alive, and apparently still in full command of his faculties. But the camp had done nothing to improve his character. 'What a tyrant!' they may have thought. 'Doesn't he realize what a fix we're in ourselves?'

Apparently he did not, since those around him who had some experience of life outside under the Nazis had not known anything similar, with the exception of the 'November Jews', but they were separated from the other prisoners by a barbed wire fence. And conversely, he probably thought his mother and sister were unable to imagine just how far the Nazis' barbarity could extend, and that they needed sharp prodding to take care of their own safety. When he asked the German Jews who had only recently arrived in the camp why they had not left earlier, given that Hitler had been in power since 1933, so many of them had replied: 'How could I have left? I would have lost my house, my store ...'[33] that he felt it necessary to tell his mother over and over again that he didn't care about whether he got a few marks more or less from the sale of his company (July 3), and that his commercial affairs were secondary (July 31). What was important was the documents that would allow him to go. It did not even matter much where to: 'If Grete has an opening for Colombia, she should grasp at it' (August 28), or again, 'Thank you for your efforts. Honduras will also do fine' (February 5). Also important were the debts to be repaid, a theme his letters constantly returned to.

On the latter question, I was not able to ascertain whether Frieda Goldstein was the wife of the German Communist whose advice was so invaluable in allowing him to organize for survival in the camp. He was later to refer to this all-important debt, which he had repaid before leaving. But if love is not enough, neither is money. After almost eleven months of concentration camp life, Bruno Bettelheim had run up another debt, a much heavier one than those 150 Reichmarks; it was a debt that he would devote the remainder of his life to paying off. On his arrival in Dachau he was already a deeply wounded man; on his emergence from Buchenwald he had become, in the full sense of the word, a survivor. That was a form of wealth, which he would now make it his duty to spread around.

On Friday April 14, 1939, after the morning roll-call, Bruno Bettelheim heard his number barked out from the loudspeaker; he was to report to the administration.[34] As Walter Poller notes, such an order, which automatically implied contact with SS soldiers, was always a source of anxiety, even for a prisoner who had hopes of being released. Those summoned had to spend a considerable time waiting, in a state of excitement, only a few feet away from the guards. An incident was always possible, especially at the last minute. Countless prisoners had already been shot dead just as they were about to be released.

Bettelheim, however, had reasons for being optimistic. His efforts, and his sister's trip to Berlin, had borne fruit. On January 26 he had finally been issued with a passport, and on February 6 his mother had purchased his ticket for New York. As for his US visa, it had been waiting for him at the consulate in Vienna for over six months.

On hearing his number read out, however, Bettelheim rebelled; he did not want to go. His hopes had already been raised too many times, only to be dashed. He thus balked; at least that was how he remembered it when writing *The Informed Heart*.[35] He had already been summoned for release twice before, he wrote, and had each time handed in his prisoner's uniform in exchange for civilian clothes, to be told at the last moment that he was not being freed. On the third occasion, he had thus rebelled against a game which he saw as being aimed at destroying him. This time, however, it was for real.

As he gives no other details, and as he survived to tell the tale two decades later, I conclude that his demurral, which is not in itself totally inconceivable, must have remained discreet. It is indeed difficult to imagine the SS obliging a prisoner to leave Buchenwald against his will. As regards the two false alarms he had been given, I was not able to learn anything more than what he wrote, as Federn has no memory of them. On the first occasion, almost all the prisoners summoned at the same time as Bettelheim were freed, he writes, but his release was postponed, 'possibly ... because I had provoked an SS official'.[36] As he gives no details of the purported incident, however, the reader can be forgiven for being somewhat sceptical. The known incidents in which a prisoner was killed only minutes away from freedom were almost all sparked by a remark that displeased the SS official in charge of the 'political interview' which preceded all releases. As for the second false alarm, it was apparently due to the fact that there was not enough money in the camp safe to pay for train tickets for all the prisoners being freed on that day; this seems a more plausible explanation.

Elsewhere, Bettelheim describes how the Gestapo had meanwhile kept Paula on tenterhooks regarding the date of his release. 'My mother was several times given a date for my release, each one untrue. Once she was told I was probably home already, waiting for her, and to hurry home. Another time she was encouraged to travel from Vienna to Weimar ... either to receive me on my release, or at least to have a visit with me. She presented herself in Weimar, where she was given a run-around for several days, until in desperation she returned to Vienna.'[37] In *Surviving*, he also mentions a Nazi lawyer whom his family had to pay to go to Weimar to meet him, once again to no avail.

In early March, Paula or Margarethe had the date of his departure for New York pushed back, from March 18 to April 29. By that time the two women could no longer count on the help of Norbert Bettelheim. On January 26, the day Bruno's passport was finally issued, a friend had warned the lawyer that he was about to be arrested, and he had immediately left for Switzerland with his family, travelling on later to France.

Other former prisoners have described the Buchenwald departure ceremony. One was Rabbi Georg Wilde of Magdeburg, one of the 'November Jews', who was freed eleven days after his imprisonment, along with around 200 others picked up during *Kristallnacht*. The prisoners were first given a lecture by a Gestapo officer, who said: 'We are allowing you to go home to make arrangements for emigration. But if you say a single word about the concentration camp, we will come back to get you, and you will stay for good. And don't go thinking that you'll be able to say what you want from abroad. We have our agents everywhere, and they will make sure you are silenced for ever.'[38]

Next, the prisoners were examined by a doctor; Rabbi Wilde immediately realized this was to ensure that they did not bear any too-obvious marks of ill-treatment. They were then made to sign a form certifying that they had been well treated, had no complaints to make, and would refrain from telling people outside about life in the camps. The group was then marched to the nearest village, where bread, cheese, mineral water and coffee were provided in the local inn. The landlord appeared to know just what the new arrivals 'from up on the hill' needed. 'He was friendly and did not ask the least question,' writes the rabbi.

There is one other point which I was not able to elucidate: exactly why Bettelheim was freed. A week after him, some 2,000 Buchenwald prisoners were to be released, in a spectacular gesture to mark Adolf Hitler's fiftieth birthday. Federn remembers that event very well; it was a Saturday and the prisoners had been exempted from work. Throughout the day the public address system barked out a series of prisoner numbers, keeping the entire population in a state of unbearable suspense. But by that day, April 22, Bettelheim was already far away. So to what did he owe his release?

Many answers have been provided to that question, all very different. Bettelheim himself always remained evasive on the subject, stressing that at the time it was often easier for a Jew to get out of a concentration camp than for a non-Jew, on condition that he promise to emigrate from the Reich without delay and leave all his possessions behind.[39] But there again, there were no certainties. In a note at the start of 'Surviving', he writes: 'The terror the concentration camps created was made even more effective by the utterly arbitrary manner in which the Gestapo imprisoned some people and set others free. There was no way to guess why one prisoner was let go after a few months, when another just like him was released only after several years, and yet again another was doomed to remain forever in the camps.'[40]

From the available documents,[41] it is clear that Agnes Crane kept the pressure on the State Department right up until Bettelheim arrived in the United States. Less than two weeks after his arrest and deportation all the red tape holding up his visa application fell away as if by miracle, which in itself shows that even in the summer of 1938, the name 'Dachau' was already enough to make an impression in Washington. At the end of July Agnes Crane mounted a new attack with a letter to A.M. Warren, head of the State Department's visa division, thanking him for his help but also asking him to press the US embassy in Berlin to seek information about her protégé. The answer was courteous but clear: as Bettelheim was not a US citizen, no diplomatic representation could be made.

Agnes Crane was not to be put off so easily, however. As soon as Bettelheim was transferred to Buchenwald, she went on the offensive again. While the American Psychoanalytic Association intervened again, via its secretary Lawrence Kubie, she was shooting off letters and phone calls to Washington. At the start of November Warren relented, asking the Vienna mission to seek information on the prisoner, but stressing that this would be in a purely unofficial capacity. He nevertheless felt it necessary to justify the move by the fact that the consulate had initially mislaid

Bettelheim's visa application. Two days later Paula and Margarethe Bettelheim were granted a meeting with the Vienna consul general, who told them that the transfer of the prisoners from Dachau to Weimar (Buchenwald) had been a purely general measure. He nevertheless sent a cable to his colleague in Berlin, seeking further information. At the end of November, in a telegram marked 'This message must be closely paraphrased before being communicated to anyone,' the Berlin consul general informed the State Department that he had 'formally asked head of secret police to release [Bruno Bettelheim] here giving the assurance that his emigration has been arranged'. The last sentence, however, was hardly promising: 'Believe in view of arrest having taken place last May, release will be difficult.' This obviously alarmed Agnes, who on receiving the message (not in paraphrased form, in fact), immediately demanded an explanation. The State Department dutifully passed on the question to Berlin: why did the consul believe it would not be easy to obtain a release? The penultimate item in the file is a cryptic cable from Berlin to Washington, dated December 12 and stating simply: 'Bruno Bettelheim referred to Vienna.' The only other item in the State Department archives is a letter of thanks to Warren dated May 16, 1939, from Bruno Bettelheim himself, by then living in New York.

This evidence thus corroborates what Bettelheim would state five years later, in his testimony for the Nuremberg Tribunal ('My release was effected through some influential friends of mine in America who were able to enlist the assistance of the State Department.'), but it does not confirm the most famous of the rumours concerning his release, carried in many newspapers at the time of his death, according to which First Lady Eleanor Roosevelt had intervened in his favour. A footnote in the opening pages of *Surviving*, while not confirming that story, at least gave it some credence. Bettelheim states: 'It may have helped that one of the most prominent public figures intervened personally and also through the American legation on my behalf.' After a day-long search through the former First Lady's private correspondence,[42] however, I am almost certain that the rumour is unfounded. Mrs Roosevelt's intervention in favour of European refugees was to come somewhat later.[43]

Another famous name has been mentioned in connection with Bruno Bettelheim's release: that of Herbert Lehmann, then governor of New York, and himself a Jew. Lehmann was one of the very few US politicians to take an active interest in the fate of the European Jews at that time. Again, however, the name Bettelheim is nowhere to be found in his correspondence.[44] One name which does feature however is that of Ernst Federn. Which is not really surprising: in 1914, when Lehmann was but a young banker, handicapped by a serious stutter, Paul Federn had travelled to New York to spend several months as his psychoanalyst.[45] So when he returned to the United States twenty-five years later, this time as an exile, he quite naturally turned to his former patient to try and obtain his son's release. It should be added however that Lehmann's archives contain only post-war correspondence with Paul Federn, so a sliver of doubt remains as regards Bettelheim.

The possibility that Agnes Crane, weary of State Department vacillation, decided to seek support from elsewhere, even if it was not from the First Lady, thus cannot be completely ruled out. That may explain why the US consul in Berlin intervened with the head of the Gestapo to seek the release of a man who after all was then considered a German national. In fact, Gina Weinmann remembers that Mr Warren himself made a trip to Vienna to try and obtain freedom for several people, one of whom was her then husband. What is certain is that the latter's family and several of his friends had paid a lot of money to the Gestapo to obtain his release, and that all the paperwork had been done to allow him to fulfil the second condition imposed by the Nazis: his departure within two weeks from the Reich, leaving all his possessions behind.

One last detail may be worth noting. In *Surviving*, again, Bettelheim states that interventions coming from too high up sometimes achieved the opposite result to the one desired. He cites the case of one of his best friends, whose release had been requested on several occasions by 'a member of a royal family', but who was in fact to remain in Buchenwald until the camp was liberated, because the Nazis had realized that his value made him a potential hostage. With the exception of one or two details, this could in fact apply to Ernst Federn's story. After his release he learned of a letter in which Himmler in person had ordered that he be kept in the camp, because a man who appeared to count so much for the Americans (but not for a royal family; that was the only difference) would make a good hostage.

By April 17, Bruno Bettelheim was back in Vienna, where he was to stay until the 27th. The two dates were recorded by Paula at City Hall and, without slipping into excessive sentimentalism, one cannot help noticing in the ledger how triumphant and vengeful the words 'New York' look in the space marked 'destination'. On the 18th, the US consulate issued Bettelheim with his immigration visa, number QIV 14560.

Ten days to obtain all the required papers, to locate all his folks and bid them farewell. Ten days in which to settle his accounts and to get ready for a departure which he knew would be definitive, a complete break with everything his life had been up until then. But above all, ten days of living in fear that they would come to arrest him again. For although nothing is known about Bettelheim's life in that short spell between Buchenwald and exile, what is certain is that he cannot have enjoyed any feeling of new-found freedom in Vienna. Hans Bandler, released three months earlier, well remembers the raw fear that gripped him every time he had to go out to make the necessary arrangements for his departure. In the street, former prisoners tried to blend into the background, but their shaved heads made them instantly recognizable. And the fact that they did not have a swastika attached to their buttonhole singled them out automatically as Jews (to have worn one would have been even more risky).

Bandler also remembers the shock he had on first entering the apartment of his aunt (who acted as his mother): it was almost stripped bare, all the furniture and other objects of value having been sold to pay for his release. For Bettelheim the feeling must have been even worse; because his mother's apartment had been requisitioned, she had been forced to go and stay with neighbours. It was probably at that point that he learned he would not be getting a cent from the 'sale' of his company. As is shown by several of his letters from Buchenwald, he must also have spent part of his spell in Vienna trying to convince other members of his family to flee.

Paula, who was not to leave Europe until September 25,[46] must have told him of the circumstances of Trude's departure. Shortly after Bettelheim's arrest, the young schoolteacher had been summoned to Gestapo headquarters at the Metropole Hotel; she had obediently gone, and had been kept there for a whole day. Between interrogation sessions she was locked up in a hotel bathroom and she thought she was never going to get out alive. To her great surprise, however, she was released that evening, and a few days later the Gestapo even sent her back her passport. Apparently they had only been interested in the Montessori school.

Until that incident, Trude had not exactly been hurrying to leave; she had made several attempts to obtain information about Bruno, or to get in touch with him. Knowing his aversion to any kind of manual labour and his lack of physical stamina, she was convinced he would not survive a spell of several months in a concentration camp. But she had come to the realization that as she was not a relative, she could do nothing whatsoever to help him. After her arrest, however, Trude never slept in her own apartment again, and started actively preparing to leave. Some cousins gave her the name of a mountaineer who could help her get across the border into Switzerland.[47] There she knew that she would no longer be alone; shortly after the *Anschluss*, the brother of her friend Emmi Vischer had travelled to Vienna to see what he could do to help. One fine day Trude therefore donned a rucksack and set out with her guide, whom she had been able to pay with a small sum donated by grateful parents of her Montessori pupils. Taking the train for the Tyrol, the two of them looked just like any couple heading out for that favourite Austrian pastime, a mountain hike. The trip over the border was not easy: they were detained by the border police, and Trude had to spend a night fending off the advances of her guide, but she had finally made it.

Coming amid so much bad news, the knowledge that Trude had escaped must have been a great consolation to Bettelheim, who had asked after her in many of his letters from Buchenwald. His sole concern at that time, however, was to get out of Europe as fast as possible, and without a backward glance, to join Gina and start a new life.

Almost all Bruno Bettelheim's family was to perish at the hands of the Nazis, notably several uncles and cousins who would be arrested in 1942. I do not know whether insufficient means or a lack of initiative prevented them from leaving the death-trap that Vienna had become for Jews. What I am sure of, however, is that as soon as he arrived in Dachau, Bettelheim had started doing everything he could to convince them to leave. He must have suffered from not having succeeded. Among the very few personal documents that he kept right to the end of his life was a long letter sent to his mother and his Aunt Jenny from their elder brother, Alfred Seidler. Dated January 1941, it tells of an unsuccessful attempt by their younger brother Rudolf Seidler, the Wagner-loving uncle that Bruno liked so much, and his wife Grete, to get over the border. Writing from Vienna while awaiting Rudolph's return to the city, Alfred was clearly trying to keep his anxiety in check, and to while away the time. It is a superb letter, full of acceptance of his own terrible situation, which he barely alludes to, and tolerance for the foolhardiness of his brother, who had himself wrecked his attempt to escape by attracting attention from a Tyrolean wedding party. Alfred's generosity even extended to expressing sympathy for the problems of Paula and Jenny, by then set up in the United States. It is the letter of a man worlds apart from the terrible Adolf Seidler, and who had clearly not inherited his father's iron determination to defeat fate at whatever cost. A man who was never to return from the camp to which the Gestapo would send him a year later.

On Saturday April 29, 1939, Bruno Bettelheim boarded the SS *Gerolstein* in the Dutch port of Flushing. The vessel, which had sailed up the River Scheldt from Antwerp, was a German ship flying the flag of the US Red Star line. Bettelheim had his own cabin. He was to arrive in New York on the morning of Friday May 11. His final departure from the Reich had come none too soon: as of August the Nazi authorities stopped issuing any exit visas at all to Jewish men aged between eighteen and forty-five.

Chapter VIII

A Short-Lived Reunion

'No, Bruno, it's over. I don't want to live with you any more.' With two short sentences, Gina had dashed her husband's hopes. Gaunt and sickly, but his eyes burning with the excitement of new-found freedom, he had just walked right across springtime Manhattan to get to her apartment. He poured out a torrent of words, pleading, coaxing and outlining his plans. He would go into politics, become a diplomat; he knew where he had gone wrong in the past, he had changed. Now he wanted a family, with children, lots of children. Gina, determined, just kept on saying 'No,' and he just as obstinately kept trying to make her change her mind. As she remembered it later, the discussion lasted for most of that day and a part of the evening.

That long and painful conversation is in fact the only memory that Gina can bring back of her reunion with Bruno. She has no recollection of having gone to meet him off the boat when he finally set foot on American soil. I wanted very much for her to recall those first moments, the first contact after a year of separation, the first glances exchanged since Bruno had emerged from hell. So I insisted ...

The SS *Gerolstein* docked on the west side of the New York Port on May 11, 1939. On the page of the passenger manifest featuring Bruno Bettelheim's name, all but one are identified as both 'Hebrew' and 'German'. This triggered my imagination; I could picture the ragged lines of gaunt refugees with the giant Statue of Liberty as a backdrop – a symbol which up until then had encapsulated their hope of deliverance, but which on arrival suddenly appeared so intimidating. Each person clutching in one hand the documents that he or she hoped – but how to be absolutely certain? – would open the door to this great New World, far from persecutions; in the other, the suitcase containing whatever they had been allowed to take with them. And, somewhere in the line, perhaps standing slightly to one side, impatient but certainly careful not to let himself be jostled or even mingle with the crowd, Bruno Bettelheim – the man with whom she had spent the previous eight years of her life, a man who only three weeks earlier had still been in Buchenwald.

Gina rummages through her memories, but finds nothing. She can only dredge up some vague recollection of a dinner at his aunt Jenny Buxbaum's apartment, a few blocks away from her own. But that in fact took place some time later. Above all, obliterating all the rest, was the memory of that long afternoon spent saying, painfully but firmly: 'It's over. I want a divorce.' More than what she said, her inability to remember those first minutes with Bruno impressed me, suggesting how traumatic the event must have been for her too. Although she hardly acknowledges it, and that only when pressed, it was not easy to turn away this man she no longer wanted, whom she knew was not for her. She could have picked a more propitious moment, giving him time to rebuild his life in the United States, but she would not. She no longer wanted to share his bed, his life or his dreams. She probably sensed that her attitude would be judged sternly by others; one does not reject a just-emerged survivor of the Nazi concentration camps. Paradoxically, she seems to have drawn the strength to break with Bruno from the uncertainty of her relationship with Peter Weinmann. He had by that time moved with his wife to Chicago, and it seemed very unlikely he would obtain a divorce. Gina's gesture was that of a woman who wants to take control of her own life, without depending on a man for security. It was a difficult, cruel but brave decision and from her point of view, the only dignified one, the only one possible.

Her first months in the United States had been tough, and at the start almost surreal. After two days in Paris at the home of Emmi and Hubert von Radanowicz, she and Patsy had boarded the *President Roosevelt* on May 17, 1938 at Le Havre, arriving in New York on the 26th. There she had immediately been taken in hand by Agnes and her latest husband, Percy 'Ed' Crane, an alcoholic whom she was rumoured to have married above all to provide Patsy with a father. The couple lived in a charming apartment in Greenwich, Connecticut. As it was far too small to accommodate two more people, Agnes had set Gina up in a luxury hotel nearby.

Although sick with worry about those she had left in Vienna, and completely unsure of her own future, Gina found herself dressing up for dinner every evening in one of the elegant evening gowns that Agnes had bought her at Lord and Taylor's. After dinner in Agnes's tiny apartment, from which one could see the ocean across from Long Island, her hostess would play her Gilbert and Sullivan operas until late into the night, while her husband nodded off. To Gina, it all seemed like a dream. Half charmed by the nonchalant and refined life of her rich American protectress, she had to keep a tight lid on her own contradictory emotions.

Almost every day the mail brought new reports of the horrors going on in Vienna, along with requests for Gina to obtain yet another affidavit that would allow a relative or friend to leave for the US. Although thanks to Agnes she was meeting quite a few people, she had soon realized that the situation in Germany was far from being the favourite topic of conversation for most Americans. They were too happy to have emerged from the Depression to contemplate the imminence of another European war. Which is not to say that Agnes or Agnes's friends had the slightest sympathy for Adolf Hitler. But discussing the political situation at cocktail parties was one thing, getting actively involved in events on the old continent, a vast ocean away, was quite another. Gina learned not to be too insistent, while taking advantage of the social events she attended to glean an affidavit here and there.

Almost immediately after her arrival, she had thought of taking a job. This in spite of protests from Agnes, who was already looking for a large house in which they could all live together – Patsy of course, but also Gina and Bruno, once the latter was free. Her dream was of a kind of extended family, in which she could go on living as she pleased while Gina would take care of Patsy. Agnes had no inkling of her protégée's affair with Peter Weinmann. Gina had revealed the relationship to no one. She probably guessed that Agnes Crane would never forgive her for thus shattering her well-laid plans. But although she was fond of Agnes, she had no desire to remain dependent on somebody as bossy and capricious, so she was determined to stand on her own two feet and start building a new life as soon as possible.

She knew only a handful of people in New York outside Agnes's circle of friends. Fritz Redl had been in the United States since 1935, but he lived in Chicago. Such was her determination to recover her independence, however, that three months after her arrival Gina found a job, thanks to one of Agnes's friends. She was taken on as a social worker with the Jewish Social Services, an agency where her knowledge of psychoanalysis and intuitive grasp of people brought her instant status among her colleagues. They were all eager to learn about the new science. So much so that it occasionally irritated her. 'These people come here because they need a place to live, not to pour out the story of their childhoods,' she would say to herself. Being thrown in at the deep end of the New York labour market was a fascinating but also a very tough experience. Her English was still very poor, but because she was good at her job, she was often assigned the most difficult cases. She then had an extremely hard time drawing up her reports, which she was meant to dictate into a tape-recorder. Later on, Wanda Willig would help her, but at first she was very alone. Luckily the head of the agency, Mrs Kamschell, was well aware of the fate of German and Austrian Jews. She gave Gina plenty of spare time in which to seek affidavits, make contacts and carry out all the formalities needed to help as many people as possible, including her husband.

For a while after she started her job, Gina commuted each evening to Greenwich, where she carried on caring for Patsy. But she soon found this schedule exhausting. At the end of June, Peter Weinmann had arrived from London, and Gina wanted some freedom to see him, if only briefly. When Agnes Crane heard of the affair, she was incensed. She had already shown some irritation during Gina's visit in 1936, when her brother Paul had taken her visitor under his wing. She had also been somewhat peeved when Fritz Redl had shown up and taken the young woman out. But finding out that Gina was being unfaithful to Bruno, even as she was laying siege to the State Department to get him released, was the last straw. A head-on clash between the two women had become inevitable; it was both brief and violent.

'Gina gave me fifteen minutes to make up my mind either to go with her or to stay with my mother,' Patsy recalls angrily. At the time she was a shy young thing just turned fifteen. She did not feel she had a choice: 'I did what seemed the proper thing to do: I stayed with my mother.' Half a century later, the hurt is obviously still there. Proper or not, for seven years her mother had in effect been Gina: it was she who had taught Patsy to laugh and to enjoy life, helping her make enormous progress. For all that time the two had been practically inseparable. After that day, they were never to see one another again.

In the fall, Peter Weinmann was invited to teach at New York's Columbia University for a semester. This procured several months of happiness for Gina, after which he had returned to Chicago. There, his wife was obstinately refusing his requests for a divorce. For a few months after that, the two lovers would spend an occasional weekend together, half-way between New York and Chicago. It was on the way back from one such meeting that Gina first came down with what she refers to as her 'immigration disease', a stomach ulcer. She had lost so much blood by the time the train arrived in New York that she had to be taken to hospital in an ambulance. As soon as Agnes heard of her misfortune she rushed over to give some of her blood for Gina, but refused to see her. Finally the same woman friend of Agnes's who had found Gina the job also provided her with an apartment, on the corner of 83rd Street and Lexington Avenue in uptown Manhattan. It was only a small one-roomer, originally intended for domestic staff, but for the young Viennese woman it was freedom itself.

It was there that Bruno came to join Gina on the day of his arrival. He had walked practically the full length of Manhattan, with his hands in his pockets as he had not been allowed to take anything with him. He was both amazed and incredulous to find himself in New York, a city he had seen so often in films and read about in books that he had the vague impression he already knew it. He was free, it was springtime, and he was on his way back to the woman he loved. All he had in his pocket was three dollars,[1] but so what? They were both young, intelligent and hard workers, so they had every reason to have faith in the future. Gina already had a job, and he would easily find one. They were going to build a new and better life together.

Their existence would be utterly different from the one the Nazis had forced them to leave behind. Was this not America, the country of the 'self-made man', where dreams actually came true? His cousin Edith was already a practising psychoanalyst, while his friend Fritz was meeting rapid success in the academic world. Fate had relieved him of his lumber business, which he had never wanted in the first place. Now he could really do what he wanted. No more unwanted burdens, or debts to be paid off. When the immigration official had asked him his profession he had shown all the required papers. But then he had insisted on also mentioning his PhD. It is scribbled in cramped longhand, squashed above the officially-typed 'merchant'.

Bruno Bettelheim talked little about his first days of freedom in America, and when he did he seldom mentioned Gina's rejection. Much later, during an evening of nostalgia at the Orthogenic School, he told a counsellor: 'When I first came to America, my wife rejected me.' Most of the time, however, he described the event with an almost detached air, explaining that he and Gina, after a long and calm discussion of their past marital problems, had decided to separate.

As any former prisoner can testify, however, the prospect of being reunited with a loved one is the one thing that can make detention bearable. Bettelheim himself was to point this out: after a while, the prisoner starts to forget about any difficulties the couple might have had, gradually replacing the real memory of the relationship with an idealized one. There could be no better illustration of this than the letters he wrote to his mother from the camps. While the first ones were mainly concerned with the settlement of urgent business affairs, as time went by an increasing number of messages for his wife crept in. 'Write to tell Gina that I'm very happy she's found a job, and that it reassures me as to her future. [Tell her] I think of her, as I do of you all, with the greatest love and the greatest nostalgia,' he wrote in July 1938. And although he added, 'She, like you, must make her own plans without thinking of me, because my future is very uncertain,' three weeks later, the emphasis had shifted again: 'Tell Gina that all my hopes rest on the future she is building for us.'

From that point on, every one of his letters to Paula contained a message for Gina. Messages of love, messages to say 'I miss you,' but also messages of hope, reined-in but nevertheless visible. Once Bettelheim had learned that there were already a visa and a passport in his name, the tone became even more pressing. He asked for her address so as to write to her directly, and wanted her to write to him. It clearly never once occurred to him that if he was lucky enough to be released, it would be to live without her. And although Trude's name also recurred, in affectionate terms, the way in which he sent her his best wishes for success and happiness clearly shows that he did not think of her as a possible future life-companion, if he had a future.

Much later, when he was about to lose Trude, who had given him the strength to go on living after the wound inflicted by Gina in New York, Bettelheim was to write: 'The strongest motive for staying alive is that one has something for which one is determined to remain alive at all costs, at all risks .... The sheer will to live cannot take the place of the strength which one derives from support from the outside, real or imagined. One of the unexpected lessons of the camps was that, contrary to what I expected and what Darwinism taught, the will to live, the life drives, the *élan vital*, the libido, or whatever other name it may be given, provided little support unless it could attach itself to some loved person, some all important idea, such as Zionism or Communism, or religious conviction. Compared to these, ideas of revenge, or the wish to bear witness, so often mentioned in the literature on surviving, carried little conviction.'[2]

Gina's rejection of him played a major role in Bruno Bettelheim's later life, however much he may have tried to cover it up. Gina remembers that during that fateful discussion in New York, she was struck by what she calls his 'grandiosity'. 'All of a sudden he wanted to go into politics,' she says. 'He even told me that, in this country, he could hope to be elected president.' If she had not been so concerned with marshalling her strength to maintain her refusal of him, she would no doubt have seen the real distress that such bravado was designed to conceal. As usual with Bettelheim, the distress was mingled with arrogance. After all, if he had had the strength to get out of Buchenwald and make it to the Land of the Free, was he not entitled to the most extravagant dreams?

When Bettelheim realized that Gina was not going to change her mind, he left his wife's apartment and walked the few blocks to his aunt Jenny Buxbaum's place. There he was reunited with his childhood bosom friend and cousin, Edith, who had also been putting in some efforts over the past few months to obtain his release. She welcomed him with open arms. Edith was pleased to get back the cousin that another woman had taken away from her, as she acknowledges in her memoirs. He was in a state of distress, and physically in very bad shape; she took him under her wing.

Edith Buxbaum had by then been living in New York for almost two years. She had fled Vienna at the end of August 1937, just as she was about to be arrested for her political activities. She arrived in New York a month later, after a trip which for her too had been a voyage of freedom. She came to the United States in her capacity as a teacher, with the Cooperative School for Student Teachers, but like Bettelheim she had insisted that her PhD be clearly marked on her immigration papers. Edith had two ambitions: to set up as a child psychoanalyst and, above all, to escape from the moral blackmail that lay behind her mother's continual illnesses. On the latter count she had obtained but a short respite, as Jenny came over to join her in May 1938. On the former, however, she had made rapid strides. Only a short time after setting foot in New York she had a sprinkling of patients, and had started consulting in social welfare agencies, notably the Community Service Society, one of the city's biggest. And in spite of the rule which excluded non-medical doctors from membership of most US psychoanalytic societies, she was even teaching at the prestigious New York Psychoanalytic Institute, headed by Sandor Rado.[3] Thanks to these contacts she was able, soon after Bruno Bettelheim was arrested, to get the American Psychoanalytic Association to write to the State Department in support of Agnes Crane's efforts to gain him a visa.

Bruno Bettelheim's first days in New York were spent simply recovering. Seeing doctors and a dentist, but also walking around, enjoying freedom, making new contacts and getting in touch with friends and acquaintances who had also managed to escape across the Atlantic. Physically, he had aged. The Willigs, who had arrived in New York two months before him after trying to settle in Sweden, noticed that he had lost most of his hair. It was probably at this time that Bettelheim met Paul Federn, to whom he was able to give news of his son.

In July, Edith Buxbaum suggested to her cousin that they set out to discover the rest of America. He agreed; although he had been looking for work, there was really nothing to keep him in New York. Edith was later to acknowledge that, unconsciously at least, she had an ulterior motive. Seeing Bruno rejected by the woman who had taken him away from her, and being herself caught up in a complicated relationship with a married man who did not appear to want to divorce his wife, she would not have been averse to an affair with her younger cousin.

So they lit out across America in Edith's old Cadillac convertible, much as years earlier they had wandered the Austrian woods together as 'young migrating birds'. She paid for everything, and as she did not have much money they often slept rough, occasionally checking into a cheap motel. Their first major stop was in Chicago, where Bruno was reunited with his friend Fritz Redl, and met a good number of other fellow Viennese who had been attracted to the city's highly rated university.

The atmosphere in the Windy City was a complete change from New York. Most of Bettelheim's friends and acquaintances lived in Hyde Park, on the campus of the University of Chicago, on the South Side of the city. A good twenty minutes' drive along Lake Michigan from downtown Chicago, Hyde Park was like a small middle-class village. With its parks, its tree-lined streets and its individual houses and gardens in full bloom, it looked much more like an English town than Bettelheim's idea of the capital of the American Midwest.

As he noted in *Freud's Vienna and Other Essays*, Bettelheim's image of Chicago had been built up from films and books: a mix of the clichés about meat-packing, money and gangsters. And then he found himself plunged into a European-style cultural environment, closer to Oxford than the Wild West. A neighbourhood in which people didn't even bother to lock their doors when they went out. Spontaneously patronizing towards America, he cannot but have been struck by the remarkable architectural harmony of the great city.

Barely three months after leaving Buchenwald, Bruno Bettelheim thus spent several days in a welcoming and cultured atmosphere, enjoying swimming in the lake, picnics and discussions with men and women whose interests and occupations were not far removed from those he had been surrounded by only a few years earlier in Vienna. With one key difference, however: far from existing on the brink of apocalypse, this was a country of boundless optimism and energy. One that was just beginning to emerge from the Depression, and was ready to fund all kinds of research into what had gone wrong, and how to avoid it happening again in the future.

Just as they had been in Vienna, Fritz Redl and his friends were swept up in great schemes for educational reform. And although the interests providing the finance were less socialist than they had been in Austria, they were almost as socially aware; the aim being to try and provide equal access to knowledge for all. The United States was in the throes of the New Deal, and for many of the young intellectuals in Chicago's very research-oriented university the key issue was to understand, and thus to find remedies for, the flaws of capitalism. One of Fritz Redl's friends got on particularly well with Bettelheim. George Sheviakov was a Russian, the son of the Czar's last education minister, who had arrived in the United States a few years earlier after a series of extravagant adventures. He and Bettelheim not only shared the same biting sense of humour, they were also capable of distinguishing between truly progressive ideas and simple naïveté. Thanks to his intelligence and dynamism, Sheviakov was fast becoming one of the best teacher training specialists in the whole country.

When Bruno Bettelheim and Edith Buxbaum visited Chicago, George Sheviakov was involved in a major project to reform progressive secondary schools across the United States. It was a colossal and long-running enterprise, as implied by its name: the 'Eight Year Study'. It involved a whole team of research workers plus thirty schools scattered across eleven states, in which both teachers and students were to act as guinea-pigs for the setting up and running of a series of new curricula. The man in charge of the overall project, Ralph Tyler, had just been appointed dean of the University of Chicago's Department of Education.

Bruno Bettelheim was immediately drawn to Chicago, and felt he could live well in the campus environment. Of course, New York was closer to his idea of what America was all about, and probably more exciting. But Chicago, or rather Hyde Park, offered the academic and cultural atmosphere he so craved, and was also warmer and less threatening. Here at least nobody was rejecting him. And although nobody had an immediate job to offer him, everyone he met, and notably Sheviakov, had promised to keep him in mind if something should come up.

After Chicago, Bruno and Edith headed west. She tried to entertain him, to snap him out of his gloom. But he was taciturn, and apparently unappreciative of her efforts. Edith tried to get him to discuss his camp experiences, thinking that this would help him get them out of his system, but he stubbornly repelled all her advances. It was only much later, in 1979, after reading the collection of essays that Bettelheim published on the subject under the title *Surviving*, that Edith Buxbaum realized how clumsy her attempts to console him had been. She then wrote to tell him so, and in his reply Bettelheim admitted that their lack of communication during the trip had also been due to his guilt at being entirely dependent on her for finance.

The purported aim of the trip, however, was to find him a job. From New York, Bruno Bettelheim had shot off letters to countless colleges and schools across the country, offering his services as a teacher. He was ready to teach almost anything: German, philosophy, psychology and art history, among other subjects. The extraordinary job résumé he sent with his applications can be interpreted either as yet another sign of what Gina calls his 'grandiosity', or as a simple indication of the dire straits in which he found himself. Here he was, a man who for so long had been used not only to earning a good living but to providing for other people, suddenly transformed into a penniless alien in a vast country of which he knew almost nothing – a status made all the more obvious by his impossible accent, which immediately labelled him either as an arrogant European or as yet another impoverished immigrant. And he was both.

Edith Buxbaum too found him both high-minded and obstinate. 'He was not about to accept second-best. He had his heart set on Chicago, which he got,' she recalled. Bettelheim himself had different memories of the period, however. As he told it, a little college in Redlands, California had responded favourably to one of his letters. So he went there for an interview and was offered a post for the following school year, with an assurance that his contract would be renewed for at least a second year. He accepted the offer immediately, even though it meant living far away from everyone he knew, and even further from those, such as his mother, who had not yet escaped from Hitler's Europe. And the only reason he did not start his American career in California, he said, was that in the meantime he received a better offer, to teach German at another college, in Oregon. Since the money for the Redlands post came from a fund for exiled Jews, he immediately resigned from it in order to allow another immigrant to take his place. At that juncture, however, Hitler intervened to change his life yet again. In September, just as he was about to leave New York for Oregon, he received a wire informing him that his post had been abolished. As war had just broken out in Europe, the telegram explained, the number of students choosing to study German was not expected to be high enough to warrant a new teacher.

Thus on October 9, 1939, when Bruno Bettelheim filed his 'Declaration of Intention' with the Southern District Court in New York City, the first step towards becoming a US citizen, he was still unemployed, and being provided for by his cousin. Bettelheim the survivor, the man who had always paid his way, sparing no effort to make sure he and those around him could live well. To cap it all, his mother – who had got her visa on August 24, barely a week before the Nazi invasion of Poland sparked World War II – was on the point of arriving in New York, and would have to live with her sister Jenny because her son could not look after her.

If Bettelheim's physical living conditions were tough, his psychological state was no better. His every night was troubled by nightmares, in which he found himself back in Buchenwald with no hope of salvation. What made things even worse was that he found it impossible to open up to anyone. Like Gina, he had quickly realized that most Americans, relieved at having put the Depression behind them, were in no mood to hear about the horrors going on in Europe. Although most of them were strongly opposed to Hitler, they found all the stories of anti-Jewish persecution somewhat difficult to believe. As for the other immigrants, who did know what was going on, they were generally too racked with anxiety about their own loved ones to be able to lend a sympathetic and understanding ear to another escapee. But most of all, Bettelheim himself found it difficult to talk about his experiences, even to those willing to listen, like the Willigs, for instance. He had become irritable. 'After the camps, his personality had changed. He had become very impatient, and of course he took it out on those closest to him,' remarks Wanda Willig.

Returning to New York after his escapade with Edith had also meant seeing Gina again. They still lived only a few blocks apart, and administrative formalities brought them together on occasion. On September 8, Gina finally obtained her US immigration papers by dint of making a trip to Havana in order to re-enter the country. After that, Bruno was able to set in motion his own naturalization process. When he did so the address he gave was his wife's.

Paradoxically, although he was very distressed during these difficult months, Bettelheim was not depressed. As he was to explain later,[4] his spell in the concentration camps and the period immediately afterwards were the only times in his life during which he did not once consider suicide. It was only later, after he had recovered secure living conditions, that the idea began to haunt him once again.

For the time being, all his energy was still devoted to a single end: surviving. One of the first things he had done on arriving in New York had been to write to Trude Weinfeld. The two had never entirely lost contact: in almost all the letters he wrote to his mother from Buchenwald, Bruno Bettelheim had asked her to pass on affectionate wishes to Trude. In the ones he sent from Dachau, he had even on occasion asked Paula to let the young schoolteacher take up a few of the lines permitted in her replies. His mother had scrupulously complied, keeping Trude informed of all news about Bruno. Thus in April 1939 the young woman had received a telegram informing her of her friend's imminent release. By that time she was in Australia, and although she rejoiced at the news, she did not for one minute imagine that the event could have any bearing on her own future, so convinced was she that Bruno's and Gina's marriage was set to last.

Trude had travelled a long way since her extraordinary voyage across the Alps. Her arrival unannounced at the home of Emmi's brother had caused a sensation in the latter's tiny village. Although he was a man of great generosity and more than happy to help refugees, he was also a bachelor living alone, and could not have put up a young woman at his home without causing a scandal. Which was how Trude came to spend three months in Basel at the home of one of Emmi's aunts. As she was later to tell her children, those few weeks of cosseting by a warm and generous family in a large elegantly furnished house with a big garden worked wonders for her. Particularly since she was also able to go and see her parents, who had settled in the French town of Tours.

Trude was still living in hopes of getting a visa for the United States; indeed Bruno Bettelheim had managed to get an affidavit in her name from Agnes Crane. But she got an even worse reception from the US consulate in Zurich than she had in Vienna. When she handed over a letter of recommendation written for her by Anna Freud and Dorothy Burlingham, the consul simply tore it up in front of her, making it abundantly clear that if she persisted in trying to gain entry to the United States, she would have to wait a very long time indeed. So Trude, ever the pragmatist, decided instead to head for Australia, an underpopulated country that still welcomed immigrants, especially women, as long as they were white.

It was to be a long and eventful trip. In Naples, she boarded a ship that was packed with Australians going home from visits to England; from them she picked up a few addresses of people to contact in Sydney. She was also armed with the address of the only psychoanalyst in the whole country, given to her by the Sterbas, whom she had seen in Switzerland. Despite her fears for her own future and for that of her loved ones, she was bowled over by the succession of extraordinary landscapes along the way. The blazing heat of the Suez Canal, followed by a stop in Aden, the first oriental town she had ever seen, and then on to Ceylon, where she spent two days viewing elephants and shrines. And finally, landfall in Perth, where she was amazed at the lushness of the southern Australian landscape.

Trude arrived in Sydney on December 14, 1938, after a full month at sea. After a number of disconcerting experiences, not the least being that of celebrating Christmas in torrid summer heat, she quickly found work. The psychoanalyst whose address the Sterbas had given her put her in touch with a school at Monavale, some twenty miles out of Sydney, where her Montessori training got her hired on the spot. It was a boarding school, run on very liberal and progressive lines, and Trude quickly felt at home with the staff. She was in charge of the youngest class, and she lived on the premises, so with her precious Montessori teaching material, which she had brought from Vienna, she was well armed both to teach and to console those children who missed their parents. Generally speaking, despite her worries, she was happy there. Being a great nature-lover, she found plenty to keep her fascinated in the outback. Above all, she discovered the happiness of living by the ocean, something she was to treasure for the rest of her life.

Not long after that, her brother and his wife also came to settle in Australia. And then in the summer of 1939, she received a visit from another young Viennese: Hans Bandler, who had been released from Buchenwald three months before Bettelheim. Thanks to him, she learned all the things that Bruno had left out of his letters: the extent of the persecution, degradation, despair, hunger and suffering of the camps. Bandler also told her of the comforting role Bruno had played for himself and other inmates. This was no great surprise for Trude, who knew what her friend was capable of. She abstained from telling Hans about her own relationship with Bruno, however.

Rediscovering youthful pleasures, Trude Weinfeld and Hans Bandler set off whenever they could for long hikes in the bush and on the Blue Mountains. Hans worked a lot, as he was both teaching and completing his engineering studies. He too had ended up in Australia somewhat by chance, because it was the first country to offer him a visa. He felt a bit lost, so far away from his aunt and his half-brother, who were all that remained of his family, and running into Trude had made all the difference. She was warm and self-confident, and gave the impression of having already made a place for herself in this strange new society, where the local accent made Hans wonder if he had ever studied English at all. She impressed him with her apparent maturity; he liked her simple way of doing things, her intelligence, her unpretentious yet energetic personality, her habit of looking straight ahead and not getting sidetracked by nostalgia for a vanished past. It was not long before he was in love. They did not see one another very often as the bus trip between Monavale and Sydney, where Hans had found a room, took three-quarters of an hour. Neither of them had much money, but they nevertheless managed to go regularly to the movies, and even on occasion to a concert.

But above all, they talked. Like Gina and Bruno in the United States, it had not taken Hans and Trude long to understand that suffering was not a very exportable commodity, and that people who were far from a conflict had no desire to hear too much about it. They also quickly realized that it was not a good idea to speak German in public, and that although open anti-Semitism was rare, it was better not to advertise their Jewishness either. Australia, like other immigrant communities, was ready to accept them as long as they blended in with the mass. And above all, as long as they kept their painful memories to themselves. Like other former camp inmates, Hans quickly learned to keep quiet about the Buchenwald nightmares that haunted his sleep. Needless to say, having Trude to talk to was a godsend.

Trude had also wasted no time in adjusting to her new environment. Even before war was declared, and thus before her nationality had her classified as an 'enemy alien', acting on the advice of friends who knew how strong anti-German feelings were becoming in Australia, she had changed her name to Trude Field. For that very reason, she almost failed to get the telegram announcing Bruno Bettelheim's release!

The love affair with Hans was a brief one. From the moment Trude received the letter from Bruno in New York, telling her that he and Gina had broken up, she could think only of going to join him. The letter had arrived while she was in hospital, being treated for a gynæcological ailment which had made her fear that she would never be able to have children. In fact, she received two pieces of good news almost at once: that Bruno Bettelheim was now free of attachments, and that she had lost none of her reproductive ability.

After having given up all hope of obtaining a US visa, she now threw herself back into the fray, writing letters and seeking appointments. Unfortunately, she had to spend the three weeks after her operation convalescing in a sanatorium, during which time war broke out, making her Austrian passport worthless. As an enemy alien, she could henceforth only leave the country with the permission of the Australian armed forces. As soon as she was up and about she went to the forces headquarters and asked to see the general in charge, who at first did not seem inclined to grant her request. Finally, after much pleading during which she mentioned her fiancé, just released from a Nazi concentration camp, and shed a tear or two, he agreed to let her go.

After another long sea voyage, Trude arrived in San Francisco on October 31, 1939. On the quayside, she was amazed to see Nuci Plank, the former head of the Grünetorgasse school, waiting to greet her, even though Trude had no recollection of having told her she was coming. The information must have filtered through the exile grapevine, which was of course buzzing with activity at the time. Nuci was working in a San Francisco school, and the arrival of a teacher with Trude's experience was a blessing for her. She invited the young woman to stay with her, and as it was Halloween, Trude was just in time for a party.

The newcomer could not believe her luck. She was so touched by her reception in San Francisco that she gave an outsize tip to the porter who unloaded her bags. Later she was also to ascribe to Nuci Plank's influence the strange and cryptic telegram she shot off to Bruno: 'Arrived safely – letter follows.' During that first evening, she raised a few eyebrows among Nuci's guests on account of her uninhibited Australian patter.

Trude awoke very early the following morning. Able to think more clearly now, she realized that Nuci Plank wanted to keep her in San Francisco. She did not quite understand what was afoot; a little later she would also find out that the Sterbas, by then living in Detroit, had hoped she would stay in the city to set up a Montessori school, to which they could send their daughters. But Trude had but one destination in view: Chicago, where Bruno had just moved. At the crack of dawn, she went down to the port to get her bags and take them to the railroad station. She was to leave San Francisco almost immediately, either that evening or the next.

Alighting in Chicago after three days and two nights of travel, she was to get another surprise: Bruno was nowhere to be seen. Instead Trude was greeted by Maria Piers, whom she had known as a fellow trainee teacher in Vienna, and her husband Gerhardt, a psychoanalyst. She had last seen them in Basel, where they had spent several months awaiting their US visas. But she was so excited at the prospect of being with Bruno again that she had a hard time concealing her disappointment. She probably did not know at that time that Gerhardt Piers had also contributed to paying for Bettelheim's release. While in Switzerland he had worked for a local psychiatrist, but his status as a foreigner meant he could not receive a salary. He had therefore asked his employer to give the money to a Nazi envoy to help free Bettelheim, 'because he was the first one of our acquaintances to get caught by the Gestapo,' as Maria Piers puts it.[5]

The Piers set Trude up in a Hyde Park hotel, only a stone's throw from Fritz Redl's apartment. She settled down to wait for the return of her lover, who had gone to Ohio for a job interview. He was travelling by bus to save money, and this was the cause of yet another frustration: knowing nothing of either Chicago or US public transport, Trude simply asked the hotel receptionist where the 'bus stop' was. She was thus waiting at the local stop when Bruno's long-haul bus thundered past, headed for the main city terminal. When she finally made it there, she was reunited with a glowering Bruno, furious at having waited so long!

By this time Bettelheim was no longer exactly unemployed; he was working, but without pay. A month earlier in New York – according to Bettelheim on the same day his mother arrived in the country, which was October 6 – he had got a letter from George Sheviakov informing him that there was an empty desk at the offices of the Eight Year Study team. Unfortunately, there were no funds to provide a salary. However this was clearly the ideal opportunity for Bettelheim to get a grounding in American work practices. It was also obvious that the job would put him in a good position to be awarded the next salaried post that came up.

It had not taken Bettelheim long to make up his mind. In New York everything had gone wrong for him, whereas only a short stay in Chicago had sufficed to give him a glimpse of a future he had long thought beyond his reach: that of a university career. In New York, it had soon become obvious that he did not have anywhere near enough experience in psychoanalysis to be able to enter the profession without starting again from scratch. The rules had been tightened since Edith Buxbaum had arrived in 1937. American analysts were feeling threatened by the sudden influx of colleagues chased out of Europe by Nazism, the more so since so many of the exiles could claim to have worked either with Freud in person or with his key disciples. Most of the exiled European psychoanalysts that Bettelheim knew at that time were caught up in a frantic chase to obtain further qualifications, as their back-home diplomas were not fully recognized. Wanda Willig, for example, was doing a stint as an intern in a

Virginia hospital, while Hans Willig was trying to get set up in business in New York. A little later, with Gina's help, Wanda was to find a job as a doctor in a reform school in upstate New York, moving on later to become a psychiatrist in a new service set up by the Salvation Army. For the time being, however, life was anything but easy for Bettelheim's friends.

Having greeted his mother and got her settled at his Aunt Jenny's place, Bruno had therefore set off for Chicago. Fritz Redl, who was teaching in Michigan and spending only two nights a week in Hyde Park, had suggested that they share his apartment there. Bruno had accepted gladly – and started work on the Eight Year Study with such gusto that only a month later Ralph Tyler offered him a paid job on the team.

In spite of the nightmares that continued to haunt him, Bettelheim thus had every reason to be satisfied. Those dearest to him were now all safely out of Hitler's reach. And he had at last been offered an opportunity to make practical use of all those theories he and his friends had been mulling over since their *Jung Wandervogel* days. What was more, people were listening to what he had to say: all that youthful intellectual ferment, that hard-won experience, had thus not been in vain.

Thanks to the gregarious George Sheviakov, Bruno Bettelheim also had a social life. He was beginning to feel comfortable with the Eight Year Study team. As for its offices, a former Universalist church building on Sixtieth Street on the south side of the campus, although he did not then know it, he was to occupy them for a very long time.

Bettelheim was as yet unaware of the speculation swirling around the building next door, outwardly indistinguishable from many of the nearby houses occupied by Hyde Park professors. Purchased by the university in 1931 as part of the Rush Medical School, it had until recently housed a school for mentally retarded children. The University of Chicago did not quite know what to do with an institution that was half-way between a school and a mental asylum, and that did not at first sight fit in with its own lofty image as a temple of postgraduate studies and a breeding-ground for Nobel Prize winners. The idea had emerged that alongside its purely therapeutic role, the school could serve as a laboratory in which to study children's development. Which was why it had been assigned to the Department of Education, with the psychiatrist Mandel Shermann, a specialist in electroencephalography, as its director. The unusual institution had also been given an unusual name, perhaps to underline its new academic vocation. It was called the Orthogenic School, from the Greek '*orthos*', straight, and '*genos*', origin.

Part Two

'Dr B'

My life is split into two parts, and each one bears surprisingly little relation to the other …. In Vienna it was difficult, complicated and in many ways unhappy; here it is fundamentally simple and happy.

Bruno Bettelheim, letter to ER, September 10, 1954

Chapter IX

From Chicago to Rockford, and Back

Chicago is a beautiful city, but a very tough one. Bruno Bettelheim had discovered it in summertime, in all its flowery splendour. Now that he was settled there, with winter coming on, he was beginning to find out why it is called the Windy, or even the Grey, City. Sixtieth Street, also known as Midway Plaisance since 1893, when it served as the central canal for the World Fair, and which he had to cross every day on his way to work, is a huge two-lane thoroughfare with a central area so wide that in summer children use it as a football ground. In wintertime, however, it turns into a conduit for the icy winds blowing off Lake Michigan, its central strip a perilous sea of mud. And Bruno Bettelheim, who had never been athletic at the best of times, had still not recovered from the year of ill-treatment he had suffered.

It had not taken him long to fit into the Eight Year Study team, however. There are differing versions as to how exactly he was finally hired. Ralph Tyler[1] insists that he found Bettelheim's name on a Rockefeller Foundation list of endangered European intellectuals. If such a list ever existed, it is no longer in the Foundation's archives. However both Fritz Redl and George Sheviakov had received grants from the Rockefeller Foundation, the former to help him emigrate and the latter to complete his training in the United States. It is likely that after Bruno Bettelheim's first trip to Chicago, they would have done everything in their power to ensure that he too could benefit from the institution's generosity, maybe even by adding his name to an existing list. Not only was he a friend, but as recent immigrants they had a good idea of what he had just gone through. Furthermore, Redl was well aware of the pain caused to Bruno by Gina's rejection.

In any case, Bettelheim had showed up at the right time. There was a vacancy on the team in charge of assessing the results of the new programmes engendered by the Eight Year Study, the one on which George Sheviakov worked. The vacancy was for a specialist in art teaching. Tests for all the other disciplines had been devised, and were already being used in the thirty schools taking part in the study. But, so far, no one had been able to come up with a working plan on how to assess the new art teaching methods.

The gaol was not to ascertain students' knowledge of art history as such, but to measure their level of appreciation and understanding of the works themselves; the aim of the new methods being precisely to make teaching less abstract, grounded more in the realities of modern life than the traditional curricula. This was a difficult task, but one for which Bruno Bettelheim was uniquely well qualified. Not only had he studied æsthetics and art history, but his work under Karl Bühler had familiarized him with such projects. Charlotte Bühler, who ran the Vienna Psychology Institute along with her husband, was a specialist in children and adolescents, and she had spent time in the United States, returning with a passion for tests. Under her influence the Institute, which was partly funded by the city of Vienna, had designed several as part of the great school reform programme set in motion by the left-wing post-World-War-I council. Indeed, that programme had been similar in a number of ways to the one being carried out in New Deal America by the Progressive Education Association. Bettelheim had probably not paid a great deal of attention to Charlotte Bühler's work during his time at the Institute, as he was then busy with his dissertation, but he cannot have been unaware of its existence.[2]

Having immediately grasped the type of tool required for Tyler's project, Bruno Bettelheim got down to work with such gusto that when the young Lee Cronbach, fresh from his graduation, was put in charge of the test statistics in the fall of 1939, he did not even realize that Bettelheim had only been on the job for a few weeks.[3] The atmosphere was just what Bettelheim needed, both friendly and stimulating. His fellow researchers were always ready to get together around a cup of coffee, to talk about problems arising from their work. Such discussions were particularly fertile, often helping someone find the solution to an apparently intractable problem. Bettelheim spent more time listening than he did talking. Although he tried not to show it, he had everything to learn about the workings of the university in particular and American life in general. His English was still hesitant, and of course heavily accented, but according to the recollections of the people he was seeing at the time he had no problem making himself understood. With Redl or Sheviakov he was even capable, on occasion, of bursts of wit in English. But he always kept a certain distance. For the young Americans who worked alongside him, he was slightly intimidating, though always very gentlemanly.

In November Ralph Tyler asked him to outline his progress for the rest of the team. Although the task he had been set was very difficult, the test that he was creating was remarkable in its simplicity. One of the hallmarks of Bettelheim's later work, his ability to put over subtle ideas with such clarity that his listeners soon forgot that they had not thought of them themselves, was already apparent in this, his first professional assignment in the United States.

The aim being to assess children's sensitivity and understanding, verbal and non-verbal, of a work of art, several pitfalls had to be avoided: in particular the results had to be independent of the children's ease of self-expression, and of their parents' tastes. This required an assessment tool which could allow the children to communicate their experiences without words or value judgements. Early on it had become obvious that these conditions could not be fulfilled if the full range of visual art forms was included. Bettelheim therefore limited his work to the field of painting. He toured the various schools involved in the project, discussing aims with the teachers and trying out his ideas on the children. The result was a test that was truly innovative. The main prop was a three-foot-eight by two-foot board on which were laid out forty good postcard reproductions of paintings, ranging from the Italian and German Renaissances up to Picasso.[4] Some of the works were famous, others little known. The cards were arranged to give a harmonious overall impression, but in no apparent order, although an effort had been made to avoid having one painting interfere with the next one.

Along with the picture-board, the student was given a form to fill in. But before he[5] began looking at the pictures, Bettelheim explained that there was no 'good' or 'bad' way of doing the test, since taste was a very personal matter that varied from person to person and should not be made to fit in to preconceived notions. Having been thus reassured, the students were asked simply to form pairs of pictures, on the basis of shared characteristics. The form had room for thirty pairs in all, but the child was free to cite only a few, and could stop whenever he wanted. He did not have to give any explanation for the choices made; at the end of the test, he was asked to write down which picture he had liked best and which least, giving reasons.

Thanks to this simple exercise, more akin to a game than an examination, the child revealed not only his stage of development (by whether he chose to 'marry' two horses' heads, two El Grecos or two chiaroscuros, for example) but also his sensitivity to colour, atmosphere and even the meaning of a work. All of this without the need for structured discourse. By giving the test to pupils both at the start and at the end of the school year, the Eight Year Study researchers could get quite a clear idea of the progress made by each child, in a field in which testing had never previously been carried out, at least not in the United States.

When Bettelheim submitted his ideas to Tyler in November 1939, the project could hardly have got far beyond its initial stages, but the latter was nevertheless deeply impressed; he has retained clear memories of the event. It was on the same day that he offered Bettelheim his first salaried post. Six months after having lost everything, Bruno Bettelheim had not only got himself a job but had also gained acceptance, at the first attempt, in the academic world to which he had always aspired.

His life was still by no means simple, however. Although he had been reunited with Trude, they were not really living together. Fritz Redl spent around two days a week in Chicago, and Bettelheim himself was often away. Trude had told him about her Australian affair with Hans Bandler. Hoping to soften the blow, she had explained that her attraction towards the young man had been mainly due to the fact that he had been sent to her by Bruno, but the latter had nevertheless found the news hard to take. The rejection by Gina was still very recent. He was wounded, traumatized. He managed to keep up appearances for the outside world but in private he had a hard time controlling the waves of anxiety and anger that rolled over him. In addition, he was still having regular concentration-camp nightmares. All of this made him difficult to live with. As Trude herself was to admit, it was a time when she wept a great deal.

Not long after Bruno got his job, she found one too, supervising the study hall in a Hyde Park Jewish orphanage. The Montessori teacher in her hated the warden aspect of the job, particularly since she lived on the premises. Somewhat later she was employed by an Episcopalian institution. There she was much happier, in spite of the presence of nuns and the religious atmosphere, because she was working directly with the children. Finally, she specialized in play therapy, working with groups set up by the Jewish social services in community centres throughout the city.

Trude was in a state of permanent anxiety about her parents. Since France's defeat in June 1940, their lives were once again under threat from advancing Nazi troops. Continuing their exodus, they had left Tours and gone south to Limoges, where her father had been hospitalized due to an intestinal ailment. He could no longer work, and Trude regularly sent them money and food parcels (most of which never arrived), while seeking all possible means to bring them to the United States. It appeared that her father's health would not allow him to make such a long journey. He was to die in April 1941, before the Germans extended their occupation to all of France. After his death Trude's mother Frederika Weinfeld went to live in the small town of Puy-Lévêque in the southwestern region of Lot. She was to remain there until August 25, 1942, when she was arrested and interned in the French camp of Septfonds. The previous day, she had written a letter to her daughter to tell her how she had been recently to the US consulate in Marseilles finally to receive her US visa, only to be told that France was no longer granting any exit visas whatsoever. In the letter, she therefore asked Trude to sell the ticket she had purchased for her, and to send the money instead. She concluded by saying that she would commit suicide if ever they came to arrest her. Trude was only to receive the letter in 1946, from a neighbour to whom Mrs Weinfeld had entrusted it at the moment of her arrest. The neighbour also gave her a few pieces of jewellery that her mother had left with her. Trude was never to know it, but her mother did not have the time to go through with her plan. Her name is on a list of 1,000 non-French Jews who were taken by train from the Drancy camp, near Paris, towards Auschwitz on September 9, 1942.

At the start of 1940, however, Trude still had hopes of saving her parents. And in any event, she was not the kind of woman to share her inner torment with strangers. True to type, she looked resolutely towards the future, quickly filing her naturalization papers, on January 23, and throwing all her energy into building a new life with Bruno. They were safe and sound, and they were together. They had friends and both of them had jobs, even if hers was not satisfying. Above all, they were secure, in a country where the Nazis could never get at them. For Trude, the top priority was therefore to learn to live with the difficult but brilliant man she loved.

It was a strange period in Bettelheim's life, at once very tough and anxiety-laden, and very exciting. Professionally, things were going well for him, even though his job was by definition a short-term one. To set up his test, he had to travel to schools all over the Midwest and along the East Coast. He was chairing workshops on the teaching of art, and his English needed to be good enough for the delicate task of reassuring teachers, many of whom were reticent about having their methods put under the spotlight in a major national study project. Bettelheim only needed to look around him, at the accelerating flow of fellow-refugees into the country, to realize how successful he had been, not only in gaining a toehold in American society, but in doing so exactly where he had wanted to. And even though he was still not assured of his ultimate aim, to become a university professor, he had got considerably closer to it only six months after setting foot in the country.

But insecurity was still just around the corner. Bettelheim was painfully aware that he would soon have to start looking for work again. And he hated that prospect; he hated what he would later describe as 'the imbalance between the newly-arrived in a country, and those who are well established there. One needs them because one has not built up a group of friends so much more than they do, who have become well-rooted in their life.'[6] Recalling his own first experiences in America, he would note that even in his work he suffered from his status as a recent arrival: 'I was much better at what I was doing than they who were old established. And they naturally resented it, grudgingly acknowledged the quality of my work, but made me pay for it every minute.' Bettelheim, who wrote these words while spending some time in Chicago after his retirement, added that these recollections had come to him the previous day, when he had run into 'a colleague from those early days, in every way far inferior to me, and much younger, [who] still continues to patronize me as a gifted but not knowledgeable newcomer, as it was true thirty-five years ago'.

Although he kept it to himself, except for the odd burst of self-deprecating humour, he was very sensitive to what he perceived as a patronizing, even possibly anti-Semitic, attitude on the part of the university establishment. This is shown in an anecdote he would later tell, concerning Robert Havighurst. The latter was a young professor who was in the process of setting up the Committee on Human Development, a unique cross-disciplinary department bringing together as wide a range of disciplines as the name suggests, and notably taking in postgraduate students in psychology, sociology and education. Havighurst also worked for the Rockefeller Foundation, and especially for the Progressive Education Association, which was the driving force behind the Eight Year Study. It was he who had discovered Fritz Redl, at a 1936 conference on childhood and adolescence in England, and brought him to the United States. But when Bruno Bettelheim asked Havighurst if he could also help him find a job, the professor reportedly answered that before aspiring to a teaching post, he would do well to familiarize himself with life in America by taking up some more modest occupation. Why not become a shoeshine boy? he added, according to Bettelheim's account of the conversation. I was unable to obtain confirmation of this story and the last quote in particular sounds like a typical Bettelheim exaggeration. But he told the story enough times and to enough people to show just how susceptible he was at the time. And, rather than simply dismissing his concern as paranoia, it is worth examining why he felt that way.

There were still few Jews at the University of Chicago, or so it seemed to Bruno Bettelheim. His best friends, Redl and Sheviakov, were not Jewish, and all the people on whom his future depended, such as Tyler, Havighurst and Robert Hutchins, the youthful president of the university, who was determined to maintain the U of C's reputation as a top-flight institution, were all WASPs, as indeed were the leading figures in all the East Coast Ivy League colleges. The U of C, however, was a particularly liberal and progressive university, despite its élitism. Its tradition was that of the Rockefeller Foundation, a prime mover in the development of the university. To make culture available to the largest possible number of Americans, to open up the roads to knowledge, to offer the opportunity of a great education to all those both willing and able were the avowed goals of many of the university's initiatives – and first among them, Robert Hutchins's famous Great Books programme, which was then in full swing. To raise the issues of racism and anti-Semitism in this context thus seems almost a heresy, particularly given the number of Jewish academics who were to find refuge at the university after fleeing the Nazis. Critics will be gently reminded that the U of C's past administrators, and notably Robert Hutchins, strove to make Hyde Park, located next to one of the biggest black ghettos in all of the United States, into one of the first racially integrated neighbourhoods in the country.

However it is fair to assume that the men on whom Bruno Bettelheim's future depended had much the same attitude toward Jews as that prevailing at the time in America's liberal élite. At bottom, it was a view not far removed from that expressed by the Count Leinsdorf character in Robert Musil's book *The Man without Qualities*:[7] a mixture of admiration for the perceived intelligence, business acumen and in some cases the artistic abilities of the Jews, and of irritated condescension at what was seen as their social climbing. And Bettelheim had only recently discovered what consequences that image of Jews could lead to. It had been confirmed to him in the most heinous way that whatever he did, his Jewishness would always stick to him, like a deadly and accursed label, impossible to scrub off. When in Vienna, he had learned to live with that image, as had all the assimilated Jews in his entourage. Now, he could no longer stand it. And he could smell it a mile off, long before people even expressed it, and while they were in many cases totally unaware of it.

He generally kept such feelings to himself, talking about them only to Trude and a few very close confidants. Many of his friends never saw that side of his personality. Others were occasionally surprised by an outburst, not knowing where it came from. One evening in 1960, Stuart Brent, a bibliophile and music-lover who owned Chicago's first psychoanalytic bookshop, was given an unexpected glimpse of this dark and very tormented side of Bettelheim's character. It was after a talk Brent had given on *The Informed Heart*, which had just been published. After the event, in the fashionable Drake Hotel on the lakefront, Bruno Bettelheim thanked the speaker profusely and then took his arm to walk with him the few hundred yards from the hotel to Brent's bookshop, on Michigan Avenue. 'You know, Stuart, there's no need in talking, really. I'm an old Jew,' Bettelheim declared sadly. He continued to ruminate on the same theme throughout the walk. What Stuart Brent found most striking was that this occurred at a time when Bettelheim was in the process of rising to fame, amid general admiration. His school was becoming very well known, he was being invited to speak all over the country, and at the university students were falling over one another to get into his classes.

The idea that Bruno Bettelheim needed to get to know the United States better was also put forward by Ralph Tyler when, as the Eight Year Study work was concluding, he recommended a vacant part-time teaching post at Rockford College, a small women's university some sixty miles northwest of Chicago. This was in the late summer of 1941. Bettelheim had finally married Trude Weinfeld on May 14, with the least possible ceremony as his bride had just lost her father. The marriage took place nine days after a Cook County court granted Bettelheim a divorce from Gina, who was ruled to have deserted him. Trude and Bruno were at last living together, at 6033 Dorchester Avenue. This was a stone's throw from the former church building where the Eight Year Study was then being wound up.

The post was for an art history teacher. Bettelheim's name had been suggested to the Rockford president, Mary Ashby Cheek, by Ulrich Middeldorf, the head of the U of C Department of Art: 'Though he was never affiliated with our department, we count him among our own people,' he wrote. Ralph Tyler provided enthusiastic support for the proposal, stating that Bettelheim not only had the required skills, including adequate English, but also that 'he comes from a wealthy Viennese family who have had fine art collections of their own. Hence, his reaction to art is that of a connoisseur as well as of a student.' That letter contained another approximation concerning Bettelheim's CV, and one that would have implications for the future. Tyler stressed that Bettelheim was highly trained in both the arts and criticism, 'although his Ph.D., I believe, is in the field of psychology'.[8]

In early September, Mary Cheek asked Bruno Bettelheim to give two classes a week at Rockford. One, an introduction to art history, would be a year-long course while the other would be devoted to the art of Antiquity in the first semester and to Byzantine, early Christian and Romanesque art in the second. He would receive a salary of 600 dollars a year for two days' presence each week, during which he would be provided with bed and board in Rockford. Bettelheim, who was in New York when the proposal came through, accepted without hesitation.

Thus, on the morning of Monday September 22, 1941, Bruno Bettelheim alighted from a train in the small town of Rockford, to be greeted by the college art studies director, a Mr Paxson. He probably did not realize it then, but this would be more than a small stop in his life. It was there in the heart of the North American cornbelt, near the point where the states of Illinois, Wisconsin and Iowa meet, that this city-dwelling Viennese immigrant was to learn how the New World into which he had been so brutally projected, and which was so different from anything he had ever known before, worked. It was also there – but how could he possibly have guessed it? – that his chrysalid-like transformation into a new Bruno Bettelheim would take place. Up to that point the circles he had moved in – psychoanalysts in New York, academics in Chicago – had borne too much resemblance to those he had known in his youth, even if many of the people he was meeting were American-born. A few months later, the entry of the United States into the war would result in other European refugees arriving in Rockford, to replace teachers who had been drafted. But in September 1941, Bettelheim was still one of a kind in the small college lost amid the cornfields and the trees.

Rockford College was at that time a girls-only institution, but it provided high-quality courses, as its links to the University of Chicago testified. The tuition fees were relatively high, and although most of its students had no intention of letting a career get in the way of their futures as mothers and housewives they took their studies very seriously. These young Midwestern women, for whom higher education was often an adventure in itself, had never met anyone quite like Bruno Bettelheim. There were occasions when his accent forced them to strain to understand a word, but that did not prevent them from appreciating the richness and depth of his teaching. He told them about art, philosophy and psychology, without much regard for the traditional boundaries between those disciplines. Rather than giving them textbooks he had them read the original texts, and whenever possible he sent them off to see the artworks discussed in class. They had never come across anyone so cultured. And once they had got used to his way of asking their permission before he took off his jacket, even in 90° heat, they began to see his manners as the very height of refinement.

Although he rarely brought the subject up himself, they had soon heard about what he had been through before leaving Europe. They discussed it among themselves, without really knowing what a concentration camp could be. But they noticed that he was sitting down most of the time. One of them, observing from a second-floor window as Bettelheim crossed the quadrangle, was so struck by the odd way he walked, holding his arms stiffly to his sides as if to protect himself from being beaten, that she wrote a poem on the subject for the college newspaper.

'It was a privilege to know such a man ....' 'He was such a remarkable, knowledgeable man ....' 'He was fascinating. Frightening too, but fascinating ....' 'His classes were very enlightening ... but he wasn't easy.' 'I was intimidated, but I worked very well with him ....'[9] Such comments, gleaned fifty years later, reflect the deep impression Bruno Bettelheim made on his students. 'Socratic' is the word they use most to describe his teaching method. And many add: 'He opened up a whole new world for me (us).' They still remember their surprise on discovering, with him, the hidden meaning of fairy-tales. They can quote from memory the names of some of the books he assigned them (notably Freud's *Psychopathology of Everyday Life*, and also works by Durkheim and Erich Fromm), and some of the films he screened for them (in particular *Le jour se lève*, by Marcel Carné).

Within a year Bettelheim gained a whole slew of new assignments at Rockford. In the fall of 1942, Mary Cheek asked him temporarily to drop his art classes to stand in for the philosophy teacher, who had gone off to the war. In that first semester, he therefore taught five classes in all: history of philosophy, history of ideas, general psychology, psychological theory and German. The following semester it was Mr Paxson's turn to be drafted, and Bettelheim reshuffled his schedule to be able to stand in for him too. He also took over running the committee which selected films to be shown on campus, a task he took very seriously.

By this time Bettelheim was spending four days a week at Rockford, for an annual salary of around 2,000 dollars. He arrived on Monday evenings and left after his last class on Friday. He also participated fully in the little university's social life. One of his then students, who did some waitressing at meal times, remembers clearly the lively conversations he took part in at the teachers' table in the large dining room, where everyone ate. Another remembers the active support Bettelheim gave to the liberal Students' Forum action committee, of which she was a member.

There was no shortage of inspiring causes to support and issues to debate, ranging from the effects of the Spanish Civil War to economic recovery and the labour situation. And of course, the World War, into which the United States had finally decided to throw its weight. At the start of the year the students had taken a Victory Pledge, and undertaken to acquire professional skills that could be of help. They were learning clerical work in case the army needed to call on them, training in emergency duties and devoting some of their time to working in a local weapons plant. Although traditionally centred on the liberal arts, Rockford University had taken in engineering students and added classes in nutrition, first aid and emergency childcare to its syllabus.[10] Bruno Bettelheim was an active participant in all the debates, urging the students to think before acting, to always weigh up the pros and cons, and encouraging them to speak up whenever they had something on their mind. That was also something new for most of them. They had been taught to give full – i.e. unquestioning – support to good causes, in other words those defined as such by the majority. And now here was Bruno Bettelheim, telling them that God, if he existed at all, could not be simply on one side.

But it was above all in his classes that the teacher built up the extraordinary influence he came to hold over his flock. He would never sit at the teacher's desk. Instead he took one of the students' chairs with its attached writing-tablet, turned it to face the class and beckoned for them to form a circle around him. Then, after a few introductory remarks, he would start shooting out questions. At first, many of the young women fell into the trap of viewing these sessions as a kind of quiz, in which the more quick-witted could get to easily show off their abilities. They soon learned otherwise. 'At the beginning, he was very tough on me, because I was rather verbal and didn't give much thought to what I was saying,' admits Ronnie Dryovage. 'Then one day, when I left the room crying, he called me back and said, "Don't be sad. I know a thousand people who think that way." So all my anxiety vanished and I thought to myself: "This man really cares about me and I am going to learn something with him." '

The components of what was to become the unique Bettelheim teaching system were already falling into place. Encouraging open discussion, getting students to think for themselves and by themselves, and the use of cutting comments to chide those who were too conformist, shallow or pretentious. If there were two things Bettelheim hated more than anything else they were stupidity and jargon, seeing the latter as a pedantic way of covering up the former. He was pitiless with students who failed to bring the same amount of intensity and seriousness to his classes as he did himself. And he would often use his exchanges with such students to demonstrate to their classmates – and to themselves, if they were strong enough to see beyond the immediate situation and understand what was going on – the very psychological mechanisms which he was trying to explain in his courses. During such verbal duels, the classroom vibrated with tension. Some students found this method most enlightening, a few others did not understand what was going on and thought it a little hard to take. Strangely enough though, few of the 'victims' of such exercises felt that way.

Bettelheim already had favourites among the students. They included the cleverer elements, those who were quickest at latching on to his train of thought, or who dared stand up to him. But also weaker pupils, the ones most in need of help. With them, he was capable of infinite patience, being attentive not only to their needs but also to their problems. They would never be the ones singled out to have their psychological make-up dissected in front of the class. For another of Bettelheim's character traits, which is very often cited by his former students at Rockford, was his kindness. 'He cared,' they say. Each of them has some tale or other that shows how he devoted time to aid a student in distress or helped them find some needed piece of information such as an address or a book reference, even before they had thought to ask him.

A good insight into the type of relationship Bettelheim developed with his psychology students can be gleaned from his article 'Self-Interpretation of Fantasy',[11] in which he reports on an experiment carried out by an unnamed psychology instructor 'in one of the smaller Midwestern women's colleges' in the spring of 1944. It involved the 'Thematic Apperception Test', or TAT,[12] which at the time was the most commonly used measure of personality after the Rorschach test. As specified in the article's subtitle, it consisted in using the TAT at once as an educational and a therapeutic device. Bettelheim further noted that the students, whom he described as predominantly 'middle class and rather conservative', were 'in the throes of late adolescent development'. They had passed that stage in years, but not in emotional maturity. 'Courses in psychology frequently attract students who are dimly aware of their own personality difficulties,' and this class was no exception, he added.

It was not uncommon in psychology classes to submit students to the very tests they were studying, but it was much less usual for the teacher to so openly take on a therapist's role. This merging of the roles of teacher and healer which Bruno Bettelheim first practised at Rockford College was to become his distinctive feature, the key to all his subsequent activity at the Orthogenic School. This is why the detailed account given in his article, which according to at least one of his former students is very accurate,[13] is particularly interesting. The TAT involves a set of nineteen cards with black-and-white pictures which look like shots from realist films. On the first, a small boy is shown contemplating a violin which is lying on a table, another features a young woman carrying books, while in the background a man works in the fields and an old woman, standing motionless, looks on; yet another shows a distressed-looking young woman leaning against a doorpost, covering her eyes with one arm, etc. There is a twentieth, white card, which is blank. The psychologist shows the cards to the subject one by one, asking him to tell the story behind each one.[14]

The TAT is called a projective test because it sets no limits on the use of the subject's imagination. Its basic assumption is that 'when interpreting a vague or ambiguous situation, [the subject] by so doing reveals significant aspects of his personality,' Bettelheim explains. For example, the desires that the subject attributes to the characters reveal those that worry him personally, while features that he does not notice point to repressed material in his own psyche. Nevertheless, as Bettelheim states from the outset, many other factors can influence the content of the subject's stories, such as his level of intellectual development, his interests and recent experiences, and also his relationship with the tester.

The aim of the article is to demonstrate that self-analysis by the subject of his or her own made-up stories not only makes it possible to avoid certain pitfalls (such as the examiner projecting his fantasies on to the resulting material), but also has a number of advantages, for the examiner, the educationalist and the therapist. After listing all those advantages, Bettelheim gives an overview of the content of the programme up until the setting of the test.

He explains that the exercise was part of a course in dynamic psychology, deliberately using the students' personal experiences. After having studied several theories of personality, illustrated by case studies, the young women were asked to write an autobiography. They were then 'introduced to an understanding of some aspects of their own behavior'. And after a study of conscious motivations, their teacher introduced them to 'phenomena ... which are in part determined by fore-conscious mechanisms; for instance ... instances of apraxia which they had recently experienced'.[15] As the discussion was based solely on the students' attempts to decipher the hidden reasons for the symptom, Bettelheim states in a footnote that 'reasoning on the basis of learned theories was discouraged in favor of spontaneous evaluation of the determining factors. Every student was able to unravel at least some of the fore-conscious determinants of the case of apraxia [she] chose to discuss.'

When Bettelheim suggested that the students subject themselves to the TAT, there was thus nothing to indicate that the experiment would be any different from what had previously gone on in the course. Then, several weeks later, he sprang a surprise by handing the class their own TAT results and asking them to analyse the psychological content of each story, summing up what the whole exercise had taught them. Once that task was completed, he asked them whether they thought the test had given an accurate picture of their personality, and in particular if certain aspects of the latter had remained hidden.

It was thus quite an experience. In his account, which he illustrated with the analysis of three cases, Bettelheim makes no bones about the fact that the results were influenced by the students' own relationship with himself (referred to in the third person as 'the instructor'). He also has no hesitation in using the psychoanalytic term of 'transference' to describe that relationship. He even acknowledges that without that transference, the self-interpretation exercise would not have given the subject any more understanding than she had already gained from the test itself.

Bettelheim had set limits to the exercise, however. Among the deviations from the standard TAT procedure, listed at the beginning of the article, he specifies that the 'instructor' did not ask the students to 'ad lib' on the stories once they had completed each one. For the creators of the TAT, such elaboration had been meant to allow the subjects to express their fantasies, and thus bring up deeper layers of repressed material. Bettelheim explains that since the plan was to subsequently have the students analyse their stories themselves, he did not want the initial versions to go too far. Citing Freud, he stresses that the unconscious material that can generate the production of stories is relatively accessible and anxiety-free, since it has been organized into a presentable form by the ego.[16] Spontaneous improvisation, on the other hand, can be much more revealing.

Despite such precautions, however, it is easy to understand the puzzlement of the young teacher who was to succeed him in psychology class. She was later to tell a colleague, during a dinner conversation: 'I don't know who this Bruno Bettelheim is, but I can't do a thing with his students.'[17]

If the Bettelheim teaching system was born at Rockford College, so too were the reactions that it was to provoke. Already, students were flocking to enrol in his classes, in such numbers that in September 1943 Mary Cheek asked him to take an overflow session on Saturday mornings.[18] And already, a number of students were dropping out only a few weeks after the start of classes, either angry and indignant or simply unable to follow. Some declared that Bettelheim was a sadist, and that they would under no circumstances be taken in a second time. Already, this strange Socrates-like figure was sparking admiration, fear and jealousy among his colleagues. And already he was creating a circle of disciples, fired with enthusiasm for the perspectives he opened up. Intelligent, idealistic, curious, imaginative and in some cases a trifle masochistic, many of them would find their vocation through his teaching.

In January 1942 it was Ralph Tyler's turn to ask Mary Cheek what she thought of Bruno Bettelheim. The Eight Year Study had been completed, and the Department of Art was considering offering him a part-time teaching job. The Rockford principal's assessment was glowing indeed: 'Everything points to the fact that [Bruno Bettelheim] is an excellent and genuine teacher, as well as a scholar of parts.' At the start of the following semester, Bruno Bettelheim thus found himself working part time for the University of Chicago. This time, he was located in the basement of the former church building on Sixtieth Street. But his job was that of an examiner, churning out exam subjects for a variety of teachers in art history, psychology and German. His friend Fritz Redl was also working there occasionally.

Bettelheim was to spend two years of weekly commuting, four days at Rockford and three in Chicago. Trude and he lived simply, devoting part of their meagre income to helping their relatives. Paula Bettelheim was by this time living in a Greenwich Village retirement home. Margarethe, who had just got married, was also living in New York.

Bruno and Trude lived well, however. They did not have a great deal of furniture but their apartment was tastefully arranged, and in spite of their heavy schedules they managed to spend a few evenings with friends. In particular at the Sheviakovs', where there was always a lot of company, with both wine and jollity in plentiful supply. Bruno was the one who did most of the socializing. For Trude had soon realized that if she wanted to find an interesting job she would have to go back to school, given that in the United States a social work diploma had to be gained at university. In the autumn of 1940 she had therefore enrolled at Chicago's Northwestern University, studying while continuing to hold down a job.

The couple seemed happy together. Bruno was very attentive with Trude, and showed a lot of respect for her energy and courage. 'Bruno and Trude seemed to take good care of each other in those days,' recalls Ruth Nedelsky, who attended one of Bettelheim's Eight Year Study workshops. At the time her husband Leo, one of George Sheviakov's best friends, was drafting physics exams in the same group of examiners as Bettelheim, and liked and admired him. He and his wife have retained the image of a courageous, very hard-working couple, a little distant but sociable, amusing and interesting. 'Bruno had the strongest Viennese accent I have ever heard. He had a lot of taste, and was a true art connoisseur, but he didn't show the slightest interest in amateur painters like myself. He used to speak his mind, but never opened up about himself,' says Leo.[19] In December 1942, Trude gave birth to the couple's first daughter, Ruth Colette.

Three months later, George Sheviakov decided to take up a post in Vanport, Oregon. And Bruno Bettelheim suggested that he pass on his apartment to one of his old friends from Vienna, Peter Weinmann. The latter had married Gina a year earlier, after finally obtaining a divorce from his wife. Curiously, the Viennese family had gradually come together again in Hyde Park. Indeed, when Paula went to Chicago to visit her son, she would often cross the street to have tea with her former daughter-in-law. She appears to have got on better with Gina than with Trude. In any case, the wounds left by the divorce were off limits for conversation. Thanks to traditional Viennese discretion or perhaps simply to the links created by exile, Trude, Gina, Bruno and Peter were all the best of friends. As Gina's birthday fell on December 24, they got into the habit of celebrating Christmas at the Weinmanns' and Thanksgiving at the Bettelheims'. They spoke mostly English together, and attended the same social events. Ruth Nedelsky, who was barely twenty at the time, has retained a strong impression of Gina's elegance and self-assurance. She had a hard time understanding how one man could have married two women as different from one another as were Gina and Trude. But that only added to the mysterious fascination exercised by these talented immigrants.

Most of the people with whom Bruno Bettelheim associated knew that he had only recently spent a year in a concentration camp, but as Ruth Nedelsky recalls today with some embarrassment, the majority did not have any idea what that meant. Bettelheim himself did not talk about it much. He was more forthcoming on his life in Vienna, relating anecdotes on art and psychoanalysis. And he talked about Patsy. Holding forth to an audience fascinated by education and psychology, he told of the progress the little American had made over the six years she spent in his household. He talked about her with the enthusiasm of a man who had followed the progress of his child from day to day, and he made it sound as though it would only have taken a few more years for Patsy to be completely cured.

He told the story in particular to one of his new friends, Benjamin Bloom, a doctoral student and assistant to Ralph Tyler. Bloom, who like Bettelheim was both Jewish and aware of being so, was more receptive than many to his tales of suffering. He got him to talk, and slowly but surely won Bettelheim's trust. As he too was very interested in the mechanisms of learning, he showed great interest in the story of Patsy. So when one day Ralph Tyler once again complained about the intractable problem of the Orthogenic School, Benjamin Bloom suggested that he talk to Bruno Bettelheim. 'He knows about disturbed children,' Bloom said, 'and has experience in the field.'

The Orthogenic School was a real headache for the Department of Education, and Ralph Tyler was at his wits' end. It was expensive to run, and although its fees were by no means low, income did not cover running expenses. Dr Mandel Sherman, who was running the place, had been continually asking for new funds ever since taking up the post. The premises were run-down and too small for the around thirty children who lived there, while the counsellors were underpaid and badly-trained. The reason invariably cited by Sherman for needing more money, however, was laboratory equipment, without which he said it was impossible to carry out serious research. As early as 1941, Tyler had told him that the solution lay not in squeezing more cash out of the univerisity but in obtaining private funding. He noted that some of the children who lived in the school had wealthy parents: why not get them to contribute?

Such suggestions fell on deaf ears. 'Mandel Sherman was a very self-centred man, only interested in his own career,' says Bernice Neugarten, who at the time was studying for her PhD and attending a seminar on child development given by Sherman.[20] She was particularly shocked one day when he asked her and around a dozen other students to visit the school to observe some cases. After having got the students to sit down, Sherman asked that a child be brought in. Then, without a single affectionate word or gesture, he had the kid plonked down at one end of the room and asked: 'Now tell us what's wrong with you.'

Bernice Neugarten's initial impression was to be confirmed a little later, when she did summer replacement work for teachers at the Orthogenic School. Sherman 'ran the place like a custodial institution,' she commented. She was thus not overly surprised, one day in the summer of 1944, to see Ralph Tyler and Robert Havighurst showing a newcomer around the premises. It was a man she had never seen before, clearly of Germanic origin, with a very strong accent. Being busy with a group of children at the time, she did not have much time to talk to him, but her first impression was a good one. 'It was a real relief. The place needed taking over,' she says.

The way he later told it, Bruno Bettelheim was practically trapped into taking on the job of director. At the end of 1941, with the institution under fire from all sides, Ralph Tyler asked Robert Havighurst to head up a committee on the problem. The resulting report was not in itself unfavourable, but it stressed one of the Orthogenic School's basic contradictions. Since its brief was now to take in children who were emotionally disturbed but of normal intelligence, its aim should have been to prepare them for a return to the mainstream educational system. But because it was so under-equipped, with badly trained and underpaid teachers, the children were in fact falling even further behind in the learning process. Havighurst's report therefore recommended that the institution be simply integrated into the Lab Schools system, which provided excellent primary and secondary education on the campus. But the idea had run into a wall of opposition from many of the university professors whose children attended the Lab Schools.

In the fall of 1942, Mandel Sherman became embroiled in a legal dispute which proved embarrassing for the university. Bettelheim said it was at about that time that Ralph Tyler asked him to draw up a report on the Orthogenic School with proposals on how it could be changed. He had been so shocked by what he had seen of the institution that he had refrained from mentioning it again to Tyler, he said. The request came at a time when he already had an extremely heavy work schedule: not only was he dividing his time between Rockford and his job as an examiner, but he was in the middle of writing and rewriting an account of his concentration camp experiences, with a view to publication. The appearance of his article a year later in the Harvard University Psychology Department's *American Journal of Abnormal and Social Psychology* gave a boost to his standing at the University of Chicago. Six months after that, the defeat of the Axis powers and the discovery of the first concentration camps would increase that authority even more.

From a purely professional standpoint, however, Bettelheim's situation was more shaky. The end of the war brought the return of the Rockford staff members who had gone off to fight, and in particular the philosophy teacher. As regards psychology, the Faculty Committee decided in the spring of 1944 that the teacher concerned needed to be present five days a week. Informing Bruno Bettelheim of the decision, Mary Cheek cited purely academic considerations, but there were probably other reasons. That at least was how his students saw it. Several of them went to the president to protest the decision, which in her eyes probably only served to confirm just how much influence this unorthodox stand-in had gained in her institution. Bettelheim was obviously a remarkable teacher, but perhaps a bit *too* remarkable for a small Midwestern women's university.[21] Whatever the reasons, replying to Bruno Bettelheim's questions about his future on May 4, 1944, Mary Cheek said that with the staffing situation as it was, she was unable to offer him a contract for the following academic year that would justify his breaking his links with the University of Chicago. She added that even if he were to work full time at Rockford College, his salary would hardly increase, and he would have to wait his turn, i.e. for many years, to get a professorship.

That letter, which in fact meant the end of Bettelheim's career at Rockford, was probably crucial in persuading him to accept the Orthogenic School offer. For a few months after he commissioned Bettelheim's report, Ralph Tyler waited, then one day he called him into his office to ask him where it was. The two men had by then been working together for five years, and had got to know one another. Bruno Bettelheim felt better able to speak his mind. As he later told the story, his reply was that 'there's only one thing to be done with that school: burn it down'. To which Tyler replied that he understood his reaction, but he was serious in wanting a detailed report on what was wrong with the Orthogenic School, and what should be done about it.

Bettelheim felt in danger of being trapped. As he told it later, he had no desire whatsoever to take on the job of reorganizing the Orthogenic School, a lame-duck institution which, as he had already seen, had brought nothing but problems for the man who was then running it. The future he saw for himself was that of a university professor, occasionally publishing lofty articles in prestigious reviews. He had had a taste of such a life at Rockford, and wanted more. Of course, conditions there had been far from ideal, but things could only improve with time. Indeed, Ulrich Middeldorf had promised to take him on as a staff member in the Department of Art at the first available opportunity. In the meantime, Bettelheim had probably been planning to work full time at Rockford. But one thing at least was clear: he could not keep up the same punishing schedule much longer. At the start of the year he had been hospitalized with pneumonia, and overwork was no doubt a contributing factor.

But then there was the letter from Mary Cheek, and also Bettelheim's reluctance to disappoint Ralph Tyler, the man who had provided him with every one of his jobs over the past five years. He therefore decided he had no choice but to accept the new assignment, while taking pains to stress that he would be acting only as a consultant. To help him assess the school, he called on Dr Emmy Sylvester, one of the best child psychoanalysts around, and like Bettelheim a native of Vienna. A former assistant to Charlotte Bühler at the Psychology Institute, Emmy Sylvester had been a patient of Editha Sterba, and when she had first started practising her supervisor had been none other than Richard Sterba.[22]

Unfortunately, Bettelheim did not keep a copy of the note he drew up for Tyler, and the original is nowhere to be found in the available Orthogenic School archives at the university. According to his subsequent account, it was around two months after he had submitted it that Ralph Tyler invited him to lunch, and then without any warning took him into Robert Hutchins' office, where the latter promptly offered him the job of running the school. Bettelheim, furious at being cornered, reportedly replied: 'All right, but on condition that you triple the budget and don't ask me any questions for five years.' To his great surprise, the president agreed on the spot.

I was not able to ascertain how much exaggeration there is in the above account. It seems particularly unlikely, on the basis of the documents I found, that Ralph Tyler could have given Bettelheim a completely free rein over such a long period. Indeed, nine months after taking up the job, the latter submitted to Tyler a detailed report on the school's requirements.

What can be confirmed, however, is that in June 1944 there was a substantial increase in students' fees at the Orthogenic School, from 165 to 200 dollars a month. And the following month, Philip Pekow, the father of one of the children, convened a meeting of rich potential donors. They concluded that the institution required at least 2 million dollars a year to function correctly. But before launching a fundraising drive, they wanted to know whether the university would be willing to provide matching funds.

In September 1944, Bruno Bettelheim contacted several of his best former students at Rockford to ask if they wanted to come and work with him at the Orthogenic School; three accepted enthusiastically while at least one refused, and now says Bettelheim never forgave her for it. On October 1, he officially took up his new job. His salary was 1,900 dollars a year, plus 1,700 dollars for courses he was to give in the Department of

Education. The latter job was no doubt used by Tyler, well aware of Bettelheim's academic ambitions, as bait to get him to accept the directorship of the school. A month and a half later, Bruno Bettelheim became a US citizen.

Chapter X

A New Man for the New World

'Bruno to head the Orthogenic School – why not? Providing he does a new spell of analysis.' Within the Chicago psychoanalytic community, Kurt Eissler was one of the few people not to criticize Bruno Bettelheim's appointment. Although very different, the two men, both Viennese, enjoyed one another's company in those days, and their wives were good friends.[1] Bettelheim had met Eissler's brother in Buchenwald and, before that, they had run into one another at the *Jung Wandervogel*. Kurt Eissler, a tall, proud yet kindly person, had also met Fritz Redl in August Aichorn's seminars, and although a medical doctor he had studied under Karl Bühler, but earlier than Bettelheim. In Chicago, however, what probably brought the two men together as much as anything was their views on all things American, and in particular on American psychoanalysis.

As events in Europe had accelerated, Chicago and its university had seen the arrival of an ever-swelling tide of refugees. The great majority were German-speaking, and desired above all to blend in as quickly as possible with the host society. But their living conditions were often extremely difficult. For some, lawyers for example, exile meant going back to square one. Others, such as doctors or engineers, had to take a number of US exams, wasting precious working months at a time when they needed money as never before. Even traders had to learn to operate in new surroundings, with different rules. All the while conforming to the 'good immigrant' stereotype: putting a brave face on things, keeping up cheerful appearances while every day brought its load of awful news concerning loved ones, and the world they had left behind.

Most of them, and notably the Bettelheims, made a point of only speaking English in public, even to one another. They had turned their backs on their old lives, and saw no point indulging in nostalgia. Nevertheless, these brand-new Americans would get together from time to time for a European-style evening, to swap experiences, news and gossip. There would be irritation at the Americans for their lack of refinement, tips on where to buy 'real' coffee or bread, or how to adapt a cake mix to bake something that tasted of home. And, human nature being what it is, there would also be snide remarks about how this or that person was getting on in the race for integration.

Bruno Bettelheim was in a class of his own. Despite his persistent accent and a none-too-advantageous past, he had been one of the quickest to understand how this dynamic new society functioned. He was again working extremely hard, but now he was succeeding in everything he put his hand to. This New World, in which he had washed up empty-handed and practically shorn of his past, appeared to be tailor-made for him. And though he found plenty to complain about in his new environment, American society's much-derided lack of refinement also made it all the easier for him to use his Old World charm. As when he amazed his young Rockford students by asking their permission to take off his jacket, for instance.

How could such a speedy adaptation not spark jealousy and even resentment in those around him? Particularly since his success appeared to be based not only on his talent and labour, but also on the modified version of his past which he had allowed to take root in the minds of his employers. The process had taken time, but it had been facilitated by the silence of those who could have told the truth. Among the Viennese exiles at least, even people who had not known Bettelheim personally had heard that his real past was different from what the Americans around him thought. If such talk went on behind his back, however, it remained within the community. One did not denounce a fellow exile. 'Especially one who had just come out of Buchenwald,' as someone who could have spoken up but didn't, and prefers now to remain anonymous, told me. What is more difficult to explain, however, is that nobody said anything to Bettelheim himself. Perhaps this was due to the desire to avoid a clash with a difficult man, and that very Viennese tendency to avert one's eyes when faced with an embarrassing sight. 'After all, it was none of my business. And my life was quite difficult enough as it was. Nobody today realizes just how tough it was for us exiles,' says Maria Piers, somewhat defensively. Meanwhile Bruno Bettelheim donned more and more openly a persona that was not exactly his.

This was indeed the period when he reinvented his past. The actual untruths on which the process was based were few in number, but they were seminal. Whatever else he would achieve, he felt obliged to go on repeating them, and elaborating on them, throughout his whole life, and they were to pursue him up to the very end. I do not know exactly when his doctorate in aesthetics turned into a psychology degree,[2] when Patsy became his patient, or Eleanor Roosevelt the person who had saved him from the Nazis. But it was in the first half of the 1940s that these myths gradually took on the appearance of solid facts. It certainly did not happen all at once, and the process was helped by a few mistakes made by others (in Ralph Tyler's letter of recommendation to the president of Rockford College, for example). But little by little, as the narrator of the fable realized that nobody was contradicting him, his tone became more and more self-assured.

The phenomenon in itself is not all that extraordinary; on close inspection many famous men turn out to have embellished their pasts. But with Bettelheim, the myth-making process is of particular interest, because it would facilitate the opening-up of a gap between the real Orthogenic School and the way he portrayed it in his books. In other words, in a country like the United States, which likes its heroes to be blemishless, the half-truths about his past ended up by sowing doubts about all of Bettelheim's achievements, including those which were indisputable. The doubts troubled not only those who knew, but Bettelheim himself. The more famous he became, the more they seemed to echo in his mind with the 'fraud' he associated with his grandfather Seidler, the forebear that he was most afraid of resembling, yet the only one who had set him an example by achieving success. Towards the end of his life Bettelheim on occasion tried to duck questions about these fables, as if he had had enough of them, as if his accomplishments in the United States should have sufficed, and he should no longer be called on to back them up with the legend of his Viennese past. But his interviewers would invariably return to the stories, and Bettelheim would end up telling them what they so obviously wanted to hear.[3]

In January 1970, Bettelheim for the first time made the cover of the Sunday *New York Times* magazine section. Whereas he should have been delighted, Bert Cohler[4] found him looking glum. When asked why, Bettelheim replied: 'There's a dark secret in my past which could destroy the school.' When Cohler first told me this story,[5] I must admit I was sceptical, believing it to be an exaggeration intended to impress me. Today, however, I feel sure it is true, if only because I have since heard the same expression, 'dark secret', from Bettelheim's own mouth, referring to his childhood fears, the mystery surrounding his family's origins and his father's illness.[6] In four years of investigation I was able to find only one possible motivation for such a dramatic statement: that Bettelheim had not undergone a proper psychoanalytic training, and that the unidentified American child (Patsy) that he refers to in all his books – and particularly in *The Empty Fortress*, the latest book he had published on the school at the time – had never in fact been his patient.

Before examining his relationship to psychoanalysis, therefore, it is worth reflecting on exactly why Bruno Bettelheim felt the need to rearrange his past. The explanation put forward by some critics, that he simply wanted to make a name for himself and therefore began telling tall stories, finally believing in them himself, does not seem at all convincing to me. Everything I have learned about Bettelheim indicates that he was not blessed with a self-serving memory, and that he knew a lie when he saw one. How, otherwise, could he have spent thirty years of his life helping children and adults alike to doggedly track down their own darkest and innermost secrets, often very successfully? Had he started believing in his own stories, he could not have understood as clearly as he did how certain memories can be deadly. And, in his relationships with others, his insistence on saying things which would often have been better left unsaid made him enough enemies, and caused him enough problems, for us to conclude that his desire to get at the truth was strong. In my view there is no doubt that Bruno Bettelheim was always capable of distinguishing between the true facts and the embroidered version of events that he sometimes gave to others.

'Dreams were given to prisoners so they could re-invent their past,' the French writer Jean-Paul Kaufman has said.[7] The three and a half years that Kaufman spent as a hostage of the Hezbollah organization in Beirut can be compared with Bettelheim's period in Buchenwald on only two counts, but they are essential ones. Both men were held arbitrarily by people who hated them not for anything they had done but for who they were, and while neither knew up until the last minute whether he would be freed, both were aware from the outset that they could be killed at any time. In such a situation, Kaufman explains, dreams and reality tend to balance one another, the prisoner drawing from one the strength he needs to face up to the other. It is only after release that nightmares come, an observation which is confirmed by Bettelheim. 'In the concentration camp, I rarely dreamed about imprisonment or captivity. I dreamed of happy occasions.'[8] As Kaufman writes: 'At night, every prisoner in the world is out and on the run. Dreams prise open the most tightly-locked door, and push aside the heaviest of iron bars.' Thus does the unfortunate prisoner remind himself that life is worth living, and that he must hang on to it. Those few hours snatched from the all-powerful jailers are a time of 'frozen happiness', of pure harmony that can never exist in real life.

And what can happen in the mind of the prisoner once he emerges to find a world that bears no relation to the one he knew before being incarcerated, when everything or almost everything in his life is new: country, wife, language, profession, environment, lifestyle? When what he had always dreamed of comes true, in a real world which is all the more credible in that, unlike that of dreams, it is by no means a bed of roses? When at the same time the real world of his past vanishes, swallowed up in a nightmare of blood and fire?

On May 5, 1939, Bruno Bettelheim lost his wife, and with her the life which he had thought was to be his in America. On July 7, 1941, he was officially stripped of the citizenship of his birth, and, more importantly no doubt from a symbolic point of view, of his PhD from Vienna University.[9] As for the Bettelheim & Schnitzer company, it had been stolen from him long before. He had no past, he was dispossessed but free. He could at last throw away the key to all the dark closets containing the terrifying skeletons of his childhood. He was in a position, or even better he was forced, to create a whole new life for himself.

Which is what he proceeded to do. Those first few years in the United States wrought such a change in him that by the end of the 1940s, one can justifiably speak of a 'new Bettelheim'. New status, new profession, new

family and new past. New also because this man who for so long had feared
that he was a carrier of syphilis had in the meantime fathered two children
(his second daughter, Naomi, was born in November 1945). A new man,
made to measure for the New World he now inhabited.

This new Bettelheim was forged from the shock of exile, coming hard on
the heels of the trauma of the concentration camps and Gina's rejection. It
probably came into being little by little, without him really being aware of
it, with the protective complicity of Trude, who above all wanted to see her
husband at last exploiting all the inner riches that she knew he possessed.
But the metamorphosis could not but leave scars on a man who desired to
be admirable and could not stand the idea that he was not. For even if the
'fairy tales' he liked to tell originated more from the basic human need to
protect one's wounds than from his desire to 'make it' professionally, he
was certainly more aware than anyone else that they were fakes. And my
impression is that the arrogance and aggressivity for which he would later
become famous had a great deal to do with the guilt feelings associated
with this awareness. As is generally the case, however, such behaviour
served only to spread doubts around him even more.

It was thus, for example, with his title of psychoanalyst, which was
continually being challenged. In France, for instance, when Daniel Karlin's TV programmes on the Orthogenic School were screened in 1974.
Writing to a Parisian friend who had made her home in Paris, and who
had expressed concern at the accusations, Bettelheim suggested ignoring
them. He nevertheless went on to write: 'I have been elected a member of
the Chicago Psychoanalytic Society. This is the only certification necessary to be officially an analyst.' He also pointed out that, as had been the
case earlier in Chicago, the Child Psychiatry Division of Stanford University Medical School had invited him to lecture in their discipline. All of
which is true, but to paraphrase Shakespeare, the doctor appears to
protest too much. As if to confirm that there is a problem, he ends his
letter: 'As if I cared whether or not I am a psychoanalyst, as if it would
prove anything. We have helped children nobody else did, that's the only
thing that counts, and we learned in the process. Who cares what it is
called?'[10]

To understand Bruno Bettelheim's complex relations with official psychoanalytic circles, and with Freud's ideas themselves, a brief historical
explanation is needed. In the United States of the early 1940s, the rule was
in theory extremely simple: contrary to the view that Freud himself had
held, only qualified medical practitioners were allowed to set up as psychoanalysts. However child analysis was viewed as an exception, tolerated
mainly because it had been invented by Anna Freud. For the profession's
official bodies it did not really count as psychoanalysis, since for obvious
reasons it could not be practised under the standard conditions defined by

the International Psychoanalytic Association (IPA): patient lying on a couch, the analyst who remained silent while the patient free-associated, sessions lasting fifty-five minutes, etc. This opened up a loophole, and one which was all the more significant in that Nazism in Europe was sending waves of psychoanalysts fleeing across the Atlantic, many of them very experienced but without medical diplomas. By opting for the analysis of children, teachers like Edith Buxbaum were able to get round the rules, and open practices right from their arrival. Even some of those with medical qualifications chose this path in order to avoid having to repeat their internships.

Bruno Bettelheim's case was different: he had not been trained as an analyst in Vienna. Which explains Kurt Eissler's remark, noted at the start of this chapter. But had he undergone a new spell of treatment in the United States, this time a training analysis, it would have been enough for him to head the Orthogenic School, as he was to be treating children there. Thanks to his studies with Karl Bühler, his contacts in the Viennese analytic community and his work in the United States, he was by no means lacking in resources. For although psychoanalysts tended to look down their noses at the kind of tests used by psychologists,[11] the borderline between the two disciplines was sufficiently blurred for him to be able to cross over it without too much trouble. Indeed, the famous Berlin Psychoanalytic Institute, which had been the model for the Chicago Institute, even demanded in the 1930s that all its candidates undergo the Rorschach test, which Bettelheim had taught his students at Rockford.[12]

The situation of psychoanalysis in Chicago was an unusual one. Elsewhere, and particularly in New York, conflicts between individuals and schools of thought generally ended in splits, and the creation of competing societies. Such conflicts were exacerbated by the wartime influx of so many European refugees, who were seen by their American colleagues as victims of Nazism but also as potential rivals.[13] In Chicago, however, an unusual institutional feature prevented such splits: it was, and remains to this day, the only city in the United States in which the body that trains psychoanalysts (the Institute) is totally independent from the Psychoanalytic Society, to which all practitioners belong. Separately, both bodies belong to the American Psychoanalytic Association (APA).

Chicago's psychoanalysts could be roughly speaking divided into two groups. One was referred to as the 'conservatives', because its members defended strict Freudian orthodoxy. The others considered that analytical techniques still needed to evolve, that Freud had only laid the foundations, and that his followers' task was to continue building the edifice while making allowances for their environment, one which bore but little relation to the world that Freud himself had known. The 'conservatives' were dominant in the Society, to which all the city's analysts belonged. The 'moderns' had as their leader Franz Alexander, the founder and first director of the Institute (where only a few members were qualified as training analysts, with the right to supervise new practitioners). It was a harsh conflict, in which real theoretical differences were mixed up with vested interests and inter-personal rivalries.

Kurt Eissler, Emmy Sylvester and most of the recent immigrants provided the bulk of the first group, the one which Bettelheim was closest to. Their figurehead was a flamboyant and highly eccentric American, Lionel Blitzsen, who had been trained as an analyst by none other than Franz Alexander. Such paradoxes are so common as to be almost the norm. Indeed, the 'conservatives' could not lay claim to the closest links with Freud, even though the Society's secretary, Roy Grinker, had spent a year in analysis with him. Franz Alexander, however, had not only carried on a correspondence with Sigmund Freud,[14] he had also counted the latter's son Oliver among his analysands.

Alexander's strong personality was an important factor. The son of a Hungarian academic, he had emigrated to the United States in 1930, at the age of thirty-nine, and had come not as a refugee but as an adventurer, in search of new challenges. Trained as a medical doctor, he had long hesitated before going in for psychoanalysis, because of its bad reputation among scientists.[15] Once he made up his mind, however, he turned out to be so brilliant that in the same year he became a member of the Berlin Psychoanalytic Institute, Sigmund Freud awarded him the prize for the best clinical essay of the year.

The Berlin Institute, set up five years before the one in Vienna, was buzzing with new ideas on psychoanalytic techniques. Thanks to the breeze of freedom blowing through the Weimar Republic, and probably also because of the geographical distance separating them from Freud, the young analysts who had early on flocked to Berlin were ready to experiment. While Vienna was still struggling to emerge from the economic collapse that had followed defeat, the Prussian capital was buzzing with cultural and intellectual activity. When Alexander left the city for the United States, the Berlin Institute included Otto Fenichel, Erich Fromm, Georg Groddeck, Karen Horney, Melanie Klein and Sandor Rado: most of the people who were to leave their mark on psychoanalysis over the following three decades, leading it along divergent paths to create widely differing schools of thought. The route followed subsequently by psychoanalysis in the United States thus had its starting point not in Vienna but in Berlin, where all the figures who would mould American thinking had spent time.

That was no accident. The Berlin Institute was the first to insist that all candidates follow a 'training analysis' before practising as psychoanalysts. The minimum duration of such an analysis was set at a year, which as Peter Gay notes betrayed 'a therapeutic optimism that now seems sheer frivolity'.[16] Nevertheless, these were the first practitioners to have started out by testing Freud's discoveries on themselves with the help of another analyst, which meant that they were more concerned than their predecessors with the purely technical aspects, and the practical effectiveness, of the cure.

Franz Alexander had thus created the Chicago Institute along the lines of the Berlin one, calling on a number of original thinkers, and in particular women, to seek ever more effective therapeutic techniques. Then, as years went by, he drifted away from Freudian orthodoxy. Having created the concept of short therapies and made many discoveries in psychosomatic medicine, Alexander gradually moved towards the very medicalization of Freudian thought which, along with Freud himself, he had contested in 1927, when he was still in Berlin.[17]

When Alexander had left Europe in 1930, Freud is reported to have commented: 'I hope America will leave something intact of the real Alexander.' Whether apocryphal or not, the statement reflects above all Freud's ambivalence regarding the future of psychoanalysis in the United States. Before discussing that vast subject, which continues to divide the various analytical schools, it is however necessary to clarify our terms of reference, if only because Freud's ideas have led to such divergent developments on either side of the Atlantic that the same words can sometimes take on entirely different meanings, as Bruno Bettelheim himself clearly showed in his book *Freud and Man's Soul.* An explanation is all the more in order in that, although Bettelheim never practised standard psychoanalysis (it was, he said, 'the icing on the cake'), all his clinical activity was based on Freud's concept of the unconscious. It is indeed impossible to understand what went on at the Orthogenic School without some understanding of that concept.

Explaining what we mean by psychoanalysis is also important because the latter is first and foremost an experience, and only subsequently a theory. This statement, which is exasperating as long as one has not oneself verified it, does not turn analysis into an initiation rite, as its critics claim ('I don't *believe* in psychoanalysis,' they say). It is a mere recognition of the fact that, by definition, the unconscious is precisely what we cannot bear to face in ourselves. As discovered and defined by Freud, it is not simply a lack of awareness, but the result of an act of repression. The ego simply refuses to acknowledge as belonging to it a desire, a representation or a voice which affects it because that desire, representation or voice is incompatible with the image it has of itself; it endangers it. But the repression of desires, i.e. the refusal to acknowledge them, cannot prevent them from seeking satisfaction. They therefore look for undercover ways of doing so, via 'symptoms' which disturb the subject's everyday life. The treatment consists of reintegrating the repressed material by repeating it via the transference, in other words through the relationship between the patient and his or her analyst.[18] If things go well, the analysand will then identify the repressed desires and thus discover the origin of his symptoms.

To build on a metaphor used by psychoanalyst Michèle Montrelay in the powerful preface she wrote for the French translation of *Freud and Man's Soul*,[19] the analysand is like a single-handed sailor who sets out in foggy weather to discover the mysterious archipelago of his unconscious. He will have to make landfalls hundreds or even thousands of times before he finally realizes that he is continually setting foot on the same islets, although each time in a different place. Only then will he be able to consider drawing a map. But the map will never be complete, since unlike a real-life archipelago the unconscious is in continual movement, doing everything it can to escape detection. It is cunning and ruthless, and appropriates the surveyor's discoveries even as he makes them, the better to confuse him.

By dint of patience, the sailor will finally learn how to get round, or see through, such tricks. With perseverance, and the help of a good analyst, he will even catch a glimpse or two of that other himself hard at work. At that point, having at last understood the shadow-play that is going on in his psyche, the lone sailor will be able to set foot on dry land and take up his rightful place, no more but no less, in the real world. He will be ready to act rather than simply react, capable of giving and taking according to his true needs and desires, rather than simply obeying phantoms from his personal prehistory.

And what part, one may ask, does the psychoanalyst play in this odyssey? That of the wind, needed for the boat to fill its sails and move forward. An elusive and mysterious wind in whose song the spellbound sailor will soon hear ancient melodies that will send him spinning round in circles or heading straight for the rocks on which he has already run aground thousands of times before. But, he will then find out, a steady and reliable wind on which he can count to help him float off again until he is ready to spot through the fog the places where underground currents he thought he knew so well collide, producing the hidden whirlpools that swallow him every time. A light, subtle wind which accompanies the sailor without directing him, ever-present yet discreet, and as intangible as the unconscious whose contours it occasionally helps to reveal, up until the point when he feels strong enough to carry on the voyage on his own.

The idea is clearly far removed from any considerations of strictly therapeutic efficiency. Sigmund Freud was a humanist, believing that knowledge could of itself engender progress. It is in that sense that psychoanalysis is effective: once recognized, the unconscious desires can find more acceptable, less debilitating, avenues of satisfaction, and the symptoms will disappear. At the end of his life, however, Freud was to admit: 'We may say that analysis, in claiming to cure neuroses by ensuring control over instinct, is always right in theory, but not always right in practice.'[20] This was an allusion to 'this quantitative element, that we do not like to acknowledge', the realization that even when a psychological problem has been well analysed, its strength and resilience can still be underestimated. This admission of relative helplessness in the face of an intractable unconscious was open to a variety of interpretations. Some people would see it simply as a noble stance, reflecting the integrity of the scholar, and his determination to pursue his research ever further towards the attainment of his aims. But others, fascinated by the verb 'to cure', would view it as nothing more than an admission of failure, authorizing research into new types of therapy, away from the path carved out by the founder. By so doing, they would often throw overboard the essential tenets of his discovery.

Replying to an interviewer's question on the treatment of psychotics, also towards the end of his life, Bruno Bettelheim would say: 'You can fix a broken arm, but you can never make it as if it had never been broken in the first place.'[21] Different subject, similar idea: people's souls can be repaired, but there is no laser beam capable of totally erasing all traces of a problem. Scars will remain, sensitive and fragile, and there is never any guarantee that the analysis has gone far enough in exploring all the hidden corners of the psyche, or that one day the whole edifice will not collapse under the force of some new internal disturbance.

However respectable they may be, such reservations are not well received in the United States, outside intellectual circles. And even there they are often welcome only if they lead to some form of certainty, to what might be seen as a 'happy ending'. That country, built on the twin myths of an ever-expanding frontier and the self-made man, is interested above all in results, the more spectacular the better. Faced with new ideas, it shows much greater curiosity than the Old World. The outsider with an attractive project will initially be given his chance, and provided with the resources needed to carry it out. But woe betide the newcomer who proves unworthy of such trust, or who takes too long to deliver. In the United States, even more than elsewhere, a loser is always in the wrong. Which explains the paradoxical reception given to psychoanalysis. Welcomed at the outset as a great discovery, even placed on a pedestal, it quickly invaded almost every aspect of life, as shown by Gina Bettelheim's experience with the Jewish Social Services in New York.[22] Almost as quickly, however, the new discipline was adulterated, falling under the competing influence of the very people whom Freud himself had identified as its two most dangerous enemies: doctors and preachers.[23] Maybe to save it from the latter, many of Freud's followers in America were the first to throw psychoanalysis into the arms of the doctors – from whose ranks many of them came, even though up until then the fact had often been of secondary importance to them. By so doing they not only gave support to the very medicalization of his theories that Freud opposed, but became the theoreticians of that process.[24] Which was why Freud could write that, in the United States, psychoanalysis had very quickly become 'nothing else but one of the maidservants of psychiatry'.[25]

And yet Freud had been the first to be impressed by American enthusiasm for psychoanalysis. In 1909, making his first and only trip to the

United States, he had been very surprised at the reception he got at Clark University in Worcester, Massachusetts. 'My short visit to the new world encouraged my self-respect in every way,' he was to write later. 'In Europe I felt as though I were despised, but over there I found myself received by the foremost men as an equal. It seemed like the realization of some incredible day-dream ... psychoanalysis was no longer a product of delusion, it had become a valuable part of reality.'[26]

When Freud made his trip, Europeans had no reason to believe that they might one day be forced to flee across the Atlantic to start new lives in America. It is thus not difficult to imagine how exciting that same experience would seem three decades later to many of his followers, who after being chased from their homes, dispossessed and humiliated, found themselves offered choice posts in American hospitals, thanks to the very science which back home in Europe had brought them only distrust and condescension from the establishment. For as Paul Roazen points out, the culture and theoretical abilities of the Europeans, plus 'their special therapeutic experience, combined with their deep sense of dedication to a common cause, placed them in the forefront of American psychiatry'.[27]

The price to be paid for this success would be a heavy one, as Freud himself had predicted as early as 1925. While the Americans showed great enthusiasm for psychoanalysis, they tended to 'water it down', to use its name to cover 'many abuses which have no relation to it', while creating 'few opportunities for any thorough training in technique and theory'. Moreover, in America, the new discipline would 'come in conflict with Behaviourism, a theory which is naïve enough to boast that it has put the whole problem of psychology completely out of count'.[28] In other words, Freud was aware that in gaining a foothold in the United States, psychoanalysis was in danger of losing both its depth and its subversive power. It was set to be co-opted, to become part of the established corpus of 'useful' sciences, the results of which can be quantified.

The main direction that psychoanalysis was to take in the United States is entirely summed up in the above quotations from Freud. Starting out with the aim of 'ensuring control over instinct' (i.e. the drives), a process which does not always succeed in 'curing neuroses', it was to lead towards behaviourism, which in fact aims to eliminate psychology altogether. The drives are the basic sources of energy of the psyche, but they have an unfortunate tendency, as soon as one begins to identify their contradictions, to go and carry on the fight in some new and unexpected region of the unconscious. Which is why Freud, after years of struggling as a clinician with the complexities of the human soul, became convinced that in order to cure neuroses, analysis had to be a long process. However, as Benjamin Franklin taught the world, in the United States 'time is money', and the maxim applies to psychoanalysis no less than to any other field. Since what was required was results, and the quicker the better, many of Freud's American followers were to relegate the drives, unpredictable and rebellious by nature, to the status of outdated accessories. Instead they would devote most of their attention to the agent in charge, the captain of the ship: the ego.

The idea that there was a part of the ego that could be considered free of conflicts between drives, and therefore more reliable than the rest of the psyche, was thus to gain ground. This proposition drew its legitimacy from a number of texts approved by Freud himself, notably some by Paul Federn,[29] and Anna Freud's book *The Ego and the Mechanisms of Defence*.[30] The conflict-free zone was said to be that of learning, and more generally adaptation. The analyst would therefore seek to strengthen it. Rather than accompanying the analysand on a deep-sea voyage into the unfathomable depths of his being, to look for mechanisms which might turn out to be irreparable, he would act as a guide. He had a function; he was also to give himself a role (and one commensurate with his status in the New World). To return to the sailing metaphor, having read the charts much faster than the voyager, the wind would no longer be a gentle breeze; it would become a steady torrent of air, and the disoriented sailor would feel a firm but heavy hand laying hold of the tiller to help him navigate.

The resulting voyage was a much shorter one, since the only job of the analysand would be to keep to the course mapped out by the analyst. More importantly, it was no longer the same voyage. The initial aim of discovery was replaced by that of efficiency. And in many cases the patient would soon be surprised to find that the most troublesome of his behavioural problems, the ones which had most impeded his day-to-day effectiveness in society, were fading away or had disappeared altogether. The changes however would often remain superficial, easily reversed by the ups and downs of life. Having not mapped out the islands of his unconscious for himself, once on his own the lone sailor was likely to get lost again at the first sign of turbulence. But then of course he could always sign up for a new spell of treatment!

This brief summary of the birth of 'Ego Psychology' is of course very schematic, taking no account either of the time that the whole process took or of its intricacies.[31] But it is enough to highlight the affinities between Ego Psychology and behaviourism, a doctrine which Bruno Bettelheim was to combat throughout his entire career. It also provides a background to some of the traits of analysis which have been frequently caricatured in the United States, for instance in Woody Allen's films. Such as the endless series of cures, the analyst who speaks in ponderous sentences (as does Bruno Bettelheim himself, appearing in a brief scene of Allen's *Zelig*), the much-ridiculed attitude of 'Do as I say, and not as I do' (illustrated, this time in *Crimes and Misdemeanors*, by a philosopher with a heavy Viennese accent, not unlike Bettelheim's, who after having preached survival, ends up committing suicide[32]). One can also see how psychoanalysis, born from Freud's desire to understand the sufferings caused to his women patients by the stifling conformism of their bourgeois backgrounds, could

turn into a technique for making people accept the established order, a
function denounced by many leftists, notably in the 1960s. Finally, by
illustrating the gulf that has slowly been created between psychoanalysis
as practised in the United States and the discipline as envisaged by
Sigmund Freud, one can understand the relative decline in its influence
over the past two decades, as patients have flocked to other, newer types
of therapy, seen as still more 'cost effective' – i.e. shorter and more
explicitly practical.

Bruno Bettelheim's place in all this is a paradoxical one. He successively went through non-Freudian psychology with the Eight Year Study,
and then dynamic psychology (a kind of passageway between psychology
and psychoanalysis). In *Symbolic Wounds*, he flirted with the culturalist
school of thought, very fashionable in the United States just after the
war.[33] The main criticism he makes of psychoanalysis in the opening pages
of *The Informed Heart* – that it concerns itself only with the neurotic
aspects of the individual and not enough with his or her strong points, and
that it is therefore of little use to anyone in a life-or-death situation – is
reminiscent of the arguments of Heinz Hartmann, generally considered
the first theoretician of Ego Psychology. (Hartmann accused classical
Freudian thought of putting too much stress on the pathological, to the
detriment of normal behaviour.[34]) Finally, in describing his work with the
children of the Orthogenic School, Bruno Bettelheim used concepts drawn
both from Ego Psychology and its offshoots, such as Heinz Kohut's Self
Psychology, and from the works of Anna Freud and the British school of
psychoanalysis, notably those of Donald Winnicott.

In all these cases, however, Bruno Bettelheim remained on the fringes
of the schools of thought within which his work could normally have placed
him; his habit of sniping from the sidelines having the effect of amplifying
the controversy that many of his statements sparked off. He has always
been a choice target for the opponents of psychoanalysis. Meanwhile most
orthodox Freudians have criticized him for focusing more on the manifest
content of his patients' discourse than on what it reveals about their
unconscious – and thus producing purely psychological rather than psychoanalytical interpretations. 'Bettelheim?' such people generally say, in
a tone that brooks no contradiction. 'That's not psychoanalysis!'

Nevertheless, after a lifetime spent exploring the various paths taken
by psychoanalysis outside Vienna, this self-taught Freud scholar was near
the end of his life to rediscover the founder of the discipline. Not the
world-famous Sigmund Freud, but the young man who waged an almost
single-handed battle against his own neuroses to discover the existence of
the unconscious. It was to that pioneer that Bettelheim would pay homage
in *Freud and Man's Soul*, published in 1982.

In this book, Bettelheim shows in-depth understanding of Freudian
thinking. Although written some four decades after his application to join
the Chicago Psychoanalytic Society, this slim volume speaks directly to

the problem which divided the body at that time, and one that had become progressively more acute, proving how fundamental the issue was. To label the orthodox Freudians as 'conservatives' and those who were seeking to make therapy more cost-effective and efficient as 'modernists' was indeed to negate the subversive, revolutionary nature of Freud's thought, and thus its very efficacy. What makes psychoanalysis different from other therapies is precisely its insistence on questioning absolutely everything, on refusing to take any kind of discourse, even that of the analyst himself, at its face value. It is because no word or form of words is exempt from scrutiny that the process of exploring the darkest corridors of the unconscious can move ahead, slowly and sometimes painfully. Without such readiness to put everything into question at any point, it is no longer psychoanalysis. And in his long essay, Bruno Bettelheim tries to show how the process of curbing the subversive power of psychoanalysis began, right at the beginning, with the translation of Freud's works into English.

Starting out from a few simple but striking examples, he stresses how the basic concepts of Freud's thought were stripped, by their translation into English, of precisely what gave psychoanalysis its power, i.e. its closeness to everything human. How Freud's 'direct and always deeply personal appeals to our common humanity appear to readers of English as abstract, depersonalized, highly theoretical, erudite, and mechanized – in short, "scientific" – statements about the strange and very complex workings of our mind'.[35] So that for such readers, psychoanalysis becomes nothing more than an intellectual construct, a system to be applied to the understanding of other people's behaviour, and not an invitation to introspection. Whereas in truth, Bettelheim stresses, the most precious contribution made by psychoanalysis, and the secret of its power, lies precisely in the fact that it was born from the struggle that Freud carried on, throughout his life, with his own unconscious.

Being uniquely aware of what Bettelheim describes as man's 'universal wish to remain unaware of his own unconscious',[36] Freud, who was a brilliant writer in his native German, always expressed himself in the clearest, most direct and simple fashion, remaining as close as possible to his reader's experience in order to get across the complex mechanisms he was trying to explain. However his English translators' desire for scientific respectability led them, for example, to use Latin words for three of Freud's central concepts, which in the original German were *Das Ich* ('the I'), *Das Es* ('the it') and *Das Über-Ich*, a composite word which could be simply rendered as 'the above-I' or 'the upper-I'. The resulting terms of 'ego', 'id' and 'superego' sound remote and technical, Bettelheim points out, whereas the original terms *Ich* and *Es* are two of the commonest words in the German language. Even more importantly, they are among the first a small child utters. And although *Über-Ich* was of course a neologism created by Freud, it could much better have been translated by retaining the 'I'.[37] Worse still is the fate reserved for the word *Seele* in the English translation, Bettelheim argues. This term, which would normally be translated as 'soul', is fundamental in Freud's writings as it refers to the very object which psychoanalysis is supposed to investigate. It has nevertheless been translated as the dry and cold 'mind', stripping the original concept of all its rich spiritual and emotional connotations. In such ways, Bettelheim writes, Freud's English translators completely distorted his ideas, and thus misrepresented his discovery.

When asked for their opinion of the book, many psychoanalysts tend to reply by saying that its arguments are generally correct, but they are nothing new, since 'Everyone knew that.'[38] It is true that all German-speakers who compare the translations to the originals are struck by the discrepancies between the two. But Bruno Bettelheim was nevertheless the first writer to offer a critique in simple, universally comprehensible terms, and in a publication that was accessible to educated lay readers. It is true that he undertook the work late on, forty years after he had abandoned German for English as a working language. However he explains this delay in his preface, noting that the first translations of Freud's work had appeared during the latter's lifetime, and that later ones had been approved by his daughter Anna, so that attacking them had seemed like 'criticizing the venerated master himself'.

There is no doubt another reason for such a long silence on the subject. Psychoanalysis is a science developed by a highly cultured man, working with men and women who were also highly educated. As a verbal experience, it is above all a science of the mind (the required route by which to reach the soul), involving much use of symbols and language, word-plays and puns. For that reason, practising it with patients whose cultural and childhood references one does not share intimately – even if one has managed to master their language – cannot but alter its nature. But for men and women whose very survival in the New World depended on their being able to make such a leap, it was obviously not easy to admit to that fact.

Bettelheim also wonders how Sigmund Freud, who read English with ease, could have allowed the publication of a translation which so clearly robbed his work of most of its humanistic content. But he does not push that argument very far either, suggesting that Freud's indifference could be explained by his animosity to the United States. That is a little too facile. Although it is clear that Freud had a rather condescending view of the place he called 'America' (that is how most Europeans then referred to the United States, which in itself is revealing; they saw it not as a country but as an entire continent, in other words as a remote, different and somewhat uncivilized place, where a much higher price was placed on survival and expansion than on culture or the art of living), he was well aware, at least towards the end of his life, that it was there that the fate of psychoanalysis would be determined. As is shown by his contributions to the debate on lay (i.e. non-medical) analysis, he was to fight to the very end to try to get across his point of view; at one point he even envisaged a 'peaceful' expulsion of the US psychoanalytic societies from the International Psychoanalytic Association over their refusal to let non-doctors practise the new discipline. But as soon as something vaguely resembling a compromise was offered by the powerful New York Psychoanalytic Society, Freud accepted it.[39] The survival of psychoanalysis was worth a few concessions. Even better, in March 1939, Freud congratulated his friend Arnold Zweig for having preferred the United States to Britain as his exile home, writing that 'America seems an anti-paradise to me, but it has so much space and so many possibilities and ultimately one does come to belong there.'[40] Without having experienced it himself, the founder of psychoanalysis had thus grasped the basic parameters of exile in the New World.

The development of Bruno Bettelheim's thinking on Freudianism has been dismissed by some of his critics as self-serving. Apart from the fact that the charge verges on absurdity, since Freud's popularity in the United States was in continual decline over the period in which Bettelheim was moving closer to his viewpoint, the criticism seems to me to be superficial. My hypothesis is that his process of introspection, begun in Dachau as a way of ensuring his survival, and carried on in one form or another throughout the rest of his life, gradually led Bettelheim to rediscover Freud on the latter's own turf.

Gina Weinmann often accuses Bettelheim of having taken himself for Freud towards the end of his life, when he was famous the world over and would often proffer his opinion on all and any subjects in an overly abrupt tone. Hidden within this cruel insinuation there is a measure of truth. 'That Freud, what a neurotic, and yet what a genius!' Bettelheim wrote in essence[41] to his friend Carl Frankenstein after re-reading Freud's works in order to write his essay. This rediscovery of a man who had spent his life struggling alone with his unconscious to try and understand its workings had clearly brought a 'shock of recognition' for Bettelheim at that stage in his life.

Anyone pursuing a psychoanalysis beyond a certain point will probably continue it as a process of introspection for the rest of their life. And the fact that so many analysands suddenly discover a vocation as psychoanalysts in the course of their treatment is symptomatic of their feeling of indebtedness, not only towards their analysts but also towards Freud himself.[42] However Bettelheim's seems to me to be a different case. First, as we have seen, his analysis with Richard Sterba was of short duration. But above all, by the time circumstances would have allowed him to resume it, it was too late. Who among the members of the Chicago Psychoanalytic Society would have been in a position to help an analysand who had just returned from Buchenwald?

It was some time after World War II before it became apparent how difficult it is for a former concentration camp inmate to gain relief from psychoanalysis.[43] Bettelheim referred in passing to this problem in a letter written in July 1980: 'If the therapist has not himself undergone the same experience, the treatment will not work. But if he has experience of concentration camps, the sessions will awaken too many psychological problems in him.'[44] As Freudian analysis concerns itself only with the patient's fantasies, it becomes well-nigh impossible to pursue it when the real world has made such a traumatic and brutal mark on his life. This is why Bettelheim suggested that such patients should follow a particular form of group treatment, in which several ex-detainees help one another to 'analyse' themselves under the guidance of an experienced therapist.

He makes no secret of the fact that this idea is based on his own experience. In his case, however, there was no collective therapy, but rather a self-analysis, forced upon him by circumstances. As we have seen, after his psychoanalysis was brutally cut short by his deportation, he resumed it in the form of introspection, for fear of going crazy. For the same reason he began observing the behaviour of his fellow inmates, and discussing his observations with Federn and Fischer. As he stresses on every possible occasion,[45] he undertook this task first and foremost to save his own life, by allowing him to defeat the Nazis' efforts at 'disintegrating his personality'.

And the effort had paid off. 'The impact of the concentration camp ... within a few weeks, did for me what years of a useful and quite successful analysis had not done,' he wrote in *The Informed Heart*.[46] What that meant is explained in the 1954 letter in which he recognized that his spell in the concentration camps 'did me good': 'Up until then, the circumstances of my life had never provided me with proof that I was able to stand up on my own two feet, even in very difficult conditions.'[47] Is that not precisely one of the main aims of a good psychoanalysis?

Although *The Informed Heart* is not exactly a song of praise to Freudian thinking, the man who had once been Richard Sterba's patient does have some scruples about this passage, and adds parenthetically, in a voluntarily lighthearted tone: 'I realize that with this admission I lay myself, and my analyst, open to the criticism that my analysis provided me with insight, but did not lead to working through.'

This is a revealing aside. First, Bettelheim admits that his psycho-analysis in Vienna only brought him an intellectual understanding of his problems. At the same time, his remark shows that he clearly knows the way to a successful Freudian analysis: through the repetition of neurotic attitudes in the relationship with the analyst (transference), the gradual discovery by the analysand of the many effects his unconscious knots have on his life, leading hopefully to his abandoning the most negative ones. Finally, with one of those intellectual flourishes that he often used to get rid of a bothersome subject, Bettelheim concludes the above statement by saying: 'Perhaps it is to the credit of my analysis that the prospect does not trouble me.'

These lines were written towards the end of the 1950s, when Bettelheim's career was really taking off. He was fully at ease in his new life as an American, the Orthogenic School was working well and his family was not causing him any problems. Above all, the book they are drawn from marked a turning-point in his life. In *The Informed Heart*, Bettelheim was laying the foundations of what would remain as his most personal contribution: the link between his experiences as a concentration camp survivor and those of the schizophrenic children in his care. His tone was one of self-confidence, that of a man who is succeeding in all his undertakings. A man surrounded by people who love and admire him, who does not yet know what it means to get old and who chooses to believe that he has once and for all put the pain of his past life behind him.

How very different is the tone two decades later, when Bettelheim is writing the introduction to *Surviving*, a collection of essays of which the main items had in fact already been used in *The Informed Heart*. The new book opens with a long meditation on the purpose of life, suicide, Faust, man's destructive impulses and death anxiety. It is as though Bettelheim, called on to select the essential writings of an entire lifetime for inclusion in the book, is once again struggling to avoid being submerged by the feeling that any attempt to leave a trace of one's existence is absurd, and that any progress man makes is doomed to turn against him to destroy him all the more effectively. Following straight on from these pages, and even before explaining why he agreed to produce *Surviving*, Bettelheim recalls the problems he faced in writing his first article on the concentration camps, 'Individual and Mass Behavior in Extreme Situations'.[48] The juxtaposition of these two passages is no coincidence.

The importance of that 1943 article in Bruno Bettelheim's life can be gauged from the number of times he was to use it. After its initial appearance in the *Journal of Abnormal and Social Psychology* in October 1943, two abridged versions were to be published, one in the magazine *Politics* in August 1944 and the other in a ten-volume supplement on the war produced by the *Encyclopaedia Britannica*,[49] in which the key passages from his article are included. Bettelheim was to use the text yet again in July 1945, in his affidavit to the office of Judge Jackson, the US prosecutor at the Nuremberg Trials,[50] and would then use it, in a modified version, in the *Informed Heart* in 1960, returning it to its original form to include it in *Surviving* in 1979.

The article is important also because it was to spread Bruno Bettelheim's reputation well beyond the confines of Chicago. In April 1945, US troops liberated Buchenwald, and the photos they took in one of the blocks, into which detainees who had survived the Nazi evacuation of Auschwitz had been crammed, showed the world what had been going on in the Nazi camps. Two months later, on June 15, Gordon Allport, editor-in-chief of

the *Journal of Abnormal and Social Psychology*, informed Bettelheim that
he had received a cable from General Eisenhower asking for permission to
reproduce his article for distribution to American officers in Europe. The
US troops had been completely unprepared for what they had found, and
at the time Bettelheim's article was one of the only existing texts in
English on what had happened in the concentration camps. Furthermore,
The Informed Heart, when it was published in 1960, was still the first
psychological analysis of the camps to appear outside specialist publications, aimed at the general public.[51] But the text is also crucial because a
little later, when Bettelheim found himself caught up in a cruel confrontation with the death camp survivors,[52] some of his detractors would take
it apart line by line in order to use it against him.

What Bettelheim's critics never did, however, was to view the article in
its context. As it was the first analytical article on the Nazi camps, it took
on instant authority, and almost everybody forgot that it was first and
foremost a simple piece of testimony. What people focused on were the
ideas it contained; nobody tried to figure out what state Bettelheim had
been in when he wrote it or what kind of theoretical material he had had
at his disposal both when he collected his observations inside the camps
and when he committed them to paper a year later. It is true that the
authoritative tone of his article militated against that kind of investigation. Once again, readers let themselves be intimidated by that facade, and
thus failed to see the personal wounds that it concealed. And yet that
article was not only the first major non-academic text that Bettelheim had
ever produced, but it was written at a particularly crucial juncture in his
life. It came after the trauma of the camps and the shock of his rejection
by Gina, at a time when exile, at once brutal and generous, offered him a
chance to start anew. To undergo, as it were, a 'second birth' – to use a
concept that he would place at the heart of his work at the Orthogenic
School.

Any examination of the circumstances in which Bruno Bettelheim
wrote that first article also needs to take account of studies into the
workings of the memory, since as I was to verify on several occasions
during the research for this book, mental recall is never completely
reliable, even in people motivated by a strong desire to tell the truth. No
reconstruction of the past is ever free of interference from the present.[53]
Above all, in the present case, the recall of traumatic memories is always
affected by the mind's efforts to try to make them less painful. The process
by which the mind seeks to cover up its wounds can be compared to the
formation of scar tissue. Among luckier victims this leads simply to
forgetting; among others it often results in rationalization and anger.

In his opening remarks Bettelheim states that he began jotting down
his recollections almost as soon as he had been released, but that he waited
until he had been able to distance himself somewhat from his emotions
before actually writing his text. The writer had, he wrote, 'hesitated for

nearly three years to interpret [his experiences] because he felt that his anger about the treatment that he had received might endanger his objectivity'.[54]

He states that he began to write down his recollections in 1940. What he does not say is that the first draft of his essay was completed shortly afterwards. That initial version had nothing impersonal about it; it was the raw and painful account of a just-released prisoner.[55] None of the psychoanalytic journals he submitted it to wanted to publish it, however. 'My story was met with utter disbelief,' he noted later.[56] Some potential publishers accused him of getting carried away by his hatred of the Nazis into painting them blacker than they really were, while others felt that on the contrary he was overestimating their intelligence and the scope of their programme. Some even criticized Bettelheim for not having taken notes, 'implicitly revealing that they had not believed a word of what I had written about conditions in the camps'. The frankest among the editors to whom he submitted the article simply admitted that they considered its contents 'unacceptable' for their readers.

It was certainly not the best of times to try and get an article published on the concentration camps. Not only did the vast majority of Americans have no idea what these were, but even those willing to listen had a hard time believing what they heard. Two recent movies had alluded to the camps: Frank Borzage's *Mortal Storm*, and above all, Charlie Chaplin's *The Great Dictator*. Although attacked by the isolationist lobby, the latter film had finally enjoyed widespread success, thanks both to Chaplin's talent and to the fact that it was a comedy. The Borzage movie, however, had been a total flop and was panned as being both partisan and slanderous. Three senators even asked the White House to ban it on the grounds that it was offensive to Germany![57] In fact, the image of the concentration camp shown in this well-put-together but not particularly subtle film on the tearing apart of a family under Nazism was far less harsh than the real thing.

In truth, Bettelheim was completely alone in trying to deal with his memories, which were much too vivid at night, and seemed all the more unreal during the day in that he could not communicate them to anyone else. And on this particular issue, having Trude by his side did nothing to ease the pain. The state of anxiety she was in over the fate of her parents could only sharpen his determination to make his voice heard. Similarly, every rejection slip, and every passing month, must have increased his feeling of guilt at not having yet kept the promise that he and Federn had made to each other one Sunday in Buchenwald. Federn had still not been freed.

The awful roll-call which had lasted all night on the *Appelplatz*, the all-pervading cold, the dirt, the smashed glasses, the screams of prisoners being flogged, the sudden silence of those who collapsed. It is not difficult to imagine how Bettelheim must have struggled with such images, which probably invaded his mind at times when he was least expecting them. Perhaps when he was watching the Illinois countryside slip by as he rode the train to Rockford, or when walking along the muddy central strip of the Midway. They were images which he must have had a hard time getting across in English, a language he had still only partially mastered. As nobody was interested in his suffering, he resorted to the one quality of which he could be absolutely sure, and which nobody had ever questioned: his intelligence. Once again, he needed to give things a meaning. He read a lot at this time, searching for theoretical tools to help him make his experiences more presentable and intelligible. It was a fruitless quest, however, as 'at the time, psychological thought had not yet developed the conceptual framework necessary for dealing adequately with these problems, so I was forced to struggle with it myself'.[58]

His article was finally published in October 1943. Bruno Bettelheim had thus spent over two years being gnawed by doubts, wondering how to organize the observations he had so painstakingly collected in the camps in a presentable fashion, and seeing in every rejection slip a confirmation of his inability to do so. It should also be noted that in the mass of unruly facts with which he was grappling there were a few memories that were even more painful than the rest, but which he had no intention of including in his article. Such as the armband for blind prisoners, for example. All of which added up to a real ordeal. He slept badly, and in the daytime, while keeping up appearances in the outside world, he was irritable and difficult to live with, as is shown by Trude's memoirs. He was angry at others for displaying such indifference to what was going on, but he judged himself more harshly for not succeeding in carrying out his mission, in spite of, or perhaps even because of, his rapid professional success. But while he could give vent to his indignation, his shame remained hidden, and thus all the more painful. It is therefore no surprise to read, in the opening pages of *Surviving*: 'My desire to make people understand received much impetus from my need to comprehend better what had happened to me while in the camps, so I could gain intellectual mastery over the experience.'[59] Once again, the aim is clearly to understand, above all in order to avoid going crazy. In other words, to give an account of the exercise he had undertaken in Dachau, he had to continue it.

In his essay, Bettelheim starts by filing, classifying, counting and generally marshalling his data. In his opening remarks he lists what he has identified as the four key objectives of the concentration camp system, stressing that his study concerns only the first one: how the Gestapo[60] managed to break the prisoners as individuals so as to transform them into a docile mass within which there was no risk of seeing the slightest act of resistance, either individual or collective.

He then distinguishes between three types of behaviour: collective, individual (occurring within the group, in relation to events in the camp) and private (relating to the individual's history and personality from before his imprisonment). He specifies in passing that the present study, which he has undertaken not out of a spirit of scientific inquiry but as a means of survival, is the only example of private behaviour he can discuss. Thus does the subject, identified as 'the author', become the object of the analysis, and his work 'a particular type of defense developed ... to protect this individual against the disintegration of his personality'.[61]

Bettelheim goes on to outline four stages in the development of detainees' behaviour: the first shock of arrest; the 'initiation' process, which generally occurs during the journey to the camp, or if this is of short duration, during the first days; the period of adaptation, during which the detainee gradually ceases to be a 'new prisoner', and finally the behaviour of 'old prisoners'.

Here again, the desire to impose order on the material can be clearly seen. Bettelheim has previously reeled off his credentials: the number of blocks and work-groups he belonged to, the number of prisoners he was able to interview, etc. (not without a measure of exaggeration,[62] no doubt aimed at bolstering his credibility with hesitant editors). He then gives his observations on each of the stages enumerated.[63] These are remarkably insightful, particularly when one considers that they date from 1938-39, and have for the most part been amply confirmed by subsequent testimony.[64]

Next, Bettelheim comments on his observations, and once again the reader is struck by his efforts to create order in, and thus derive meaning from, his data. For example, he classifies the types of reactions prisoners had during the first phase according to their socio-economic background, noting that the people who came off worst were the apolitical 'middle-class' prisoners, who had always been law-abiding. Unlike criminals and political activists, for whom arrest had always been on the cards, they were wounded in their dignity and self-esteem by what had happened to them. They clung to the idea that it must have been the result of an error, and although they were ridiculed and insulted for this by both their jailers and their fellow prisoners, it was a long time before they realized that there had been no mistake.[65] When they finally did so, they generally went to pieces. Bettelheim also notes that it was almost exclusively among this middle-class, non-political category (which in fact made up a minority of prisoners at the time when he was interned) that most of the suicides occurred during the early period of detention, and that the most flagrant examples of antisocial behaviour (theft, denunciations of fellow inmates, etc.) were observed later on.

Leaving aside the overall scope of such a remark, two features stand out for anyone who is aware of Bettelheim's own life prior to his arrest: the severity of his judgements, and the fact that they are delivered against precisely the category of prisoners to which he himself belonged.

When he comes to discuss the differences of behaviour between 'new' and 'old' prisoners, and explains how the latter adapted to life in the camp, his tone becomes even more critical. Whereas the 'new prisoners' were above all concerned by the world they had left behind, spending all their money on keeping in touch with their families and obtaining information about the political situation outside, he writes, the 'old' ones were interested only in improving their lot within the camp.

As we have seen, Bettelheim's own behaviour was somewhere between the two: while keeping in touch with his mother, and striving through that contact to remain present in the lives of friends and relatives, his everyday efforts in the camp were directed towards avoiding conditions in which he would not have survived. This does not invalidate his observation; many subsequent writers have confirmed the hardening of camp detainees as they adapted to their new environment.[66] But his own example does show that the process was a gradual one, that it started earlier than he stated and that for a long time the prisoners were neither completely 'new' nor definitively 'old'. Above all, Bettelheim's description expresses his inability to accept his own weaknesses. In judging other people's behaviour so harshly, he is above all judging himself. One can also see how a man who is so demanding manages to turn even his most precious qualities against himself; had Bettelheim been less observant of the signs of adaptation in his fellow prisoners, he would surely have been less terrified by the process as it occurred in himself. And, being less aware of every tiny detail of his own adaptation, he would no doubt have been more indulgent towards others.

Clearly Bruno Bettelheim was not one of those happy mortals who, on reviewing the events of their lives, invariably cast themselves as the good guy. The above two examples give the measure of the battle he must have waged against himself in order to write his article, at a time when he could still hope to save lives by alerting US public opinion to what was going on in the camps in Germany. If the burden of responsibility had been less heavy, or the struggle less arduous – if, for example, Bettelheim had been able to enlist the aid of an analyst to unearth the origins of the 'debts' that he was also seeking to pay off by writing it – then perhaps the essay that was to make him famous around the world would not have returned to haunt him until his dying day. It would have taken up its rightful place in the history of concentration camp literature, and only the remarkable accuracy of most of his observations would have remained in people's minds. Instead of which his article, the record of the painful self-analysis which he was obliged to resume after his release, is now only ever quoted for the extreme severity of some of its judgements.

Most of the criticism levelled at Bettelheim for his article centres on his use of the concept of 'identification with the aggressor' to describe the behaviour of some of his fellow detainees, and his remarks on their 'regression' and 'infantilization'. These terms shocked people more than anything else. What right did this man, who had had the luck and the wherewithal to get out of the camps, have to take such a patronizing view of others? To this question, which was asked of Bettelheim in many ways and on many occasions, sometimes in the most insulting manner, I feel like replying with another: how can people who profess their devotion to the memory of the camp victims be so lacking in compassion for the struggle that one of those victims had to wage in order to bear witness? After all, the Nazis took their prey as they found them, neuroses, physical handicaps, warts and all. And when some of their victims miraculously escaped their clutches, they had to contend with those same handicaps and neuroses in trying to deal with the experience.

Which brings us back to Bruno Bettelheim's relationship to psychoanalysis, a question upon which his use of the concept of 'identification with the aggressor' throws a certain amount of light. At the time of his deportation, that relationship was in its early stages, made up of a combination of book-learning and a shortish analysis undertaken in somewhat exceptional circumstances. In the second stage, in Buchenwald (probably much more than in Dachau, as he only met Ernst Federn in the second camp), he found himself in a position strangely akin to that of an analyst in training. On the one hand he had his 'patients', Hans Bandler and the other people he interviewed, and on the other his 'supervisors', Dr Fischer and above all Federn. For although the latter was not an analyst, he knew enough about the subject for Bettelheim to engage in a fruitful dialogue with him about what he had heard from his 'patients'. The two men used the theoretical concepts at their disposal to try and understand their observations, in particular Anna Freud's book on the development of the child's psyche, *The Ego and the Mechanisms of Defense*, which had appeared just over a year before their arrests. For it was clearly from that work that Bettelheim drew the concepts of 'regression' and 'identification with the aggressor', to try and understand the behaviour patterns he was witnessing.

The fascination that the Nazis inspired in many of their victims is as undeniable as the repulsion that they simultaneously stirred in them. Expressed in its most simple form, the least affected by shame, it resulted in reactions like that of the seventeen-year-old George Clare, a Jew and a socialist, on observing the arrival in Vienna of the *Wehrmacht* on March 13, 1938. 'The exhibition of perfect discipline and splendid equipment made a great impression on me. The men were mostly, or so it seemed to me, tall, young, handsome, elegant and well-turned out, and incredible as it may seem, I suddenly realized that I admired these soldiers and was even proud of them.'[67] Clare was shocked to find himself experiencing such feelings, and immediately sought to justify them by telling himself that the real enemies were the SA and the SS, and not the regular army. However he was only half convinced by this argument at the time, and when he came to tell the story a few years later he had seen through it completely.

At Buchenwald, of course, things were more complicated. There was no way of dissociating the handsome soldier that one admired in spite of oneself, and the feelings of horror and terror he inspired. The SS troops of the *Totenkopf* unit were the very incarnation of evil, and as if to underline the point they had a death's-head symbol on their caps. I shall not however try to analyse the unconscious mechanisms through which Bettelheim may at some point have identified with the Nazis who were torturing him, or how he may have felt himself slowly regressing to infantile forms of behaviour when subjected to their ill-treatment. Such work can only be validly carried out from the inside; the observer can but draw up a list of clues, and put forward hypothetical interpretations. Bruno Bettelheim was a middle-class intellectual who disliked any form of disorder, albeit idealistic and revolutionary, an assimilated Jew who had a hard time accepting that he belonged to the same category as the religious, sidelock-wearing *Öst-Juden*, whose bigotry he condemned as obscurantist. He was also a frail man, very conscious of his lack of physical courage ('a cowardly lion' is how he would describe himself later, in better days[68]). It would seem logical that he initially perceived in himself the mechanisms that he was to describe in such detail in other people, but it is impossible to be any more conclusive than that.

If one does consider that hypothesis, however, it is easy to imagine the anxiety that such a discovery would have sparked in him, to picture how his need always to find the meaning of things would once again have served only to feed anger directed against himself. The opening pages of *Surviving* then take on an extra dimension, and one can better understand why, after describing the intellectual difficulties he had in finding a framework for his article, he writes: 'even harder was trying to deal with the anxiety-provoking and otherwise deeply upsetting memories which constantly intruded .... Trying to be objective became my intellectual defense against being overwhelmed by these perturbing feelings.'[69]

In a way, it was a good thing for Bettelheim that people did not believe him when he told them about the camps. In his case, indignation was a good coach; it allowed his anger and aggressive feelings to be directed outwards. It gave force to his writing. Once the article had been published, he could at last relax, freed of his feelings of remorse. His efforts had finally proved useful. And it was the man whose very name symbolized victory, 'Ike' himself, who had declared Bettelheim right against the sceptics. That was something he would remain proud of for the rest of his life.[70] He had accomplished his mission; he had succeeded in transforming his sufferings into a useful message. He could thus get on with his new life.

All would have been well if Bettelheim's old enemy within had not been lurking, on the lookout for any opportunity to come welling back up again. Perhaps his story-telling did it, or simply his growing renown, since the feeling of being a fraud seems always to have been at its strongest when he had scored some new success. Or perhaps it occurred when the first heaps of corpses were found in the camp that he had been able to get out of six years earlier.[71] Whatever the reason, the feeling is clearly apparent in the first letter Bettelheim sent to Ernst Federn when the latter was released from Buchenwald.

The letter was written from Chicago on July 11, 1945, the day after Bettelheim had been in Washington at the invitation of the War Department to record his affidavit on the camps for the Nuremberg Tribunal. That visit is the first thing he mentions, telling his former fellow-inmate that he is to be 'one of their main witnesses'. Interestingly, the letter is written in English. Even if, as Federn puts it, this was a way for Bettelheim to signify that he no longer wanted to have anything to do with the country that had persecuted him, I cannot but see it as also an affirmation of his new status as an American, *vis-à-vis* a man who had just spent seven years in the camp about which Bettelheim was now being viewed as an expert by the US government, even though he had only been there a few months.

Only in the second paragraph does Bettelheim seek to make real contact with his former camp companion. 'I do not know whether you still remember me. We spent some time together in Buchenwald. I was much more fortunate than you by being able to leave the camp.' The arrogance of the first paragraph is thus offset by the modesty of the second, into which one could even read an implicit acknowledgement that Federn would probably have been better placed to testify than he was.[72] '*It so happened* that I published an analysis of the concentration camp as a social institution, a study which received quite some attention (I think *undeservedly*) by such persons as, for example, Victor Serge, to mention only one name with which you still might be familiar,' the letter goes on (my italics).

'Undeservedly': here it is, the ugly whiff of fraud. As we have seen, the success of Bettelheim's article was anything but undeserved; not only did it display remarkable intelligence, but it was no doubt the most difficult piece of writing he had ever done, the one which had caused him the most painful soul-searching. But none of that effort and suffering had any intrinsic value for him, as the more important fact was his inner feeling that he had in some way cheated to gain the mantle of expert. Whence the extraordinary understatement: 'It so happened that ....'

Bruno Bettelheim had two ways of reacting to the nagging feeling that he was enjoying undeserved privileges. One was arrogance, which required him to be continually seeking further successes, distinctions and important names to drop. And the other, at the opposite extreme, was an excessive modesty, which those close to him sometimes found difficult to bear. With Federn, who was more experienced than he was in politics and camp life, but who was eleven years his junior, he would constantly switch from one to the other. In the letter, having both staked out his territory and acknowledged what could be seen as his 'fraud', he adopts a fatherly tone, stressing how pleased he is at his correspondent's release. He takes care to add that he went to see Federn's father (a celebrity, at least in psychoanalytic circles) as soon as he set foot in New York to make a few suggestions on how his son's release could be obtained. He also offers his services, mentioning in passing that he has given Ernst Federn's name to Judge Jackson's assistant as that of 'a reliable witness', and then tells him that he is now in charge of a school for disturbed children. In backing up this second 'admission' (subtext: 'Now I'm a psychoanalyst'), as with the first, he goes on to list his distinctions (U of C faculty member, head of the Orthogenic School), while skating over what makes it really important for him in just a few words: 'A job which interests me very much.'

Like Bettelheim's fellow Viennese exiles, Ernst Federn was never to betray his friend's little secrets. Being more tolerant of Bettelheim's failings than the latter was himself, he would simply stress on occasion that their views did not always coincide. As for the increasingly warlike tone that Bettelheim would adopt as the controversy over the camps intensified, Federn simply smiled, being better placed than anyone else to know that his former companion in misfortune would himself have been incapable of putting up a real fight. This was no doubt an amicable and understanding attitude, but one which left his friend alone, once again, to face his inner demons.

Much later, in his last book on the Orthogenic School, Bettelheim would write that the therapist for psychotic children is someone who can 'bridge the gap' between reason and the chaotic world of insanity. 'The difference between the patient and the therapist is that the therapist can at will walk back and forth across that bridge,' he went on.[73] And by then he had indeed spent three decades working tirelessly to cultivate that ability in the school's counsellors. In his own way, with obstinacy, severity and even brutality, but always attentively, encouraging the reticent and holding back the foolhardy. And above all, profoundly reassuring in his role of 'bridge-keeper'. However nobody else would be capable of crossing that bridge as spontaneously as he was, even though he had never benefited from anyone else's guidance. During the process through which he as it were trained himself, those around him had remained silent; just as, in his childhood, his well-meaning father had never reprimanded him. I believe that training process took place during those two years in which he wrestled with himself in order to get across a message that nobody wanted to hear. If the research he undertook while in Dachau as a means of survival was a way of carrying on the work he had begun on Richard Sterba's couch, its 'working through' was impossible while he was still in the camp. That process took place, through much suffering, when Bettelheim was obliged to analyse his experience to try to communicate it to other people. Little by little, and through much struggling with self-doubt, he was able to locate his own inner 'bridge' between madness and sanity, and thus the vantage-point from which he could address others. Thus did he in effect bring about his own rebirth, through self-analysis. The 'new Bettelheim' was indeed a psychoanalyst.

In any case, the idea of self-analysis was not as far removed from established psychoanalytic thinking as it is today. There was much discussion of its pros and cons, with those in favour often drawing their arguments from one of Freud's last texts, *Analysis, Terminable and Interminable*.[74] in which Freud recommended that once a young analyst had completed his training, he should continue to keep up with his own unconscious. *Self-Analysis*, by Karen Horney,[75] was published just at the time Bettelheim was writing his article. Horney, a Berlin-trained German analyst, had played a role in setting up the Chicago Psychoanalytic Institute along with Franz Alexander. At the time, she had just left the New York Psychoanalytic Society to set up a breakaway group, which diverged from orthodox Freudianism on several questions, notably the concept of 'penis envy'.[76] Bettelheim's friend Wanda Willig had in fact joined her group. While stressing its pitfalls and difficulties, Horney believed that self-analysis could be very fruitful, especially when carried out as a follow-up to a classic psychoanalysis.

Unlike most other critics of *The Informed Heart*, Franz Alexander acknowledged Bettelheim's self-analytical approach. 'This is a dignified book, convincing because it is not derived from textbook knowledge, but from insights gained in the laboratory of the author's own life,' he wrote, in an article which also noted the writer's unusual detachment from his subject, and saluted his 'fine introspection'.[77]

Bettelheim's approach to psychoanalysis was thus not entirely iconoclastic. What was rather special, however, was the way that approach meshed in with his concentration camp experience. This 'marriage', brought about in the extreme conditions of the camp, was to last throughout his life. It would colour Bruno Bettelheim's therapeutic work at the Orthogenic School, and as we shall see it also opened the way to his progressive rapprochement with Freudian thinking.

On November 27, 1946 Roy Grinker, secretary and treasurer of the Chicago Psychoanalytic Society, informed Bettelheim that he had been admitted as a non-clinical member. This meant that the Society authorized him to apply his psychoanalytic knowledge in the field or fields of his choice, with the exception of conventional treatment itself. His admission had been approved unanimously, on the basis of Bettelheim's presentation of his work on the concentration camps.

Bettelheim's relations with the official institutions of psychoanalysis were quickly to become tangled, however. A few months after his admission, the Society's Commission on Membership and Education, set up in

September 1946 in a bid to end the ascendancy of the 'moderns' over the training of new analysts and thus settle the main conflict between the two arms of the Chicago establishment, moved that he be admitted to the Institute. But Franz Alexander was against this, and Bettelheim never became either a training analyst or a member of the Institute. From 1951 to 1955 he was nevertheless allowed to hold a training seminar for child psychoanalysts. Very much later, in November 1973, six months after Bettelheim had retired and moved to California, he was to be made a life member of the Chicago Psychoanalytic Society thanks to Dr Charles Kliegerman, its president in that year. To have the decision adopted, Kliegerman had however to get round the violent hostility of many of his colleagues towards Bettelheim. And as if to underline the ambivalence of the decision, the letter informing him of it was mailed to the Chicago address he had been living at in 1946!

Chapter XI

Orthogenic School:
The Magical Years

So there you have the story of my life, and also the explanation why I
could devote it so single-mindedly to work strenuously to help children
overcome the damages their childhood experiences did to them.

Bruno Bettelheim, letter to
Carl Frankenstein, November 19, 1986

Meeting the former inhabitants of Bruno Bettelheim's school is rather like
visiting the members of a once-large family that is in the process of dying
out, or encountering an indigenous tribe in the final stages of assimilation.
There are memories that the interviewee at first hesitates to dig up,
fearful that they will not be understood, and that surge back after a while,
surprisingly intense and emotionally charged. Former loves and moments
of tenderness, jealousies and other scars that have lost little of their edge,
in some cases even hatreds. Full of shared references, jokes, and a common
language. 'That day, I was behaving very orthogenic.' The sentence just
slips out in the middle of the story: no need to translate. After four years
of investigation, the writer has indeed become used to the lingo. 'Orthogenic': that ugly word which Bruno Bettelheim inherited but which he
never liked, had over the years taken on for his charges (he rarely used the
word 'patient', preferring 'kid' or 'student'[1]) a meaning somewhat removed
from its etymological one. 'Orthogenic behaviour' was that of people who
took life seriously, who were, as we would say today, 'in touch with their
feelings', and who never did anything without thinking about why they
had done it. An idea which is somewhat too redolent of virtuous effort,
of playing the good student, to be very much fun. The kind of idea that
you laugh at, while suspecting that it may be good for you. For some
people, of course, it smacks of the straitjacket. They are among the
younger ones. For the others, who are more numerous, recalling it
sparks the amused, slightly self-mocking reactions that often come with
a childhood memory.

What is most striking when one meets a large number of former 'O.S.'
people is that, whatever their position – for or against Bettelheim – they
are all thinking men and women, who seek to understand and go beyond
surface appearances. Some will on occasion use flat-footed arguments

against Bettelheim: 'Do you realize that we weren't allowed to play base-ball?', while some in the opposing camp are a little too quick to reel off quotations from his books to be entirely sincere. But such facile weapons are merely polemical. What all these people have in common is a readiness to question received wisdom and never to take things at their face value. I did not meet a single one who could remotely be described as either a fool or a timeserver. Bruno Bettelheim did not believe that happiness could be achieved by simply closing one's eyes to reality; for him there was no such thing as a happy moron.[2] And the people who surrounded him for some thirty years certainly prove his point.

Like other tribes, the Bettelheim community has its clans and its outcasts. The former tend to be defined chronologically; as the time-span stretches from 1944 to 1973, the first recruits were long gone when the last generation entered the school. Some, however, kept in touch, returning to visit from time to time. They were held up as examples for the younger generation, rather like older brothers or sisters. Others would never ever go back, preferring to cross the street rather than risk bumping into anyone who might remind them of their time in that most unusual school. And yet others never got to make such a choice; they had left the school one day for a psychiatric institution, after which the tribe had lost track of them. This did not mean that they had been erased from people's memories. Some former students still cite the names of those lost sheep with great anger, seeing their fates as incontrovertible proof of their arguments. Others recall them with sadness, occasionally blended with fatalism and always with a dose of guilt. Again, what is striking is the existence of a link between all these people. Those who became outcasts, either voluntarily or involuntarily, have remained present in the collective memory, but more like ghosts than some kind of 'dark secret'. For although Bettelheim did seek to minimize the number of failures at the Orthogenic School, he never concealed the fact that such failures existed.

Now definitely grown-up – the oldest among the 'ex-kids' are going on sixty – the school's former students and counsellors are scattered all over the United States, and in some cases abroad (in France, Switzerland and Italy, for example). It is a rather quirky tribe, the members of which are not always easy to approach. The men tend to be abrupt, highly logical and somewhat aggressive, at least on first contact. The women are more varied. Some are very down-to-earth and 'up front'; warm, reassuring and practical. But although they are generally forthcoming about their expe-riences, unlike the men they are rarely categorical in their judgements. Other women are more reserved, waiting for the interviewer to bring up a subject before discussing it. But all have interesting things to say, and often raise questions which are difficult to answer.

It will not be possible to write the full history of Bruno Bettelheim's Orthogenic School until legal restrictions protecting the privacy of its former students no longer prevent the University of Chicago from declassifying all the relevant documents. Until then, with the exception of a handful of administrative papers released under the university's thirty-year rule, the researcher is reduced to relying on and comparing individual accounts. Which in most cases means trying to choose between the statements of people who have at some point in their lives been declared 'mad', or at least 'disturbed', and those of people whose entire careers were often founded on their experiences alongside Bruno Bettelheim. With both types of witness, the interviewer finds it at first near impossible to give an impartial hearing, fully respecting what everyone has to say. Faced with former students she finds herself veering between sympathy and a kind of unhealthy curiosity (*'If he was really crazy when he entered the place, what amazing progress he must have made there! But then was he really crazy at all?'*). And the second category of witness tends to inspire suspicion (*'Even if there were abuses, he (she) wouldn't tell me about them, of course, to avoid sullying his (her) reputation.'*).

The purpose of this book is to tell Bettelheim's life-story, not that of his school. However interesting the stories of his individual patients may be, they have no place in it. And indeed, to talk about them they would have to be handled as 'cases', which would mean hiding them under false names,[3] and that would be contrary to this writer's approach. Having ploughed through countless case studies, I can see all too well how the use of an alias allows one to take liberties with the truth and overlook awkward details. Bettelheim himself pointed this out in his second book on the school.[4] This may be of little significance for the specialist, whose only concern is with clinical technique. But for the man whose history I am trying to trace, the 'cases' he was surrounded by, day in, day out, were real live people. Each with his or her own face, way of talking and moving, smiling or crying. Their movements were often disorderly, they shouted or screamed, made unreasonable demands or suffered from irrational fears: in short their actions triggered off strong reactions in him. They were human beings, children; anything but 'cases'. Which is why, rather than adopting a pseudo-scientific stand to discuss them and their problems, I think it better to enter the world that was Bettelheim's during a good third of his life as a voyager free of preconceived dogmas but with ears, eyes and heart wide open to the discovery.

A number of impressions quickly harden into certainties. For example, that the tribe's patriarch was feared by all its members. He was always there, omnipotent and ubiquitous. Some worshipped him; a few hated him. But was that quite as true at the time? It is interesting to discover, for example, that at least two of the people who now number among his most virulent detractors suffered when they were students from not being among his favourites (the researcher seeking to understand what went on in the O.S. is continually being faced with such dilemmas). Before setting out to explore the strange universe of the Orthogenic School, those whose image of it has been shaped solely by reading *The Empty Fortress* and the three other books that Bettelheim devoted to it will need to jettison a few received ideas.

First and foremost Bettelheim did not love children – he understood them. And he used all the means at his disposal to try to unlock the mental universe which not only prevented them from leading normal lives, but also caused them great suffering, as he was one of the first writers to point out. He did however love *some* children. At the school, as in his classes, he always had his favourites. Those were more often girls than boys, but not always, and they could generally twist him round their little fingers. On one occasion, for example, he spent hours feeding an anorexic girl who had arrived at the school on a stretcher. By patiently getting her to swallow one raisin at a time, he literally saved her life.

But the fact that Bettelheim laid great stress on listening to and understanding the children in his care does not imply that he was brimming over with love for all of them. Nothing could be farther from the truth; indeed the mawkish image of Bettelheim projected by many of his admirers does a terrible disservice to all concerned. First, it is damaging to some of the former children whom he tried to help, because it presents them with a distorted picture of that essential experience in their lives, and thus affects to this day the very relationship to reality that Bettelheim tried to foster in them. Secondly, because it is simply untrue, the fairy-tale image tends to obscure the true value of Bettelheim's contribution. When passing through the famous yellow door that leads into the Orthogenic School, at 1365 East 60th Street in Chicago's South Side, this is one preconception that the reader must leave behind.

In its place, let's pick up the very large 'white pebble' that forms the title of Bettelheim's first book. *Love is Not Enough*, Bettelheim tells us; in other words, 'What I give these children is something else.' Implied meaning: 'You, with your love, have all too often done them more harm than good.' In an article published in 1949, he put it in a nutshell: 'With the exception of love at first sight, an adult's immediate love for a child can only be due to emotional starvation and keeps the child from one of the most maturing experiences – that of a slowly developing, mutually satisfying personal relationship.'[5]

Another certainty that the researcher acquires on speaking to people who worked with Bettelheim throughout his life – not only the counsellors, but also the mothers whom he brought together every Wednesday over a four-year period to advise them on bringing up their children, and the young psychologists and psychiatrists that he helped, first in Chicago and then later in Stanford, to understand how to treat their patients – concerns his power of insight. Bruno Bettelheim had the rare gift of being able at a glance to read through someone's behaviour, and even more to grasp the internal workings of a relationship between two people. He could feel instantly where the pain was. He was sometimes wrong, but rarely. It was this intuition that allowed him, for thirty years, to do everything in his power, everything he believed appropriate, to help the children in his charge become independent and responsible individuals. Here again, the word 'everything' has implications which sit uneasily with the kindly and rather harmless image that his books may give of him. Curing his charges was, and remained to the end, his number one priority. This led him on occasion to use controversial methods, and to systematically exploit his counsellors. Most of the latter have no regrets on that score: they see it as the price to be paid for a unique formative experience which, they all agree, they have used ever since. It is nevertheless essential to point out that Bettelheim, while being capable of great compassion, was not a 'Mr Nice Guy'. He was a man with a mission, a survivor who had made a choice and stuck to it.

One last observation: the Orthogenic School was a living organism, in continual motion and development throughout the thirty years that Bettelheim spent as its head. That period can broadly speaking be broken down into three stages, each lasting roughly a decade. They are the years of discovery, the years of fame and the run-up to Bettelheim's succession. The evolution obviously corresponds to developments in his own life, but it also reflects deep social changes in the world outside, in people's hopes and in the moral climate. Such changes could not but affect the tiny world of the school, which for a time was to be in the forefront of the age: a model and a unique experiment.

The early years were an extraordinary, almost magical time. In spite of his reluctance at taking over the school, Bettelheim was quick to grasp its potential. Although a heavy responsibility, it did provide an opportunity to try out all those ideas that he and his friends had been talking about over the previous twenty years. And of course the opportunity for him to show his true mettle, to put his past far behind him. He was not alone, and Trude's influence had been decisive in persuading him to take on the new job. Not only had she, as usual, reassured him that he could do it, but she was able to contribute her years of experience as a Montessori teacher. Bettelheim also turned for advice to his faithful friend Fritz Redl, whose reputation in the treatment of disturbed adolescents was by now well established in the States – a collaboration he duly acknowledged in his first book. 'My long and close friendship with Fritz Redl has helped me immensely in developing the School's working philosophy and in setting it into practice. Our many conversations and our constant exchange of ideas have now created a situation in which I no longer know exactly where his ideas end and mine begin,' he wrote.[6]

For practical help, Bettelheim also called on Emmy Sylvester, who was already acknowledged as a brilliant child psychoanalyst, and whom he soon had appointed psychiatric consultant at the Orthogenic School. In her, Bettelheim found an interlocutor on a par with himself. Although seven years his junior, she possessed the very academic qualifications that he lacked. A medical doctor, she had also earned a PhD in child psychology at the University of Vienna in 1932, while working both as an assistant to Charlotte Bühler in the Psychology Institute and in the university's paediatric clinic. She had been in analysis with Editha Sterba and followed seminars at the Psychoanalytic Institute, taking on her first patients under the supervision of Richard Sterba and a member of Freud's circle, Jeanne Lampl-de Grot. After leaving Vienna at the time of the Anschluss, Emmy Sylvester had continued her psychoanalytic training at the Chicago Institute, supervised by Franz Alexander, while doing an internship in psychiatry at Michael Reese Hospital.

Although Emmy Sylvester's qualifications and experience were no doubt reassuring for Bettelheim, the key to their close working relationship lay elsewhere. They had the same type of intuitive intelligence, the same need to go straight to the point, the same Viennese charm and arrogance. And even the same way of being aggressive. In the early days of her work at Michael Reese Hospital, for instance, Sylvester had been introduced to a patient who was distractedly wandering the corridors, repeating: 'Oh, I feel guilty, I feel so guilty.' The man had been interned after murdering his father. She took one look at him and shot back: 'And you're damned right, because you *are* guilty.' Her colleagues, who had always used the opposite tactics to try and pacify this clearly violent patient, were stunned. Telling the story later to a few friends, Emmy Sylvester confessed, a little sheepishly, that her reaction had been completely spontaneous. But she added that, far from disturbing the patient, it had calmed him down instantly.

Working with Emmy Sylvester, Bettelheim was to lay the theoretical foundations of the Orthogenic School. Drawing on the way August Aichorn had used psychoanalysis to treat juvenile delinquents in Vienna,[7] they would carry out the first real-life experiment in total 'milieu therapy' – i.e. the creation of a living environment in which every single detail of everyday life was designed with a view to the treatment of its occupants. The latter's needs, as well as the therapeutic methods, were conceived entirely on the basis of Sigmund Freud's teachings. As Bettelheim and Sylvester would write later, once practical results had started to back up their theory, 'Milieu therapy is not new as a psychotherapeutic technique. It is no more than the application of psychoanalytical concepts to the specific task of creating a setting for emotionally disturbed children who are in need of residential treatment.'[8] The Orthogenic School was therefore designed as a place where 'psychoanalytic concepts [were put] in action'. It offered its occupants what they could not get from individual psychotherapy sessions – a life in which their psychological development was catered for twenty-four hours a day, seven days a week. That idea was the cornerstone of the whole edifice.

'Don't forget, at that time mad children were seen as bad children,' says Patty Pickett, who worked as a counsellor at the Orthogenic School from autumn 1946 to summer 1952.[9] To write psychoanalytic theory into the constitution of an institution for severely disturbed children was indeed a revolutionary act. It was to state that people labelled as insane were not in fact fundamentally different from the rest of us, that their difficulties in life were due to damage sustained during their emotional development, rather than to some original sin in their or their parents' past. The mentally ill were no longer monsters, but simply sick people. Their condition resulted from neither a curse nor divine punishment; it was simply a type of malfunction, and could thus be repaired.

The idea was simple enough, but its implications for everyday life in the school were not. If the mad were not evil, but simply sick, then they should no longer be punished or locked up, but treated. Which involved trying at every point to alleviate their suffering and to determine the inner reasons for their strange behaviour. Accepting that when a child attacked another, bit his counsellor, beat his head against a wall, ran away, screamed without apparent reason, wet his bed or excreted into his bathwater, threw furniture out the window or into the stairway, he was not doing this to annoy other people, but simply because he was suffering. And that this behaviour was the most effective way he had found to alleviate his inner torment. Which was the reasoning behind the two golden rules of the school, incumbent on everyone from the director down to the maintenance staff: to make life as easy and pleasant as possible for the children and to try to understand what lay behind their 'crazy' behaviour, rather than seeking simply to make it go away. Even though such ideas were implicit in Freud's thinking, they had never before been implemented in a residential institution for the mentally ill.[10]

'There was an atmosphere. You could feel it: "something is working here." It was like a great big stew, with the emotions and everything, and something was holding it together – his conviction, the dedication of the staff.' Patty Pickett was twenty-one, and had four years in college behind her when she knocked on the door of the Orthogenic School, looking for a job to help her pay her way through her studies in the Committee for Human Development. Having grown up in the very conventional setting of small-town Illinois, and being unused to hearing people raise their voices, she was amazed at the way the children were allowed to behave in this very strange school. 'We didn't judge them, we tried to understand them. To create an environment in which they could feel accepted. Dr B was always telling us: "These kids have a right to be here. They have a right to their behavior, given the way they've been treated." And after a while, because we were kind to them, because we accepted them, you could see it: the kids were getting better.'

In order to get to that point, however, Bettelheim first had had to move mountains. But he had to use tact, and be careful not to scare anyone – least of all the children, but also the university and the handful of rich donors who supported the school. The latter, although shocked by the parlous physical state of the institution, were not ready to fund a revolution. At that time, the school was home to around thirty full-time students, all boys, plus a handful of day-pupils. For a full decade already it had stopped taking in mentally retarded children, and accepted only those with psychological problems. But most of these did not correspond to the type of child Bettelheim and Sylvester wanted to carry out the experiment with. They were either too deeply disturbed, or had already spent too much time in institutions for there to be any reasonable hope of curing them before they reached the age limit for the school, which at the time was fourteen. And in spite of his lack of experience, or perhaps because of it, curing his charges was Bettelheim's only objective. He had no intention of presiding over a holding centre for incurably sick children. However, he could not simply eject in one day all those children or staff members who did not fit in with his project. In fact, he spent a lot of time finding adequate placement in other institutions for the former. The departure of the adults too was gradual. Finally, only one teacher, a Miss Lukes, stayed on.

In recruiting his counsellors, Bettelheim was able to harness the university's aims for the school – seen as a training centre as much as a therapeutic one[11] – to his own ends. Rather than taking on counsellors who were already set in their ways and working methods, he preferred training the people he would work with himself. His three years' teaching at Rockford College had shown how good he was at getting through to, and stimulating the enthusiasm of, young women students keen to serve a worthy cause. And that was the kind of help he needed for this adventurous undertaking. Financial considerations no doubt also played a role in his decision. For the school was poor and what Bettelheim had in mind for it required money.

Betty-Lou Pingree and Marjorie Jewell, two of the three psychology students who had accepted Bettelheim's job offer, had arrived at the school in early September 1944. Inexperienced, but eager to please the man they referred to since Rockford only as 'Dr B', they immediately took a group of boys out to play football on the Midway. With the best of intentions, they plunged into the game, kicking at the ball with as much energy as their charges. In the space of a few minutes, the latter had become angry and totally unruly – one of them had even torn a sleeve off Betty-Lou's blouse. When the two young women finally managed to return to the school with all the boys, Bettelheim was waiting for them in the hall. The two were completely shattered. Weighing up the situation at a glance, Dr B got a nurse from the previous team to look after the children, while Betty-Lou and Marjorie retired to their room in tears. They felt humiliated by their failure. Later that evening, Bettelheim took them to his apartment, a few yards away from the school. There, they sat with Trude, and he explained where they had gone wrong. By behaving in the same way as the children, Betty-Lou and Marje had triggered the anxiety of their charges; by becoming like them they had given up their control of the play, and with it their ability to protect the boys. Which was why, he explained, the children had got into a rage with them. 'Day one, lesson one,' concluded Betty-Lou Pingree, recalling the incident forty-two years later.[12]

The first change Bettelheim ordered was that even regular bedwetters were not to be woken up during the night. In the morning, he wanted their sheets changed without any fuss or any remark likely to make them feel guilty. One day, in one of the children's bathrooms, he noticed a chart on the wall. 'What's this?' he asked. Betty-Lou explained that the night nurse wanted the children's bowel movements recorded daily, in order to determine their laxative doses. Bettelheim snatched the chart off the wall, and 'that was the end of that,' says Pingree. Then, he had the locks of the various doors changed so that one key could open them all and that the counsellors stopped looking like prison wardens with bunches of keys dangling from their belts.

During the first month, Mandel Sherman and his students continued to come and go, while the incoming team gradually eased into the driving seat. In the basement of the building was a large laboratory full of forbidding-looking machines, which intrigued the newcomers. Bettelheim's first act, after the surgical bed and the EEG and other electrical gear had been moved out, was to rip down the black drapes covering the windows, and replace them with patterned linen curtains. He then had a ping-pong table installed in the place, which was designated the games room.

Ronnie Dryovage, the third Rockford student to respond to Bettelheim's invitation, arrived at the school soon afterwards. One of the first tasks she undertook was similarly to spruce up the children's dormitories. But it was no doubt the hiring of the fourth counsellor, Gayle Shulenberger,[13] a few weeks later, that best sums up the way the school operated during that transitional period. Gayle had come to Chicago with her depressive sister-in-law and the latter's baby, while her brother was away fighting in Europe; she did not dare abandon the two of them. She was looking for an office job, preferably 'somewhere with children'. The university had thus put her in touch with the Orthogenic School, where the secretary asked about her experience. As she had practically none, Gayle mentioned that when in high school, she had occasionally been sent to watch over some younger children when one of the teachers was absent. The secretary dutifully noted 'a little teaching'. The only job available was a fill-in for the night nurse, who was leaving for two weeks' vacation. 'So I met this woman, who looked like the Wicked Witch of the West in her uniform. And I thought this was the craziest place I'd ever seen in my life. There were children with epileptic seizures, there was a mixture of all kinds of kids. It didn't make any sense. But I was fascinated. So I slept there and my only job was, if a kid came and knocked on my door at night, I'd jump up .... There was one very disturbed boy who looked like he belonged in a mental hospital and who had been there forever. They were trying to find a placement for him. He had a complete set of keys that he had had made and the nurse told me disapprovingly that the director didn't want them taken away from him. Knowing nothing, I thought, "Good for the director." '

'So, that night, everybody was asleep, except this kid who was walking around the hall. I followed him around and he locked himself inside the broom closet. So, I sat outside the closet, and I heard him say: "Don't take away my beautiful keys, my beautiful keys, my beautiful keys .... Don't take away ...." I didn't have anything to do, so I counted how many times he said it and it came to about seventy times. Then, there was a pause and he started again: "Don't take away ...." So I said: "I won't take away your beautiful keys." and this went on for a long, long time. But, each time he said it, he said it less. I asked: "Are you hungry? I'll get you some food." I don't think he talked to me. I went down and got him some food and went away. And when I came back he'd eaten the food and left me the plate. Then, later, I would go and check that he was asleep.'

The same scenario was played out on every night of the two weeks. When the night nurse returned, Gayle was offered a job as an assistant counsellor, which involved looking after the handful of children who opted to stay behind at the school when the others went on an outing. She had met Bettelheim only once, on the first evening. He had asked her where she was from, and she had told him a little about her childhood on a farm in South Dakota, amid a flock of cousins. With his strange accent, he had remarked that she was the first native of that state he had met, and that had been the end of the conversation. But Gayle continued exploring her new world. Among the children she occasionally cared for in the afternoon was a certain Nicky, who had been described to her as mentally retarded. Without telling a soul, she started observing him; he played the piano a little, and also spoke on occasion. She became so sure that he was not retarded that on returning home each day she made notes on his behaviour. Later, when she had got to know Bettelheim more, she raised the subject with him. He burst out laughing: 'Of course he isn't retarded. Why do you ask?' When she told him that she had filled up several notebooks on him, he chided her for not having brought them straight to him. At the time, though, Gayle would not have dared.

It was when she sat in on her first staff meeting that the penny finally dropped. 'We were all in the living room and this man comes in and he starts talking about everything that's wrong in this place and how he's changing it. And I thought, 'My God, he knows it!' and I remember walking home that night: I was walking on air. Because that was the most exciting time in my life.'

This account not only tells a lot about the empirical way staff were recruited in the early stages of the school, but it also gives an insight into what was to make those first years such a magic time. Into Bruno Bettelheim's charisma, and the way he could, with only a few words, make each person who worked with him feel like a true pioneer. 'We were convinced that we were doing something very revolutionary, something that had never been done before,' Gayle recalls. 'I wouldn't have changed places with anyone, even if I had had to work twenty-four hours a day.' Forty years on, all the first counsellors have retained similar impressions.

Through her recollections, Gayle also gives an insight into the personalities of many of the young women on whom Bettelheim was to rely to help him build his school. Although often both shy and naïve, they were sharp-witted, and not about to swallow just anything they were told about their charges. It was not in their nature to throw in the sponge when faced with a case they had been told was incurable; instead they would draw on all the resources of their imagination to detect the chink in the child's armour, and thus make contact. These young women had grown up during the Depression, and many of them came from families which had known bad times. They were hard workers, and wanted to feel that their labour was doing some good. Nicky and the 'key boy' did not stay at the school; they had already spent too much time in institutions, burdened with an 'incurable' label. But with the help of two welfare agencies whose officials had soon been impressed by his eloquence, and probably also by his camp experience, Bettelheim went about choosing new students, as and when he found placements for the ones he had inherited. It was a very slow process. According to *Truants from Life*, which was published in 1955, it was only in the fall of 1947, three years after his appointment, that the Orthogenic School was running in full accord with his ideas.

If the counsellors were at first recruited more or less by chance among the young people drawn to the university but not sufficiently well off to pay for both the tuition and their living expenses, the children, on the other hand, were carefully selected. The diagnosis was not the most important factor. Psychoanalysis, psychology and psychiatry were all in fashion, and words like 'schizophrenic', 'schizoid', and 'disturbed' were bandied about somewhat loosely. Kanner had recently provided a clinical definition of autism, but in those first years the school was not yet taking in such severe cases. On the criteria for selection, Bettelheim himself spoke of 'primary behavior disorders'. Whether they were delinquents or runaways, hyperactive, suicidal, sufferers from hospitalism[14] or afflicted with truly schizophrenic traits, however, the first students generally had two things in common: intelligence that was at least normal and in many cases above average, and behavioural problems affecting their lives in several areas. 'If they'd simply had problems at school, they could have been treated in connection with their families. If their problem had been at home, another type of therapy would have been possible. We took them only when they didn't succeed anywhere,' says Gayle. They were basically 'problem children', either rejected by, or incapable of living with, their parents, and who, if admitted to an orphanage or other residential centre, quickly found themselves in trouble because of their uncontrollable violence or their inability to form normal relationships. In other words, children unwanted by the rest of the world, and who had nowhere to go.

In each case, nevertheless, somebody somewhere, be it a social worker, psychiatrist, psychologist, doctor or teacher, had reckoned that the child could be cured, if provided with appropriate treatment, and that he or she had a fighting chance of one day becoming an autonomous adult. In which case the child would be referred, generally by either the Jewish Children Bureau or the Illinois Child Services, to the Orthogenic School. There was a trial period of a few weeks. After meeting the child, the staff and Bettelheim would decide in which group to put him, while leaving open the possibility for him to change to another one if he felt more comfortable with it. The aim was to see if at least one adult was able to establish contact with the newcomer. That was the basic condition for his admission. 'We wanted kids that we could help,' says Gayle. In fact, rejection at this stage was rare, and would generally be viewed by the counsellors as a failure on their part. 'On paper, they always looked sicker than in real life,' says Gayle, true to form.

The aim was indeed to achieve a complete cure for the children. 'We expected them to make it .... It was going to be hard. It's never easy to give up an old way and all growth is painful, as he said lots of times. But I was absolutely convinced that he knew what he was talking about,' says Patty Pickett of Bettelheim. 'And when we started to see results, we were hardly surprised at all.' That was indeed what made the school magical; these inexperienced, but intelligent and courageous, young women pouring all their energy and imagination into serving a challenging idea which was given shining clarity by the way in which Bruno Bettelheim and Emmy Sylvester developed it. What was meant by 'cure' was understood by all to be the ability to take control of one's own life, to behave as a responsible, independent adult. 'To stand up on one's own two feet,' as Bettelheim had learned to do in the camps.[15]

The method was to be created empirically, step by step over time, with each one making their own contribution. The team built up around Bruno Bettelheim did not simply apply his instructions; they played a role in elaborating them. It was a process of mutual exchange which went on twenty-four hours a day, seven days a week. And indeed Bettelheim gave credit where credit was due, warmly paying homage to his collaborators in all of his books on the school. He and Emmy Sylvester were the theoreticians and the guides, but the counsellors were in constant contact with the kids. So Bettelheim had asked them to record their observations on their charges. Not their ideas or analyses, but simply what they had seen and heard. Nothing should be left out, as even the smallest detail could be significant. He wanted this done every day if possible, while the impressions were still fresh.[16] He would then read everything, and if he did not feel he was getting the full picture, he would make it known. Like the day he showed up at a staff meeting and said: 'I have read all your dictations with great attention, and I have some important news for you.' With all eyes fixed on him, he concluded: 'None of our children has been to the toilet for the last two weeks!'

Some counsellors had a real gift for drawing up their reports. Gayle, for example, clearly had an eye for detail, and jotted down her impressions in a spontaneous, lively and often amusing style. Others found this part of their duties an ordeal, and their dictations were much less detailed. But the mere fact that they had to pay attention to every detail made them much more conscious of the children's behaviour, deepening their understanding. At the same time, their observations provided grist for the theoretical mills of Bruno Bettelheim and Emmy Sylvester.

The latter came to the school every Friday, and saw two or three children individually, after which a meeting would be devoted to those children, with their respective counsellors. All the former staff members I was able to interview recalled those meetings as a revelation; for many of them Emmy Sylvester became a role model. The effect of her remarkable intelligence, extensive culture and cutting wit was certainly enhanced by the fact that she was both beautiful and an elegant dresser; Bettelheim himself was always very attentive to her. But she impressed them above all with her ability, whatever the subject under discussion, to turn things round so as to see them from the child's viewpoint. Bettelheim would engage her in discussion, and their young American listeners would be fascinated by a dialogue that blended intuition, wit, concern for the children and scholarliness. Little by little, even the most obscure of vistas would become clearer, and explanations would emerge for the strangest types of behaviour. Listening to the two Viennese, the counsellors felt they were discovering, week after week, the essential meaning of what they had just lived through, but which had not struck them at the time as significant. Yet Emmy Sylvester continually insisted on the key role being played by the counsellors. 'She made us feel like queens,' says Gayle Shulenberger. 'She was always telling us that what we were doing with the kids was marvellous. Nobody else ever showed so much respect for our work. Listening to her, you'd think it was us who were the real therapists.'

So it appears that Emmy Sylvester played a leading role in getting Bruno Bettelheim to develop, or at least to make use of, what was to become his most distinctive quality, the one which would impress all the young therapists who were to work with him, and which can still be detected in the seminars that he was giving shortly before his death.[17] To wit, his ability to surmise instantaneously where a child's suffering was coming from; the famous 'empathy' which he would make into the corner-stone of his therapeutic method. Sylvester would kick off the conversation and he would listen, respectful both of what she had to say and of the relationship she had with the counsellors. Then he would take up where she left off, pushing the analysis a little farther, bringing in a new piece of interpretation. Their relationship appeared to be based on mutual respect and involvement, and devoid of any trace of the rivalry that some of the same young observers could often detect in conversations between Bettel-heim and Fritz Redl, who was another frequent visitor to the school during the early years.

Nevertheless, at the start of the 1950s Emmy Sylvester was abruptly to break off all contact with Bettelheim, accusing him (not publicly, however) of having appropriated all the credit for what had been their joint under-taking, and which he was in the process of turning into a famous institution. 'He's a monster,' she is even rumoured to have said, within the small circle of Bettelheim's early collaborators.[18] Nobody, however, was able to tell me exactly which incident, if any, sparked her decision to up and leave for California. Among other differences of opinion, one con-cerned authorship: she apparently wanted to restrict their publications to academic journals, while he was already keen to reach out to the widest possible audience. In all, they were to co-sign six articles, all of which appeared in psychoanalytic reviews.[19] Indeed, their articles are, of all Bruno Bettelheim's writings, the most classically psychoanalytical. And the split did occur when he was bringing out *Love is Not Enough*, a work aimed at reaching beyond specialist circles to everyone interested in children's problems. That being said, it is also noteworthy that, although Emmy Sylvester was undoubtedly both brilliant and creative, she in fact published very little in her own name. So, obviously, Bettelheim too brought something to their relationship.

As regards the Orthogenic School itself, the question is no simpler. This was another of those situations in which Bruno Bettelheim, while having a pressing need to feel reassured as to his ability (or maybe his moral right) to carry out a task, at the same time possessed all the abilities needed to do so. For although Emmy Sylvester may well have shown him how to use his intuitive understanding of other people in order to help his young patients, it is clear that that faculty had to be there in the first place. No doubt having her at his side in 1947 when they first presented their work to the American Orthopsychiatric Association's Annual Meeting helped give him self-assurance. But once he had received confirmation that he had the right to do what he was doing, his innate therapeutic gifts were there to let him advance under his own steam. Indeed, although Bettelheim and Sylvester were very similar in their way of looking at problems, their practical approaches were markedly different. Ronnie Dryovage, who had great admiration for Emmy Sylvester, nevertheless says: 'She was very intuitive and very learned. More intellectual than he was. But I never felt warmth emanating from her, whereas Dr B was real, warm and very concerned.' An opinion shared by two of Emmy Sylvester's former patients. 'She didn't have the same empathy as Dr B. She was very sharp and knew all the theory. She was a very good teacher. But she asked intrusive questions and didn't give me the feeling that she wanted me to get better the way he did. In fact, I hated my sessions with her,' says Bert Cohler, for example.[20]

For as Patty Pickett also points out, there was much more to the school than meetings and analyses: above all there was everyday life, with upwards of thirty very difficult children. And once Emmy Sylvester, Fritz Redl or any other outside consultant had left the premises, it was Bruno Bettelheim who stayed behind, in charge and always available, ready to seek the most 'orthogenic' solution to the problems that never failed to arise. For behind the lofty principles of the school, the actual nitty-gritty of putting the children first, even the least attractive amongst them, was a tough discipline, forcing one continually to question one's reactions, however spontaneous. Such as the day when Patty complained to Dr B about a new child who had been assigned to the older boys' dorm, of which she was in charge. As usual, outings for the group had been suspended until such time as the newcomer felt sufficiently at ease with the others to be able to take a bus or a train without anxiety, or without behaving in too disorderly a way. What drove Patty to exasperation was that the new boy continued to be very aggressive, and she found the situation unfair. Not only were the other boys, who had learned so well how to behave in public, being deprived of their regular outings to the Science Museum, the Observatory or the movies, but they were also having to put up with continual attacks from the newcomer, who had been sparking fights in the dormitory every night since his arrival. Patty was expecting a little sympathy from Dr B, or at least some advice, but certainly not the response she got. 'And what have you done for him recently?' he asked. Being a good counsellor, she had immediately got the message: her complaint proved that she was more worried about the overall functioning of the group than by the needs of the new boy. And the latter's aggressiveness was probably caused, at least partly, by what he saw as a rejection on her part. Indeed, after a lot of attention from her, a few weeks later the boy's behaviour had calmed down sufficiently for the group to be able to resume its outings.

Letting children's symptoms express themselves freely, day after day, was by no means easy. Gayle, for example, was in charge, among others, of a seven-year-old boy to whom Bettelheim gave the name of 'Harry'.[21] His particular problem was running away, which meant that for six weeks Gayle spent every evening ('except two', she specifies, discussing the affair as if it had all only happened yesterday) waiting up for him to come back, which would usually be between midnight and one in the morning. Then she would feed him, give him his bath and put him to bed. Until the day when Harry suddenly showed up at three o'clock in the afternoon, just as Gayle was starting her afternoon shift!

Another of Gayle's charges, identified in Bettelheim's writings as 'Paul',[22] recalls the atmosphere in the school dining room. 'A lot of antics went on during the meals .... Everybody was together in a room, eating, and there were different tables and there were lots of distractions. Some kid would pick up his dish and throw it on the floor and that would upset the next table, and they would spill their milk and some kid would go into his shell and crawl underneath the table sucking his thumb, and it was a kind of an abominable thing .... He [Bettelheim] would say: "What's going on here? Get up, sit down!" – just like any parent at the end of his tether. And things would calm down.'[23]

At all times the children had to be reassured that they were safe, shown that they were accepted as they were and that nobody in the school saw them as monsters, even when they screamed, bit, kicked, soiled or wet themselves day and night, flooded the bathrooms or the stairway, or even if they stole (Bettelheim was merciless with any adult who had money stolen, accusing them of having exposed the children to temptation by leaving it lying around). At the same time the children had to be shown that although their behaviour was being accepted, because it was a comfort to them, it was not the best way for them to escape from their suffering and solitude. Little by little, they had to be convinced to give up their defensive behaviour, so inadequate for living in society.

All the adults in the school were steeped in this philosophy, which was at the time even more revolutionary than now. That meant all the staff, including the cook and the maintenance man (who for example had on one occasion to repair all the toilets in the building several times a day for several weeks, because one newly arrived boy could only overcome his terror of losing part of his body by stuffing the most varied objects down them), plus the secretaries, the cleaning women and the switchboard operator. 'Very few people said "I" in the school: it was "we". We were all working together toward that very important goal, each one in our own way,' says Mary-Ellen Cowan, who headed Bettelheim's secretariat, acted as his administrative liaison with the university and supervised the kitchen and all the maintenance staff for six years. She never hired anyone without first making sure that they could put up with such conditions. 'Anybody self-centred or who thought they knew it all, I turned down immediately. I made it clear to them that the school was run for the children, but I added that if they stayed the course they would find a lot for themselves too,' says Mary-Ellen, who also did the first screening of prospective counsellors. 'I knew the type of people Dr. Bettelheim was looking for. It is not easy to verbalize .... There was a feeling about them, a dedication, a caring, a desire to be part of it .... Sincerity was paramount. More so than experience. Because he had an innate ability to see in each of us what we could do, far beyond what we had achieved before or thought we could achieve. Dr B also had the reputation for liking pretty girls, and he did. But that was never enough.'[24]

At that time the school was housed in a single building, a good-sized house but one that had to accommodate both the children and their counsellors (the teachers in general did not live in). There were thirty-two full-time boarders and three day-pupils. Groups of six (and later eight) children were formed on the basis of dormitories. As well as the child's own choices, and his relationships with at least one counsellor, the team was also attentive to the influence that the children had on one another. It had only taken a short time for them to realize how important that influence was. One day, as 'Harry' was coming back from yet another escapade, one of his dorm-mates, himself a former runaway, whispered to the others: 'Remember guys, "thin air"!' Gayle, who overheard the exchange, was baffled. When 'Harry' entered the room, instead of listening to the fantastic adventures he claimed to have had during his outing, the seven boys simply kept on talking amongst themselves, as if 'Harry' was indeed 'thin air'. This went on for the whole evening, and happened a second time, after which 'Harry' finally got the message. 'They talked through him .... And he was so furious. I had nothing to do with it,' says Gayle. 'But they too were mad at him for behaving so stupidly. In my view, that was the most amazing thing; the tremendous investment the children had in each other. It was as though the progress made by one child showed the way to the others. And they weren't about to let it go to waste.'

In the evening, when the children were at last in bed, the adults would get together downstairs, in the kitchen. However late it was by the time the last counsellor had tucked up the last of her children, Bettelheim would always be there to greet her with a cup of tea. They would go over the events of the day, and if it was not too late, someone would often ask: 'Dr B, tell us about Vienna.' And Bettelheim would always have some interesting story to tell about Anna Freud, Wilhelm Reich and so on. Then, he would go back to his office; it was the only time of day when he could write. He would often not get home before four in the morning.

He was nevertheless back at the school every morning around ten thirty (and earlier still, in the first months). His smallish office was located next to the secretaries' on the ground floor. It was open to all, children and adults, and to prove it, the door stayed ajar, except when he had visitors. Close by there was a small bench for people who wanted to wait, or simply to cool down before going in to see him. On his desk, which was always tidy and almost empty, was a pink pig-shaped cookie jar, from which each child who came to see him was invited to help himself. Which did not in any way prevent Bettelheim from giving his charge a good dressing-down immediately afterwards, if he deemed it necessary – if he thought it would be reassuring for the child to have clear limits laid down for his behaviour. 'Bruno was a wonderful actor. He could put on an act of being terribly angry, while at the same time giving a wink to whatever adult was present in the room,' recalls Gayle, echoed by both Patty Pickett and Bert Cohler. The latter adds: 'In my opinion, even in later years, he never got carried away with a child. He always knew exactly what he was doing.' Not everyone agrees on that last point, however.

But Bettelheim was certainly the ultimate source of discipline in the school. 'I am the Big Bad Wolf here,' he used to say. And indeed there was a need for one. In order for the counsellors to devote all their efforts to being caring mothers, there had to be someone they could rely on to let out a growl or two when things got out of hand. The very early counsellors are unanimous in saying that they never saw him actually hit a child. But even at that time, his comments could be extremely hard to take. Patty remembers a child who was about to leave, having reached the age limit of fourteen. One day he went wild, shouting, 'I'm going to my father's! I'm going to my father's!' She tried to calm him down, but nothing would do it. He was brandishing a suitcase when Bettelheim walked into the dormitory. 'And just when did you last see your father?' he asked him coldly. That stopped the boy in his tracks: for several years already he had stopped hearing from his father. The incident left Patty almost in tears. On reflection, however, she now believes that the reason Bettelheim appeared so cruel was that the boy was about to find himself confronted with the real world, where he would not be able to survive if he kept on deluding himself. She is convinced that he would not have spoken to him in the same way two years earlier. But most of the time Dr B did not even need to raise his voice; his very presence was enough for calm to return. Gayle also recalls that on certain occasions one or another of the boys would go up to his office, not even to talk to him, but just to check that he was there. The children feared him, but they were not scared of him. On the contrary, his presence was reassuring for them. At mealtimes, it was common for a child to go over to the staff table, to chat with Dr B. Some of them even made a point of doing so, as the act gave them kudos with those who were less daring. Bettelheim would answer all questions and respond to all expressions of anxiety, often with a story. And when he made his evening rounds in the dorms, he would willingly play a game of checkers or chess if a child should ask him to.

Alongside his role as the Big Bad Wolf, Dr B was also Santa Claus. His generosity is legendary among those who worked with him. He never forgot a birthday, and would always have a carefully chosen gift, often brought back from his travels. Beautiful gifts, which always had a meaning for their recipients, and which he took the time to wrap himself. Whenever he was away, he would send postcards to the children, as well as to the counsellors. The message was often a short one, but always meaningful. Regardless of the time at which they knew him, everyone marvels at his ability to remember all those dates, and to find the time to seek out each gift or write each message. Bettelheim did not much like receiving gifts, however. Lou Harper, who holds the absolute record for length of service at the school – a total of twenty-two years, briefly as a counsellor, then as a teacher – still squirms on recalling the time the team decided to offer Dr B an electric drill, in the year when he moved house. 'I don't want you to spend money on me. It's for me to give you presents, not the other way round.' Bettelheim's expression was even more eloquent than his words, Lou recalls. Nevertheless, the young man later undertook to build him a table – but never got round to finishing it.

During those first years the atmosphere at the school was still very relaxed, and even if everyone worked very hard there was plenty of laughter. Bettelheim's heavy accent and his linguistic idiosyncrasies were a regular source of jokes among the staff, such as when he would gravely announce that 'something's perspiring in the playground'. But his charisma was such that on occasion some counsellors were not sure whether to laugh or not. For instance, when he mixed up the metaphors he was so fond of using, saying 'Hook, line and barrel,' or 'Lock, stock and sinker.' Gayle was so fascinated at Bettelheim's ability to bring out the hidden meaning in things that she sometimes found herself seriously wondering what such strange-sounding expressions could refer to.

Others, however, were able to take a more distanced view. Betty-Lou Pingree, perhaps because she had known him when he was a beginner at Rockford, was much more aware than Gayle of how much insecurity still hid behind Bettelheim's apparent self-confidence. She has even kept documentary evidence, in the form of an invitation to a party at his home that he pinned up in the fall of 1945. It was addressed to the whole O.S. staff and read: 'My dear friends: You have suffered during this last year, and the gods know, so have I. Don't you think it is time that we all get together for one big lament, so that we can get the horror and sorrow of this first year of suffering out of our system and get ready for the horrors and sorrows of the second year?' He had obviously typed the invitation himself and it was complete with typos, and much, much too long: '... There won't be enough chairs, or things to eat and drink, but I assure you there will be enough people who will join you in swearing at me. This is an occasion (namely to be able to swear at me) which no self-respecting staff member of this institution can afford to miss .... Don't you worry, I'll get even with you during the rest of the year.'

The candy closet in which any of the children were allowed, at almost any time, to stock up on M&Ms, KitKats, Hershey bars, Reese's Peanut Butter Cups, Chuckles fruit pastilles, Kraft cheese paste, salted peanuts, Hollywood chewing gum, etc.; the doors that freely opened on to the outside world only, so that the kids knew they could leave if they wanted to, but at the same time felt protected against intruders; the cuddly toy that each child was given on arrival and then on each anniversary of that event; the special relationship that grew up between each child and one adult (counsellor, teacher or social worker) in particular; the way children of different ages and with different problems were mixed together in each dormitory and classroom; the freedom each one had to take part or not in group activities; the beautiful tiles and painted wallpaper decorating staircases and corridors to alleviate the anxiety brought about by transitional periods.

The later workings of the Orthogenic School, those of its legend, have been described often enough by Bettelheim and others to require no detailed introduction here. In the first book he devoted to it, *Love is Not Enough*, Bettelheim explained the school's philosophy, illustrating it with concrete examples taken from the children's daily life, ranging from the bathrooms and toilets to bedtime, classwork or meals. Published in 1950, this easy-to-read work rapidly became a bestseller in the United States. Five years later, *Truants from Life* outlined more detailed case studies of four children (including a number of indications as to what had become of them after they had left the school). Forty or so introductory pages summed up the precepts of the first book, although in a much more abstract style. In them, Bettelheim specified that the last part of the trilogy would deal with the school's staff, and their selection and training. However that third volume, *A Home for the Heart*, was to appear only in 1974, almost twenty years later. In the meantime, Bettelheim had brought out *The Empty Fortress*, his bestseller on autism, which, although not dealing directly with the Orthogenic School, had made it famous the world over.

In spite of this prolific output, and notwithstanding the 200 or so pages devoted to the staff in *A Home for the Heart*, there is a fundamental aspect of life in the Orthogenic School that Bettelheim never dealt with directly in his books, even though it was often raised implicitly. And that is the relationship between him and the young people, predominantly young women, who were in day-to-day charge of the children. And yet, all the people who ever worked with Bettelheim at the O.S. freely admit that it was precisely that relationship which made the experience so different from any other they had known. Bettelheim's enemies fully agree with this, since they depict him as a guru, and his institution as a sect. But, above all, those who continue to this day to draw on the inner riches that they found at the school in all their activities, be it teaching, therapy or simply living, stress that the knowledge they gained was not so much discovered in his books as in their everyday exchanges with Bettelheim. For his therapeutic work translates poorly into theory. As is so often the case, his talent as a clinician sprang from his personality, his history and his wounds. It was not best expressed in words, or at least not in the kind of words that one can commit to paper.

Contrary to what one might expect in an institution run by such an autocratic man, the counsellors enjoyed considerable autonomy in the way they carried out their duties. Bettelheim very rarely interfered between them and their charges. They alone decided what activities their group would take part in, and how to manage their relationships with the children. When it came to deciding whether or not a child should be allowed to go home during a holiday, it was their view that carried the most weight. The bulwark against errors or abuses lay in the eyes of the others, both counsellors and children – and indeed a well-adapted student would not hesitate for one moment to criticize a counsellor whose behaviour was not 'orthogenic'. And above all, it lay in the regular exchanges with Bettelheim. But to grasp how the system worked, it is necessary to understand first what the counsellors' daily life was like. And as their working conditions were particularly tough, it is also important to understand what made them stay.

A key document for this is by Jules Henry, a social anthropologist who had specialized in the study of hospital structures and who spent almost a year in the school as an observer in the mid-1950s. Henry wrote about the O.S. in several essays and he also participated in Bettelheim's study of autism.[25] In 1957, comparing the workings of the O.S. with those of other psychiatric institutions, he gave a detailed account of a counsellor's daily life.[26] It is written in the third person feminine, for as he notes at the outset, during his time at the school all but two of the counsellors were women.

> At seven-thirty in the morning she goes to the dormitory to get the children up and ready for school. Once there she dresses or helps dress the children who cannot do this themselves, she comes to grips with the emotional problems of children who are not able to get out of bed, she helps wash children who are not able to do it themselves; she sees to the toileting of children who are in a similar situation. She breakfasts with the children, continuing the process of guidance as necessary. Shortly before nine o'clock she goes with the children across the play yard to school. At every point the counselor brings the insight, empathy and understanding she has acquired to the resolution of the emotional problems at issue.

Then it is back to the dormitory, where there are always toys to put away, clothes to leave out for the laundry, wet sheets or pyjamas to take to be washed, etc.

> At about ten o'clock, the counselor begins to see her children in therapy sessions. Experienced counselors see from one to four children for one hour several times a week. If a counselor is not otherwise occupied, she may take one of her children out for a walk during school recess. It may now be time for one of the regular staff meetings, in which the children are discussed by the assembled counselors

in consultation with one of the two visiting psychoanalysts and the Director.

Then comes lunch, which is in principle a free period for the counsellors, as the children eat with their teachers. But as their meals make up a non-negligible part of their salary, and as the food is excellent (Bettelheim insists strongly on that point), they often prefer to eat at the staff table, in the same dining room as the children. On three days each week the staff meeting continues after lunch, for discussion of the counsellors' own problems, and general issues affecting the school.

... If it is a Monday or a Friday, the counselor has about an hour between the end of the staff meeting and the time she goes on duty, and this may be taken up with any of the following: dictating records, writing to parents, making a quick trip to a store to buy something for a child or for the dormitory, or looking after her own personal affairs. Shortly before three the counselor is in the staff room, ready with her after-school snacks for the children, and making arrangements with the counselors of other dormitories for use of the play facilities at the School [such as the swimming pool, gymnasium and sandpit].
... At three o'clock sharp the counselors are in their dormitories awaiting the return of their children from school. The return of the children, bearing their schoolroom tensions or pleasures with them, at once presents the counselor with therapeutic problems that may be handled on the spot. Then plans for the day's activities are discussed among children and counselor, with the occurrence of behaviors [*sic*] one might expect in a group of psychotic children. This again is an opportunity for therapeutic management. The afternoon ends at a quarter to six when children and counselor enter the dining room of the school and sit down together at supper, each dormitory at its own table.
After supper is activity time, until about eight-thirty, when the children get ready for bed, lights go out and the counselor reads the evening story by flashlight. At this time anxieties often well to the surface, and the counselor spends much time in the darkness by the children's bedsides giving help, although avoiding 'deep' explorations. She may remain until ten or after; when a child is overwhelmed by anxiety she may stay in the dormitory far into the night. While long night vigils are relatively infrequent, some counselors, especially when a seriously disturbed child is newly admitted to the dormitory, may undergo a long and wearing stage until the child grows calmer. There is no sedation, no packing, no mechanical constraint and no isolation.

Although laborious and detailed, this description omits the entire housework dimension of the counsellors' tasks, which in spite of the fact that the school possessed well-qualified domestic staff was considerable, since Bettelheim could not stand seeing a broken toy lying around. Whatever the time of day, the children were expected to be able to find their dormitory neat and pleasant, in a state which testified to their counsellor's concern for their well-being. Apart from her regular duties, one of the counsellors was responsible for the menus: every month, she went round all the dorms, asking for each child's preferences and then carefully planning the month's meals with the cook. Another was in charge of the candy closet; she had to make sure that it was at all times stocked up with everyone's favourite snacks. Jules Henry also omits to point out that it was the counsellors who organized all school parties, of which there were a lot, since celebrations played a key role in the therapeutic environment created by Bettelheim. In addition to the standard US public holidays, and some of the Christian ones, notably Christmas, each child had two birthdays; his real one and one marking the day he had entered the school, the latter being seen as his 'second birth'. On such days leave was cancelled for the staff members in charge of the child's group; one counsellor would devote herself entirely to the birthday child, while the other would take care of the other children. Furthermore every party would be accompanied by a large number and variety of gifts, all of which had been carefully selected and wrapped.

Each group had two counsellors assigned to it, which meant that the latter had to share out their working time, including weekends, when each had a twenty-four hour shift. Scheduling systems changed over the years, but during the entire period of Bettelheim's stewardship working hours were extremely long, the more so in that it was during their 'free' time that counsellors usually found it easiest to develop the close relationships with their children that the school's therapeutic methods demanded. At other times, when they were in charge of the whole group, they found it difficult to make themselves available enough. The one exception was often at bath-time. This latter was seen as an important moment in the children's day, since most of them suffered from an inability to come to terms with their own bodies. It should also be noted that every Wednesday evening there was a general staff meeting at 10 p.m. To attend it, the counsellors were often obliged to speed up the bed-time routine.

Although they received full bed and board plus laundry services, the counsellors received a mere pittance in terms of salary. In 1950, the last full year in which she worked at the school (she had by then become an assistant to the director), Gayle Shulenberger earned just 1,600 dollars. In 1970, when Geneviève Jurgensen was taken on, Bert Cohler, who was then in the process of taking over Bettelheim's job, proudly told her that given her experience – she had already been practising as a speech therapist for four years in her native France – he could offer her no less than 3,000 dollars a year! That was 500 dollars more than the starting salary for a counsellor.

It is clearly worth asking just what, in that age of full employment and rapid economic growth, could incite young students to accept such sacrifices, of both money and time. Gayle says laughingly: 'I often told myself that if I'd been Catholic, I could just as well have been a nun! It was practically the same – I was there twenty-four hours a day.'

Jules Henry answers the question in the same impersonal, matter-of-fact style he uses to describe the counsellors' working day. Their workload was so heavy, he writes, that a process of self-selection took place in the first months, with people only staying at the Orthogenic School if they had 'rather special inner needs'. 'Rather than impose upon the counselors a transparent mask of adjustment, routine and frozen professional competence, as often occurs in American institutions,' he goes on, 'the School recognizes the existence of powerful inner needs and uses the resultant energy in a training and guidance program which takes these problems into consideration and works to resolve them. But note that the process is circular. Only those who perceive that the resolution of their problems lies in this direction, who need possession of and can help young children in this way, are motivated to remain.'[27] To back up this statement, Henry notes that the school's director was giving psychotherapy to several of his counsellors.

Behind the sympathetic explanations provided by this academic – Henry's analysis points to the conclusion that the Orthogenic School is vastly superior to the other structures that generally take in psychotics – one can easily see how critics can discern a very different pattern: that of an institution in which one needs to be oneself afflicted by serious psychological problems in order to cater to the children's disorders, and in working conditions that are not much better than slavery.

That is indeed the way Bill Blau, one of Bettelheim's most implacable enemies, portrays the school. This avowed enemy of psychoanalysis spent almost a year as a counsellor in the institution, and the experience left him with a burning hatred of Bettelheim. He considers it his duty even now to denounce him at every available opportunity, and he devoted considerable time to doing so on the occasion of his death. His testimony is interesting for several reasons. First, because Bill Blau is perfectly sincere in his crusade against Bettelheim. He tells no lies, and does not try to edit his memories selectively to make them fit his story. He acknowledges, for example, that he never saw Bettelheim actually hit a child – or rather, he corrects himself, that he does not remember seeing him do so. When the interviewer points out that, if he had, it would therefore not have shocked him particularly, he ends up by admitting it. His testimony is also interesting because it helps to highlight the origins of the misunderstanding that sprang up around Bettelheim's method. Particularly since his experience of the Orthogenic School dates from that early, enchanted period.

In essence, Bill Blau accuses Bettelheim of having been an impostor, and of having done a great deal of harm, particularly to parents of autistic children. Interestingly enough, Blau claims to have seen through what he believes to be a 'fraud' not at the school itself, but during Bettelheim's classes. On being demobbed, he had enrolled for psychology courses at the U of C, and ended up working at the Orthogenic School to complement his veteran's scholarship. He had been working there for several months, in charge of a group of young boys called the 'Pirates', when Bruno Bettelheim invited him to attend one of his lectures. There, the young man was shocked at the way Bettelheim treated his students. 'He was really a brute with them. He'd pile on the readings, of Freud and others, with no concern for how long it takes to read. Later, his technique was to call a student and ask all these questions about the Freudian texts and then to ridicule him with his answers. He'd savage them.'[28]

The moment of truth for Bill Blau came when he himself came to answer a question. Far from ridiculing him, Bettelheim congratulated him for his answer, and that was precisely what made Blau furious. 'I didn't know any better than the others. In fact, much less, because I didn't have much time to read. Only, as I worked for him, I had to be right ... in order to prove what a good teacher he was!' Unfortunately, Bill Blau has now forgotten both the question Bettelheim asked and his answer to it, so it is impossible to try and see with him why his reply might have been worthy of the teacher's praise. Perhaps because, unlike those of the other students, it was based on experience, and did not seek to conceal woolly thinking behind a wall of jargon. But even if one were to attempt such an explanation, Bill Blau would probably not accept it.

From that day on, Bill Blau began feeling suspicious of everything Bettelheim did. He saw the staff meetings as unjustified exercises in tyranny; he felt that some of the young women looked on Dr B as a kind of god, that they only told him what he wanted to hear and furthermore that they were being disloyal to the children by 'squealing' on them to the director. He started to see Bettelheim as such a tyrant that he even suspected him of abusing his position to obtain sexual favours from some of the young women.

Bill Blau also believes that the children who attended the Orthogenic School were no sicker than many of the kids he had rubbed shoulders with when, at the age of twelve or thirteen, during the Depression years, his mother had put him into an orphanage after his father had committed suicide. He sees Bettelheim as a coward. 'He had little experience of life. We had just returned from the war; we were tougher, meaner, than him. He was very intelligent, but he was sick, and more interested in his own image than in the truth.' On listening to Blau, one cannot help but wonder what he was looking for when he joined an institution the principles of which were so diametrically opposed to everything he believed in. To which he replies that at the time, psychoanalysis was all the rage at the

University of Chicago, the subject on everyone's lips, and that Bruno Bettelheim and the Orthogenic School were considered the ultimate experience in the field.

Here then is a witness who puts the picture painted by Jules Henry into perspective. For if the latter argues that 'inner needs' are essential to the make-up of a successful counsellor, it is clear that Bill Blau had just as many such needs as those for whom the Bettelheim method worked wonders. It is simply that, for reasons of his own, he reacted with repulsion to what others found invaluable. It is true, however, that Bettelheim usually felt more comfortable with women than with men, but that did not prevent the school from having some very good male counsellors among its staff. It is also true that at the time Bill Blau was there, looking after children was still considered by the great majority of people to be a woman's job. Indeed, as the school's students still numbered four groups of boys for only one of girls, finding more male counsellors was one of Bettelheim's major concerns. But that is not the crux of the matter.

Let us return to the question of what motivated the counsellors who stayed the course. The top specialist in the field is Ben Wright, professor of statistics at the University of Chicago's Department of Education. He not only devoted his doctoral thesis to the subject, but also wrote the first drafts of two articles that he was to co-sign with Bettelheim on it. He is also responsible for all the data and some of the writing in the section of *A Home for the Heart* devoted to staff training – around 200 pages in all – although the commentary is Bettelheim's.

Like Jules Henry, Ben Wright stresses at the outset the heaviness of the counsellors' workload. They had to act both as parents and therapists for the children in their charge, since they started to see an individual child in one-hour sessions two or three times weekly, after about a year at the school. The sole function of the psychoanalysts who succeeded Emmy Sylvester, coming to the school once a week, was in fact to guide the counsellors in their work, and not to treat the children themselves. Wright (with the blessing of his co-signatory, Bettelheim) explains this system by the seriousness of the children's condition. 'Being repeatedly bitten, kicked, defecated upon or otherwise abused results in defensive or punitive actions, cold indifference, emotional distance or superior looking down on such "animal-like" behavior. Though these may be rationalized as necessary interference, as the setting of healthy or socially required limitations, such attitudes interfere with rehabilitation. They can be avoided only if staff members know it is their responsibility, and only theirs, to help these children, if they receive all the narcissistic and interpersonal rewards that derive from being the children's main therapists.'[29]

Ben Wright, who had spent several years as a counsellor at the school before becoming its analyst, then points to an important characteristic of staff members: due to their young age and lack of experience, they had a different type of relationship with the children than did the other adults of the school. 'Still basically in opposition to (what to them appear to be) the oppressive mores of adult society, the young staff members, far from experiencing the children's anti-social behavior as a threat, tend to enjoy it,' he and Bettelheim wrote.

Bettelheim had noticed early on how some counsellors clearly got a thrill out of seeing children cursing and swearing, breaking toys or crockery, in a way they themselves had never dared to do. He observed the fascination, concerned that it should not reach the point when a child might be tempted to exaggerate his symptoms to please his counsellor. But he noted that 'Such common feelings, unspoken and not acted upon by the workers but acted out by the children, permit the severely disturbed child to feel understood and appreciated in his rejection of the world.'[30]

Just like the children in their care, the counsellors were still seeking their way in life, and as they were young, they still believed that anything was possible. It was a hope that bore in it the seeds of healing, and the young folk were better placed than anyone else to transmit it to their charges, since they had so far led normal lives, and been successful in their studies. (Very quickly, the criteria for recruiting counsellors became stricter, with Bruno Bettelheim demanding that they have a university degree.)

Anyone surprised by this parallel drawn between the school's students and their counsellors has either forgotten, or not accepted, the basic tenet of the Bettelheim approach, which was that the difference between crazy and sane people is one of degree only. The validity of this affirmation was being demonstrated every day at the school. Gayle clearly recalls the day when this dawned on her. 'I remember walking into his office. He was writing, so I waited. But I was boiling inside. Then, finally, he looked up and I said: "Dr B, everybody is crazy, is that it?" and he said: "Did you just discover that, my girl?" For me, it was a revelation.'

Reaching that moment of understanding was no doubt the decisive event in the training of a good O.S. counsellor. As long as the recruit had not got to that point, taking care of the children was just another job, and a gruelling and badly paid one at that. Work that one carries out without conviction or imagination; as Bettelheim would have said, without passion. To put it another way, until counsellors realized that by working with the children they would learn as much about themselves as about their charges, as long as they had not accepted with humility that they had to sort out a few things in their own heads, and that they could get the help they needed from the very people they were trying to assist, they would not be good counsellors in Bruno Bettelheim's eyes.

And to help them get there was Bettelheim's most essential role at the school. It is true that he also acted as a father and a reassuring symbol of authority, doing his rounds twice a day, one in daytime and the other in the dormitories just before lights-out, ever ready to respond with a story, a kind or an angry word to the continual requests for help he received from both children and adults. But he could quite well have fulfilled those functions in another setting. What was really different about the Orthogenic School was the way he gradually got its counsellors and teachers to become aware of their own problems, their own quest in life, thereby making therapists of them too. How he taught them to 'walk back and forth across that bridge'.[31]

Bettelheim carried on this work on two levels simultaneously: individually, during the one-to-one talks he had regularly with all his counsellors, and collectively in the daily staff meetings. Of all the memories of the people who worked at the school, those assemblies remain among the most vivid. Their tone could vary from the warm, family-like atmosphere of the early days to what some witnesses refer to as public torture sessions. There are as many different recollections as there are people, but all are intense.

In this area as well, the system evolved gradually, over time. In the early years, any time that a counsellor had a problem, or simply an idea that seemed important, he or she would drop by Bettelheim's office. As Gayle says, 'Everything was a bit mixed up. I would go to see him about a kid, and I would end up talking about myself.' And it had not taken long for Bettelheim to realize that the only really intractable problems that arise in an adult's day-to-day relationship with a child, whether disturbed or not, are those which touch on some painful memory from the adult's own childhood. They are memories of which the adult is often unaware, but they offer him the opportunity to either punish the child he once was, or give him what he had been deprived of, by force if necessary. For he is then convinced that he knows better than the child himself what the latter needs. This in other words is the 'blind spot' in the relationship, when the adult ceases to see the child as a different person.

When a counsellor came to discuss a problem with him, Bettelheim would ask a few questions, and soon get round to: 'How do you feel when …?' '… when he starts screaming, biting, smashing everything?' for example. In most cases, the answer to that question contained the solution to the conflict with the child. A typical reply might be: 'I don't really know – it scares me. It shocks me; I know I should stop him, that he's bothering the other children …. But I feel he needs to do it, after all those years spent at the orphanage, where he wasn't allowed to do anything at all, where he was nothing but a retarded child. He needs to scream out that he exists, make others acknowledge him, even if it disturbs them …. As a kid, I never screamed, because I lived with my aunt, and she was so good to me that I never felt I had the right to …' etc. With the smartest or the best trained among his counsellors, Bettelheim would often not need to push the conversation much further. They would immediately detect the repetition in their mental images, see what was getting in the way of their relationship with the child. With others, Bettelheim would have to be more forceful, probing them with questions, and reassuring them as well, until the penny finally dropped, and the counsellor understood why that one child struck more of a chord in her than the others, or why she was unable to establish contact.

But it was in the staff meetings that the technique took on its full force. A recent recruit would explain in detail how she had been unable to handle a child's erratic behaviour, expecting a few words of advice. Instead, with the others looking on, Bettelheim would ask: 'Imagine what could make you act that way?' Surprised, the new counsellor would often mumble, searching desperately for the 'right' answer, and then come out with something like 'Oh, I understand. If I was in his shoes ....' She had fallen into the trap! The aim of the exercise being not to put oneself in the child's place, but to dig down into one's own emotions to find what could bring about such behaviour in oneself. As Karen Zelan, one of Bettelheim's all-time favourites among the counsellors, says, this is almost the opposite of putting oneself in the other person's shoes. For unlike compassion, which involves a movement of one person towards another, empathy, which is what Bettelheim sought to foster, is an encounter with the other person inside oneself. In order to accept him, first. And then to hold out the hand on which he can lean to help him cross the bridge toward reality. A firm hand, that no fear, no repulsion, can push away.

It was a tough training. Trying to identify within oneself the child who, after defecating on the floor, is in the process of methodically smearing your blouse with excrement, or, even more terrifying, the murderous child struggling with his desire to kill someone, either you or himself, is by no means easy. It took time, and gritty determination, to graduate. Indeed, many people never did so; they left the school after a few weeks or months. In May 1986, when the University of Chicago organized a small conference in honour of Bruno Bettelheim, Josette Dermody Wingo gave a very lively account of her first months spent as a counsellor at the school forty years earlier. Speaking in the presence of her former boss, she explained how she never knew exactly what Bettelheim expected of her, and thus was continually nervous that she would make a mistake, and say or do something that would thwart the progress of a child towards recovery. 'Since most of the time I was flying blind, I never knew when I would be blindsided,' said Wingo, who had joined the school in 1946, after being demobilized. She went on to describe the continual fatigue, and her struggles to dictate her reports on the children in her care: 'Anxiety over owed tapes hung like a guilty albatross around my neck all the time .... The requirements were for a flat narrative style with no interpretations but with an emphasis on what children and counsellors said and did.'[32] Josette Wingo then quoted an extract from one of her dictations:

Pete walked into the dormitory and threw his model airplane on to

the floor. I said: 'If you don't like it any more, Pete, I'll be glad to keep
it for you.' He kicked the pieces to flinders.

Daniel said, 'He's always breaking things. He's just trying to *uproar*
you, Josette.'

The other kids gathered round the table for their snacks. 'Want a
piece of chocolate cake, Pete?'

'You know I hate cake. You know I hate chocolate. It's shitty. You're
shitty, shitty, shitty, shitty!'

I shrugged my shoulders.

And then, Wingo reported on the next staff meeting:

Dr B: 'Why did you shrug your shoulders?'

Stupefied silence. I thought I had been doing well just to have Pete
not get to me.

Dr B: 'He was being hostile to you. Why?'

Resisting an impulse to shrug my shoulders and riposte with
something clever like 'Beats the hell out of me,' I bit my lip. There
was more to come – there usually was.

Dr B: 'I saw Pete yesterday, wearing that ridiculous, poisonous-
green hat. He looks like Happy Hooligan. Even our most neurotic
parents would never let a child looking like Happy Hooligan out of
the funny papers.'

By this time, Dr B was mad and it was perfectly clear to me that it
was up to me to 'Do Something' about Pete's hat, but whether the
sound psychological reasons were Pete's self-image or Dr B's dislike
of arsenical yellow-green plaid wool hats with ear flaps are beyond
the scope of the discussion. Lots of things were. When to shut up,
when to speak up, when to put up: I spat on my finger and held it up
to the wind, trying to decide whether to tack or to jibe, but mostly
staying the course.

Bruno Bettelheim was never an easy man to get on with. The originality
of his technique and ideas only seemed to enhance the idiosyncrasies of his
character, including an innate irascibility which was to increase over the
years, giving him a reputation for being completely unpredictable. Some
people saw this as nothing more than fickleness and a lack of self-control;
for others it was yet another proof of his remarkable talent – psychoanalytic wisdom residing precisely in the capacity to acknowledge that no two
people are ever alike, and that, in dealing with human beings, everything
must remain flexible, for it is the overly rigid rule that negates the
individual. For Josette Wingo, as for all those who both gave and received
a great deal during their time at the school, the two images of Bettelheim,
as an ill-tempered man and a talented one, corresponded to successive
stages in her perception of him, as she gained a better understanding of

her own role ('Technique, if that was what it was, became almost second nature by the beginning of the third year. No longer did fear hobble me at work ... [and] the lessening of fear freed the intuition. Like Gayle, Joan, Patti, Ping and Florence White,[33] I became a living feedback loop for what was going on with the children.') without one ever completely blotting out the other.

While many things changed at the Orthogenic School during the thirty years of Bruno Bettelheim's stewardship, the training of counsellors remained the same throughout. Geneviève Jurgensen, joining the staff a quarter of a century after Josette Wingo, gives a vivid account of the hell she went through in her first two months in charge of a group of adolescent girls. As she was about to start her shift, she often fantasized about slipping on the steps, which would give her an excuse to go home.[34] Each time, however, she kept at it. The same feelings of discouragement and revolt can be found in the account of Candace Hilldrup,[35] who started at the school in 1969. But there is also the same determination to overcome her powerlessness, to get in control. In a word, to understand.

Another thing that Dr B was well aware of, probably because he had experienced it himself during his cohabitation with Patsy, was just how much anxiety disturbed children can generate in the adults who live with them. Anxiety about not being able to help them, or fear of being similar to them. Dr Ugo Formigoni, who today heads a psychiatric hospital for children in the Chicago suburbs, also has vivid memories of the first staff meeting he attended at the Orthogenic School, in 1960. Aged twenty-nine at the time, Formigoni had come from his native Italy to complete his medical degree with some experience of US hospitals. He was then a psychiatric intern in Oklahoma and somewhat disillusioned at what he saw as the depersonalization of the treatment in the two institutions in which he had worked since his arrival. Having read *Love is Not Enough*, he wanted to spend some time at the Orthogenic School. Bettelheim did not welcome live-in observers but he had finally agreed to Formigoni spending a month there as a counsellor.

At the first staff meeting he attended, Dr B had spoken at some length about the difficulties counsellors experienced when a child made them lose their tempers. The problem, he explained, had to do with their self-image. 'We like to see ourselves as St Georges helping children to get well. To be confronted with the negative feelings those kids can evoke in us, and especially anger, is totally unacceptable to us.'

As Dr Formigoni was reporting on the meeting,[36] I could not resist interrupting him: 'But don't you think Dr B was really talking about himself?' And this competent sixty-year-old man, who has spent over thirty years treating people with mental problems, paused in the middle of a sentence, reflecting. Then, he said: 'You're right, I can see it now. He must have been talking about himself .... But it did not even cross my mind at the time. To me then, he was talking about me, about us. About feelings that we were struggling with, feelings that we were trying very hard to repress.' Such was Bruno Bettelheim's impact as a therapist, and such was the influence he wielded over those who worked with him.

That meeting made such a deep impression on Dr Formigoni that when Bettelheim suggested he continue to work at the school, not as a psychiatrist but as a simple counsellor, 'to learn', hinting that there could be better prospects in the future, he accepted almost immediately.

However one wishes to label it, as therapy, psychoanalysis or (more appropriately) as 'supervision', this was the core of Bettelheim's work at the Orthogenic School. It was the same task that he was to carry out, in a more classical fashion, with a group of young lay analysts, who started attending seminars with him in 1959. On Tuesday evenings, they would come to the school to discuss their most difficult cases. The sessions were taped, and the unedited transcripts make fascinating reading.[37] Each case unfolds somewhat like a detective story (Bettelheim liked to compare the role of the therapist to that of a lawyer[38]). A particular case would be outlined, with Bettelheim interrupting from time to time to ask for more details. Then there would be a period of discussion between him and the analyst presenting the case. On reading the transcripts, it quickly becomes apparent why some people who attended his courses (where he used the same technique with his students) use the word 'sadism' to describe them. Bettelheim's questions would of course probe the most sensitive area of the psychoanalyst's relationship with his or her patient. If the former then stiffened, failed to give a direct answer or tried to hide behind a ready-made theoretical one, the dialogue could become painful. Bettelheim would keep up the pressure, finding different ways to ask the same question. Other participants would join in and their contributions often seemed to convince their unfortunate colleague that he was the only member of the group who had failed to see what was so glaringly obvious for everyone else. Secretly, the person 'in the hot seat' probably felt foolish for holding out so long. In each case, however, the discussion has a constructive ending, generally with the laying bare of some hidden wound in the analyst's own make-up, which could well be the cause of his problem with his patient.

The whole process is almost too perfect. When one reads several such accounts one after the other, one is forced to conclude that Bettelheim could not possibly have got it right every time. And indeed, he did not really claim to do so. He offered hypotheses and opened doors, but rarely put forward his interpretations as the only possible ones; the recipient was free to do what he or she wanted with them. When his interlocutor was clearly very ill at ease, Bettelheim would on occasion extend a helping hand to get round an obstacle. But his tone could also be very harsh, and the authority he wielded over the group was indisputable. 'With his glasses that made his eyes enormous, he could look very intimidating. I felt I was face-to-face with Erich von Stroheim!' Ugo Formigoni admits.

'Socratic' is the term most often used by Bruno Bettelheim's former students to describe his courses or supervisory sessions. For throughout his whole career, from Rockford to Stanford, via the Orthogenic School and the University of Chicago's lecture halls, his working method never varied. A glimpse of it can be obtained from *The Art of the Obvious*, a work compiled by Alvin Rosenfeld from seminars the two men ran jointly in California, and completed after Bettelheim's death.[39] An even better illustration is to be found in *Dialogues with Mothers*. At first view, this little book reads like just another childcare manual. But it is not. The actual content of the book is of little importance; what is significant is the exchange itself, the path taken by Bettelheim to bring the mothers (and sometimes fathers) to become aware of what they are actually saying. When read from that standpoint, the book not only illustrates its author's method, but it also reveals what was remarkable about his way of looking at children.

The dialogues started at the end of the war. To cater for the huge influx of demobbed GIs who wanted either to start or to complete studies in Chicago with their grants, the university had a prefabricated village built at the end of the Midway, a few hundred yards from the Orthogenic School. Many of the couples who moved in had their first children there, and so many of Bettelheim's students asked him questions about child-rearing during his regular classes that he ended up organizing informal meetings with them or their spouses every other Wednesday. For, as he states in his book, 'the most appropriate advice, the most carefully-explained theory, is of little use when it comes to handling specific everyday events with a child'.[40] Within only a few months the experiment proved so successful that he made the meetings weekly, and began recording them. The sessions ran from 1948 until 1952, when Bettelheim gave them up for lack of time. *Dialogues with Mothers* was compiled from the resulting tapes. He was to resume the meetings, only on a less regular basis, later on, and he would use them to feed a monthly column in *Ladies' Home Journal* which ran from 1965 to 1975.

An example of the 'detective work' side of his technique was filmed by Daniel Karlin during one such session in April 1973. The scene opens with a mother telling how her daughter, aged almost five, is incapable of persevering in any difficult task, becoming discouraged and giving up at the very first hurdle. What should the mother do – keep on encouraging her to try harder, or on the contrary ignore her, leaving her to manage on her own? Bettelheim asks for an example, and she tells how her daughter gave up trying to learn 'Mary Had a Little Lamb' on the piano, becoming irritated and lapsing into thumb-sucking. 'Try again! You know very well that, in order to learn something, you have to work at it,' the young mother had told her child. Bettelheim interrupts her: 'Suppose you were crying and upset; what would someone have to say to make you feel better?'

The mother replies: 'Something like: "Try again, it'll be better next time." '

Dr B: 'I'm trying to find something in your own experience .... Suppose that your husband had tried in vain to climb a mountain, and then gave up, saying: "It's too hard, I'll never make it." What would you say to him?'

' "Sure, you can make it!" '

'I wouldn't like to be married to you, my dear lady. I would never have succeeded in life if my wife had reacted like that. Do you know what she has always said to me about the school?'

Several other mothers volunteer answers: 'That it wouldn't work?' 'That your ideas are excellent, and that ...?' 'That it's a tough job, but she's there to help you ...?' At each reply, Dr B waxes ironic, with comments such as: 'Between you and me, all your husbands should be filing for divorce! You are quite unbearable.' Then he finally gives the answer, pausing for dramatic effect to emphasize his punch-line. 'For twenty-four years she has been telling me to ... give the whole thing up!'

The mothers express surprise. 'You think that's so marvellous?' To which Bettelheim replies: 'Yes, because she doesn't want me to tire myself out!' At that point he becomes gentler and tries to explain to them, in a few sentences, the difference between encouragement and pressure. Between things that one is forced to take, such as a medicine, and things one chooses to do (play the piano). Another mother suddenly points out that maybe the little girl is only playing the instrument because it is important *for her mother*. 'Exactly,' says Bettelheim. 'She doesn't really know what importance it could have for her .... But when you tell her to "try again", you show her clearly that you want her to make the effort. But why?'

'Because I want her to be successful!'

'Precisely. That's exactly the point! ... Your child's frustration and anxiety are caused by your insistence that she has to *succeed*.'

From this point on, the whole plot unravels. 'It's even worse than that,' the mother starts. Now feeling guilty, she blurts out the 'truth', which is that she is trying to keep her daughter a baby because she fears the day when her children will no longer need her. She doesn't know why, but she has never allowed herself to be successful in life. Bettelheim interrupts her again. 'What did you study in college?'

'English literature.'

'And what did you want to do with it?'

'I didn't have the faintest idea. It seemed the best thing to do, given my abilities. I was interested in other things, but I wasn't gifted for them ....'

'Which things?'

'Music.'

'Ahah – interesting!' This last remark brings a burst of general laughter.

If the above dialogue were not there on film, it would seem too good to be true. And in a way, it is. The exchange is typical of the way Bruno

Bettelheim operated towards the end of his career in Chicago.[41] The technique was more abrupt and less analytical than in the earlier dialogues, with Bettelheim using a heavier hand to steer the conversation the way he wanted. Cathy Kaiser, one of the first mothers to take part in the meetings, even before Bettelheim started recording them, remembers him as much more considerate and kind than the person who emerges from the above exchange. More concerned by his listeners, and probably also more optimistic as to the progress that the discussion could yield.

She remembers the sessions very clearly; the war had just ended, and Dr Benjamin Spock had revolutionized classical paediatrics with his *Common Sense Book of Baby and Child Care*. This was supposed to be a reassuring book, since its basic message was that mothers should not worry, that they in fact knew their children better than did any of the books they consulted. However, as it also went against the precepts of strictness which had dominated child care up until then, its initial effect was in fact to throw its readers into a state of anxiety. Young mothers were suddenly being told that all those key decisions on feeding, weaning, potty-training, etc. – which the new psychology manuals described as being of crucial importance – were in fact up to them. As a result, they were continually worrying whether they had done the right thing. Their husbands had just returned from saving Europe (Cathy Kaiser's had been involved in air operations over Germany); they did not have the right to mess up their sons' upbringing. 'What I got out of those meetings was not recipes, but a way to be with my children. Thanks to Dr B, I was no longer afraid to make mistakes,' says Cathy.[42] The mother of the young pianist, however, may feel differently. Yet, the latter discussion does have one advantage: it points very clearly to the enemy that Bettelheim continually had in his sights.

The pain that a mother, however loving and devoted, can inflict on her child with her own unfulfilled desires was indeed one childhood misfortune that he knew at first hand. How she can become blind to what he really is, negate him without even realizing it, by projecting images from her own past on to him. After all, was the empathy that Bettelheim tried to foster in his counsellors any different from that which little Bruno had been craving when he insisted on doing his homework next to his mother on the dining room table, at the end of a day when he had been made fun of in the school yard or beaten up on the way to school? Was it not the understanding that he never got from her? For as far back as he could remember, Paula had burdened him not only with taking on the role of the father who had been found wanting, but also with opening the doors that had remained closed to her. He had to be a real man and a family breadwinner, to take the place of Anton. He also had to be rich and influential, like Grandfather Seidler, and like the businesswoman that she had not been allowed to become. What he, Bruno, really was, with his own ambitions, pleasures and fears, she did not see (would she otherwise have made such a noisy entrance when he was giving one of his first lectures in English?).[43]

The worst of it was that he could be in no doubt that she loved him. Her devotion to her children, and especially to her son, was a subject of universal admiration. Did he have any right to blame her for the suffering that, unknowingly, she caused him? And if he felt that he did not measure up to what she wanted, whose fault was it? Certainly not hers. 'My parents … tried their very best to be very good parents …. So we could not blame them, and if we occasionally questioned their depressive way of life, we had to feel guilty,' he was to write later.[44] And, on his own 'relative success', he said that although his mother had lived long enough to see the start of it, 'her long life of sorrows did not permit her to really enjoy it.'[45] Upon reflection, if those early dialogues with mothers were kinder and more optimistic in tone, it may also be because Paula Bettelheim was still alive at the time, and her son had not given up all hope of changing the way she too saw her son.

Bettelheim was said to be merciless with mothers. And, on occasion, he was. But all he was ever trying to do was to give back children their identities in their mother's eyes. 'I don't remember ever being afraid of him,' says Cathy Kaiser. She was fascinated by the way he managed to get even the shyest young women to speak, always with delicacy, and can remember only one situation in which he would really become harsh with a mother. That was 'when it became obvious that she didn't really want to help her child'. It was the same at the school. If Bettelheim demanded of his counsellors that they be at all times attentive to what the children actually said and did, it was because the latter had to learn how to become themselves, rather than the model child, or more commonly the monstrous child, that their mothers saw in them. To break out of the model they had always been trying to conform to, at the cost of forgetting to live for themselves, which resulted in self-hatred, and self-destruction.

With the young women whose children were growing up normally, and whose desire to get it right was manifest, Bettelheim had undertaken preventive work. He would remind them of a few obvious truths. 'Never again in your life will you be so important to a human being. And if you don't enjoy that, you're sunk,' he tells a mother, who has been complaining that her four-year-old son tyrannizes her. She nevertheless insists:

'But before Christmas he would play around the house and he could entertain himself for hours. He was very quiet and very happy.'
  Dr B: 'Who told you he was happy?'
  'Well, he seemed to be. He wasn't demanding; he wasn't crying.'
  Dr B: 'That's right. The mother is ignored and that's identical with the child being happy. Isn't that a funny kind of attitude?'[46]

Bettelheim was not unaware that a young mother's life is often difficult.

During the discussions, he notes in the introduction to *Dialogues*, 'they began to see and hear for themselves how others felt and – encouraged by me, whom they considered an authority – they could admit to themselves that caring for a small child is not always wholly blissful and entails genuine hardship. It was a relief for them to learn that all mothers are sometimes exhausted from the labor of caring for babies, the home, and a husband distracted by the desire for professional advancement and the need for making ends meet.' Yet while reassuring these young mothers, he also tried to get them to glimpse what they were keeping silent; the hidden side of their maternal love. The repressed desires that they imposed on their children, and also the aggression, anger and even hatred that the latter could trigger in them at times. He never tells them, 'You should do this,' but always asks, 'What do you expect from your child?'; 'What sort of child do you want?' In other words, he seeks to pin down their unconscious. In the hope that, once they have been confronted with the ambivalence of some of their desires, they will stop making their children pay for conflicts that they themselves have not been able to resolve. His aim is not that they should change, but that they should accept themselves as they are.

Over the years, however, the tone of the dialogues was to evolve, as did Bruno Bettelheim's relationship with the Orthogenic School counsellors. The magic of those early years was that of jointly made discoveries, the excitement of the first results, the joy felt by pioneers who set out on the right track. Then, the first counsellors began to leave. Marjorie Jewell first, followed by Betty-Lou Pingree and Ronnie Dryovage in 1947. Gayle Shulenberger, who had become Dr B's assistant, had stayed on until 1951, but even she had finally moved on. During 1946, Bettelheim had struck up a friendship with Morris Janowitz, a young sociologist from New York who had spent the war in London, analysing the content of German radio broadcasts in the Psychological Warfare Division of the Supreme Allied Headquarters. Deeply affected by the war, Janowitz had come to Chicago with a demobilization fellowship to read for his doctorate. Soon thereafter, he had started work on a book with Bettelheim,[47] and he had become a frequent visitor to the school. Encouraged by Dr B, Gayle had started dating the young sociologist. They had become engaged, a result of which Bettelheim was very proud, even though the prospect of Gayle's departure filled him with anguish. He was best man at their wedding, along with Jeremiah Kaplan, his (and Janowitz's) publisher.

Josette also got married, in September 1950, with the whole school attending the ceremony. Enraged at seeing their counsellor taken away by another male, the boys in her group were furiously energetic in bombarding the couple when they stepped out of the church. And Josette was clearly relieved that it was only rice, and not stones, the boys held in their fists.

Chapter XII

Dr B the Enchanter

The publication in 1950 of *Love is Not Enough* was rapidly to make Bruno Bettelheim well known across the United States. The years of discovery thus gave way to years of success. He had been admitted as a member of the American Psychology Association, and had even been awarded a diploma in clinical psychology. He was now a fully fledged university professor of psychology and education. He had achieved his ambition, and, as he was to tell Bert Cohler twenty years later, he was starting to be bored.

The world around him had meanwhile changed. In the US, the victory over Nazism had been seen as confirmation of the superiority of the American system, in terms of both justice and strength. American children also had to be the best. Mental illness, which had never been well accepted in the United States at the best of times, had to be defeated at all costs. Some people even blamed all the horrors of the just-ended war on the madness of a single man, Adolf Hitler. If mad people could not be cured then they needed to be got rid of; there was no place for them in American society. This was the time when some states had laws on their books providing for the putting-away, or in some cases the lobotomization, of people who did not fulfil the basic conditions required of a good citizen. Meanwhile the Department of Health and private foundations had started funding innumerable psychiatric research projects. In 1952, a federal law banned from US territory aliens suffering from psychotic symptoms.

The mood of rabid anti-Communism which set in within months of the end of the war could only increase the pressure for conformity. Stalin's mind, like that of Hitler, was analysed for signs of madness. For many people it seemed clear – and some said as much – that if mankind could rid itself of mental illness, there would be no more wars, atrocities or totalitarianism.[1] Needless to say, by no means everyone in psychological or psychoanalytic circles shared these simplistic views. But intellectuals were the prime targets for the McCarthyists, and the European immigrants in particular were not about to risk their new-found security by defending progressive ideas against the 'reds-under-the-bed' consensus. Even committed Marxists like Otto Fenichel gave up discussing social or political issues in public.[2] Ego Psychology, with its individualistic and reassuring message, was in its heyday.

Anti-Communism was not a problem for Bruno Bettelheim, who had in fact become aware of it well before the rise of Senator Joseph McCarthy. In September 1945, in a letter to Ernst Federn, he apologized for not being able to send any of the documents on Marx or Freud his friend had asked him for. The reason was simple, Bettelheim wrote: such literature simply did not exist. He went on: 'Wilhelm Reich is living and working in Brooklyn, New York. He is the only one who is really concerned with Marxism, but he is by now so confused that nothing comes from it. The only somewhat more interesting contributions were made by some of the sociologists, but they again don't understand Freud. You will have to learn that in this great country there is not a single real Marx scholar, and probably with the exception of your father and a very few old analysts no Freud scholar either. They publish all right, but it does not amount to anything.'[3]

While the view that mentally ill people had no place in American society was diametrically opposed to everything Bettelheim believed in, the two philosophies did have one idea in common: the possibility of a cure. And on reading *Love is Not Enough*, it was easy to become convinced that Bruno Bettelheim had indeed created a method that could cure mentally ill children. Even better, it was a humane, kindly method; just the ticket for the liberal, well-meaning donors who were eager to devote a little of their wealth to the betterment of their community by fighting mental illness. And Bettelheim was to benefit greatly from the largesse thus made available to those in the front line of that war.

From day one of his tenure, the quest for funds was a major part of his job. He had first met, and won over, Philip Pekow, a rich industrialist and the father of a former student, who chaired a Concerned Parents' Committee. In July 1944, Pekow had offered to raise the funds needed to refurbish the school's crumbling infrastructure. Having lost confidence in Mandel Sherman, he said he could find 2 million dollars for the construction of a new building, on condition that the university appoint a new director and match what he raised. Ralph Tyler still remembers the first meeting of the Foundation, which was to be named after its most generous donor, Sonia Shankman. He jokingly refers to the event, in January 1945, as 'the extortion meeting'.[4] The auctioneer had also clearly been won over by Bruno Bettelheim's charm. 'Come on, you can do better than that,' he told the assembled donors. 'You can give more, I know. Remember: I'm also your lawyer!'

Despite the relatively high fees – which were paid either by the parents themselves, or in the case of orphans or children from poor families by sponsoring charities – the school was chronically short of funds. All the university paid for was the upkeep of the building, maintenance and the director's salary.[5] All other expenses had to be found by the school itself. Staff costs were high because the institution employed a lot of people, and the only ones who were so underpaid, in relation to the amount of work they put in, were the counsellors. The building was dilapidated and cramped, so funding was also required for refurbishment and enlargement. Last but not least, Bettelheim needed to hire students to carry out the research which was also part of the school's charter.

And he was a very good fundraiser. The wives of several members of the Sonia Shankman Foundation set up an Auxiliary Branch, running a thrift shop to raise money. Bettelheim kept them under his spell, dropping in to see them from time to time with one or two of the children, and occasionally inviting them to visit the school. These ladies provided day-to-day help; it was they for example who bought the school its first station wagon, a second-hand Buick, used for picnics and other outings. Bruno Bettelheim's skill in raising funds, from private individuals but also from government agencies and major foundations, earned him the admiration of the university authorities, as is shown by the presidential archives stored in the Regenstein Library.[6] With the exception of one or two missives referring to his books, all the congratulatory letters to Bettelheim relate to cheques of 10,000 or 20,000 dollars or more, in donations to the Orthogenic School. In some cases the funds were intended for a particular project or child, in others their utilization was left up to the director. But the money always transited through the university's accounts.

As the university's aim was to spend as little as possible on the O.S., Ralph Tyler was delighted at the successes being chalked up by his protégé, and gave him strong backing. For example, at a Sonia Shankman Foundation fundraising dinner in November 1947, held to try to raise a million dollars for the construction of a new building, he gave a glowing speech in which he rated Bettelheim's work just after that of Enrico Fermi, the Los Alamos physicist who five years earlier had achieved the first controlled nuclear reaction, in an underground lab only a short distance from the school. He also told the assembled donors that, in recognition of their efforts, the school would henceforth bear the name of their foundation.

Bettelheim had very quickly grasped the workings of the US system, and understood how to use it to the school's advantage. But in exchange, he was forced to bow to the system's demands. The constant search for funds took up a huge amount of his time, which gave him the impression, when he was feeling depressed, that when Tyler and Hutchins had chosen him to run the school it had been above all for his skills as a businessman. That at least is how I interpret the disillusioned comments he would mutter on occasion to Ben Wright, Stuart Brent and a few others.

As we have seen,[7] his ruminations were unfair, but behind them there lurked a misunderstanding which was to poison Bettelheim's existence: it concerned the meaning of the word 'cure'. For the successful industrialists and businessmen who financed him, men who were lords of all they surveyed, from Third World dictatorships to the workers in their plants, the word could only have one very simple meaning. But it was not the same as for the therapist, faced every day with the suffering of children, and for whom each new word spoken, each gesture achieved, was a victory in itself. As Bruno Bettelheim belonged to both those worlds at the same time, he was aware of that difference. He played on it for the benefit of his school, but the price to be paid would be a high one.

This misunderstanding was to affect the way he presented his work, or at least the results of that work. For in reality the four books he was to devote to the school were all reports on the use of the grants he had obtained. Their real value, of course, lies elsewhere, but the financial dimension was important, and Bettelheim took care, in each publication, to thank his sponsors. On reading his correspondence, one sometimes gets the impression that almost up until the end of his tenure, he too was always late with some report or other. *Love is Not Enough* and *Truants from Life* resulted from a grant provided by the National Institute for Mental Health, a newly created branch of the Department of Health. The funds were for a study into 'the institutional treatment of emotionally disturbed children'. As for *The Empty Fortress*, its publication in 1967 was the culmination of a research project into infantile schizophrenia, sponsored by the Ford Foundation in 1956.

The latter grant, for 342,500 dollars, was to have a considerable influence on the development of the O.S. Due to the five year study it was inititially intended to finance, the general public would learn to associate the name of Bettelheim instantly with the psychological condition that at the time was seen as the ultimate form of schizophrenia in the child: autism. And because it amounted to a huge sum of money, the Ford Foundation grant would place a huge burden on its recipient's shoulders. An outsize grant called for outsize results; that, it seems to me, is the conclusion Bettelheim drew. Why otherwise would he have felt obliged to assert, in *The Empty Fortress*, that with the children involved in the study, he had achieved 42 per cent of 'good' results, 37 per cent of 'average' ones and only 20 per cent of failures, thus shattering all known records in the treatment of autism up until (and indeed since) then?

This huge exaggeration, which would prove detrimental both to the school and to Bettelheim himself, was but the logical conclusion of a process which had started well before. For although *The Empty Fortress* is the most striking example, it was not the first book in which Bettelheim had given an overly perfect image of the school.

'Your book's great, Bruno,' Fritz Redl said. 'But why did you turn it into a fairy story?' The comment was made during a visit to the school in 1950, just after *Love is Not Enough* had appeared in print. Redl was lunching at the staff table. Having thus got everyone's attention, he went on: 'Why didn't you talk about the most difficult? Why didn't you address the issue of discipline?' Ben Wright, who told me of the exchange, does not remember exactly what Bettelheim said in reply, but he believes it was something along the lines of: 'Because people wouldn't understand what I was trying to say. Because they would use it as an excuse to mistreat their own children.' Whatever his exact response, Wright adds, Bettelheim looked very irritated, and nobody else at the table said a word.

Before examining in depth the issue of discipline,[8] the above exchange is worth considering, for it throws light on at least one aspect of the Orthogenic School's development. I have found no one else who recalls that dining-room conversation, but it is perfectly believable, as other examples of such behaviour by Bettelheim can be cited. For him, certain things were better left unsaid. And contrary to what his enemies say, this was not only for the wrong reasons. The most explicit example I found does not directly concern the school. It occurred in July 1981, when Macmillan, Bettelheim's former publisher, was about to bring out *Mother Love, Myth and Reality*, by the French writer Elisabeth Badinter.[9] As its name suggests, the book examines what is generally known as the 'maternal instinct', and concludes that it does not in fact exist. Bettelheim had been asked to write a preface for the US edition, but he refused, explaining his decision by letter in the following terms: 'All my life I have been working with children whose lives have been destroyed because their mothers hated them .... The demonstration that there is no mothering instinct – of course there is none, otherwise there would not have been the many children who needed my professional services – and that so many mothers reject their own children will remove these guilt feelings which were the only brake which saved at least some children from destruction, suicide, anorexia, you name it. So I can not lend my name to remove this last barrier which offered many unfortunate children a chance against being destroyed.' Shortly afterwards, he was furious to learn that his letter had been published in the French daily newspaper *Le Matin de Paris*.[10] Badinter had indeed been amazed by his reaction, and had decided to make the debate public. While paying tribute to Bettelheim's work, and acknowledging that his position was coherent with the therapeutic rescue mission in which he had been involved for the previous three decades, she described his letter as 'an appalling admission of failure'. It was absolutely essential to tell the truth, Badinter wrote. This was 'perhaps the only way to ensure that psychiatrists, historians, thinkers and moral philosophers are forced to think in new ways about the mother-child relationship.' In a subsequent unpublicized letter, to Madeleine Chapsal, another French writer, Bettelheim dismissed Badinter's riposte as 'an intellectual reaction'.[11] In his view the idealism of her position was simply irresponsible, and was above all self-serving.

It is difficult to take sides in such a debate. On the one hand, it is normal and right for a young woman, whose life has so far spared her any extreme experiences, to believe in facing up to the deepest recesses of human nature. On the other, one cannot deny an old man who has spent his life fighting the demons hidden in those recesses the right to have given up hope of winning the battle by fair means. Nor the right to state that, given the tenacity of the enemy, all possible subterfuges may be used in order to defeat it. The debate between these two viewpoints has been going on ever since human beings started living in society.

However, when that debate is moved from the theoretical level of whether the maternal instinct may or may not exist to that of the need for discipline in the day-to-day running of an institution housing some forty seriously disturbed children, then without talking about 'truth', the need for simple frankness becomes obvious. For by too often demanding that others should 'do as I say, not as I do', Bettelheim not only gave his enemies a stick with which to beat him, he also disarmed his friends.

'He was so goddam moral!' says Gayle (Shulenberger) Janowitz, as if still amazed at the fact. Diana (Grossman) Kahn, who arrived at the school fifteen years later, puts it another way: 'He had such a strong sense of duty.' The disquiet that the accusations of brutality made against Bettelheim after his death inspired in the early counsellors illustrates the impact that the books had on the development of the school. Gayle never saw Bettelheim strike a child. Look angry, shout, yes, but strike, no. Or at least, she has no memory of that. It is true that at that time the occasional slap, or a smack on the behind, was nothing exceptional; perhaps it happened, when the situation required it, and she simply didn't notice. She finds the doubt infuriating. She knows that the school changed after she left it, and she strives to get a clearer, more accurate, idea of what it really became.

But she also knows that the picture of the school given in the books, even in *Love is Not Enough*, in which she features prominently, was a bit too glossy. 'The books were the ideal. The ideal we were all aiming for,' she says, a view expressed by all the early counsellors. *Love is Not Enough*, which is packed with photos, described a host of events that they had lived through. Perhaps a little differently from the way they had experienced them, but as usual, what counted in their eyes was the meaning Bettelheim was able to draw out of those events, this time for public consumption. In its essentials, the picture was true, and the school being described was the one they had lived in. If he had omitted to mention certain aspects of its workings, it was because he was only describing what was new, and important. And it is undeniable that Bruno Bettelheim's books changed the way people viewed disturbed children. Countless institutions, all over the world, were inspired by them, and notably by *The Empty Fortress*, at long last to pay attention to such children's suffering.

However, Bettelheim never saw anything wrong with being economical with the truth in order to promote a good cause. In 1947, for example, staff at the school became worried about the windows of the dormitories, on the first floor of the building. A child could jump out of one of them, possibly breaking a limb. Bettelheim therefore had bars put up. But as this was clearly contrary to his 'open door' policy, he immediately got the children together in the living room and told them that the reason for the barriers was that the neighbourhood was changing (which was true), and he wanted to make sure nobody could climb in through one of the windows. Bettelheim believed it was more reassuring for the children to think that the threat he was protecting them from came from outside, rather than from themselves.[12]

The counsellors were well aware of Bettelheim's taste for neatly packaged, exemplary stories. Josette Wingo called them his 'teaching stories':

This was long before I discovered Sufi stories, Elijah stories or Zen stories; the parables in the New Testament I had heard as a child had lost their zing through overfamiliarity. Dr B's Teaching Stories were special. They usually involved a friend who had had a similar problem and had reached such and such conclusion or resolution. Dr B was never at a loss for an appropriate anecdote, which usually had the satisfactory feeling of reducing anxiety, freeing energy to live through it, if not to resolve it, perhaps to become a protagonist in another story told to some other suffering soul some day .... It took a while to tumble to Dr B's stories as his masterful technique – some of the stories may even have been true – [was] crafted to fit the current situation. They were certainly psychologically true.

When the scandal broke after Bettelheim's death, Gayle and her former colleagues found it impossible to square what they were hearing with a certain number of facts, of which they were completely sure. They knew, for example, that the counsellors were not allowed to strike the children – because that was unusual – and that some newcomers had been immediately dismissed for doing so. The rule was so well established at the school that the children would sometimes use it to tease a recently arrived counsellor who had still not got her bearings. ('You're going to get fired, you know, when Dr B hears that you hit him!')[13]

The case of Gayle Janowitz is significant, as she is a solid, no-nonsense person who after being Bettelheim's assistant at the school, and having married one of his friends, never lost touch with him. She knew who he was, both his good and bad sides. But the gap he helped create between the reality of the school and its public image has made it very difficult for her to defend him against accusations concerning events that occurred after she had left. It is the same for the others. Fae Tyroler, Betty-Lou Pingree (Rellahan), Ronnie Dryovage, Joan Little Treiman, Jean Brown, Patty Pickett, Ben Wright, Shelton Key, George Kaiser, Adrian Kuypers, Lou Harper, and even those who were not there during the early years, such as Karen Zelan, Luitgard Wundheiler, Ugo and Maurie Formigoni, Kathy Lubin, Diana Grossman Kahn, Leslie Cleaver, Nina Helstein, Candace Hilldrup, Julie Newman, Elio Fratteroli, Geneviève Jurgensen and Marylin Garner: all the former counsellors and teachers I was able to speak to expressed, in their own different ways, the difficulty that Bettelheim's writings created for them in their attempts to defend the school from its detractors. Those who do not say so outright express their unease in their way of talking about the school, or in the way they brush off certain objections ('I didn't read that one. You know, I didn't get time to read ...'). Each person has their own way of seeing things and their own opinion; some are harsher than others. Some are aggressive, others philosophical. Many feel that each time they tried to explain what they had lived through in the school, and what Dr B had taught them, their statements were distorted. Somewhat as if, by playing games with the school's image, Bettelheim had prevented them from ever being able to pin it down. One of the few among them to have tried to, Jacquelyn Sanders, described an Orthogenic School that had very little in common with Bruno Bettelheim's description, save for the physical setting.[14] Which is hardly surprising, given that Bettelheim had left her his post, but nothing more.

On first hearing the charges laid against Dr B, some former counsellors wondered if maybe these things had taken place when they were on vacation, or while they were so absorbed by their group that an incident in another part of the school might have escaped their attention. But after thinking about it, and talking to a few other people, they realized that was impossible. Every issue was always raised at least once, and more often several times, in staff meetings. But their initial doubts cast a revealing light on the complexity of their relationship with Bruno Bettelheim.

The gap between the reality of the school and what Bettelheim wrote about it also made it more difficult for the children themselves to accept what he said about them. Several years after *Truants from Life* was published, one former student ('Paul') paid a visit to the school. Bettelheim asked him what he had thought of the book, and his reply was, 'I didn't know I was so bad.' Dr B first sought to reassure him: 'No one is bad.' He then asked 'Paul' to explain, and the young man told him that when he had arrived at the school, his only problem had been that he felt the orphanage in which he had been living was not the right place for him. 'Precisely,' said Bettelheim. He went on to remind 'Paul' of the anti-social behaviour he had used to express that feeling, and explained that in order to be understood by his readers, he was obliged to use labels. This cleared up the problem for 'Paul'. He points out however that some of his former schoolmates never came to accept the way Bettelheim portrayed them in his books.[15]

Writing about the school nevertheless involved a real difficulty: that of describing unconscious phenomena in a way that was at once comprehensible for lay readers, and convincing for specialists. Bettelheim's texts

were packed with examples, and they did indeed, on occasion, use psychiatric concepts. Inside the school, however, Bettelheim had from the start
made it clear that there should be no diagnoses. Of course, the children
arrived with medical records, which their counsellors and teachers could
consult if they so wished. But during the everyday life of the school, labels
were never used. People would refer to Richard's running away, Sandy's
bouts of rage or Linda's refusal to eat, but such behaviour was never given
a clinical name – at least not during the early years. The school thus felt
hardly at all like a psychiatric hospital, and as much as possible like a
home. So that even without Bettelheim's habit of adjusting his stories to
match the conclusion he sought to draw from them, the intentional,
therapeutically determined vagueness that surrounded goings-on at the
School made the latter difficult to describe. To understand this, one need
only dip into the books that Fritz Redl devoted to his own work with
problem adolescents.[16] While he, unlike Bettelheim, devotes much space
to the question of discipline, he does so in an abstract, theoretical way,
with a dryness of tone that does not do justice to his remarkable talents as
an educationalist and therapist. In both cases, the picture is incomplete,
but Bettelheim's books at least have the advantage of reaching a broader
public, and not just the specialists, who are always suspicious of new ideas,
particularly when they are put forward by someone from outside their
charmed circle.

   To help him get his ideas across, Bettelheim had found a talented
assistant. Ruth Soffer (later Marquis), the daughter of Jewish immigrants
from Russia, was an editor in the Chicago offices of the *Encyclopaedia
Britannica*. In August 1944 she was working on a ten-volume supplement
on World War II, to be published three years later. A subscriber to *Politics*,
a left-wing weekly, she was deeply impressed on reading Bettelheim's
concentration camp article there. She immediately suggested that he be
asked to write the entry on concentration camps. Ruth lived in Hyde Park,
and had on occasion run into Bettelheim socially. 'I have no time. But if
you can get something out of this, go ahead,' he told her, holding out the
original version of his article, much longer than what had appeared in
Politics. Seeing the young woman's worried expression, he added, 'Don't
worry – I'll read over what you write.' When he did, he was very pleased
with the result, and soon afterwards asked Ruth to become his personal
editor. Without hesitation, she accepted. At first, she restricted herself to
correcting his mistakes in English, and cutting out repetitive passages.
Then, as she gained self-assurance, she started chopping out passages she
thought redundant or complicated, resolving contradictions, and generally
transforming the rather repetitive and imperious prose of the German-
speaking intellectual, a little too eager to convince his readers, into
something more accessible for a broad English-speaking public. Of course,
Bettelheim always had the last word, but he had great faith in Ruth

Marquis's judgement, and agreed readily to cuts which made his writing better and more effective.

Ruth Marquis shared the first counsellors' enthusiasm for Bettelheim's ideas and approach. She was pretty, intelligent and hard-working and she enjoyed a relationship with Bettelheim that many at the school envied. When she was there, the two of them would shut themselves away in his office to work. Although she admired Bettelheim greatly, she would not hesitate to raise any disagreements she had with him. They talked a great deal; he opened up new worlds for her, introducing her to books such as *Civilization and its Discontents* and *The Psychopathology of Everyday Life*. She would drop in at the school in the morning to take what he had written the previous evening, and after her day's work at the *Encyclopaedia* she would come back at around 11 p.m. with her corrections. On occasion, he would hand her a sheaf of papers with a request such as 'Please get thirty-two pages out of that.' Today, Ruth Marquis still wonders whether it is possible to communicate to someone else the magnetism, vitality and energy that Bettelheim then radiated.

Bettelheim's first books owe a great deal to their work together. Although she would not say so herself, I believe that his exchanges with Ruth Marquis were decisive in moulding Bettelheim's very special style, and that her admiration freed him from a tendency to labour his points and assert his credibility, letting him exploit his true talent as a story-teller to describe phenomena that are not easily explained. Writing about the unconscious is indeed a thankless task. Many have tried, without much success. The reason is always the same, circular one: if something could be easily said, then it would not be unconscious, and if it is unconscious, that is because it is crude, basic and not very pretty. Freud was the first to acknowledge that the best way to describe unconscious phenomena was through fiction. Like him, Bettelheim frequently regretted that he did not have novel-writing skills. And if both of them nevertheless succeeded at least partly in their attempts, it was because they both knew how to spin a good yarn. By stimulating their readers' imaginations they helped them to feel, through what was being said, the depth of what was not being said.[17]

In 1948, Bruno Bettelheim met Jeremiah Kaplan, who had just founded The Free Press, a small company producing academic works on social science. He promised to write him a monograph on the school. Almost two years later, when Bettelheim handed over the manuscript of *Love is Not Enough*, Kaplan was dumbfounded. Although the two men, who both lived in Hyde Park, had often met in the meantime, Bettelheim had not told him that he was working on a real book, rich, exciting and easy to read. As he would with all the books that Ruth Marquis helped him with, he had done all the work beforehand, providing the publisher with the finished item, ready to go to the printer. Kaplan tore up the initial contract, not very favourable to the author, and replaced it with a regular one. *Love is Not*

Enough was to launch The Free Press into the wider world, beyond strictly academic publishing. For his other books with Kaplan, Bettelheim followed the same method of only signing a contract when he handed in the manuscript, without any prior agreement.

Some of Bettelheim's detractors have accused him of not having written his books himself. Later, he would even be accused of plagiarism.[18] The issue is worth examining in more detail. The accusations generally come from former O.S. students, from Bettelheim's colleagues or from journalists, but not from people who worked directly with him in his capacity as a writer. The latter speak differently: 'There's no doubt about it. He wrote his books himself. Even though ....' The qualifier is an allusion to the fact that most of his books were tacked together from pre-existing parts, such as essays, articles, case studies, etc. Using these as building-blocks, Bettelheim would play the architect. With the search for meaning as a plumb-line, he designed the overall structure, stood back and took a look, then produced the cement and the missing parts. He left to his editor, at least during Ruth Marquis's tenure, the task of fixing the details. Once that had been done, he would revise the whole thing, switching a few bits around or adding on new ones.

That was particularly true of his books about the school. For raw material, Bettelheim used the dictated reports of the counsellors and teachers, transcripts of staff meetings or any other document which he considered useful.[19] It was all the more easy for him to do in that he had already put his name to the monthly reports that counsellors and teachers had to write as well as their daily dictations. Those reports often constituted the only news parents would get from their children. Each month, and for each of the students, Bettelheim would edit one of the reports, adding his own comments and signing them. He did this to prevent any direct contact between parents and counsellors, be it only through a name. The counsellors belonged entirely to the children's world and he did not want certain parents to use the reports, during vacations, to undermine the relationships that their child was developing in that world. This tradition, which was the rule during all of Bettelheim's tenure at the school, was well understood during the early years. Some of the later counsellors, however, did not find it so easy to accept.

As regards his other books, there is no doubt that the material is his own. Which does not mean that every one was made up only of original material, for Bettelheim was a champion of the 'cut and paste' technique, recycling parts of his old essays and other texts, such as conference addresses (of which he produced a considerable quantity). Here again, his editor played a key role. As the editors who succeeded Ruth Marquis appear to have been less bold about making changes than she was, one can get a pretty good idea of how Bettelheim really wrote. *The Uses of Enchantment*, the first of his books produced without Marquis's help, and subsequent works, have one thing in common: they are repetitive, and that is true even of the very brief *Freud and Man's Soul*. The structure is in places more tangled, and less direct, than in the earlier books. In places only, for it is clear that when Bettelheim was gripped by the force of his demonstration, his ideas flowed on to the paper without one word too many. One day, he admitted to Ruth Marquis that he would have liked to have written novels like those of Trollope or Jane Austen, but added that he was unable to because the desire to write only ever came to him when he was carried away, either by anger or the desire to outwit a rival. (This latter aspect is nowhere more apparent than in his book reviews, of which he produced many. Most of them were ferocious.)

Heaviness and repetition do not in fact detract from the fundamentals of his texts, nor even from their progression, since Bettelheim liked to stoke his readers up, leading them step by step to the uncovering of some hidden mechanisms, as though telling a detective story. But they do make reading more difficult. The ideas remain powerful, and the climaxes striking, but the effect is often diluted by the rather obsessive way the writer returns to hammer at the same subject. This is particularly notice-able in *The Uses of Enchantment*, in which, having first laid out his overall analysis of the role of fairy tales, Bettelheim launches into a review of the best-known stories, repeating in each particular case what he has already outlined in general terms.

The start of the 1950s was a very fertile period for Bruno Bettelheim. Two of his books appeared in 1950: *Love is Not Enough*, and *Dynamics of Prejudice*, the latter written with Morris Janowitz. His second book on the school, *Truants from Life*, appeared in 1955, a year after *Symbolic Wounds*. He was also starting to be in demand from periodicals, such as *Parents Magazine*, the *University of Chicago Magazine* and the *Elementary School Journal,* for contributions on child-rearing. *Scientific American*[20] published a few of his case studies, while the Jewish press wanted him to write on children's reactions to anti-Semitism. And weightier publications, such as the *American Journal of Sociology*, printed his book reviews.

Altough Bettelheim's contribution to the ideas and analyses of *Dynamics of Prejudice: A Psychological and Sociological Study of Veterans* is undeniable, the book owes too much to Morris Janowitz to be a good example of Bettelheim as a writer. An analysis of racial prejudices among a group of freshly demobilized Chicagoans, it was published as one of the five parts of a project on the roots of anti-Semitism commissioned just after the war by the American Jewish Committee.[21] The aim of the huge study was to try and determine what kind of society could give rise to Nazi-type persecution, and to see if any of those social features were in evidence in the United States. In 1944 the Frankfurt philosopher Max Horkheimer, then living in exile in New York, and who headed the committee's Department of Scientific Research, asked Bettelheim to take charge of one of the projects. Several ideas had been put forward, including a study comparing racial prejudice among a group of psychotics to that among a control group. Bettelheim, who was then just getting started in his job as head of the school, did not want to undertake such a task on his own. He therefore asked the sociologist Edward Shils, whom he had met when he worked as an examiner, to help him. Having agreed in principle to take part, Shils was then posted in London by the military and had to stay there longer than planned. He sent Morris Janowitz to help Bettelheim out and the two of them went ahead with the book. Having taken part in the initial discussions and sent several long essays from London, Shils was taken aback when the book came out without his participation – even though the authors paid tribute to his contribution in their introduction.[22] He remained somewhat bitter about that, although he never said so publicly.

The meeting of Bruno Bettelheim and Morris Janowitz, who had spent the previous two years monitoring and analysing *Wehrmacht* radio transmissions for the OSS (US secret service), was to be the start of a real friendship. The young man was already specializing in the sociology of the military, a field in which he was to be a pioneer.[23] Bettelheim helped him deepen his understanding of, if not actually discover, psychoanalysis. The input data they used for *Dynamics of Prejudice* was Janowitz's, gathered for (and used in) his PhD dissertation.[24] Bettelheim's influence could be felt in the use of Freudian concepts (inspired by Anna Freud as well as by her father) to analyse the data. That influence consisted in 'reminding the reader that an individual's childhood experiences have an effect on the way he confronts the ups and downs of his existence, for example during military service', and that 'the more self-assured the ego is, the less the individual needs to bolster his own sense of self by hatred that identifies another ethnic group as evil'.[25] The study's conclusions are indeed quite close to those Bettelheim had reached as regards the anti-Semitism of the SS in the concentration camps.

With *Symbolic Wounds*, in contrast, Bruno Bettelheim wanted to make his mark in the realm of ideas. It was the first time he had set out to write a fully fledged book from almost the moment he put pen to paper, and it was one of his works to which he felt the most committed intellectually. The Orthogenic School was running the way he wanted it to and his ability to get results was beginning to be generally acknowledged. With the excitement of the early breakthroughs having somewhat subsided, Bettelheim was in need of new challenges. He felt the time had come for him to produce an original work, for despite his new role in the world of therapy, this had remained his prime ambition. Many of those who, like him, had fled the old continent, such as Heinz Hartmann, Erich Fromm and Otto Fenichel, were hard at work creating a sequel to the history of psychoanalysis. As also was Erik Erikson, whom Bettelheim had known in Vienna, at a time when he was a penniless artist.[26] After a brief psychoanalysis with Anna Freud, but without any academic training, Erikson had launched into a brilliant career in the United States. His *Childhood and Society*, published in 1950, was already seen as a landmark in the developing relationship between psychoanalysis and the social sciences. The time had come for Bruno Bettelheim, in his turn, to make a contribution to the growing edifice. He was to do it with an idea that had been in his mind for a long time, but which he had not been able to formulate clearly until he saw it confirmed by his observations at the school.

It was one of the children in Gayle Janowitz's charge who first aroused his curiosity. 'Harry', as Bettelheim was to call him in *Truants from Life*, had arrived at the school at the age of seven. He was a perpetual runaway, and his behaviour was provocative in every other way, but particularly on the sexual level. He was continually showing off his erect penis, chanting 'Look at my beautiful ....' He also had an obvious fear of castration; on one occasion he threatened to emasculate a superb snowman he had built, because, he said, it had run away. On another, sitting in his bath, he held his penis with one hand and pretended to saw it off with the other, asking Gayle: 'Do you think any mother would do this to her little boy?' Speaking of his mother, 'Harry' also used to say, 'She has no tits. She's a man.' In his most agitated moments, he often also asked his (female) counsellors to show him their penises. What struck Bettelheim most was the pleasure 'Harry' procured, a little later and when circumstances such as Halloween allowed him to do so without being ridiculed, from dressing up as a girl. At first sight, this might be due to the fact that his mother had treated him ever since his birth as a 'mean boy', with all the ambiguity the idea contained, while showing loving and maternal behaviour towards his sisters, who were born after him. But Bettelheim suspected that there was something else. A little later, his attention was drawn to a kind of initiation rite invented by a group of four adolescents. When two of the girls began to menstruate, the boys took to each cutting their fingers every month, with the intention of mingling their blood with that of the girls.

In 1949 Bettelheim published a long case study on 'Harry', who by then was well on the way to recovery.[27] Presenting it to fellow analysts, he produced a number of hypotheses suggested to him by the behaviour of his young charges. Stressing that, within the safe boundaries of the school, children often allowed themselves to express crude feelings that are generally repressed in society, he said he had observed expressions of a desire to belong to the opposite sex in all pre-adolescent children, under one form or another. He suggested that Sigmund Freud had not paid sufficient attention to this factor in his theory of the Oedipus complex.[28] His listeners' reactions had been so aggressive and patronizing – or so, at least, he felt – that Bettelheim immediately set out to prove he was right. It was a time when many social anthropologists were flirting with psycho-analysis. Having explained his idea to Ruth Marquis, he asked her to sift through the rich ethnographic literature of the period to find data that would complete – and confirm – his observations from the school.

Symbolic Wounds is a treatise on puberty rites, particularly those centring almost entirely on circumcision. Having noted that this is a universal rite, found in one form or another on all continents and at all periods of history, Bettelheim refused to see in it only the symbolic castration of sons by fathers that Freud had portrayed in his *Moses and Monotheism*. In line with the positive approach of Ego Psychology, he criticized the Freudian interpretation for putting too much stress on the aggressive, negative aspect of the rite. In order for it to have survived everywhere, circumcision also had to have a positive function, he wrote. According to Freud, its purpose was to ensure observance of the incest taboo by generating castration anxiety. Bettelheim wondered whether it was not, on the contrary, a relatively effective way of mastering the fear that arises in a young boy's mind when he discovers that only women can bear children.

His survey of primitive societies provided him with evidence of that fear from all over the world, and of the rites aimed at surmounting it when boys reached the age at which society expected them to fulfil their sexual role. However as the goal of such rites (to provide men with mastery over reproduction) could never be achieved in reality, they were always surrounded with a dense aura of mystery, designed to cover up that failure. That was what he called 'the secret of men'. The most astonishing example he quoted was 'stopping up the rectum', performed at puberty by the Chaga of Africa, as described by O.F. Raum.[29] Shortly after being circumcised, a young boy was dressed up in women's clothes, and then taken into the 'Men's House', where his true initiation would take place. This was not a physical act, but only the simulation of one, a secret he learned only at that moment of becoming a man. From that time on, he was supposed to stop defecating. This was seen as a proof of his virility, just, Bettelheim stresses, as the halt of menstruation at the start of a pregnancy was seen as a proof of womanhood. Nobody of course really believed the men's story; the older men would give the initiate tips on how to relieve himself without being seen, while the women would joke among themselves on the men's secret, all the while pretending to believe in it in their presence. But the fiction created an illusory parallelism between the sexes. Just as the act of circumcision provided the young boy with both the appearance of a vaginal opening, and, by exposing the head of the penis, a permanent affirmation of his virility, thereby helping him overcome his fear at not mastering the act of procreation.[30] Here once again is the Bettelheim for whom every symptom, even the most apparently incomprehensible, has a meaning, and is the most appropriate way the subject has found to fight his or her anxiety. The subtitle of *Symbolic Wounds, Puberty Rites and the Envious Male*, elegantly sums up its central idea.

The tone of the book, however, is not peremptory. It is that of a prudent seeker of truth, carefully opening up avenues of research but refusing to close any off. The work is solidly documented, and Bettelheim is careful to stress his ignorance as regards anthropology. As for his dialogue with Freudian ideas, it is more subtle than one might expect. He does not see 'vagina envy' as excluding castration anxiety, but simply as the other side of the same coin. However, he writes, 'it seems that in any society, envy of the dominant sex is the more easily observed'.[31] And though the book's central thesis may seem incompatible with that of *Moses and Monotheism*, Bettelheim nevertheless bases himself on Freud's ideas to demonstrate it, as he stresses in his dedication: 'To the memory of Sigmund Freud, whose theories on sex and the unconscious permit a fuller understanding of the mind of man.'[32]

Such precautions were to no avail. Although *Symbolic Wounds* attracted a handful of enthusiastic reviews, and even today retains a small number of unconditional supporters who consider it unjustly neglected, the overall reaction to it was not very good. The anthropologists accused Bettelheim of paternalism and ethnocentrism, since he appeared to be lumping together the rites of primitive societies and the outlandish behaviour of the schizophrenics in his school. (It is worth noting that at precisely that time, the 'culturalist' tendency among Freudian dissidents was attacking psychoanalysis for seeking to make the Oedipus complex a universal model.) The psychoanalysts, meanwhile, were hardly less critical of Bettelheim's book, which they saw as betraying 'vaginocentrism'.[33]

Bettelheim may have been prepared for criticism, but he was nevertheless hurt by the book's failure to convince his peers.[34] He attempted to reply to the anthropologists' arguments in a second edition, revised to take account of certain criticisms. He stressed, for example, that his use of the expression 'primitive' to describe desires was in no way pejorative, as he was referring to the original desires of human beings, whoever they may be. And that if he lumped together children, schizophrenics and 'primitive' peoples, that was simply because those desires were more visible in such people than in 'normal' adults in Western societies. This did not convince the critics, however. Jean Pouillon, in his appendix to the French edition of *Symbolic Wounds*, described Bettelheim's statement as 'ambiguous', noting that 'primitive societies, just like our own, contain children, schizophrenics and adults, and they should not be confused with one another'.[35]

The book however deserves better than the disdain with which most experts have continued to view it. Some observers still see it as being ahead of its time. Whatever the case, it at least had the merit of asking an original question, from an unusual viewpoint, in a field in which research and theory had always been, with a few notable exceptions, dominated by the masculine viewpoint. *Symbolic Wounds* marked an important stage in Bruno Bettelheim's life. As Ruth Marquis notes, it summed up 'all he thought about men and women'. Ben Wright confirms that Bettelheim was 'not angry, but hurt' by the incomprehension which greeted it. This time, he had tried to state the whole unvarnished truth, as he really saw it. He had indeed tried to do away with 'fraud', since he had gone so far as to reveal 'the secret of men' – that phallic superiority is a myth, one that can only be perpetuated with the at least tacit acquiescence of women. And his conclusion was above all an appeal for tolerance, for the acceptance by our societies of the individual's polyvalent tendencies 'would go a long way to lessen the negative effects of the antithesis between the sexes'. He goes on: 'If we could give greater recognition to boys' desire to bear children, to the desire of male adolescents and adult men for the more passive and leisurely enjoyment of life, instead of having always to "fight and to strut", our boys and men might feel less envy and anxious hostility toward girls and women.' They would then also have less need to 'assert power through destructive inventions', Bettelheim concluded.[36]

For anyone interested in Bettelheim's life, and not just his ideas, these words take on a somewhat tragic dimension. This appeal made to society to recognize, behind the deceptive image of the all-powerful phallus, the right of men to also be fragile, can indeed be heard as a cry from the too-powerful and too-responsible director of the Orthogenic School, seeking to make people realize that he too was only human, under the magician's costume that he could don to such convincing effect.

'If I had to sum up in one word what I learnt from him, I would say: autonomy,' says Ruth Marquis. That indeed was Bruno Bettelheim's aim, to turn the children in his charge, his students and the young people who worked for him into autonomous, responsible, self-respecting adults. People who were capable of running their own lives, fully aware of the choices facing them and in full possession of their faculties. Capable of loving and working, as Freud said when summing up the aims of psychoanalysis. Throughout his life, Bettelheim would respect people who were capable of standing up to him and maintaining their integrity, whatever treatment he meted out to them. He did not much like meeting resistance, but if that resistance sprang from real feelings, he respected it. What he really hated was what he called 'passive aggressivity'; hostility that dared not speak its name.

Being able to stand up to him, or at least resist being overwhelmed by him, was a question of temperament, not one of age. Adrian Kuypers, who was a student at the school for a long time before returning as a teacher, adored Bruno Bettelheim, and the feeling was mutual. But even as a child, she never let him affect her to the point where she lost sight of her own identity. 'Dr B thought I was anorexic. I didn't think that was true. But I didn't say anything, because he seemed to like the idea.' And indeed, on the photo published in the US edition of *Love is Not Enough*, where the eight-year-old Adrian is seen reading a book, her arms are far from skinny. But the exact diagnosis was not very important.[37] What counted was that, while acknowledging that Bettelheim was doing a great deal for her, and admitting that she was afraid of him ('he could see right away what you were thinking and all the terrible things you had done'), she was aware that 'there was always that softness inside of him', and never believed him to be infallible.

That was by no means the case for everyone. The spreading fame of Bruno Bettelheim's books had started to affect the people around him. Now the mothers who brought him their children were expecting miracles; they had read *Love is Not Enough*. And as the years of war and depression had given way to a new affluence, the profile of the students who applied to work at the school had also changed. No longer were most of them tough, hard-working young women who saw Bettelheim as an immigrant who had lost everything, and wanted to do something useful before having children of their own. Those who came knocking on his door now had a very different view of life. They had grown up in better times, and had more diplomas, as over the years Bettelheim had become more demanding on that score. But they were also more malleable and more fragile. And for some of them the fact that a woman's role was now less clearly defined than before, which meant that their spell in the school could be seen as the start of a career, only added to their anxiety. Psychoanalytic jargon was now all over the media, and the once-poor immigrant had become a public figure. The desire to do good was still there, but applicants for counsellors' jobs now no longer came to help Dr B as much as to seek help – and answers – from him.

Just when did Bettelheim first encourage one of his counsellors to lie down on the couch in his office for a session? It is difficult to say with any precision, since as Gayle Janowitz points out, the distinctions were blurred from the outset. Those one-to-one discussions in the director's office could be seen as debriefing sessions on the counsellor's work, supervisory activity, personal talks, or all of the above. Some of the counsellors who had regular appointments with Bettelheim would see them simply as an opportunity to deepen their professional understanding. As Diana Grossmann Kahn, a counsellor from 1961 to 1969, puts it: 'It was the one occasion when an incident could be analysed, not in terms of the child's welfare, but of mine.' It is true she had been in analysis before arriving at the school, and was thus able to tell the difference. Others, however, were certainly convinced that the regular meetings they had with Bruno Bettelheim in the privacy of his office amounted to an analysis, or in any case to psychotherapy.

During the early years, Bettelheim encouraged his staff to undertake therapy outside the establishment. And right up until the end, he would hand out the names of analysts to anyone who asked for them. But quite soon, it seems, he stopped broaching the subject. In fact, practical considerations – the low pay and long working hours – ruled out any external therapy for even the most determined members of staff. In the unlikely event that he or she could set aside the money to pay for it, as most analysts practised downtown, the counsellor would have to find the time to take a half-hour subway ride in each direction, plus the time for the treatment, several times weekly. A few brave souls tried it, but threw in the sponge after a few months. As Bruno Bettelheim was on hand, and as the young people had the daily opportunity to witness his astonishing gifts of understanding, it was difficult to resist his helping hand, whenever he honoured them by offering it.

Bettelheim did not in fact call it analysis, or even therapy, but rather 'dynamic supervision', which was how he explained this aspect of his work to Bert Cohler, when the latter was about to succeed him as director. He liked to say that psychoanalysis was 'the icing on the cake', implying that people at the school were still at the stage of making the cake itself, rather than icing it. Bettelheim also explained that although milieu therapy was everyday life organized according to Freudian principles, it was not psychoanalysis. For his staff, however, a regular appointment in his office became a status symbol. There was strong rivalry between the counsellors, and those who were 'in therapy with Dr B' most certainly earned extra points with their colleagues. He knew this, and at times he used it. On a few occasions he even offered sessions to a counsellor who was about to leave the school. Some of those who accepted were glad they did so; others now regret that they did not go through with their decision at the time. Yet others simply said 'No.'

George Kaiser, who was at the school from 1948 to 1952, was one of the latter. It is a subject he still finds embarrassing, as he has retained not only a lot of affection, but also a profound admiration for Bruno Bettelheim. Having instinctively perceived the incident as manipulative when it occurred, he finds it difficult to talk about it. And yet Bettelheim's relationships with men were simpler than those with the opposite sex. What had first impressed Dr B about Kaiser, a twenty-seven-year-old Jewish American, was the fact that he had served in the US Air Force during the war. When taking visitors through his class, he would always introduce him with the words 'This is George Kaiser, who dropped bombs over Germany.' Kaiser had been attracted to the school by the stories his wife, Cathy, brought back from the mothers' meetings. He had quickly realized, however, that although one could learn a lot at the School, it was very clear who was boss. He went to offer his services as a teacher, but Bettelheim insisted that he first take charge of a group for six months, 'so you can see what the school is all about'.

One day during his first week, Kaiser was taking over his group after class. 'What are we doing this afternoon?' the children shouted, jumping all about him in the hallway. 'Let's go into the dorm and talk about it,' was his reply. But Bettelheim, who was observing the scene, interrupted him.

'You tell them now, George,' he said sternly. A few minutes later, softening his tone, he added: 'You see, Tom and Bobby can wait till they get to the dorm. But Billy can't. That's why you've got to tell him now.' Like other counsellors, George Kaiser was faced with the sudden realization that he had a lot to learn before he could respond spontaneously to these children's needs. But he also could not forget that the incident had taken place in public. Later on, Bettelheim gave him the impression that he would like to groom him to be his successor. In June 1952, he made George Kaiser his deputy director. He was thus in charge of receiving the parents, and chairing staff meetings during Dr B's absences, in particular his August vacation. Kaiser found the position uncomfortable, however. As the staff meetings were always tape-recorded, Bettelheim made a few critical remarks on his return. Even in the subsidiary tasks he was given, George felt that he did not have any real scope for initiative. For while Dr B allowed his counsellors plenty of leeway in dealing with the children, he could exercise his prerogative on any detail, however minor, from the colour of the curtains to the contents of the candy closet. George therefore decided to take up a post at the Lab School, on the other side of the Midway. It was then that Bettelheim made the offer of therapy sessions, which George turned down.

Here again, it is easy to rush to judgement and condemn Bettelheim over appearances, but much harder to reach a truly informed opinion. From a formal point of view, things are relatively clear: an arrangement in which one and the same person acts as both director and psychotherapist is subject to criticism. Fantasies are one thing, reality another, and to mix them up is to open the door to all sorts of manipulatory behaviour. In practice, however, things are more complicated. Bettelheim was certainly neither the first, nor the only, head of a psychiatric institution to wear both hats at once. And the way he worked with, or rather through, his counsellors did indeed create a relationship of transference, not unlike the one an analysand develops with his or her analyst. The fact that in some cases he considered it useful, either for the counsellor herself or for the children in her group, to analyse that relationship during one-to-one sessions is not in itself shocking. It is certainly not very orthodox, but then was not the function of the Orthogenic School precisely to seek new solutions? Furthermore, the authority that Bruno Bettelheim wielded over most of his counsellors was such that it would have necessarily interfered with any transferential relationship they developed with an outside analyst.

Conversely, if a counsellor had developed a strong analytical relationship outside the school, it would probably have interfered with Bettelheim's power; it should not be forgotten that the counsellors themselves saw the children in one-to-one sessions, and it was absolutely essential that Bettelheim retain his ability to supervise those relationships. After all, the children had been put in his care. Being well placed to appreciate the power that the process of transference gives to the analyst, he knew that if his counsellors were to undergo analyses outside, 'his' children would in effect be falling under the authority of other analysts. Could he, who continually criticized his fellow practitioners, accusing them of being mainly interested in money, allow that to happen?

The school's therapeutic system had two tiers: children – counsellors, and counsellors – Dr B, and one could not work without the other. Although some counsellors, here again, laboured under an illusion, their function as Bettelheim saw it was not really to act as therapists. If he asked them to see two or three children for regular one-to-one sessions, the aim was for them to deepen their relationship, to give the students an opportunity for individual contact, and not to engage in analysis. That was his job (which he carried out both via the reports of the counsellors, and, precisely, through his relationship with the latter) and, secondarily, that of the consultant psychiatrist. The former counsellor Leslie Cleaver, who is herself an experienced psychotherapist, explains the difference well: 'We didn't analyse the transference as you would in a regular session, because we also had a parental function with the kids. The point in milieu therapy is that you deal with what actually happens and how the kid feels about it at the time. So that the kid can get organized around you, and the other kids in the dormitory and Dr B, and that they become aware of how they feel. But you don't deal with it as if it was from the past. You deal with it in the present.'[38] Bettelheim indeed provided implicit confirmation of this in 1971, when after leaving the school in the hands of Bert Cohler, he returned nine months later to resume control. In his absence the psychoanalyst Al Flarsheim, consultant at the School, had started giving the counsellors a little training in therapy, explaining certain mechanisms of the unconscious, and how to deal with them. Although Bettelheim was very fond of Flarsheim, a young psychoanalyst who had attended his seminars and was also in frequent contact with Donald Winnicott in London, he immediately wanted to put a stop to the courses. He was prevented from doing so by strong opposition from a handful of counsellors (one of whom was Leslie Cleaver, who was in analysis with Flarsheim). But that only went to show that the school had already started slipping out of his hands.

That then was the Bettelheim system. The specialists will no doubt hand down their verdicts, if they can. One can simply hope that their judgements will be based not on preconceived ideas, but by comparing the principles with the practical results, and without forgetting the conditions under which the system operated. Besides, Bettelheim's therapeutic practices were not a secret in any real sense; it was not because he had asked them to keep quiet that the counsellors did not talk much about them to people outside. From the early 1960s, the fact that he played therapist with his counsellors was an open secret in Chicago's psychoanalytic and psychiatric circles. It was the object of much whispering, generally with suggestive overtones. Ugo Formigoni's wife Maurie experienced this after leaving the school. 'So you worked at the Orthogenic School? And were you in therapy with Bettelheim? On the couch?' She got tired of answering such questions from colleagues of Ugo's, whom she had married after he left the School. As she found them both unpleasant and unfair, she would refuse to reply, a fact that probably only gave more currency to the rumours.

Depending on who one speaks to, the end of the 'magic' period at the school can be situated between 1951 and 1956. In a letter congratulating Gayle Janowitz on her marriage, in 1951, Bettelheim already expresses nostalgia for the old days. Then he backtracks: 'They weren't [better]. We have now a better school,' adding: 'But I was younger and had more idealism.' 1952 certainly seems to have been a turning-point in his life. In that year, Bettelheim had a son, and he also achieved tenure as a professor in the Education Department. Meanwhile the extension and refurbishment of the school were completed. With an extra building and new play areas, the environment changed completely, and the number of groups rose from four to six.

Soon, the rule under which students left the school at the age of fourteen was also dropped. Early experience had shown that results could only be obtained over time, and it was often just when a child was beginning to improve that he had to leave. Although Dr B had devoted a lot of energy to finding suitable families to look after such children, many would stop improving, or even regress, on leaving the School. Some asked to return, others experienced their departure as a rejection, and suffered from it. Meanwhile the break between the children and their parents became greater. Now when a child was admitted, Bettelheim demanded that he not see his family at all for at least the first nine months. In the early years, the children had often spent all their vacations with their parents, except in too-serious cases.[39] But they would frequently return disturbed and filled with anxiety once again, as if months of effort had been wasted. Of course the children were allowed to receive mail, but for the same reason this was read by the counsellors before being given to them. In the mid-1950s the idea that parents were responsible for the psychological problems of their children was very widespread in professional circles; Bettelheim was simply putting it into practice.

The six-month trial period, during which the counsellors tried to see if they could get through to a child, had been dropped. It no longer had much meaning now that the school was beginning to take in children who were more and more seriously disturbed. On passing through for a visit a few years after her departure, Betty-Lou Pingree told Gayle Janowitz that the school looked much more like a psychiatric institution than it had in their time. Thanks to the inflow of donations and grants, however, the surroundings had been greatly improved. From the start, Bettelheim had done everything he could to ensure that the children had pleasant living conditions; now he wanted them to be luxurious. The old flower-patterned sofas were replaced by velvet-upholstered items, and the plastic crockery by fine china. At some point Bettelheim even brought in red crystal drinking glasses. The theory being as always that surrounding the children with beautiful objects was a way of showing them that they were accepted, and that their well-being was the number one priority for both himself and the staff as a whole. Both Gayle Janowitz and Bert Cohler think he went too far, however. 'It was more to please himself than the kids. Besides, the old furniture was much more comfortable,' says Cohler, who after being a student at the school up until 1956 went back to live there in 1969, when Bettelheim asked him to be his successor. Bert Cohler adds that in his view the change can be read between the lines of the books Bettelheim wrote about the school. As he sees it, the last of them, *A Home for the Heart*, is devoted mainly to architecture and interior decorating.

At the university, Bettelheim's reputation was by now well established. His aggressiveness towards his students was legendary, but far from driving away recruits, it tended to attract them. Bernice Neugarten, who ran the Committee on Human Development, recalls that two or three times as many students would be enrolled for Bettelheim's courses at the start of the year as for any other teacher. This did not worry her overmuch, however; she knew that after a couple of weeks, many of them would be asking to switch.

He was respected for his results, but was also in conflict with many of his peers. He was an indefatigable worker, who seemed to be everywhere at once, forever churning out courses, lectures, articles or travelling, while still managing to read hundreds of pages of reports and dictations every month in his capacity as director-cum-therapist. But the latter task provided him with the opportunity to know every last detail of what was going on, and thus the temptation to exercise universal control. And although he had demonstrated the necessary limits to such omnipotence in *Symbolic Wounds*, the tendency increased over the years. After the lukewarm reception granted to that book, in which he had sought to state his own personal truth, but one which hardly anyone had wanted to hear, Bettelheim returned to writing about the school.

Ruth Marquis had left Chicago, but she and Bettelheim stayed in touch by letter. At her request, she put together *Dialogues with Mothers* (because Bettelheim did not really believe in the project). She worked from the transcribed recordings of the meetings, which she had attended before becoming a mother herself. She also played an important part in putting together *The Informed Heart*, insisting that Bettelheim put more of his own feelings into the work and interviewing him to help him recall the inner tumult he had experienced in Buchenwald.

Once a book was finished, she would shut herself away at home for a few days and dip into her favourite writings, in particular the poems of

William Blake. Then she would draw up a list of twenty or so possible titles, from which Bettelheim would make his choice. Sometimes she would use an expression drawn from the text itself, such as *Empty Fortress*, which had been used by one of the teachers at the school, Luitgard Wundheiler, in a report on an autistic boy in her class. Ruth Marquis provided Bettelheim with the titles for all his books, with the exception of *Symbolic Wounds*. They were such good titles,[40] showing such a subtle understanding of the text, that they became as it were common property, testimonials to the memory of Bettelheim. As shown by an anecdote from a former student, who told me of a conversation with Bettelheim he had, as he was about to leave the school at fourteen. He was discussing his mother with Bettelheim, and said: 'Oh, you know, everything she did to me, she did out of love.' Then, after pausing for a few seconds, he blurted out: 'But love is not enough.' The incident no doubt occurred – after the book's publication. But such is the power of words, when they suddenly take on their full meaning, that the former student is convinced that he gave the phrase to Dr B.

Ruth Marquis's role in helping Bettelheim shape his ideas was sufficiently important for him to not only provide the standard acknowledgements in each of them, but also to dedicate a volume to her. That was *The Empty Fortress*, which came out in 1967. It was the last but one of the books on which she was to work, for towards the end of the 1960s, Ruth no longer agreed with all of Bettelheim's ideas. The divergence was initially political: their opinions on issues such as the Vietnam War and the student revolt were at odds. Then, more subtly, she began to observe that sometimes the effect of her friend's books was the exact opposite of what he had been aiming at. One day, she found one of her neighbours in tears. 'I did it all wrong,' the woman wailed, having just read a few pages of *Love is Not Enough*. Ruth tried to calm her down, explaining that Bettelheim did not provide recipes to be applied word for word, but that his aim on the contrary was to encourage young mothers to be freer and more spontaneous in their relationships with their children. At the same time, she felt somehow responsible for her neighbour's distress. So that in the early seventies, when she received his latest manuscript, she blurted out: 'Oh no! We're not now going to start telling mothers how and when to read fairy tales to their children!' Bettelheim did everything he could to get her to change her mind, but to no avail. While declining to work on the book, she nevertheless gave him a title for it: *The Uses of Enchantment*.

Chapter XIII

The Ultimate Limit

My task which I am trying to achieve is, by power of the written word
to make you hear, to make you feel – it is, before all, to make you *see*.
That – and no more, and it is everything. If I succeed, you shall find
there according to your deserts: encouragement, consolation, fear, ...
and, perhaps, also that glimpse of truth for which you have forgotten
to ask.

Joseph Conrad, *The Nigger of the Narcissus*, quoted by
Bettelheim as the last lines of *Surviving*

'My life is my work, Trude and the children. And, if I am completely honest,
in that order,' Bruno Bettelheim wrote in September 1954.[1] The director
of the Orthogenic School had indeed little time to devote to his family.
When he woke up, at around nine thirty, his wife and children had already
left. On weekdays, he would return home between six thirty and seven.
After freshening up, he would join the family for the evening meal.
Dinnertime was sacred in the Bettelheim household. It was a European
affair with a tablecloth and napkins; a formal style that used to grate a
little on Bettelheim's daughters. They were forbidden to leave the table
before the meal was over, a rule which was relaxed somewhat in the 1960s,
when it was their brother Eric's turn to fidget with impatience while
waiting to go outside and play.

After dinner, Bettelheim would relax for a while. He would sometimes
play cards or another game with the children, especially when Fritz Redl
was there. While Trude was busy bathing Eric, or tidying up the kitchen,
he would also help the girls with their homework when needed. Or else he
read the counsellors' dictations while drinking his coffee. Then, around
nine thirty, he would return to the school. This was the routine six days a
week, for Bettelheim also worked Saturdays. On Sundays he would get up
a little later than usual, and the family would enjoy a leisurely brunch.
But in the afternoon Bettelheim would be off again to the Orthogenic
School.

People who dined informally at the Bettelheims' home, such as Gina
Weinmann, her daughter Catherine, or Ruth Marquis, all recall that the
conversation was lively, and that one had to fight to get a word in. Bruno
and Trude would discuss world affairs, or their respective jobs, which both
were totally caught up in. And their elder daughter Ruth would try very

hard to catch their, or rather her father's, attention. Her younger sister, Naomi, was the only member of the family to remain aloof, lost in day-dreams and playing little part in dinner-table conversations. 'She was like Cinderella,' says one eyewitness. It might be more accurate to describe her as a wild flower, growing free without needing to be tended. 'I have two daughters,' Bettelheim liked to say; 'one of them had to be continuously pampered throughout her childhood, the other one would have been top of her class, no matter what.'[2] And when a psychoanalyst friend of his once asked him why he was 'so hard on Naomi and so lenient on Ruth', he did not feel guilty at all – or so he would write later.[3] Of his three children, Naomi was the one who most resembled him, both physically and intellec-tually. Lively and intelligent, she had the same biting sense of humour as her father, and her little face was often screwed up into a frown. Some observers even thought they could detect some rivalry in Bettelheim's attitude to his younger daughter.

Caught between an elder sister who did everything she could to mono-polize her father during the rare moments he spent with them, and a kid brother who was the pride and joy of his mother, Naomi had decided early on that she had better make her own life for herself, independent of the family dramas. She had her own interests, her girlfriends, her books and her school life. She was not quite eight years old when the Bettelheims moved into a house at 5725 Kenwood Street, but when asked which bedroom she wanted for herself, she had no hesitation in picking one on the top floor. In early childhood, her best friend had been Catherine Weinmann, who was born a month after her. And when Gina and her family left Hyde Park to set up in faraway Highland Park, one of the affluent suburbs to the north of Chicago, Naomi would often go and stay with the Weinmanns during weekends and school vacations.

Bettelheim's relationship with his elder daughter was more compli-cated. Later he would attribute his problems with Ruth to the fact that she had been born when he and Trude were still recently arrived immigrants, struggling to make their way and living in precarious conditions. To make up for the time he was unable to spend with her, he was continually buying her gifts. Which was why, he would explain, she had turned into 'a grabby little girl'.[4] Although this explanation sounds a little self-serving, there is ample evidence that Ruth was indeed what is called a spoilt child, moody and difficult. She needed to be loved and admired, and to be constantly reassured that she was loved and admired.[5] For example, she hated having to wear the clothes her mother picked for her. Pragmatic above all, and conditioned by her Montessori training, Trude did not share the enthusiasm of many American mothers for ribbons and frills. When she found comfortable and sensible garments at the school's yearly jumble sale, she had no qualms about buying them. As Trude worked a great deal, Ruth also had to learn to dress herself very early on. One day her nursery school teacher made a disparaging comment in her report card about the way she was dressed, which left Ruth with a deep feeling of injustice.

Ruth was nevertheless the eldest child, adored by both her parents and particularly by her father. In her early years, she was often a source of worry, due to a series of minor problems. According to an unconfirmed story Bettelheim told some friends, he took her to the hospital one day to check whether she was suffering from a urinary ailment, as she had suddenly started wetting her bed again. Such was the vogue at the time for psychological explanations of everything that the doctor burst into laughter: 'What, even you, Dr Bettelheim!' But, the latter concluded triumphantly, Ruth did indeed have a urinary ailment.[6] Then, in an article entitled 'How to Arm our Children against Anti-Semitism',[7] he recounted how his daughter had at a very early age wondered aloud why a friend had called her a 'Shoe' and, a little later, how she had been very upset by more explicit racist comments (and how he had managed to defend her). Later on, he became worried that she did not have any friends; and both Trude and he devoted much energy to remedying that situation. Later still, he worried about the company she was keeping, particularly during Ruth's hippie phase. He introduced her to other young people, and at one point he reportedly even tried to convince an already-married Ben Wright to spend more time with his elder daughter. And in 1968, when his younger daughter, then living in Mexico, announced her engagement, he said to Gayle Janowitz: 'Naomi should have waited for her elder sister to marry first!' However advanced his ideas may have been in his work, at home Bruno Bettelheim was quite simply a father like other fathers, and a rather old-fashioned one to boot.

One weekend in 1947, the Bettelheims were visiting the Sheviakovs when somebody suggested going for a walk. Everyone was in favour except Bettelheim. And as two-year-old Naomi was likely to slow the party down, it was decided that she should stay behind with her father. The latter immediately dropped into a rocking chair and started reading, while the little girl soon became bored, and started playing with her nappy. When the group returned, some two hours later, they found the infant busily smearing excrement over the living-room walls, while her father was rocking furiously back and forth. The story unfortunately does not tell at exactly what point Bettelheim looked up from his book and discovered what was going on. Too late, no doubt, for him to imagine that he could actually do something about it!

'At home, he was a different man,' Ruth Marquis recalls. 'He was always apologizing. For being late, for not being able to start the car, for not having done this or that.' She remembers Trude Bettelheim bossing her husband around occasionally, sometimes with a measure of irritation. Her description seems at odds with those of other eyewitnesses who paint an almost contrary picture, with Bettelheim often being rather off-handed with his wife. This may be simply due to the fact that Ruth Marquis left

Chicago in the early fifties, but it could also have to do with her being one of the very few people who saw Bettelheim at close quarters in both his worlds: the Big Bad Wolf usually shed his coat on leaving the school for home. However it is true that the relationship between Bruno and Trude Bettelheim seems to have undergone quite a change after he started running the Orthogenic School. The very early counsellors remember a day when Trude arrived at the school in tears and closeted herself with Bettelheim in his office. It was not in keeping with her character, and the onlookers automatically assumed that she was at the end of her tether, having to wait endless hours for her husband, alone with their young daughter. The cause of her sorrow may well have been something else entirely, but that was the explanation that seemed obvious.

Bettelheim ended up behaving somewhat like a guest in his own home, leaving the running of the house entirely to Trude. She took care of everything: the children, the housekeeping, his clothes, the car and even the family dog and the garden (at which she became very proficient). The only practical aspect of the family home that Bettelheim took an interest in was the decoration and furnishings. With the exception of the children's bedrooms, which were left up to them, he made all the decisions in that field, and even built the family's bookshelves himself.

In the mid-sixties, Bettelheim was to spend some seven weeks in an Israeli kibbutz, researching what would become *The Children of the Dream*. After his departure, on entering the little apartment in which he had stayed, the woman who had made sure that he received a change of sheets every week was shocked to discover the six pairs, untouched, and piled up on a chair![8] In Chicago, however, Bettelheim's dislike for any type of housework was well-known and he made no mystery of it. 'Most of us are quite happy to master one of two environments (professional and domestic) and let the other marital partner take care of the other,' he would say.[9]

That statement, of course, did not apply to Trude: she had her own professional life to deal with, along with her domestic functions. Now a trained paediatric social worker, she worked full-time for the Chicago Child Care agency. Although her specialty was play therapy, she was in charge of adoptions. She found adoptive families, carried out checks on them and monitored the children once placed. It was work she loved, and she did it with total dedication. To help her with the housework, she had Lillian, a black woman from the South. Intelligent, skilful and devoted, Lillian had quickly become an indispensable member of the Bettelheim household, acting as a stand-in mother for the children during the day. She was to stay with the family until Eric left home to go to college, towards the end of the 1960s. Later, when Lillian fell ill, Naomi made sure, from faraway Vienna where she was then living, that she was well taken care of until her death.

Trude's heavy workload probably grew heavier with the realization, from day to day, of just how much her husband was getting drawn into his work, in a frenzy of activity that excluded practically everything else. If that was the case, however, she never said so publicly and, even in private, it is doubtful that she ever expressed it fully either, for she knew how much his work meant to him. But the situation no doubt left its mark on her. Some people now tended to interpret her natural reserve as a sign of coldness.

Others on the contrary had huge admiration for her courage, intelligence, boundless energy and the great compassion she brought to her work. But Trude Bettelheim was so good at hiding her feelings that nobody was able to give me the slightest idea of what it must have meant to her to see her husband spending more than half his time surrounded by often attractive young women, over whom he had almost absolute power and most of whom idolized him. If she did feel jealous, she must have had an extraordinary strength of character, for nobody I interviewed would even venture a hypothesis on the subject. But quite early on, Trude stopped going to the Orthogenic School, except to admire some new fixture or extension, at the invitation of her husband.

At first, the barrier between the two halves of Bettelheim's world was not absolute. Most of the first counsellors even did some babysitting at his home on occasion. They have clear memories of his first apartment, which was simply but tastefully appointed in European style. Their relations with Trude were straightforward and friendly; only Paula Bettelheim, on her occasional visits to her son, intimidated them. After the first two or three years, however, Bruno Bettelheim stopped inviting his collaborators to his home, except for the party he threw each New Year for the school staff.

Shortly after Naomi's birth, in 1945, the Bettelheims moved into a larger apartment. The best bedroom was assigned to the children and the smallest was Bruno's, which was separate from that of Trude. To anyone who dared ask him why, he would explain that in his view a man should enter his wife's room only when she invited him to do so. Later, his teenage daughters would often joke on the subject, expressing amazement at the fact they had even been conceived, and wondering at what time of night such an event could have taken place. Bettelheim's lair was tiny, and crammed with books, statuettes and other items purchased on his various travels. The children would go there in summer to play Monopoly, as it was the only air-conditioned room in the house. Bettelheim was meticulous in his personal habits, and Naomi liked to observe him as he groomed himself, clipping his fingernails, or wielding a small circular mirror and a pair of tweezers to pluck out stubble that had escaped his razor.

It would be mistaken to conclude, as some mainly male visitors did, that Trude no longer counted for much in Bettelheim's life after he took over the Orthogenic School. As he himself said in the letter quoted at the start of this chapter, and as he would repeat countless times in the five and a half years between his wife's death and the day he killed himself, his relationship with Trude was the most important thing in his life, apart from his work. In that same epistle, in which he summed up the preceding two decades of his life, he also wrote that: 'My first years in America were not easy, but they were nevertheless much better – not materially, but emotionally – than what I had before (in Vienna).' And as his correspondent knew Trude well, he added: 'I am convinced that our marriage is the best one possible, the best I could ever have had.'

The statement is interesting, for although the first impression it may give is one of lukewarm feelings, what it expresses above all is the poor image Bettelheim continued to have of himself, in spite of all his success and the arrogance he could display in public. The letter is that of a man who knows how to count his own lucky stars, a man who truly appreciates what life has given him. 'Back there, I rarely admitted it to myself, but in fact I always wanted to be a university professor .... It can therefore be said that I have fulfilled my childhood dream. I still have a hard time believing that all these good things have really happened to me: Trude, the children, my job. And I am happy that I am not so arrogant as to believe that all this was my due. I have been incredibly lucky.'

A far cry indeed from the public image of Dr B, the rising star of child psychology and a man renowned for his stinging remarks and short temper. And a far cry even from the warmer image the school's counsellors had of him, that of a man of such towering authority that it left no room for any kind of doubt. Very few people ever met that pacified, almost serene Bettelheim, a man at peace with himself. A man who was no longer haunted by feelings of illegitimacy. And I believe it is on that level that Trude's influence was essential in his life. As if to prove it, she indeed comes first in the above quotation.

From the young women he worked with, Bettelheim gained reassurance on two important points: the value of his work and his power of seduction. But deeper still there remained a gnawing doubt which only Trude seems to have been capable of silencing, concerning his very right to exist. What he saw reflected in the admiring eyes of his counsellors was an image of the larger-than-life person he wanted to be. But he needed Trude, who really knew him as he was, warts and all, and beyond all his clever stories, to help him truly accept himself. On his own, he was incapable of finding such reassurance. As was shown in the last years of his life, the flattering image reflected back at him by his entourage, far from satisfying him, only served to strengthen his own lack of self-respect. The more he appeared great and beautiful, the more he felt small and ugly inside.

During a conference on the student revolt of the late 1960s, Bettelheim was to give a very simple explanation of what he saw as the role of the family: 'We all need a place where we can let our hair down, where we can expect understanding, generous acceptance of us as we are, including our failings. Our perfections everybody will appreciate. For them we do not need a family. What makes a family is the readiness with which it accepts our failures and shortcomings.'[10] As usual, Bettelheim drew from his own life a lesson filled with humanity and wisdom. But as was often the case, the ideal he put forward was in fact unattainable. Parents capable of accepting everything without passing judgement: that was the role he had conferred on the counsellors of the Orthogenic School, and no doubt the role that Trude played in his life. But once again it was a role that he, as a father, had a hard time fulfilling.

Bettelheim's relationship with his own children is often questioned by his critics: 'He was so hard with other parents,' they say in essence, 'but what kind of a father could he himself have been, spending as he did all his time with the school kids?' The question may also be asked at a less strictly material level. For the outside world, Bettelheim was a magician and a leader, a creator of rules and a wielder of authority. At home, the presence of Trude allowed him to be simply a fallible human being, with weaknesses that could be accepted. And indeed this set-up did not leave much room for his own children. The way he himself saw it can be found in a letter written to Ruth Marquis in 1973: 'Many things I did wrong, as does any parent, but I never felt guilty … I was always convinced that we as parents had to live our own lives, were doing the best we knew by our children, convinced that this would be enough.'[11] The family spent a month of vacation together each year, generally in the Rocky Mountains or on the New England coast in the early years – later, it would often be in California, and occasionally in Europe. What is certain is that Bettelheim did not behave towards his children in the same way he behaved towards the students at his school. He was at once more absent-minded and more indulgent – perhaps like Anton, his own father. Later, after Trude's death, he was to maintain something of a 'buddy' relationship with his son, to the extent that some eyewitnesses occasionally wondered which one was the father.

But although Bettelheim's children can justifiably accuse him of having always given a higher priority to his work than to them while they were growing up, those critics who describe him as an absentee father are mistaken. Family was extremely important for him, as can be seen from his correspondence throughout his life. His children were part of his life, even though he did not look after them very much. He talked to them when he was there, took an interest in what they had to say and although each of them at one time or another felt anger towards him, none of them appears to have at any time doubted the strength of the links between them and him.[12] Once again, the point is not to pass judgement on whether or not Bettelheim was a 'bad father' (each person is free to draw their own conclusions on that), but to try and understand what made this complex man tick. His absences did show that he had more exciting things to do with his time than to spend it with his children, but not that they were not important to him. He knew they were in good hands, with Trude and Lillian to look after them. He may even have feared, consciously or not, reproducing with them the errors that had overshadowed his own childhood. On Trude's side, there was no family curse to worry about. Her childhood had been a happy one, in spite of her mother's preference for her brother. She at least had enjoyed a rich and strong relationship with her father.

Bettelheim had lost his mother. Paula Bettelheim died in 1953, and he had her ashes sent back to Austria, to be buried alongside those of her husband.

'My life is my work, Trude and the children ....' When he drew up that list, in September 1954, Bruno Bettelheim omitted to mention another important aspect of his 'second life', and one which, as he stressed a little earlier in the same letter, bore 'surprisingly little relation' to the previous one. This was the inner work he was pursuing about the key experience that had catapulted him into his second life: his period in Dachau and Buchenwald. Gayle, however, remembers clearly: 'He read everything that was published on the concentration camps. His desk was stacked with books.' For alongside his professional work, Bettelheim continued all through his life with a process of self-analysis to develop his thinking on these subjects which, given the circumstances, had triggered in him a highly personal struggle. And that process never ceased to enrich his work as a therapist.

The first long text he wrote on his own after his arrival in the United States was to be devoted to his camp experience, and the final chapters of his last book, published half a century later, were to be on the same subject. The very construction of *Surviving*, which came out around ten years before his death and can be viewed as his testament on the subject, confirms that Bettelheim continually reworked and thought about the camps and the Nazi genocide all through his 'second life'. For this collection of essays, drawn up forty years after that first article on the camps, he included the latter *in extenso*, stripping it of the personal anecdotes he had added for *The Informed Heart* and returning it to its impersonal third person form. Even more simply, one can reflect on this to-ing and fro-ing between the 'I' and the 'he', of which another example is the article about his frostbite.[13] Why was it always when he was writing about the concentration camps that this practice occurred? What were the memories he was wrestling with, what fear was he trying to conquer, what was the 'dark secret' he wanted to free himself of?

In order to unravel this painful inner process, which had indisputable repercussions on his work as a therapist, and to try and answer the above questions, we need to temporarily step outside the chronology of his life to follow the thread of his thinking. An examination of the main texts he wrote on the subject, in the order in which he wrote them, reveals three main periods.

Following the publication of his first article on the camps, the views of Bruno Bettelheim had become the benchmark for a handful of progressive newspapers on issues relating to the Nazis' persecution of the Jews. His articles were appreciated because they were different from others, they always provided food for thought, questioning received wisdoms and raising new questions. For example, when in 1945 the American occupation forces obliged groups of Germans to visit the concentration camp sites with a view to educating them, Bettelheim did not join in the general applause, but instead pointed out the dangers the approach entailed.[14] To blame an entire people for a crime was undemocratic, he explained; it would be better to identify those responsible and publicly punish them. Showing piles of dead bodies to Germans selected at random may have no other effect than to convince them that they had been right all along not to try and oppose the Nazis![15]

Writing in the run-up to the Nuremberg Trials, he tried to show his American readers how the German people must have felt, exhausted by the war, weary of politics and suspicious of their victors. For the trials to make an impression on them, he pointed out, the notion of individual responsibility (a concept they had become unfamiliar with over twelve years of Hitlerian rule) was not enough: they would have to be made conscious of their own involvement in the Nazi machine, for example by the indictment of organizations which one or more members of every German family had joined. At the same time, it was important that Nuremberg should not appear as the trial of a whole nation, which could only unite all Germans against the prosecutor. Mission impossible, Bettelheim concluded.[16]

Then, as his first writings on the Orthogenic School were appearing in print, Bettelheim published his two articles on frostbite, and the incident at the Buchenwald infirmary.[17] To illustrate the dangers of stereotyping one's enemy, as we have seen, he was harsh in his judgement of his fellow prisoners. In 1948, he was to turn on the American Jews, accusing them of irresponsibility for supporting the ill-fated voyage of the refugee ship *Exodus*.[18] 'I doubt that many American Jews who insist on the Jews' *right* to Palestine would be willing to give America back to the Indians,' he wrote.[19] Rather than inciting the Nazis' victims to break British laws, and in the process to endure more suffering, Bettelheim went on, American Jews would do better to spend their money on bringing them to the United States, 'the land where they would be safe from persecution, and where history has shown they can be integrated into an existing community of power and culture'. He added: 'I cannot help feeling that this anger against the British was a projection of the anger of American Jews against themselves for not doing their duty towards the Jews in Europe.'

It can be seen that Bruno Bettelheim had got into his stride as a writer during those first years of exile. His tone, one of intelligent remonstrance, based on acute observations and the constant questioning of what others took for granted, grew firmer and more self-assured with each article. There was always a strong moral undertone, and he was generally more concerned to attack the complacency of his friends – or those who saw themselves as such – than the crimes of his enemies, which were frequently disposed of with a few words such as: 'It is not the purpose of this statement to recount once more the horror story of the German concentration camps.'[20]

In 1947, noting that the Germans had definitively lost the war, Bettelheim wrote that the time had come to speak out frankly about what had gone on in the camps. Reviewing books on Buchenwald by the Austrians Benedict Kautsky and Eugen Kogon, he focused his article on the class structure in the camps, i.e. the power relationships between inmates. He in particular stressed the cynicism of the Communist prisoners, who had been all too ready to sacrifice the lives of innocents to save their own. And while acknowledging the merits of Kogon's book, he accused the latter, who had acted as a medical secretary in the camp, of having been one of the 'élite prisoners', and of taking in his book a patronizing and contemptuous view of the lower class of inmates. Indeed, he went on, 'almost all those who survived the camps and could therefore report on their experiences had in one way or another been beneficiaries of a class system whose lowest strata rarely survived'.[21] He even acknowledged that in Buchenwald, an inmate's awareness of his superiority over other prisoners was an important psychological defence mechanism against his own fear of falling to the lowest level, even though this class system could only serve the interests of the SS. Here again we see a subtle and clear-sighted analysis, focused not on the failings of the oppressors but on those of their victims. It is a convincing, intelligent and uncompromising piece of writing. Yet a great deal of its strength and appeal is due to the fact that its author himself belonged to the very category of inmates whose behaviour he takes apart in such a robust manner. For the reader, the harsh, peremptory tone is at least partially cancelled out by the implicit 'we' that lurks behind the 'they' in every paragraph.

This was the first stage of Bettelheim's post-concentration camp thinking; the positive phase, during which he strove, and successfully so, to derive lessons from his experience. It was the phase during which Bettelheim wrote that his year of detention 'did me good'. It ends in 1956, with the publication of the first article in which he drew a parallel between the hell experienced by the children in his charge, and the hell he had been through in Buchenwald.[22] At the school, meanwhile, he was continually urging the counsellors to learn and progress from their worst experiences. 'When something bad happens to you, turn it around and use it,' he would say. 'Make a project out of it.'

At the same time, Bettelheim was involved in the debate over Germany's reconstruction, which exposed divisions among American intellectuals. On the analysis of Nazism, the denunciation of Stalinism, the Marshall Plan, etc. Are there ways of preventing any relapse into barbarity? Are certain peoples anti-democratic by nature? The debate had drawn in many people who in the past had been interested in Marxism, and in particular the members of the Frankfurt Institute for Social Research,[23] many of whom had found refuge at Manhattan's Columbia University. By then, however, the label 'neo-Hegelian' had replaced all intellectual trace of the now-infamous epithet 'Marxist'.

At the University of Chicago, the discussions took place in the Chaos Club, so called because it kept no roster of its membership. One evening Max Horkheimer, who along with Theodor Adorno had chosen to return the Institute to Frankfurt almost as soon as the war was over, had just concluded a talk in which he argued that Germany was a profoundly democratic country, as shown by developments there at that time, in the early 1950s. Although still only a graduate student, the sociologist Albert Reiss Jr. (who was at the time sharing an apartment with Morris Janowitz), spoke up: 'But how can you say that after the death camps?' David Reisman, who was chairing the debate, icily tried to put him in his place. 'That statement is unworthy of the brilliant speech that we have just heard,' he said in essence. At which point Bettelheim stood up and shouted: 'You'd do better to listen to him. He's the one who is right.'

He was never one to be swayed by ideas just because they were in fashion. Towards the end of the 1950s Luitgard Wundheiler, a young German woman who taught mathematics to Naomi's Lab School class, offered to work at the Orthogenic School. She had just lost her husband, a Polish Jew whose brother had died in the Warsaw Ghetto, and she could not get over her feelings of guilt at having grown up in Nazi Germany. Bettelheim's reaction astounded her: 'You shouldn't feel guilty for being German. If you blame all Germans, you're like the Nazis: you're condemning human beings on the basis of what they are as a group, not of what they do as individuals.'

As early as 1954 Bruno Bettelheim agreed to return to Germany, to spend three months in Frankfurt running a teacher-training seminar on the subject of democracy. Trude was firmly against the idea. 'I don't know how you can go back to Germany,' she told him. And indeed, the experience was a difficult one, as he confessed to the Janowitzes, who were also in Frankfurt at the time. Morris had received a Fulbright Fellowship to spend the academic year at the Institute for Social Research, and Bettelheim was very thankful for the occasional dinner at the home of these close American friends. He found himself again dreaming in German, about the concentration camp. He was deeply upset to see how limited the process of denazification had been, but was at the same time struck by the well-meaning attitudes of the young teachers who attended his seminars. But even they, he noted, had the utmost difficulty understanding that one simply cannot use authoritarian methods to teach democracy.[24] Nothing seemed to have changed in Germany's educational methods, and not even those who most sincerely wanted to believe in democracy could rid themselves of the notion, which Bettelheim detected in most of the people he met, that it had been the Weimar Republic, and later on the Allied democracies, which had plunged Germany into the state of chaos that it was then struggling to emerge from. Bettelheim also met young Germans from the Soviet-occupied zone, and although he was shocked by their political indoctrination, he was also struck by the breadth of their philosophical, æsthetic and sociological interests, compared to the materialism of their western counterparts.

One day, he returned to Dachau, alone. The visit was to result in one of the most serene of all his articles on the subject.[25] It focused on memory, and the impossibility of keeping the trace of such a tragedy alive. It was a highly personal, simple and descriptive text, in which Bettelheim did not seek to lecture anyone, but just related his impressions during the visit, as they evolved from cold anger at the indifference of the local populace, to a final feeling of inner calm which came with the realization of the heavy burden the Germans had to bear in order to simply go on living there, next to what had once been a concentration camp. Whatever he had suffered inside, he did not envy them their situation.

In the same year, with the help of his cousin Norbert, who had returned to Vienna after the war, Bruno Bettelheim undertook to obtain war reparations for the loss of his business and his deportation. He spent two years fighting doggedly for this, going so far as to file a lawsuit against the Austrian state, which had pointed to the highly restrictive time-limit it had set on requests for compensation by the victims of Nazism.[26] Finally, the Austrian administration gave him partial satisfaction, and he dropped his suit. He was given a deportee's pension and, later on, compensation for 'interruption of professional activity'. However, in spite of unceasing efforts, carried on with the help of both his cousin and the latter's son, up until 1969, Bettelheim never obtained any reparation for the loss of his company.[27] (There is a repetition here that may be of interest to a psychoanalyst: Anton had fought in vain to gain compensation for the stocks of wood he had lost during World War I, and a little later his brothers had striven, also to no avail, to prove the existence of blood ties between their father and the Bettelheims of Pressburg.)

At the same time, Bettelheim was honing his ideas on the issue of totalitarianism, in a direction not unlike that taken by the Frankfurt School.[28] Like them, he attached particular importance to the notion of individual autonomy. In October 1952 the *American Journal of Economics and Sociology* published his 'Remarks on the Psychological Appeal of Totalitarianism', a brief text devoted to the psychological conflict that the modern totalitarian state imposes on all those who oppose it. For him, the specificity of twentieth-century totalitarianism lies in the way it bases its power on the disintegration of the independent ego in all its citizens, by penetrating every nook and cranny of their lives, including the most private ones.

For the purposes of his argument he discusses the Nazi salute, an everyday gesture that was required of all citizens. Several times a day, the anti-Nazi was thus confronted with an inner conflict, the outcome of which could only weaken his ego. Either he refused to give the salute, thereby following his conscience (the superego), but at the same time risking his life. And as Bettelheim points out, the conservation of life is the most basic of all the ego's functions.[29] Or he went through the motions, while telling himself that the gesture was of no importance, thereby demeaning himself in his own eyes by failing to live up to his own moral precepts. 'Thus, the opponent of the totalitarian regime, who must have a strong ego in order to survive in an inimical society, found himself, because of the very nature of this society, continuously in a situation that forced him to work on his ego's own destruction.' Bettelheim went on to note that for most human beings, the desire for conformity was a very strong one. To resolve a conflict between their ideals and their survival, little by little they would quite naturally adjust their ideals. 'In the final analysis then, the ego can protect the individual in a totalitarian society only by accepting the system as it is.'

Three years later, Bettelheim's thinking on totalitarianism had evolved further. As if his stay in Europe had opened his eyes to the shortcomings of his country of adoption, he published in 1955 a hard-hitting critique of American society. In a long essay, of which large extracts feature in *The Informed Heart*, he used the concept of individual autonomy to draw out correlations between the totalitarian state and mass society.[30] Expressing for the first time a lot of ideas which a few years later would have achieved such widespread currency that they would become clichés, he demonstrated how man gradually became alienated in the modern world. A world in which an apparent plethora of choice in fact only served to conceal the limited scope left to each individual's responsibility. Practically the only areas in which modern man still enjoyed some freedom to define and appropriate his own identity were the most private ones. There were people to tell him what to drink, what to eat, which car to buy and how to furnish his home. He was even advised on how to spend his leisure time, by those who stood to make money thereby. Of course he appeared to enjoy freedom of choice, but in fact he listened to the same radio station (the article dates from 1955) and read the same books as his neighbour. 'Thus, in exchanging opinions, they enjoy the comfort of conformity until they suddenly realize the emptiness of a life which offers no experiences particular to themselves.'

Like the Nazi state, mass society thus presupposed the weakness of its subjects' personalities ('When life activities are not selected on the basis of internalization of the values of cherished persons, but solely on the basis of the wish or need to earn a livelihood in a convenient fashion, doubts, insecurity and inability to integrate are the consequence.'). Perversely, it nevertheless maintained the illusion of great freedom, thereby reinforcing the feeling of failure in the subject who did not succeed in fulfilling his or her desires. Being unable to truly exercise his personal choices, he invests

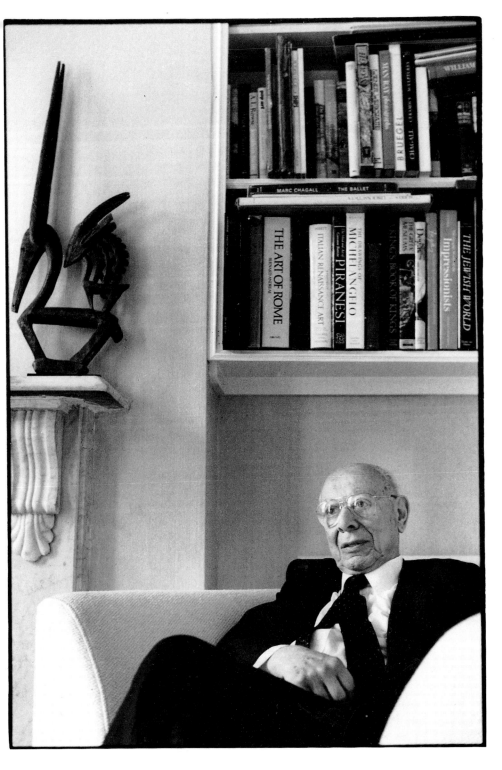

African art, Bruegel, Impressionist painters, Jewish history and Italian Renaissance: the world and images of Bruno Bettelheim.

Anton and Paula Bettelheim.

9/6 1915

Adolf Seidler and his wife
Franziska.

Bruno Bettelheim as a child.

July 1921: *Matura*
'What do you want to do later?'
'Philosophy.'

With Gina Altstadt.

1932: BB's first driving licence, requiring him to wear 9 diopter glasses before taking the wheel.

In 1930, Gina Altstadt became Mrs Bettelheim (right). On BB's shoulder, Wanda Willig, whose husband Hans, BB's schoolmate, is taking the picture.

Raum für amtliche Eintragungen (besondere Bedingungen, Ausdehnung der Fahrerlaubnis nach Ergänzungsprüfungen u. dgl.).

Die Vorschreibung einer Brillenverpflichtung für Gläser mit beiderseits 9 Diopt. sph. 1.9 cyl. zur Kenntnis genommen.

(Fahrschule Buresch Gr. Enzersdorf)

P. B. Lager-Nr. 928. — Druck und Verlag der Österreichischen Staatsdruckerei, D. B., in Wien. (St.) 7870 31

(Name der ausstellenden Behörde. — So

Zahl   859

Führerschein

für Herrn   Bruno
    Frau

Bettelheim

in Wien

geboren am   28. Aug. 1903

geboren in   Wien

Die Führung von Kraftwagen zum Erwerb im Hauptberuf ist an das vollendete 21. Lebensjahr geknüpft.

Patsy on holiday with Editha Sterba, at the Sterba family residence in Gmunden.

February 2, 1938: one of the last PhDs awarded a Jew at Vienna University before the war.

Summer 1932: holiday camp in the Shalaburg imperial (but derelict) castle. Sitting, from left to right: Annie Hatchek, Fritz Redl and Gina Bettelheim.

Patsy

Letters from Dachau and Buchenwald: debts to be paid, visas, tickets and various other papers to be obtained. Deceptively practical and stern at first glance, they tell a very different story when set against the events taking place in the camps at the time.

'As regards myself, I haven't got very much to tell you. My life is filled with work, and the nostalgia I feel for you . . . . Think of yourselves, not of me, for over time that would be too heavy a burden.'

Konzentrationslager Dachau 3 K

Meine Anschrift:
Name: Bettelheim Bruno
geboren am: 28. August 1903
Block: 22   Stube: 3

Dachau 3 K, den: 3. Juli 1938

Meine Allerliebsten!

Euren Brief und die Gld-
sendungen dankend erhalten. Bitte schickt
mir weiter in den selben Abständen regelmäßig
je RM 15.– Wenn es Euch schwer fällt soll Frieda
es vorstrecken. Bitte sofort durch geeigneten Anwalt
alle Steuersachen in Ordnung bringen lassen auch
Steuerunbedenklichkeits-Erklärung sowie alle im
sonst noch fehlenden Papiere. Wenn Euch
Geld fehlt, kann vielleicht Fritz bei Freunden

Liebe und Sehnsucht denken. Sie auch ebenso wie
Ihr, alle Pläne, ohne jede Rücksicht auf mich
machen, da meine Rückkunft ganz ungewiss ist

Konzentrationslager Weimar-Buchenwald

Meine genaue Anschrift:
Bettelheim Bruno
Nr. 9036
Block 17
Konzentrationslager Weimar-Buchenwald

8. Jänner 1939

Liebste Mutter!

Anbei Photos, die
für Pass- und
Visumsausweise
zu verwenden sind. Sollte eine be-
glaubigte Unterschrift auf ihnen
nötig sein, so wendet Euch an den
Notar, der Bildeneuter in Kleiner
vertritt, damit er diese besorgt.
Statet diesen Notar mit allen

meinen Papieren, auf, damit die
zu fertiggestellt werden. Haltet
sich genau nach seinen Anwei-
sungen und übergebt ihm auch
insbesondere meine Schiffskarte.
mit meiner Unterschrift auf dieser
geholt werden kann. — Dank für
Geld und Geld; bitte jede Woche je
10.– schicken. — Bitte an Frieda Gla-
Berlin, N, Fehrbelliner Straße 19
10.– überweisen, diese Überweisung
auch Ehrensache und dann wiek-
Euch Allen, Gruss! – viele Küsse Bruno

A ticket to freedom, which Paula Bettelheim had to have extended several times, while BB remained in Buchenwald.

Right: October 1939: application to become a US citizen.

April 1939: BB's last certificate of residence in Vienna (he is now Bruno 'Israel', in compliance with Nazi regulations).

LIST OR MANIFEST OF ALIEN PASSENGERS FOR THE UNI

ALL ALIENS arriving at a port of continental United States from a foreign port or a port of the insular possessions of the United States, and all aliens arriving at a port of said insular possessions from a foreign port, a port of contin...
This (pink) sheet is for

S.S. " Gerolstein " Passengers sailing from Antwerp, Belgium , April 29th , 1

No. on List	HEAD-TAX STATUS	NAME IN FULL Family name	Given name	Age Yrs.	Mos.	Sex	Married or single	Calling or occupation	Able to— Read	Read what language	Write	Nationality (Country of which citizen or subject)	Race or people	Place of birth Country	City or town, State, Province or District	Immigration Visa, Passport Visa, or Re-entry Permit Number	Issued Place	Date	Data concerning verification	*Last permanent Country	
1		BAUMANN	Erika	18	1	F	S	Clerk	yes	German	yes	Germany	Hebrew	Germany	Vienna	QIV 14613	Vienna	4/21/39		Germany	V1
2		BASZ	Leopold	63	36	M	M	Printer	yes	German	yes	Germany	Hebrew	Germany	Vienna	QIV 14123	Vienna	4/11/39		Germany	V1
3		BASZ	Berta	55	2	F	M	Housewife	yes	German	yes	Germany	Hebrew	Germany	Vienna	QIV 14122	Vienna	4/11/39		Germany	V1
4		BASZ	Kurt	25	11	M	S	Clerk	yes	German	yes	German	Hebrew	Germany	Vienna	QIV 14135	Vienna	3/4/39		Germany	V1
5		BASZ	Adele	21	4	F	S	Student	yes	German	yes	Germany	Hebrew	Germany	Vienna	QIV 14125	Vienna	4/4/39		Germany	V1
6		BETTELHEIM	Bruno	35	6	M	M	Merchant	yes	German	yes	Germany	Hebrew	Germany	Vienna	QIV 14560	Vienna	4/18/39		Germany	V1
7		BUTTERKLEE	Samuel	19	10	M	S	Student	yes	German	yes	Germany	Hebrew	Germany	Vienna	QIV 14387	Vienna	4/13/39		Germany	V1
8		CHALFON	Hans Joachim	27	5	M	S	doctors orderly	yes	German	yes	Stateless	Hebrew	Germany	Berlin	QIV 13918	Berlin	4/24/39		Germany	Be
9		DEUTSCH	Sofie	54	8	F	M	None	yes	German	yes	Germany	Hebrew	Germany	Schleining	QIV 14248	Vienna	4/6/39		Germany	Vie
10	UNDER 16	DEUTSCH	Margarete	13	7	F	S	Student	yes	German	yes	Germany	Hebrew	Germany	Vienna	QIV 14246	Vienna	4/6/39		Germany	Vie
11		DONATH	Sofie	26	1	F	M	Housewife	yes	German	yes	Germany	Hebrew	Poland	Stanislau	QIV 5110	Vienna	4/5/39		Germany	Vie
12		EPSTEIN	Felicitas	17	3	F	S	Student	yes	German English	yes	Germany	Hebrew	Germany	Vienna	QIV 22562	Vienna	3/24/39		Germany	Vie
13		FRENKEL	Anna	29	2	F	M	Housewife	yes	German	yes	Germany	Hebrew	Germany	Basel	QIV 12282	Stuttgart	3/27/39		Germany	Ba
14	UNDER 16	FRENKEL	Inge	2	5	F	S	child	no	-------	no	Germany	Hebrew	Germany	Godesberg	QIV 12281	Stuttgart	3/27/39		Germany	B.G
15		FRITSMANN	Chaja Esther	55	9	F	Wd	none	yes	German	yes	Poland	Hebrew	Poland	Warsaw	QIV 4642	Berlin	2/2/39		Germany	Ber
16		FUCHS-SCHNAUTZER	David	25	3	M	S	Painter	yes	German	yes	Stateless	Hebrew	Germany	Vienna	QIV 14395	Vienna	4/13/39		Germany	Vie
17		GOTTFRIED	Lina	41	7	F	S	Seamstress	yes	German	yes	Stateless	Hebrew	Poland	Monasterzyska	QIV 6131 6151	Vienna			Germany	V1
18		GUENTHER	Paul Israel	25	5	M	S	Student	yes	English German	yes	Germany	Hebrew	Germany	Berlin	QIV 14331	Rotterdam	4/17/39		Germany	V1
19		HERSCH	Walter	31	1	M	M	Merchant	yes	German	yes	Germany	Hebrew	Germany	Nuernburg	QIV 12865	Stuttgart	3/10/39		Germany	Stu
20		HIRSCH	Moses Leib	48	7	M	M	Clerk	yes	German	yes	German	Hebrew	Poland	Tlumte	QIV 6197	Vienna	4/6/39		Germany	Vie
21		HIRSCH	Anna	42	7	F	M	Housewife	yes	German	yes	Germany	Hebrew	Poland	Monasterzyska	QIV 6198	Vienna	4/6/39		Germany	V1

May 11, 1939: BB arrives in New York with 3 dollars in his pocket and a PhD scribbled in as a bonus.

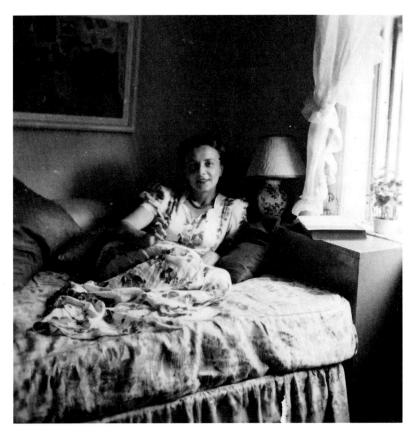

Gina Bettelheim in her Manhattan apartment: 'No, Bruno. It's over . .

...ss, or a port of another insular possession, in whatever class they travel, MUST be fully listed and the master or commanding officer of each vessel carrying such passengers must upon arrival deliver lists thereof to the immigrant inspector
RST-CABIN PASSENGERS ONLY

No.	The name and complete address of nearest relative or friend in country whence alien came, or if none there, then in country of which a citizen or subject	Final destination		By whom was passage paid?		Whether ever before in the United States, and if so, when and where?			Whether going to join a relative or friend; state name and complete address, and if relative, exact relationship	Condition of health, mental and physical	Deformed or crippled. Nature, length of time, and cause	Height		Color of —		Marks of identification
1	father:Nathan Beumann 108 Maerastr.Vienna,Germ.	PA. Phila. yes self 25 no					cousin: Nathan Deitelbaum 1508 Allegheny Ave,Phila	no	good	no	5 3	fairbld.gr.	none	M20
2	frd.:Jennie Rothstein,40 OP.Mohrengasse,Vienna	NJ Kenilw.no self 25 no 1908 1912 NY				cousin: Abraham S.Lewitt 19121 Michigan Ave.,Kenilworth	no	good	no	5 3	fair br. gr.	none	M20
3	-------"dto-------	NJ Kenilw.no husband no				-------"dto-------	no	good	no	5 1	fair gr. br.	none	M20
4	-------"dto-------	NJ Kenilw.no father no				-------"dto-------	no	good	no	5 5	fair bld gr.	none	M20
5	-------"dto-------	NJ Kenilw.no father no				-------"dto-------	no	good	no	5 0	fair bld.gr.	none	M20
6	mother:Paula Bettelheim, Neubaugasse 66, Vienna	SUNNGreenw. yes self 25 no				friend: Mrs.Agnes Grans Greenwich,Conn.	no	good	no	5 7	fair br. bl.	none	M20
7	father:Nisson Butterklee Vienna,17 Florgasse	NY Wh.Plai.no self no				cousin: Davy Gross, 92 Grant Ave.,Buffalo,Plain,N	no	good	no	6 0	fair br. br.	none	M20
8	uncle:Isaac Chalfon,285 Neptune Ave.,Brighton,NY	NY Bright.yes self 25 no				uncle:Isaac Chalfon,285 Neptune Avenue.Brighton	no	good	no	5 7	fair blck.br.	none	M20
9	Deutsch,Sigm.Husband,26 Vienna,Fr.Hochallingstr.	NY Bronx yes self 25 no				sister: Helene Feldinger 2052 Grand Ave.,Bronx	no	good	no	5 3	fairgr. br.	none	M20
10	father: ------dto	NY Bronx yes mother no				aunt: -------dto-------	no	good	no	5 4	fair br. br.	none	M20
1	parents:Josef Taub,7/73a gerlgasse,27,Vienna,Germ.	NY Brookl.yes self 25 no				husband:Karl Donath,87 Stockholmstreet,Brooklyn	no	good	no	5 7	fairbr. gr.	none	M20
2	mother:Helene Epstein, Singerstr.27,Vienna,Germ.	NY NYC yes self 25 no				fath':Helmrmh Epstein, Hotel Paris,97thStr,NYC	no	good	no	5 7	fairbr. gr.	none	M20
3	mother:Barbara Cahn,74 Bonnerstr.Godesberg,Germ.	NY MYE yes self 25 no				husband:Bernhard Frenkel, 560 Westchestdraw,Pt.Che ster,NY	no	good	no	5 2	fairbr. br.	none	M20
14	gr.mother:------dto------	NY dto yes mother no				-------dto-------	no	good	no	3	fair bld.bl.	none	M20
15	acqu.:B.Finkelstein,201 Millaastr.,Berlin	NY NYC yes self 25 no				cousin:Dr.Rosenkranz,1905 RHO Bldg.,Rockefeller,NYC	no	good	no	5 10	fair blckgr.	none	M20
16	mother:Regine Fuchs, 17/1o Baulergasse,Vienna,Germ.	NY Brookl.yes self no				uncle:Moritz Schnautzer, 64 Blake Ave.,Brooklyn,NY	no	good	no	5 1o	fair br. br.	none	M20
17	acqu.:Walter Sternberg, I felmfaltostr.3,Vienna	Tex Houston no self 25 no				cousin: Sam I.Mass,3820 La Branch Str.,Houston,Tex	no	good	no	5 0	fair br. br.	none	M20
18	stepsister:Terese Guenther 18 Tabzostr.,Vienna,Germ.	NY NYC yes self new no				father: Dr.Felix Guenther 230 Riverside Dr.,NYC,NY	no	good	no	4 7	fairbld.bl.	none	M20
19	mother: t.1.rLilly Sottohen, Gr.Haldg.1o,Seligmstatt	NY NYC yes self 50 no				brother: Willi Hrschm, 529 W.157th Str.,NYC	no	good	no	5 11	fair br. br.	none	M20
20	br.Enk.: Maier Hirsch,22 Heinzelmanng.,Vienna,Germ.	NY Brookl.yes self 50 no				cousin:Joseph Margulies, 1clo Lincoln Pla,Brooklyn,NY	no	good	no	5 2	fair gr. br.	none	M20
21	Dr.L.:----------dto-------	NY Brookl.yes husband 25 no				-------dto-------	no	good	no	5 1	fair br. br.	none	M20
	parents:l.:Jonas Fraund 108 Ottakringerstr.,Vienn	NY Buffalo no self 25 no				uncle: Frederik Pollok, 96	no	good	no				

Edith Buxbaum, BB's
cousin, soul-mate and guide
on his first trip of discovery
across America.

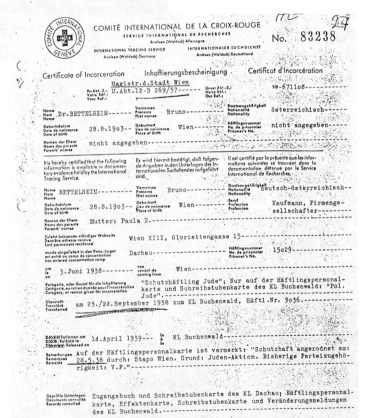

HARVARD UNIVERSITY
DEPARTMENT OF PSYCHOLOGY

PSYCHOLOGICAL LABORATORY

Emerson Hall
Cambridge 38, Massachusetts
June 15, 1945

Dr. Bruno Bettelheim
Orthogenic School
University of Chicago
Chicago, Illinois

Dear Dr. Bettelheim:

You will be interested to know
that we received a cablegram signed by
Eisenhower asking for permission to translate and reprint your article on "Individual
and Mass Behavior in Extreme Situations."
The Headquarters had only the mimeographed
edition but we authorized the reprinting
and hope that your contribution will play
an active part in the education of occupation authorities. From returning army men
who have seen conditions first hand I judge
the psychological direction taken in your
article has been wholly validated.

Sincerely yours,

Gordon W. Allport

Gordon W. Allport

June 1945: Bettelheim's article on the
concentration camps is distributed to US
occupation forces in Europe.

The International Red
Cross Certificate of
Incarceration.

December 1945: Trude Bettelheim and her two daughters.

Christmas 1946 at the Orthogenic School: Gayle (Shulenberger) Janowitz is sitting (behind the candy house) between 'Paul' and 'Harry', once more playing truant – this time under the table. Dr B is on the right.

Thanksgiving 1949: Dr B is in the shadow under the 'N'. In front of him, Gayle and Fae Tyroler (under the 'H'); Patti (Pickett) McKnight is third on the right (under the 'I').

The Orthogenic School's famous yellow door. Above: in 1945, only a few months after BB's appointment; below: some thirty years later, after he had left (the colonnade was built in the early 1960s).

1950s: Trude Bettelheim, Fritz Redl and Bruno Bettelheim, with the daughter of Dr Jerry Kavka, a consultant at the Orthogenic School.

Early 1980s at Portola Valley. Sitting: BB and his old friend Hans Willig. Standing on the left is Gina, by then Mrs Weinmann. Trude Bettelheim is second from the right. With them are a couple of friends, also from Vienna.

Bettelheim with Heda Bolgar, shortly before he was to leave Los Angeles: 'He was depressed, but not suicidal. He just wanted to be sure . . .'

March 11, 1990: last Sunday at Naomi's. BB reading and re-reading *Just Me and my Dad* to his grand-daughter.

more and more in the power of the mass, in the society of which he is a part. Just as the Germans were led, by the Nazi régime, to place more and more faith in the reputedly magical powers of their leader.

Bruno Bettelheim was no revolutionary, however. He was not against the American system, he simply sought to underline its inherent dangers, to point out that too great an imbalance between society's ability to control and each individual's internal autonomy was a source of emotional disturbance. He cited the Nazi state and its concentration camps as the ultimate form of a process at work in all mass societies which based themselves on technological progress but failed to measure all the implications of that progress. The instruments that science made available to the managers of society were never neutral, he wrote. One should never 'neglect the powerful modifying forces which flow from any external control of man and [deny] the individual responsibility in which man's dignity resides'.

The second period in Bettelheim's writings on the camps began at the end of the 1950s. That was when, after having discussed Buchenwald, he started to write about Auschwitz, and in the same lecturing tone. In May 1960 he agreed – not without much hesitation, he stressed – to write a foreword for the memoirs of Miklos Nyiszli, a Hungarian doctor who had survived the extermination camp only by agreeing to collaborate in the sinister 'medical research' carried out there by Joseph Mengele.[31] The importance of accounts on the death camps lay 'not in their all too familiar story but in something far more unusual and horrifying,' wrote Bettelheim, in paragraph four. 'The unique feature of the extermination camps is not that the Germans exterminated millions of people – that this is possible has been accepted in our picture of man, though not for centuries has it happened on that scale, and perhaps never with such callousness. What was new, unique, terrifying, was that millions, like lemmings, marched themselves to their own death.'

He was not the only Jew to be putting forward that argument. The following year saw the publication of the first edition of Raul Hilberg's minutely detailed analysis of the Nazi killing machine, which the historian had been working on for over ten years. The conclusion of *The Destruction of the European Jews*[32] was that the Nazis' Jewish victims, prisoners of their history, had precipitated themselves into catastrophe. The philosopher Hannah Arendt, in her writings on totalitarianism and anti-Semitism, also pointed the finger, although a little less harshly, at the role played by Jewish traditions in determining the scope of the Holocaust. In their different ways each writer, Bettelheim, Hilberg and Arendt, was trying to hold the disaster out at arm's length in order to understand it. And thereby, as Bettelheim repeatedly stressed, to try and prevent any repetition.

One evening Naomi, then almost fourteen, came home from school with

The Diary of Anne Frank, which she was studying in class. Surprised, Bettelheim read the book overnight. The next day he was filled with indignation, and in November 1960 *Harpers* published his fulminations under the title 'The Ignored Lesson of Anne Frank.'[33] In Bettelheim's view the acclaim that greeted the writings of the little Jewish girl – worldwide, but especially in Germany – proved only one thing: the tendency we all have to deny the reality of Auschwitz and the existence of the gas chambers. He agreed that the story of Anne's two years in hiding with her family in Amsterdam, before she was taken to Bergen-Belsen where she died, was touching, and was aware of the risks he was running in taking on such an emotional symbol. However, the real reason for the success of Anne Frank's diary, he went on, was to be found in her insistence, right up to the end, that human beings were basically good, i.e. in her denial of the reality of Nazism.

Instead of taking measures that could have saved them, the Frank family had opted for the most dangerous plan possible: hiding all together in a closed space with only one exit, from which they could not escape even if alerted of danger, Bettelheim wrote. In other words, they had put their desire to remain together – to carry on 'life as usual'[34] – above what they should have known to be going on in the real world. The family had thus refused to believe in the Nazis' barbarity, that human beings could be so inhuman. Which was why the public liked them so much, even though, with the exception of the father, they had all perished.

This article sums up to perfection Bettelheim's ideas on survival, and also sheds light on the title of the book in which it appears, *The Informed Heart*. In all circumstances, and particularly in extreme situations, survival is a question of balancing the yearnings of the heart against the strictures of reason. By giving priority to the latter, and using his professional pride as a doctor to avoid seeing what he was doing, Miklos Nyiszli had ended up taking part in experiments that were so appalling that Bettelheim asks: 'How could he do it and live with himself?' At the opposite extreme, Anne Frank's father, by choosing to listen only to his heart, had led his family into the arms of their executioners. Clinging to one's previous life – or, in the case of those Polish Jews whom Bettelheim accused of having carried on with business as usual even though they had been informed of the advancing German troops, to one's house and other possessions – was like believing that one had only to close one's eyes for the danger to disappear.

Although his argument was built on convincing foundations, in backing it up, Bettelheim went too far. He was particularly unjust with Otto Frank, a German-born Jew who had in fact left Frankfurt with little Anne and the rest of his family just six months after Hitler came to power, to seek refuge in the Netherlands, a country that had remained neutral in World War I. Overlooking the fact that Mr Frank's minutely prepared plan had come within months of succeeding (the family were only arrested by the Gestapo on August 4, 1944), Bettelheim blithely asserted that if he had acted otherwise, as 'thousands of other Jews in Holland (as elsewhere in Europe)' had done, he could probably have saved his family. Adding insult to injury, Bettelheim went on: 'There is little doubt that the Franks, who were able to provide themselves with so much while arranging for going into hiding ... could have provided themselves with some weapons had they wished.' As they were going to die anyway, they could at least have killed one or two of the SS men who came to arrest them; they would thus have 'sold their lives for a high price instead of walking to their death'.

A little over a year after the Anne Frank article, Bettelheim published an even more provocative text, under the title 'Freedom from Ghetto Thinking'.[35] This came at the height of publicity over the Eichmann trial, at a time when many Jews felt it was time for their people to close ranks. The man who was seen as one of the key orchestrators of Hitler's 'Final Solution' had been abducted by Israeli agents in Buenos Aires in May 1960; the story of his capture and subsequent trial in Jerusalem between April and December 1961 had been followed in its every detail by the thousands of Nazi victims then living in the United States. Up to that point, few of them had spoken out, and their feelings about the case were pretty straightforward. After having been disappointed by the Allies' refusal to deal separately with anti-Jewish persecution at the Nuremberg Trials of Nazi leaders, they found in the Eichmann trial the opportunity to have their sufferings at least recognized, if not avenged. The fact that it had been the fledgling Israeli state which had undertaken to hunt down Eichmann, thumbing its nose at international law in the process, served only to amplify their feelings, which were played up in their most simplistic form by the media. For most of them, it was a contest of Good versus Evil, with the Jewish people once again alone in defending its victims.

The death sentence against Adolf Eichmann had been handed down and the Israeli Supreme Court was due to hear his appeal when Bettelheim's piece appeared, in *Midstream*, a Zionist magazine. The article opened with a discussion of the phrase 'innocent victim', which had been heard countless times from witnesses during the trial. Why was it, Bettelheim asked, that this label was invariably applied to Jews murdered by the Nazis, but never to the German gypsies, who had been completely wiped out, even if they were less often talked about? He then launched into a long analysis of how centuries of living in ghettos, bowing down before oppressors and pretending not to notice, carrying on with 'business as usual' as if nothing was wrong, waiting for the storm to pass, etc., had led to some Jews opting to 'remain "innocent" in the jaws of disaster' when Hitler came to power.

Those not affected by 'ghetto thinking', Bettelheim contended, had believed the dictator when he announced that there would not be a single Jew left in Europe by the end of the war; they had got out in time. Most of the others had perished. But 'ghetto thinking' was not to be found solely among inhabitants of the *shtetls*; he also detected it in the United States, for instance among the Jewish friends who refused to believe him when he told them that most of his fellow inmates at Dachau and Buchenwald had in fact not been Jews at all. 'Only what happened to Jews counted: they were not aware of what happened to others. Lacking interest, they could not learn from others' experiences.' The ghetto Jew, Bettelheim went on, was typically an exiled Jew. And the main reason he indulged in 'ghetto thinking' was to avoid having to act. 'It is a type of deadening of the senses and emotions, so that one can bow down to the mujik who pulls one's beard, laugh with the baron at his anti-Semitic stories, degrade oneself so that one will be permitted to survive.' In other words, 'to believe that one can ingratiate oneself with a mortal enemy by denying that his lashes sting, to deny one's own degradation in return for a moment's respite'.

Bettelheim had never gone this far before. Once again, several of the points he discussed raised real issues, but once again it was his tone which for many people verged on the unacceptable. There was the same blend of arrogance – people have to fight, like the Israelis today, or the Warsaw Ghetto Jews yesterday – and condescension – as seen in his definition of 'ghetto thinking'. Even Hannah Arendt, whom Bettelheim was clearly seeking to get on his side (his article praised the way she had escaped from the French camp of Gurs, where she had been interned as a foreign Jew after the defeat of France in 1940), felt it necessary to distance herself from his remarks, which she considered anti-Semitic. In a letter published in the following issue of *Midstream* she acknowledged that she too had found the huge success of Anne Frank's diary to be suspect, particularly in Germany, but added: 'There is such a thing as an inverted chauvinism, and when discussing the wrongs of the Jewish people one should be careful not to fall into that trap.'[36] This from an assimilated Prussian-born former student of Karl Jaspers, Edmund Husserl and Martin Heidegger, who since those years had never ceased to question what it meant to be Jewish, and had placed the Holocaust at the heart of her philosophical thinking.

Due to that concern, Hannah Arendt had offered to travel to Jerusalem to report on the Eichmann trial for the *New Yorker*. Whatever her personal views of Bettelheim may have been, the resulting articles, published in February and March 1963, were to get both of them lumped together by many critics in the category of anti-Semitic Jews. On attending the trial, Arendt had been astounded to discover that far from being a monster, Eichmann was no more than a petty, vain civil servant who spoke only in clichés. While seemingly ready to co-operate with the court, he could only clearly remember the acts which had sent thousands of people to their deaths inasmuch as they had coincided with key points in his career. He seemed to be nothing more than a small-minded bureaucrat, who looked sincere when he claimed that he had never killed anyone other than by passing on orders. The way she portrayed him, the fact that she challenged the judicial validity of the trial, and above all that she raised questions about the role played by the Jewish Councils in the occupied countries in helping with the deportation programmes, brought a storm of protest from all over the world. The controversy rose to new heights a few months later, when Arendt published an edited version of her articles in book form. The title, which her adversaries considered scandalous in itself, was *Eichmann in Jerusalem: The Banality of Evil*.[37]

When the weekly *New Republic* asked Bruno Bettelheim to review the work, the resulting article only added fuel to the flames.[38] He who was so adept at demolishing the credibility of a book in a few lines, and who did so more often than not, had almost nothing but praise for Arendt's work. He started out by trying to show that the trial had in fact been a misunderstanding, because it was not Eichmann as an individual who was being put in the dock, but anti-Semitism through the ages. This explained why it had been necessary to portray the man as a monster, Bettelheim wrote. What should have been on trial was the totalitarian state, rather than a man who was in fact only one of its cogs, and not a very interesting one at that. To show what he meant, he quoted an expression which Eichmann frequently used to justify his acts: *Kadavergehorsam*, which he translated as 'the obedience of a corpse'. Although inherited from Prussian army traditions, the term only took on its full meaning in Hitler's Germany, Bettelheim noted. 'The obedient servant of Hitler and the prisoner who walked to the gas chamber became alike as true symbols of the total state. The rewarded servant and the prisoner to be murdered, each had lost his free will, his ability to act out of personal conviction.'

Following on from Arendt, Bettelheim stressed how much the Jewish organizations in the Nazi-ruled countries had facilitated the extermination programme, even if their actions had only been aimed at easing conditions. 'Arendt's point – and it is well taken – is that any organization within a totalitarian society that compromised with the system became immediately ineffective in opposing it, and ended up helping it,' he wrote, bolstering his own argument with that of the book he was reviewing. Only active resistance to the oppressor, either open or underground, could possibly have changed the course of events, he went on, if only because it would have made it more difficult for the rest of the world to act as if nothing was happening. Bettelheim illustrated this argument with an example that his readers were then seeing every night on their TV screens: 'Many of us were impressed by the way Negroes in Birmingham marched, singing and upright, to jail. But much deeper feelings were aroused in us when we saw pictures of a solitary Negro being dragged down by policemen because he refused to march to jail on his own.' This was certainly a telling point for the liberal readership of *New Republic*, but although the great majority of US Jews were at that time supportive of the Civil Rights movement and Martin Luther King, not all of them identified the fate of their people with that of American blacks. A few lines further on, Bettelheim denied that Eichmann's trial had been the trial of the century, which it should logically have been since it dealt with the crime of the century. Instead, he preferred to retain the title for a *cause célèbre* of the 1920s, the trial of Leopold and Loeb, two Chicago students who had murdered a third one in a completely gratuitous act, 'to see how it felt,' as one of them said. Theirs had been a crime committed 'because of the most inhumane principles and to assert their superiority,' Bettelheim wrote. But their trial had been historic because, thanks to defence attorney Darrow, 'the incredible inhumanity of their deed was put within the broad context of human nature. The result was that ... enough empathy was aroused with these errant human beings so that the trial ... aroused in us the determination to create a better society, one that could not and would not produce another Leopold and Loeb.' This argument was not likely to endear Bettelheim to those who had accused him of anti-Semitism: Leopold and Loeb were Jews.

This time, for those who demanded total respect for the victims of Nazism, Bettelheim had really gone over the edge. 'From the comfort of Chicago, Bettelheim presumes to award patents of heroism and/or cowardice to Hitler's martyrs,' wrote Alexander Donat, a former Maidenek inmate.[39] Noting that Bettelheim had chosen 'to start a war against Anne Frank' and her family for hiding in a place with no exit, he wrote: 'Doesn't the man know that hundreds of thousands of Jews perished because they had *no* place to hide, with or without an outlet?' But it was the condemnation of Otto Frank's failure to get himself a weapon that most enraged Donat, who had taken part in the Warsaw Ghetto uprising. He recalled that the Jewish Fighters' Organization, set up in July 1942 to organize the revolt, had only been able, in six months of existence, to obtain a total of fifty revolvers from the Polish underground. 'In Bialystok and Vilna, the Jewish fighters received nothing.'[40]

For the death camp survivors, and even more for the relatives of those who had perished, Bettelheim's statements were unbearable. It was tough enough for them simply to tell of their experiences, but to find their story being hijacked by a group of German Jews who had been lucky enough to sit out the war in the United States, and who dared to blame them for their own sufferings, was simply too much to take. This was made even worse by the fact that, while Bettelheim and his fellow detainees had mostly been German, the majority of those gassed at Auschwitz, Treblinka or Sobibor had been *Öst Juden*, who from time immemorial had had to contend with the arrogance of their assimilated brethren in Vienna, Berlin or Frankfurt. For them, Bruno Bettelheim's credentials as a deportee did not carry the same weight as they did for his other readers. 'He forgets that by comparison to the later camps, the camps in 1938 were like summer resorts,' Donat wrote.

Initially confined to the letters columns of Jewish journals and a few New York papers, the controversy now widened, affecting Bettelheim even in his professional life. In 1964 a debate on Hannah Arendt's book was held at the University of Chicago branch of the Hillel Foundation, a Jewish cultural centre. It was chaired by Hans Morganthau, himself a former concentration camp inmate and a friend of both Arendt and Bettelheim. When the latter stood up to speak the hissing, shouting and heckling were so loud that he had to sit down again without saying a word. Although his stormy character was already well known on campus, and though the subject was emotionally charged, several of Bettelheim's friends and colleagues were shocked to see so much hatred directed at him in an academic debate. A professor from a neighbouring university even waved his bare arm, carrying a tattooed Auschwitz number, in Bettelheim's face, while another shouted: 'We knew about you in the camps; we knew you had a visa in your pocket.'

Bettelheim did not even try to answer the accusations but 'pooh-poohed them off,' as one witness recalls.[41] Indeed, he generally feigned to be unaffected by such displays. He could afford to: *The Informed Heart* had won him support from thousands of readers, who admired his lucidity and viewed any attack on him as but further proof of the correctness of his ideas. And to brush off most of the objections, all he had to do was to return to his central argument. Alexander Donat, for example, was the first to admit that, right up to the end, nobody in the Polish or Ukrainian ghettos had been able to imagine just how far the Nazis' murderous folly had taken such a civilized people as the Germans.

Privately, however, it is hard to believe that Bruno Bettelheim could have taken this controversy lightly. The mid-1960s was precisely when, at the Orthogenic School, he was forced to acknowledge that despite all his efforts, the results achieved with autistic children were not as conclusive as he had hoped. It was also when he chose to go to Israel to study kibbutz children, a trip which stirred intense and contradictory feelings in him.[42] Bettelheim had by this time achieved celebrity status. He was writing on almost any subject: education and children of course, but also the role of women, violence, jealousy, sexuality, racism or John F. Kennedy's assassin. He had just embarked on a new, highly ambitious, extension programme for the Orthogenic School, which involved a lot more fundraising, as well as accounting for funds already received. He was autocratic, irritable, and liable to take offence at anything and nothing. Such as when the American Association of Orthopsychiatry failed to publish his contribution to its twice-yearly conference, in precisely the year when his friend Fritz Redl was its president: Bettelheim decided to stay away from its next meeting.

Why should this man, who was otherwise so busy, have plunged into such quarrels, which after all related to a previous chapter of his life? To answer that question, one has to consider the major development that had occurred since he had first written his article on the camps: the return of the death camp survivors. During an initial period, they had remained silent, or at least, nobody had listened to them. Then, towards the end of the 1950s, their accounts had started to appear in print, and the story they told was worlds apart from what Bettelheim had described. He himself stressed that difference in *The Informed Heart*, which was published at about this time, stressing that in the death camps 'no effort was made to modify personality since their only purpose was to exterminate prisoners as efficiently as possible'.[43] The distinction was of prime importance, since his entire study was concerned precisely with changes in prisoners' behaviour during their internment. It also made it clear that, however hellish Buchenwald had been, Bettelheim had not experienced the most extreme of situations. Nevertheless, the remark was consigned to a footnote.

When he wrote *The Informed Heart*, Bettelheim had thus not yet realized, or else refused to see, that the conclusions he had drawn from his period in Buchenwald were not applicable to the people who had returned from the death camps – that he no longer had the right to use the first person plural to speak in the name of all the survivors of the Nazi camps. And what had he in fact learned at Buchenwald? Quite simply that life meant a lot to him, which is how I interpret his decision to turn down the opportunity to wear that destructive armband. And that when his enemy was clearly identifiable, when he could hate him without feeling guilty, or without having to punish himself for doing so, he was no longer depressed. As he was to tell the French journalist Daniel Karlin, the period he spent in the camps was the only time in his life when he never had thoughts of suicide.[44]

Hardly had Bettelheim been released than he found himself faced with a conflict between his now explicit desire to live, and to live well, and the old burden of responsibilities and unpaid debts, made even heavier by the memory of those he had left behind in the camps. They, who were neither any better nor any worse than he was, had not been lucky enough to get out. Lucky? That was a dangerous word, evocative of the accidents of birth, sex, physique, race or family. A taboo word for a man who felt responsible for his own fate, the heir to a tradition in which everything had to be earned, either through work or fraud, because it was never free. A man who had never been granted the right to be unlucky, to be simply a victim. No, luck had no place in this process. As he was to endlessly repeat at the Orthogenic School, there are no accidents.

The work of interpretation that Bettelheim carried out to write his first article on the camps therefore consisted of uncovering the hidden necessity behind the chance events of deportation and internment. This was his way of shouldering his share of the responsibility for those who had stayed behind in Buchenwald. No wonder he was so hard on them, since he was deriving his understanding from what he discovered in himself. To do this he was forced to wrestle not only with his memories, but also with the ever-present pessimistic, nihilistic streak in him, that old enemy that Freud had called the 'death instinct' but which Bettelheim, who knew it well, then referred to as inertia. It was the force that whispered in his ear that nothing was worthwhile, that was bolstered by his reading of Oswald

Spengler. The drive he had always combated by trying to draw meaning out of every event, and finding a 'happy ending' to even the most awful among them, so that they could serve some useful purpose.

The trouble is that in seeking at all costs to give a meaning to events, some of which are literally beyond human understanding, one may find oneself asserting as truth anything one is not in a position to prove, and on occasion rearranging the facts a little. Such as when Bettelheim switched the time of his story on the broken glasses, or attributed to himself a role he had not in fact played, so as to lend more weight to his story. As long as the ultimate goal is just, though, what does it matter? If the end(ing) is to be a happy one, it must surely justify the means – the story – used to arrive at it. But, when one has been haunted from childhood by the idea of fraud, the story-telling exercise is fraught with risks. All it takes is for the legitimacy of the ending to be suddenly called into question for the whole edifice to collapse, leaving behind it nothing but guilt and shame. If this happens, what started out as mere inexactitudes and omissions can, over time, turn into unatonable crimes.

However strong his convictions, and whatever the validity of his arguments – and it is clearly essential on this point to distinguish between the content of his statements and their tone – it is inconceivable that being plunged into such a furious and even hateful confrontation with the death camp survivors could not have affected him personally. After having spent over two years locked in struggle with himself because he felt it his duty to alert the world to what was going on in Buchenwald, how could he have faced the reproaches he saw in the eyes of the Auschwitz survivors without shame?

An echo of the inner turmoil that Bettelheim must have gone through at that time can be found in his review of Jean-François Steiner's book *Treblinka*,[45] his first piece on the camps after four years spent writing on completely different subjects. One might have expected him to like this book, which tells the story of the uprising by the last thousand prisoners in Treblinka, a camp built for the sole purpose of exterminating Jews. Before that, it briefly relates the arrival of the Nazis in the Lithuanian capital of Vilnius, and the first mass executions in the nearby woods, showing how the Vilnius Jews refused until the last minute to believe the people who tried to warn them of the impending disaster. The book is written like a novel, based whenever possible on the first-hand accounts of survivors, and this triggered Bettelheim's first criticism. 'Steiner turns the story of this deepest of horrors into a gripping escape fiction,' he wrote. In a further criticism of the form of the book, he accused the writer of failing to make a choice between fiction and the telling of history, thereby creating inauthentic-sounding dialogues. For example, when the prisoners discuss the need to survive in order to tell the world what they had seen, he commented: 'The truth is that to tell about the horrors of the camp was a very strong motive. Certainly it was for me, for my friends at some moments. But our goal was revenge; to bring the world down on the SS, not to warn people against "making decisions lightly without knowing where they will lead them" .... [That] came typically as an afterthought ... the prisoner wanted to scream out against an abomination so that the world would take action against the Nazis .... He did not care about any lessons to be learned from the camp. In fact they took years for me to learn.'

What is striking in this article is the way Bruno Bettelheim's thinking on the subject has deepened. He has clearly read all the testimonies published about the camps, and reflected on the difference between his own experiences and those of the death camp inmates. At several points he is careful to underline that difference. Meanwhile, he also uses the article on Steiner to distance himself from Raul Hilberg's position: it is not Jewish traditions *per se* which are to blame for the Jews' passivity *vis-à-vis* the Nazis, he stresses, but specifically ghetto-related traditions. The reason for this was that since Napoleonic times all Jews who had a spark of rebelliousness in them had left the *shtetls*. The lack of reaction was not due to some atavism but to the impoverishment of certain characteristics in a historically defined group.[46] Bettelheim does not believe in innate racial or national characteristics. For him a human being, be he Jewish or German, is above all an individual, and reacts as such to his surroundings. But, he writes, in order for Martin Buber, Marc Chagall or Isaac Bashevis Singer to create such touching portrayals of the *shtetl*, they first had to leave it. Despite the phrase that traditionally marked the end of anti-Jewish pogroms, 'The Jewish people lives,' Bettelheim went on, Hitler had succeeded in wiping out the *shtetl* with its very specific customs and culture. The state of Israel, whose mentality he saw as diametrically opposed to that of the ghetto, only existed because a totally assimilated Viennese Jew, Theodor Herzl, had launched a movement that had been taken up by the most active elements in the Jewish community. 'It is precisely the absence of this activist element, and the many hundreds of years of "compliance" that explains ghetto mentality, and not any racial inheritance of the Jews.'

In the space of four years, the tone has become firmer and the ideas clearer and better laid out. In this new article Bettelheim seems more concerned to explain, and less aggressive; his severity towards the book is even tempered by the recognition that its author, whose father died in the camps, had been driven to write to fulfil a sacred duty. He nevertheless criticizes Steiner for wanting to save everyone: both those who, like his father, fought, and those who submitted to their fates in the name of what the author presents as their philosophy. In passing, Bettelheim gets in a dig at the French philosopher Simone de Beauvoir, for writing in her preface on things she knew nothing about, and at General de Gaulle, for having misunderstood the book's message. But his aim there was probably to stress that the book was a French one, and that its success among non-Jews could not be seen as a vindication of the ideas it expressed.

More importantly for our purposes, this is the first text in which Bettelheim places insistent emphasis on the guilt of the survivors. He criticizes Jean-François Steiner for concentrating his narrative on the inmates who plotted and carried out the uprising, thereby allowing the reader to forget that in the same period some 700,000 people had let themselves be gassed. In order to turn the few into heroes Steiner had drawn a distorted picture of them, pushing into the background the fact that if they were in a position to revolt, and that only at the last minute, when their own lives were threatened, it was only because up until that point they had agreed to be collaborators in the extermination programme. And although nobody who has not experienced death camps has the right to condemn them for having sought to survive, even for a few days, and having thus accepted the horrendous tasks they were given (even before the death camps, 'prisoners in the concentration camps were often in situations where their survival may have cost the lives of others,' he notes), they were not heroes, but rather 'desperately ashamed men'.

Further in the same article, Bettelheim comments on the relative lack of success of accounts written by survivors of the death camps, compared to the acclaim that greeted Steiner's book, suggesting that this was because survivors' accounts had been written by 'people who were broken by the knowledge of how they had let themselves be degraded, broken by the knowledge that they had taken part in destroying their brothers in order to live another day of such a life'. Clearly Bettelheim had finally understood that no survivor from Auschwitz, Treblinka or Sobibor could ever have written, as he had, that 'the impact of the concentration camp ... within a few weeks, did for me what years of a useful and quite successful analysis had not done'.[47]

From that point on, everything he would write about the camps would include in some form or other the ideas of shame and guilt. Almost as if, having come to such a painful realization of the gulf that separated his experience from that of the Holocaust survivors, this was the only bridge he had found between himself and them. Or even better, as if their testimony had finally helped him to confront what had been haunting him since his own release, and which was the source of so much of his aggressiveness.

The guilt feelings, which run like a continuous thread through *Surviving*, are indeed a distinctive feature of accounts by Auschwitz survivors. But they do not permeate in the same way the testimonies of former concentration camp inmates. Ernst Federn, for example, does not recognize any such feelings, and they cannot be detected in the accounts of Kogon or Walter Poller, who were also in Buchenwald at the same time as Bettelheim. Guilt feelings do not obsess Hans Bandler, either. The experiences of all these men left them with feelings of rage, of enormous pity for the weaker inmates who did not survive, and sometimes, as Bettelheim reports, of shame at having been reduced to such a state of powerlessness and degradation. On occasion they also express feelings of injustice because they survived while others did not. But such feelings do not form a backdrop for all their memories, as they do for example in the accounts of Primo Levi,[48] or in those of Bettelheim towards the end of his life. 'Being one of the very few who were saved when millions like oneself perished seems to entail a special obligation to justify one's luck and very existence,' the latter wrote in *Surviving*. This was a problem 'which one cannot solve, but with which one must live'.[49]

And yet, from all we know about the conditions of Bettelheim's incarceration, it is hard to see why he should have reacted differently to the experience. As we have seen, the 'sins' he committed while in the camps (wearing a blind man's armband which he was almost, but not quite, entitled to, and more generally using his money to purchase a few advantages without which he would probably not have survived) could not be viewed as detrimental to other detainees, except in the general sense, stressed by Bettelheim, in which a privilege accorded to one inmate was thus not available to another. But it was precisely in Auschwitz that that kind of privilege became automatically deadly, when simply staying alive meant that other people died. In Buchenwald, when Bettelheim was there, conditions were horribly tough, degrading and extremely dangerous, but the logic was not one of extermination. It was easy to die there, as could be seen from the regular passage of coffin-bearers, but one could also survive, if one had strength, the clear will to live – and luck.

The unease that Bettelheim no doubt felt about his minor compromises with the camp system must have been aggravated by the contradiction between his own past behaviour and the lessons in survival he had retrospectively handed down to Anne Frank's father and other victims. Although he did not of course admit it publicly, he could certainly not have forgotten that he himself had not been very much smarter than the people he was criticizing. Once arrested, he had indeed thrown all his energy into being able to leave. Before that, however, he had, like many others, sought to put his affairs in order before fleeing, without realizing what the resulting delay would cost him. Why therefore did he so obstinately refuse to admit that human beings, however well informed, simply could not imagine the death camps until they had seen them? Why did he absolutely have to point the finger at the victims? He, who at the same time as he was embroiled in this controversy, was every day demonstrating his extraordinary ability to understand the sufferings of the children in his care?

. But that is precisely the point. If, as I believe, it was in Buchenwald that this chronic depressive discovered the strength of his own will to live; if he owed his survival to that discovery and if it was what led him to devote himself to helping others, then his first encounter with the death camp survivors must have been quite simply unbearable. For their experiences meant the absolute negation of all the positive conclusions he had drawn from his Buchenwald sojourn, and thus the negation, at a critical juncture, of his life's work, notably at the school. In Auschwitz he would never even have had the choice of whether or not to wear an armband, for there blind people were simply and immediately gassed. Before his self-analysis had allowed him to assimilate this new reality with all its implications, he had reacted precisely in the way which he himself so often denounced in others – by denial. In somewhat the same way as he would, thirty years later, angrily suggest that Aids sufferers ought simply to refrain from sex, this miraculously healthy child of a syphilitic father had banished the Auschwitz survivors to their 'ghetto thinking'. Why couldn't they have fought? By shifting the blame for the main part of their suffering on to the victims themselves, Bettelheim had rid himself of a dangerous threat to his own hard-won equilibrium.

But, to go a little further, is this not precisely what made Bettelheim's message on the genocide so appealing to the younger generation, who while not wishing to deny the past, wanted above all to look towards the future? In the mid- and late-1960s these young people were faced with much more immediate dangers than those which obsessed their parents: the Kennedy assassinations, that of Martin Luther King, the Vietnam War, a changing society, etc. For many of them the appeal of Bettelheim's message was no doubt that his status as a former camp inmate gave him the right to say what they, who had never known Nazism, did not even dare to think. That, horrendous as it was, it was not their problem, and that no, they were not responsible for Hitler's crimes. It was indeed tragic, but precisely, it was too much so for them to be able to do anything about it. The only thing they could do, apart from feeling compassion for the victims, was to try and make sure that it never ever happened again. Which is exactly what Bettelheim was continually saying. A preoccupation that he pithily summed up in the opening sentence of one of his very last essays on the subject: 'My business is not with the dead but with the living.'

This text, one of the most forceful he wrote on the subject, is entitled 'The Holocaust – Some Reflections, a Generation Later'.[50] It is essentially a long reflection on the death instinct and it figures prominently in *Surviving*. For the first time, Bettelheim stressed that the denial of such a monstrous crime could only have been unconscious. This time, however, the bulk of his criticism was not aimed at the victims. Instead, he concentrated on how, since the war, everything possible had been done, particularly in the United States, to avoid facing up to the reality of Hitler's crime. Denial, he wrote, begins with words. The Nazis were the first to try and disguise what they were doing, by calling it the *Endlösung*, or 'Final Solution'. But as early as 1944 the Allies had also helped in the process by choosing the neologism 'genocide', half-Greek, half-Latin, to designate what was in fact the mass murder of Jews. A similar motivation inspired the Americans, who opted for the word 'Holocaust', borrowed from the liturgical vocabulary and referring to sacrifice by fire, Bettelheim pointed out. While it was true that Hitler's victims had ended up as ashes in the camps' crematoria, the religious reference was 'a sacrilege, a profanation of God and man', because its ultimate effect was to 'rob the victims of this abominable mass murder of the only thing left to them: their uniqueness'.

So, after all those years, Bettelheim's inner travails had finally brought him back to the only position he could occupy without betraying himself in his own eyes: that of authentic defender of the memory of the victims. Authentic because the defence was based not on sentimentalism, which he considered to be blind and therefore guilty, but on extreme clear-sightedness. On a lucidity which pierced into the depths of the soul, to the point where it hurt the most, to dig out what had been denied, what could not be expressed. To reach that point, however, he first had to express the rejection that the victims inspired in him, too. 'My business is not with the dead, but with the living.'

But how could a man whose own father had been reduced (through his 'fault') to spending two years hidden away in a Viennese clinic, like one of the living dead, consciously entertain such a thought? From that instinctive rejection, Bettelheim had thus arrived at guilt. Not the superficial emotion of social convention, but remorse that cut into the soul like a scalpel. In 1968, he had pointed out that, in extreme situations, the guilt of the survivor was not the noble sentiment that it was sometimes made out to be. 'I believe, on the basis of my experience, that this guilt is not for the death of the other but for how one felt about it.'[51] For that feeling was not just one of relief at still being alive when others were dead, it was 'the morally unacceptable feeling of happiness' that wells up incontrollably when one discovers that it is the next man who has drawn the unlucky number.

Facing up to such feelings had not been easy. But he had to go through with it in order to overcome the terrible conflict between his desire to live – a powerful drive but one that he had difficulty accepting unless he could justify it by passing on to others what he had learned in the camps – and what he could read in the eyes of the men and women who had found themselves locked in a confrontation with death from which no one could emerge a winner. People for whom surviving was not, and could not be, a victory. For whom no 'happy ending' was possible.

The last phase of Bettelheim's thinking about his concentration camp experience, which was to lead him to undertake *Surviving* at a time when he thought he was through with Nazism, was certainly the most disturbing for him. It started with the shock he experienced on seeing the film *Seven Beauties*, by the Italian director Lina Wertmüller. In the text he devoted to this, Bettelheim's indignation is also directed at a book called *The Survivor*, published at around the same time.[52] The criticism of the two works is so tightly intertwined, however, that the reader has a hard time realizing that they in fact have nothing to do with one another. An intellectually questionable procedure, as the author of the book, Terence Des Pres, was to point out.[53]

In the United States, Lina Wertmüller had shot from obscurity to quite extraordinary popularity in just two years, and when *Seven Beauties* opened in January 1976 it was greeted with widespread critical acclaim, as her masterpiece. This tragicomic, baroque and expressionist film starts in Fascist Italy. The central character is the seductive but totally amoral Pasqualino, a young Neapolitan thug, who rapes, robs and murders his way through life until he finds himself thrown into a concentration camp. There, in the hope of winning his release, he decides to try to seduce the camp commander, a massive German woman. Pasqualino's plan works, but not exactly as he had intended: the commander, who is no fool, offers him a good meal and a good night's sleep to recover, at the end of which if he fails to get an erection with her he will be killed. He accepts the bargain. There follows what is obviously the high point of the film: a burlesque scene in which the frail and sickly youth struggles to carry out his side of the deal – finally with success. 'Your thirst for life disgusts me, you shitty little Neapolitan,' the woman spits out, sadly ruminating that for that very reason her 'master race' will probably not survive the war. All the idealists in the film end up dead: the one who dreamed of a new man in a better world commits suicide by throwing himself into the open latrine pit, while Pasqualino, promoted to the rank of *Kapo* after his sexual performance, ends up shooting his friend, a socialist and man of principle. The film ends in Naples after its liberation by US troops, where the wretched hero, now free, is reunited with his girlfriend. She has in the meantime become a prostitute, and will remain one; Pasqualino tells her that he wants to have lots and lots of children.

Even leaving aside those details which must have particularly affected Bettelheim by recalling painful memories, it is easy to see why he found the work so disturbing. Whatever else he thought of her film, he had to acknowledge that Wertmüller, a former assistant to Federico Fellini, had talent. She had also done her homework; the film portrays many of the known features of Buchenwald, such as the *Bock*, the hanging of inmates by the arms, and the majestic surrounding forest. The central character is also remarkably acted, by Giancarlo Giannini, who often manages to win the audience's sympathy for the contemptible Pasqualino. The shots of the camp even feature the bluish fog often mentioned by survivors; by contrast, Naples is shown as a riot of colour.

After attending a private showing of *Seven Beauties*, Bettelheim immediately informed the *New York Times* that he would not be able to comply with their request for a review. Still upset about the film two weeks later, he agreed however to see it again. On that second viewing he found it even more disturbing, but better understood why, as he recounts in the introduction to *Surviving*. This resulted in the article which three years later would form the title-piece of that book.[54]

Bettelheim had in fact been expecting to see one among the spate of films, like *The Night Porter*, which exploited Nazism for erotic purposes. That would have been easy for him to deal with. To gain pleasure from hurting others, or from pain inflicted on oneself, was clearly not 'decent', to use a word Bettelheim was fond of employing to assess human behaviour. But Wertmüller's film was not erotic but philosophical; it did not glorify sadism as a means to pleasure, but simply as an essential component of the survival instinct. That is precisely what makes it so disturbing. It shows a crude, grotesque and despicable lust for life that carries all before it, triumphing in particular over all forms of ideal. The film portrays the life instinct as essentially obscene, grasping, sadistic and above all power-hungry. Message: forget all the rest, this is what really makes the world go round. The absolute negation, in other words, of everything that Bruno Bettelheim had been teaching for thirty-six years. A Bettelheim who had spent his entire life struggling against just those unacceptable elements in his own life instinct (and those of the children in his care), to try and channel them (or, as a psychoanalyst would put it, sublimate them) into the most productive, the highest life-enhancing actions. Wertmüller's film did not just negate such efforts, it actively ridiculed them by emptying them of meaning.

In his article, which first appeared in August 1976, Bettelheim accuses Wertmüller of being confused. He does not doubt that, consciously, she is against fascism and the concentration camps, but at the same time she is fascinated by their brutality and power, their 'rape of man'. All the noble characters are shown to be losers, good is feeble and only evil triumphs. Unconsciously, she is seeking to justify the world that has spawned the camps, writes Bettelheim. 'Pasqualino is not a person whose experiences have added to his depth; understanding, compassion, the ability to feel guilty, all of which were lacking in him before, continue to be lacking in him, despite world-shaking experiences that one feels should have changed him completely. It is this depiction of the survivor that robs survivorship of all meaning. It makes seeing the film an experience that degrades.'

But the worst aspect of all for Bettelheim was clearly the acclaim which greeted the film in American intellectual circles – precisely those where many of his admirers were to be found. One cannot help but feel that this success appeared to him as a betrayal, as evidence that his efforts had been in vain; that almost a half-century of trying to point out the road away from barbarity had failed, that absurdity had won out over meaning, ugliness over beauty. This impression is strengthened by what he then goes on to write about *The Survivor*: 'By quite different routes Professor Des Pres ... and Wertmüller ... arrive at parallel conclusions about what is required for survival in a world dominated by the concentration camp or standing under its specter .... The main lesson of survivorship is: all that matters, the only thing that is really important, is life in its crudest, merely biological form.'

There is no need to delve too deeply into the debate between Bettelheim and Des Pres – carried on solely through their writings, since they never actually met – to see that its significance, for Bettelheim at least, had little to do with details of the camp life provided on each side. Indeed other writers have already pointed out that their descriptions do not in fact differ very much.[55] What is important in the confrontation is that Bettelheim appears to have reacted to it with absolute bad faith, thereby showing just how deeply this new controversy had affected him.

For *The Survivor* bears little relation to the description given by Bettelheim. Terence Des Pres in fact shows that in order to survive in the camps, inmates could not afford to consider their own individual needs alone. If they did not help one another, they were lost. And although he does defend a viewpoint which could be described as 'biologist', it has nothing to do with the cynical 'thirst for life' of Wertmüller's anti-hero. For Des Pres, the lesson to be drawn from the concentration camps is that what keeps men alive is not great ideas, but their awareness of their condition. 'The survivor is evidence that men and women are now strong enough, mature enough, awake enough, to face death without mediation, and therefore to embrace life without reserve,' he writes. The message is that one should beware of all ideologies, religions and other beliefs (among which he includes psychoanalysis), because while claiming to save humanity they often end up annihilating it.

It was a message that was in tune with the times. In the mid-1970s idealism was on the wane, with Watergate and the Vietnam War forcing the United States to reassess its world role. Rather than the victory over the self proposed by Bettelheim, Des Pres preached observance of Voltaire's famous 'We should take care of our own gardens.'[56] This was not a new debate, and it could have remained a simple difference between two humanist views of man, explicable in part by the difference in age between its protagonists (Des Pres was thirty-seven, Bettelheim seventy-three). Furthermore, Bettelheim would probably not have found it very hard to counter Des Pres' arguments, and show up the misunderstandings in his book. The latter was indeed not a work of history: Des Pres was a professor of English at Colgate University, New Hampshire, and his work had grown out of a research project on the theme of the survivor in literature, a figure he viewed as the epitome of the anti-hero. On studying the accounts of survivors, he had become fascinated, and decided to write a book on the subject. In it, however, he lumped victims of the Soviet Gulag together with those of the Nazi genocide, and he failed to clearly make the all-important distinction between concentration camps and death camps. Above all, Des Pres' work was purely textual, and his analysis of what constituted a survivor was therefore strictly intellectual. The work is nonetheless moving in places, and frequently brilliant and insightful, being well documented and built around a clear idea. But although it remains nothing more than a textual analysis, it takes upon itself to decide which of the survivors' accounts are right and which are wrong.

Among the former inmates whose accounts Terence Des Pres dismisses are most of those who sought to analyse camp behaviour from a psychological standpoint, and first and foremost Bruno Bettelheim. He criticizes him for using the concepts of infantilization and identification with the aggressor, which he sees as meaningless within the framework of a camp. He also condemns Bettelheim for imposing his own interpretations on the behaviour of his fellow inmates, in particular that of Eugen Kogon, without seeming to realize that that is precisely what he, Des Pres, is doing to Bettelheim. With a key difference, however: Bettelheim had actually been in Buchenwald, while Des Pres, who had not, considered himself entitled to play the testimony of one inmate off against that of another. More generally, Des Pres accuses Bettelheim of always portraying his own actions in a favourable light, and above all attacks his position as that of an uncontested authority on the subject, going so far as to write that Bettelheim's 'first analysis of the camp experience – "Individual and Mass Behavior in Extreme Situations" – appeared in 1943, adding the weight of precedence to a position which has never been challenged and which has influenced all subsequent study'.[57] It does not appear to have occurred to him that its precedence was precisely what gave it authority.

According to some of his friends, Des Pres had in fact been an admirer of Bettelheim's, until his reading of other survivors' accounts led him to question his writings.[58] He thus veered from admiration to hostility, as did many of Bettelheim's detractors, and ended up in effect denying Bettelheim his validity as a witness, without any regard for a man who, whatever his position, was but a human being and therefore fallible. All of which, coming from the author of the above-mentioned lines, was paradoxical to say the least!

That Bettelheim should have been angry, not to say furious, at being so criticized by a disillusioned young man who felt himself entitled to judge him without taking into account the fact that before becoming an authority on the Nazis he had been one of their victims is easy to understand. Bettelheim was an irritable person, who while preaching autonomy, did not much like to be challenged. But that fact alone does not explain the way he couched his article, shooting down Des Pres with images from Wertmüller's film, and without ever informing the readers of the *New Yorker* that this same Des Pres had previously attacked *him*.[59] Bettelheim was very protective of his reputation in academic circles. This was not the first time he had been criticized. He could very well have answered Des Pres by pointing out the omissions and contradictions in the latter's book, not to mention its literary effects, which on this issue could be seen as a little out of place. He could also have decided to ignore the attack altogether. So why did he choose a path which, if Des Pres had decided to reply in a mass-circulation paper, could have led to his being very publicly accused of intellectual dishonesty?

In a letter to Carl Frankenstein, Bettelheim admitted that he had had a lot of trouble penning his article, but that he had felt it to be his duty. 'Although in opposite ways – Des Pres attacked me personally, but this is beside the point – the film and the book, in my opinion subtly, in camouflaged ways, preach fascism, glorify, as Des Pres calls it, "living by the crude demands of the body, beyond the compulsions of culture".'[60]

So Bettelheim's attack on Des Pres was not in fact merely for revenge, as Des Pres himself, and a few others after him,[61] believed. Bettelheim was sincere; he was even shocked that others had not seen the same hidden danger he had detected ('Even Jewish magazines reprinted Des Pres, so much were they taken by his thesis,' he wrote to Frankenstein). In his view all of this was to be lumped together with the popularity at the time of the memoirs of Albert Speer, one of Hitler's former ministers, and of other books on Nazism. Not long afterwards, while browsing in an antique store, he would get a similar shock, as he told his friend in another letter.[62] On examining a medal bearing Goethe's head, which he thought would make a good gift, he suddenly noticed a Nazi symbol on the back. The object was extremely expensive. Repressing a desire to hurl the medal in the dealer's face, he simply stated that he would not want it even if it was going for free. Surprised, the man replied: 'But the Nazi sign is precisely what makes it valuable!' Bettelheim commented sadly to his friend: 'So the catastrophes in our lives have acquired rarity value, so far has this time removed itself from them.'

Here we see an ageing, weary Bettelheim (he had recently had a mild heart attack, and among other ailments was suffering from arthritis), waging one last fight against what he saw as the creeping revisionism of the period. But that is not all. His reaction to the book and to the film seems too passionate, too based on gut feeling, to have been entirely rational.

It could be that the source of his discomfort is to be found in the lyrical closing words of *The Survivor*, when Terence Des Pres appeals to his readers to be content with being simply human beings, rather than supermen: 'A biological wisdom exists, prompting us to know that in life's own needs the spirit can find a home. Not noble or god-approved, not especially dramatic or sublime as in the old days, but rooted in the plain happiness of work and communion with others, and in the small shared universe of physical joy which is our due as creatures of flesh.'[63] In both his article and his letter to Frankenstein, Bettelheim singles out that last expression as evidence that Des Pres is 'glorifying living by the crude demands of the body'. Such insistence on a few fleeting words of conclusion is worth a second look; it seems to indicate that Bettelheim is reading more into them than meets the eye. Perhaps they reminded him of 'the crude demands of the body' which, seventy years earlier, had deprived him of a father he could respect, a moral authority he could lean on, leaving him all alone, and much too young, to face up to his own actions. At one and the same time an inflexible judge, and an eternally guilty party.

In addition to the reminder of Anton, or rather of Anton's weakness, that it may have stirred, this reference to 'physical joy' in the conclusion of a book on Auschwitz survivors is indeed somewhat shocking. On that point Des Pres does have something in common with Wertmüller. Indeed, unless someone has been forced by circumstances, and thus by a feeling of duty, to spend a large part of his or her life studying the Nazis' cruelty, there is always something a little suspicious about such an exercise. Something that has to do with the sadistic dimension of the life drives. For man's aggressive instincts are indeed on the side of life, which is what all survivors, in one way or another, discover – precisely in the horrible jubilation one feels, in spite of oneself, when it is the other guy who draws the short straw. A jubilation which is immediately tempered by a strong feeling of guilt, except perhaps in people for whom 'in life's own needs the spirit can find a home'. But one needs to have lived through such an ordeal truly to understand. And the writer who does not realize this can do no more than string out empty statements, which once again only serve to camouflage the reality of man.

What Bettelheim had been trying to get across for the previous forty years was that in the extreme situation of the camp, the continual struggle that Freud described between the life drives (including sadism) and the death instinct (that force which aspires not to victory but to the simple ending of the battle, i.e. to nothingness), was liable at any moment to reach the 'ultimate limit', the point beyond which there is no turning back – the point at which the aggressive instincts line up their forces on the side of death. In the early days those were not the words he used, but the idea was already there. He used every possible avenue to try and get it across. Over the years, as he carried on the inner struggle to understand these things, to put an end to the pain they caused him, the idea became clearer in its outlines. In his last texts on the subject, written to mesh together the articles published in *Surviving*, it came into sharp focus.

As he had already noted in his preface to Nyiszli's book, the specificity of the Nazi genocide had less to do with the murderous wish expressed by Hitler himself than with the echo it found in the minds of so many of his victims. Which did not mean that those victims had consented to their fate. Once again, Bettelheim was talking about the unconscious (but in such a peremptory, and often such a convincing, fashion that his readers did not realize it). What he was trying to say, because he had felt it in himself, was that the real danger point is reached when the deadly desire of the killer touches on the hidden feeling that lurks in every human being, the feeling of having no right to be alive. It is a feeling which is stronger in some people than in others; there are even people who deny its existence.

Bettelheim, for his part, knew it only too well. Since his childhood days, when he would shut himself away in his room, not exactly unhappy, but convinced that his life was not worth living. He had heard that same feeling echoed in every anti-Semitic remark – for what a racist is in fact saying is that the other person does not have as much right to be (here) as he has. And he may also have detected it in some rather obsequious attitude displayed by one or the other of his parents.[64] Which would explain his anger at 'ghetto thinking', and also his fascination with the state of Israel.

One day in Jerusalem, Bettelheim asked Carl Frankenstein why he had chosen to reside in Israel rather than in the United States, where his life would have been so much more comfortable. His friend smiled at him, and replied: 'Because here, I'm not a Jew.'

To glorify the life instinct, whether it be with intentional vulgarity like Wertmüller, or by dressing it up in natural lyricism like Des Pres, while ignoring the constant struggle that it has to wage against its toughest enemy, the death drive, in the murderous environment of the camp – that was the true obscenity. And that, for Bettelheim, was real negationism, the denial of the camps' reality. What right did these two *goys*[65] have to preach to him about survival? What did they know about the camps? Did they not realize that, for someone who has spent time in the hands of the Nazis, nothing can ever be the same again? That indeed, he had experienced sadism in its most naked forms; other people's sadism but above all his own, without which he would have died? Was it not for precisely that reason that he, Bettelheim, had devoted his life to telling people how to make good use of that sadistic component of their life instinct – by turning it not against themselves or their own kind, but against the enemy? Was that not the purpose of all his writings? Was it not precisely because it was 'death which gives meaning to life'[66] that he sought always to provide the happiest possible endings to his stories?

But already the public appeal of those stories appeared to be waning; or at least was no longer strong enough to satisfy his need to feel useful. Since the Chicago campus revolt of 1969, Bettelheim had appeared to many students as no more than an aggressive and reactionary old man. At Stanford, where he was by then teaching a few courses, many viewed his ideas as old-fashioned. The California campus was the temple of behaviourism, and psychoanalysis was not in favour. Bettelheim's teachings no longer appealed to most students, and neither did his style. And when he went to Chicago, for three months of classes in the spring, he was brought face-to-face with the loss of the Orthogenic School. True, the rest of his life was still going well, and copies of his book *The Uses of Enchantment*, published in 1976, were selling like hot cakes. But not even a best-seller could make up for what he perceived more and more as a rejection on the part of his young audience, the prime targets for his message. As he wrote shortly before this period, 'I always felt that teaching students, although

at times trying, is so very important because the personal contact is
something no written word can replace.'[67]

Bettelheim wrote in *Surviving* that when the title article of that book
was first published, in the *New Yorker* in August 1976, it resulted in a
large number of grateful letters. However he cited only one, from a
German woman who had been saved by a Dutch clergyman during the
war, and who asked him to write more on the guilt felt by survivors, a
feeling which had dogged her ever since. The space Bettelheim devoted to
the letter, which he quoted practically *in extenso*, suggests that it had had
on him the effect of a badly needed antidote to the poison that *Seven
Beauties* and the Des Pres book had pumped into his system. Someone still
needed him, and what she wanted to hear about was guilt, the psychological mechanism that he understood best of all. The instrument that had
served, throughout his whole life, to give a meaning to his existence.

Six months after the appearance of his article, Bettelheim took part in
the San Jose conference, to which he submitted his beautiful piece on the
death instinct, 'The Holocaust – One Generation Later'. In it, he stressed
how important it was for prisoners to feel that they were being heard, and
the role that the silence of the outside world had played in the Holocaust:
'Murderers can only kill; they do not have the power to rob us of the wish
to live nor of the ability to fight for life. Degradation, exhaustion and utter
debilitation through starvation, sickness and mistreatment – all these
seriously weaken our will to live, undermine our life drives, and with this
open the way for the death drive. But when such conditions – in which the
Jews found themselves because of Nazi persecution and degradation – are
worsened by the feeling that the rest of the world has forsaken us, then we
are totally deprived of the strength needed to fight off the murderer, to
refuse to dig our own grave.'

To illustrate this state of despair, Bettelheim quoted lines by the
Austrian poet Paul Celan, a Jew whose parents both died in the death
camps, and who was himself a camp survivor:

> *There was earth in them, and*
> *they dug.*
> *They dug and dug, and thus*
> *their day wore on, and their night ...*

He stressed the final lines of the poem:

> *Oh someone, oh none, oh no one, oh you:*
> *Where did it go, if nowhere it went.*
> *Oh you dig and I dig, and I dig myself towards you,*
> *and on our finger the ring awakes us.*[68]

Bettelheim added: 'The Nazis murdered the Jews of Europe. That nobody but the Jews cared, that the world, the United States, did not care, was why Jewish life drives lost the battle against death tendencies. This was why the camp inmates had already relinquished life as they dug their own graves, and why, as the poet put it, "there was earth in them".' Then, finally acknowledging that his place at that point had been in the outside world, he noted: 'We ought to have been their someone, but we were their no one. This is our burden. Just because we cannot atone for it, it is wrong to deny or obfuscate it.'

This time, Bettelheim was fully accepting his position in relation to the camp victims, no more and no less. No longer needing to fight against himself, he stopped pointing the finger at them. A little later, on the publication of Miep Giese's book *Anne Frank Remembered*, he even implicitly made peace with the little Jewish girl's father, through his tribute to the woman who had saved her diary. 'It was Miep's courage that made her ignore the risk to herself and her husband, and her wish to protect Anne's privacy that alone preserved Anne's diary .... Her courage, her humanity and her decency give us hope for humanity,'[69] Bettelheim concluded.

It had been a long and painful voyage, as he acknowledged when putting together *Surviving*: 'The basic motive for both writing these essays and assembling them now has been at work in me for some forty years, dominating my private thoughts and feelings during all that time.'[70] Indeed, the compilation of *Surviving*, which he initially thought would require around six months, since it was mainly a question of selecting essays and writing a few connecting texts, in fact took him two years.

It is worth noting in passing that in the course of his long and painful self-analysis, Bettelheim had little by little moved away from the triumphalist assertions of Ego Psychology, to rediscover the importance of the drives, or instincts. Indeed, his next book after *Surviving* (with the exception of a work on teaching children to read which he had been engaged in on and off for a decade, and which he was to co-sign in 1981 with Karen Zelan) was to be *Freud and Man's Soul*.

In one of the last pieces he was to write on Nazism, one of the three linking chapters he wrote specially for *Surviving*, Bettelheim again quotes Paul Celan:

> *Black milk of dawn we drink it at dusk*
> *we drink it at noon and at daybreak we drink it at night*
> *we drink and we drink ...*

These are the opening lines of *Todesfuge* ('Death Fugue'), the poem that made Celan famous in Germany. After pointing to the small word that is changed in the final stanza:

Black milk of dawn we drink you *at dusk,*

Bettelheim makes a terrible confession:

> When one is forced to drink black milk from dawn to dusk, whether
> in the death camps of Nazi Germany, or while lying in a possibly
> luxurious crib, but there subjected to the unconscious death wishes
> of what overtly may be a conscientious mother – in either situation,
> a living soul has death for a master.[71]

Two years after *Surviving*, Bettelheim was to write a preface for a
French book based on accounts of Jews who as children had been taken in
and protected from the Nazis by Christian families, *Je ne lui ai pas dit au
revoir* (I didn't say goodbye).[72] Bettelheim found here an opportunity to
write about the terrible silence of those whose parents had disappeared at
the hands of the Nazis. In their deepest recesses, he said, these people
'realize, or at least think, that others wish that they could make their
peace with what had happened to them; and this, they know, is impossible'. Because, he said, 'in order to be able to continue to live, to do well in
school, to pass exams', and later to hold down a job and build a family, 'the
victims hid their true feelings so deeply, in the innermost layers of their
very being, that they can hardly reach it themselves ... [so that] all they
know is that life is extremely difficult for them, and that in the deepest
sense it is empty'.[73] In a letter to the writer Madeleine Chapsal, he added
that the accounts by the deportees' children tell us 'once more how the sins
of the generation of the parents destroy the lives of their children'. Which
was why, he added, 'I devoted all my life's work to helping children,
because this chain of one generation destroying the next must be broken,
or one must at least try to do whatever one can to break it.'[74]

Chapter XIV

The Big Bad Wolf

Actually, all my life, I did what came simplest to me; and what is praiseworthy about that? It is true, what to me seems obvious does not seem so to many other people.

Bruno Bettelheim, letter to
Madeleine Chapsal, June 24, 1977

'Joey' arrived at the school in early 1952. He was nine years old and fragile-looking, with something imperious in the expression that played around his large eyes. 'Something a little sadistic, like a two-month-old sitting on the throne,' his counsellor recalls. He spoke a little, stammering heavily when he did, and balked at uttering certain words, such as 'sugar'. He did not pronounce any names, and particularly not his own. 'Joey' could spend hours sitting silently in a corner, rigid and immobile. From time to time he would explode, running around in all directions screaming 'Crash!' and smashing the light bulbs and vacuum tubes that he always managed to hoard in large quantities; then he would revert to his apathetic, switched-off robot mode. Before eating, playing or going to bed, he would unroll imaginary cables connected up to a large electric motor that he carried with him everywhere, plugging them into equally illusory wall sockets. In the early days, he could do nothing without his motor. When 'switched on', however, his gestures were so precise and convincing that, in the dining room, it was not uncommon for counsellors or children to step carefully over his connections as if they were really there. His bed was festooned with electrical circuits and dials, and if he should happen to knock one of them over in his sleep, somebody would always be sure to put it back in place, so that 'Joey' did not switch off on awakening.

The boy held a special fascination for the Orthogenic School staff and was well accepted by the other boys in his dorm. His elaborate rituals could get on their nerves at times, notably when they held up the start of some group activity or outing, but his companions were also impressed by his extraordinary grasp of all things electrical – at least 'when we had time to think about it', as one fellow student says, adding that most of the time they were too wrapped up in their own problems to take much interest in the other boys. When he got into one of his periodic panics, 'Joey' could be extremely violent, but the rest of the time he was a shy, retiring child who caused no trouble at all. A fascinating blend of emotional distress and almost superhuman technical skill; a crazed scientific genius locked up'in the body of a terrified child. For Bruno Bettelheim, 'Joey' was a living metaphor for the profound imbalance he found in the technological society around him.

One Memorial Day, four years after entering the school, 'Joey' made a banner for the parade. It read: 'Feelings are more important than anything under the sun.' He still had a long way to go, but he was clearly on the road to recovery. Today he lives like millions of other people. He still stutters, but he has a regular job – in electronics, of course. He is single but he has friends and manages his life himself. The first article that Bruno Bettelheim published about his case[1] upset him: he thought the description of his symptoms was exaggerated, and was shocked by Bettelheim's portrayal of his mother. He nevertheless paid regular visits to Dr B after leaving the school, and was saddened on hearing of his death.

On the phone, the slightly hesistant voice which politely declines to answer my questions is indeed that of a man responsible for his own life, who knows what is best for him: 'I am sorry, but I have had some bad experiences. I would rather not take part in your project ... I'm sorry you're calling from so far away.'[2]

'Joey the Mechanical Boy' was to become the most famous of Bruno Bettelheim's patients. He emerged as a touching little victim of the technological age who, deprived of human love, could trust only machines and barricaded his own emptiness behind a fortress of electrical wires. 'The most telling case of autism in all the literature,' as summed up by Geneviève Jurgensen.[3] It should however be pointed out that 'Joey''s problem would probably not be diagnosed as autism today. He had indeed arrived at the Orthogenic School with that label, but it seems likely that even by the time Bettelheim was writing *The Empty Fortress*, in the mid-1960s, he no longer considered him as such. As early as 1956, in a report for the Wiebold Foundation,[4] he described an unidentified child with symptoms very like those of 'Joey', but categorized him as 'delusional with autistic features' rather than simply autistic.

Why then did Bettelheim decide to use 'Joey' as one of the three cases of autism described in *The Empty Fortress*? The simplest answer to that question is probably the right one. Not only did 'Joey''s symptoms offer great material for analysis, but Bettelheim needed a success story to validate the results cited in the book. And 'Joey' was indeed a true success of the school, and of the Bettelheim method. Which could not be said of 'Laurie' and 'Marcia', the two other cases described in *The Empty Fortress*, both of whom were undoubtedly autistic, even under the stricter definition prevailing today.

'Laurie', as Bettelheim himself reports, was taken away from the school by her family too early, before the astonishing progress she had started to make could lead to a durable improvement in her condition. The case of 'Marcia' is more complex, and may illustrate insurmountable barriers to the treatment of autism, as well as the school's own limitations. At first, the young girl made spectacular progress, as evidenced by miles of film of her, shot month after month, at Bettelheim's request.[5] After four years of constant care and attention, 'Marcia' could carry out simple household tasks, look after herself, and had above all started to communicate with other people. Unfortunately, by the time she emerged from her isolation, she had already reached fourteen, and she was sufficiently intelligent to understand just how much of a gulf separated her from other girls her age. Realizing that she would never catch up with them, she became discouraged, and her rate of progress slowed considerably. Three years later, she stopped making any progress at all, after Karen Zelan, her counsellor, left the school. 'Marcia' then went back to her family. Her condition was immensely better than it had been on her arrival, but she was not capable of looking after herself alone. 'We did everything we could for her; we helped her to go half the way,' Bettelheim told Ruth Marquis one day.

Much later, in Stanford, Bettelheim would admit to the young therapists attending his seminar that 'Nobody knows how to treat these children.' And when one of them reacted with surprise, saying, 'But you yourself have treated some autistic children rather successfully,' he replied honestly: 'We did the best we could .... Unfortunately, in quite a few cases, our success was limited.'[6] That was not, however, the way he described things in *The Empty Fortress*, his seminal work on autism.[7] And when interviewed by Daniel Karlin in 1973, he asserted that the school 'cured eighty-five per cent' of all autistic children admitted before the ages of seven or eight![8]

Of all Bettelheim's exaggerations, this is clearly the most serious. Not only did it offer false hopes to families already suffering greatly from their child's handicap, but it distracted attention from the school's genuine achievements, notably with autistic children. Furthermore, in the minds of those who knew that the claim was false – and there were quite a few – it sowed a seed of doubt about *The Empty Fortress*, a book whose remarkable insights and observations should have earned it an unquestioned place among the standard references in child psychology. There again, Bettelheim's need to be the best, and to have the last word, succeeded in casting an aura of 'fraud' around his work, thus confirming the deepest fears of this man who could not bring himself to believe in his own legitimacy.

It should however be noted that in the early 1950s, when the Orthogenic School began taking in 'the non-talking kids' as the other children called them (even though some were not completely mute), the accepted definitions of schizophrenia and autism were vaguer than they are today.[9] The first such children admitted were simply stranger, and more difficult to get through to, than the others. It was somewhat later that the school started deliberately to take in autistic children; around 1956, and the obtention of the Ford Foundation grant.

At that time the term 'autism' was applied to the most severe forms of infantile psychoses – which were then referred to as schizophrenias.[10] In the first publication to distinguish between autistic and mentally retarded children, the psychiatrist Leo Kanner had, in 1943, drawn up a list of symptoms that gained general acceptance.[11] In the early fifties the psycho-analyst Margaret Mahler further distinguished autism from another form of extreme mental disturbance in children, 'symbiotic psychosis'. She described the autistic child as one who, in spite of an intelligent and even thoughtful facial expression, never looks anyone else directly in the eyes. He is often believed to be deaf, since he behaves as if he cannot hear anything. Typically, he is mute; if he does speak, the words are unintelligible. Unlike other psychotic patients, he only appears content when left completely to himself. In his relations with the outside world, he often acts as though he were a magician, signalling in a robot-like fashion to others to do things that he cannot do himself. His only emotional attachments are, in some cases, to a single object, or to some stereotyped gestures, which he repeats indefinitely. He is totally intolerant of any changes in his environment, apparently impervious to pain, and subject to crises of extreme violence. Rather than auto-eroticism, he often engages in self-mutilation – such as bashing his head against a wall, or biting himself and drawing blood.[12]

According to Fae (Lohn) Tyroler, who was both 'Joey''s counsellor and Bettelheim's assistant at the time he decided to take in a number of autistic children, he had long hesitated over the move. Emmy Sylvester, with whom he had discussed the issue before she left Chicago, had been against it. From the first experiences with very sick children, Bettelheim knew that it would profoundly change his school, which up to then had been doing very well. But his wariness had finally been overridden by his need to continually expand the limits of what he could achieve, combined with his intellectual curiosity and his unending quest for funds. These kids were said to be incurable, and yet he knew that he could help them: that they were no different from the ones he had helped up until then, just a little sicker. Providing he was given the proper means, he felt certain that work, dedication and intelligence would allow him and the staff to meet the challenge. Bettelheim thus decided that the Orthogenic School would become the laboratory in which the great psychological riddle of the age would be solved, and that he would devote most of his own time to it. The message was implicit in his 'Application for a grant permitting a research program in therapy of infantile autism and dynamics of early ego development', submitted to the Ford Foundation in 1955.[13]

The new challenge had immediately stimulated Bettelheim's creative intuition, as is obvious from both his grant submission and the first of his annual reports. Autistic children often look both beautiful and intelligent

(Kanner thought them of above-average intelligence), which may explain the fascination they generally hold for those who work with them. Despite their inability to communicate with others, their appearance creates the illusion that it would not take much to reach them; that if only one could break through that shell, one would find an intact human being beneath it. The impression is so strong that it is not unusual, even today, to find traces of it among people looking after autistic children, who should know better than anyone else just how unrealistic it is.[14]

In that pioneering age, the autistic child also seemed to hold out the hope that psychologists and other specialists could one day understand just how the personality is formed. Those who did not see autism simply as resulting from an organic, genetic or chemical defect, but rather as an accident in a child's emotional development, thought that studying it could reveal the stages in the formation of the ego. As Bettelheim stressed in his application to the Foundation, most of the theoretical models of personality development up until then had been inferred from memory traces elicited during therapy on adults. If, however, one was able to observe autistic children twenty-four hours a day, as they emerged from their isolation, one would in fact be witnessing the process by which the ego becomes integrated in the first years of life under ordinary circumstances. He therefore proposed to study six boys and six girls in the six-to-eleven age group. 'Since these children are old enough to talk,' he wrote, 'and begin to talk as they acquire an ego, they can convey much more to us about this process than the observation of infants only' (the latter method being the one adopted by some psychoanalysts, notably in Britain, to try and answer the same question).

The arrival at the school of these deeply disturbed children immediately led him to exciting discoveries. As early as July 17, 1958, in his second report to the Ford Foundation, he noted that, rather than suffering from arrested development, as many thought at the time, autistic children seemed to have acquired 'isolated islands' of specific experience, both sensory and motor. But that these islands 'do not merge to permit formation of a continuous internal structure'. As if they had been able to acquire a few of the bricks needed to create a normal ego, without being able to start building one.

Treatment and observation of the children selected for the study were only one part of the programme. Bettelheim also asked George Perkins, the School's consultant psychiatrist, to analyse the mothers of three of them, while supervising the corresponding children's therapy. Jules Henry, the social anthropologist, was to observe a number of families in their home life, while Ben Wright would pay particular attention to the counsellors' interactions with the most disturbed children. The school's psychiatric social worker, Florence White, also worked for the Ford Foundation's project. And the new funds allowed Bettelheim to take on a few psychologists and psychiatrists on a part-time basis to participate in the research. His reports to the Foundation, which he would later use in the opening chapters of *The Empty Fortress*, were therefore packed with notes on the children's families, and hypotheses about the causes of autism. But what made them truly remarkable was the way they portrayed the children.

To this day, it is not uncommon in psychiatric manuals to find 'autists' classified under the heading of 'mentally retarded', and described solely in terms of their deficiencies. In Bettelheim's reports, however, those same children appeared as living human beings, acting and even reacting to their environment. They were individuals, who although they had problems, were described in terms of what they actually did rather than what they could not do. This is above all why *The Empty Fortress* was to be a revolutionary book, which would have an impact on the way psychotics were viewed and handled the world over. Once again, for Bettelheim 'mad' did not mean 'deficient', but simply 'ill'. As he did with his other patients, he gave autistic children 'the benefit of the doubt',[15] working on the assumption that, however disturbing or obnoxious, their behaviour had meaning for them. That it was the best way they could find to express their pain, and maybe alleviate it. As he says in *The Art of the Obvious*: 'Freud taught the rest of us to suspend our disbelief – our refusal to believe – that patients, whether neurotic, psychotic, or autistic, act with intelligence or good purpose. I think we ought always to proceed on the assumption that the other person's thoughts and actions are worthy of being considered in the most positive way possible.'[16]

'Positive' is not the most explicit word, for it may be interpreted as moralistic. Whereas it is clear that Bettelheim is not referring here to the purity of the child's intentions, but simply to the intelligence of his actions. Good or evil are not part of the equation when a psychoanalyst is seeking to decipher a patient's behaviour. And it is precisely because unconscious motives are never pure that people have so much trouble accepting them. The therapist's role is not to pass judgement, but to discover exactly what the patient is trying to achieve, and the fears that prevent him or her from doing so. Which is why Bettelheim never used drugs, even with the most disturbed children. 'Maybe it would help to add what medication means to the child,' he once suggested to a former counsellor writing about her work at the O.S. 'To some it means that they are being poisoned. But all know that through medication one wants to force them, or their bodies, not to do what they otherwise would do (not to be too active, etc.). That is, if one gives them medication, they can't believe that one wishes them to be as they feel like being. In this way their bodies are manipulated. How can they believe that one does not also wish to manipulate their minds?'[17]

Between what he believed to be a meaningful intent and the crazy behaviour it resulted in, Bruno Bettelheim detected a blind terror he thought he recognized. What triggered the connection in his mind, he explains in *The Empty Fortress*, was the arrival at the Orthogenic School of 'Anna'. By the age of ten, the little girl had already tried to kill her younger brother several times, and no psychiatric hospital would keep her for more than a few hours. She resembled the popular image of the 'wolf-child': she would suddenly scream, run and jump around in all directions, rip off her clothes and attack both children and adults, often biting them until they bled.[18] The rest of the time she would crouch in a corner, totally withdrawn from her surroundings.

Although she had not been in a concentration camp, 'Anna' was also a victim of Nazism. Born to Jewish parents in occupied Poland, she had spent her infancy living in hiding in a windowless basement owned by a farmer, for whom her father had to work all day as a weaver in exchange for protection. Her parents did not get on together, and her mother was extremely depressed when she was born. Worse still, as the slightest noise could have cost the family their lives, as soon as the baby gave signs of starting to cry, one of her parents would rush to gag her with their hand. 'Through her, the phenomenon of the camps which had long occupied much of my personal and theoretical interest became somehow linked with my daily work, the treatment of severely disturbed children,' Bettelheim writes.[19]

Observing the little girl with her crises of rage and despair, he concluded that: 'Some victims of the concentration camps had lost their humanity in response to extreme situations. Autistic children withdraw from the world before their humanity ever really develops.'[20] He too had once been in a situation of total powerlessness, in the grip of a world uniformly hostile and unpredictable. That is when he realized that the expression he had used to describe the most terrible experiences of his spell in the camps was also applicable to these children. And he defined it · for the first time in *The Empty Fortress*: 'This, psychologically, is what constitutes an extreme situation: when we ourselves respond to an external danger – real or imagined – with inner maneuvers that actually debilitate us further.'[21]

Two pages earlier, Bettelheim had engaged in an extraordinary exercise: that of describing madness *as seen from the inside*. If very few people seem to have noticed this, it is probably because he did not distinguish between the various types of mental disturbances, but only between their levels of intensity, so that each pathology corresponded to a different stage in the patient's alienation from the outside world. The picture Bettelheim thus builds up ranges from the kind of temporary withdrawal from reality that most of his readers may have experienced at one time or another, to the permanent and dramatic isolation of the autistic child. And what does he find *inside* the deranged mind? The 'overwhelming anxiety' of someone who feels completely powerless to defend himself in the face of a world seeking to destroy him. For as he also points out, what makes a situation extreme is that one cannot escape from it, and does not know that it will ever end.

But there is no need to fall into the hand of the Nazis to experience such a situation: 'It makes little difference whether the anxiety began because of real or imagined dangers in the world, or because of some inner psychic process.'[22] Because 'inner hostility, for example, can arouse tremendous anxiety if we are convinced that giving vent to it will cause our destruction'. There is a difference, however: 'As long as the person views his anxiety as caused by something on the outside, he remains in some distorted contact with reality.' Panic-inducing anxiety, in which the subject's links to the outside world truly break down, occurs when he no longer experiences his own aggressiveness as such. As a result, he feels totally unable to exercise any control over the dangers that his very anxiety generates. The world then ceases to have any meaning at all, and reality becomes absolutely terrifying. 'Living in such an unreasonable, unpredictable world, the best thing, the only protection, lies in doing nothing.' A strictly unvarying environment, and zero feelings, thus become the subject's most urgent needs. 'This is autism as seen from inside the person,' Bettelheim concludes.

Bruno Bettelheim first drew a comparison between his concentration camp experience and the condition of the children in his care during a symposium on infantile schizophrenia in 1955, some ten years before he wrote *The Empty Fortress*. What then struck his listeners – and a little later the readers of the *American Journal of Orthopsychiatry*[23] – were above all his conclusions, which could be summed up as follows: If an unrelievedly harmful environment can push a hitherto normal subject into schizophrenia, a uniformly beneficial environment may offer a schizophrenic the opportunity to be 'reborn' out of his madness and eventually take his place in society.

This exciting idea made a strong impression, but it also aroused some scepticism. Ernst Federn himself saw it as no more than an effective literary flourish, which had come to Bettelheim through hindsight. However, examination of his work at the school, based on the testimony of former counsellors and students, and even including the criticism that followed his death, demonstrates that the connection was real in his mind. But here too, Bettelheim's desire to put a gloss on his work, to round off its awkward angles and retain only the 'happy ending', did him a disservice. Its effect on the world outside the school – but not, however, on most of the people who actually worked with him – was to attract a following of unconditional admirers. And when they finally found out that the reality had not been quite as smooth as Bettelheim's picture of it, they were the first to put him in the dock.

For Bruno Bettelheim's concentration camp experience truly was at the heart of his work as a therapist, and probably even before he himself realized it. This was inevitable, given how intimately the course of his self-analysis had been bound up with it. If he could show so much intuition into the problems that tortured sick children, it was because they found an echo within him. Only, playing to his audience in the well-meaning, liberal climate of the period, he kept certain things quiet. He dropped hints, particularly towards the end of his life, but he never clearly stated what he had discovered at Buchenwald: that nothing is more effective in defeating self-destructive anxieties than a high-profile, visible enemy; someone one can hate without reservation. And that although a closetful of candy can help convince a child that life is worth living, it will not suffice to strike down the monsters that haunt his psyche. As he muttered to Fritz Redl that day in the school dining room: 'People would misunderstand what I was trying to say.'[24]

This is indeed where the issue of violence at the school comes in; but not in a scandalous or simplistic way. Bruno Bettelheim was not a hypocrite, preaching one doctrine and practising another. One can disagree with his way of thinking, but it was consistent. And if nobody took him up on the reply he gave to his friend, it was because it made sense to the people who worked with him.

That Fritz Redl raised the question was certainly no accident. He himself had invented a system of physical restraint, using force but no violence, in his summer camps for problem adolescents, and he had written a great deal on the subject. He and Bettelheim must have discussed the issue at length, and they agreed to make a clear distinction between punishment and discipline. Both of them were against the former, which they saw as being aimed mainly at calming the adult who administered it. 'The child nearly always knows that he has done wrong,' wrote Bettelheim. 'Isn't guilt – the pangs of conscience – a much better and more lasting deterrent than the fear of punishment?'[25]

He was thus opposed to corporal punishment, not because he believed it was too tough on the children, but because he thought it only resulted in Pavlovian-type reactions. And as there are situations in which such conditioned reflexes can be necessary, he made exceptions to the rule. Cathy Kaiser recalls one of them, from the early meetings with mothers: 'If a child starts to run across the street without paying any attention to cars, a smack on the bum, saying "Don't you ever do that again!", is protective of the child. But don't overdo it – do it for emphasis,' Bettelheim used to say.

Discipline, on the other hand, was something Bettelheim valued. He saw it as indispensable in giving life a meaning, in shaping an autonomous adult. He liked to point out that the word is derived from 'disciple'. In the 1960s, nothing irritated him more than seeing his name linked to the permissive mores of the time. 'What was wrong ... with old-fashioned, authoritarian education was not that it rested on fear. On the contrary, that is what was right with it. What was wrong was that it disregarded the need to modify the fear in a continuous process so that irrational anxiety would steadily give way to more rational motivation,' he wrote in 1969, about the student leaders of that time.[26]

Never did Bettelheim preach unbridled permissiveness; on the contrary, he continually insisted on the need for limits. If the children's good was the school's highest law, the reasons for that were strictly therapeutic. Depressed, self-destructive or suicidal children had to be given the taste for life which they had never acquired, or had lost, in their infancy. They had to feel accepted, along with their symptoms, and be allowed to regress to the point at which the derailment in their development as healthy human beings had occurred. This implied specific living conditions, which had nothing to do with permissiveness. In *Truants from Life*, Bettelheim explained it this way: 'To put our philosophy in practice we had to create a very specific environment .... This particular society has developed mores of its own .... For example, tolerance and even temporary encouragement of asocial or regressive tendencies often takes preference over the encouragement of academic progress. In respect to sex behavior, verbal expressions, orderliness and cleanliness, polite conventions yield to emotional honesty. Protection of property takes second place to emotional needs.'[27]

But in this uniformly well-meaning universe, among these good mothers who, unlike others, were not likely to either abandon their children or project unbearable feelings on to them (Bettelheim made sure of that), there was also a need for a fighter. Someone invested with force, capable of guaranteeing the children's safety. Not only against external threats, or against one another,[28] but also and above all against their own internal demons. That fairy-tale world needed its Big Bad Wolf to confront the monsters which lurked in the children's heads, and had brought them there in the first place. A 'reassuring enemy', as Leslie Cleaver would put it.

In defining his role at the school, Bruno Bettelheim would occasionally replace the Big Bad Wolf image with a more Freudian one: 'Here,' he would say to the counsellors, 'the children are the id, you are the ego, and I'm the superego.' For anyone accepting his stated intention to put psychoanalytical concepts 'into action' at the school, this is even clearer. For the superego in each of us is indeed the 'Big Bad Wolf', the part of us that adopts the values of our parents, and thus 'identifies with the aggressor' to become our internal law and order agent.

Sigmund Freud himself describes the superego as 'obscene and ferocious'.[29] Why 'obscene'? Because nothing escapes the intransigent superego and it knows all of the id's most unacceptable desires. Which is why it can be so ferocious. But that ferocity remains internal. If tempered, it results in guilty feelings; if exacerbated, it can turn into the 'overwhelming anxiety' which little by little cuts the subject off from the real world. This translates into depression, suicidal tendencies, aggressiveness: in a word, self-destruction – such as remaining hidden behind a blind person's armband that one is ashamed of. Bettelheim's concentration camp experience had clearly taught him that his worst suffering came not from the outside world, but from his own inner forces. From the ferocity with which he himself judged his own acts, rather than from the pain his enemies inflicted on him. Indeed, when his torturers appeared explicitly as such, in the uniform befitting their role, it was a relief (during the terrible Buchenwald roll-call, for instance). To allow his charges to get better, he had to free them, for the time it took them to sort out their own desires from those inherited from their parents, of the merciless judge who prevented them from living. And to allow them to undergo this type of 'rebirth', he had to don the appearance of the aggressor who was torturing them from the inside. Punishment was not the object.

'Dr B knew,' says Tom Lyons. He is telling me about the occasions – 'approximately two or three times a year,' he says[30] – when Bettelheim slapped him. One was soon after he arrived at the school, at around the age of eight. He had let the bathtub overflow, and he even recalls that this caused some damage to the wall in the stairway. 'I was old enough to run a bath. I had done it many times at home. But I figured that since my counsellor had turned it on, she might as well turn it off,' he says. He was always talking about his rights and thought this was fair. When the accident was discovered, the counsellor indeed took full responsibility for it. But Bettelheim knew that young Tom had purposely kept quiet about the overflow, and that this had little to do with fairness: 'I don't want you to take revenge on your counsellor,' he said after giving him several slaps.

Discussing the incident some forty years on, Tom Lyons remembers perfectly well how enraged he was that his counsellor insisted on always taking his hand when they were outside. He was not treated that way at home.

Similarly, Bert Cohler clearly remembers the slaps he got from Dr B one day when he returned from class with an excellent grade for a German essay. I had heard the anecdote mentioned in a radio programme as an example of Bettelheim's sadism, shortly after his death, by one of Cohler's former dorm-mates. The story sounded so unbelievable that I felt certain there had to be some mistake, some malice or some distorted memory somewhere. But when I asked him about it, Bert Cohler burst out laughing. 'Dr B knew exactly what he was doing: in my essay I attacked Arthur Schnitzler. And I knew Schnitzler was one of his favourite authors.'

So the story was true! It took me a long time to understand it, to go beyond its shocking appearance. After a very serious trauma suffered in early childhood, Bert Cohler had lived, until his arrival at the Orthogenic School, in constant terror of expressing even the slightest amount of anger. For he had been led to believe that if he dared to show the aggressiveness he felt towards one of his relatives, he would be killed.[31] Being highly intelligent, he had opted to escape into a dreamworld, where he settled his conflicts in thought only, or in puppet shows, at which he was very good. Attacking Bettelheim via Arthur Schnitzler was more sophisticated indeed, but it was a repetition of the same mechanism. And since the incident occurred just as the young man was preparing to leave the Orthogenic School, Bettelheim no doubt considered it useful to show him what he was doing. By acknowledging the aggression implicit in Bert's act (the essay), by showing that he knew that it was aimed at him, and by replying with overt violence, Dr B was playing his role as a lightning-rod, ensuring that the dangerous charge was mortal neither for its originator, nor for its recipient.

Whatever one may think of the method, Bert Cohler's and Tom Lyons' reactions, and the fact that both spontaneously remember, forty years later, the unconscious motives which had inspired Bettelheim to slap them, at least show that the latter had been right on target. And that his action had allowed them to face up to their own aggressiveness rather than feeling guilty, unworthy and therefore bad, over their deviousness. To return to the example of Bert Cohler, whose affection for Dr B is very deep, it is easy to imagine how, if Bettelheim had merely congratulated him for his essay, he would later have felt ashamed of his underhand attack, particularly since he had got an 'A' for it. He may then have concluded that the praise was undeserved, and instead of gaining satisfaction and encouragement from it, he may even have become convinced that he was nothing but a fraud.

'Murderer', 'obscene', 'monster': such words may seem excessive when applied to overflowing bathtubs, or essays with hidden agendas. Viewed by outsiders, they are indeed disproportionate. Which is just why writing about the unconscious is near impossible. For the unconscious does not work with kid gloves, and it does not reason. It expresses and represses, desires and punishes, without nuance. And it always takes its wishes for reality. At the unconscious level, when we hold a grudge against someone, we do not retaliate proportionately; we kill him.[32] Or at least we believe we have killed him. The task of adapting outrageous desires to the real world is that of the ego (and therefore no longer totally unconscious). The captain of the ship decides what is possible and what is not – and occasionally makes mistakes in doing so. It is the ego that decides in what more-or-less presentable form an unacceptable hatred can be expressed, such as letting a bathtub overflow (which does not prevent Tom's 'id', forty years later, from boasting about the damage done to the stairway!).

For that is the most frightening thing of all: the hatred we can feel for those we love. The ambivalence of love is probably the most difficult of all Freud's discoveries for us to truly come to grips with, and therefore the one most often denied. Bettelheim experienced this himself, since commentators generally present him as 'the' accuser of the mothers of autistic children. Whereas if one places *The Empty Fortress* in the context of its time, one finds that on the contrary he was the first author to stress the mutual nature of the mother-child relationship, pointing out that there is no such thing as a perfect mother (which is fortunate, since otherwise children would never need to learn the ways of the world), and stating clearly that the problems of the autistic child cannot be blamed on an external cause (such as the mother's behaviour). 'I would stress that the figure of the destructive mother (the devouring witch) is the creation of the child's imagination, though an imagining that has its source in reality, namely the destructive intents of the mothering person,' Bettelheim writes in *The Empty Fortress*.[33] Indeed, in that book he constantly refers to the (unconscious) death-wish that a mother can feel for her child. After Freud, he indeed believes that all mothers (and fathers) from time to time feel an unconscious desire to see their offspring disappear. And he therefore stresses that it is not the mother's attitude that produces autism, but the child's spontaneous reaction to it.[34] He does not claim to know why one child should be more receptive than another to the unconscious ill-wishes of his mother, and even leaves open the possibility that such hypersensitivity could have organic causes. Yet, the idea that a mother can desire her child's death, even unconsciously, is so difficult to accept that it is this image which has stuck in most of his readers' minds.

Similarly, Bettelheim often mentions murderous instincts that can be so powerful in certain children that they could kill others, or more commonly, themselves. That idea too is hard for people to accept. It is easier to talk about madness than to recognize, within ourselves, such terrifying vestiges of infancy. And yet there was a time when each of us experienced the raw and irrepressible desire to eradicate someone else, be it a parent or a sibling, because he or she had denied us what we wanted, or reprimanded us, or usurped our place. In growing up, most of us have learned how to transform such primary instincts into more acceptable traits, such as a competitive spirit, a love of hunting or even creativity. But it does not prevent them from occasionally flaring up, almost as violently as before, and stirring painful guilt feelings. Indeed these instincts were clearly so familiar to the readers of Tom Lyons's novel *The Pelican and After* that many wondered why its protagonist, Tony, had to live in a school for emotionally disturbed children!

Tom Lyons, who had himself spent almost twelve years at the Orthogenic School, had put the problem up front, with the subtitle, *A Novel about Emotional Disturbance*, featuring prominently on the dust-jacket of his book.[35] For *The Pelican and After* is a perfect illustration of the inner violence with which most of the young pupils at the school were struggling. Indeed, the unconscious is never more unbridled, or more ferocious, than when one is young. Before he arrived on Bruno Bettelheim's doorstep, the author, a hyperactive boy of eight, had been diagnosed as incurably 'schizophrenic', and even the Menninger Foundation's Southard School had declined to admit him, suggesting to his mother that he be institutionalized for life.

Pelican is a droll and well-written novel which although a bit long in places is somewhat reminiscent of J.D. Salinger's *The Catcher in the Rye*. It is, to date, the only book published by a former Orthogenic School student on his or her experience. The central character is Tony, a fourteen-year-old boy who is spending a few days' vacation in Mexico with his mother and brother. During the rest of the year, he lives in a Chicago school for disturbed children, run by the fearsome 'Dr V', whose thick Austrian accent is rendered with graphic detail by the author. The book is a mine of information on the Bettelheim method from one of the people whom that method helped to become an autonomous adult.

It is all there. The violence, of course, because it was at the heart of Tom Lyons' problems. But also the warmth, the devotion of the counsellors and teachers and their ways – for instance around Christmas, 'a time when the staff was always on the lookout for feelings'. The moments of great emotion and the crises, such as the departure for a psychiatric hospital of Mark, a boy with whom Tony had spent time trying to play. Tom Lyons gives us the whole story, because he is trying to see it clearly himself (thus giving us a good idea of what an 'orthogenic' attitude may be). There too is his youthful desire to be a grown man, a tough one, who commands respect from women – such as when he meets a little girl who closely resembles the terrible 'Anna' of *The Empty Fortress*, and finds himself secretly hoping that she will attack him, in order to check whether he can overpower her this time. Occasionally, Tony also gets an inkling that this may in fact be just a Hollywood-style image of a man. He wants to get out of this goddamn school, in which he feels treated like a baby, where, although already a strapping youth, he has no real privacy. Deep down, though, he knows that he is not quite ready to leave, and he has a strange feeling of pride whenever he can help a fellow student more unlucky than himself. Such as little Freddy, who has formed an attachment to Tony, and is making progress, or even Mark, who spits out everything he is given to eat. Tony is provocative, sarcastic and aggressive; he flies into rages. One day, while under the shower, he has a flash of insight: 'Hate is a killer of fear.' Whenever he does something really stupid, he regrets it immediately, but more often than not his efforts to make amends only make things worse. He knows that he is at the school to break out of his isolation, and he is becoming aware of the barriers of aggressiveness and sarcasm that he keeps erecting between himself and others, but he is not yet able to rid himself of them.

But the book is also about the complexities of love. The ambivalent feelings of its youthful hero for his grandmother, whom he adores, but about whom he once fantasized that he had killed her, by leaving her and her wheelchair out in a rainstorm. When the grandmother is really dying, she gives Tony the blue porcelain fox that her own mother had given her before dying. They had often played with it when Tony was small, and he knows how much it means to her. Once back at the house, Tony picks up the little fox, which he has not touched for years, and is once again struck by the loving expression on the animal's face. Then his hands slip, and the little fox smashes into myriad pieces, at the very moment when Tony's mother calls from the hospital to tell him his grandmother is dead. The boy collapses among the shards of blue porcelain. ' "Oh Granny! No! I love you! … I didn't mean to hurt poor Fox!" ' But then another, familiar, inner voice cuts in: ' "What do you mean, you bastard. You know you don't love anyone but yourself." '

Unfortunately, that passage went unnoticed by most critics when the book came out. What attracted all the attention were the events depicted inside Tony's school. The first of them, for example. During a game of dodge-ball involving around forty children, Ronny, one of Tony's dorm-mates, elbows a little girl in the eye. Ronny and Ted, another older boy, were the only two left in the game, and Ted has just been eliminated. Ronny mockingly congratulates him, shaking his hand with exaggerated emphasis. Then, as he jumps one last time to dodge the ball, his elbow hits the girl standing behind him. In short, a typical accident.

This brings the game to an immediate halt. The counsellors utter suitably 'orthogenic' instructions as they gather the children. Tony's group returns to its dormitory in an atmosphere of tense expectation. In the courtyard, Tony 'walks' his hand along the low wall between the two buildings. 'He pretended his fingers were the legs of a man being walked to execution deep in the recesses of a large prison somewhere in a small alien country. Surrounding this country there was another country to which the man belonged, but from which he was now totally isolated.'[36] Suddenly, he finds himself thinking about the Midway, only a few yards away from the building, where there were 'people who knew nothing about Dr V's anger, who had never heard about hidden feelings and accidents that weren't accidents. Tony envied these people, but he also felt that they missed out on something basic to life although he was unable to say just what.'

Then comes the anxious wait in the dormitory. As the young counsellor continues to talk to Ronny (' "Have you tried to think about why you did that?" "Yes," he answered. "I jumped up and my elbow went out. I didn't *see* her." ') the five other boys busy themselves in their own areas. An unusual calm reigns in the room. Igor, sitting on his bed, is making himself as unobtrusive as possible. He turns a knob attached to a piece of cardboard, one of the innumerable electrical contraptions affixed to the wall by his bed (this is indeed 'Joey', who was one of Tom Lyons' dorm-mates). When Tony, who chooses to go to the bathroom before the storm, passes by his bed, Igor whispers to him, indicating his electrical set-up. ' "Do you know what it's for?" ' No, Tony indicates softly. 'Igor became a bit more bold. "Th-this switch is to turn down the voltage power in that robot so that when he comes in here, Ronny won't get into too much trouble."

' "Look, Igor," Tony said sympathetically, "if he were really a robot, you would have turned him off long ago."

' "No, y-you can't do that," Igor smiled. "That would ruin his batteries and we don't want to kill him." '

Then follows the description, also very colourful, of Dr V's arrival in the dorm. After having copiously slapped Ronny, he suddenly stretches out his arms in front of him, palms upward, shrilling in mock imitation of the boy: ' "I didn't mean to! It vas an accident!" ' Then, resuming his normal voice, Dr V asks: ' "Does zat make it feel any better?" ' Ronny shakes his head. ' "All right, zhen, remember zat ven you have accidents, I vill have zem also. Is zat clear?" '

Once things have calmed down, Dr V points out that the act of congratulating a companion who has just lost a game can be very aggressive, and suggests a connection between this and the incident with the girl. Tony wants to say that the congratulations and other forms of foolery are due to the 'electric mix of boys and girls', but he does not say anything; he is afraid of Dr V. The latter meanwhile alludes to the resentment older boys may feel at having to play with younger children, especially girls, and he invites the other boys to join in the discussion. Behind the caricature – for the reader should remember that the whole episode is being seen through the eyes of a kid who is crazy about movies, and who himself is struggling with strong surges of violence – the young Tony never forgets that things are not as simple as they seem.

Very few former school staff members admit to having read *The Pelican and After*, and among those who do, few liked it. The reasons given range from 'It's a not a good book'; 'I couldn't get hold of it'; 'After leaving the school, I didn't want to read anything about it'; 'Oh, I know what Tom thinks, I don't need to read his book', to the extreme 'He wrote it to get back at Dr B.' And, strangely enough, such reactions appear to verify Bettelheim's prediction that 'People would misunderstand what I was trying to say.'

For Tom Lyons's book is in fact a striking tribute to the Orthogenic School in general, and to Bruno Bettelheim in particular. It is telling that Fae Tyroler, who spent five years as counsellor to Tom and 'Joey''s group, the 'Pandas' and later the 'Panthers',[37] did read the book, and that she liked it. Not only does *The Pelican and After* prove that Tom Lyons was able to master his inner demons to write it, but behind the verbal aggressiveness it is also full of feeling and hope. The book demonstrates a great deal of self-knowledge, and the biting humour that runs through it is indeed the expression of a violence that has been conquered and channelled into constructive activity. Even the strongly caricatured Dr V character clearly testifies to the 'lightning-rod' function fulfilled by the real-life Dr B, as viewed 'from the other side', from that of the child. Tom had clearly understood the system so well that he felt he could tell all.

When his book came out, far from using the resulting interviews to settle scores, Tom Lyons persistently stressed just how special a place the Orthogenic School was, even talking about 'the magic' of the experience. Asked about autism, he replied that he only heard the word after leaving the school. For him, the children thus referred to were simply some of his childhood companions, only 'more unlucky' than him. And when radio host Studs Sturkel asked him: 'When did you feel that you were cured?' he spontaneously replied, in vintage Bettelheim style: 'Well, let's take you for an example. You'll agree with me that you are more mature now than when you were three years old. But you didn't wake up one fine morning and realize "I'm big." You were always the same person. Well the process at the school was as gradual as growth itself.'

All my own discussions with Tom Lyons indeed show that he has remained the same, even though he has learned to live with himself. The ambivalence of his feelings for Bettelheim ('Did he save my life, or did he ruin my childhood?') come out in practically every conversation. As does his 'ferocious superego', which although it no longer prevents him from leading a normal life, still makes it difficult for him to simply enjoy things as they come. The day I met him, he told me: 'I think that one of the deepest hurts at the School was the constant belief that [Dr B]'s brutality was therapy .... Because then, the kid was in limbo.' Three years later, when listening again to the tape, I finally understood the full meaning of that statement, and congratulated him for it during our next phone conversation. He expressed shock. 'Brutality? No, I didn't use that word, it's too strong .... You've got it on tape, really? I meant his violence. No, brutality is too strong a word. Dr B wasn't brutal .... Look, I really don't want to interfere with what you write, I'm a firm believer in freedom of expression. But, in this particular case, maybe, you should let me check my quotes.' Similarly, Tom is clearly uneasy at the way Bettelheim portrayed his friend 'Joey' in his book. He knows that it caused hurt in 'Joey''s family. Careful not to breach his former schoolmate's privacy, he tells me nothing at all about him, but encourages me to speak with him directly (while at the same time refusing to give me his phone number), and with his mother. Then, the day after he has criticized *The Empty Fortress*, Tom sends me a fax: 'I stand by my reservations. But recently it occurred to me that there is a real difference between BB's case histories and those of Freud. BB's are almost like love stories in which it is very easy to care about the central character .... Is BB the first to [have] put "soul" into his cases?'[38]

Unfortunately the circumstances surrounding the publication of Tom Lyons's book served only to exacerbate the ambivalence of his feelings towards Bruno Bettelheim. For he suspects, without being sure, that Bettelheim had something to do with Macmillan's decision to turn down his novel, after initially accepting it.[39] Having studied the voluminous file gathered by Tom Lyons, and discussed it with some of the protagonists, I am not sure that that was the case. What seems more likely is that the publisher himself decided to play safe by avoiding a book which he thought might be offensive to one of his star authors. Whatever the case, the affair seems to indicate that, once again, Bettelheim was pretty close to the mark when, on the publication of Lyons's novel, he answered a journalist who asked him if he had ever hit his charges: 'That's between me and the children.'[40] He and Tom Lyons were practically alone in having truly understood what *The Pelican and After* was about.[41] As soon as he had read it, Bettelheim wrote to Tom, saluting his 'very considerable talent as a writer' and adding: 'I am sure it is a true picture of how you saw things when you were fourteen.'[42] When the book came out, almost ten years later, the two of them had lunch in California. The atmosphere was relaxed, and the conversation lively. That was the last one-to-one meeting Tom Lyons was to have with Bettelheim. Some time later he heard of a lecture during which Dr B had predicted that a lot of his former students would publish books accusing him of the most terrible things; but he was never able to confirm the information. And he still has a hard time accepting that Bettelheim could at once be truly proud that he had been able to write his book, fearful of the damage that it was likely to cause him, and hurt by the caricatured image it gave of him.

'I much prefer that he should hate me than himself,' or 'I can never hurt him as much as he hurts himself,' Bettelheim would say to the counsellors who showed surprise at seeing him slap a child. And when, thanks to a timely smack, a child stopped banging his head against the wall or biting himself, the argument carried weight. In other cases, the effects would be less immediately obvious, but noticeable over the longer term. But as Bettelheim never publicly admitted to the use he made of violence at the school, even those who were thus convinced by his arguments have a hard time facing up to the problem.

I do not know exactly when the Big Bad Wolf went beyond simply baring his teeth at the children. The number of incidents requiring his intervention appears to have increased substantially after more seriously disturbed children entered the school. The change in staff also played a role, for it was almost always at the request of a counsellor who could not cope that Dr B used force. Some people, such as Ugo Formigoni, made it a point of honour never to call on him. But as situations could degenerate very rapidly, few counsellors could do without Dr B's occasional help. Whenever an incident occurred, it sparked a great deal of discussion, amongst the staff and the children. Generally, the counsellor who had called on Dr B considered this to be an admission of failure, and felt guilty about it. During staff meetings, Bettelheim and the counsellors would try to work out what had sparked the crisis, probing the anxieties of both the child and the adult involved.

In this area, however, even the most sincere testimonies can be deceptive. Often, such incidents are mentioned to the interviwer by third parties. At first this seems a good thing; the accounts are therefore likely to be more objective. But after a while, one begins to realize that things are not that simple – that, for instance, when X mentions slaps administered to Y, the situation described has in fact more to do with X's own feelings about the event (pity, guilt, unavowed satisfaction at seeing a fellow student punished, etc.) than with what really happened. In most cases, the onlooker had in fact no idea of what was going on between Y and Dr B (as with Bert Cohler's dorm-mate reporting the incident involving the German essay). This is particularly true when X considered Y to be weaker or 'less lucky' than himself. For example 'Paul', a sturdy, muscular man, told me that he felt Dr B was harder on the girls than on the boys. This turns out to be untrue; there is no doubt that Bettelheim resorted to force more often with boys. Similarly, I was told by a few former students that he was harder with the autistic kids, but this was denied by many, and particularly by the counsellors who had some of them in their groups. What is undeniable, however, is that those impenetrable children, given to extraordinarily stressful forms of behaviour, could arouse in those around them a cocktail of feelings, exasperation mixed with pity and guilt, that were often difficult to control, and even to express.[43]

Problems involving those children were indeed the ones which upset people the most. The incident which led Nina Helstein to leave the Orthogenic School occurred in 1970, on a day when an older boy had had to be sent off to a mental hospital. The atmosphere was gloomy, with everyone wondering what could have been done to avoid such a failure. In her class, Nina Helstein had a seven-year-old autistic girl who was beginning to break out of her isolation. On that day, however, Nina had not been able to get anything out of her. 'Erin' had spent the whole morning lost in her own world, rocking backwards and forwards and muttering the name of the departed boy. Nina had tried to reassure her, but to no avail. During lunch, when Dr B came up to her table, she told him about it. He thereupon turned to the little girl, who was sitting next to Nina, and gave her a series of slaps, repeating, 'That's enough. Stop that right now!' 'Erin' did not say another word, but Nina Helstein was shocked. Later that night, during the staff meeting, Bettelheim questioned her: 'Why did you think Erin was upset?' 'She wanted to be told that she wasn't going to be sent away too,' the teacher answered. 'That's right. So why did you want me to hit her?' Nina, who is very small, stood up and looked him straight in the eye. 'Dr B, it was you who hit Erin. I didn't ask you to.' The meeting was coming to a close, and he did not reply. The next day Nina Helstein discovered that she was suffering from mononucleosis. After two months of sick leave, she decided not to return to the school again. Today, while affirming that what she learned with Bettelheim is unique and has enlightened her entire working life as a therapist and consultant to social work agencies, Nina Helstein remains convinced that during his last years at the school he on occasion lost his self-control. She believes that, on that day, he was very disturbed by the boy's departure and, later, feeling somewhat ashamed at having struck 'Erin', he was seeking to shift the blame for his action on to her.

That is not the way the incident is viewed by other counsellors from that period with whom I discussed it. They stress that because of her background,[44] Nina Helstein had an unusual relationship to Dr B, seeming constantly to question his power – something she does not deny. They wonder why Nina felt the need to call on Dr B to reassure the little girl. Nina's answer is that, as she did not live at the school, she did not feel in a position to guarantee to 'Erin' that she would not be sent away, that only Dr B had the authority to do so. As can be seen, the arguments are not on the same plane. For implicit in the counsellors' comment is the idea that Nina, troubled by 'Erin''s behaviour, had kept a distance between herself and the little girl, which was anything but reassuring. But this does not rule out the possibility that Bettelheim was indeed upset by the day's events, or that he had simply misunderstood Nina's remark to him, accustomed as he was to counsellors only calling on him when they needed help with a hopeless or potentially dangerous situation. He may have thought that 'Erin' had spent the whole morning shrieking, since that was one of her symptoms. This is lent credence by what he said to her; for 'his slaps were always accompanied by a clear message', stresses Diana Grossman Kahn. It is also likely that later, having realized his mistake, Bettelheim regretted having acted so fast. Whatever the case, this disturbing incident seems characteristic of his final years at the school, when the ground-rules were less clearly delineated.

The message to 'Erin' however seems clear to all, although each one expresses it in his or her own words: 'Since I am disciplining you, that means I intend to keep you. Now it's up to you to get a grip on yourself, to stop behaving like a mad girl, if you don't want to be treated like one.' Kathy Lubin, one of Bettelheim's favourite counsellors, had already left the school when the incident with 'Erin' occurred; when I asked her for her view, she replied with another recollection.

One day, a woman was murdered only a few yards from the school. At three o'clock, when the children were due to return from the classrooms, the body was still lying where it had fallen, visible from all the windows at the rear of the building. The counsellors did not know what to do. Should they bring the subject up, or should they try to make sure that the children did not see the body? Informed of the situation, Bettelheim told them to do nothing. He then went round all the dormitories and talked to the children about the crime, addressing more specifically those who had strong homicidal tendencies. He told them that what had happened to the woman could one day happen to them if they did not make any progress. Kathy Lubin was dumbfounded. 'His speech was completely on target. For each one, he picked up what would concern her the most. Whereas we were terrified by that corpse, he had brought it inside the school and was using it with remarkable efficiency.'

That was indeed where Bettelheim's real violence lay – in his ability to look straight at the darkest recesses in the psyches of those around him. And much more than his slaps, that was what scared them. For the violent incidents were not very frequent. Bettelheim did not in general need to resort to force to inspire fear in his charges; so explicit was his function that his simple presence was enough. Only one of the counsellors has tried to explain that function publicly. Like Fae Tyroler, Leslie Cleaver was in charge of a boys' group. In 1986, during a conference in honour of Bruno Bettelheim, she described him as 'a worthy enemy – unflinching, highly visible, ultimately absolutely responsible and reliably undestructible'. She took a dig *en passant* at his accent ('Vell, how are sings?') and verbal tics ('Oh, it vas an accident? I can't control my hand,' or the more serious 'Permit me to disabuse you of zat notion'). To describe the general feeling at the school that Dr B saw and heard everything, she quoted two counsellors vacationing in a remote part of Ireland. Passing a local cinema, they saw that a film called *The Most Dangerous Man Alive* was playing. 'He's here! He's found us,' one of them shrieked. And, concerning the children, she alluded to 'the high jinks that went no further because there was someone in Hyde Park besides Muhammed Ali who could glide like a butterfly and sting like a *B*'.

Far from being offended by Leslie's speech, Bettelheim thanked her for it. His relations with her had never been very close. Arriving at the school in 1969, a difficult year for Bettelheim, she had immediately seen through 'the goofy stuff', as she calls the rivalry that his attitude generated among the counsellors, and had remained outside the charmed circle of his favourites. Unlike her friend Nina Helstein, however, Leslie Cleaver had played the game of the school fully. While she was not in therapy with Dr B, she had been willing to 'face the mirror' – the expression is hers – in search of the 'monsters' within her that could help her understand what was going on inside the children in her care. She simply took care not to let her work drag her into a relationship of complete dependence on Dr B. And that is why, on that day when the University of Chicago was paying homage to a figure whom Bettelheim knew not to be totally himself, the testimony of this young woman was a precious gift. For Leslie Cleaver's candid and realistic words were clearly addressed not to the legendary Dr B but to the real flesh-and-blood man, warts and all. She went beyond describing Bettelheim's role as the school's bogeyman; she also tried to explain it. 'I want to stress that many potentially "dangerous" feelings and "dangerous" actions were able to be experienced in their full vigour, as high-spiritedness, fun-loving, loving and hating, because Dr B was willing and able to fulfil his enemy function.' She also explained how Dr B was always on hand, ready to deal with even the slightest fears and needs of everyone, and above all to stand protectively beside a counsellor when the mirror revealed that the monsters lurking in a child's unconscious were also present in the recesses of her own mind. She described his unique way of passing on his experience; never through ideas, always through lived feelings. She cited his 'strong sense of original sin', but also his 'almost religious faith' in human beings' adaptative capacity. And in comparing her experience at the school with that she had had in other institutions, she did not balk at using the word 'perfection'.

This testimony on the later years of the Orthogenic School, coming from someone who was never one of Bettelheim's uncritical fans, is important. It confirms that even in that most difficult period, when his behaviour could be incomprehensible and apparently lacking in self-control, and when most of the incidents occurred that were to be held against him after his death, the essential kernel of his teaching and his method was still intact. This conclusion is supported by other testimonies, but they come from people who were too close to Bettelheim for their statements to carry as much weight.

The third and final period of Bettelheim's stewardship at the Orthogenic School started around the middle of the 1960s. This was when he began to realize that, in spite of the best efforts of himself and the staff, the progress being made by the autistic children was not up to his expectations. Nor to his promises, since in his 1956 article he had put down Margaret Mahler's pessimism on their chances of recovery to the fact that she only saw her patients in consultation, rather than in residential care.

The biggest change at the school since the arrival of the first autistic children had been precisely on that point: the staff's faith in their capacity to cure. The gritty determination of the first counsellors ('We're going to pull them out of this') had gradually given way to a more realistic view, at least for those in direct contact with the most disturbed children. It had not happened all at once. Karen Zelan, who started at the school in 1956, just when Bettelheim obtained the Ford grant, took care of 'Marcia' and two other autistic girls during the eight years she spent there. And she had hopes of completely curing at least one, the little girl she was to call 'Vivienne' in her Master's dissertation.[45] Aged five on her arrival at the school, this child was extremely violent. She spoke only rarely, inverting her pronouns when she did, and manifested all the other symptoms then associated with autism. After a year in the school, however, 'Vivienne' was behaving more or less like a normal child of four.

It was a little later that the intractable stubbornness of autism started to become apparent to those who were grappling with it. In 'Marcia''s case, that happened when her awakening to the world showed her just how much she had to catch up with, a discovery which plunged her into depression. More generally, it was when Bettelheim was forced to admit that what he had termed 'isolated islands of experience' could in most cases not merge to form a whole. It appeared clearly in 1964, when Karen Zelan left the Orthogenic School. For in spite of the progress they had made, none of the three girls she had looked after continued getting better afterwards, mainly because they were not able to strike up the same kind of relationship with another counsellor. 'Marcia' returned to her family a few months later; 'Vivienne' stayed at the school until 1970, but regressed seriously. As for the third girl, she suddenly had a psychotic breakdown around a year after Zelan's departure, forgetting even her own name, and had to be interned shortly afterwards. The same type of problem is being encountered today, over forty years after the first autistic children arrived at the Orthogenic School. Through constant care, a single individual can prise open a crack in the shell-like defences of the autistic child, but that does not often have much effect on the child's relationship with other people. There is no real opening-up to the rest of the outside world; and when there is, specialists now tend to conclude that the case was therefore not one of genuine autism.

That type of circular argument makes Karen Zelan see red. Having continued her career as a psychotherapist, and having always treated young psychotics, she has read all the specialized literature, and points to the continuing discrepancies between the various definitions of autism. Even 'Joey' could still be categorized as autistic today by some authors, she stresses. Rather than get involved in a specialist debate, let us simply examine the influence this issue had on Bruno Bettelheim's life. It is clear that although those first results were very encouraging (according to Zelan, they were in some cases better than those achieved today, if rated in terms of overall progress rather than simply in modified behaviour patterns[46]), the hope of any complete recovery was gradually abandoned. The arrival of the autistic children marked the end of the school's ascendant phase, the period in which even the most extraordinary dreams seemed within reach.

His experience with very disturbed children seems also to have reinforced Bettelheim's belief that healing is not achieved by ideas, but by harnessing one's own psychological problems to the task. With autistic children, even more than with others, the progress achieved depended on the personality of those who looked after them. It had hardly anything to do with the counsellor's intelligence, learning or even the depth of his or her devotion; it was a question of intuition, or as Bettelheim put it, of communication between two unconsciouses. For he had noticed that, whatever overt attitudes people took to them, the most seriously disturbed children were above all receptive to their unconscious motives. And as was shown by the story of Karen Zelan, who is widely acknowledged to have a special gift for communicating with the most impenetrable of children, such intuition often goes with somewhat whimsical temperaments.

Karen was twenty-one when she arrived at the Orthogenic School. Originally set to be a pianist, she had dropped her music studies for psychology after an attack of stage fright prevented her from playing in her senior recital, at Oberlin College, Ohio. Reading *Love is Not Enough* had sparked a strong desire to work with Bettelheim, but lacking self-confidence she had called at the school to offer her services as a secretary. Dr B himself had interviewed her. After a few questions about her life, he had asked: 'Well, do you want to be a secretary or a counselor?' 'You mean I could start looking after children right away without any training?' she asked back, in amazement.

Her first month as a fully fledged counsellor[47] was very tough. The girls in her group gave her a hard time, mocking her for all her mistakes and threatening to tell Dr B. The latter also kept her under pressure. She still remembers how he screamed at her, one Wednesday night when a pillow-fight started in her dorm because, eager to be on time at the ten o'clock staff meeting, she had left it before everyone was asleep. At first, she thought that Bettelheim was only pretending to be angry; but he was not. At the end of the month, however, things had improved, and then she had received her first newcomer. The little girl was deeply disturbed, and quickly became very attached to Zelan, who at last had an opportunity to show off her psychological finesse and intuition. They were skills partly founded in experience: Zelan's sister, nine years her junior, also had serious emotional problems, and a few years earlier, she had spent a lot of time teaching her to read. She had retained a fascination with children who, although clearly endowed with intelligence, were unable to put it to constructive use. After three years at the school her talent as a therapist was so widely accepted that she dared on occasion to challenge some of Bettelheim's diagnoses. He would accept this, because he recognized that her objections were based on a genuine understanding of the children she worked with. In the early 1960s, he would write nothing about autism without first discussing the issues with her. And, later, Karen Zelan was to be the only member of the school's staff with whom Bettelheim would co-author a book.[48] She had become in his eyes the epitome of what a good counsellor for very disturbed children should be.

Without claiming to draw up a balance-sheet of the Orthogenic School's achievements in the treatment of autistic children, it can be said that although Bruno Bettelheim's results were not the triumph that he claimed, they were not so far removed from those obtained today, thirty years later, by those therapists who seek to do more than simply train such children to eat, wash up or take a bus. As says the novelist-cum-therapist Howard Buten, who has been working with autistic children in the US and France for over twenty years: 'With a real autistic kid, there's only one alternative: either you train him like an animal, and some are very good at it, going so far as to use electroshock treatment, or you can try and make him suffer less.'[49] At the Orthogenic School some autistic children made great progress, others did not; but all lived better there than elsewhere in that they were treated as fully-fledged human beings whose sufferings, rather than their deficiencies, were the object of everyone's attention. That is in itself no mean achievement. It was not enough, however, to satisfy Bruno Bettelheim.

It was around 1963 or 1964 that some of Bettelheim's co-workers, such as Diana Grossman Kahn, began to detect a subtle change in him. Something that looked like discouragement, with perhaps a hint of depression. It is difficult to be more precise than this, since very few members of Bettelheim's entourage could stand back far enough to view him as a simple, vulnerable mortal. And his fame was then very great, making him more flamboyant and autocratic than ever. The Orthogenic School was now catering to some fifty children, and parents were ready to wait years to have their offspring admitted. In the wake of *The Informed Heart* he had published *Dialogues with Mothers*, and mass-circulation newspapers were vying with one another to carry his words of wisdom. He was also starting to appear regularly on TV. 'Now I've seen the canonization of a saint,' quipped a columnist for the *Chicago Daily News*, emerging from a press luncheon with Bettelheim in February 1963.

A close examination of the dates, however, reveals a different story. In 1964, Karen Zelan had informed him of her intention to follow her husband to Boston. Some three years earlier, the school had lost another of its key members, Inge Fleischmann. She was not only Karen's co-counsellor but a remarkable group therapist, adored by the children, and also a woman of powerful organizational skills, on whom Bettelheim could rely blindly to run the school when he was away. Perhaps more importantly on a personal level, was the fact that the period covered by the Ford Foundation grant had expired and Bettelheim had still not written the book which he was announcing back in 1960, when he had asked for an extension of the deadline.[50] He was caught at his own game. Having arrogantly promised so much, what definitive answers could he now provide to the puzzle of autism; what happy end could he find to a heartbreaking story, whose victims failed to respond to his best efforts to understand and heal them? And at the very moment when Bettelheim was faced with that dilemma, Auschwitz survivors were clamouring to tell him that the vital lessons he had drawn from his camp experience were worthless; that he had in fact understood nothing. It was then that he decided to go to Israel.

Chapter XV

Israel: Understanding is Not Enough

The relationship between Bruno Bettelheim and Israel resembles one of those exasperating love affairs, dogged by endless misunderstandings and missed appointments. They seemed to have been made for one another, but in fact they were forever squabbling, until it was too late, Bettelheim was too old and Israel seemed like a faraway friend, or rather like a grown-up son, whose father can only follow his development from afar, worried and nostalgic but powerless to influence events – which was the tone of his last letters to Carl Frankenstein. Meanwhile *The Children of the Dream*, the fruit of their mutual hopes, a book which in spite of some criticisms is largely a defence of the kibbutz system of education, was received in Israel like a slap in the face. And no publisher would bring it out in Hebrew!

Bruno Bettelheim arrived at Tel Aviv airport in the first days of March 1964. The aim of his visit was to study the psychological effects of the communal upbringing of children, as practised in kibbutzes, and to see how the example could be adapted to underprivileged American city kids. His destination was Ramat Yohanan, one of the oldest of the collective farms Israel was then famous for; in *The Children of the Dream*, he was to call it *Atid*, the Hebrew word for 'future'.

The first incident occurred right at the airport; it was of no practical importance but it gives the flavour of the whole visit. Bettelheim had brought with him three large boxes of toys for the children of Ramat Yohanan. And he simply could not understand why the Israeli customs officials insisted on inspecting them. Meanwhile, his hosts did not see why he should be so upset by what they saw as a necessary, if tiresome, formality in a country that had lived under the threat of terrorism ever since its creation.

Bettelheim's decision to make the visit had come all at once, but the idea was not a new one. Since the end of the 1940s many Western psychologists and educators had been taking an interest in the kibbutz children. The oldest of them had by then reached adulthood, and they provided a unique sample for a generation of researchers haunted by the question 'Does man mould society, or is he moulded by it?' They had been raised from infancy in homes specially designed for them, in a system in which everything – housing, resources, tools, etc. – was collective, yet in an open and democratic society. Bettelheim's curiosity was aroused; he had often discussed the question with his friends and colleagues, in particular with David Rapaport, a Chicago psychoanalyst who knew Israel well: What happens when a child grows up outside the three-sided nuclear family – dad, mom, baby – of Freud's theories?

In addition to that theoretical question, Bettelheim had another, more practical concern. Since November 1963 he had been chairing a weekly seminar with a group of Chicago teachers on the problems of children from poor urban backgrounds.[1] It appeared that drug-taking and delinquency were practically unknown among kibbutz children. Was the reason for this to be found in the social model that was handed down to them by their parents, as Rapaport appeared to think, or was it perhaps, as Bettelheim hypothesized, the fact that their development had not been based on the oedipal conflict?

Ramat Yohanan had been founded by immigrants from Central Europe in 1932. Located in Galilee, Israel's most fertile region, it was one of the richest kibbutzes in the country. At the time Bettelheim visited it, the population consisted of around 300 adults and 170 children. They were all living in permanent housing, rather than the large tents and huts which took in new arrivals and visitors in other kibbutzes. Having by then abandoned the Marxist credo of *Hashomer Hatzair* (the young guard), the Zionist youth movement which had founded it, Ramat Yohanan was politically on the right of the kibbutz movement.

The first settlers of *Hashomer Hatzair* had arrived in Palestine in the 1920s. They brought with them two books: Marx's *Capital*, and Freud's *On the Interpretation of Dreams*, and they designed their kibbutzes to be the realization of those two sets of ideas.[2] Their Zionism aside, their concerns were much the same as those of the German youth movements, and notably of the *Jung Wandervogel* to which Bettelheim had belonged. They sought to create a new, egalitarian and just society by freeing the individual from the oppressive weight of tradition as regards education and sexuality, by sharing work and resources and by going back to nature.[3] Whether he admitted it to himself or not, Bettelheim was also revisiting his own youth, and at a particularly troubled period of his life, by going to Israel.[4]

The country he was arriving in was one where men and women he could have met in Vienna, inspired by the determination to set up a Jewish state which they saw as the only adequate response to anti-Semitism, and faced by geographical conditions forcing them to start from scratch, had tried to build the ideal society they had all discussed passionately as students, often seated around a camp fire – the same type of camp fire that was generally used to illustrate life in the kibbutz.

Yet by 1964 Israel had already evolved away from the project of those young idealists. While 7.3 per cent of the population had lived in kibbutzes at the end of World War II, now less than 4 per cent did so. Labour was still in power, but it had become clear that Israeli society had opted for the Western democratic model, that of capitalism. While young Israeli-born *sabras* continued to claim the spirit of the pioneers, more and more of them aspired to the comforts of middle-class life. Born in the Middle East and raised under the Mediterranean sun, in often harsh conditions, they were already very different from their parents. Less idealistic probably, but also less ambivalent about their own Jewishness. On that score at least, Zionism had succeeded perfectly. Being a Jew, for an Israeli, had little in common with the feelings of a *Jung Wandervogel* member in Vienna, or an inhabitant of a *shtetl*. And that difference would be a source of incomprehension between Bettelheim and many of the Israelis he would meet.

In opting for Ramat Yohanan he had chosen one of the kibbutzes where the flame of the pioneers still burned strongest. But his own contradictions would make communication difficult with its inhabitants, men and women shaped by thirty years of simple and hard communitarian life. Intellectually, he may have admired the ideal of the kibbutz, in which everything belonged to everyone and nothing to anyone in particular, where nobody was at anyone else's service and the common good was more important than individual needs. But it was not his way of life, and he had a hard time accepting it during the weeks he spent in Galilee. A few months before his arrival, during a major conference on the aims and practice of rearing children in kibbutzes,[5] his friend Fritz Redl had described in his characteristically frank manner the ambivalence of his own feelings about the first kibbutzniks he had met. His initial feeling, he said, had been one of 'admiration for such selfless people, living with so much restraint, as far as egotistic demands for privacy, etc.' were concerned. But quite rapidly, he added, he had begun to feel a measure of anger at such saintliness. 'There must be someting wrong,' he thought to himself. 'Besides, what's that got to do with me?' Redl also underlined the kibbutzniks' defensive attitude, stemming from a deep-seated impression that outsiders could not possibly help them. At the same conference Yehuda Messinger, the director of a kibbutz teacher training centre and a member of Ramat Yohanan, had expressed the fear felt by the pioneers of the early farming communities at the way Israeli society was developing around them.

Bettelheim knew Yehuda Messinger, as he had spent a sabbatical year at the University of Chicago in 1957-58, and assiduously attended one of his classes. He had great admiration for Bettelheim, and during his stay in the kibbutz the latter frequently visited him in the evenings. They talked of education, of course, but for Bettelheim the visits were above all an escape from what he felt as the stifling atmosphere of the kibbutz, into a less foreign environment. Yehuda Messinger, twelve years his junior, was from Saarbrücken, in Germany, where he had headed the Zionist

youth movement. He had emigrated to Palestine in 1936, after his mother
had bought his freedom from a Nazi jail.

The first real *sabra*[6] that Bettelheim had got to know well was also from
Ramat Yohanan. Nechama Edelman was the principal of the kibbutz's
primary school; it was she who had organized his stay, neglecting husband
and children to be his interpreter, driver and general guide for a little over
six weeks. Although in her fifties, she had at least as much right to the
title of *sabra* as did the children of the pioneers, if not more: her mother's
great-grandfather had left Lithuania for Palestine back in the eighteenth
century! She was born in Jerusalem in 1908, and unlike most of her fellow
Israelis, she grew up speaking Hebrew as her native tongue. For her, exile,
diaspora and assimiliation are abstract notions, and the Bible is not a
religious text but a history book. 'I was born with the sky over my head
and the ground under my feet,'[7] she says simply, a statement which neatly
sums up the complexity of her relations with Bettelheim.

In 1956 she had written to ask him whether everything she had read in
Love is Not Enough was in fact true! This was not impertinence, but a
genuine question. Nechama Edelman had delicate psychological problems
to tackle in her own pupils, of whom there were around fifty, aged from
nine to eleven and coming from eighteen different countries, with as many
languages. All were separated from their parents, and they had trouble
understanding one another. Some had survived Nazism in Europe, others
came from Arab countries, where Israeli agents had spirited them away
to protect them from the reprisals that Jews had suffered since the
creation of the Jewish state. If what Nechama Edelman had read in *Love
is Not Enough* was true, she had a lot to learn from Bettelheim. It was not
until the end of the war that she had found out what the Nazis had done.
For two days she had been unable to teach; if such crimes could be
committed in the twentieth century in the country of Goethe, Beethoven
and Schiller, what point was there in trying to transmit culture?

'Come and see for yourself,' Bettelheim had written, in reply to her
letter. A year later she got the opportunity, when Eleanor Roosevelt
visited Israel, and was so impressed by Nechama Edelman's work that she
gave her a grant to spend a year at New York's Columbia University. From
there, Nechama wrote to Bettelheim to ask if she could visit the Orthogenic School during her holiday. When she arrived in Chicago, Fae Tyroler
met her at the airport and there was a room waiting for her at the
International House, a students' residence just opposite the school. At
dawn the following day, Nechama rang the bell on the yellow door, and
was shown into the staff room. There she sat down to wait. And wait.
People came and went, and nobody seemed to notice her. She watched, but
said nothing. Not out of shyness, but because she was simply satisfied to
be there. 'I know that great men have great *mishugenes*,' she says, using
the Yiddish word for 'follies'. 'But it doesn't worry me: I also know what I
can learn from them.' In the afternoon she left, quietly and without

making a fuss. The next day she came back, and sat at the same place. A man brought her a bundle of reports to read; she found them fascinating. 'The more I read, the more I was impressed. Everything was so serious, so much thinking went into it,' she says. She did not feel that she was wasting her time, she was ready to wait for as long as it took.

Whatever the reason for Nechama Edelman's long wait – Bettelheim could have been away, or there could have been a crisis, or perhaps simply a difference between her scheduling and the school's (in a kibbutz, work starts very early, so that labour in the fields is over by the time the sun is at its hottest) – the way she reacted to it is sympomatic of her personality. She is calm, determined, knows what she wants and is not easily deflected from it. Finally, on the third day, Bettelheim met her and asked her what she wanted to know. 'Whatever I can learn from you will be a benefit,' she told him. He looked at her, and then asked Margaret Carey, one of the school's two psychiatric social workers, to show her round. Nechama was struck both by the seriousness of the condition of many of the children and by the fact that the school felt like a real home, even in the classrooms. She was deeply impressed. The next day, without further ado, Bettelheim asked her whether she would like to take charge of a group. Thus the principal of the Ramat Yohanan primary school had been, for two months in the summer of 1957, a counsellor at the O.S. The experience had taught her a great deal. Her relations with Bettelheim were direct and straight-forward; he never gave her a hard time in the staff meetings. One day he even asked her to talk about the School to members of the Sonia Shank-man Foundation. When she left, she invited him to visit Ramat Yohanan. But for the following six years she had no news of him.

As early as 1959, however, Bettelheim had joined in the debate about communal child-rearing, with a critique of the book *Children of the Kib-butz*, written by Melford Spiro after he had spent a year in Bet Alpha, the *Hashomer Hatzair*'s first kibbutz.[8] While praising Spiro's observations, Bettelheim considered his conclusions to be ethnocentric, betraying an unconscious bias in favour of the middle-class American child-rearing model. Three years later he wrote a new article, reviewing the by-then abundant literature on the subject.[9] He notably criticized John Bowlby for writing that it was 'essential for mental health ... that the infant and young child should experience a warm, intimate, and continuous relation-ship with his mother,' by comparing the anxiety-stricken mother who spends all her time with her child and is often too busy, too demanding or simply exasperated, with the continuous and attentive care provided by a maternal substitute, whose only task is to look after the child's well-being. In other words, before he actually set foot in a kibbutz, Bettelheim's image of it was a blend of his youthful ideals and what he himself had tried to accomplish at the Orthogenic School. As he notes in *The Children of the Dream*, however, the more he thought about the issue, the more he felt the need to go and see for himself.

He therefore wrote to Nechama Edelman. He proposed to do his research at Ramat Yohanan because he knew people there, and also because Ron Polani, who had set up Bet Alpha's educational system, lived there.[10] In *The Children of the Dream* he adds that as all previous studies had focused on the more radical kibbutzes, i.e. those in which the split between parents and children was the most complete, he thought it interesting to see how things worked in the others, particularly since the trend within the movement was then towards greater flexibility in family relations.

As soon as she received his letter, Nechama Edelman got the kibbutz leadership to lay on a welcome befitting Bettelheim's reputation. He was assigned a small apartment comprising a bedroom, living room, kitchen and shower, of the type normally reserved for a couple. The kibbutz would cover all his expenses, and he was invited to stay for as long as he wished, with everything possible being done to facilitate his research. Nechama was to place herself at his disposal.

Their day started at 6 a.m. Visits to nurseries and day care facilities, observation of infants' behaviour, interviews with *metapelets*, in charge of the children's quarters, interviews with parents, exchanges with children of various ages, seminars at the Oranim teacher training centre, visits to two other kibbutzes plus group discussions and communal meals in Ramat Yohanan's huge dining room. Thanks to Nechama Edelman's energy, and Bruno Bettelheim's appetite for work, the project moved along at a furious pace. In principle it was he who decided on each day's schedule. But there were just so many things to discuss with this 'Jewish genius', as Nechama puts it, so many things to show him.

'They are very nice to me, but actually make it impossible for me to do what I set out to do. My entire day is so regulated by them that I have no time to take notes. I must do this and that, and most of all I must not have time to think on my own. Either one gives in to them and then one cannot do what one wants, or it is impossibly oppressive. In short, it is a totalitarian society populated by basically lovely people, but totalitarian nevertheless,' an exhausted Bettelheim wrote to Ruth Marquis just over a week after his arrival.[11] A few days later, when he had settled in a little, his tone would soften a little. For although Bettelheim always loved to travel, he in fact found it difficult to live away from home for any length of time, and the beginning of every new trip would always find him looking on the dark side. In the exciting yet cramped environment of the kibbutz that tendency was exacerbated by other contradictions. He was touched at so much hospitality, but at the same time felt hemmed in, manipulated and stifled.

The kibbutz leadership had placed great hopes in Bettelheim's visit. Nechama Edelman and Yehuda Messinger were influential members of the community, and their reports on him, his books and his reputation all had combined to give him an exceptional aura. He was mostly spared the instinctive suspicion of outsiders mentioned by Redl, and even the slight bitterness that Israelis usually feel about Jews who have resisted the call of Zionism. When his visit had been announced, there had been a few protests from former camp inmates living in the kibbutz, angered by his recent writings on 'ghetto thinking' and Anne Frank's father. But their complaints had had little effect. Nechama and most of the kibbutz leadership were convinced that Bettelheim's study would be useful to them.

There was nothing manipulative in that view; they were proud of what they had achieved and wanted to show it off, in the hope that Bettelheim's advice would help them to make improvements. For the kibbutz had always made the education of its children a top priority, and as Rahel Messinger, Yehuda Messinger's widow, confirms, Bettelheim's visit had sparked off an intense process of brainstorming among the teaching staff. 'On the way to school, we would talk about what we were about to do with the children. On the way home, we talked about what we had done, and in the evenings we would take part in discussions with Bettelheim. We had never asked ourselves so many questions.'[12] She was a nursery school teacher at the time, and she recalls with a smile the day when she asked him whether having two strong feminine influences in their lives – that of the *metapelet* and that of their mother – could be damaging to infants. 'Who said that to be loved by two people is bad for you?' Bettelheim shot back.

So much enthusiasm and goodwill left Bettelheim trapped in his own contradictions. For he was very disappointed. He liked and even admired the people, but the defects of their society were obvious to him. 'I feel like a traitor because I will have to come out with critical evaluations, but I can't help it,' he wrote to Ruth Marquis. 'I do not want to hurt them or their cause. Maybe I'll write only a report for the Foundation[13] and never publish anything. And maybe I'll even write a book on it. I just don't know. I must give myself time to digest it all from far away,' he added a little later.[14]

He was not impervious to the charm of kibbutz life. In his letters, he even admitted he found it 'tempting' in its simplicity, in spite of its harshness. But he was simply allergic to the conformism imposed by the group. 'What would you like to see changed in the kibbutz?' he asked a group of seventeen-year-olds one day. 'To have two movies a week instead of one,' one replied. Surprised by the stony silence of his friends, he quickly added: 'Oh, it was only a joke.' Bettelheim remarked that even jokes have reasons, but everyone in the group, including the teacher and the boy who had spoken, emphatically disagreed. The worst of it was, Bettelheim stressed in a letter, that nobody saw any reason why the kibbutz should not show two films a week. But it did not, so there was no reason why it should.

As regards the conclusions of his study, he felt he could sum them up in one sentence: 'The educational system works simply because the children grow up in a closed society that feels itself, as [do] all utopian societies, vastly superior to the rest of the world. This solves a great many questions with which our children have to struggle.'[15]

Bettelheim had soon noticed that there were people who flourished in the egalitarian kibbutz environment, clearly fitting in and full of enthusiasm for their chickens or carp, the latest crop or some new factory being built. But there were others. 'The kibbutz is full of people who are sullen, talk to nobody, do their work and don't want to be bothered. They would be driftwood in the big cities, if not worse. Here, they are useful members of their community. But short of that they are as persons as unhappy as they would be anywhere else,' he wrote.[16]

In spite of the language barrier, Bettelheim was, as usual, very aware of the psychological tensions between people, and maybe even more so of their efforts to try and deny those tensions. 'As I told them yesterday: since they have voted to abolish jealousy they really believe it no longer exists among them. The result is that the kibbutz is fine for the very strong who run and dominate it, and for the weak, who in all ways are protected and taken care of by the community. But it is very tough for the large middle group who have to stay and can't help themselves, and they pay for it with a depletion of their personalities, a self-destruction imposed by the fact that they have to repress so much,' he wrote.[17]

He did not doubt the sincerity of the kibbutzniks, but he could not accept their determined efforts to convince him of the superiority and justice of their form of society. He even began to doubt the veracity of Nechama's translations (needed mainly with the children, as most of the adults could converse with him in German, English, French or even Yiddish, which he understood a little). Assailed by contradictory feelings, Bettelheim, true to form, took refuge in hard work. The light often burned in his room until 1 or 2 a.m., to the admiration of his hosts, and particularly of Nechama Edelman, who on several occasions found him up and at work at six in the morning.

Relations between them were not what they had been in Chicago. Bettelheim was grumpy, demanding and tyrannical. Nechama, being determined to show him everything, underestimated the degree to which he needed to be alone from time to time.[18] She did not understand the distance he always placed between himself and others, nor his abrupt way of refusing whatever was offered him. 'He didn't even say "No thank you," but simply "No, I don't need it," ' she notes. As a convinced kibbutznik, she could not grasp the doubts he had about the system. She found him moody, disagreeable and subject to childish tantrums when he did not immediately get what he wanted.

One Friday evening, his tape recorder broke down, and he asked her to accompany him to Haifa to get it fixed. 'But Dr B, it's Sabbath, everything is closed,' she protested. To no avail; he insisted on leaving right away. In the town, they had driven around until they found a shop that looked open. He got out of the taxi without a word, and waited for three hours while the device was being repaired, as Nechama paced up and down outside. When he finally emerged, still without a word, he hailed a taxi and they returned. 'I don't think he even thanked me,' she says.

'If I hadn't been convinced that his research would be beneficial to us, I would not have let him treat me like that,' she adds. After Bettelheim's departure, Nechama was amazed to find all the fresh bed-linen that she had taken him each week still neatly piled up on a chair in his room. 'I wasn't going to make his bed for him as well, was I?' she mutters. She speaks without bitterness, an emotion which is clearly foreign to her, but she was obviously hurt by Bettelheim's attitude. And also intrigued. Although it is not her style to indulge in speculative interpretations, after six weeks of being subjected to his moods and tyranny, her guess was that, as a child, he must have been not spoiled, as so many people believed, but mistreated, and deprived of a real childhood.

Bettelheim did have an 'official' reason to be disappointed. Only days after his arrival, he realized that he had been mistaken as to what he would find in Ramat Yohanan. Although they did not sleep in the same houses as their parents, the children enjoyed a very strong relationship with them, which was contrary to the model he had set out to study. This was a genuine reason for concern, and one that his hosts could understand. Rahel Messinger recalls how, at the start of his stay, Bettelheim would often come to see her husband and lament: 'This is terrible – I'm going to have to return the grant. The example of the kibbutz just isn't applicable to American ghettos.' In his letters, he went further. Writing to Ruth Marquis, he explained how a communal upbringing did not protect children from the 'pathogenic impact' the parental relationships could have on them. It simply prevented their neuroses from breaking out into the open: 'The neuroses do not become fulminant, because for that you have to be an individual and not all your life part of a group .... Sure, they feel very secure within their group, there is much less tension, anxiety.'[19]

If Bettelheim chose his editor to vent his disappointment on, it was because she had been closely involved in planning his trip. Ruth Marquis was then working as academic advisor to the Psychology Department at Michigan State University, where Albert Rabin, the author of an important study on kibbutz children, also taught. The two men knew each other. Having edited the *Dialogues*, and being a mother herself, Marquis was personally curious about the outcome of an upbringing in which the maternal influence would not be preponderant. She had encouraged Bettelheim to go to Israel. He could unburden himself to her because they had both invested great hopes in the trip, and he could count on her not to let anyone know how disappointed he was. For his letters were the epitome of ambivalence. Leaving aside his feelings of guilt towards his very welcoming hosts, his doubts can be summed up as an opposition between individual and security. The strength of the kibbutz was that it offered its members total safety; its weakness was that it prevented them from developing fully as individuals. Except, that is, for the élites, i.e. those who regularly left the kibbutz to go to work or to travel. The very people with whom Bettelheim was in contact.

Things began to improve, a couple of weeks later, with the arrival of the film-maker Charles Sharp, who was to shoot a documentary on Bettelheim's research.[20] 'A fellow American is a blessing,' the latter exclaimed.[21] 'I received him as a saving angel – a person with whom one could say whatever one wanted, and who also would not stand to have his own life in all minutiae run for him. Since I can unloose my frustrations with him, it's OK.'[22] Not long after Sharp's arrival, Bettelheim went to spend a week in Jerusalem, and his mood improved even more: 'I am glad now about the experience: even though sixty, I could still learn and change opinions.'[23]

Simply being able to get away from the closed world of the kibbutz and return to the more familiar environment of a university did him good, and allowed him to sum up his impressions. 'My research, for all practical purposes, could be finished now,' he wrote.[24] '[The kibbutz] is very much a class society, like all others. Only they share property and that's fine .... As I see it, the kibbutz is a most noble experiment – it had its great moments, but now it's an anachronism.' On his hosts, he added: 'Still they are very fine people and I love them as soon as we meet outside the confinement of the kibbutz, and that tells the story, theirs and mine.'

It was during those few days in Jerusalem that Bettelheim first met with Carl Frankenstein, who was then Dean of Education at the Hebrew University. Up until then the two had exchanged a dozen or so letters on their respective writings, and Frankenstein had published one of Bettelheim's articles on the O.S. in his review, *Megamot*.[25] As a PhD in philosophy, a psychoanalyst and an educator concerned with the problems of children from under-privileged backgrounds, Frankenstein had a lot in common with Bettelheim. He had been born in Berlin into a highly assimilated family, just over a year after his friend. The two spoke the same language and had the same cultural references. They had both experienced the arrival of Nazism as an unforgivable betrayal by a culture which they had always considered their own, and therefore as a deeply personal wound. And although Frankenstein had emigrated to Palestine in 1935, he liked to tell people that he was not a Zionist, but had simply gone where he could be useful. In spite of their academic qualifications, both men were intellectual free agents, despising all forms of pretence and pedantry. Both were suspicious of religion and all forms of orthodoxy. One of their common references was Vaihinger's philosophy of 'as if ',[26] and it would recur frequently in their later correspondence, as they vented their disappointment at either the political situation or the prevailing thinking of the time. Carl Frankenstein, however, would never become as conservative as Bettelheim.

Above all, he was less pessimistic and more at peace with himself. In spite of their shared interests, the two men were in fact very different.

Having lost his father at an early age, Frankenstein had spent his youth defending what he saw as just causes – such as fundraising for young artists who had come to Berlin to study – while his mother, although protesting about such idealistic dilettantism, continued to pay for his upkeep. After the war, he had never returned to Germany, and never claimed the damages which were his due. He was the kind of man who gives up a post just before retirement, simply because he has found something better to do; at age sixty-five, he would indeed step down from his job at the Hebrew University to found a school for culturally deprived children. As his widow puts it, 'He had a very peculiar sense of money. Like Bettelheim, only the other way round.'[27]

But there was more. Frankenstein was also very tall and handsome (his female students used to refer to him as 'Prince Charming'). He was a lively, witty character, clearly in love with life. His wife, also very beautiful, was a nurse with psychoanalytic training. Like Gina, she hailed from one of the eastern provinces of the Austro-Hungarian empire, in her case Bukovina.[28] Between her and her husband, however, these differences of origin, and the prejudices they generally give rise to, were treated as jokes. They never had children, and carried on a close, often playful, relationship right up until his death. On viewing photos of the couple together, hearing anecdotes of their encounters with the Bettelheims and reading the correspondence between the two men, one begins to realize that beyond the strong intellectual bond and the mutual admiration, Frankenstein was probably the man Bettelheim would have liked to have been, rather like a brother who had chosen happiness. This aspect of their relationship would gradually become more apparent as time passed, until Frankenstein, who had never been a father, took on more and more of that role *vis-à-vis* his friend, who had never been allowed to be a child, trying to inspire Bettelheim with the taste for life that was leaving him.

In 1964 the relationship was only just beginning. But the encounter probably contributed to Bettelheim's regaining some inner peace during his trip to Jerusalem, in particular by helping him to decipher some of his complex feelings about Jewishness, his own and that of others. Everyone who met him during the Israel trip was indeed struck by those feelings, which some people rather hastily interpreted as a rejection of his origins.

On the first night of Passover, Bettelheim announced to Nechama Edelman that he did not want to attend the traditional dinner, or *seder*. She was amazed: he must really hate his Jewishness, she thought, to refuse to share the joy of the festival commemorating his people's exodus from Egypt and the end of their slavery. Furthermore, at Ramat Yohanan, Passover also marked the beginning of the early spring harvest. Having finally convinced him that his absence would truly offend his hosts, she was surprised to note that during the ceremony he was murmuring the prayers, although he continued to look furious. When I suggested that Bettelheim, as an atheist who had been forced in his youth to learn prayers which meant nothing to either himself or his parents, probably had a hard time sitting through any religious event, Nechama exclaimed: 'But Passover isn't a religious festival! It's like the 4th of July in America; it's our Independence Day.'

For Nechama, born and bred in Palestine and a Hebrew speaker from birth, 'Jewish self-hatred' is an alien concept. The only oppression she has experienced is that of colonization, the same as that suffered by her neighbours, Christians or Moslems. A type of oppression which one faces with both feet firmly on the earth which one knows to be one's own, against people who have come from elsewhere. How could she understand the inner conflicts of a man who had grown up in Vienna, a city which while offering some of its Jews prominent positions had continually undermined their own self-image, turning them against one another and then exterminating them? An early incident had left her perplexed. Before his arrival, Bettelheim had asked her to set up only one appointment for him, with the philosopher Gershom Scholem. But when Nechama, who had been one of Scholem's favourite students, contacted him, he replied in no uncertain terms: 'Nechama, if you go around with that man, we will no longer be friends.'

Bettelheim should have known better. He should have guessed that his articles on Eichmann and 'ghetto thinking' would not be to the liking of Scholem, a Berlin-born historian of Jewish mysticism, who had always seen assimilation as the worst of all pitfalls. He seems on the contrary not to have understood it. For him, Israel appeared as the country of Jewish warriors, the ones who had opted to get out of the *shtetl*. It was a clear-cut opposition in his mind: submission on the one hand, combat on the other. The man who bows his head to try and hold on to the trappings of his narrow existence, versus the one who courageously tackles the desert to build a new life.

Bettelheim's image of Zionism had been forged in Vienna. It no doubt closely resembled that of his compatriot and near-contemporary, George Clare, who wrote that above all, 'it held out the promise of the rise of a new and different type of Jew, different from the insecure assimilants and different from the ghetto-created perversions of Jewry. The Jews who killed themselves rather than surrender at Massada, the warrior-Jews described by Flavius Josephus ... were proud men and women, different from the downtrodden, cringing, ghetto-Jews. The return of a whole people to its true nature, that was the ultimate aim of Herzl's Zionism, that was and is the greatness of his vision.'[29] Being forced to compare that vision to the real world, as he found it at Ramat Yohanan, reignited in Bettelheim both the dreams and the doubts he had felt deep within himself ever since childhood.

The cypress grove that graced one's first view of the kibbutz, the sight of muscular Jews, with skins tanned by working in the fields, Jews proud of what their labour had drawn from the soil, and ready to die for it, all these scenes must have deeply affected the Viennese-born visitor, whose mind had been filled with images from the age-old canon of anti-Semitism. The myth of the rootless, landless Jew had indeed been laid to rest by the kibbutz. Yet this closed world, made up of ordinary people with ordinary feelings, in which their common good demanded a kind of conformity troubling to Bettelheim, also evoked the old images he knew: those of the *shtetl*. As he was to write in *The Children of the Dream*: 'What I did not find stressed in the literature was how their poor preparation as colonizers forced kibbutzniks to repeat, though in a deeply different way, the close unity that had characterized the ghetto, and for similar reasons: because it helped them survive in a basically hostile environment.'[30]

Real memories also interfered with his view of this world which was strange to him. They were brought home to him one day during a visit to a school outside the kibbutz along with Haim Hadoumi, a regional educational official. 'Mister, what difference is there between a kibbutz and a concentration camp, if there too the clothes belonged to everybody?' a child asked him. Haim's wife Leah recalls that Bettelheim came back to that question with her husband continually during the following days.[31] In Jerusalem, Bettelheim also visited Yad Vashem, the great Holocaust memorial. Nechama Edelman decided not to go with him, knowing he would be shown around by the director, but she was struck by just how overwhelmed he looked on his return. At the same time, in his letters, he often spoke of the low price put on life in a country living in a permanent state of siege.

Two weeks after Passover, one or two days before he was due to leave, Bettelheim once again tried to duck out of a holiday banquet, wanting Nechama to go with him for one last interview instead. But once again, he had to give in. On this occasion, however, the festival was not a religious one – it was the annual Day of Remembrance, on which Israelis recall the victims of the Nazi genocide. Nechama was not the only person present to notice his expression during the ceremony: it was not the same as at Passover, that of the obstinate child dragged into something against his will, it was a look of profound suffering.

As is shown by the correspondence he carried on with Frankenstein, right to the end of his life Bettelheim never quite managed to see either Israel or Israelis in realistic terms. Despite his ever-strengthening attachment to the country, and all his efforts to understand it, he never completely accepted that having 'the ground under one's feet', as Nechama puts it, had turned Israelis into a new type of Jews, different not only from himself but from the 'dream' referred to in the title of his book. When France's Pompidou Centre asked him to write about the city of his birth for the 1986 *Paris-Vienne* art exhibition, he made the following remark to his friend: 'In rethinking those years, some before my birth, others I lived through, I realized how hopeless the situation of Vienna-Austria really was, and how this led to an internalization, introspection if you want, in thinking (Weininger), writing (Schnitzler), music (Mahler, Schoenberg, etc.), in painting (Klimt and Schiele) and, of course, Freud. I saw these connections better than ever before. So my question: Why does not a parallel situation in Israel lead to a parallel introspection? This would seem particularly appropriate to the Jewish temper.'[32] A year later, he remarked sadly: 'Israel just went the way of all nations. It was silly of us to hope for anything better.'[33]

After shortening his stay by a few days and spending a week in Paris on his way home, Bettelheim arrived back in Chicago at the end of April 1964. *The Children of the Dream* was to come out five years later. His Israeli friends – who did not know he would write a book about his visit – had expected Bettelheim to get back in touch with them. During all those years, he did not. Once away from the object of his study, he mulled over his ambivalent feelings. The rise of youth protest and the anti-Vietnam War movement made him more aware of the advantages of a kibbutz education. Haim Hadoumi was Israel's cultural attaché in Detroit for a time, and he occasionally discussed the issues with him. Then the Six Day War helped him overcome his doubts. Between his trip to Israel and the publication of his book, he had completed *The Empty Fortress* and published a lot of articles. But up until July 1967 and his critique of *Treblinka*, he had not written anything else on the concentration camps, Jews or Nazism.

How his trip to Israel had brought back images from his youth is made clear in *The Children of the Dream*. In particular, in a long introduction analysing how all relations within the kibbutz, notably child rearing, had been moulded by the founders' determination to free themselves of ghetto ways and thinking. The migrating bird (*Wandervogel*) is by definition one which flies away, and the desire to flee the cloying atmosphere and authoritarianism of the family unit was indeed one of the main motivations of the youth movements. According to Bettelheim, the pioneer women, even more than the men, were determined to sweep away the old structures. Having come to Palestine to be free, they demanded absolute equality, particularly in work, and had no time for the role of mother that tradition assigned to them. But Bettelheim went deeper. Insisting again on the profoundly misogynist nature of Judaism,[34] he pointed out an unresolvable contradiction that could explain the first female pioneers' desire not to raise their own children: 'Deep in the Jewish girl's unconscious, from earliest childhood, the idea was embedded that the good daughter is the one who grows up to be a good mother. She is the daughter who repays the mother's outpouring of love by giving her a grandchild. And at this the daughters rebelled.' And yet, 'Much as they were ready to cast off their mothers' role in practice, psychologically they remained beholden to an image of their mothers who had instilled in them the unconscious feeling that only giving all is enough,' he wrote.[35]

While other authors before him had presented the kibbutz as the antithesis of the *shtetl*, Bettelheim was the first to highlight the survival of unconscious patterns of thought. His insistence on this point was to anger both his Israeli hosts and, even more, the leadership of the kibbutz movement, notably that of *Hashomer Hatzair*. 'His book shows, I think, that blending Marx and Freud is an impossibility. His idea that one could not simply change people's personalities made them mad; the book was seen as an attack on the "new Jew",' says Moshe Kerem, who was the principal of Western Galilee high schools for kibbutzes at the time of Bettelheim's visit.

For although *The Children of the Dream* was never published in Israel, extensive extracts circulated within the kibbutz movement. And needless to say the English-language edition was read all over the country as soon as it came out. It sparked expressions of anger that were out of proportion to the book's actual contents, which are in general favourable to the kibbutz upbringing. But Bettelheim's tone was considered too dogmatic, and his attitude condescending. He was accused of not knowing his subject-matter: 'How can one write such a definitive work after only a few weeks of research?' said many critics. Others accused him of relying too much on psychoanalytic explanations. Those who had been against his trip from the start felt vindicated. At Ramat Yohanan itself the reactions were a little less harsh, but the disappointment was greater. As Bettelheim had read everything he could find about the kibbutzes while working on his book, his arguments at times seemed more fitted to the more radical ones, which had been studied more often. And yet the incidents he cited were those he had gleaned at Ramat Yohanan. Many people felt somewhat betrayed, even among those who, like Yehuda Messinger, considered *The Children of the Dream* to be an important work containing many useful ideas.

The critics focused mainly on what Bettelheim had to say about adolescents. As is confirmed by his letters to Ruth Marquis, he found no fault with the education provided for small children. The burden of conformism and its effects had become apparent to him on listening to the older children. And he gives a very convincing portrayal of the malaise felt by the kibbutz's young people. His book, which has the advantage of high-lighting the mythology, ethics and historical role of the kibbutzes before discussing his findings, makes a clear distinction between generations, and subtly brings to light the gulf that had grown up between them. It shows in particular how the children of the pioneers were weighed down by the auras of their parents. As the founders of a new world, the latter did not realize how heavy a burden they were placing on the shoulders of their offspring. For them, every new skyscraper or factory built in Israel was a reason for pride, a proof that they had won their battle. For their children, however, every such development was but another threat to the survival of the world they had grown up in, the only world they knew, that of the kibbutz. A world from which they could not dream of escaping, since

'The fast growing new nation around them with all its turmoil, competition, expansion – [had] been depicted to them as one of injustice, inequity, sometimes pure evil,' wrote Bettelheim.[36]

For her part, Nechama Edelman is convinced that Bettelheim had genuinely tapped into, and correctly interpreted, the deepest feelings of the young people. When, at the end of the five years, she received a copy of the book, she read it attentively. She was first in line for the protests, for 'Bettelheim was Nechama's project,' as another witness said – thereby involuntarily confirming what Bettelheim had felt: that their concern for the common good pushed the kibbutzniks to restrict their own personal ambitions without even realizing it.[37] And what did Nechama feel on reading the book? 'Jealousy! How had he managed, in such a short time, to see so clearly what had escaped me during forty years of experience?' the former primary school teacher admits frankly. 'He was right, even though many of us didn't want to admit it,' she adds.

What is most striking is indeed that twenty-five years later, even those who had most strongly criticized *The Children of the Dream* on its publication now acknowledge that many of its observations were well founded. Rahel Messinger, for example, had been all the more upset by some of Bettelheim's assertions in that her husband had played a decisive role in the warm welcome he was given in the kibbutz. Today, however, she admits that *The Children of the Dream* allowed her to understand at least one important thing about her own children: the very specific relationship that develops in a communal nursery between a baby and his 'crib-mate' – the child in the next crib, the first person he sees on opening his eyes and who, unlike the mother or the *metapelet* coming and going, is always there.

One of Bettelheim's remarks was particularly offensive to Israelis. When stressing the pragmatic, down-to-earth attitudes of the second generation, which he contrasted with the idealism of the pioneers, he described the younger kibbutzniks as lacking in depth and 'emotionally flat' compared to their contemporaries reared in families. That remark is but the logical result of the book's opening analyses on the origin of the kibbutz: feeling unable to give enough to their children, Bettelheim wrote, the pioneer women had created a system in which they would get less in return. And indeed, once in adolescence, their children no longer showed the same kind of attachment to be found in a traditional family. But along with the neurotic aspects of such a relationship, the dynamic aspects had also disappeared.

In his introduction, Bettelheim stresses the exemplary role played by kibbutzniks during the Six Day War. Not only were many of them among the officers, but they had been predominantly in the front lines. Twenty-five per cent of the 800 Israelis killed during the conflict came from the kibbutzes, although they provided only four per cent of all troops. 'This was the true measure of their heroism, courage and devotion to duty,' wrote Bettelheim. 'Once more, as in the settling of the land and in the war of liberation, the kibbutz ethos gives special meaning to the lives of Israelis today.'[38] In his book, he did not discuss the issue any further. But privately, he had more to say. Moshe Kerem has a vivid memory of a discussion on the issue with three army officers, that took place at a Tel Aviv sidewalk café in 1972. 'Don't be so proud of them,' Bettelheim said. 'This may have been simply a consequence of their inability to take the last-minute decision that could have saved their lives' – a reference to the kibbutzniks' habit of making group, rather than individual, decisions. Needless to say, the remark had made Bettelheim's companions very angry. As soon as they got back to their offices, nevertheless, they had commissioned a study to find out whether there was any truth in his statement!

Although himself a member of the kibbutz 'establishment', Moshe Kerem is convinced of the value of Bettelheim's book, and has used it in his classes at Haifa University. He also believes that *The Children of the Dream* was the determining factor in changes that were subsequently made to the kibbutz system of child-rearing (today, children live with their parents). Having mainly frequented Bettelheim when the latter returned to Israel in the winter of 1972, he thinks the misunderstanding arose in large part because of his tone. A patronizing Bettelheim, who felt he had put himself out to serve the cause of the kibbutzes, faced with hosts who were over-sensitive. He was also able to see just how much Bettelheim had been hurt by their negative reactions to his book: rather like a father who has given his son a gift, only to find it spurned because he also tendered a few pieces of advice.

That wound was to remain hidden, however. Bettelheim would never express it to the people who had caused it. When he returned to Israel it would no longer be to the kibbutz, but to Jerusalem, where he ended up feeling almost at home, between Carl Frankenstein and Seymour Fox, a former student who invited him to run seminars in the Milton Centre for Education he had set up at the Hebrew University. When the leaders of the kibbutz movement invited him to come and debate with them after publication of his book, he did not go. But three years later he willingly took part in a discussion at the teacher training centre in which Rahel Messinger worked. She would hear him speak once again in 1987, during an international congress on Early Childhood Education held in the suburbs of Tel Aviv. And she would be astonished by the very pro-kibbutz tone of his address, on the 'Effects of Industrialization and Technology on the Family'. As for Nechama Edelman, on the occasion of a visit to the United States in 1973, she decided to end the silence that had set in between herself and Bettelheim ever since his visit. Bruno and Trude received her with great kindness, showed her round Chicago and showered her with gifts (for her grandchildren, since she insisted that there was nothing she needed for herself).

Chapter XVI

The Bad Guy

There'll be courses, even in your own field, that will bore you. Don't try to make A's in them just because it'll look good on your record .... Concentrate instead, and give your very best to those courses that excite you. ... Play with knowledge.... Most of all, don't forever be preparing for something else. Today counts too. ... When Einstein and Freud entered college they started out with no more than what each of you can bring to your college career: all they had to go on was the conviction that the creative mind of one single person can revolutionize the field he makes his own, and because of that, the whole world.

Bruno Bettelheim, graduation speech,
Wayland Academy, May 30, 1973

In 1966, Anna Freud came to Chicago at the invitation of Heinz Kohut, the then-director of the Psychoanalytic Institute. During her stay, she paid a visit to the Orthogenic School, and Bettelheim granted her the rare privilege of taking part in the three o'clock meeting with the children.[1] Seated on the floor as usual, the students felt very intimidated while waiting for the old lady whose visit was visibly important for Bettelheim. They knew that she was the daughter of the man he admired the most, and that she had come all the way from England to visit them. But, as soon as she arrived, Anna Freud, with characteristic kindliness, put them at ease. As someone was getting her a chair, she pointed to the large wooden rocking-horse in a corner of the room. 'That's what I'd really like to sit on. But it wouldn't be sensible. I'm too old for that.'

At the end of the meeting, she spoke a little about her father, saying in essence: 'As you know, my father only treated adults, but he thought his teaching could be extended to children. I hope you will honour his teaching.' Diana Grossman, as a typically Bettelheim-trained counsellor, was outraged. 'What right does she have to use the children like that?' she recalls saying to herself. 'They are at the school to get better – not to honour her father!' But Kathy Lubin was deeply moved by the whole event, in particular by the fact that each time the old lady said 'my father', she was referring to Sigmund Freud himself. She above all recalls Anna Freud's closing remarks: 'His dream was for psychoanalysis to be used to cure children. And today I see that his dream has come true.'

Only one false note soured the brief but memorable visit. When Bettelheim took his guest on a tour of the school, and they arrived at the famous candy closet, for the first time in two decades, it was locked! He was furious, and once she had departed, he went into a rage. The incident, due no doubt to the well-meaning desire of a counsellor or a housekeeper to ensure that the school's most famous closet should be impeccable for the much-awaited visitor, sums up pretty well the atmosphere at the school during the later years. It was a situation characterized by excessiveness of all kinds, creating the impression that Bettelheim was weary of it all, and no longer completely in control of either his desires or his impatience. On the material level, the end of the 1960s was the Orthogenic School's age of splendour. There was a reflecting pool with contemporary sculptures, great to look at, but definitely not intended for the children to bathe in, as Diana Grossman was to learn to her cost on a very hot day. There was fine china, cut-glass beakers and contemporary furniture; the children's surroundings had become truly luxurious.[2]

In October 1966, Bettelheim organized a lavish reception for the inauguration of the 'Adolescent Unit'. Meant for children who were getting ready to leave the school, this wing had been designed to provide a half-way house between the over-protected atmosphere of the dormitories and the harshness of the 'out there', as Bettelheim generally called the world outside the school (it was an expression he used with increasingly menacing emphasis as the years went by). The Adolescent Unit had been five years in the making, and as planning went ahead it had become progressively more ambitious. It was separated from the rest of the school by a long corridor, complete with statues and an artful lighting system. The one-person bedrooms looked like monastery cells; the overall impression was one of cold elegance. 'Bruno has built his mausoleum!' Morris Janowitz commented to Gayle Shulenberger, on the inaugural evening. A little later, Bettelheim was himself to adopt the expression, self-mockingly. For this costly architectural adventure turned out to be a fiasco; the building was inconvenient and above all generated much anxiety in its occupants. It was not long before the walls between the bedrooms were being knocked down to create new dormitories.

Bettelheim had become more and more touchy, unpredictable and irascible. His classroom style had also become much more rigid, as was noted by Ruth Nedelsky, when she returned to Chicago and enrolled once again for the class in psychoanalytic theory that she had so loved in the 1940s. She was astounded to find a completely different Bettelheim. 'I was so disappointed. He was tired. He no longer invested anything of himself in the class.' His habit of holding up one student's errors as an example from which the whole class could learn, which had earlier been luminous, had become frankly unpleasant. 'Can't he see that he is defeating his own purpose?' thought Ruth Nedelsky. The Bettelheim who had been so good at laying bare the mechanisms of people's power was now clearly wedded to his own. Nedelsky was also troubled by the way he spoke to Trude. She had a hard time accepting that anyone could change so much.

This testimony is important, for few people were thus able to compare Bettelheim's teaching over a twenty-year gap. One should add however that among those who did not have that chance, and who discovered Bettelheim's classes during the later period, many still found him to be an exceptional teacher. Such as Geneviève Jurgensen, who was his student between 1970 and 1972. 'I find it difficult to talk about this teaching, which made such a strong impression on me,' she writes, in the book she devoted to the school.[3] 'That was probably because the teacher did not use anything that could really be described as a method. Depending on the day of the week, his mood, the students and the atmosphere in the lecture hall, he would deal with one subject rather than another. It would be too easy for me to draw up a list of his witticisms, or to count the points he scored at our expense. To show how he emerged the victor from each and every debate ... in a word, to concentrate on his style. But that would not be serious, and his courses were nothing if not serious. They may often have taken the form of a duel between the teacher and one of his students, yet they were as fundamentally interesting as life itself. And indeed life was always what they were about.'

This paradox explains why the students or counsellors of the later period found it so difficult to discuss Bettelheim after his suicide. Ruth Nedelsky herself had still not found a way out of the dilemma when I met her in 1993. For towards the end of the 1960s Bruno Bettelheim was indeed still the same person, but he had become quite simply impossible to get on with. That fact was obvious to everyone, even those who were still benefiting to the full from what he had to offer. Such people simply told themselves that the difficulties were the price to pay for a unique learning experience.

Inside the school, Bettelheim tended to play more and more with the boundaries. For instance when he took in as a student the grandson of his earliest and most faithful sponsor, Philip Pekow – after whom, a year later, he would name the new Adolescent Unit. That was a dangerous mixing of roles, for whatever the reasons may have been for Charles Pekow's admittance to the school, he always felt that he was there more as his grandfather's descendant than as a patient of Bettelheim. He was convinced that he had no valid reason for being there, and resented Bettelheim's authority all the more in that he was sure that if he tried to tell his family about some of the things that went on in the school, they would not believe him. It is certainly no coincidence that the young Pekow, although a somewhat puny child, remains in many of his fellow students' memories as the one who dared to punch Dr B back.

It happened one Monday in 1968, during lunch. Charles Pekow was then fourteen and his counsellor had become worried about his sudden loss of some 15 pounds – due, Charles claims, to his becoming tired of 'institutional food'. Those were days of intense political agitation in the world outside the school, with the recent political assassinations of Martin Luther King and Robert Kennedy, and the young boy felt very concerned about it all. His sympathies went to the Left and the Palestinians and he resented his political views not being taken seriously. So, when Bettelheim went over to his table and instructed him to eat, after explaining to his teacher that he was losing weight because he was jealous of a couple of anorexic girls, Charles denied it vehemently. According to him, this is when Dr B slapped him (although, he adds, he had seldom been hit up until then). Charles whirled around and pasted Bettelheim in the jaw. Visibly surprised, Dr B grabbed his hair with one hand and continued to slap him with the other until the boy got hold of his arms, while kicking Bettelheim in the leg and in the groin, causing him to scream in pain. Pekow says he repeatedly offered to stop fighting if Bettelheim agreed to stop too. In return, Bettelheim told him to let go of his arms. When Pekow complied, the fight ended.

Later, someone asked Bettelheim why he had not done anything about Charles Pekow after that incident. He replied that he had been too angry.

Bettelheim returned to Chicago from Israel at the end of April 1964. In spite of all his agonizing, the trip had given him a boost. But before deciding what to do with his kibbutz findings, he had to put the final touches to *The Empty Fortress*, on which he had been working for years. The manuscript was practically finished, and yet he was not satisfied. He was unable to complete the job. In his everyday practice, he had come to more or less accept that autism was not as easily curable as he had earlier hoped; the rate at which such children were being admitted to the school had slowed. In the writing of the book, however, he appears to have had a much harder time coming to terms with his relative powerlessness. His public statements on autism were no doubt triumphalist, but his critics were saying things that he considered dangerous, and even despicable. Asserting that the condition resulted either from genetic problems or from a defect in brain development, they recommended forms of treatment which amounted to nothing more than conditioning, treating human beings as if they were animals to be tamed (drugs, punishment/reward therapies, etc.). Whereas Bettelheim's experience proved that a genuine therapist was dealing, not with mental or behavioural disturbances, but with children in difficulty. That was the message he simply had to get across, above all else. The trouble was that the results in themselves were not conclusive enough to see off the arguments of his enemies. He needed incontrovertible evidence. Bettelheim was dissatisfied with himself, furious at his inability to score the knock-out blow that would force the whole world to finally show respect for autistic children – and to acknowledge that he was right.

What appear to be details of the cases quoted in the book are contained in a small index file, discovered somewhat by accident during the research for this book.[4] That document gives a good idea of how Bettelheim must have had to grapple with the feeling of fraud as he wrote his book. The cards indeed correspond to forty-six children, as stated in *The Empty Fortress*, and the percentages relating to the number of successes and to the intellectual level of the children's parents are the same as those given in the book. The problem is that in order to achieve the success rate announced, he had boosted his sample with the cases of some children who had never been autistic. In March 1965, one of his main critics wrote to Bettelheim to ask him for his results to quote in his own book. Bernard Rimland was the father of an autistic child and a vigorous campaigner against all forms of psychological approach. Bettelheim replied curtly that he refused to have anything to do with a work that was 'ill-conceived and based on erroneous and biased judgements', and referred Rimland to the book he was about to publish. A year later, *The Empty Fortress* had still not appeared, and Rimland repeated his request. He felt so confident about his own conclusions that he offered to give Bettelheim five pages in which freely to contradict him at the end of his book, on condition that he, Rimland, could do the same in *The Empty Fortress*. Manifestly pleased with this suggestion, Rimland went on to regret that Karl Marx had not thought of doing the same thing. Anyone else might have been touched by such naïveté. Not Bettelheim. He once again turned Rimland down flat, adding haughtily that the proposal only showed just how little its originator understood of human emotions. On the latter point he was probably right, but the tone of his reply betrayed how embarrassed he was by the request itself.

These were but surface conflicts, however. On a deeper level, on the fundamental issues, Bettelheim did not cheat. Although unable to provide anything like a recipe for the curing of autism, he needed to give an account of his method in order to demonstrate why those of Rimland and his ilk were mistaken. 'Much of modern psychology seeks to know about others; too much of it, in my opinion, without an equal commitment to knowing about the self. But I believe that knowing the other – which is different from knowing about the other – can only be a function of knowing oneself,' he wrote.[5]

To discover meaning in the children's crazy actions, and thus find the responses capable of calming them without shutting them up, the therapist has no need for batteries of tests and assessment charts. He can count only on his own self-knowledge, on condition that he has pushed that self-knowledge down to the deepest and most archaic mechanisms of the unconscious, those that only appear once defences and rationalizations have collapsed, when all adaptative attempts have failed. Bettelheim had gone through that painful exploration in two ways, in his analysis and in the camp. The former experience had helped him perceive the fortress which, in protecting him from his childhood fears, was keeping him from self-fulfilment and love. And then, just when he was beginning to emerge, the Nazis had hurled him back, with the greatest possible violence, into a world of death and hatred. They had even sold him the miserable armband, which by providing a few pathetic improvements to his daily lot could only push him towards abandonment. That was how he had been able to understand and describe 'autism as seen from inside the person'.[6] With an upsurge of determination, he had refused the illusory protection, and carried on the fight to survive, while remaining himself. Autistic children were just like those inmates that other camp prisoners referred to as 'moslems': those in whom the crucial upsurge simply did not take place. Neither drugs nor carrot-and-stick forms of treatment could pull them back. However someone who had experienced both states, who had crossed the 'bridge' in both directions, could perhaps, by dint of much obstination, find the way to spark off the required jolt of energy.

There was a detailed description of the emerging to the world, to others, of an autonomous human being. The central importance in that process of the infant's gradually acquired feeling that his actions can affect his surroundings. The couple that the newborn baby forms with its mother, and the role played by the latter in fostering, or failing to foster, in her child the conviction that life is something of value. The stages and critical points in that development; the possible deviations, and their consequences, such as turning in on oneself, or the decline of the self.[7] The opening pages of *The Empty Fortress* are so rich, so packed with crucial observations and original remarks that they inspired the following slightly irritated comment from the British psychoanalyst Donald Winnicott: 'I find [Bettelheim] difficult to read simply because he says everything and there is nothing to be said that one could be certain has not been said by him. But one must read him because he can be exactly right, or more nearly right than other writers. This applies especially to his opening chapters of *The Empty Fortress*.'[8]

Next, Bettelheim illustrated his method with the case histories, of 'Laurie', 'Marcia' and 'Joey', at once exciting and moving, showing how even the worst-case clinical situation could be modified or amended. Stories capable of inspiring new hope in even the most despairing parent or clinical practitioner. Nevertheless, on his return from Israel, Bettelheim was still not satisfied. Once again, he plunged frenetically into the literature on his subject. With the aid of Ruth Marquis, he had read all the material on the infantile psyche or on autism, from Piaget to the most recent studies. He had also entered into correspondence with some of the researchers who, across the world, were studying children. He explored every possible direction in the search for the conclusive and incontrovertible answer that his clinical research had failed to provide. And then one day, he suddenly called a halt to the research (which makes up the third part of his book). His editor had dug out some lines from William Blake, which summed up his beliefs in a nutshell:

Thought is life
And strength and breath
And the want of thought
Is death.

He made them the final words of his book.

The mid-sixties also saw major changes in the staff line-up at the school. One after another the counsellors of the 'second generation', those who had arrived when the school was in full growth, had left. The team was now made up of young men and women born after the war, at the time when Dr Spock's influence was spreading. Only the really good counsellors stayed on; anyone who did not fit in soon found themselves shown to the door. Bettelheim still had his favourites, such as Kathy Lubin, and those on whom he knew he could count, such as Diana Grossman. The latter had taken over the managerial responsibilities previously discharged by Inge Fleischmann and Jacquelyn Sanders. These counsellors were by now the only ones to have individual sessions with him. Some critics accused him of having created a class system within the staff, of having built himself a praetorian guard.

Bettelheim had turned sixty. He was now extremely famous, and in the habit of handing out advice in the form of aphorisms. 'I know only three things ...' was his usual opener. There were many more, of course. Some of them never varied, such as 'The end is in the beginning,' his favourite one and a key concept in his thinking. It had a double meaning. It was an obvious reminder that people's psychological make-up is shaped in the early years of life. But it above all meant that even if it took years to bring it out, the very first contact between a therapist and his patient contained within it the outcome of the treatment. On the basis of that observation, reached through years of experience, Bettelheim advised the psychologists who followed his seminars, and the counsellors in his school, to only consult a patient's file after they had met him or her at least once.[9] As for the other maxims, each counsellor has retained memories of specific ones. There was: 'If a person does something it's because they have a need to do it,' recalled by Karen Zelan, or: 'Better a wrong decision than to remain hung up in ambivalence' (Maurie Formigoni). In Zelan's recollection, the latter maxim becomes: 'Don't be afraid of making mistakes.' Bettelheim also liked to paraphrase Aristotle: 'Do everything in moderation.' The one Diana Grossman Kahn recalls is 'The patient is always right.' With some counsellors, the promised third aphorism never came. Dr B would tell them: 'You'll learn it when you've spent enough time at the school.'

The departure of a counsellor, above all a good one, was always a difficult process. For the children, of course, but also for the rest of the team, which had to find a new balance. And for Bettelheim himself, who found it less and less easy to accept the loss of those on whom he could count, and who counted for him. There was no satisfactory solution to the problem, only palliatives. Departures were never announced more than a month in advance, to avoid creating unnecessary anxiety. But, as Bettelheim said, the children could always feel whatever the adults tried to hide from them. And the children in the school were particularly observant and sensitive.

The slightest incident could spark off a crisis. Karen Zelan had been gone for two weeks when one of her former charges, 'Vivienne', then aged ten, broke into uncontrollable screams one evening, hitting her head against the wall. Maurie, who had built up a good relationship with the little girl, was unable to do a thing. She sent for Dr B who calmed the child down, and then asked Maurie what had happened. The counsellor had not the slightest idea; she had been reading a bedtime story to the children, and everything had been going fine until the screaming started. 'What story?' asked Bettelheim. Nothing terrifying, said Maurie, simply an Arabian tale, set in the Persian Gulf, on an island. The name of the island? 'Karan.' The sound of her former counsellor's name had been enough to send the little girl into a frenzy.

Over the years, a tradition had gradually set in: the person who was leaving became identified as the 'bad guy', thus providing a kind of scapegoat on to whom the children, and to a lesser extent even the counsellors, could project their aggressiveness whenever things went wrong. Here again, the idea was to prevent the children from turning the pain of the departure against themselves ('It's my fault if she's leaving,' or, more crudely, 'If she's not here any more, that means I killed her'). Bettelheim's overriding concern remained to relieve the children of their self-directed destructiveness. On occasion, he would back up this concern by quoting Freud, who indeed saw the origin of melancholy – deep, deadly depression – in the subject's turning against himself the aggressiveness that he cannot direct against its true target, the lost love object. 'Our job is to help our patients to feel angry,' Bettelheim would tell the students in his Stanford seminar.

The 'bad guy' did not have an easy time. Bettelheim would be the first to make her or him feel the odd one out, notably during staff meetings. Everything the future departee said might suddenly be judged either stupid or uninteresting. The change was all the more striking in that it was often Bettelheim's favourites who were subjected to the treatment. And it was very cruel given that, after devoting several years of their lives to the school, the good counsellors generally had a very hard time taking the decision to leave. Abandoning children who had such a great need for them, and to whom they had given so much, was always a painful and guilt-ridden process. Some of them accepted the rite of passage as something inevitable. Others, such as Karen Zelan, refused it. After witnessing the change in Bettelheim's attitude to another of his favourites, she went to seek him out. He was busy in the basement, wrestling alone with the editing of the film about 'Marcia', and apparently having a hard time of it. Feigning to ignore the funny side of the situation (he was tangled up in strips of film, moaning 'I can't! I can't!'), she barked angrily: 'You're not going to do it to me too, I hope.' Putting on his 'doctor' voice, Bettelheim replied: 'Tell me what you're feeling.' 'You know perfectly well what I'm talking about,' shouted Zelan before calming down and finally helping him to untangle the mess of film. Later, when her time came to leave the school, Bettelheim made no attempt to turn her into the 'bad guy'.

Strangely enough, although many people testify to the existence of the 'bad guy' rite of departure in the last years of the school, a few counsellors from the period energetically deny that it even existed. Kathy Lubin and Diana Grossman, for example, both say that they were not subjected to it when they left; nor did they ever witness it being inflicted on others. This could have been because they found leaving the school such a difficult process in itself that they did not notice that particular aspect of it. But although the reason for this discrepancy between different people's reports remains a mystery, the fact that it exists at least highlights the ambiguity of the practice. For all those who have recollections of the rite of departure are torn between an understanding of its aim, and resentment at the cruelty it involved. This touches on the central contradiction in Bettelheim's behaviour in the period leading up to his retirement: in those last years, it looks as though he was less and less able to clearly distinguish between the children's good – which he had made into the school's *raison d'être* – and his own. Rather as if, through years of understanding the children from within, he had somewhat lost the ability to hold in check the child inside himself. He knew he should not be trying to prevent his counsellors from going, but he could not resist doing so. He respected those who stuck to their decision, but made them pay for it. This was indeed because he was aware of the children's needs, but not only. And he used all his powers of seduction to dissuade those he wanted to keep from leaving.

Nonnie never managed to leave. By the spring of 1969, she had spent thirteen years at the school. She was a strange girl, very bright and sensitive, with a somewhat ethereal manner. With her tall, slim figure and her blonde looks she could have been very beautiful if she hadn't always seemed to be apologizing for being there. She continually stooped, and paid no attention whatsoever to her appearance, with the result that she looked twice her age. Nonnie's relations with Dr B were very particular. He was not charmed by her, but deeply moved by her obvious distress, and her fierce desire to calm the sufferings of the children in her charge. Later, Bettelheim would say of Nonnie that of all the people he had known, she was 'the one who came closest to being a saint'. That was not exactly a compliment; it was a reference to Nonnie's self-sacrificing tendency. For a long time, the young woman had refused payment, considering that the personal progress she was making at the school was ample compensation for her work. When Bettelheim finally did persuade her to put the cheques in the bank, she promptly donated the money to charity.

Nonnie's and Bettelheim's backgrounds had enough in common – a painful childhood, a desire to make amends for some perceived sin, physical self-hatred, great sensitivity and intelligence – for him to have seen something of himself in her. More importantly, Nonnie's own condition when she arrived at the school was such that she could in fact have been admitted as a patient, and hers seems to have been the first case in which Bettelheim thought he could actually heal a counsellor at the same time as she was healing children. This was not always to the liking of the other counsellors. Karen Zelan, for example, recalls a time when Nonnie was off sick. Not only did the others have to take turns looking after her group, but Dr B also asked them to sit at her bedside. When Zelan went to him in exasperation and told him she had had enough of listening to Nonnie talking about the wonderful vacation she would take once she was better, Bettelheim shot back: 'If the school can't take care of a Nonnie, then I wonder what the point of it is? Don't you know that that's the way one gets better, by fantasizing about better times?'

At the same time, Bettelheim was by no means easy on Nonnie. She was in therapy with him, but he never let her get off lightly, and she came in for more than her share of singling-out in staff meetings. Over the years, she had become a very good counsellor, showing particular skill with the more severely disturbed children. One of her dreams was to open a school for autistic children only – an idea which Bettelheim disliked because he felt that for the latter to be surrounded by less deranged children helped bring them out of their isolation. In the summer of 1969, Nonnie went off on vacation with her boyfriend, another counsellor. Bettelheim disapproved of the relationship, considering that the young man was not good enough for her (he often reacted that way when one of his favourite female counsellors took an interest in another member of the team). Then, on their way home, the two had a car crash. The young man, who was driving, survived, but Nonnie died.

Sorrow, guilt or anger: it was difficult to tell which of these three emotions was uppermost in Bettelheim's mind. His first reaction was to call Nonnie's boyfriend to tell him never to set foot in the school again. 'The children might kill you,' he told him. Geneviève Jurgensen, who arrived at the school the following year, adds: 'And not only the children.' In fact, that crash marked a turning-point in Bettelheim's life. Needless to say, he could never accept that it had been simply an accident. Even in front of the children, he hinted that the counsellor had deliberately killed Nonnie. A short time afterwards, during a TV interview, he also complained about the indifference shown by the other members of the staff to the young woman's death, asserting that in a kibbutz, the whole community would have gone into mourning. Much later, in California, he told Karen Zelan that he had been trying out a new method with Nonnie, which gave Zelan an insight into why her death had plunged him into such a crisis.

Nonnie's death came at a time of great agitation in Bettelheim's life. Ever since his sixtieth birthday, three years earlier, he had been worried about who would succeed him as the head of the school. And while he had always been given to hypochondria, he was now beginning to have some serious health problems, notably circulatory difficulties in his legs. In 1966, he had also been operated on for a cataract. Just before the operation, he had taken aside, one at a time, some of the most experienced counsellors and told them that if he came out blind, which was possible, he intended to commit suicide. He asked them if he could count on them to see the school through the inevitable transitional period should that occur.

Politics was another source of worry. First there was the Middle East, where Israel's lightning victory in the Six Day War had indeed given the lie to the image of the helpless Jew, but had also increased the country's isolation.[10] In the United States, the protest movement was building up and, the previous year, the Democratic Convention had attracted to Chicago the entire spectrum of its components – anti-Vietnam War activists, Black Panthers, hippies, etc. The violence of the clashes with the police had shocked America.

The University of Chicago was far away from the city centre, where the convention was held, and for five months after the event it seemed that the campus would remain untouched by the fires of protest sweeping the rest of the nation. But at the end of January 1969, the flames took hold in the Sociology Department now chaired by Morris Janowitz. The spark that set them off was the university's refusal to renew the contract of a young lecturer. She was one of two women in the department, and she was a radical.[11] The decision triggered off a sit-in by a group of students. Janowitz, caught off guard, spent a whole night negotiating with them, but to no avail. It was not long before the protesters were also occupying the administration building, an unheard-of event in the U of C. The crisis was finally resolved after two weeks; a number of students were expelled but Edward Levy, the university's president, refrained from calling in the police. That fact is still a subject of pride for many a faculty member.

Bruno Bettelheim was not directly affected by these events, either in the Orthogenic School or in his classes. He nevertheless jumped into the arena right from day one. At a press conference, he described the protesting students as paranoid, and went so far as to compare them to the members of the Hitler youth movement who were storming the faculties of Germany when he was still in Vienna! Up until that point, his name had not even been mentioned in the protests. From then on, he became a prime target for the protesters.

The reasons for Bettelheim's thus placing himself in the forefront of the opposition to a handful of students, whose demands hardly went beyond the framework of campus affairs, were no doubt many. There was the fact that his friend Morris Janowitz was in the students' firing line. And there were his memories. The University of Chicago and, beyond, the United States had saved his life and allowed him to fulfil his childhood dreams. He could not stand to see them be attacked. It is also possible that he was genuinely afraid. A few months later, on a visit to a former student then living in Cambridge, Massachusetts, Bettelheim suddenly let drop: 'All of this will be bad for the Jews.'[12] He was not the only Holocaust survivor to have a gut reaction to the 1968-69 events. Others, both in Chicago and elsewhere, reacted instinctively and irrationally to the wave of unrest which all of a sudden seemed to threaten all the major democracies. In France, the leading sociologist Raymond Aron, who was also Jewish, admitted later that the May 1968 student revolt had frightened him. But, above all, Bettelheim's reaction to the campus occupation – a mere tea-party compared to what was going on in other US colleges – seems to be symptomatic of his state of mind in the last years of his tenure at the O.S. It was a disproportionate, passionate reaction, testifying first and fore-most to his state of anxiety. It is however worth noting that, once he succeeded in channelling it, that anxiety encompassed most of the themes he was to work on after leaving the school, and which would figure in *A Good Enough Parent*.

Once calm had returned to the campus, Bettelheim outlined his view-point in an interview with the *Chicago Sun-Times*.[13] The protesters' anger resulted from their own self-hatred, he said. 'They are so unable to make a go in this world that they feel the only way they can [do so] is by destroying it – so the chaos in the external world will be comparable to the chaos in the internal world.'[14] Their behaviour was thus 'an extreme defensive maneuver to avoid a total, a complete break with reality'. These shocking assertions were only for starters. What made Bettelheim really angry was what he saw as the failure of the young people's parents. They had brought up their offspring both spoiled and unloved, and had thus failed to play their required roles. It was in such terms, going far beyond the events of Chicago, that Bettelheim was to discuss the youth protest movement over the following three or four years. He would repeat his viewpoint in the newspapers, on TV, in lectures, and also in testimony to the many committees that would be set up to study the problem in both houses of Congress.

If the leaders of the movement reminded him of the fascist students he had known in his youth, he explained,[15] it was because he was struck by their blanket condemnations of the 'Establishment', just as the German youth had lashed out at *Das System*. He was also shocked to hear of books being once again burned, thirty-five years on, in Berlin. He saw other parallels between the present-day student leaders and those of his youth: their anti-intellectualism, and their 'moral absolutism', the unshakeable conviction that they held the high ground. Even though the aims of the two groups were very different, he saw both as 'true believers', rather than as adults who had made a reasoned, thought-out choice. 'Revolution without a definite picture of what the future would be like when the revolution is over, can only contribute to the creation of a well-founded anxiety,' he wrote.

Bettelheim believed the young people rebelled because they felt the new technological society had no need for them. 'It is unnatural to keep a young person for some 20 years in dependency,' he said in the *Chicago Sun-Times* interview.[16] 'I think this may be a way of life for a small élite which always in the past went to universities .... In the past, the vast majority of young people, when they were at the height of their physical strength – which is around 20 – were active meeting life outside, proving themselves as men or women .... Now we pay them all to go to school. Which makes them dependent when they should be, psychologically speaking, independent. And this is a very hard thing to take.' The post-war generation of young people was generally believed to have been brought up according to liberal and permissive principles, but that was in fact an illusion, he went on. In reality, their parents only 'indulged them when it was convenient [for them]'. And there had been a price to pay, as the parents were in effect saying to their children: ' "I indulge you now. But for that you have to be the brightest kid in school. Haven't I let you have the bottle? Now you go and be a whiz in school." '

What Bettelheim found particularly striking among the student leaders was the discrepancy between their over-developed intellects and their lack of emotional maturity. Many of them were still at the stage of temper-tantrums, Bettelheim said. He saw such immaturity and unease with society as resulting from repressed desires, the absence of strong role models (fathers working far away, spending what little time they had at home hiding behind a newspaper or watching TV), and a failure on the part of authority figures fully to accept their authority. On the grounds that children should not be repressed, modern parents had failed to teach them to deal with either their desires or their aggressivity. And to avoid having to incur their offspring's displeasure, they had not been strict enough when giving orders. Victorian-style education had at least had the merit of being coherent, whereas its modern counterpart was shot through with contradictions. Even worse, what repression there was was carried out in the interests not of the children, but in that of their parents.

Politically, this period saw Bruno Bettelheim lining up once and for all with the conservative camp. He defended the US involvement in Vietnam, was outraged by the exposure of the Watergate affair and the impeachment of Richard Nixon, and was later to become an active Ronald Reagan supporter. On all major political issues, he thus found himself in the opposite camp from many of the people who were most attracted to his theories about madness; the contrast is striking. Yet, Bettelheim's political views nevertheless point to a central tenet of his thought. After having spent a quarter-century trying to heal those left behind by the liberal methods of upbringing, fed on half-digested notions of Freudianism, that were then in vogue among the middle classes in the United States, Bruno Bettelheim was convinced of one fundamental thing: a good parent is one who fully accepts and plays out the role of an adult in relation to his or her child. This may sound obvious, but it is not. A good parent, according to Bettelheim, is someone who lets the child be a child by not forcing him to think when he should be playing, or to try and deal with the problems of the adult world before he is mature enough to do so. A child should not have to grapple with the problems of his parents, to share their concerns or try and console them, Bettelheim believed. The child's role is to grow up, to take advantage of his childhood to learn about life, and become a strong individual. The parents' role is to create an environment in which that process can best take place, and to set limits to that environment by exercising authority. And also, at every opportunity, to seek out the 'happy ending' to each problem, which will foster the child's desire to live and to grow.

This idea, so apparently simple but so difficult to apply in practice, in fact sums up the whole of Bettelheim's theory as regards upbringing. The role he thus assigned to parents was a tough one, as he deprived them of the right to themselves act like children, i.e. to demand understanding and indulgence from their offspring. To play such a role unfailingly at all times is impossible. Parents are also human beings, liable to be overcome by their emotions and behave in ways detrimental to their children. To pretend otherwise was to show excessive intransigence and once again to put forward valuable advice in too rigorous a tone, as Bettelheim was to do in *A Good Enough Parent*. But that exasperated, peremptory tone was probably the expression of an inner vicious circle: that impossible adult role was the one his family had assigned to him from the earliest age. It was the only role Bettelheim knew how to play spontaneously – and the one he had once again felt compelled to adopt when faced with the student revolt, at a time when many of his colleagues preferred to line up without a murmur alongside those who were attacking them. He was incapable of abandoning that role with anyone but Trude. With other people he never allowed the child within him to express itself – except by moaning about his health problems. And now, at the end of the 1960s, when he was weighed down with both responsibilities and honours – celebrations of the twenty-fifth anniversary of his arrival at the school, various distinctions and titles – it was as though the balance between the responsible adult and the inner child had finally collapsed. As if, for having been too long repressed, the child in Bettelheim would on occasion take over, making him demanding, megalomaniac, provocative and determined to ignore all 'boundaries'.

The day Bettelheim learned of Nonnie's death, the Orthogenic School was practically empty. Kathy Lubin, who had stopped living in after her marriage, had invited most of the counsellors to a bridal 'shower', or pre-wedding gift party, for Diana Grossman. As the event was mostly for Diana's friends, she had not invited the latest arrival at the school, who had been there only a few days. Her name was Candace Hilldrup and she was an unusual girl. Pretty and very intelligent, she hid a secret personality behind an outgoing exterior. She was petite, and her long red hair stretched down below the waist. She would pin it up when with the children, but at other times she let it loose. Coupled with her bouncy way of walking this gave her something of a wild-animal look.

Candy, as she was known, had abandoned a budding career as a modern dancer[17] to come to the school. Her real age was twenty-one, but within herself she felt no more than fifteen. (Her first impression on meeting Dr B was that he looked like Mr Magoo; but, 'as soon as he came in, his presence filled the living-room'.[18]) She had been born into a modest family in rural Virginia and felt very naïve and very lonely in trying to cope with growing up. Beside dancing, Candy had been studying psychology at the University of Virginia, when one of her teachers had brought to her attention a job offer from the O.S. Neither dancing nor her classes had succeeded in helping her sort out the very violent and conflicting emotions that her mother's recent death, after a long and harrowing illness, had triggered in her. Then she read *Love is Not Enough* and two other books by Bettelheim and felt that a door had suddenly opened, and a void been filled. In the short life-history she had to send with her application to the Orthogenic School, she chose to be totally candid about the mixed feelings that made life so hard for her to face.

Perhaps it was the fact that Candy happened to be around when he received the news about Nonnie's death that made her so special in Bettelheim's eyes, as Kathy Lubin seems to think. Or perhaps it was her undeniable physical resemblance, in spite of differences in age and complexion, to his first wife Gina. It could have been that she also had something of Karen Zelan, or again the fact that she was a dancer, just as Karen was a pianist. Or else her straightforwardness in asking questions about the things that worried her, or her obvious intuition. Or it may have been the combination of all of the above in one young woman who was very ill at ease with herself and yet proud, lively and amusing. What is certain is that the complicity that developed between Candace Hilldrup and Bruno Bettelheim was special. It was clear that she needed him: 'I should not have come here as a counsellor,' she kept thinking, 'but as a child.' As he had done with Nonnie, he would care for her, teaching her to respect herself, while she was caring for the children. But with Candy, he would succeed. Because, with her, things were different: she could make him laugh, she moved him, in short he loved her.

Candy Hilldrup thus became his baby, his favourite child. She was good at imitations, and she could easily amuse him by mimicking the voices or gestures of those around them. They shared a passion for the Middle Ages, and would tell each other marvellous stories about knights, princesses and dragons. They would leave one another little messages, or spring surprises on each other. Some people suggested that maybe other things went on as well, after the last staff meeting, when Candy would go into Dr B's office for her daily session, occasionally dressed in the cotton jump-suit which served as her pyjamas, and obviously impervious to the black looks she got from the other counsellors in therapy, who had only weekly appointments with him. Such suggestions however show a total misunderstanding of the nature of Candy's relationship to Bettelheim, or rather they project on to that relationship fantasies which were alien to it. Bettelheim felt that Candy needed to regress to get at the source of her problems, and she was totally, avidly, ready to do so. She had blind faith in the man she still refers to as her 'Poppa'. He, while remaining in control of the exercise, found in it the opportunity he badly needed to indulge the child in himself. Having since become a psychoanalyst herself, Candace Hilldrup sums up the situation as follows: 'The relationship between us was pure affect, a meeting of spirits. There was no intellectualization, and therefore no resistance. Dr B had that type of relation with some children, girls in particular, the ones he could feed by hand, hold, rock, etc.'

For all that, Bettelheim had not lost sight of his role as head of the Orthogenic School, and thus the good of his children. Candy was totally devoted to the latter. At the time, her life had but one focus, Bettelheim, and two fields of expression: the children and her therapy with him. As had Karen Zelan and Geneviève Jurgensen among others, she found the first few days at the school very tough. 'The children were getting so much emotional attention there, people were so involved with them, that they treated newcomers with arrogance, almost with scorn, and they verbalized it. They didn't need you, and you had to prove that you had something to offer before they came to you. It took months.' Very soon, however, she had created a strong relationship with a group of girls. It was not Kathy's group, which Bettelheim had singled out for her at first, but the dormitory next door. After a couple of weeks, therefore, she was exceptionally allowed to switch groups. This was not the first time Bettelheim bent the rules of the school for Candy. He had already done so by allowing her to keep her nickname, which under normal regulations she would have had to change, as it carried too much of a symbolic charge. But Candy had not wanted to drop it, and Dr B had yielded.

Food in fact played an important role in their relationship. At the end of Candy's second day in the school, Bettelheim asked her for her impressions. 'It's the eatingest place I've seen,' she commented. That was the first thing she could think of. Since the morning she had enjoyed three full meals with the children, plus three snacks and a late-evening drink with her fellow counsellors. At lunch, she had been seated next to an anorexic, and had watched another girl vomiting into her plate and then eating her own vomit. Candy, who was herself prone to anorexic attacks, had found that pretty hard to take. She had nevertheless resolved to carry on eating, being determined to show willing – and also being greatly impressed by the food at the school. She not only completed the piece of German chocolate cake she had been eating, but helped herself to another one. 'If they don't keep me on, at least I won't have missed out on that,' she told herself, between mouthfuls.

Bettelheim was clearly delighted at her 'eatingest' neologism. 'That's a good sign,' he told her. He himself was fond of his food, although he tried to keep an eye on his waistline. In particular, he had a pronounced sweet tooth ('When I was a baby, my nurse used to put a piece of chocolate under my tongue to help me go to sleep,' he once told Candy). He was interested in 'oral' problems, and was particularly skilful at treating anorexics. Their manifest will to achieve total control over their bodies struck a chord in him, and he was often the only person capable of finding the word or gesture that could persuade them to give up their life-threatening abstinence.

Candy had several anorexic girls in her group, and she too knew how to get through to them (as, indeed, did Karen Zelan and several of Bettelheim's favourite counsellors). In fact, she had the type of intuition which Bettelheim valued most; the kind which short-circuits the mind's reasoning system to act directly through gestures and affect, from unconscious to unconscious, as he used to say. Shortly before her arrival, the school had taken in 'Erin', and Candy soon became the only person capable of calming her down when she started shrieking, attacking and biting herself. Step by step, the little autistic girl began to take an interest in the outside world. She would learn to read and write. But she could not bear being held by anyone other than Candy.

Bettelheim was convinced that Candy had the potential to be a truly great counsellor. His affection for her probably blinded him to the climate that their highly exclusive relationship created around them. But he would never have devoted so much time to the young woman if he had not been convinced that her influence on the children was beneficial. A few years earlier, he had brought to the school an Israeli poetess to whom he was clearly very attached. But she had not survived more than a couple of weeks, as it soon became clear that her over-excited behaviour was detrimental to the kids. His powerful sense of duty had come into play and he had not hesitated to ask her to leave.

Candy was unstinting in her devotion to her girls. After a year, she was seeing three of them, including little 'Erin', for individual sessions. A few other girls were attracted to her, and she found time for them too.

Bettelheim had also asked her to give the children dance classes. Some of the boys, notably Charles Pekow and Ronald Angres, found this humiliating. But there again, Candy threw herself wholeheartedly into the task, fascinated by the new possibilities that Dr B's teaching opened up for her even in that field. The two of them also shared a passion for festivals and parties, and notably for Christmas, which was Dr B's favourite holiday and a major event at the school, because it celebrates a birth – that of the child in each of us, as he put it.

One Monday evening, a few weeks after her arrival, Candy was suddenly gripped by severe anxiety, for no apparent reason. Bettelheim was not at the school, and she found herself unable to calm down and shake off the feeling that something terrible was happening. Finally, she went into his empty office and left a little note on his desk, saying 'I'm very frightened. Please, don't die.' The following morning, during the staff meeting, Bettelheim suddenly announced: 'Do you know we have a psychic person among us?' He went on to explain how, the previous evening, a group of angry students had knocked on his door at home. When he opened up, he had found himself face-to-face with a gun! 'At the very same time, that person felt that my life was theatened,' he concluded, enigmatically. The following summer, while on vacation in Europe, Candy sent him a postcard of *Eva*, a painting by Ernst Fuchs. And on her return she found that Bettelheim, who was also on vacation, had sent her the very same card!

A few of the other women counsellors liked Candy, but others detested her. Many of them from jealousy, as Bettelheim's attachment to her was so obvious.[19] But others disliked her because, while acknowledging her qualities, they thought her too unstable and too much in need of help herself to carry on wholly beneficial relations with the children. What is sure is that Candy, wrapped up as she was in her relationship with Bettelheim and her work with the children, was a walking, talking provocation. She appeared unaware of other people, and was both excessive and exclusive. She saw herself as a fifteen-year-old, so she wore schoolgirl-style skirts. To other eyes, however, she was a young woman with miniskirts so skimpy as to border on indecency. And Dr B, who was generally so prudish on such issues, said nothing. One year, Candy went to the regular New Year party at the Bettelheim home decked out in an extraordinary medieval princess's dress, with long skirts and a Tyrolean-style bodice covered with hearts. She had chosen it for him, of course, but the other guests found it shocking. Being ill at ease with what she saw as idle chatter, Candy vanished in the course of the evening with Eric, Bettelheim's son, providing yet more grist for the rumour mill. In fact, the two were upstairs, thumbing through family pictures and, later, jumping up and down on the Bettelheims' bed having a mighty pillow fight!

Leslie Cleaver arrived at the school a month after Candy, at the same time as two other newcomers. She does not harbour animosity towards Candy, but nevertheless considers her presence at the school to have been disturbing and detrimental for the children. She cites Bettelheim's 'mega-lomania' at that time, which led him to believe that he could handle everything at once: taking care of both Candy and the children, while also ensuring respect for the very limits which he himself was flouting. As for what this end-of-an-era atmosphere may have revealed about Bettelheim's own inner anxieties and psychological needs, although she acknowledges them today, Cleaver feels that such considerations had no place at the school. Dr B's role did not include sharing his own problems with the staff.

In August 1963, Ruth Marquis visited Bettelheim at the school on his sixtieth birthday. On entering his office, she was thunderstruck at the sight of his desk: there was not a single scrap of paper in sight. 'I have to settle all my affairs. Now that I'm old, I must retire,' her friend told her, in a lugubrious tone of voice.

Six years later, however, the issue was still pending. Over the years, Bruno Bettelheim had hinted to several of the men who had worked with him that they could become his successor. Notably George Kaiser, and a few of the psychoanalysts who had worked at the school as consultants. In 1964, when Ugo Formigoni, tired of spending his days changing sheets and putting children to bed, decided to leave and seek a post more in line with his qualifications, Bettelheim had told him as he passed the door: 'When I think that I wanted to make you my successor!' He was very fond of the charming Italian. In 1962, he had devoted much effort to getting him a permanent residency permit, citing his exceptional and irreplaceable activities at the school. And Formigoni had the added advantage of being a qualified doctor. But Bettelheim was angry at him for his departure. After leaving the school, Formigoni headed a psychiatric service in which Bettelheim worked as a consultant, and the resulting inversion of their roles did not help matters. Ugo Formigoni was no doubt hoping that Bettelheim would call, but he did not.

There was also Lou Harper, head of the teaching team, who had been at the school for twenty years. Bettelheim trusted him totally. He was everything that he was not: tall, fair-haired and calm. With Harper, most problems got solved via peaceable means. 'That's the way it is: I'm slow at getting angry,' he says, matter-of-factly.[20] All the children loved him and found him a reassuring figure. But Lou had never taken the time to get a PhD.

When the time came, it was Ben Wright whom Bettelheim tried to persuade to succeed him. He fitted the bill perfectly: he had the required diplomas, was perfectly at ease with the university hierarchy, knew the school very well and was loyal to it. Bettelheim did everything in his power to persuade him to take on the job, telling him that the school's future depended on it. But Ben Wright knew what the task involved. He did not feel capable of taking on Bettelheim's mantle, and was in any case not prepared to make the required sacrifices in his private life. He stood firm in his refusal.

In the meantime Bert Cohler, one of the school's great success stories, had obtained his PhD in clinical psychology from Harvard, something Bettelheim knew about from Cohler's regular visits. In April 1969, Yale University had just offered him a lectureship, when Bettelheim came to Boston for a conference. Afterwards, as Bert was driving him to the airport, Bettelheim, looking gloomy, suddenly told him that the school was going to have to close unless he, Cohler, agreed to step into his shoes. The young man, then aged just twenty-nine, barely hesitated. Although he knew full well that a teacher's life at Yale would be far easier and more pleasant, his devotion to Dr B and the Orthogenic School won out. His wife agreed with the choice.

The Cohlers thus returned to Chicago in the fall of 1969. At first, Bert's position was a strange one. In the university directory and on his pay slips, he was identified as the school's deputy director, but Bettelheim had not breathed a word about that to the counsellors. He took Cohler with him everywhere he went, introducing him to the managerial sides of the job, but clearly wanted him to impose his authority on his own. Or perhaps he was simply probing him. In the end, it was Cohler himself who informed the staff of his status. Little by little, Bettelheim began to bow out, leaving Bert to take the major decisions on his own, even if he laid the groundwork for them. In December 1970, for instance, it was Bert Cohler who officially hired Geneviève Jurgensen. But it had been Bettelheim who had spotted her at the university, and asked her if she would like to come and work for the school.

In the event of disagreements, however, Bettelheim now let Cohler have the last word. The director-to-be thus admitted, against Bettelheim's advice, the little autistic girl whom Geneviève was to care for. As he stated in a staff meeting, Bettelheim considered that to begin with, Bert Cohler should concentrate on less serious cases, so as to start out with a few successes and thereby gain self-assurance. But of course Bert wanted to measure up to his mentor, by undertaking the same impossible tasks as him, and without delay. Had not Bettelheim called on him in an emergency, giving him the impression that the school's survival depended on him?

Even before Bettelheim left for Palo Alto, in California, where the Center for the Advanced Study of Behavioral Sciences had invited him to spend a sabbatical, the trap that was to doom the Cohler directorship had already been sprung. Unlike some of his critics, however, I do not think that Bettelheim had created it intentionally; he may have become very manipulative, but he was never Machiavellian. And although he had a hard time handing over the reins of what he often called, in letters from this period, his 'life's work', he had no desire to see his school disappear. Far from it: at a time when his authority was being noisily challenged by people who, a few years earlier, would no doubt have been the first to be enthused by his ideas, and when psychoanalysis was beginning to lose ground in the United States, he ardently desired to see the school accepted once and for all as a respectable and unchallengeable university institution.

It was shortly after Cohler's return to Chicago that Bettelheim made his comment about the 'obscure secret' in his life. It came around Christmas, after Bettelheim had just seen an advance copy of the cover story that the *New York Times Magazine* would devote to him and the school in early January. He had been very agitated, asserting that he risked being ejected from the university, or even from the United States altogether. In Bert's recollection the incident has certainly been over-dramatized, since it disturbed him considerably. But considering this anecdote in the light of others that betrayed Bettelheim's inner turmoil at that time, it seems likely that he was once again grappling with his feeling of fraud. In fact the article, in which he was presented as 'Dr No, the anti-Dr Spock', contained only the usual exaggerations (about his psychoanalytic training, Patsy, Eleanor Roosevelt). However, seeing them put together in a newspaper that was read all round the world, Bettelheim must suddenly have been confronted with a terrible mirror-image of himself, at the very time when he was preparing to leave for ever the sanctuary that he had spent twenty-six years of his life creating. To shelter children who suffered, but also to shelter himself. A sanctuary – the term is also used by the writer of the article – which he could only hand over to someone who knew it from the inside, as it also contained a few secrets.

Bert Cohler had the required diplomas to put the school firmly on the academic map, awarded by the most prestigious US university of all, and he had undergone a regular psychoanalysis. This is why, contrary to what he himself appears to believe, I doubt that Bettelheim ever saw him as a second-best choice to succeed him. Nor was he used as a sacrificial lamb, sent to the slaughter for the sole purpose of proving that Dr B was irreplaceable. Far from it; the daring yet splendid idea of handing over the school to one of its former students was an extraordinarily ambitious one. If it had worked out, it would have proved not only that Bettelheim was a remarkable therapist, but also that his analysis of psychological ailments was exactly right. The wheel would have turned full circle, and his mission been accomplished beyond his wildest dreams: the perfect 'happy ending'. That he had this in mind is confirmed by his correspondence with Augusta Wallace Lyons, Tom's mother. He referred to Cohler's appointment to run the school as the fulfilment of a dream, and expressed genuine joy at the young man's decision to accept the proposal.[21]

Bettelheim could not but have realized that Bert Cohler was too young to be his successor. He must have known that he would not be able to keep the counsellors in line as he had done, possessing neither his authority nor his experience, and being fresh out of university. But Bert's progress since his departure from the school, not only in college but also in his private life, had impressed Bettelheim. Cohler was uniquely qualified to take over. He was intelligent, loyal and good. He knew the school's philosophy almost as well as Bettelheim did himself: the constant attention to the children's well-being, the need to make them feel that their actions had an impact on the outside world, the use of empathy, etc.; it was all totally familiar. And family, too, as it was how he had himself grown up. Bettelheim could count on him. Sure, he was young, but that could prove to be an advantage in giving the school a more up-to-date image. Over time, he would find his own style and impose his authority.

Of course, these thoughts – reconstructed from confidences Bettelheim made to various people around him – did not prevent him from being very disturbed about having to abandon his school to another man. But his ambivalence expressed itself more through Bettelheim's relations with his chosen successor than through his acts. As regards introductions, and the responsibilities that he gradually handed over, he did the necessary for Bert Cohler, much more than he would do for Jacquelyn Sanders later on. But when he had been a student, Bert had had to come to terms with the fact that, even though Dr B liked him well enough, he would never be one of his favourites. He did not have enough charm, or was not sufficiently sick, for that. In his group, Dr B's favourite had been Sandy Lewis, who was tall, fair-haired and arrogant. Bert had learned to live with the disappointment, but twenty years later by making him feel that he was only his second choice, at precisely the time when he was asking him to assert himself, Bettelheim could only undermine him.

1970 had been a year of intense activity for Bettelheim. With Bert Cohler easing himself into the job, he was undertaking ever more lectures and trips. He was interviewed about the student revolt and *The Children of the Dream*, which had just come out. *The Empty Fortress* had been published in France, where it had achieved enormous success. He was being showered with honours and appointments, and invited to speak all over the country. But he was still not freed from his obligations, conflicts and other problems. This was the time when he had learned of the existence of Tom Lyons' manuscript, without having yet read it, and also the time of the incident with little 'Erin'.[22] When he was in Chicago, Bettelheim was still very much the director, while he was also giving his classes and even seeing a group of mothers every three weeks. He let Bert chair the staff meetings, but it was still he who had the last word, and to whom people turned with their really tough problems.

Bert Cohler had begun changing the rules somewhat, to adapt them to his own management style. As of January 1970, he informed the staff that there was to be no more hitting the children: 'Control must remain verbal.' Shortly after that, he announced that tears were to be proscribed during counsellors' meetings. 'That type of exhibition is unnecessary between responsible adults,' he stated. As of July 1970, Bettelheim formally handed over the reins of power. A year later, on June 27, 1971, after a few moving yet discreet farewell dinners, he left the school in the evening, as usual, but did not return the next morning.

Just over a week later, Candy got a postcard showing the 'Lady and the Unicorn' tapestry from a Paris museum. 'In a fashion the only way I can put my second life behind me is to return to the first one, in Europe, only I am no longer at home there either,' Bettelheim wrote from that city. He had tried to hide it, but although he had finally allowed himself to retire, he was very frightened by the prospect. No more children to look after or counsellors to train, no more of the responsibilities that had weighed him down. The only remaining one being to enjoy life. Having Trude at his side, discreet in public but dynamic in private, was a great help. After the trip to France, they visited Central Europe, and then spent a few days in Vienna at a psychoanalytic congress. ('Life here is so much more relaxed than in the States, but unfortunately it is a dying city, living on the glories of its past .... To be and feel a stranger in the place where one has spent more than half one's life, I find this time particularly difficult as I am surrounded by American analysts who rave about the city that so utterly expelled and robbed me,' he wrote.[23]) Then on to Salzburg for the festival, a visit to Emmi and Bertel von Radanowicz in Switzerland, and a two-week safari in Kenya, the last requested by Trude but enjoyed by Bruno more than he had expected. In all, the longest holiday the Bettelheims had ever taken together.

Arriving in Palo Alto in early September, Bruno Bettelheim was clearly in a better mood. He was rested, and generally pleased with the house the couple had rented on the Stanford campus, even though he remained harsh in his criticism of American ways. ('In Europe, even poor people manage to make their home very comfortable. In the house we rented, there isn't a comfortable chair, and the light is so miserable that one hardly sees what one eats, not to speak about reading. The only two places with good lighting – and that is neon which I hate – is the kitchen and the study. Obviously where one works (the wife in the kitchen, the prof in the study) one can have some semblance of adequate equipment, but where the family supposedly lives, no.'[24]) Delighted with the garden, Trude had immediately dismissed the Japanese gardener who tended it, and busied herself once again with hoes and rakes.

Being located just far enough from San Francisco to avoid the ever-present mists of that city, and even further from the heat and smog of Los Angeles, Palo Alto has offered many a stressed-out East Coast or Midwestern academic the ideal venue for a sabbatical. Not even Bruno Bettelheim was entirely immune to its villagey charm. The climate was easier on his aches and pains than that of Chicago and he was not alone in the area. Several of his former colleagues or students were teaching at Stanford University, and others, such as Fritz Redl or Morris Janowitz, had preceded him as fellows at the Center for the Advanced Study of Behavioral Sciences. Janowitz had been his sponsor for the sabbatical, but that had been a mere formality, as the Center had in fact been founded by Ralph Tyler, in 1954, with a Ford Foundation grant that was part of the same programme from which Bettelheim had benefited for the Orthogenic School. The premises of this high-level 'think-tank' were located slightly away from the university, on a small wooded hill overlooking the campus. Each year it took in around fifty fellows, selected on the basis of their potential complementarity, in the hope that their interdisciplinary contacts would advance the cause of knowledge. In addition to their scholarships they were provided with typists and researchers, leaving them completely free from material considerations, with nothing to do but think. As if to underline the fact, their small studies were not even fitted with telephones, something of which Bettelheim frequently complained in his letters. The only formal obligation for fellows was to produce a report on their stay, but Ralph Tyler took great pride in the large number of books written, either wholly or in part, while they were his guests.

'Being out here with no other purpose but to write, I find writing nearly impossible and I realize how closely all my writing was really connected with the daily clinical experience. Suddenly nothing comes to mind.'[25] A week after his arrival at the Center, the fact that he was now in retirement, far from his school, was finally brought home to Bruno Bettelheim. He had initially planned to devote the year to the last volume of his trilogy on the school; after *Love is Not Enough*, which dealt with general principles, and *Truants from Life*, which discussed the children, he wanted to focus on the counsellors, explaining how their understanding of their own problems helped them to better care for their charges. Before leaving Chicago, he had gathered all his notes and writings on the subject, and ordered them sent to him, first class mail and recorded delivery. But his orders had not been followed and the package had got lost.

Fortunately, Bettelheim was by then interested in another project. 'What I would really like to do here,' he wrote to Ruth Marquis on his arrival, 'is the book on children and how to raise them. More and more I feel a need for it, and particularly of a book that sees the kid in contact (or, if you want, emotional back and forth) with the parent. That is, I would like to write something that is impossibly difficult to bring off, though it makes such good sense to me in theory: We know perfectly well what makes the child tick. We know preciously little of what it does to the parent, though this is what has the greatest impact on the child. Analysts seem to have studied adults only as children, and never as parents, or if so, only in respect to their own childhood residues. But there is in addition a great chunk of reality in a parent's attitude to the child, and today more so than ever because parents are so dumbfounded by their kids though they understand them so much better than other generations. So there is a problem: We know so much better what makes them tick, and are so much less able to live with them.'[26]

So the book which was eventually to appear as *A Good Enough Parent* in 1987, could just as well have been called *What Makes a Parent?* – indeed a question which is very rarely asked. As he is writing here to his old friend and former editor, with whom he has already discussed the issue, Bettelheim's form of words is too concise for us to see exactly where he is heading. We can nevertheless surmise that he is touching on one of psychoanalysis's grey areas. Alongside the image created in the child's mind, who exactly is the parent, how does he or she function as such (and not simply as former child) when communicating, consciously or unconsciously, with the child? Was he inspired by the proximity of the Palo Alto Mental Research Institute, the cradle of 'family therapy'? Or was it that, being deprived of his school, he had begun thinking about his relationships with his own children? The book, which was to be over twelve years in the writing, unfortunately does not provide explicit answers to the questions raised in that letter. But once again Bruno Bettelheim's vigorous drive to forever further his quest for understanding human relations, as disrespectful of labels as he was of the boundaries between disciplines, is worth noting.

Almost as soon as they had moved into their new home, the Bettelheims undertook to visit the many friends, both working and retired, they had in the Bay Area. Three weeks later, Bruno was writing to Ruth Marquis about another idea. He had recently seen two friends who were no longer able to write due to strokes, and as he was still suffering from writer's block, he had been moved to 'put my literary house in order' by compiling a collection of essays. 'I haven't put much thought into the selection, but here are some articles I liked when I wrote them .... Maybe I'm looking for an easy way out. If so, what's wrong with that?'[27] he asked, as if trying to convince himself. The selection he went on to make was highly eclectic and lacked a common thread, but it contained many of the essays which would eventually make up *Surviving*. It would be another six years before he actually put together that work, however, which highlights the fact that for Bettelheim, the longest and most difficult part of any book was always the ordering of ideas, the drawing out of meaning. The gift that struck everyone who knew him, and for which he was most admired – that of intuitively sizing up a situation and the essence of human relations – was 'what came simplest to me', as he told Madeleine Chapsal.[28] That part was therefore not work in his eyes. Which explains, at least in part, the errors of judgement he was to make in handing over his school to a successor.

Finally, he opted for his initial project to work on during his stay in Palo Alto. The book, his last on the school, was to be titled *A Home for the Heart*, thanks again to Ruth Marquis, who vetoed his idea of calling it *The Secular Cathedral*! Bettelheim had however gone beyond his original plan to focus on the counsellors, and was considering his work as a teacher and therapist as a whole. Perhaps this was simply another way of giving form to the idea he had outlined to Ruth Marquis, or perhaps he was trying to understand his role as 'parent' to the school, to students and counsellors combined. Whatever the case, his approach betrayed a concern for coherence and order which is reminiscent of his first article on the Nazi camps. In his introduction, he reviewed all his writings, with *The Informed Heart* and *The Empty Fortress* interspersed between the books dedicated specifically to the school, and seen as necessary stages in the deepening of his understanding of mental illness, as based on his own experience. Until, that is, he cut out part of the manuscript. The book also provides an explanation for his torments while writing *The Empty Fortress*: as autism was the most serious form of mental ailment caused by non-physiological factors, he wrote, 'Success in helping autistic children would, more than anything else, establish the merit of the school's philosophy and of its methods.'[29]

He wanted to cover everything, the school's principles, its premises, method, staff, etc., in what would in effect be an appraisal of a quarter-century of work. 'A book of this sort is as much intended for the reader as it is an account to oneself. It is even more of the latter when it reports on work concluded,' he noted, in a comment he later crossed out. For as usual with Bettelheim, what was important was to make the exercise useful for others, to draw lessons from it. 'The soul of an institution is not its philosophy as such, but only as it is set into practice by the staff,' he wrote. Which was what he set out to prove.

But Bettelheim did not enjoy the peace of mind needed to carry through such a project, which implied not only reflection but also a process of mourning over the loss of the school. At the end of September he returned to Chicago, for a visit which sparked off deep anxiety, and even paranoia. Candy was by then desperate, convinced that Bert was destroying her 'Poppa''s school and that the children and herself were no longer safe. With Bettelheim gone, some of the other women were taking their revenge on her for past jealousies, and Candy's distress was contagious. That was enough to bring to the fore Bettelheim's ambivalence towards his successor. Once back in California, he kept in almost daily telephone contact with Candy, and a few others among his favourite counsellors. The situation rapidly got out of hand, with him wanting to know everything, and countermanding Bert Cohler's decisions from afar. By December 1971 Cohler could not take it any longer; he went to the university authorities and asked them to choose: Bettelheim or him. When they hummed and hawed, clearly embarrassed, he tendered his resignation, agreeing never-theless to stay on until the end of the academic year.

Bettelheim had in fact tried to fight the temptation to interfere in the school's affairs, as is confirmed by his letters to Candy: 'I think that much that happened to and around you has to do with the feeling that I am not really gone and may return any day. But after a while it will sink in that the days of my running the school are over, and what they now fight against will become the memories of the good old days.'[30] Being aware of her self-destructive anxiety, and no doubt feeling guilty at having aban-doned her too early, he sought to calm her fears, telling her he was sure that Bert would finally get it right.

In January 1972, when the University of Chicago persuaded him to return for at least a year, the time needed for another successor to be found, he sent her a long and beautiful letter to warn her that he would definitely not be staying any longer than that. For once, he talked about himself, explaining how the preceding six months had changed him. 'For a quarter of a century I lived only for the school, which meant in practice a group of people, children, staff – not everybody, some very much more than others, such as you – but I did not live, not a life of my own. Suddenly, I discovered that I do have such a life, that I want it, and equally important, that unless I do, I won't live one, as I was damn close to it last winter.'[31] It was as though he had suddenly woken up an old man. He still had things to do, useful and even important things, but he had realized that he could no longer work with the same intensity. He had started taking an afternoon nap. He regretted not having taken more care of his health earlier on, and acknowledged that when he had left the school he had been in an alarmingly run-down state, physically and also mentally. He had no intention of going through all that again. 'I do care very much about the school, but I care differently. It was "I have to do it, even if I die." Now I want to live a little longer, and do a few things in life. I no longer want to die for the school to keep it going, because as the example shows, sooner or later it will have to go without me, or become something very different.'

Which is precisely what happened. On his return to the school in July 1972, Bruno Bettelheim announced that Jacquelyn Sanders would be taking up the directorship from the start of the following academic year. Having failed in his improbable attempt to have the school run by one of its former children, he had turned to the woman he knew he could count on to play the role of the mother. He had first made another attempt to persuade Ben Wright to take up the job, but when that failed he contacted Sanders in California, where she was then bringing up her son alone after a brief, failed marriage. It was not an exciting choice, but it appeared to be a safe one. Jacquelyn Sanders had started at the school in 1952,[32] and had spent almost fourteen years there. She was the youngest child of a large family of Russian immigrants, and had been able to study at Radcliffe thanks to a scholarship. In terms of qualifications and breeding, right down to her Boston accent, she was impeccable. During their first meeting, Bettelheim had criticized her for speaking too softly, and had remarked that her photograph did not look like her. He had however approved of one thing: she did not wear red nail varnish. That at least was Sanders's recollection of their first meeting, as she was to describe it at a funeral service held for Bettelheim at the University of Chicago's Rockefeller Chapel. She recalled that he had also asked her to dress more simply when she returned the next day, and she of course obeyed. She always obeyed, and she knew how to get obedience from others.[33] Gradually, she was thus able to carve out a quite special place alongside Bettelheim. She was in charge of a boys' group, and she looked after several autists. Her devotion to the children was acknowledged by all; Karen Zelan recalls how, during her training period, she despaired of ever being capable of spending three or four hours silent and motionless while waiting for a child to get to sleep, the way 'Jacqui' did. Within a few months, however, it was Jacquelyn's turn to envy Karen, for in spite of being less rigorous and more temperamental, the latter was getting better results with her autistic children. It was also clear that Bettelheim was very sensitive to Karen's charm. Unable to be the favourite, Jacquelyn Sanders had chosen to make herself indispensable. Little by little, she had become the 'law keeper' whenever Dr B was away. When he was there, she was the faithful number two, totally devoted to him, and always putting his every wish before and above her own needs and those of others. Although a few of her colleagues called her 'the snitch' behind her back, she got on well with most of them, but with the exception of Inge she had no close friend at the school. Her desire for power was already manifest, but she had placed herself entirely at Bettelheim's disposal, going so far as regularly to make the sandwich that he usually called for at around eleven at night. Jacquelyn Sanders was intelligent, a hard worker and a good manager. As a potential director, she thus had all the qualities needed to reassure Bettelheim as to the running of the school.

As regards the rest, it is more difficult to reach an opinion. For myself, after having spent four years questioning people who knew her at the school, both during and after Bettelheim's tenure, and having met her on two occasions, Jacquelyn Sanders remains one of the institution's great enigmas. From our very first encounter, everything about her seemed to me to be at odds with what I had found important in Bettelheim's books.

It was in November 1990. Having arrived in Chicago in the midst of 'the Affair' and spoken to several of Dr B's critics, I was forced to realize that my image of him was idealized, but just how much I did not know, since I had barely started my research. In other words, I was hoping to get from his successor a more balanced, objective view of the work accomplished. After having given me a whirlwind tour of the school, Jacquelyn Sanders took me into her office for a brief discussion. She was seeing me only reluctantly and had made that very clear. A few days previously, in Washington DC, I had met Ronald Angres, the author of one of the most strongly critical articles on Bettelheim,[34] and he had shown me the dissertation that Jacquelyn Sanders devoted to him after being his counsellor for over seven years.[35] I therefore asked her: 'Would you still maintain today that Ronald was autistic?'

'Of course not,' she replied spontaneously. Then, with a start, she stated: 'I shouldn't have told you that.' Surprised, I asked her why not.

'I had warned you that I wouldn't discuss the children.'

'Don't worry. It was Ronald himself who gave me your dissertation to read. He certainly wouldn't be offended at your talking to me about it.'

She thought for one moment, and then said, with due concentration: 'If Ronald asks me – but only if he *does* ask me – I shall authorize you to go public with this.' While listening to her, everything I had read about the Orthogenic School, about the use of empathy and the creation of a very special relationship between each child and a particular adult, was racing through my mind. Unable to keep quiet any longer, I blurted out: 'Are you telling me that you, who were his main counsellor for seven years, could doubt for one minute that Ronald would like to have that awful label, which he has had to live with for the past thirty years, removed from him?' I remembered the tall man I had met in Washington, so intelligent and yet so obviously ill at ease with himself; the way he had uttered that terrible word 'autistic', both indignant and shameful, drowning the hurt in a torrent of brilliant rationalizations. Struck by my reaction, Jacquelyn Sanders gazed intently at me for several seconds, then, in the voice of a little girl who has just been caught out doing something naughty, said: 'Oh, anyone can make a mistake!' and I was unable to tell whether she was referring to the original diagnosis, or to what she had just said. Very shortly afterwards, she terminated our discussion.

The hand-over of the school to Jacquelyn Sanders did not take long; she did not require any training. On returning from California, Bettelheim had behaved too abruptly in resuming his powers, at the expense of Bert Cohler. He had straight away cancelled most of the reforms, in particular the creation of wage differentials among the staff. 'If you need a boyfriend, an analyst or an apartment, you don't belong at the school,' he had told Leslie Cleaver, after finding out that she was in therapy with Dr Flarsheim. He had also vetoed the arrangements set up by Cohler to allow counsellors to undergo therapies outside the school.

An anecdote shows just how much his forced return to the school had knocked him off balance. When he had ordered Flarsheim to stop the training for counsellors,[36] some of them, including Leslie, had written to Flarsheim to ask him to try and persuade Bettelheim to relent. Flarsheim had raised the request with Bettelheim, but without naming the counsellors who had contacted him. At the next staff meeting, Bettelheim was in a state of great agitation. 'There are traitors among us, people who are trying to destroy the school,' he said. 'Dr Flarsheim has received an anonymous letter.' He went on to say that he would seek out 'the culprits' and throw them out of the school. Leslie Cleaver called Flarsheim and asked him to try and do something.

The next day a delivery boy arrived from Marshall Fields, the big Chicago department store, with a large package addressed to the school staff. It contained a superb assortment of candies and other delicacies, along with a note from Flarsheim thanking the counsellors – without naming anyone – for their letter, and telling them that he would raise the issue with Dr B. This clever move had the required effect of calming people down, and notably Bettelheim himself, who never mentioned the question again.

A few weeks after Jacquelyn Sanders's arrival, in September, he had started withdrawing from the day-to-day running of the school, giving his classes, working in his office, but leaving her, his deputy, to keep things ticking over. Many of the counsellors had resented his imperious and erratic comeback, and had taken to avoiding him. That hurt him; he felt alone and rejected. Part of him was already no longer there. He knew that this time he would have to finally let go of his school, that he could not make a second false exit. As if to make the break more definitive, he was working flat out on his book about the school. In December, with the first draft completed, he had wanted Ruth Marquis, who had visited him in Chicago, to take the manuscript. He had the feeling he had written it all too fast, 'more to free myself and not enough to communicate with others'.[37] He expressed regret that Ruth's successor as his editor did not have her capacity for dissent. 'I need somebody who can really question my ideas,' he stressed. But Ruth Marquis had agreed only to look for a title for him. Shortly afterwards, he sent her the contents page, plus, 'since the end is in the beginning and the end is the end',[38] the first and the last two pages.

In early January, Bettelheim returned to Israel, this time with Trude. One of his former students, Seymour Fox, was in the process of setting up the Milton Centre for Education at Jerusalem's Hebrew University, and he had asked Bettelheim to head a three-month seminar on the training of teachers. Once again, Israel had an invigorating effect on him: 'Israel is exciting, tense, upsetting and all-consuming as [it was] the first time. Much has changed, and not all for the better, though people are much better off than before. I visited Ramat Yohanan, so far only for a day, and still feel the kibbutz is the most exciting thing in Israel.'[39]

Despite the controversy sparked off by publication of *The Children of the Dream*, he had received a warm welcome, and had also had the pleasure of being reunited with Carl Frankenstein, who was taking part in Fox's project. The six months he had just spent in Chicago had left him exhausted; after his arrival he was sleeping fourteen-hour nights. A couple of weeks later, however, he was taking an active interest in his friend's problems in the school for culturally deprived children (mainly from Arab countries) that he had set up. The two friends were comparing its pupils with the children of US ghettos, and discussing the best ways to harness psychoanalysis to the learning process. A whirl of debates and conferences, interspersed with tourism, helped him feel he was once again being useful, which was all Bettelheim needed to get him back on track. When the French film-maker Daniel Karlin, who had just read *The Empty Fortress*, called him in Jerusalem to request a long interview, he immediately agreed, and set an appointment for April. Karlin, who also wanted to film inside the school, offered to send Bettelheim a copy of one of his pro-grammes so he could get an idea of his work. The answer surprised him: 'No need, I know you're a good one,' Bettelheim replied.[40]

Back at the Orthogenic School, Jacquelyn Sanders was consolidating her power. After having tried to get Candy on her side, and having briefly thought she had succeeded, she abruptly decided, at the end of February, to fire her. She had learned from Bert Cohler's experience; she was unable to keep the young woman in line. She probably also resented in the latter's eyes the implicit judgement on the way she was running the school. In the space of twenty-four hours Candy had to pack her bags and say goodbye to her children. She found refuge at Adrian Kuypers's home for a few days. She was shattered; it felt as if her entire life had been taken away from her. From Jerusalem, Bettelheim could not do much, except worry himself sick. He tried to calm her down, both by phone and mail, reminding her that she had plenty of resources to fall back on, pointing out how her too-high expectations of others always ended up pushing them away from her, and telling her how much she meant to him. But as he would explain to Geneviève Jurgensen a few months later, he had already realized that with him gone, Candy could probably never have been happy at the school.

On returning to Chicago at the end of March, Bettelheim had a new problem on his hands: the imminent arrival of Daniel Karlin and his film crew. At the school, the announcement was seen as Bettelheim's latest extravagance. Never before had he allowed TV cameras at the school. Jacquelyn Sanders and most of the counsellors were opposed to the project, fearing the negative impact the intrusion would have on the children in that troubled period. Right up to the last moment, Karlin was not sure he would be allowed to film the children. In the end, Jacquelyn Sanders, realizing how important it was for Bettelheim to have his life's work immortalized at the moment of his departure, had relented. She had however set very strict limits: the shooting should be of short duration, people should only take part if they agreed to do so (for the children, with written approval from their parents), and Karlin should undertake both to conceal their identities and to ensure that the film was never screened in either the United States or Canada.

The French team had three weeks in which to get to know the premises and their occupants, and one in which to shoot. Their presence set off a storm of controversy, but even the loudest critics now acknowledge that the disturbance had no lasting effect on the children. In fact, the person the most deeply torn by the event was probably Bettelheim himself. Coming on the heels of so many other upheavals, the project was indeed at odds with the philosophy he had tried to instil in everyone he had worked with. He felt guilty about it, but the filming provided a welcome distraction at a very difficult juncture for him. In the preface[41] he was to write for Karlin's subsequent book he would claim that if the French film-maker had contacted him in Chicago, rather than in Jerusalem, he would never have accepted. The fact that he was in Israel, he said, had reminded him of how radically the Nazis had eradicated the first half of his life. 'That someone should offer to prevent a repetition of that annihilation by making a visual record of my work, produced by a person who seemed to me to be as sincere as possible in his approach; that was a prospect that suddenly seemed very attractive to me,' he wrote.[42]

That statement seems to me to be both very true, yet deceptive, in that it glosses over more complex feelings. True, because the meeting of minds between Bruno Bettelheim and Daniel Karlin, who is both Jewish and the grandson of a concentration camp inmate, was as much about Nazism as about the Orthogenic School. As for Bettelheim's more complicated feelings, they related to the man Karlin was, to his Marxist convictions, his long hair and the fact that, between laying the groundwork for shooting at the school and the actual filming, he chose to take his team to the Wounded Knee reservation, then beseiged by the federal police. In short, the young Frenchman was providing the elderly director of the Orthogenic School with a unique opportunity to sort his thoughts out on the eve of his departure.

Contrary to what Karlin seems to believe at times, Bettelheim never lost sight of the fact that he was a Communist, as is evidenced by his correspondence. He also sensed that Karlin was in the midst of a personal crisis, thus interpreting the intensity of the relationship that the young man immediately established with him. But he seemed to forget that he too was undergoing a crisis, a fact that did not escape Karlin's attention ('The King is dying,' Bettelheim told him, in French,[43] to explain the limits to his power within the school). In fact the arrival of the film-maker, who was at once close to and different from the movement leaders whose psychology he had been dissecting from afar over the preceding five years, offered Bettelheim an opportunity to verify *in vivo* (and indeed *in situ*, as the event took place within the school) his analyses. Bettelheim was aware of the influence he had over Karlin, and he knew what he was doing in granting him a right he had always denied to American television journalists. However conservative he may have become, the ideals of the young Frenchman remained familiar to him. And while he was lashing out at the liberals and leftists who at the time were besieging the Nixon administration, he also knew that his theories about mental illness were generally better understood and accepted by those who questioned the existing social order.

He had just completed an overview of his life's work, one he had hoped would be definitive, but with which he was only half satisfied, when Karlin appeared on the scene. The journalist was intelligent, and he appeared to have read Bettelheim so well that he might be able to transpose his ideas on to film. He came from France, a country whose culture Bettelheim admired, and where *The Empty Fortress* was being hailed as a seminal work. Moreover, Karlin was untainted by all the controversies that had been dogging Bettelheim for around a decade. He could listen to him with an open mind, and hear only what was essential.

A year later, after Karlin had come to San Francisco to show him a preview of his films, Bettelheim would write: 'There is no doubt that no American TV man would have been able to produce anything approaching it. He has put a lot of himself into it, and it shows ... [But] it is amazing how much he saw, filmed and understood in these few days.'[44]

I have often wondered what it is about Karlin's films that gives them their magic quality, so different from other documents. For once, Bettelheim appears at peace with himself on film, neither overly dogmatic nor aggressive. He even looks happy, unusually so for him. And today I can find only one explanation for that: this dialogue with the grandson of a former death camp inmate, someone who like him was looking for a meaning to life, is the very image of Healing. Illustrated by shots of real flesh-and-blood children who are in the process of returning to the world, and say so on camera, it is tangible proof that man's humanity has survived Nazism and that we have the right go on living and hoping.

It was indeed a testament.

Looking at the broader picture, when Bettelheim's life was about to take him away from the Orthogenic School, the same question keeps recurring. It transcends the obvious point that a great clinician is irreplaceable, or the issue of his own personal weaknesses, the confusion surrounding his retirement or the scandal that followed his death, and concerns the type of cult that grew up around him. Why is it that this psychoanalyst, who spoke in rather stern terms, disliked social niceties and decried fads, became such a unique reference for so many people – and that instead of being sent into purgatory after his death like most famous writers, he was instantly forked into hell? Why did Bruno Bettelheim inscribe himself in the imagination of so many people in so many different countries, as some sort of a secular saint, untouchable and unquestionable?

Critics may answer that if he had not painted such an idealized picture of his school, he would never have achieved such celebrity. But that is precisely where the Bettelheim mystery lies. If good self-promotion was enough to gain the respect, even the love, of the multitude, the list of idols would be long indeed. Kurt Eissler once told me: 'Bettelheim had all the trappings of a genius, without being one.'[45] Although judicious, the remark still does not explain the man's worldwide fame. Many may call themselves magicians, but few are recognized as such. Here was a man with no particular psychiatric qualifications other than his birth in the same city as Sigmund Freud, who without a medical degree or support from the psychoanalytic establishment, said: 'I am going to cure people who have been identified as incurable. And I shall do it without drugs, straitjackets or electrical shocks; I will do it by simply listening to them, and showing them that I love them.' Why was he believed?

Paradoxically, Bettelheim's attitude to the student protesters of the late 1960s helped me to answer that question. Having been one of those protesters, I felt personally concerned by it: how could this man whose ideas about madness – but also about the ghetto mentality and personal autonomy – were so attractive to us, so in line with what we were demanding, have totally rejected our revolt? Was he hypocritical, neurotic, or simply inconsistent, to the point that he no longer knew what he had said twenty years before? Then Mark Lubin mentioned the 'This will be bad for the Jews' comment, so typical of the *shtetl*, and which had so surprised him in Bettelheim's mouth. I realized that there was something else, and that it had to do with the question of 'What is a Jew?' – a question that had run through Bettelheim's whole life like a continuous thread, one for which he had been robbed, humiliated and almost killed, and to which he had tried to provide an answer in each stage of that life.

There are two types of Jew. One who sees himself as one, based on his beliefs, culture or lifestyle, and another who, as was shown by Jean-Paul Sartre,[46] is identified as a Jew by the anti-Semite. Whatever the latter does, or does not do (respect the Sabbath, circumcise his sons, eat kosher, attend synagogue, etc.), he will be stuck with a yellow star from generation to generation. Even if he converts, or if he and his sons marry non-Jews, his grandchildren will always run the risk of hearing (or, perhaps even worse, of not hearing) themselves insulted as 'yids', suspected of avarice or social climbing, etc. And, to add insult to injury, they will be labelled as ashamed of their Jewishness. Thus humiliated, they will be called upon to defend themselves (if only in their own eyes), even if, knowing nothing of Judaism, they have not the slightest idea what they are supposed to be ashamed of (or proud of – but it comes down to the same thing). Even in apartheid South Africa, it was easier for a coloured person to cross the racial Rubicon and be reclassified as 'white', on condition that he or she had a pale enough skin, straight enough hair and passed a number of other legally defined tests. In our democratic societies, however, the descendant of a converted Jew remains one for ever.[47]

As numerous writers have pointed out, that type of Jew, the one who never sets foot in a synagogue, inspires the most virulent hatred, precisely because he is so like those around him.[48] He is perceived as the 'enemy within the walls', generating all kinds of fantasies – in the anti-Semite first, and soon in all those who hear him rave. He becomes the object onto which they can project everything they hate, or are frightened of, in themselves. Bettelheim was not the first writer to point this out, although the particular case he discusses (the Jew as perceived by the Nazi guard, inside the concentration camp) is strikingly unique, because it is located in the very place where anti-Semitism reaches its ultimate limit, where the fantasy became reality.

After the war, or more specifically after the discovery of the Final Solution, it was possible for a while to believe that a page had been turned. That, having witnessed the ultimate in inhumanity, 'informed' people had learned to recognize the limits beyond which they could not go. There was thus a naïve belief that phantasmagorical anti-Semitism was dead, and that the Jews could finally take their place among other minorities. That they would henceforth suffer only from 'ordinary' racism.

And indeed the Holocaust engendered a taboo. For years, there were epithets and ideas which were no longer heard in public. The first post-war generations thus enjoyed 'protected' childhoods. Coincidence or not, it was precisely those generations that in the late 1960s were to take to the streets all over the globe chanting 'We want the world, and we want it now!' The demand of course was expressed differently in different countries (in Paris, a former centre of collaboration with the Nazi régime, it became at one point: 'We are all German Jews!'[49]). Nevertheless, in Chicago as in Berlin, Milan and even Prague, the thirst for social justice and authenticity was the same. And everywhere, the voices of Jews, half-Jews and 'Jew-lovers' of all types were preponderant.

This was just the time when Bruno Bettelheim chose to reveal his deep pessimism. Turning his back on Herbert Marcuse, Jean-Paul Sartre and many others among his fellow academics, he attacked the leaders of the revolt head-on. And what exactly did he call them? 'Spoiled children!' The lover of Goethe and German Expressionism, who had one day had to consider himself privileged to be allowed to haul pails full of excrement to fertilize SS officers' gardens, had immediately sensed that such an appetite for freedom, equality and truth could only be 'bad for the Jews'! For if these young people had been 'spoiled', it was above all because they had grown up in a world in which the anti-Semites had been silenced. As a result, they knew the truth without knowing it, without understanding what had really happened. And they wanted to be told everything, secure in the illusory belief that national or international laws and courts were there to protect them against any repetition of a past which they viewed as dead and buried.

Bruno Bettelheim appealed to these 'spoiled children' of anti-Semitism, those whom the Holocaust had paradoxically protected against the traumas of hatred – and, when they were Jewish, against self-hatred; that is to say in the final analysis that, thanks also to the creation of Israel, they had been given the opportunity to assimilate successfully elsewhere. They liked to hear a Jew speak out proudly to say that everyone has a duty to protect his own life, and that of his family. Whether he actually had the courage of his convictions was beside the point; what mattered was his tone. It was the tone of a man who was not waiting for God to determine his destiny.

And they also liked his way of handling what others called madness. There appeared to be parallels between Bettelheim's ideas on mental health and those of the 1968 movement on politics. In both cases, a simple desire to repair the world's unfairness, providing it was sincere, seemed to be all that was needed to change it. To chant 'Make love, not war', '*Sous les pavés, la plage*',[50] 'Do it!' or 'Workers and students, unite!' seemed to make it all come true. It was an idea that the French writer Marguerite Duras summed up neatly with the slogan: 'Be realistic; demand the impossible.'

In fact there was a misunderstanding: Bettelheim, who was speaking as a psychoanalyst, was not saying that madness does not exist, but simply that it is alien to nobody. That the ossified categories of classical psychiatry, like the institutions they had engendered, are prisons, within which human beings are trapped whose only crime is to suffer. To transpose his ideas into the social or political realms was already to distort them. Yet those who did so had an excuse: the place from which Bettelheim had chosen to speak out. It was a place so real that it transcended psychoanalysis – the concentration camp. Once Bruno Bettelheim had drawn a parallel between his experience in the camps and his work at the Orthogenic School, that parallel had come to life in his readers' minds, endowing him with a role which went well beyond the field of psychoanalysis.

Having experienced the worst that human nature can devise, Bettelheim appeared to have the right to demand, and therefore to promise others, the best that humanity can give. He would wipe away the injustice he had suffered, by requisitioning the enemy's weapons to destroy another menace, every bit as arbitrary as the one that had struck him: mental illness in children. It was a just aim, and a good one. After the return to peace, and its unavoidable compromises, its omissions ('Life must go on') and its pettinesses, Bettelheim-the-magician offered a hope as daring, as immense, as the crime had been monstrous. If out of the horrors of the Holocaust could come a way to save insane children, then God had not died at Auschwitz. It was the message that everyone had heard, the one that had set Bettelheim apart. The young protesters, just because they were 'spoiled', were simply demanding from the adult world what everyone was expecting of him, overlooking that he was merely another fallible human being, and more severely wounded than many.

After his death, people started calling him to account. As if, in the field of mental health, results could be summed up in figures. The impossibility of obtaining documentary evidence of his therapeutic effectiveness fed suspicions. Yet, in psychology, what answers can material data provide? With the right type of tests, one can claim to measure scholastic aptitudes (but not really the qualitative factor in teaching), and one can evaluate a person's effectiveness in certain types of action (personal hygiene, eating, mobility, etc.). But only the subject himself can provide the overall picture, and answer the only truly interesting question: 'Am I happier than before? In other words, can I make more effective use of my energy to become the person I would like to be, and achieve my aims?'

Only the testimony of those who attended the Orthogenic School can thus provide a valid reply about what Bettelheim accomplished there. Of the fifty-odd individuals I talked to, two-thirds were there as adults, either counsellors or teachers. For it requires a great deal of courage – or a lot of pain – for someone who has since created a whole new life, perhaps with family and children, to stand up and say: 'I was once a student at the Orthogenic School.' The interviews took place between November 1990 and December 1994. In many cases, I spoke several times to the same person, and sometimes noted changes in his or her feelings over time. Of the former staff members, only one was totally hostile to Bettelheim. Two others, while acknowledging the value of his teaching, consider that during the final years he was so distracted that he on occasion acted in ways that hurt the children. All the others, without exception, are convinced that the mistakes he may have made with them were negligible, weighed against the good he did. Most of them also think that, even today, there are very few places in the world where disturbed children have as good a chance of recovery as at the Orthogenic School under Bettelheim.

Among the former students, the picture is less clear-cut, the ambivalence greater. Bittersweet memories often surface, even as someone is recounting a breakthrough. Five of those I spoke to expressed anger with Bettelheim, in two cases even hatred. Those who acknowledge their need to go to the Orthogenic School say in general that they learned to overcome several of their problems while there. Some even say they were happy. Many speak of Bettelheim with true affection, some do not. With a single exception, all those who vehemently denounce him were still at the school when he left, at least the first time. One is reminded of the 'bad guy' ritual, while being aware that it is only part of the story.

Such testimonies must indeed be taken 'as is', without looking for hidden meanings or omissions in each person's story. Nobody is deliberately lying and, overall, nobody challenges the truth of the events related. It is simply that the same incident recounted by two different people sounds so different as to be unrecognizable. The story of Alida Jatitch in the shower, for example,[51] was told to me by half a dozen different witnesses, including two of her dorm-mates, and it thereby lost a lot of its power to shock, and all of its indecency. Nobody is right. In matters psychological – for that is indeed what is at stake here – there are no bad marks to be handed out. Just feelings to be recovered.

The fifty-six-year-old man who says, with a lump in his throat: 'Dr B saved my life. Without him, I would never have made it into adulthood' certainly knows what he is talking about better than the former counsellor who, filled with hate for Bettelheim, shrugs his shoulders and says: 'That kid was simply a little difficult. He was no more crazy than you or me.' The life of which the former student speaks is precisely what other people do not have access to, other than occasionally, by intuition or empathy. It is the realm of his personal phantoms, of his closets full of skeletons, and also of his dreams, acceptable or not. It is the life that Sigmund Freud gave back to us, the life of the mind, or as Bettelheim might have called it, the inner life. It is the life behavioural therapies seek to smother with conditioned reflexes.

Hence most of the misunderstandings and doubts about Bruno Bettelheim's work. His aim was not to adapt the unhappy children in his care to their parents' social mores. It was not to make them 'well behaved'. His aim was not even to make them happy, but to get them gradually to understand, because that discovery had once saved his life, that even the most miserable of lives ('even the life of a Jew in the hands of the Nazis', he used to say) is valuable as soon as one succeeds in giving it meaning. This is what recovering, or being cured, meant for him: finally to acknowledge the value of one's own life. And to get there, he always worked with the inner lives of those around him. For, in spite of appearances, that is the only life that matters to individuals, because it is the only one that produces meaning.

'He saved my life.' This is the statement that occurred most often in the testimonies of the people I spoke to, both former students and counsellors. It takes time to understand what it means. Time to recognize the existence of that inner life, which is not parallel to the other, but woven into it giving it texture. Time to become aware of it in oneself – the time it takes for a good psychoanalysis – and also time to learn to respect it in other people. When I heard those first 'He saved my life's, armed with my microphone and the certainties of one who knows all about the 'real world', I interpreted them as the expression of total loyalty coming from sect members. But I heard it too often, from too many different people and, every time, in a tone that commanded respect. The people who use the expression know what they are saying. However their behaviour appeared to an outsider, the phantoms with which they had to struggle in their minds were indeed killers. And it was Bettelheim who helped them to put those killers out of action, just as he had once removed his blind man's armband in Buchenwald. Put them out of action: that is to say return them to their rightful places in the past, so that, ceasing to be phantoms, they became memories, and stopped cannibalizing the present.

'Everything is perfect in your films, except that awful character – the old director,' Bettelheim told Daniel Karlin, in late March 1974, when the latter showed him his work in Francis Ford Coppola's studios, in San Francisco.[52] He was not just being coy. By now retired and in his seventies, his self-image was harsher than ever. Six months after having made California his new home, this time for good, he was making great efforts to free himself from his lost school. In a letter written to Candy nine months earlier, on the very day he was saying goodbye to the children, he had these comforting words for her: 'That it now all seems unreal to you is how it has to be – it's too painful to accept that it was real and now is no longer .... This is part of the process of separation, when it all has to become shadowy so that one can take it.'[53] The advice was drawn from Freud, but it was aimed as much at himself as at her. Karlin had come back too soon. To see the children looking so very alive on film, with the school and himself in the middle, had been a painful experience indeed.

A few days after the screening, Bettelheim was due to travel back to Chicago to give two months of classes, under the contract that still tied him to the university. He was filled with apprehension at the idea of returning, and once there, he was overwhelmed by feelings of loss and abandonment. There was no longer a place for him at the school. When he visited, he felt that many people were avoiding him. He understood their need to push ahead, without him, but he suffered from it. He nevertheless enjoyed seeing former colleagues and some O.S. children on campus, in that other world to which he now belonged, and he also enjoyed the teaching. The following year, he no longer really felt like going at all. Although he had had a tough time settling in, he had got used to a life of active retirement in the California sun. He had also just finished *The Uses of Enchantment*, and had no desire to take another trip into his Chicago past. In the middle of that stay, he in fact returned home for a week's rest. And in 1976, the last year he made the teaching trip, the whole exercise had become a burden, shouldered solely for financial reasons. He hated staying in a hotel in the city of which he had been a resident for so long. He found the climate, which was exceptionally hot and humid that spring, particularly disagreeable. Six months earlier he had had a mild heart attack during a trip to France. It had taken him a while to recover, and his overriding desire was to turn the page on what had once been his work. Candy, by now living in Paris, had sent him a manuscript of some 700 pages on her experiences at the school. After reading it attentively he sent her seven pages of comments and suggestions. In the accompanying letter, he wrote: 'I was glad to read what you wrote because reading it was kind of a communication with you. For the rest my desire is not to hear another word about the school. It is all over for me. I did it, we did it, it is no longer mine – may the others have it, but please they should not bother me with it when it is not mine.'[54]

That last wish was to be granted him beyond all his expectations. After his departure, his relations with Jacquelyn Sanders had remained cordial, even though it was clear that the way she was running the school did not have much in common with what he had created. When people criticized her, he would express faith in her, and say it was normal that she should adapt the institution to what she herself was able to do with it. 'Without Jacqui,' he once told Candy, 'the school would already have fallen in the hands of the behaviourists.' Indeed, during the first year, Bettelheim continued to rely a great deal on the school for material support in his own work. He had one of the secretaries type out his texts, while Jacquelyn Sanders took care of procuring books he required. Up until 1975, she continued regularly to seek his advice on new admissions. But their relations gradually soured. Finally, in April 1982, as Bettelheim was about to pay a flying visit to Chicago, he received a note from Jacquelyn Sanders telling him she no longer wished to see him. With that he had felt that the door of the Orthogenic School was closed to him once and for all. Although hurt, he had not taken it too badly at the time, as he was too busy dealing with Trude's illness. Over the years, however, the loss of the school would rankle more and more, combining with his other troubles to cast a painful shadow over his final years.

Neither Bettelheim nor Jacquelyn Sanders herself had fully realized just how much bitterness lay behind the new director's devotion. She indeed acknowledges the fact. After Bettelheim's departure, she chose for an analyst the man against whom he had warned her. Little by little, the reasons for her resentment started to come out. She was angry about the power he had wielded over her in his role as director-cum-therapist; this she would later tell him, in a letter. As she freely recognizes, she was also bitter that he had not helped her in her career. She became particularly aware of this on seeing Daniel Karlin's films.[55] She felt insulted by the short passage in which Bettelheim refers to her. Karlin asks him if 'out of all the counsellors you have trained, there is a single one of whom you can say: "I have managed to make him or her capable of replacing me." ' 'Yes, a few,' Bettelheim answers. 'But they have chosen less difficult jobs. One of my best staff members is now one of my colleagues at the university, where he teaches. I had wanted him to succeed me, but he refused.[56] Those long hours, every night .... He could have done it, even though he chose not to do it. I think Dr Sanders, who has succeeded me, will manage very well. But of course, it's always a personal creation.'[57]

Jacquelyn Sanders did what she thought best. She very carefully preserved the school's overall framework, and even wrote a book, entitled *A Greenhouse for the Mind*, in which she explained the need for it.[58] She stopped admitting autistic children, banned all forms of physical violence and ended in-house therapies. In other words, she knocked off the rough edges and made the school presentable. She also got it in tune with the times, bringing in co-ed groups and allowing teenagers to go downtown alone for medical or dental appointments. But, in that irreproachable institution, what had happened to psychoanalysis, to empathy, to the fantasies and phantoms that made living so unbearable for the children? To all those awkward, not-so-presentable feelings? One asks such questions in vain. Once Bruno Bettelheim had left, the Orthogenic School stopped seeking out and confronting hidden 'killers'. Instead, it tried to lull them to sleep.

As this is a biography of Bruno Bettelheim, and not a history of the Orthogenic School, we will leave the matter there. It is nevertheless worth noting how conformism, the desire to be presentable and an apparent concern for justice, can camouflage feelings and deeds that are anything but nice. How the suppression of all physical, i.e. visible, violence can be used for ends that are no less violent, while remaining hidden.

It is one thing that Jacquelyn Sanders decided to place in the publicly available Bettelheim archives, without any explanation, a copy of the letter in which she informed him that the children at the school were no longer being hit, and that she had put a stop to in-house therapies.[59] It was not exactly an elegant move, but it remained within the framework of their professional relations. It was a reply to the secrecy which Bettelheim had maintained about his therapeutic methods. He had never clearly faced up to his use of violence, and she was thus refusing that part of his heritage.

The role that Sanders played in 'the Bettelheim Affair' is quite another thing, however. For several of the former students who publicly attacked Bettelheim after his death contacted her before doing so. 'I didn't want to prevent them from expressing their reality,' she told me, clearly convinced that she had done the right thing. From the outside world, it sounded convincing; did not these 'former children' have the right to shout from the rooftops that their lives at the school had been very different from what Bettelheim described in his books? However, having spent fourteen years working alongside Dr B, how could Jacquelyn Sanders not have known how difficult it would be for these former patients to handle the public expression of their hatred for him, now that he was dead? Was this not jeopardising everything he had always tried to do to calm their inner conflicts? How could she have let these former O.S. students, towards whom she professes such devotion, go out alone to face a public crying out for sensational revelations, and lay into the corpse of the man who had for such a long time served as a lightning-rod for their own internal storms? All of this knowing that he could no longer stand up to prove to them, even by growling at them, that they were not murderers, that they had not killed him, that they were not responsible for his suicide?

It is difficult to answer such questions. I have no doubt as to Jacquelyn Sanders's good intentions, or rather as to her ability to turn the other way at the precise moment when Dr B would no doubt have encouraged her to face up to the motives lurking behind her so proper attitude. For nothing helped me to understand Bettelheim's therapeutic method better than the scandal that broke out after his death. Shortly thereafter I spoke to several of the people who had publicly attacked him; I was to see a few of them two years later, and speak to others again on the phone. Over time, the vigour, often mingled with jubilation, of their recriminations had dissolved. All that remained, obsessive, obsessing and disturbing, was the complaint. Words, lots of words, and reasoning that kept turning over. But the Big Bad Wolf was indeed no more. The words, echoing in the void, fell, vengeful, hurtful, painful and sterile, back on to those who had uttered them.

And yet even the scandal could serve a purpose. Like the dead body, lying near the school. Like the revolting soup at Buchenwald. It was Myles Gordon ('Paul' in *Truants from Life*) who showed me how: 'On reflection, I think the scandal helped me to overcome the anger I felt when I heard of his suicide. I had never felt so let down in my life. I was so angry at him. Then, those nasty letters began to appear and I started to think back at all the things he had done for me. So my anger fell,' he said. It is true that 'Paul' was lucky enough to be able to rely on a great therapist, up until the day when he was able to recognize on his own that his life had meaning.

In May 1986, the University of Chicago decided to stage a conference in honour of Bruno Bettelheim. Putting her feelings to one side, Jacquelyn Sanders undertook to organize it. Although she was on a sabbatical, she did her duty. The programme was laid out like clockwork, with only one afternoon out of two days devoted to the workings of the Orthogenic School, and six former counsellors invited to speak.[60] It was above all to Bettelheim as a writer, thinker and academic that homage was being paid. With the exception of Bert Cohler, the only former student invited to speak was at the time a high-ranking academic in another university. But feelings disrupted the nice arrangement. Former staff and students flocked from all over the country, and even from abroad (Geneviève Jurgensen, for example, travelled from Paris). The atmosphere that was lacking on the podium was spontaneously recreated on the floor, with former students gravitating naturally towards their former counsellors. The ambivalence of people's feelings was also in evidence, and at least one person who was violently to attack Bettelheim after his death attended. To sum up, it was warm, occasionally difficult, but always moving and enriching, bringing a bit of life into the existence of a depressed old man, who had just lost his wife. A gift from some of the people whom he had earlier helped to recover their own love of life.

On this occasion, Leslie Cleaver once again found simple words in which to bring back to life, beyond people's fantasies, something of what Bruno Bettelheim's Orthogenic School had once been. 'When I started to write this paper, I wrote down a number of anecdotes in apparently random order,' she said. 'The last one was an exchange between a twelve-year-old boy who had been at the school for two years and me, who had been there six years, about an autistic boy of five, who was then just, joyously and very movingly, learning to talk. Billy, the older boy, was very jealous of the fragile and desperately ill younger child to whom he behaved in a very tender and protective way. Quite properly (a range of feelings, not a range of actings out) he directed his angry and jealous feelings towards me .... Then he said: "The thing I'm most jealous of is ... I wish I had learned to talk at the school like Jonny. I wish I learned to talk to express myself, instead of to protect myself. My life would have been so different." To know that, to be able to say that, to be able to say how things really are, didn't make all the difference, but it made enough difference for Billy, for me, that there aren't enough words to say "Thank you, Dr B".'

Epilogue

Modern technology has produced lack of respect for the unknown and unknowability. The terrible arrogance of the technicians, the mathematicians, the measurers, the consumption addicts, the status-seekers, all these dervishes of the rationality and consciousness cult. They have superbly succeeded in turning the external aspects of life into the sole contents of man's mind. And what makes this perversion even more painful is the fact that the one revolution that could have brought about a real change, depth psychology, has helped distort human truth into the falsity of denying unknowability. They have misinterpreted Freud, who knew the malaise of civilization. But Freud is not free from guilt for his sons and daughters, his disciples. At least he did not do enough to counteract this dangerous superstition of seeing the unconscious in terms of potential consciousness.

Carl Frankenstein, letter to Bruno Bettelheim,
August 31, 1975

Chapter XVII

Trude and the Children

It took us a long time, Trude and I, to get ourselves free of Vienna, and
in spite of that we haven't become Americans. In a way, we are between
the two, perhaps a little more over here than over there; at least that's
the feeling I have.
                    Bruno Bettelheim, letter to ER, September 10, 1954

'Which Dr Bettelheim do you wish to speak to?' The question, and even
more the hard tone in which it was asked, took Geneviève Jurgensen
aback, leaving her ill at ease. It was early spring in 1988, and the young
woman was calling from Paris to ask her former teacher for an interview,
on the occasion of the publication in French of *A Good Enough Parent*.
Since leaving the Orthogenic School she had seen Bruno Bettelheim only
twice – at the Chicago conference two years earlier, and in the fall of 1975,
when he had dined at her home in Paris.

But they had kept in touch by mail, and this had always meant a lot to
Geneviève. Her life as a writer and journalist in France was worlds away
from the one she had led in Chicago, and over the years their correspondence had become that of old friends, discussing everyday life with no
didactic or philosophical pretensions. But when the going got rough,
Geneviève Jurgensen had always found in Bettelheim that same combination of clearsightedness and compassion that had earlier helped her to
become an adult. She had told him of all the major events in her life, and
his comments had often proved very helpful.

In 1980, when a reckless driver killed both her young daughters, Bruno
Bettelheim had been the only professional to approve of her seemingly
crazy desire to become a mother again as soon as possible. Doctors,
psychoanalysts and others had all told her to wait awhile, until she had
finished mourning her lost children. Otherwise, they said, she would not
be able to love the newborn for itself, she would burden it with a load of
suffering too heavy to bear. Only the author of *The Empty Fortress*, the
man who had so often been accused of unfairness to mothers, had fully
understood her instinctive need to create a new life immediately. Only he
had trusted her ability to love and give anew. And fifteen years later,
Geneviève Jurgensen can still quote from his letters almost word for word:
'So, what I trembled for during the thirty years I ran the school has
happened to you ....'[1] And then the sentence which 'cut through all the

complications', as she puts it today: 'Of course you will raise your children with great anxiety. It is perfectly natural, and it cannot be avoided.'

Having made an appointment with Bettelheim, Geneviève Jurgensen arrived in Los Angeles in April 1988. He was then living in a beautiful hacienda-style house in Adelaide Place, a tiny and exclusive street running up a hill near the ocean, in Santa Monica. He greeted her in what looked like a small library, adjacent to the front door. She was struck at how old and frail he now looked. He had always dressed with care; now he had stains on his lapels. He had lost a lot of weight, and walked with difficulty. Above all he seemed constantly afraid of making too much noise, of causing a disturbance. He looked somehow diminished, humiliated, and she got a feeling of satisfaction at seeing how her visit quickly gave him back some of his old bearing.

Geneviève Jurgensen had no way of knowing it, but she had arrived in Los Angeles at a tragic juncture in Bettelheim's life. He was just recovering from a pancreatic infection and, now unable to ingest any solid food, was in a state of near starvation. But, most of all, he was in a deep depression. After a year and a half of cohabitation, relations between the old man and his daughter Ruth – the other 'Dr Bettelheim' – were past breaking-point. She had just bought a new house, a few streets away from Adelaide Place, and she had not given her father either the address or the phone number. He was himself looking for an apartment. The atmosphere in the house had become unliveable; the two were no longer on speaking terms and Bettelheim was convinced that his daughter wanted him dead. He felt horribly alone, abandoned and hated, as he confided in letters and verbally to a few close friends.

His distress even showed through in the interview he gave Geneviève Jurgensen.[2] It was a bitter irony for the old man to have to defend *A Good Enough Parent*, a book which often adopts a peremptory tone to discuss the raising of children, at a time when his own relationship with his eldest child was falling apart. When he could not but be aware of all the mistakes he himself had made as a father.

In reply to Geneviève Jurgensen's opening remark – 'The thing that strikes one most on reading your book is that bringing up children today is not exactly simple' – he mentioned the owner of a hardware store in Harlem, who ran his business with the help of his seventeen-year-old son in perfect harmony. 'That has become extremely rare,' Bettelheim commented. He went on, betraying his own concerns: 'It has always impressed me very much that of the Ten Commandments only one, the fifth, refers specifically to parents and children. And it does not say "Love thy father and mother," which would be in line with the expectations of modern parents. It says "Honour thy father and thy mother." To honour one's parents is very easy if one works with them, alongside of them. It doesn't take any commandment to tell a blacksmith's son to honour his father when he sees him pulling the iron out of the fire and beating it into shape!

Seeing how skilled the father is automatically inspires admiration, and the father feels great gratitude to the child for providing him with such narcissistic satisfaction.'

Although Geneviève Jurgensen could feel the bitterness in those remarks, she could not imagine how deep it ran. She did not know that it was that of a man who had been forced to succeed his own father in a trade he didn't like and thus to give up – or so he believed at the time – all hope of ever occupying the noble position he aspired to. And that because of his father's 'sin'. Neither could Geneviève Jurgensen know how painful was the wound resulting from the break with Ruth, the only one of his three children to have chosen the same career as himself.

This latest drama in Bettelheim's life, from which he would not recover, indeed appeared to be a replay of all the preceding ones. As in a nightmare, it showed traces of all the worst fears and crises of his life. The fear of being a 'fraud', with his book on child-rearing coming out just when his own life was revealing his failures as a parent. The issue of paternal impotence, as he had proved unable to provide his elder daughter with the support she expected when she had found herself alone with two children. But also the grandfather's despotism and his illnesses, as Bettelheim's last years were punctuated by emergency hospitalizations, heart attacks, strokes and other ailments. And lastly, there was the feeling of being despoiled. Firstly of his school, which like his former company, had been taken away from him – or so he felt. But also of his money, as he now had the impression that Ruth wanted more than her share. The family curse had indeed returned. Only this time, Trude was not there to help him defeat the ghosts that haunted him. To help him live.

The Bettelheims' move to California had been anything but easy. From an Austrian engineer, they had bought a house poised spectacularly on a hilltop in Portola Valley, a few miles west of the Stanford campus. Access was by Sierra Lane, a winding road which led to a short track with only one other house. Theirs, number one, was at the top. It was like another world: lush vegetation all around, near total solitude and the ocean far off in the distance. A little too wild, perhaps, as if man did not really belong there. The wilderness even got the better of Trude's passion for gardening. 'The deer come every night and eat all her flowers, and what the deer don't do, the rabbits, gophers, raccoons and what not finish off. All which they don't touch – like cacti – we don't like,' Bettelheim wrote.[3] There nevertheless remained a few laurels, oleanders and rhododendrons scattered among the pines, cacti and orange trees that surrounded the house.

'City-dwellers just shouldn't suddenly try to live out in the country, least of all in California, which is less a state of the Union and much more a state of mind, and not our type of mind,' an exasperated Bruno Bettel-

heim wrote to Ruth Marquis on his arrival.⁴ The slightest shopping trip
was a major expedition. He appeared to doubt whether he would be able
to stand living in such an out-of-the-way place for long, and he raged
against his and Trude's willingness to be won over by their stay in Palo
Alto. 'The difference between the year at the Center which seduced us to
move out here is fantastic, exactly the difference between a lovely vacation
and settling down in a vacation place to live and work. It was a crazy
idea.We should have known better,' he added.

In spite of such recriminations, the Bettelheims gradually got used to
their Californian retirement, as Bruno would realize on his first trip back
to Chicago. Although he missed the city atmosphere, the balmy climate,
plus, once they were settled, the comfort and convenience of their new life,
had their charms. There was also the life on a campus free of noise, traffic
snarl-ups and dirt, yet famous enough to attract a good number of interesting visitors each year. Although he would only admit to it when he felt
uncomfortable somewhere else, he had become used to California.

Their house was far enough from Palo Alto to protect them from the
crowd, yet they had enough friends in the environs to provide an enjoyable
social life. There were musical evenings and pleasant dinners, at other
people's places and even at theirs. Since his leg operation, Bettelheim was
supposed to walk as much as possible. He and Trude took a daily one-hour
stroll in the big natural parks that dotted the region. Trude had joined the
Sierra Club, a ramblers' group, played regular tennis and even began
riding a bicycle given to her by Naomi. And Bruno was still very active,
although it did not feel like much compared to his workload in Chicago.
He gave a few hours of classes each week at Stanford, held regular
meetings with a group of local psychiatrists and psychologists, plus an
occasional meeting with mothers. Soon he was holding a seminar at the
Child Psychiatry Division at Stanford University Medical School. And of
course there were lectures and conferences, both across the United States
and abroad. The couple travelled a lot, now most of the time together.

Above all, Bettelheim wrote. Long before retiring, he had already
started worrying about how inactivity would affect him. As he told
Frankenstein, 'I miss my old work very much. I know I had to give it up,
but I also know what is right for others was the wrong thing for me to do.
As long as I was busy all day running a clinic I did not have time for
thoughts which are only depressing. In one's work one has to be optimistic
or it won't work. Now nothing forces me to be optimistic, and that makes
things much more difficult.'⁵

Before leaving Chicago, Bettelheim had thus made plans for work to be
done in Portola Valley. He was thinking about his planned book on
child-rearing, a project he mentioned in most of his letters to Ruth
Marquis. But at the same time he had been awarded a 123,000-dollar
grant from the Spencer Foundation for a study on the role of the unconscious in school learning. The programme, for which he planned to carry

out field work, was due to take three years. He wanted to find out how psychoanalysis could contribute to teaching, or 'what little kids think when they sit in classes and are being taught .... How does their preconscious support or interfere with what goes on in class, and how should they be taught, so that their preconscious will support the learning?'[6] Bettelheim had long denounced the inanity of American schoolbooks. His seminars with elementary school teachers in Chicago had only confirmed what he had known all along: that children growing up in neighbourhoods racked by drugs, violence and poverty, often in single-parent families, would not learn to read, even at the age when the appetite for knowledge is the strongest, so long as their textbooks contained only bland, non-controversial stories, happening to well-behaved children living in middle-class suburbia; that a child's appetite for reading stems from his desire to understand what is happening to and around him.

Bettelheim therefore started organizing visits to local schools, and he asked Jacquelyn Sanders to have him sent all available US readers, and also French, British and German ones for comparative purposes. Meanwhile, being especially interested in the child's initial contacts with the written word, he began re-reading the first texts which most children are confronted with: fairy tales. He starts mentioning this work in his correspondence in October 1973. The subject enchanted him immediately. All the feelings and emotions that he found lacking in the modern textbooks – anger, jealousy, curiosity – were there in the fairy stories, in all their raw intensity. Like the unconscious itself, the characters in *Grimms' Fairy Tales* do not bother with nuances. Evil parents or hated rivals are killed, often with great cruelty. Love expresses itself orally most of the time. Good mothers often vanish, to be replaced by evil stepmothers, while brothers or sisters are invariably wrong. Things are simple: if one is not good, one is bad. And when one is bad, if one fails to repent, one is doomed. All of which is perfectly clear to a child. With generally a resolution of conflicts and a happy ending that are just right for his age.

As his correspondence shows, the two years that Bruno Bettelheim devoted to writing *The Uses of Enchantment* were certainly the happiest in the later part of his life. Deciphering the meaning of the stories was a source of delight to him, and he even wondered aloud to some friends, almost embarrassed, if he was not going through 'a second childhood'. It was a huge relief for him not to have to write about either autism or the concentration camps any longer. It felt like being reborn. He thought of his mother, and regretted not having told his own children any fairy tales, 'because, in our then rationalistic period, we thought that they were bad for them. What fools men be.'[7] When Carl Frankenstein sent him a volume of his poetry, Bettelheim compared his own work to that of writing verses – something of which he felt totally incapable. 'There is really quite some poetry in these tales .... I just finished *Cinderella* and now have only one more, *Beauty and the Beast*,' he wrote in January 1975.

There was *Hansel and Gretel*, the story featuring a gingerbread house and a little boy whom the witch fattens up in order to eat him, teaching very small children how to get past the oral phase of development. *The Three Little Pigs* illustrates the three stages in a child's development. *Jack and the Beanstalk* shows young boys how to grow out of their Oedipal conflicts, while *Little Red Riding Hood* warns pre-pubescent girls not to let themselves play seductive games they are not old enough to handle, and *Goldilocks* tells of a little girl's search for her identity in the house of the Three Bears. There is the dormant period of adolescence, during which *Sleeping Beauty* is getting ready for marriage. *Cinderella*, a more complex tale, touches on sibling rivalry, ambivalence and the castration complex.

The ideas in *The Uses of Enchantment* are well known. It is Bruno Bettelheim's most famous book, the one which reached the largest number of people – with the usual misunderstandings, by those who read it as a book of instructions ('My daughter wants me to tell her about Cinderella, but she's only five. It's too early, isn't it?') encouraged by Bettelheim's often dogmatic tone. It also drew some critical fire. Apart from those who challenged the psychoanalytical approach *per se*, some found it too long, and poorly structured. He was also criticized for leaving aside Hans Christian Andersen and modern children's stories, and, almost immediately, a few writers accused Bettelheim, if not of plagiarism, of having failed to cite his sources correctly.[8]

The accusation is partially justified. In his book, the first he wrote without the scrupulous and demanding assistance of Ruth Marquis,[9] Bettelheim failed to take all the precautions required in academic writing. He quoted the names of the authors he had consulted, but not always at the right place, and sometimes even with errors in his references. It is also true, as pointed out in 1978 by Joan Blos and by Alan Dundes in 1991,[10] that his text contains around half a dozen sentences which are very similar, both in form and content, to those of Julius Heuscher.[11] The latter's book is indeed cited, but only in order to position it half-way between the Freudian and Jungian standpoints. All of which creates an unpleasant impression of negligence.

But nothing more. 'All of this is not to say that Bettelheim's book is not infinitely superior to Heuscher's,' Alan Dundes acknowledges. Bettelheim indeed took the analysis of fairy tales much further than those he is accused of having plagiarized. As Alison Lurie points out, Erich Fromm was the first writer to note that the colour of Little Red Riding Hood's clothes is that of menstrual blood.[12] But his analysis is sketchy and does not explore the whole range of the child's unconscious desires, or the ambivalence of her feelings, as Bettelheim's does. It is difficult to tell whether Bettelheim's borrowing some of Heuscher's expressions was due to sloppy notetaking, or whether, as Jacques Lacan before him, he 'took his assets where he found them', considering that what mattered was not so much where he picked up an idea, but what he did with it (in my view, the erroneous references, Bettelheim's pride and the stupidity of such a 'theft' lend credence to the first hypothesis). What is clearly established from his correspondence, however, is that the book is indeed the result of original thinking that he had pursued passionately for over two years.

That work seems in fact to have sparked off the train of thought that would lead Bettelheim, five years later, to write *Freud and Man's Soul*. After expressing regrets for not having introduced his children to fairy tales, he wrote to Frankenstein: 'The interesting thing is that in rejecting them I followed the psychoanalysts, who should have recognized how deep these tales really are. But in a strange way, Freud and his followers are really afraid of the unconscious. They say it contains the mainsprings of our strength, but somehow they all shied away from it, even Freud. Before him we did not know what it was ... so we did not defend ourselves against it. Freud taught us what it is all about, and I guess instead of teaching us how to use it, he taught how to live without it. As any other prophet, his teaching bore its own defeat within it. What a topic this would be for a book on psychoanalysis. But I am too old for it.'[13]

At around the same time Bettelheim wrote to Candy, who had asked his advice: 'About reading: I have to include in their reading lists things so that the students feel that they know the field. For yourself, read only old man Freud, you'll spend your time much better with him than [with] anybody else.'[14] That summer he read Paul Roazen's book *Freud and his Followers*,[15] recalling with nostalgia and just a hint of bitterness 'all the struggle and all the excitement of the early days of psychoanalysis and how we hoped that it would be another important step toward freeing man and making this a better world'.[16]

His correspondence with Carl Frankenstein was becoming more regular, and also more intimate and varied, ranging from psychoanalysis to politics, Vaihinger to the Yom Kippur War, Watergate to French intellectuals.[17] The two friends understood one another; they shared the same references, the same past and the same Spenglerian pessimism as to the way the world was going. But, above all, what they had in common was, as Frankenstein put it in reply to Bettelheim's observations on fairy tales: 'I feel I always have understood where your love for children and where the tenacity of your refusal to take a "No" (or a seeming "No") for an answer comes from, when it comes to helping a badly mishandled youngster. Your anger at "growing up at any price", that seldom if ever leaves some remains of sincerity and humanity intact in us, has always been mine .... We belong, I feel, to the same company of fools who have managed to remain children, to some extent at least. Imagination is still a value for us. And we are angry with "them", as only children can be angry with "omniscient" adults.'[18] And among those whom Frankenstein referred to as 'the dervishes of the rationality cult', one of the two friends' favourite targets was the psychoanalytic establishment, which they found guilty of having fallen into 'the dangerous superstition of seeing the unconscious in terms of potential consciousness'.[19]

Bettelheim found regular confirmation of that at Stanford. What the young psychiatrists and psychologists who attended his seminars were looking for, even those most interested in psychoanalysis, was above all technique. And not his 'philosophy', as one of them, albeit well disposed towards Bettelheim, called it.[20] They were seeking practical advice drawn from his experience as director of the Orthogenic School, not what most of them saw as outdated reflections on man's soul; and even less to have to go through the inner work that was at the core of his teaching. With these students, Bettelheim did not go in for much Socratism; he simply gave them what they wanted.[21] At Stanford, he noted, 'all is drug-related research and treatment and nothing longer than the ninety days the insurance pays for'.[22] Meanwhile his letters to Frankenstein were becoming more and more pessimistic. He was not yet mentioning suicide, but his reflections on the impotence that comes with old age, and the vanity of even the most noble human undertakings, were those of a man continually asking himself 'What's the point?' It was around this time that the controversy with Des Pres and Lina Wertmuller's film moved him to resume his writing on the concentration camps, to produce *Surviving*.

Each year, the Bettelheims made at least one trip to Europe. They had in fact briefly considered retiring to Switzerland, where Emmi Vischer-Radanowitz and her husband Bertel lived. The couple had had an eventful time since they had left Vienna in 1935. After the Anschluss, they had refused to emigrate to the United States so as not to deprive Austrian Jews of two places in the strict US quota system. But when the Siemens company asked Bertel to run its Tehran office, just before war broke out, they gladly seized the opportunity to get out of Paris. In Iran, apart from some friction with the German embassy, which did not understand why the local representative of such a major company was not a Nazi party member, and from the sad news they received from their friends, they led a relatively peaceful existence until the Anglo-Soviet offensive against Iran that was sparked by Hitler's decision to attack the Soviet Union in June 1941. The Soviets too felt that the head of the Siemens office had to be a card-carrying Nazi, and they immediately arrested Bertel von Radanowicz as a German spy; he was thrown into the Lubianka prison in Moscow, tortured and then shipped off to Siberia. Emmi and her three young children took refuge with her family in Basel, and she spent the next fourteen years not knowing what had become of her husband, nor whether he was still alive. Once the war was over, Trude Bettelheim made contact with her again, and helped as best she could. Emmi's situation was made more difficult by her refusal to declare her husband dead, which would have allowed her to regain her Swiss nationality, and many material advantages along with it. 'I don't know that he's dead,' she kept answering, to civil servants bemused by such lack of practical sense. And then, one day, her many efforts paid off; Bertel came back, emaciated and in terrible shape, but alive.

Bettelheim, who had been very attracted to Emmi in Vienna, even though he had kept it to himself, was now also deeply impressed by her and Bertel's courage. Over the years their friendship had played an increasingly important role in his life. And now that he was retired, he rarely went to Europe without stopping off in Basel. He also had some acquaintances in Vienna, at least one school friend who had never left the city, and a few, like Ernst Federn, who had returned after exile. But each time he went back it was with mixed feelings, of nostalgia and resentment. He now knew a lot of people in Germany, France and Israel. He was often invited to lecture, and each time he was clearly delighted to find abroad some of the respect for his ideas that he felt his home state was denying him, turned as it was towards the Pacific and fascinated by technology. He had a good life there, but felt more than ever like an exile. 'What will we all do, when other forms such as retrieval systems and computers will have taken the place of books?'[23] wondered the old man, perched in his eyrie just a few miles from what was soon to become Silicon Valley.

An even greater dose of culture shock was in store. In September 1976, just after his article 'Surviving' had appeared, and he had begun compiling the book of the same name, Bettelheim received an invitation to spend a year as a guest professor in a Japanese university, from the education minister, Michio Nagai. After hesitating a great deal, he agreed to give three months of classes, providing it was at Kyoto University. So, after a failed trip to Israel, in the autumn of an emotionally charged year, which had started with the San Jose conference on the Holocaust and also seen *The Uses of Enchantment* win the National Book Award, Trude and Bruno Bettelheim flew to Japan, in September 1977. The experience shattered him: 'After the concentration camps these were for me personally the most difficult times in my life, as far as external conditions were concerned,' he wrote on his return.[24] During the first weeks, he had dreams of dying every night. The couple were then staying with a Japanese family; after a few weeks they moved into a hotel, and his letters became calmer. He expressed amazement at a people he found incomprehensible: 'I soon ... realized that all that we had been told about [the Japanese] and read was simply nothing but the fantastic wishful projections of Westerners who [can] project so well.'[25] He nevertheless was very receptive to the charm of the old imperial city, its decorative screens, gardens and traditions, whereas he found Tokyo uninteresting, if easier to handle. He was particularly baffled by the impossibility of entering into a real dialogue with his hosts. 'Despite their superficial attempts to resemble the Western world, everything here is different in the deepest sense. The structure of the language and, with it, the thinking are fundamentally different. The ego, which to us is the centre of all human experiences, is almost forbidden here. One doesn't say "I" even though the word does exist. Verbs don't have past or future tenses .... One word is used to designate both the singular and the plural .... This is to show how timeless events are. Every word has several meanings, so one is never sure of what the other means exactly but mustn't show it. For example, I had to analyse the behaviour of a little boy. The main word that he said was "*kami*", which among other things means "army", "the spirit of a dead person", or else "paper". The therapist thought that the child meant "army", but other elements clearly indicated that he meant "the spirit of a dead person". It was however impossible to check with the child, since one mustn't ask questions. And, like everyone else, he mustn't say "No." The closest thing he may say is: "It would be difficult",' Bettelheim wrote to a friend.[26] To show what he meant, he drew the ideogram for 'a man', which consists of two lines, one leaning on the other. 'Beautiful, isn't it? It means that one does not exist without the other. And that is why there is no ego,' he noted.[27]

By the end of February 1978 Bettelheim had completed *Surviving*. He was exhausted and felt completely empty, doubting that he would ever be able to write another book. The perpetually sunny California weather only added to his gloom. 'If the climate is harsh, one's energy goes in fighting it and in surviving. When the weather is always pleasant, no energy is eaten up by surviving, and one is robbed of the feeling that one accomplished something by sheer staying alive.'[28] He envied his friend Frankenstein, who was still teaching and working with children. His nostalgia for the school had been reawakened during the Christmas period, and he had dreamed about it several times. He had just penned a short preface for the US version of Janusz Korczak's book *King Matt the First*.[29] He felt himself getting older, and remarked sadly that 'If one stops being a therapist, this leaves an emptiness one must fill out some other way.'[30] His health problems were becoming more numerous: a cataract operation, a minor heart attack during a trip to France, trouble with a hip joint and his neck (for which his doctor told him to do an hour of swimming each day), then dental problems, new heart problems, an intestinal infection, etc. None of which were very serious, but he tended to dramatize them. This made him very demanding with his family (Naomi still remembers the panicky tone in which he asked for her help when he was stricken by a raging toothache while in Japan). In his letters he often referred to his age, although in generally calm terms, and more and more often he mentioned his no longer distant death.

At the beginning of June 1979, Trude discovered that she had breast cancer. That his wife, who was eight years his junior, might die before him was something Bettelheim had never envisaged. It was a local tumour, and Trude did not want to die. She would fight. Stanford was at the cutting edge of research into X-ray therapy, and the head of the department was one of the Bettelheims' friends. Although mastectomy was the usual method of treatment in the United States, Trude decided not to have it. She underwent three operations, had to fight an infection and put up with a long series of X-ray sessions. But, four months after the initial diagnosis, Bettelheim was able to write: 'I am happy to report that thanks to this complicated treatment my good wife is completely cured.'[31] Trude was very tired, however, and so was Bruno, after a summer filled with anxiety and hospital visits. But as the therapy had had no side effects, they both reckoned that the alert was over.

As is shown in his correspondence, this is the time when Bettelheim started to realize just how much he depended on his wife. Their relations were not very tender. They argued at times, and when no stranger was around, Trude was not the self-effacing wife that many of his friends remember. She indeed put up with a lot, but she occasionally let him know how she felt about it. Although always polite with her in public, Bruno could be less than tactful. Karen Zelan, who lived in Berkeley, remembers a concert in San Francisco when Bettelheim abandoned his wife at the interval to go and sit with Gina. For the Viennese threesome had got together again in Northern California. Twenty years earlier in Chicago, when Peter Weinmann had died, the Bettelheims had helped Bruno's first wife, even offering to have her and her daughter move in with them. They had later met up again in San Francisco, where Gina had made her home and set up as a psychotherapist. They saw one another on occasion, and Trude sometimes joined Gina for outings with her experienced hikers' group. At Bruno's lectures, Trude was often the first to stand up and reply to his critics, in lively and incisive terms. And it was not unusual to see Gina figuring prominently in the ranks of those critics.

Bettelheim still had a need to charm people, be it only via letters. He obviously enjoyed chatting with Gina, or rather, arguing with her. But the only woman with whom he could live – and who could live with him – the only one who understood and accepted him as he really was, was Trude. 'From time to time, I feel very tired of life and I would not mind if it came to an end. Without Trude, I could not and would not go on. But I would not like to abandon her either, so I go on,' he wrote in the fall of 1979, in reply to an old friend's birthday greetings.[32] He seemed surprised to find that at seventy-six, in spite of his many ailments and a sickly childhood, he had lived longer than both his parents and any of their sisters or brothers. He noted the effects of ageing with some detachment: 'Without knowing it or without wanting it, one starts to withdraw from life, so that it is not too hard to leave it. But, please, do not be mistaken: I say all this without sadness. I am quite happy with my life, particularly now that Trude is again in good health.'[33]

Ever positive, the latter had quickly returned to her normal pace, and wanted to hear no talk of her recent illness. Freed from his anxiety over her, and having overcome the empty feeling that had invaded him on finishing *Surviving*, Bettelheim once again plunged into work with his usual ardour. In the space of two years he was to write *Freud and Man's Soul* and finally complete the project on learning to read. Not alone, this time, but with Karen Zelan. When he was beginning to work on *The Uses of Enchantment*, she had mentioned to him that she wanted to write a paper on the psychological meaning of children's misreading and he had asked: 'Why not do it together?' Flattered, she had agreed immediately. At first, she had mostly analysed and written up the data and, while he was finishing the book on fairy tales, she collected most of the observations that they would use.[34] As he liked what she was writing, he had asked her to do some editing on his texts and, in the last year, urged her to contribute some discursive writing of her own to the project.[35] They ended up co-signing the book, with Bettelheim specifying in the preface which chapters were his, at his agent's suggestion.

Despite affirmations to the contrary in his letters, he was still taking a lively interest in world affairs, and particularly in events in the Middle East. He hated the Carter administration, and blamed his liberal Jewish friends for having voted it into office after having celebrated the fall of Nixon, a friend of Israel. '*Judische Selbsthaß à la Lessing, wie immer,*' ('Jewish self-hatred *à la* Lessing. As usual,') he noted in a letter to Frankenstein.[36] He nevertheless detested the very term 'Jewish lobby': 'The self-importance of Jews combined with the paranoia of the anti-Semite had created the image of this lobby. Actually the Jews here are exactly as powerless as they were in Weimar. But the gloating of the populace that the Jewish lobby was defeated is worthy of a Goebbels, whose diaries are now the hot issue in the liberal literary magazines,' he wrote.[37] Not even the signing of the Camp David agreement calmed him down. He saw the fall of the Shah of Iran and the advent of an Islamic Republic in Tehran, to applause from the same liberals, as yet another terrifying result of the West's, and especially the Americans', self-destructive tendencies. 'It is sad to see a great power tottering into impotency because nobody is willing to make any sacrifice. I guess nobody ever does .... For a few more fat years we gamble away the freedom of man. Well, what is this, the freedom of man? To live free to think, to express ideas, or whatever we value? Or is it to live in as much comfort as one can, the devil may take the hindmost? ... Carter wants to be reelected for four more years, and if he can get that, the world may fall apart after it. And the American people want to drive their cars for a few more years, if this means to sell out to the Arabs, who cares?'[38]

It is clear that such letters, often written under the influence of raw emotion late at night,[39] do not express thought-out ideas, intended for public consumption. Indeed, their tone varies considerably from one recipient to another. When writing to Candy, for example, Bettelheim remained very much the therapist, the provider of friendly advice. The tone was paternal and attentive, and the letters centred almost exclusively on her problems. With other friends, when he complained about his health and age, it was in an almost philosophical mode, most often with a tinge of hopefulness. When writing to women his tone was always chivalrous, sometimes even flirtatious. His old Israeli friend was probably the only correspondent with whom he thus gave free rein to his profound pessimism. In a way, Bettelheim's letters to Frankenstein were a perfect illustration of the process of turning in on oneself which he described in them as being ineluctable in old age. More and more frequently, ruminations on anti-Semitism and the futility of life suddenly came in between often highly interesting observations on psychoanalysis or education. The old wounds and obsessions had never healed despite a lifetime spent trying to help others.

The letters also show Bettelheim's children occupying a growing place among his concerns. Ruth had been living in the Los Angeles area since the mid-1960s. After taking a long trip to the Far East and then gaining a PhD in early childhood education, she had set up as a child therapist. In 1974 she had married a city planner. He was a Mennonite and very good-looking. Although he disapproved of his elder daughter's choice of husband, Bettelheim had financed a lavish wedding ceremony, celebrated in a church. Ever since, he had provided generously for the young couple, who were living well and had just had their second child. Naomi was more independent of her father. After graduating from college she had lived in New York for a time and then spent a year in London, where she had worked for Thames & Hudson, the art books publishing house founded by Bettelheim's old friend Walter Neurath. In 1968 she had married a Mexican, but the relationship did not work out. After barely a year, to Bettelheim's great relief, she had left Mexico City to enrol in a master's program in city planning at the University of North Carolina. In 1981, after spending a year in Palo Alto, she got married again, this time to a former teacher at Berkeley University and a practising Jew who now worked for the government. After a honeymoon trip to Israel, the couple moved to England, where her husband had been posted. As for Eric, after graduating in law studies at Oxford in 1975, he had, at his father's urging, obtained an equivalent degree from the University of Chicago the following year. He preferred life in England, but Bettelheim had persuaded him to ensure that he could also practise in the United States. He had just joined a San Francisco law firm. The prospect of having two of their children nearby had in fact encouraged the Bettelheims to move to California.

Bettelheim was thus seeing his children quite often. Wherever they might be, the family would come together at Christmas, and sometimes also at Thanksgiving. Relations between them were relatively easy, even though he could on occasion be quite tactless with his children. Naomi remembers one Christmas, for example, when he informed them that, the night before their arrival, he had dreamed that the Nazis were coming!

But even when he disapproved of their choices, be it of spouses or of studies, he tried to convince them, not to impose his will. Meanwhile, their reactions and beliefs loomed ever larger in his thinking. During the summer when Trude was under treatment, he wrote the preface for Claudine Vegh's book on Jewish children who were hidden in Christian families while their parents were taken to concentration camps.[40] That made him wonder at the very different attitudes his two daughters had adopted towards their Jewishness. He saw Ruth's marriage as quite simply a rejection of it, and was intrigued that an atheist like Naomi had ended up choosing a husband with such firm beliefs. He was not displeased at his second daughter's choice, and always had a good word to say for that son-in-law. He rarely mentioned the other one. But of his three children Eric was the one whose whereabouts seemed to interest him most. Ten years younger than his eldest sister and very much Trude's boy, Eric had had little to do with his father when he was a child. Now, he had become a subject of wonderment for Bettelheim. He often mentioned his witticisms and his pranks in his letters, and gently poked fun at his certainties. After visiting him in England he reported, with more than a touch of pride, that 'Eric is playing the gentleman scholar in Oxford.'[41] Another time, he was struck at hearing the young man attribute his bouts of anxiety to the fact that his parents had been persecuted by the Nazis.

During all those years, Bettelheim had gone on thinking about his planned book on child-rearing. He had come to see it as a summing-up of all his experience; so it weighed heavily on him, and he would put it aside each time another one turned up. Yet he was continually thinking about what it took to be a good parent. The development of his two daughters took him back to his reflections on the role of women, and of mothers. Once Ruth Marquis made a remark about psychoanalysts exacerbating parents' guilt feelings concerning their children. He replied vehemently: 'I cannot accept that psychoanalytic writings have created parental guilt. Sure, they have added to it and given it substance. But guilt comes from way back when, way back deep down. If you are secure within yourself, nothing anybody writes is going to give you guilt feelings .... I have been saying for years that the worst you can do is to feel guilty about what you did to your kid, because this is such a tempting weapon in their hands to act out all their oedipal resentment that they practically cannot help using it. And then, they feel miserable about having done so, and you invited them with your guilt to do so. But here I go again making the parents feel guilty, so what's the end [of it]?'[42]

In the year after Trude's cancer was diagnosed, Bettelheim was continually ill himself. A first operation, followed by a serious allergic reaction, put him out of action for two months; he lost over twenty pounds. Shortly afterwards, he required treatment for a lung infection, caused by the diverticulum in his oesophagus which was to plague the last part of his life.[43] He ended the year with his right leg in a plaster for a month, after a fall on the front steps of the San Francisco Opera House. In the spring, he had caught a nasty case of bronchitis in Vienna's main library, where he had loved to study in his youth. On that occasion, he was a guest of the Austrian government, for ceremonies marking the twenty-fifth anniversary of the treaty which finally settled Austria's post-war status. In spite of the honours bestowed upon him, the trip to the city of his birth was not a pleasant one. Trude, who had not been back since 1938, was outraged at how much the Austrians were denying their Nazi past. During a TV interview, Bruno was asked not to mention Hitler in a discussion on fairy tales; the name should only be used in historical programmes, he was told. On the same trip, however, Bettelheim was pleasantly surprised by his meeting with Manfred Rommel, the mayor of Stuttgart, who spoke to him about his father's relationship with Hitler. On the whole, he found the Germans much more ready to face up to their past than the Austrians were.

He was also rereading Freud, and asking himself iconoclastic questions about psychoanalysis – which he only mentioned to his friend Frankenstein, but which others have discussed publicly since then. 'I have come to see to what degree Freud's work is a defense against his pathology, the work of a true genius, but at the same time full of reactions against his own pathology. And I believe psychoanalysis will become what it could be only after these two elements have become separated,' he wrote.[44] Or again: 'Will psychoanalysis survive Jewry? .... Maybe it takes millennia of persecution to have enough compassion with man's deep misery to be a good analyst, I do not know. But in my latest work I was continually appalled [to see] how America made a therapy of adjustment and adaptation out of it, and how the British simply do not understand it, because to them it is but a rather questionable method of therapy .... They still are convinced that decent Englishmen simply do not have any of these dirty problems. So we are back [with the idea] that only Jews have such dirty minds.'[45]

In 1981, the Bettelheims spent another month in Europe, notably in England with Naomi ('We found Britain in very bad shape, but still probably the most civilized country in the world,' he wrote[46]). He had reread Arthur Schnitzler's *Der Weg ins Freie*,[47] and been surprised to discover in it so many new insights into the world around him. As both of them were by now feeling better, they laid plans to travel to Israel the following spring.

In mid-October, however, Trude Bettelheim suddenly collapsed, unable to move. She had been complaining of back pains for some time; now the doctors diagnosed bone cancer, which had caused one of her vertebrae to crumble. With X-ray treatment plus chemotherapy on a permanent basis, she could hope to live a few more years. Just before Christmas she was able to leave the hospital for home. She could sit up for a few minutes at a time, and the doctors assured her that within two months she would be walking again, although only with the aid of a frame. But her suffering was such that she still had to take pain-killing drugs all the time.

At the beginning of March, Bettelheim wrote: 'Despite it all we are in pretty good spirits. The reason is that the first month of it was so horrible, that everything since has been such an improvement (little as it is, seen objectively) that we are quite cheerful. The last two weeks we even went out for dinner a couple of times .... I work a little, we play music and watch a little TV, and so the days pass. Last week we were able to take Trude to a heated pool for swimming which helps her a lot. Since then, she has been able to walk a few steps in the house without cane or help. As she says, one measures her improvements like those of a baby.'[48]

The next three years were thus dominated by Trude's fierce struggle against terrible pain – aggravated at times by the aggressive way in which Bruno expressed his own panic at the possibility of being left on his own. Sometimes his outbursts reduced her to tears, but she never let herself slide into depression. Among the people who knew her, Trude's courage is legendary and there remains at least one trace of it: the three auto-biographical tape cassettes that she recorded at her children's request, when she learned that her days were numbered.

The tapes are heart-breaking in their precision and clarity. In them, Trude is obviously carrying out a mission – that of handing down to her children, who live in such a totally different world, some of the memory that will disappear with her, about their ancestors and the city she came from. So, she gives a host of concrete and striking details about her family and education, and what it was like to be a young woman growing up in Vienna at that time. She is less forthcoming about her feelings, but behind her matter-of-fact tone, the listener quickly senses a lively human being, full of emotions. The effect is heightened by the way this dying woman tells her story, without faltering or hesitating over a single word. When her voice breaks, she switches off the machine until she has regained her breath. To produce an account of such clarity, she must have stopped and rewound the cassette hundreds of times. And even though it obviously costs her dearly to do so, she carries her mission out to the end.

On hearing of Trude's relapse, Naomi returned from England to spend a few weeks in Portola Valley. The remoteness of the couple's home made life very difficult under such circumstances, particularly for a man as incapable of performing the simplest household task as was Bettelheim. To accommodate a home help, he had an extra room built on to the house. But when they finally found somebody they considered suitable, cohabiting with a stranger proved to be unliveable for everyone concerned. Eric travelled from San Francisco each weekend to help out. Both of Bettelheim's daughters proposed to put the couple up in their homes, but Trude and Bruno, not wanting to infringe on their family lives, declined the offers. They preferred in any case to remain independent for as long as possible. Bettelheim inquired about retirement homes in the area, but none of them suited. Either he was too old, or Trude was too ill, or there was a five-year waiting list, etc.

1982 was a busy year. Hardly had Trude got back on her feet again, walking a little each day, than Bettelheim resumed his activities. *On Learning to Read* and his *New Yorker* article on Freud[49] came out within two months of one another, and he was in demand for interviews and lectures. At Eric's urging, he even agreed to play a short role in a Woody Allen film, *Zelig*. And starting in January, he got seriously down to work on the writing of *A Good Enough Parent*. It was to contain 'no advice: on the contrary, a warning (to parents) not to look for it, nor to accept it, but an effort to show them how they could and should go about analyzing each situation as it comes about,' he wrote.[50] In April, he spent a few days in Chicago, the first visit on which he did not set foot in the Orthogenic School. In June, however, he was obliged to stop work. He underwent an operation for a detached retina, and the anaesthetic caused a serious blockage of his prostate. A second operation a few days later lasted seven hours, and took a heavy toll on him. 'Only now, two months after it all, have I somewhat recovered. I can now walk for some ten minutes without pain, although in a snail's tempo .... So right now both Trude and I are more or less crippled. We manage to take care of each other and ourselves, but our life and what we can do has become severely limited. Still, we manage, and only hope it'll stay this way for a while,' he wrote in mid-August.[51]

At around this time, Bettelheim made a first contact with the Hemlock Society, set up two years earlier in Los Angeles by a Briton, Derek Humphry, to promote assisted suicide and the right to die in dignity. He and Trude agreed on the issue; neither of them wanted to ever find themselves helplessly forced to stay alive when they had lost all ability to act for themselves. They had seen too many of their friends thus reduced to the status of vegetables. And, despite his great affection for Fritz Redl, Bettelheim had not been able to bring himself to visit his friend since a stroke had severely incapacitated him a few months earlier.

What is most striking about this whole period, however, is the way the Bettelheims would bounce back, as soon as a respite in their health problems allowed them to. For despite his tendency to dramatize his own ailments, Bruno also showed great courage, as can be seen from his correspondence. As his strength gradually faded, as simple everyday acts became more and more difficult, he would go through the same cycle: initial discouragement and bitterness, followed rapidly by an attempt to accept the new situation, to compare it to others which were even more difficult, and then to overcome it by plunging into something interesting. That year, following a visit from Naomi and her husband, a chess enthusiast, Bettelheim discovered the joys of playing against a computer ('which lacks compassion – it beats me all the time,' he lamented). He marvelled at the progress he was able to make in a game which he had not played since his teens. He also enjoyed rereading the novels of Jane Austen and

Trollope: 'Their quiet irony, combined with their gentle acceptance of the foibles of man touch me more than the qualities of other writers.'[52]

At about the time Anna Freud died, in 1982, he read Aldo Carotenuto's *A Secret Symmetry*,[53] based on the letters of the psychoanalyst Sabina Spielrein, who had been both Carl Jung's patient and for a time his lover before embarking on a dialogue with Sigmund Freud which played a role in his elaboration of the death instinct concept. The previously unknown story of the relations this pioneer of psychoanalysis (who was to be Piaget's analyst for nine months) entertained with the two giants inspired Bettelheim to write a long essay, in which he expressed some of his ideas on Freud's weaknesses – and therefore his humanity – and also showed what a poor opinion he had of Jung. 'I would not trust anything Jung says about Freud. Unfortunately ... neither of them was open to the other, both dissimulated, only Jung much worse. The friendship with Jung is a sad chapter in Freud's development, while Jung lies outright,' he wrote.[54] The *Atlantic Monthly*, which had commissioned the article, turned it down. Which did not surprise Bettelheim: 'Since the New York intellectual establishment is in the hands of either Jungians or Freudians, the only chance one has to be published is to side with one against the other – not to criticize both,' he remarked.[55] Only to be forced to eat his words three months later, when his article appeared in the *New York Review of Books*![56] His sarcasm however was probably triggered above all by the frosty reception given to his *Freud and Man's Soul* in the psychoanalytic community which, while it was to be expected, hurt him. He was understandably amused, a few months later, when the Hogarth Press, the British publisher of Freud's Standard Edition, contacted him to seek his advice on how the translations could be improved.

On March 22, 1983 in San Francisco, Bettelheim also had the pleasure of receiving the Goethe Medal, an annual award for service to German culture. In telling his friends of the distinction, he usually mentioned Sigmund Freud's great pride at being awarded the Goethe Prize, reserved to the best writers in the German language. While stressing that the two honours were not at all comparable, he never forgot to point out that the president of the Goethe Institute was at that time a descendant of Bismarck.

Their determination to live life to the utmost right to the end led the Bettelheims to undertake, at the end of August 1983, a European tour that was too much for Trude. 'A few days in New York to break the long trip, then on to London for a long week and another in Venice, and then a few days to visit with old friends in Basel. That's all,' Bettelheim announced modestly, just before leaving.[57] What he omitted to say was that the couple had decided to cross the Atlantic aboard the *Queen Elizabeth II* rather than by plane. His eightieth birthday was coming up, and in order to avoid the inevitable festivities, they had arranged to be in mid-ocean at the time. Naomi, who was in New York, gave them a *Sacher-törte*[58] for the crossing;

as it turned out, that was the only thing they could eat on the whole trip, which was marred by a huge storm. It was an ordeal for Trude, but being reunited with Eric and a few days of rest in London put her back on her feet. When the couple arrived in Basel, after Venice, however, her friend Emmi was shocked to see what efforts Trude was making to keep up with her husband and avoid disappointing him. The couple were in a taxi in Zurich, on their way to see a movie after visiting Emmi's daughter, when Trude collapsed from a heart attack. At the hospital the doctor asked Bettelheim: 'You're opposed to extraordinary measures, I believe?' After a moment's hesitation, Bruno muttered: 'Yes, I am.'

'You'll be sorry for this!' Emmi, who had rushed from Basel, thought to herself. Bettelheim had to be helped with everything, while Trude's condition was critical. Then, having met up by chance at the airport even though they were all coming from different directions, their three children joined them. Emmi was struck at how instantly Trude perked up when Eric arrived. She sat up in bed and smiled; an outside observer would never have guessed what an ordeal she had just been through.

About a year before that trip Sandy Lewis, who had been one of Dr B's favourite students, had written to tell him of his success on Wall Street since he had left the Orthogenic School. He wanted to thank Bettelheim and see if he in turn could do anything for him. From Zurich, Bettelheim now sent him an SOS; Lewis offered to send his private plane over for Trude, but the Swiss authorities would not allow her to travel home on it. Instead, she was flown out to Frankfurt on a Red Cross plane, nine days after her heart attack. From there she returned to San Francisco, accompanied by Bruno, Eric, a doctor and a nurse, arriving at the Stanford University hospital on a stretcher. A few days later she was allowed to return home, and a month after that Bettelheim told his friends that Trude was recovering her strength and morale. 'We are determined to try and live as well as we can and try not to let things get us down,'[59] he added.

'Trude never believed she was as ill as she was really – it's often the case with cancer patients …. Three months before she died, she told me about a trip they had made to New York, where she went to see four plays, went shopping, etc. After Zurich, even Bruno thought she would live for another two years,' says Emmi Vischer-Radanowitz.[60] It was not to be. Trude Bettelheim struggled on for just over a year, in spite of agonizing pain, with the times when she could sit out on the terrace and enjoy the sun in relative comfort becoming progressively rarer. Their children took turns coming to see them. In April, the Bettelheims made a trip to New York to see Naomi, who was leaving for Vienna; her husband had been given a four-year posting in the city. At the theatre, in spite of what Trude wrote to Emmi, they never made it to the end of the play, as she could not remain sitting for such long periods. A little later, they spent a week by the sea. Bettelheim was working on his book about child-rearing, and writing letters. He too had tried to commit his memoirs to tape, but had soon given up. He could not talk to Trude about her approaching death, and how he would manage without her. His will, and all the plans he had laid up to that point, had been based on the assumption that she would outlive him. He had not changed anything, and she resisted all his attempts to raise the subject.

In mid-September, Trude underwent a new course of X-ray treatment. The cancer had spread, and now affected her back and one of her feet. She was now in continuous pain. 'Please, keep all this to yourself, but I have almost no one to discuss it with. Here, we don't have any very close friends and, even if we had, I would not tell them anything, for fear Trude would hear how sick she really is,' Bettelheim wrote to a friend, after summing up the medical situation.[61] On Thursday October 25, Trude turned seventy-three, and Eric came over to spend a few days with his parents. On the Sunday evening, after he had left, the couple started a game of Scrabble, but Trude felt too unwell to complete it. Shortly afterwards she had another heart attack, and Bruno accompanied her to the hospital in an ambulance. 'But even there she made plans with me for the next morning. A few hours later she died. The end was relatively easy and relatively painless, and one must be grateful for that.'[62]

As soon as he could summon the strength to do so, Bettelheim wrote to Carl Frankenstein. 'We had been loving each other for the last fifty years. Ours has been a very good life, despite the horrid experiences we shared under Hitler. Despite it, our life turned out much better than we had any reason to hope. I owe to her all I am. It was she whose love encouraged me finally to finish my doctorate and which made it possible for me to overcome my latent depression to make a success here in the US. She was a wonderful wife and mother. I do not know how I shall be able to carry on without her ... but I shall try since this is what she would have wanted.'[63] And to Candy, with whom he usually mentioned Trude less often, he added: 'We were the center of each other's lives much more than anybody knew, because we kept what we had gone through together to ourselves.'[64]

Unlike her husband, Trude Bettelheim did not wish to be cremated. She had picked out the Skylawn Memorial Park, where both of them are buried. Located in Half Moon Bay, some twenty miles north of Portola Valley on a hilltop overlooking the Pacific, it is a place of strange beauty. Stark, like the eucalyptus forests that surround it, abrupt like the steep fall to the ocean, yet calm. There the two exiles have found a suitable resting place. Every evening at sunset, when the fast-moving fingers of fog that are the region's hallmark slide in menacingly off the ocean, this little corner of California looks for all the world like an Austrian forest.

On the day of Trude's funeral, Wanda Willig called from New York: Bettelheim's sister, Margarethe, was in a deep depression. She suggested that Naomi stop off in New York on her way back to Vienna to spend a little time with her aunt. But Bettelheim instructed his daughter to fly directly to her husband. Two months later he had to make the trip himself: Margarethe had tried to kill herself, and was now in a semi-coma. He spent Christmas week trying to persuade the doctors to let her die. She was in pain, and complaining continually.

Since Margarethe had arrived in New York, some six months after her brother, the two siblings had kept in touch with one another, but from afar most of the time. They got on well at a distance, never forgetting each other's birthdays and other festivals. But their lives and interests were very different. Whenever Bettelheim was in New York he would have dinner with Margarethe, but he often asked the Willigs to join the party. For he felt that Margarethe lived in the past, which depressed him. In the United States, she had never managed to build the kind of social life she had had in Vienna. Early on, she had tried working in radio, but her strong accent and declamatory style did not go down well. This left her bitter. She and her husband lived well, but they had opted very early on to move into a retirement home. Since she had become a widow, Margarethe had taken to complaining a great deal, about her rheumatism in particular and life in general.

During the week he spent watching her suffer, with death as her only possible escape, Bettelheim felt guilty, according to Wanda Willig, who helped him get over this new trial coming so soon after Trude's death. He no doubt recalled all the things his sister had done for him in the past, since he made a point of telling his children about them. When he was a young man, he had been both proud and a little jealous of her successes on the stage. He remembered how she had introduced him to her friends in the press and the theatre world. And how she always arrived just in time to drag him away from the gaming table when he was about to lose more than he could afford. And, of course, all the efforts she had made to obtain his freedom from the concentration camp.

A story came back to him concerning his brother-in-law, a Hungarian who had served as an officer in the Imperial army during World War I. He had then been engaged, but with the collapse of the empire, his fiancée's family no longer considered him a good match and the marriage was called off. In despair, he resolved to take his own life. He rented a room in a grand hotel, put on his best uniform, and shot a bullet into his heart. He was still conscious when a chambermaid burst into the room and found him lying in a pool of blood. 'My God – and that beautiful shirt completely ruined!' she cried. Having thus realized how little a life could be worth, he pulled through and survived. He met Margarethe later, and dated her for almost twenty years in Austria before finally marrying her, in the United States. In 1974 he died from heart failure, probably caused by the bullet, which had never been removed.

On New Year's Eve, Bettelheim arrived late at Maria Kramer's party.[65] He was obsessed with his sister's fate, and could talk of nothing else throughout the evening. Two years earlier, his cousin Edith Buxbaum had died in Seattle, only shortly after getting in touch with him again. A few days after that New Year's party, his friend Hans Willig was to suffer a serious heart attack. One by one, his last childhood companions were deserting him.

'It is nearly six months that Trude died – I can still not believe it, but with the passing of that much time ... patterns slowly begin to adjust. Unpleasant and sad as such adjustments are, they no longer cut so deeply and so acutely. It is rather a general depressive feeling that life has become utterly pointless. I am glad you can write, and write heretical articles. I still cannot write. As I sit down and try to do so, sadness floods me to the degree that I become incapacitated. But one goes to bed in the evening, and hesitantly but nevertheless gets up in the morning, although I do not know what for. And so the days pass,' wrote Bettelheim in April 1985.[66]

After Trude's death, he seemed suddenly to have lost the ability to bounce back, to counter his pessimism and attacks of anxiety with the certainty, acquired through years of experience, that out of every catastrophe a new strength can be gained. Up until that point, even when he was very depressed, his letters always reflected such a movement. In fact, they probably offered him the best opportunity for it. During the day, Bettelheim was not able to hold back his flashes of anger, the hurtful phrases that earned him a bad reputation, and also made him feel guilty (which usually pushed him to behave even more provocatively). But late in the evening, when he sat down to write, he could at last break out of this vicious circle, returning to the world of ideas and lofty feelings which calmed him down.

As time went by, Bettelheim became more and more aware of the role Trude had played in that process. A year after her death, he wrote: 'Trude knew how to enjoy life so much better than me. Despite all my analyses, I was never able to overcome the depression which followed me all my life. The fact that, relatively late in life, I fully understood its origin helped me to master things intellectually, but not on a deeper emotional level. It was Trude who helped me the most to pull out of my depression at times and it was she alone who, despite all my self-doubts, made it possible for me to achieve what is known as the work of a lifetime (I try to continue working, because when I work, I think of nothing else).'[67]

By the end of 1985, Bruno Bettelheim had completed the first draft of *A Good Enough Parent*. Despite his depression, he had never been completely inactive. During that year, in addition to the book, he had notably produced four articles, including 'Freud's Vienna', written for the catalogue of the *Paris-Vienne* art exhibition.[68] He had also penned a short preface for the British paperback edition of *The Informed Heart*, dipping into the texts written for *Surviving* to re-use the passage in which he stressed that the death instinct gets the upper hand when one no longer feels the desire of others. That was indeed his problem. Although handling ideas and giving a meaning to things helped calm him down, his own work did not have enough value in his own eyes to give him back his love of life. He had admitted as much to Ruth Marquis one day, when he encouraged her to send a note to the author of a book she admired: 'That's why one writes, you know.'

In August, Bettelheim spent a month with Alvin Rosenfeld at Bellagio, in Northern Italy. Rosenfeld had been appointed director of Child Psychiatry training at the Stanford Medical School in 1977, and it was he who had invited Bettelheim to hold a seminar there. Now he had undertaken to produce a book from the resulting material. He was by then based in New York, but his respect for the old psychoanalyst had grown as his work in child psychiatry brought him daily confirmation of the usefulness of his teaching. There was real affection between the two men, although Rosenfeld was forty-two years Bettelheim's junior. The book was his idea. Bettelheim did not believe that collections of dialogues had much sales potential, and cited *Dialogues with Mothers* as a case in point. As the project was lagging, Rosenfeld had obtained an invitation from the Rockefeller Foundation to spend a month in the Villa Serballoni, a retreat for writers on an island in Lake Como.

The trip to Europe did Bettelheim good. On his way to Italy he stopped off for two weeks in London to stay with Eric, and then went on to Vienna to visit Naomi. He could not get over the fact that she was living in the city of his youth, and took her on a tour of his old haunts. 'But as soon as I returned to the empty house where everything reminds me of my terrible loss, I am back in a depression, maybe not as deep as before, but still serious enough so that nothing I do makes any sense .... Still, I try to keep busy,' he wrote later.[69]

Not only was he still teaching a little, but he was constantly being invited to take part in conferences or run seminars. He was called on for interviews and for advice, and universities lined up to bestow honours on him. The conservative Hoover Institution, based in Stanford, offered him a fellowship. In the spring, he travelled to New York State to receive yet another honorary doctorate and spend a weekend with his son. From there he went to New England, where two renowned boarding schools wanted his advice on how to deal with their drug and sexual delinquency problems.

Such activities were a welcome source of distraction for Bettelheim, and also flattering. In each case, he did what he could to help. As regards the boarding schools, for instance, 'I tried to convince them that a disciplinary board would only be recognized by the children if they were part of it, and also that they should think about the causes, and ask themselves why these children are so desperate that they choose to poison themselves.'[70] But nothing could shake off for very long the feeling of solitude and uselessness that now plagued him. Only the weekly consultations that he gave in the Child and Adolescent Psychiatric Inpatient (CAPI) Unit of San Jose Hospital still gave him an occasional feeling of being useful. The first time he had met Saul Wasserman, the head of the unit, Bettelheim had called him naïve. But over the years a relationship had grown up between them, which in many ways resembled those he had entertained with the school counsellors. The CAPI, which until Wasserman's arrival functioned according to behavioural 'punishment-reward' principles, took in a lot of severely maltreated children, and Bettelheim's teaching proved providential with them. This brought about a complete rethinking of methods.[71] 'We were very well meaning and we were convinced that the kids knew it. He helped us to see through their eyes, to understand the deep mistrust they felt towards all adults – including us!' Wasserman says.[72] But the young doctor also got the old man to talk about his life, his love of art, the concentration camps and his youth.

When considering Bettelheim's final years, it is striking to see how this man who had previously surrounded himself with women, finding in his exchanges with them the desire and the punch to keep going, now relied mainly on young men, heirs in whom he seemed to be seeking the strength of a father. Sandy Lewis, who was protective in one of the fields through which his anxiety often expressed itself, money. His literary agent, Theron Raines, who shielded him in the publishing world. Alvin Rosenfeld, Saul Wasserman, and a few other spiritual heirs, whose turn it was to act and to heal. And, of course, his son Eric.

After Trude's death, memories of the Orthogenic School returned to haunt Bettelheim even more frequently, and he was no longer able to combat the feelings of loss and resentment that came with them. When Karen Zelan paid him a visit with her children one day, she was shocked to find that he could talk of nothing else. On his trip East, he had stopped off for two days in Chicago, to give a lecture. 'Since it was known all over Chicago that I would be there, Jacqui more or less forced me to pay a visit to the school, mostly to give the world the impression that we are on the best of terms. It was an ordeal,' he reported to Candy.[73] He got the impression that the only people pleased to see him again were the domestic staff.

His increasing inability to distance himself from his emotions even affected his view of former students. On learning that a few had said publicly that they should never have been sent to the school, Bettelheim – who only a few years earlier would have viewed this as a healthy reaction[74] – now only saw it as ingratitude. What allowed him to overcome such bitterness was the marks of affection he received from other former patients, and they were numerous. One brought him an academic distinction; Sandy Lewis made a donation to the University of Chicago to top up his retirement pension; Myles Gordon was to contribute 10,000 dollars to the funding of the 1986 conference in his honour; a former anorexic came by to show him photos of her children, etc. Hardly a week went by without either a phone call or a visit from a former student or staffer, reminding him that his work had not been in vain. And perfect strangers wrote to him from all over the world, either to ask for advice or to thank him for the effect one of his books or lectures had had on their lives. In France, a psychologist whom he did not even know had undertaken to write a book about him; this at first irritated him greatly, then touched him.[75]

But on each such occasion, the soothing effect quickly wore off. The death of his wife had also left Bettelheim even more aware of the ravages of ageing. This returned again and again in his letters. 'So, you are reaching eighty years of age. You'll see how everything becomes difficult,'[76] he wrote to one friend. He found it profoundly humiliating that so many of his everyday acts, previously taken for granted, had now become difficult or impossible. The time it took simply to wash or get dressed. The shoelaces he could no longer tie, as he could not bend down. He also suffered from the obstruction in his oesophagus, which now prevented him from eating practically any solid food. Even with help from his neighbours, Bruno Bettelheim soon realized that there was no way he could go on living in the remote Portola Valley eyrie. Less than a month after Trude's death he was writing: 'I've just got over a pretty nasty case of flu ... and it made it obvious that I need to change my living conditions. This is very painful to me, as I am very attached to everything which reminds me of our life together. But here I'm really a long way away from everything.'[77]

His daughter Ruth reiterated an offer she had made before her mother's death. As the grounds of her house in Pasadena were large, she proposed to add on a wing in which her father could live. He would thus remain independent, while no longer being alone. Bettelheim hesitated before accepting. He did not like Los Angeles, and he was aware that he would be a burden for his daughter. He once again considered entering a retirement home. He was not enthusiastic about it: 'As for the possibility of living over there with three hundred other old people who like me are awaiting death, it's not very pleasant, but of course it would be more reasonable.'[78] He soon found out however that the Palo Alto establishment he had in mind could not accept him, on account of his liquid diet.

His daughter's offer was all the more attractive in that, in the months following Trude's death, Ruth had sought to replace her as the family's pole of stability. Physically, she indeed resembled her mother.[79] By the end of February 1985, Bettelheim's mind was made up: he would move in next to Ruth. Not without misgivings; when announcing the decision to his friends, he also listed the proposals that he had recently received (a fellowship at the Hoover Institution, the chair of a committee set up to study the working of high schools, etc.), all of which would have required his continued presence in San Francisco or its environs! But the architect was already at work on the Pasadena house, and when Eric joined him there at Christmas (Naomi, who had just had a baby, stayed in Vienna that year), the blueprints were ready. 'Of course the children miss their mother a great deal, as it was always Trude who gave us a marvelous Christmas.

But Ruth tries to emulate her, and she is also a wonderful mother to her children. So one generation follows on from the next, and one must try to hold on to that to avoid losing all courage,' he wrote.[80] Bettelheim suddenly seemed ready to emerge from his depression: 'I'm finally getting a grip on myself and beginning to try and go on living, mainly for the children's sake. I can't replace their mother, but I can at least try and put off the day when they also lose their father.'[81]

A month later, his tone had changed dramatically. He had gone down to Pasadena to make final arrangements for the construction work, and heard from Ruth that she wanted to divorce her husband. The couple's relationship had been shaky for some time. And yet, 'had it not been for my project, the marriage would have gone on for a while. But her husband, who at first was in favor, didn't want to know about it after a while. This implicates me in the break-up, which is something that weighs heavily on my heart .... If Ruth obtains her divorce and custody of the children, then I'll go to help her.'[82] That is Bettelheim's version of events. Although it probably exaggerated his responsibility in the couple's break-up, it heralded the last act of the drama: his feeling accused of having destroyed Ruth's marriage. Such is the implacable logic of family feuds. This view of things presented as obvious an outcome whose dangers were apparent to all concerned. It gave Bettelheim an altruistic excuse for not choosing the exile of an old people's home. And it provided Ruth with a home, as her husband was refusing to move out of their house in Pasadena.

Everyone tried to dissuade Bettelheim from moving in with his elder daughter. They were too alike, in both their demands and their needs. Initially, Eric and Naomi managed to persuade their father not to move right away. Then, as he appeared more and more determined to do so, Naomi canvassed his old friends, notably Gina and Wanda Willig, to try to get him to listen to reason. 'We all knew it was going to be a disaster,' she says. Gina, who saw similarities between Bettelheim's relationship with Ruth and the one he had had previously with his sister Margarethe, suggested that he instead move into a home in San Francisco. That way, she added, they could go to concerts together and she would be able to take care of him. Bettelheim had been to see the establishment, but the visit only strengthened his determination to move in with Ruth.

He was feeling somewhat better. He had been moved by the birth of his second grandson in Vienna, which he mentioned in all his letters. He was also pleased because Eric had become engaged. He believed that the timing of the two events, like that of Ruth's divorce, was no coincidence. 'The death of a parent triggers a psychic revolution in children. Naomi, who had been wanting a child for a long time, became pregnant only after her mother's death. Our lives are so strangely woven with that of our parents,' he wrote.[83] He had another, more down-to-earth reason for feeling better: the white Mercedes that Sandy Lewis had offered him for

Christmas. He may have feigned indifference, but he was clearly proud of it.

While waiting for Ruth's divorce to go through, before moving to Los Angeles, he had a busy schedule. In April he went to Europe, starting with four days in London. The BBC had organized a debate, 'For or Against Psychoanalysis', between him and the writer George Steiner. It was a taxing experience for Bettelheim. 'Steiner's arguments against psychoanalysis were really silly. He even stooped down to say that the Oedipus theory can't be true, because he never had sexual desires for his mother. This I hadn't heard since World War I. It was so obvious that he is scared to death to discover his unconscious that one can only have *Mitleid*[84] with his towering neurosis – if he would just not be so intellectually arrogant. So I was sorry that the debate proceeded on such a low level.'[85] Although in full possession of his intellectual powers, Bettelheim had lost some of his nimbleness in out-manoeuvring debating opponents. The day after the BBC discussion he was due to lecture in Stuttgart, at the invitation of the Robert Bosch Foundation. Feeling upset, and suffering from an intestinal ailment, he took too many pills before leaving London, with the result that he had to stop in the middle of his address. The incident turned out not to be very serious, but it shook him. He then went on to Vienna, where his memories of Trude, and the election posters for president-to-be Kurt Waldheim, marred his pleasure at meeting his Viennese grandson – whom, as he liked to point out, his father had named Immanuel, after Kant.

In May, Bettelheim travelled to Chicago for the university's conference in his honour. Despite the tensions with Jacquelyn Sanders, he found it a heartwarming experience to see so many of the people who had made up his life of thirty years. And yet, he had a hard time getting close to people. Adrian Kuypers, who held a party for him, found herself spending most of the evening by his side: people would come over to him full of effusive enthusiasm, but after chatting for a while, they drifted away. Bettelheim seemed to have lost his ability to reach out to others. He did not even go over to greet his friend George Perkins, who had been the school's consultant psychiatrist for years, even though a stroke had left him paraplegic, and he had to be carried up in his wheelchair. Former staffers and students had indeed flocked to see Dr B again, but they did not have with him the kind of relationship which could have given them an insight into his depression. He had for so long played the father figure for them, the figure of authority, that they were unable to see things the other way round. They could not possibly imagine how deep the feelings of solitude and loss ran in him, or the ever-stronger impression of slipping into physical decay; that humiliation of the body that ends up by also enslaving the mind. Like what had happened to his father Anton in the Tulln clinic; and what threatened him when he was in the hands of the Nazis. Like what was then happening to Morris Janowitz, who at the age of sixty-seven was in the final stages of Parkinson's Disease. After seeing him delirious and helpless, Bettelheim kept saying to Gayle: 'It can't be .... He's too young, too young. I'm the one who should be dying, not him.'

Once back in California, Bettelheim started sorting through his posses- sions, and this depressed him even more. 'With each piece of paper that one throws away goes a bit of one's life, or so at least it feels.'[86] He was apprehensive at having to meet new people in his new home. 'True friends, one makes only relatively early in life, and best before and during adoles- cence. It seems after puberty things become frozen, at least emotionally, to the degree that one can no longer give so freely of oneself, nor take the other into oneself, as true friendship requires.'[87] He was convinced that he owed to Trude the few acquaintances he still had in Palo Alto. In deciding how to share out his possessions among his children, he also betrayed his apprehension at the prospect of living with his daughter in Los Angeles, a city whose climate he feared, and which he saw as superficial and materi- alist: 'As for Ruth, she does not want anything that she cannot put in the dishwasher!'[88] Meanwhile he was correcting the manuscript of *A Good Enough Parent*, and reading the proofs of Robert Jay Lifton's book on Nazi doctors, which he was due to review for the *New York Times*.

In mid-June he went to visit the house that Ruth had found in Santa Monica. It was beautiful. With its tiled roof, its large arched windows with leaded panes and its sculptured door in reddish wood, however, it looked more like the home of some latterday Mexican grandee than that of an ageing Viennese psychoanalyst. The interior, with its immense vestibule and double staircase, would have suited a movie star. In other words it was, as Bettelheim would later admit, anything but *gemütlich*.[89] 'Every- thing for show, and nothing for a comfortable life; all of California only worse.'[90] Needless to say it was also very expensive; much more so than Bettelheim had anticipated, particularly as he was going to have to pay for it on his own. Being unable to sell her Pasadena home, still occupied by her husband, Ruth could not pay her share.

It would be pointless to list the financial squabbles which from that point on were to poison relations between the old man and two of his children (Naomi remained out of them, except for trying from time to time to find a solution – just as, when a child, she had preferred to stay out of family conversations). Bettelheim himself said and wrote on many occa- sions that when people quarrel about money, the real reason lies elsewhere. He would see that principle at work here, attributing his son's warnings against the investment he was making to the fact that he had chosen to live with his elder daughter. But it was too late. All the time that Bruno Bettelheim had failed to devote to his children in the past was to be counted out, in dollars and cents, each child convinced he or she was being cheated. Which is maybe what he had in mind a few months before his death, when in reply to a question from David James Fisher, he remarked, as if making a painful discovery, 'You know, my children are children of a Holocaust survivor.'[91]

What Bettelheim appears to have grasped less clearly, judging from his letters, is the complexity of his own relationship to money, beyond his legendary generosity. Money: for the lack of it, as an adolescent, he had seen his beautiful city ravaged; to it, as a young man, he had had to sacrifice his most noble dreams; without it, he would almost certainly have died at the hands of the Nazis. Money of which he would one day be stripped, or so said the family curse. He may have despised it, but he was always terrified of it. And he had spent his life trying to dominate it – i.e. trying not to let himself be dominated by it – because he was all too aware of its destructive power.

At a time when he feared that his health might require major outlays, in a country in which serious illness could mean financial ruin, Bettelheim was obviously nervous at pouring all his resources into this opulent house, which he knew was not meant for him. His anxiety was aggravated by the fact that the Hoover Institution fellow to whom he had sold the house in Portola Valley was having a hard time getting together the sum. Eric, whom he had asked to watch over his financial security, advised him against the purchase. But Bettelheim went ahead and signed, accusing his son of selfishness.

He finally moved into Adelaide Place at the end of September 1986. Two weeks earlier, he wrote: 'I am naturally somewhat apprehensive at the thought of moving and living with Ruth. Of course, she too has anxiety. But we are both determined to try and make it work. It will not be easy, but one can assume that it is not for a very long time.'[92] Yet on the very day of his arrival, Bettelheim understood that living with his daughter would be even more difficult than he had expected. Ruth and her children had already been settled in for a month. The young woman had taken the master bedroom, on the first floor, leaving the other large room to her father. Just like the arrangement in the old days, in Chicago. Except that she was not Trude, and her children were not Bettelheim's children. And, even more seriously, he no longer had the Orthogenic School in which to go and work, and spend his days.

'Ruth is trying, but there is no doubt that she feels I am an imposition on her life,' he wrote to Gayle Janowitz, two weeks after his arrival.[93] From that point on, the tone of his letters becomes more and more poignant. Although they are often detailed, they do not allow the reader to get a proper understanding of what was going on between father and daughter, they simply show him sliding inexorably into the deepest depression. Not surprisingly, it was at this time that he started telling Frankenstein about the origins of his anxiety, referring implicitly to his father's syphilis, and stressing how much his childhood fears had been reawakened when Trude was dying.

These letters are moving also because in them Bettelheim never tried to put all the blame on his daughter. On the contrary, he stressed how tough Ruth's life was, and how, after a year-long process of divorce, she had to rebuild it completely. He always mentioned the efforts she was making to help him. But as he told Candy Hilldrup: 'There was a misunderstanding right from the start. Ruth thought I was going to come and take care of her. Instead, she saw a tired old man show up who himself needed to be taken care of.' He felt like an intruder in his own home. He thought that his grandchildren held him responsible for their parents' divorce. He felt bad about that, but at the same time had little in common with them, finding them noisy and intrusive. The two small rooms that his daughter had assigned him on the ground floor were located on either side of the main entrance, and separated from it only by heavy curtains; he had no place in which he felt comfortable working. Ruth complained that he frightened her young patients; he was afraid of disturbing someone each time he moved from one room to the other.

Having been unable to obtain Ruth Bettelheim's version of events, it would be dishonest for me to try to describe their quarrels in greater detail. It is indeed easy to imagine how impossible Bettelheim was to live with. How, torn between love and dashed hopes, both father and daughter could be convinced they were doing their utmost, and resented the other for what they saw as ingratitude. How much each must have felt wronged and betrayed.

Bettelheim was to live at Adelaide Place for twenty months. With some ups and some terrible downs, a lot of illness, a few trips and even some brief moments in which he thought that the arrangement might work out. In spite of his antipathy for Los Angeles, he had found there a lot of acquaintances and even some friends. Within a few months of his arrival he was running a training seminar in a clinic for psychotic children. A little later Seymour Feschback, a professor of psychology at UCLA, invited him to come and discuss psychoanalysis twice a month in his classes. He was regularly being asked to teach on other campuses in the region. And he went on giving lectures, running workshops and replying to the dozens of requests for help he received each month. ('The parents' despair is really terrible … I spend almost all my time answering them, so that they feel that one has at least a little compassion for them,' he wrote).[94]

Eric came to spend Christmas with him, helping him settle in and unpack his books and papers from the boxes in which they had been left. Bettelheim was happy at the closeness he felt to his son; the two discussed politics, art and literature and felt they understood one another. Another piece of good news cheered him up: Naomi and her husband were returning to the US, to settle in Washington DC. Nevertheless, Bettelheim had by now realized that his life was over. 'My children are good children, but we have brought them up to have full lives which occupy them fully. So I don't really feel I serve much purpose any more. We all live too long for our own good.'[95]

This was when he started to seriously look into ways of ending his life before it became too late – i.e. before a stroke or some other such accident reduced him to helplessness, which he feared most of all. The memory of his father's last two years was now haunting him, and as he told his son-in-law one day, he was determined to ensure that his children did not go through what he had endured. At first, he only discussed the issue with a few friends who were able to understand. Such as the psychoanalyst Heda Bolgar, a fellow Viennese whom he had known in Chicago, and with whom he enjoyed socializing in Los Angeles. 'He was very rational about it. What he wanted was to know what to do when the time came. Because the most striking thing was that he didn't actually want to die. He was depressed, but not suicidal. If someone had been able to guarantee that, when the time came, he would be there to help him go without suffering, I don't think he would have killed himself,' she says.[96] Dr Al Flarsheim had once made that promise to Bettelheim but, in 1980, he had taken his own life.

On account of his eating problems, the slightest ailment now took on alarming proportions. In February 1987 a bout of influenza, complicated by bronchitis and the after-effects of a fall on his hip, kept him in bed for two months ('This illness has shown me that I was right to come here, for Ruth did all she could to assist me'[97]). After a new series of tests, one of his doctors now recommended an operation on his oesophagus. He neverthe-less pushed ahead with his travels and speaking engagements, going notably to Detroit in June to be the key speaker at a dinner held to mark Richard Sterba's ninetieth birthday. The following month found him in Ramat Gan, in the suburbs of Tel Aviv, for a debate on 'Childhood in the Technological Era'. On that occasion, unconcerned by possible charges of sexism, he questioned the role of day care centres in an infant's develop-ment.

The lull in his relations with Ruth was short-lived. Each time he returned to 'what I now must call home, although it does not feel like one',[98] he soon was invaded by the same impression of being of no use to anyone or anything. In the outside world, he was fêted, respected and thanked. At home, his life was empty. But it was now taking him progressively longer to get over the strain of each trip. On his return from Israel he was hospitalized for a serious attack of gastro-enteritis, and fed through a drip for four days.

In October 1987, Bettelheim nevertheless resumed his travels, this time for a heavily booked tour. After a dozen or so lectures across the United States, he flew to Vienna for a major conference on 'Fifty Years of Exile', attended by prominent Austrian expatriates from the whole range of scientific and cultural disciplines. He spoke on 'the transfer of culture from Austria to the United States', and as the two other participants older than him had declined the honour, it was he who gave a reply to the Chancellor's address on behalf of the gathering. The Austrian Minister of Universities awarded him a 'Cross of Honour' to mark the fiftieth anniversary of his doctorate. And Vienna's Freud Society invited him to address a gathering of its members. Bettelheim's fame being what it was, however, the small room in the *Rathaus*, or City Hall, that was generally used for such gatherings soon proved too small, and the organizers had to get the main meeting room specially opened. It was thus that, without realizing it immediately, the author of *The Informed Heart* spoke under a large portrait of Karl Lueger, the famously anti-Semitic politician who had been Vienna's mayor at the time of his birth! Very much on form, Bettelheim described his first contacts with psychoanalysis.

After evoking his rivalry with Otto Fenichel for the favours of Lisl Lazarsfeld, and his first encounters with Richard Sterba, he told the story of little 'Johnny', the metaphor which best sums up what a life spent in the service of psychoanalysis had taught him.[99] 'Johnny', he said, was a young psychotic being treated by Editha Sterba,[100] and Bettelheim used to meet him in the Sterbas' common waiting-room. He had tried on several occasions to strike up a conversation with him, but without success; the child would either remain silent or reply with incomprehensible mumblings. 'Johnny' had an obsession which disturbed Bettelheim: on arrival he would rip a leaf off a prickly cactus on a windowsill and start chewing it. He did not appear to feel any pain, even when drops of blood appeared on his lips. One day, unable to stand it any longer, Bettelheim blurted out: 'I don't know how long you have been seeing Dr Sterba, but it must be at least two years ... and here you are still chewing these awful leaves!' Whereupon the child looked at him and said: 'What are two years compared with eternity?'[101] Bettelheim felt humbled.

He drew a first lesson from the incident immediately, which was that his apparent concern for 'Johnny' in fact expressed a very personal worry: he was afraid that his own analysis was not progressing quickly enough. He felt guilty at the hypocrisy, but it took him much longer to decipher the little boy's deeper message. This was that physical pain over time is nothing, when compared to psychological suffering which knows no time limit. 'Johnny' had also showed him in his own way that when people are in deep distress they care nothing for making polite conversation. When suffering is great, the only exchanges worth having are those in which the speaker is truly implicated, those which convey meaning, not conventions.

After Vienna, Bettelheim spent a weekend at a psychoanalytic seminar in the Tyrol, and then flew to London for three more lectures. He then went on to give a week of courses in Florence, before returning to the US. It had been, he wrote, 'a beautiful journey. It does one good to be celebrated in old age, and ... I was truly pleased with it. It is the first time since Trude's death that I felt good, even though I missed her all the time.'[102] In the US, Bettelheim spent a few days in Washington with Naomi and her family.

He felt giddy a couple of times and, the last morning, had some trouble holding up his right arm. But he paid no attention to those symptoms and flew on to Orlando, Florida, where he was due to give a last address. The next morning, he woke up with his right arm and hand paralysed. It was a mild stroke, and he would never fully recover the use of his hand. But, above all, the incident fed his anxiety: What if the next stroke were to leave him completely paralysed?

Once again, Ruth rushed to her father's bedside, bringing her children with her on the night flight to Orlando. It was to be the last time they would return together to Adelaide Place. A month later, Eric came from London to spend Christmas with his father, while Naomi stayed behind in Washington. Discussions about the house had become impossible between father and daughter, and Bettelheim had repeatedly asked for his son's help. Ruth had finally sold the Pasadena property and, for tax purposes, she had to re-invest her money in another home. Since an agreement on Adelaide Place could not be reached, Eric agreed to arrange for the sale of the house. A few months later Bettelheim once again had to be hospitalized, for a pancreatic infection. The day he was due to come out, tied up by her obligations, his daughter only came to get him in mid-afternoon, rather than in the morning as he expected. In the meantime, he had had a nervous breakdown which left him severely depressed.

'After much thought, I have come to the conclusion that life with Ruth is too difficult, for her as well as for me. I feel physically constrained and psychically overwhelmed by being such a burden for her. I am convinced that she will live much better without me.'[103] Once again Bettelheim was putting a good face on things. As he had done with Gina: if they had divorced after their arrival in the US it had been 'by mutual consent' and for material reasons, he generally explained. As he had done also with Paula: if his mother had abandoned him to a wet-nurse, it had been because of her social obligations.

'I am stuck between Scylla and Charybdis,' Bettelheim wrote to Frankenstein in January 1988. The idea of ending up in a retirement home, making conversation with people he had not chosen to be with, horrified him, but he was by now afraid of living alone. He wondered if he should not move closer to Naomi. He recalled that before dying Trude had exclaimed: 'Poor Bruno!' and the thought tugged at his heartstrings. He felt guilty at not having done enough for her; he missed her more and more. 'Your last letter expressed your anguish and desperation about things in Israel .... My own desperation is with this flesh of mine which will not die,' he wrote in March,[104] apologizing for no longer being able to take an interest in world events. He was reading Primo Levi.

At the end of May, Bettelheim finally moved into a small elegant building on Ocean Avenue, which Eric had found for him, about a mile from Adelaide Place. Through the large bay windows of his apartment he could see the eternally blue sweep of the Pacific, dotted with many-hued funboards. He hardly ever went out any more; he was in a terrible state, being cared for by a nurse. 'I now have more peace, but no desire to live,' he wrote to Candy.[105] His letters were now very short, around ten lines. And indeed, what could he tell his friends? 'My life is my work, Trude and the children,' he had written in 1954. He had lost almost all those things, and in that same order. He did not even know that his daughter's new house was located three streets away.

'So intricately, so inextricably interwoven are death and life's meaning that when life seems to have lost all meaning suicide seems the inescapable consequence .... Very few suicides are due to the wish to end insufferable pain .... More frequently suicides are the consequence of an unalterable conviction that the person's life has completely and irremediably lost all meaning,' he had written ten years earlier.[106] Now, suicide was constantly on his mind. He mentioned it to all the people who took turns in helping him. To Josette Wingo, who on his arrival in Santa Monica had thrown a party to introduce him to people he could work with, and who deployed all the energy of a former Orthogenic School counsellor to try and pull him out of his depression. To George and Kathy Kaiser, who lunched with him on a visit to LA. And to many others. He even put his son in an impossible position by asking him if he would accompany him to the Netherlands, where a doctor had promised to assist him with his suicide. He finally got Connie Katzenstein, who often went with him on outings, to make the promise.

Among the people he saw frequently, the most knowledgeable on the question was undoubtedly Edwin Shneidman, professor of thanatology at UCLA. A former student and friend of Henry Murray, at Harvard, Shneidman was fifteen years younger than Bettelheim, but he shared several interests with him. He was Jewish, conservative and iconoclastic, a lover of *Moby Dick*, and he too had begun his career by working on personality tests, notably Murray's TAT. His first patient as a therapist had been a psychotic veteran who was so violent that he had been scheduled for a lobotomy. Shneidman had cured him by convincing him that he respected him. But his reputation had been made by a study of several hundred suicide notes that he had stumbled across somewhat by accident in the early 1950s, in a forensic pathologist's archives. Edwin Shneidman had since become an authority on the psychological mechanisms associated with death, which he was teaching in UCLA's Department of Psychiatry and Biobehavioral Sciences at the time he met Bettelheim in 1987. He had soon had the latter hired as a visiting professor and invited him to join the regular Wednesday lunches he held informally with around a dozen elderly, high-level professors (including two former university presidents, he points out), for free-ranging discussions. Somewhat in the manner of a confidant, or a therapist, Shneidman refuses to divulge the content of his conversations with Bettelheim.[107] But it is clear that they saw a lot of one another, particularly after Bettelheim had left Adelaide Place. He speaks of him with affection and a lot of respect. He was struck by the large portrait of Trude hanging over Bettelheim's bed.[108]

But the most worried of Bettelheim's friends in Los Angeles was no doubt the psychoanalyst Rudolf Ekstein. He was ten years younger, and had not known Bettelheim in Vienna before the Anschluss, but he had trained as a Montessori school teacher at the same time as Trude. A committed socialist, Ekstein had emigrated to the United States in 1938. Later, he had worked for some ten years at the Menninger Foundation. During that period a solid friendship, built on both complicity and rivalry, had grown up between the two men. They exchanged their articles, and on Ekstein's bookshelves Bettelheim's works are lined up just beside his own. 'He was always one book ahead of me,' he said, clearly brimming with emotion, when I visited him in December 1990. He had then just published a new book, thereby evening up the score after his friend's death. Each year, Bettelheim would invite Ekstein to visit the Orthogenic School, and after asking him to speak during a staff meeting, he would cross swords with him in a lively debate. One of their favourite jokes was to argue about which of them had been married to the most beautiful woman in Vienna.

It was notably thanks to Dr Ekstein that Bettelheim was for once in his life well received by a psychoanalytic society, that of Los Angeles. Warm and nostalgic, and a collector of objects owned by Freud, Ekstein had introduced Bettelheim to the society of which Otto Fenichel had once been a prominent member. As he was not an MD, Bettelheim only became an honorary member. But that ceremony, on May 18, 1989, saw the inauguration of a bust of Bettelheim by the Swedish sculptress Jane Ullman, financed by a donation from Sandy Lewis.[109] Ekstein was deeply concerned by Bettelheim's deteriorating state when he was living at Adelaide Place. As a Freudian analyst fully aware of the complexities of family ties, he was not interested in assigning blame to anyone. But he could see how ill and miserable his friend was, spending his days wandering between two small rooms. He often took him out to lunch in a small deli close by. There, while Bettelheim would eat a bowl of soup, which was practically the only thing he could by then swallow, they would talk about Vienna, about what America had done to psychoanalysis, and also about death. 'Rudi is like me, he believes in Thanatos,' Bettelheim used to say.

Ekstein often discussed his friend's plight with David James Fisher, a former patient who had become a colleague. Fisher, who was very interested in the history of psychoanalysis, had first made contact with Bettelheim in 1982, on the publication of *Freud and Man's Soul*, which he had reviewed. When Bettelheim moved to Los Angeles, he had offered to help. He visited him at weekends. They went for walks and talked a great deal, Bettelheim of his problems and Fisher of his difficult cases. At one point he had even considered asking Bettelheim to be his supervisor. After he had moved out of Adelaide Place, Bettelheim finally agreed to let Fisher record five hours of interviews, on condition that nothing should be published before his death. Well before the break with Ruth, Ekstein and Fisher had been wondering who could help pull Bettelheim out of his depression. They finally opted for a woman who had trained as a psycho-analyst with Anna Freud in London. Bettelheim followed their advice, and visited the colleague for several months, once or twice a week, sometimes more in times of crisis. Psychologically, it was once again a struggle for survival. He was so lacking in self-love, so full of resentment against himself. For not having done more for Trude, not having been as good, as disinterested, as considerate as he wished he had been. He spoke of women he had known, who had desired him when he was married but were no longer interested now that he was alone. And he continually returned to his own unattractiveness, to the body that he hated.

One day Bettelheim got a call from Hans Bandler, whom he had not seen since the latter had left Buchenwald and emigrated to Australia. Bandler was passing through California for a congress, and he longed to see his former fellow inmate. He had already tried once to contact Bettel-heim, during a visit to London, after reading in the newspaper that he had given a lecture in the city. He had telephoned Eric, but it was too late. This time, too, Bandler's efforts were in vain. 'I don't feel well enough to see you,' Bettelheim said, obviously very depressed. Bandler insisted, feeling sure that he could bring some cheer to the person who had once aided him to recover his own human dignity.[110] He called back the next day, but to no avail; he was not able to see his friend.

Around the middle of July 1988, Bettelheim was feeling somewhat better. He was taking a daily half-hour walk along the ocean front, and speaking on the phone every evening with Naomi, who was about to give birth to her second child. On his doctor's advice, he had finally decided to risk the operation on his oesophagus. He had resumed his correspondence with several of his friends. He was even working on some of the seminars he and Alvin Rosenfeld had selected, and thinking about the essays to be included in one last book, a more personal work, as his publisher had asked.

'Our job is to help the patient to feel anger.' He had repeated this axiom to a group of psychologists only a few months previously; now he seemed to have succeeded in applying the therapy to himself. He finally accepted his own anger against Ruth, which he had previously always sought to temper with understanding. Hints of this appear for the first time in his letters, and also in his interviews with Fisher. To express it, he often linked it to his contempt for Los Angeles, which he saw as an artificial city. 'Here so many people live in opulence and without any goal; it's really awful to see how empty they are.'[111] To Fisher, he said: 'I saw changes in my own daughter from the girl she was in Chicago to the woman she became once she made her home in Los Angeles, which in terms of my values, were undesirable ones. Now, I cannot blame it on the city. It might be her personally. It might be what drove her to move here. I cannot sort it out. I'm much too close to her. There is a concern with possessions which I consider external. But I would have liked to see her develop other qualities.'[112] To a very close friend, he gave a detailed description of his clashes with Ruth, adding that in the end she did not even talk to him or visit him in his room when he was 'mortally ill'.[113] He had decided to disinherit his elder daughter.

The operation on his oesophagus was fully successful. But although his vocal chords were not affected, he caught pneumonia in hospital, due to his weakened state. On returning home, early in September, to replace his nurse, he hired a Polish refugee named Wanda, who did everything in the house for him. He found her a little strange, and complained about her cooking, but acknowledged that she was very devoted to him. As she spoke little German and even less English, he would on occasion call Wanda Willig in New York to ask her to play the interpreter. While he was in hospital, the psychoanalytic division of the American Psychology Association had awarded him its Distinguished Scientific Award. He continued to receive a large number of invitations, and at the beginning of October he gave his first lecture after the operation. The next day, however, he was so exhausted that he could not do anything all day.

Physically, Bettelheim was by now extremely weak. He had become very thin, and could only walk with a stick. Getting up, shaving, washing and dressing took him all morning; typing even a short letter left him worn out. He was going to the hospital three times a week for rehabilitation sessions, but they took a huge toll on his energy. He was no longer able completely to control a tremor that had developed in his right hand. And at the beginning of November, after two minor accidents, he had to face the fact that he could no longer drive his beautiful Mercedes; his foot did not respond quickly enough. At around the same time, Naomi visited, bringing his new granddaughter.

His relations with his second daughter were much simpler than those with Ruth, but also more brusque. When he started talking of suicide again, she interrupted him to say: 'I can't stop you from killing yourself if you want to. But I don't condone it. And, so long as you will live, I'll try to convince you not to.' She had been horrified to find out that he had disinherited her sister and she tried very hard to make him change his mind, but to no avail. Her efforts at bringing about a reconciliation between her father and sister also proved unsuccessful. After speaking to Bettelheim on the phone, Ruth asked Naomi not to give him her address. Bettelheim's disappointment comes through in his letters, although he kept adding: 'If that's the way she wants it, I'll have to come to terms with it.'[114] It was the year when he blurted out his statement about his father's syphilis, at Connie Katzenstein's Thanksgiving party.[115] That Christmas he travelled to Washington to be with Naomi, as did Eric. He returned from the trip feeling contented, regretting only that he lived so far away from Washington, not to speak of London.

The lull in his depression was to last around six months, during which Bettelheim resumed his seminars, gave a few more classes and attended several speaking engagements. At the end of March 1989 he addressed 900 people in San Francisco. He was amusing, incisive and thought-provoking. Daniel Karlin was there with a small TV crew; Bettelheim had contacted him to suggest giving him one last interview. It lasted five hours, stretched over two days. Although the old man tired quickly, he had lost none of his verve. When the Frenchman asked him why, given his age and condition, he had not yet committed suicide, since he often thought of doing so, Bettelheim smiled and said: 'As long as I can still do things that interest me, such as talking to you, I'll keep going.' When Karlin mentioned the nickname of 'Brutalheim', which was going the rounds among his students, Bettelheim replied frankly: 'It's true, I've always been very irritated by stupidity. It's one of my failings. But whenever I was brutal with a student or counsellor, it was always to try and make him grasp something. There was always love behind it. To mean something, an experience has to be forceful.' Karlin pushed the question further: 'But didn't you ever get a kind of pleasure from such brutality?' After pausing to think, Bettelheim murmured: 'Yes, certainly. There is always pleasure in dominating intellectually – not physically.' He also acknowledged that such brutality was a way of getting his own back for the physical oppression he had once suffered.

In May, Bettelheim finished compiling *Freud's Vienna and Other Essays*, and as always when he completed a book, felt empty. This time round, the feeling was amplified by his uncertainty over his future. He felt oppressed by loneliness, yet he found it harder and harder to put up with Wanda's constant presence. He complained that she was treating him like a baby, was furious at having to let her drive the car, and accused her of spying on him. His oldest friend, Hans Willig, had just died, leaving him the only survivor of his trio from the *Gymnasium*. Being so far from his family was another source of anxiety; Eric was urging him either to come and live in London with him or to move to the East Coast to be nearer to Naomi. The young lawyer was now travelling to New York on business five or six times a year. He repeated both suggestions in Washington that April.

As for Naomi, while she was ready to help her father as much as she could, she above all wanted to avoid making the same mistake as her sister. She knew that with two small children to care for, she could never devote the amount of time to him that he would want. She therefore did not suggest that he move in with her, but offered instead to inquire about lodgings in her vicinity. Bettelheim hesitated. Although he carped at California's perpetual blue skies, he appreciated their effects on him. And while he gave his distant correspondents the impression that he was very alone, he had in fact built up a good circle of friends in Los Angeles. Why become an exile yet again, and risk yet more disappointments?

As soon as he had moved in with Ruth, he had realized that 'although both my daughter and I try to do our best to make living together possible and bearable, it is a most difficult and complex task, given the feelings of a daughter for her father and those of a father for his first-born daughter. I think Freud and his daughter managed, because she was the last born, and his favorite had been the oldest daughter who died early, at which point he transferred his attachment to his youngest daughter.'[116] His trip to Washington had shown him just how busy Naomi was. But he was also touched to see how, behind her brusque tone and detached exterior, she was concerned about him. He felt at ease with his son-in-law, found their relationship harmonious and their children charming, even though he was too taken up with his own problems to pay much attention to them. By mid-July, he had finally made up his mind; he would move to Washington in the fall. 'The decision to move to an old people's home is a hard one to make, but I can no longer look after myself alone .... For the moment, though, these are only dreams – or rather nightmares,' he wrote.[117]

His friend Wanda Willig could tell, when they spoke by phone, that Bettelheim did not really care to make this new move, and that he was not really all that miserable in Los Angeles. She strongly advised him to stay put. He replied: 'But the children want ....' Rudolf Ekstein also did all he could to dissuade his friend from moving, even suggesting that he move into the apartment that he had arranged for his own father, on the first floor of his house. But Bettelheim declined the invitation. In the fall, he went to visit some of the places that Naomi had selected for him in the Washington suburbs. 'Each one has its pros and cons .... It is a painful blow to have to give up one's independence ... but I do not know how long I still have to live .... The moving worries me greatly, and I also wonder whether I will not regret having left here .... It will very much depend ... on whether I find somebody with whom I can develop some kind of a friendship over there. My requirements on that score are very modest .... I have thought many times about suicide, but I decided against it on account of the children, and I have made up my mind to try and live in Washington for a while, however difficult it may be,' he wrote.[118]

At the end of October, Bettelheim granted an interview to the writer Celeste Fremon.[119] She noted how his shoulders were hunched, and how he shuffled when, courteous as ever, he showed her to a chair. His right hand, the writing one, trembled and jerked a little. She was however struck by the clarity of his ideas. The interview, which was supposed to deal with previously unknown aspects of Bettelheim's life, such as his marriage, psychoanalysis and his friendship with Wilhelm Reich, had not got off to a very good start. He was clearly preoccupied. He answered her questions (on Reich: 'Few people were as stubborn as he was'), but his mind was clearly elsewhere. 'It was as if asking him to talk about his life and ideas was equivalent to asking him to look through a scrapbook from a now-inconsequential journey,' wrote Fremon. After a while, exasperated, she asked him in a somewhat aggressive tone: 'Are you afraid of dying?'

'No,' he said, 'I fear suffering. The older one gets, the greater the likelihood that one will be kept alive without purpose.' Having noted how the question had made him perk up, she tried to get him to elaborate, but Bettelheim dodged her questions. She had switched off her tape recorder and was getting ready to leave when he suddenly turned to her. 'There is something you should know,' he said. 'I am planning to take a trip to Europe from which I may or may not come back.' From that point on, a real dialogue began. Celeste Fremon was to go three times to 515, Ocean Avenue, recording a total of six hours of conversation, of which at least half was devoted to death and suicide.

Clearly touched by Bettelheim's distress, Celeste Fremon found herself torn between 'the illogical and unjournalistic urge to bring him a dozen brightly colored balloons in the childish hope of cheering him up' and her respect for both the ideas he discussed with her – paradoxical, thought-provoking and always interesting – and his considered decision to die at a time of his own choosing – a dilemma that everyone who sought to help Bruno Bettelheim at the end will recognize.

In his interviews with Fremon the psychoanalyst touched on a multitude of subjects, but his most incisive comments were those on old age, mourning and depression. They were remarkably frank. For example, after running through the list of his physical ailments, he remarked: 'I always found that I understood a problem much better after I began to write about it. I can no longer do that.' He stressed that in other countries, old people could still make themselves useful, that they were not shunted off to specialized institutions in which to await death, either in opulence or poverty, as they were in the United States. When Fremon pointed out that a lot of people still came to him for advice, Bettelheim admitted: 'People do seek me out …. Perhaps not as much as I would like. But there are some to whom I am important and to whom I feel I make a contribution. That certainly is what is attractive about life.'

'Let's not talk about depression. It's depressing,' said the old man, almost gaily, at the start of the third interview. His doctor had just prescribed a new anti-depressant, which appeared to be working wonders. But then a few sentences further on, the names of Primo Levi and Paul Celan came up. 'I don't think that one ever really fully masters this experience of having been a prisoner in a German concentration camp,' he said. He went on to reflect at length on the specificity of the camps. 'It is an experience that makes one lose one's belief in mankind.' He then started talking about Eros and Thanatos: not, says Fremon, as psychoanalytical concepts, but as living forces within himself. 'I believe that Freud is right that we have both a life drive and also a death drive. As long as the life drive, or the libido, is in ascendancy – certainly as long as we are sexually active and we want to procreate – we are going to live. But it can also reach a point in old age where one must accept that one withdraws the libido from the world because otherwise one couldn't face death.' The reporter probed him further: 'Then is the waning of the libido, the waning of life, a consequence of the loss of love?' Bettelheim started to reply. 'Loving and being loved ...,' he said. Then, his face flooded with emotion, he turned away. 'Maybe we could talk about some other topic,' he concluded.

In November, Bruno Bettelheim went to Washington to spend Thanksgiving with two of his children, and visit some more retirement homes in the area. As one of the homes selected by Naomi agreed to take people on a trial basis, he decided to stay there for the duration of his visit. Naomi had carefully prepared things. A chauffeured car was available to take her father wherever he wanted to go, and notably between the home, located north of the city in Bethesda, and her place in Virginia, to the west. She had also inquired about the house next to hers, which was for sale. Well laid out, with all the basic amenities on the same floor, it seemed ideal for her father. He could be at once independent and close by, as initially planned with Ruth. But he did not seem very interested. Her neighbourhood was very peaceful but somewhat distant from the city. Naomi had also contacted as many of her father's friends as possible. She had even found work for him: as soon as he moved to Washington he could start training social workers for the Jewish Social Services, giving two or three seminars per week, as he wished.

During the visit, Naomi was dismayed at the state her father was in. He even seemed to have lost his legendary courtesy. When they passed by a florist's store, she suggested that he buy a bunch of flowers for the friend of a friend who, at her request, had managed in two days to get together a large dinner in his honour, to be held that same evening. 'There's no need. I'm past that,' Bettelheim replied. He was indeed in a gloomy mood. The more retirement homes he visited, the more awful he found them all. And Naomi had to threaten never to have him in her house again to make him stop discussing his suicide plans in front of his grandson, now aged four and able to understand. She also informed him that if he insisted on disinheriting Ruth, she would side with the latter to attack his will after his death. Bettelheim finally gave in and had the document amended. On the evening before Thanksgiving, Eric arrived, and Bettelheim returned to the subject of his death. Feeling uncertain that Connie Katzenstein would go ahead with their plan, he had found another couple who had agreed to accompany him to the Netherlands. But, he explained, they wanted to have his children's agreement before committing themselves. Naomi replied that, if they asked her, she would advise them to check with a lawyer on the risks they were taking for themselves; Bettelheim was furious. Finally, Alvin Rosenfeld, who had exercised a pacifying influence during the holiday, told him: 'Listen, kill yourself if you really have to. But don't try and get your children to approve.'

'I have now decided to move at the end of January,'[120] Bettelheim wrote on his return to California. The Dutch doctor on whom he had been counting to help him to die had just succumbed to a heart attack. That was one more reason for leaving Los Angeles, as he was convinced that his Polish housekeeper would prevent him from killing himself. He complained that she got up in the middle of the night to spy on him. Which was not to say that he was about to act; for the time being he was waiting for his book to be published, and to move house. In the letters he had written for Christmas and the New Year he even used the future: 'We'll see ...', 'Perhaps it might be possible to ...' and 'I hope to receive better news from you there'; the last to Carl Frankenstein, who had been hospitalized following a heart attack and was to die before reading his letter. In early January, on hearing that Tübingen University in Germany had awarded him its prestigious Lukas prize, Bettelheim expressed great pride, and added: 'I don't think I will be able to attend the ceremony .... But maybe the move will give me new strength and I will be able to go ....'[121]

He spent that Christmas with Eric and his new girlfriend. The latter made a very good impression, and revived an old dream of attending his son's wedding before he died. Then, at Rudi Ekstein's request, he agreed to be interviewed with the latter for UCLA's archives on the history of psychoanalysis. He finally left Los Angeles for Washington on January 19, after several farewell dinners. A few days previously, David James Fisher had dropped in with a bottle of champagne to celebrate the publication of *Freud's Vienna and Other Essays*. Bettelheim was happy. He found the book handsome, with its dust jacket featuring a black-and-white photo of Freud's building at Berggasse 19 on a rainy day, set off by a brown Art Nouveau pattern found in the Austrian Museum for Applied Arts. However Fisher could not help but notice the effort it cost him to scribble a few words of dedication.

His furniture took two weeks to follow him across the country, and on February 2, 1990 he finally moved into his new apartment, in the Silver Spring residence, Charter House. The place was roomy and comfortable, with a large living room, two bedrooms, a large terrace, two bathrooms and a kitchen. Naomi and her husband had spared no effort to fit it out to the old man's liking. Eric had hired an interior decorator. Curtains, carpeting, bookshelves; everything had been done up or replaced with him in mind. They had hung the engravings and lithographs and arrayed his books on the shelves themselves; they had also bought him a personal computer. Naomi had made sure that her father would have all necessary medical assistance on hand, and that when he took his meals in the common dining room his special needs would be catered to. Charter House, a select establishment for the well-heeled, was proud to be taking in such a well-known guest. A party had been laid on for Bettelheim's arrival.

'I am terribly disappointed. I cannot find one person to talk to here and

I am very lonely, much lonelier than in Santa Monica. The moving has been very traumatic, several pieces of my old furniture were damaged on arrival and I regret very much having left California,' he wrote only ten days later.[122] His signature was now little more than a shaky scribble, with only the 'B' vaguely legible. The few lines typed under the letterhead of his new home were full of typographical errors. They show clearly that the 'cowardly old lion', as Bettelheim had once described himself to Alvin Rosenfeld, had hardly any life left in him. All that remained was his 'terrible roar'.

At Charter House, it had not taken long for Bettelheim to gain the reputation of an appalling old grump, who complained about everything. In the dining-room, he could not stand any of the people who proposed to share his table. He railed against the food, the service, and all the rest. After much effort, the management started to despair of the situation. The other residents were turning away from Bettelheim. Charter House was not the Orthogenic School, and nobody had explained to them that, like disturbed children, desperate old people often express their suffering only through unpleasant behaviour.

Elsewhere, his hangdog look did not always inspire compassion either. 'What's your excuse for being here?' he was asked at a Washington dinner, by a woman he did not know.

'I've just moved to this area,' he replied.

'How do you like it?'

'I'm not happy,' said Bettelheim.

'How old are you?' she asked.

'Eighty-six.'

'Well, then you might like to be introduced to my friends at the Society for the Right to Die.'

Shocked silence around the table.[123]

Bettelheim did not need any such advice. After all those years spent studying the question, he now knew exactly what to do. He had had the pills since Trude's death. And since he would have to act on his own, he had to make sure that neither vomiting nor the arrival of another person would 'save' him at the last minute. He wanted to end it all painlessly, and had finally found the answer in a book by the founder of the Hemlock Society. In 1986, Derek Humphry had explained how he himself would commit suicide when the time came.[124] To speed up the process and vastly increase the chances of success, he would put a plastic bag over his head after having taken the required dose of sleeping pills. As an added bonus, the carbon dioxide thereby inhaled was said to have a soporific effect.

It took over a month for Bettelheim finally to throw in the towel, even though everything in his new life seemed hopeless. He had traded in the California sunshine for Washington's rain and fog, and his view over the Pacific for the sight of a few trees, scattered among buildings and a parking lot. After so often condemning the way American society treated its senior citizens, he found himself surrounded by people his age, in a place which in spite of its flowers and neatness was for all of them a last halt before the grave. He who so feared illness was surrounded by wheel-chairs and walking frames, and he who hated polite conversation found himself with no one with whom to discuss the ideas which he could no longer work on through writing.

The few friends he had in the Washington area all lived far away, and Naomi's house was even further. He no longer even had Wanda to look after him and drive him around; a bitter price to pay for his past carping. But as he pointed out in his letters, there was now no turning back. He tried to come to terms with his new life. He agreed to give a few lectures, and there were even plans for a meeting with mothers. As news of his presence in the city spread, invitations began to flood in. And, when his agent visited towards the end of February, the phone was ringing so often that they hardly managed to talk.

Theron Raines was there to hear his life story. For in 1984, Bettelheim had finally agreed to his requests to let his biography be written. Until that point, he had rejected all such demands. With Geneviève Jurgensen, whom he respected, he had, in 1974, backed his refusal by an explanation. 'In truth, I am a very private man. All the world has a right to know is my work, my ideas about matters on which I feel I can speak with confidence. My own children and the rest of my family have suffered enough from the fact that I am fairly well known ... I do not wish them to suffer from the fact that their father, and as far as my wife is concerned, her husband, becomes known as a person. To them I always was and wish to remain just another father, just another husband, and not somebody who is public property.

'There are many aspects of my life and personality – though nothing I am ashamed of, or have any reason to be – which persons who did not have the same experience would not, could not, should not understand .... It would have to be a work of fiction, a work of art, and of those there are enough around. As a person, I belong to another century and world, but not in my work. There are factors in my life of a most private nature which made me go into my work, and made me good at it. I do not wish that these should become public – in order not to become an actor, or conceited, or self-important, one must keep private things private. Accepting to be interviewed for a book about myself, I would feel a cheater if I didn't speak about those things which were most important in my life. But these very things I wish to keep to myself .... So, I would have either to do things which I did not want to, or to pretend to say all, while not doing so.'[125]

By 1984, things were very different. His three children were grown up, and living far away. Trude was in the terminal stages of her illness. And Theron Raines was far more than a simple agent; he was a loyal friend who for close to fourteen years had done a great deal to defend his rights and his works. Bettelheim therefore let himself be persuaded, on condition that Raines do the work himself. He wrote to his friends and oldest colleagues to ask them to take part in the project, and at irregular interviews he began telling his life story.

As Theron Raines for obvious reasons did not want to answer my questions on the subject, I can only fall back on a last hypothesis, based on over four and a half years of trying to understand Bruno Bettelheim. It seems to me that although he may at some point have enjoyed the project, by early 1990, plunged into a depression on which no drug appeared to have any effect, he was finding it a burden. Theron Raines was the last person with whom he could unload the 'dark secrets' which had led him to try and heal others. What Bettelheim thought this unconditional and devoted admirer expected from him was his legend. The stories with the happy endings, which inspire love of life. And yet, coming at a time when he could think of nothing but death, how could such an exercise not confront him once again with the awful feeling of 'fraud', which had plagued him since his childhood? 'What a bore!' he muttered on Sunday March 11, when he was due to have another session of recollections.

Bettelheim spent that Sunday with Naomi and her family. In the afternoon, he took a brief walk with his son-in-law. Passing by the house next door, he asked: 'Is it still for sale?' As the answer was 'No,' he dropped the subject. Later, Naomi offered him some new tape for his typewriter (he had not tried to use his new computer), but he did not take it: 'Keep it,' he said, 'I won't need it.' His physical condition was neither better nor worse than it had been in the preceding weeks. What really surprised Naomi to the point that she decided to take a picture is that Bettelheim sat reading and re-reading a little book called *Just Me and my Dad* to his granddaughter. Then, he went back to Silver Spring.

He could no longer read very much for himself. He was too depressed, and his attention wandered. There were exceptions; he had re-read *Moby Dick*. The opening line of Melville's novel – 'Call me Ishmael' – still fascinated him. He felt that, by implying the depth of an unrevealed past, it summed up to perfection the attitude of the foreigner, the outsider. He was also re-reading Goethe, and particularly *Faust*, which took on a completely different meaning to the one he had found in it in his youth. At the beginning of March, Ruth Marquis sent him *Soumchi*,[126] a children's story by Amos Oz, an Israeli writer Bettelheim was fond of. It was the kind of tale that makes adults think; he got through it in two hours and enjoyed it greatly.

He often spoke with Ruth Marquis by phone. But before calling her, he would take some Ritalin, a children's tranquillizer which can have a paradoxical effect on adults,[127] to sound cheerful. He knew she could not bear to hear him so utterly depressed. When he moaned, 'I'm nothing but an ugly old Jew,' it upset her so much that she did not know what to say. She was no more able than any of his other friends to understand how this man whom she had seen display such strength and accomplish such miracles, and to whom she owed so many of the ideas that had helped her to live, could have sunk so far. Why he was so difficult, demanding and miserable, nor why he so needed reassurance.

Two years after Bruno Bettelheim's death, one fine summer afternoon on Long Island, I was sorting out what I had learned about him with his old friend Wanda Willig. After exhausting the specifics, we were down to trading impressions and interpretations. Although she had known him better than most, Wanda was puzzled and cautious in her judgements. Looking back, what particularly baffled her was the extraordinary gap in Bettelheim between the man eager to cut a fine figure, in constant need of admiration, and the almost embarrassing humility which he could sometimes display. She had been particularly struck by his miserable tone of voice on the answering machine shortly before his death: 'He sounded so self-effacing,' she kept on saying. The remark stuck in my mind – maybe because it took a while for me to realize that he had indeed 'effaced' himself, in the most literal sense.

That fault-line in Bruno Bettelheim's personality, that lack of love for himself, which was apparent to everyone who ever cared for him without falling under his spell, is called shame by some psychoanalysts. They say the yawning chasm in the self-image originates in a wound suffered before the personality becomes structured, a wound caused by the mother's disappointed look upon first seeing her baby. She does not recognize him; he is not the child of her dreams; she looks away from him. Sometimes, feeling guilty, the mother tries to make up for that unconscious antipathy with impressive displays of devotion.

The baby is not beautiful ('Thank God, it's a boy!'), not worthy of interest (or at least not as interesting as the 'social obligations' requiring that she abandon him to the care of a wet nurse). Yet, he cannot even be angry at her, she is so devoted – even spending the whole night at his bedside when he is sick. So, there can be no doubt in his mind; if he cannot get her to 'devote her full attention' to him, it must be his fault, a consequence of what he fails to be. He is obviously unworthy of the love that he misses so much that he could die. And this lack, this self-doubt, this shame rooted deep in the child's psyche before he has developed the means to overcome it, to turn it into something else, is almost impossible to cure.

Later, during the Oedipal phase, the child discovers guilt, under which he sometimes manages to bury his shame; in other words, he begins to hope that he can 'repair' it. He no longer feels the lack of love as resulting from what he is, but from what he does (or does not do). In the best of cases, he will then spend his life trying to lift the curse, to turn the shadow under which he has lived into light. In Bruno Bettelheim's case, for example, by identifying the shame in his young patients' hearts early enough to hope that it could be erased at least there, or else by helping them to develop guilt, thus giving them the means to live.

But it is a gigantic mission, because shame begets self-contempt. It happens all the faster when the self-imposed goals set for the 'repair' are unattainable. When merely helping incurable patients is not enough, actually curing them is required to silence the self-doubt. And any relief is short-lived. To proceed with one's life, to give that life meaning, shame must be silenced over and over again; it is always ready to spring back, at the first mistake, at the first shortfall between what one has wanted (to be) and what one has managed (to do). Between the image of the magician which one has held out as a promise and the too-often disappointing results of one's most determined efforts.

In that gap, that 'abyss' as Bettelheim himself called it, depression looms. The kind of depression that makes it impossible to get out of bed, that makes one hate the dawn, and only dare to express oneself – to write, i.e. to bare the bottom of one's soul – when everybody else is asleep, in the reassuring dark of night, the time of dreams, the time stolen from the gaze of others, when there is nothing to prove. It is the kind of depression that kills all desire to struggle, to build, to live.

We shall never know how far Bruno Bettelheim's own psychoanalysis helped him recognize those mechanisms in himself. He often said that although it revealed the reasons for his depression, it did not help him to overcome it. The way he chose to die seems to confirm this. But the way he lived, and his life's work, also show that, whether it was on Dr Sterba's couch or at Buchenwald, he had discovered what he most needed to go on: in someone else's eyes, the look that could erase his shame.

In Buchenwald, he had found it in the eyes of Hans Bandler, and of others for whom his listening and storytelling had restored self-respect and the taste for life. But, there, paradoxically, things were simple, since reality came down to a stark choice between life and death. Later, in his 'second life', Bettelheim was able to validate his existence in the eyes of some students, counsellors and readers. And each of his books, each of his essays, was new evidence not only that he deserved to be, since it bore his name, in black on white, but also that his ideas and exemplary tales could earn him, even more than admiration – love.

Above all, he found the look that he so much needed, the look that effaces shame, in Trude's eyes. By replacing Gina's critical stare with Trude's reassuring and constructive gaze, Bettelheim displayed his instinct for survival; he showed that his love of life was stronger than his fascination with his internal chasm. It was no easy task. For the shame so deeply engraved on the child's soul by the 'not good enough' mother[128] cannot be erased by an outpouring of empty flattery. On the contrary, that only makes things worse, by adding the suspicion of fraud to the initial self-doubt ('Not only am I unworthy of love but that I managed to win her love for the wrong reasons only goes to show how bad I really am –

monstrous or even mad, depending on the form of self-contempt involved. And, incidentally, this shows that she isn't worth much either, that I can turn my contempt on her, since she couldn't see through me.').

Bettelheim was immediately ready to trust Gina, because the contempt he saw floating in her eyes merely mirrored the contempt he knew only too well; it was forever echoing inside him. But that Trude managed, with patience and perseverance, to get Bruno to accept the validity of her vision of him shows not only her love but also her great intelligence. And, if his outbursts of harshness when she was dying no doubt reflected his pain at being reminded of his father's agony, they above all expressed his panic at the thought of seeing Trude's eyes close, of losing the image of himself he had come to trust more than his own. That loss was more than unbearable, it was literally unliveable, as he would write to his children just before his death.

That admission was to be the last little white pebble, the one which brought Bruno Bettelheim, like little Hansel, back home – where the good but fallen father had never succeeded in standing between him and his mother. True, she had not abandoned him deep in a hostile forest. On the contrary, she had done all that she could to save him from the deadly world where he had one day found himself, because of the origins she had passed on to him without pride, rather like his face. In that world he had nevertheless learned 'to stand up on his own two feet'. And he had summoned up the courage to reject a protective blindness, which he had perhaps embraced to spare himself above all from the sight of his own plainness – a plainness which he could never forget he had discovered 'when his mother first beheld him'.

On Tuesday March 13, at 8.15 a.m., the Charter House janitor called down to reception for help. On using his passkey to enter apartment 1007, he had found Bruno Bettelheim lying in the hallway, behind the door, with a plastic bag over his head. He was shirtless, and a pair of glasses lay on the grey carpet next to his body. The bag was secured around his neck with elastic bands. In the bedroom, the old man had left a brief note to his children on the typewriter. He bid them farewell, and reiterated that he simply could not go on living without their mother.

Police Officers Laney and Wass arrived shortly after 9 a.m. to confirm the death. Bruno Bettelheim had apparently died at around 2 a.m. He had taken barbiturates and a small amount of alcohol.

The same day fifty years earlier, *Wehrmacht* tanks had rolled into Vienna flying Nazi flags, greeted by a crowd chanting, 'Death to the Jews.' The coincidence was probably not intentional – that at any rate is the view of Bruno Bettelheim's children, and others frequenting him then. But the memory of the unconscious works that way. Coincidences are no accidents.

Notes

Foreword

1. Karlin later published the soundtrack, plus his comments on the shooting, under the title *Un autre regard sur la folie* (A different view of insanity), Editions Stock, Paris, 1975, with a postscript by Bruno Bettelheim – which later became the preface of the paperback edition.

2. Published by Editions Robert Laffont, Paris, 1973.

3. See Chapter X.

4. Reviews published in the *American Journal of Sociology* in January 1957 and in the *New Leader* on May 1, 1958, both of which were later reworked and included in *Freud's Vienna and Other Essays*.

5. See Chapter XVII, p. 460.

6. Freud referred to this in a letter to his fiancée Martha Bernays dated April 1885.

7. When Bertram Cohler, Bruno Bettelheim's former student and successor, who went on to head the Committee on Human Development at the University of Chicago, looked up the latter's file to write an obituary for the in-house magazine, he commented: 'His must have been the shortest résumé in the history of the university!'

Prologue 'The Affair'

1. *New York Times*.

2. *Washington Post*.

3. Notably the *Guardian* in England.

4. Interview published in the *Connecticut New Haven Register* on April 8, 1984, on the publication of Tom Wallace Lyons's book *The Pelican and After*. Cf pp. 341-4.

5. Issue dated September 10, 1990.

6. Bettelheim often used the term 'shock of recognition', coined by the literary critic Edmund Wilson.

7. 'A case study of a brilliant autistic boy with total reading disability; an investigation of the causes of this condition and the steps that led to his being able to overcome it'. University of Chicago Department of Education, September 1964, by Jacquelyn Seevak (Sanders's maiden name).

8. A small boy who forgets to put hands on the drawing of a person may be unconsciously seeking to hide an activity which he believes to be reprehensible. A psychoanalyst would think in particular of masturbation.

9. The psychologists who examined him before his entry to the Orthogenic School at the age of six and a half credited him with an IQ of 168.

10. Bettelheim believed that competitiveness was damaging for his charges, and diverted them from their key task at the school, which was the reconstruction of their egos.

11. On this extraordinary affair, see *In the Freud Archives* by Janet Malcolm (Alfred A. Knopf, New York, 1984) – the book which made Masson widely known, but which he later accused of misrepresenting his position.

See also what Masson himself has written about it, particularly in *The Assault on Truth: Freud's Suppression of the Seduction Theory*, as well as his comments in *The Complete Letters of Sigmund Freud to Wilhelm Fleiss* (The Belknap Press of Harvard University Press, Cambridge and London, 1985), which he published in unexpurgated form for the first time, and which were at the origin of his falling out with the psychoanalytic community.

12. *Washington Post*, October 6, 1990.

13. *On Learning to Read*.

14. Interviewed in Chicago in November 1990.

15. *Journal of American Folklore*, vol. 104, no. 411, winter 1991.

16. *Los Angeles Times*, February 7, 1991.

Chapter I. Vienna: Once Upon a Time

1. *Freud's Vienna and Other Essays*, p. 133. This book was published in London under the title *Recollections and Reflections* (Thames & Hudson, 1990).

2. In *Moses and Monotheism*.

3. In his doctoral dissertation, submitted in 1937, Bettelheim cited the study by Kris, which had been published in 1934 as *Die Legende vom Künstlere* (*Legend, Myth and Magic in the Image of the Artist*, Yale University Press, 1981).

4. Budapest was created in 1873 from the merger of Pest with Buda, on the other side of the Danube.

5. Cf *Die Juden und die Judengemeinde Bratislava*, in which one Samuel Bettelheim, a native of Budapest, wrote the chapter entitled 'History of the Yeshiva of Bratislava'. A Yeshiva is a Talmudic school.

6. The Yiddish word *shtetl* means 'small town'. The word 'ghetto' is strictly speaking incorrect in this context, since it implies an obligation to live in a certain place. In fact, in the Austrian empire at least, there was no law obliging Jews to live in the *shtetl*, even though their material conditions made it very difficult for them to live anywhere else.

7. Even Anselm von Rothschild, the emperor's banker, was for many years forbidden to buy a house in Vienna.

8. It is worth noting that this was not out of any affection for the Jews as such, but from a desire to 'de-Judify' them, and make them into ordinary citizens. Cf vol. II of Léon Poliakov's *The History of Anti-Semitism*, Vanguard Press, New York, 1965.

9. 34 per cent in 1910 (Pollak, op cit).

10. Stefan Zweig, *The World of Yesterday*, Viking Press, 1943.

11. As outlined in particular in *Freud's Vienna and Other Essays*.

12. Ibid, p. 134.

13. It was customary among the Rothschilds for men who had proved themselves trustworthy by educating the family's children to be rewarded with posts of responsibility. In France, for example, this was more recently the case for Georges Pompidou, who was to become president after Charles de Gaulle. He served in his youth as a tutor to Guy de Rothschild's son, and was then appointed head of Banque Rothschild, before going into politics.

14. A post which carried more responsibility in the Rothschild bank than it would elsewhere, since unlike other bank owners, the Rothschilds generally declared their private fortune as security for their liabilities.

15. Although Morris's death certificate mentions tuberculosis, there is in this case every reason to believe the family's version of the cause of death. As was confirmed to me by the official in charge of the records at the Vienna *Israelitische Kultusgemeinde*, disguising the cause of a death was a common practice at the time, and in Jewish families there was no glory attached to being killed in a duel.

16. Non-Jews, in Yiddish.

17. In March 1883, a month after Morris Bettelheim's death, Herzl was to resign from the prestigious Albia club as a result of a violently anti-Semitic speech delivered there by Hermann Bahr on the occasion of Wagner's death. Herzl thereby avoided the indignity of being thrown out of the club.

18. Lueger, who was to remain mayor through until 1910, made a lasting impression on the young Adolf Hitler, who saw him as a model. Hitler arrived in the city in 1907 in the hope of gaining admission to the Fine Arts Academy. Although he failed in both of his attempts, he was to remain in Vienna until 1913.

19. Arthur Schnitzler, *My Youth in Vienna*.

20. The first performance of Schnitzler's play *Reigen* was to take place at the Burgtheater in 1903 – a few months after the birth of Bruno Bettelheim.

21. To use the phrase coined by the novelist and essayist Hermann Broch.

22. Knopf, New York, 1979, and University of California Press, 1972. The list of books devoted to this question is too long to be presented *in extenso* in the present work. In addition to Stefan Zweig's *The World of Yesterday* (Viking Press, 1943) and the works of Arthur Schnitzler and Martin Buber, I made considerable use of two studies published in France: the regrettably brief *Vienne 1900* by Michael Pollak (Gallimard/Juillard, 1984) and the very erudite *Modernité viennoise et crises de l'identité* by Jacques le Rider (Presses Universitaires de France, 1990). Both books were invaluable in explaining the complexity and ambiguity of the world in which Bruno Bettelheim grew up. Also worth mentioning is the very rich catalogue to the Pompidou Centre's *Paris-Vienne* exhibition (Paris, 1986), for which Bruno Bettelheim first wrote the essay which opens his book *Freud's Vienna and Other Essays*. Other works, such as *Freud, A Life for Our Time*, by Peter Gay (Macmillan, 1988), *Anna Freud* by Elizabeth Young Bruehl (Summit Books, 1985) or *Les Rothschild* (Stock, 1989), gave insights into particular historical issues. Other works are cited in following footnotes.

23. *Freud's Vienna and Other Essays*, op cit.

24. One example: when the Austrians chose Kurt Waldheim as their president, in spite of his wartime service in Nazi uniform, he snapped: 'Bah! They deserve each other!' (interview in *Illustrierte Neue Welt*, Nov-Dec 1987.)

25. *Freud's Vienna and Other Essays*, p. 46.

26. An idea which conveniently overlooks the fact that until the start of the nineteenth century most Jews lived in *shtetls*.

27. To quote the title of the pamphlet Wagner was to publish, first anonymously in 1850, then under his own name in 1869. In it Wagner, who according to his autobiography had agitated for the emancipation of the Jews during an earlier revolutionary period, for the first time expressed his anti-Semitism openly. For more on this question, see *Wagner et la Question Juive*, by Jacob Katz (Paris, Hachette 1986).

28. Quoted in L. Poliakov, op cit.

29. There is a huge corpus of work devoted to this question also, among which the study by Poliakov (op cit) stands out.

30. Cf the remarkable thesis on Robert Musil by Laurence Dahan, to whom I am indebted for much of the material in this chapter. It was published in 1994 by Presses Universitaires de Vincennes under the title *La rime et la raison, savoir et fiction chez Robert Musil*.

31. As Jean Clair points out in his subtly argued introduction to the catalogue of the *Paris-Vienne* exhibition (op cit), there is a considerable difference between the artistic movements of the period in the two cities. Rebellious artists in Paris organized the *Salon des Indépendants*, while the comparable phenomenon in Vienna was labelled the Secession. In the first case, independence implied breaking out of chains to move ahead, in an outward-looking movement. Secession, on the other hand, meant turning in on oneself, breaking away while remaining within existing boundaries.

32. Including Albert Einstein, who found part of the inspiration for his theory of relativity in Mach's lectures.

33. Including a number of people who were only half Jewish, and many Jews who had converted to Catholicism, which at the time was a fashionable thing to do. It is worth recalling, for example, that before the young Theodor Herzl drew up his theory of Zionism, one of his dearest wishes was to see the emperor presiding over mass conversions of Jews in St Stephen's Cathedral!

34. See for example *Philosophie de l'antisémitisme*, by Michel Herszlikowicz (Presses Universitaires de France, 1985).

35. 'Class, Color and Prejudice', in the *Nation*, October 19, 1963.

36. Lessing's book of that name, *Der Jüdische Selbsthaß*, was published in 1930. It was hated by most assimilated Viennese Jews, and notably by Sigmund Freud. However the latter was to write, in a letter to Kurt Hiller dated 1936: 'Don't you think that the type of self-hatred depicted by Theodor Lessing is a typically Jewish phenomenon? I really think it is.' (Quoted by le Rider, op cit.)

37. Cf Jean-Paul Sartre's *Reflections on the Jewish Question*, the central idea of which is that the 'Jew' is essentially defined by the anti-Semite.

38. It is somewhat ironic to note that Germans, then as now, tend to look down on the Viennese accent, which is somewhat 'singsong' in tone. It would be tempting to conclude that the entire Viennese population, like that of New York, in fact 'talks Jewish' without realizing it.

39. Robert Musil, *The Man without Qualities*, Secker & Warburg, London, translated by Eithne Wilkins and Ernst Kaiser, vol. III, ch. 20.

40. Cf *Le cas Otto Weininger*, by Jacques le Rider (Presses Universitaires de France, 1982). Practically all the works devoted to turn-of-the-century Vienna discuss the Weininger case, seen as symbolic of the period as a whole. A particularly subtle analysis is to be found in Michael Pollak's *Vienna 1900*, op cit.

41. *Sex and Character* was in fact to serve as the catalyst for the split between Freud and his confidant Wilhelm Fleiss. The latter claimed to have first elaborated the concept of bisexuality, and he accused Freud of having divulged the idea to a friend of Weininger's.

42. *The History of Anti-Semitism*, op cit.

43. On this point, see Arthur Schnitzler's fine novel *Der Weg ins Freie*. For a particularly interesting analysis of the different forms that *Selbsthaß* could take, see the well-documented *Modernité viennoise et crises de l'identité*, by Jacques le Rider (Presses Universitaires de France, 1990).

44. *Freud's Vienna and Other Essays*, p. 47.

45. *And the Bridge is Love* by Alma Mahler-Werfel, Harcourt Brace, New York, 1958.

46. Interview in *Illustrierte Neue Welt*, Nov-Dec 1987.

47. *Freud's Vienna and Other Essays*, p. 108.

Chapter II. One Big Family

1. This information is drawn from a letter of recommendation sent to the Chamber of Commerce in 1921 by another lumber merchant, in support of Anton Bettelheim's application to be elected to the status of *Kommerzialrat*, or commercial adviser, as his father had been before him. The application was unsuccessful.

2. In 'Freud's Vienna', a text written for the catalogue of the *Paris-Vienne* exhibition at Paris's Pompidou Centre in 1986 and republished as the title piece of *Freud's Vienna and Other Essays*.

3. Stefan Zweig, *The World of Yesterday*, op cit.

4. In *A Good Enough Parent*.

5. *A Good Enough Parent*, pp. 307-8.

6. The title of this book is derived from the English psychoanalyst Donald Winnicott's concept of a 'good enough mother', as Bettelheim explains in his acknowledgements. The idea being, as he also notes, that 'perfection is not within the grasp of ordinary human beings', and that 'efforts to attain it typically interfere with that lenient response to the imperfections of others, including those of one's child, which alone makes good human relations possible'.

7. *A Good Enough Parent*, p. 306.

8. Ibid, pp. 40-1.

9. Letter to ER, September 1980.

10. *A Good Enough Parent*, p. 305.

11. Ibid, p. 348.

12. A recollection that Bettelheim told to Denise Bombardier, who published it in the French magazine *Le Point* on May 28, 1988.

13. *A Good Enough Parent*, p. 340.

14. Ibid, p. 341.

15. Ibid, p. 304.

16. Letter to C. Frankenstein, November 10, 1986.

17. *A Good Enough Parent*, p. 306.

18. 'Women: Emancipation is still to come', in the *New Republic*, 50th anniversary issue, November 7, 1964.

19. Edith Buxbaum, unpublished memoirs.

20. According to Bettelheim, the idea originated in an anecdote reported by Lou Andreas Salomé around 1912, and which is cited in H.F. Peters's biography of her, *My Sister, my Spouse*. The story goes that Salomé was knitting while attending one of the first psychoanalytic gatherings. One of the other participants remarked jokingly that Salomé 'seemed to enjoy herself by indulging in continuous coitus, as symbolised by the movement of the knitting needles. She just smiled, and kept on knitting,' Bettelheim writes, quoting Peters.

21. Initially, most of the reports I heard of the knitting incident were second-hand, along the lines of 'a friend who attended one of Bettelheim's lectures told me that ...'. I was beginning to think the whole thing might be a myth until I met Professor Al Reiss Jr., who confirmed that he had been personally present at a lecture during which Bettelheim rebuked a woman student for knitting, and referred to masturbation. The young woman did not reply, however.

22. Letter to the *New York Times Magazine*, February 8, 1970.

23. Unpublished memoirs.

24. *A Good Enough Parent*, p. 120.

25. Ibid, p. 112.

26. Ibid, p. 187.

27. 'Learning to Read: a Primer for Literacy', in *Harpers*, April 1978.

28. The opening sentence of *On Learning to Read*, p. 3.

29. See p. 28.

30. *Dialogues with Mothers*, p. 165. Bettelheim's handwriting is not only firm, regular and perfectly legible but also elegant, in the old-fashioned European style.

31. *On Learning to Read*, p. 30.

32. Information provided by the present headmaster.

33. He was, for example, to strongly condemn the creation of special schools for gifted children, which he saw as educational ghettos, cutting their pupils off from their peers. (See 'Segregation: New Style', in the *School Review*, April 1958, and 'Sputnik and Segregation' in *Commentary*, October-November 1958.) See also 'German Schools Revisited' in the Chicago-based *Elementary School Journal*, November 1955, written after a three-month spell of teaching in Germany.

34. In *Freud's Vienna and Other Essays*, he gives his age as thirteen, but according to his friend Wanda Willig, he was a little older.

35. Op cit, p. 24.

36. Interview with Wanda Willig in New York, November 1990.

37. *A Good Enough Parent*, p. 80.

38. Ibid, p. 84.

39. He could in fact have been slightly older. When telling his children of the incident, he gave his age as fourteen or fifteen.

40. Stefan Zweig, op cit, p. 98.

41. Edith Buxbaum, unpublished memoirs.

42. *Peurs et Terreurs face à la Contagion*, Ed. Fayard, Paris, 1988, p. 331.

43. Ibid, p. 425.

44. 'The Social Studies Teacher and the Emotional Needs of Adolescents', published in the *School Review* in December 1948. All the quotations in this and the next paragraph are drawn from the same source.

45. With the exception of his son Eric Bettelheim, who broached the subject without my having mentioned it, it was only in Los Angeles that the illness was mentioned without my first having to ask about it. Elsewhere, and particularly among the people who knew him best, i.e. those who had known him in Vienna, the subject was never raised unless I first brought it up. Gina Weinmann (the first Mrs Bettelheim) reacted by saying: 'That's something I wouldn't have mentioned if you hadn't known about it ....'

46. S. Zweig, op cit.

47. 'The Right to Privacy is a Myth', article published in the *Saturday Evening Post*, July 27, 1968.

48. Published in the the *Saturday Evening Post*, March 11, 1967.

49. The quote is from *Peurs et Terreurs face à la Contagion*, op cit, p. 330.

50. This was in particular the case for the French writer Maupassant, and also for his compatriots Stendhal and Flaubert. In Germany, many people suspected that Nietzsche had syphilis.

51. *Peurs et Terreurs face à la Contagion*, op cit, p. 322.

52. The text, published in *Freud's Vienna and Other Essays*, was originally a lecture Bettelheim gave at the University of Southwestern Lousiana. In a shorter form, it was also published as the preface to an American edition of Korczak's book *King Matt the First* (Farrar, Straus & Giroux, New York, 1986).

53. Henryk Goldszmit was Korczak's original Jewish name. He changed to the Gentile Janusz at the age of twenty in order to be admitted to a literary competition.

54. *Freud's Vienna and Other Essays*, p. 196.

55. Betty Jean Lifton, *The King of Children, A Biography of Janusz Korczak*, Farrar Straus & Giroux, New York, 1988.

56. *A Good Enough Parent*, p. 86.

57. Source: Edith Buxbaum, unpublished memoirs.

58. *The Empty Fortress*, p. 6.

59. S. Zweig, op cit.

60. 'Essential Books of One's Life', published in a Swiss magazine in 1987-88 and reprinted in *Freud's Vienna and Other Essays*, p. 106.

61. In particular in his book *Geschichte als Sinngebung des Sinnlosen*.

62. Paul Watzlavik, of the Palo Alto Mental Research Institute, offers a splendid example of this technique in his books. Before dying, a father tells his three sons that after his death he wants the eldest to have half of his estate, the second a third and the youngest a ninth. But as his estate amounts to seventeen camels, they see no other way to carry out his wishes than to cut some of them up. They are about to do so when a mullah passes by on camelback. They ask him for advice. 'I give you my camel,' he says. 'Now that you have eighteen, you the eldest can take nine, i.e. half of them. The second brother can take six, or a third. And the youngest can take two, or a ninth of the estate. They add up to seventeen. So one is unaccounted for. It is mine, and I take it back!'

63. After having written these lines, I learned that the Folklore Studies Centre at the University of Tel Aviv had carried out a comparative study of Jewish tales and fairy tales. The team, under Dov Noy, found that in 80 per cent of cases there was close correlation between the themes of each type.

64. Out of a total Austrian population of 8 million, 1.2 million were to be killed and 3 million injured during World War I.

65. *Larousse Mensuel Illustré*, August 1919, p. 866.

66. *The Informed Heart*, ch. 1.

67. As regards workplace legislation, Austria had already proved itself progressive in comparison with other empires. As early as 1883, a labour inspectorate was set up by law to ensure respect for restrictions on working hours, including a ban on Sunday working and limits on the employment of women and adolescents. And in 1887, Austria created an early form of health insurance, including measures to compensate employees for accidents at work.

68. A similar phenomenon was noted in countries allied to Austria. As Léon Poliakov (op cit) notes, in October 1916, with the war in full swing, the Ministry of War in Berlin ordered a census of all Jews serving in the armed forces, with information on whether they were at the front or in the rear. The official reason for the survey, the results of which were never published, was to disprove a widely believed rumour according to which most Jewish soldiers managed to get themselves cushy non-combat postings in offices or in the rear lines.

69. As Bruno Bettelheim himself was to point out in his article 'Class, Color and Prejudice', published in the *Nation*, October 19, 1963.

70. It is worth noting that the father of Austrian Social Democracy, Victor Adler, who was Jewish, was in his youth a supporter of the pan-Germanist party of Georg von Schönerer, only changing his opinion when the latter openly declared himself an anti-Semite.

71. The order was in fact never to be carried out, for lack of transport.

72. Letter to C. Frankenstein, November 19, 1986.

Chapter III. Gina

1. Interviews with Gina Weinmann in December 1990, July 1991 and May 1993.

2. Op cit, p. 25.

3. Bettelheim was to confirm his love affair with Lisl Lazarsfeld much later, during a lecture given in 1987 in Vienna, at the invitation of the Freud Museum.

4. Paul Lazarsfeld was later to emigrate to the United States, where he became a leading proponent of social psychology.

5. Quoted by Russell Jacoby in *The Repression of Psychoanalysis*, University of Chicago Press, 1983, p. 59.

6. *Freud's Vienna and Other Essays*, p. 26.

7. Ibid, p. 27.

8. According to Naomi, the younger daughter, Bettelheim only informed the two girls of the situation because Gina had told her own daughter about it, and he was afraid that they would learn it from her before he told them.

9. *Öst Juden:* eastern Jews. At the end of World War I, when Galicia became part of Poland, there were still some 700,000 Jews recorded as living there, most of them in ghettos.

10. 'They didn't speak Jewish,' is how she puts it.

11. *Freud's Vienna and Other Essays*, p. 20.

12. The auto salesroom which now occupies its ground floor no doubt makes it look a little more bourgeois than the butcher's store which was there in Freud's time.

13. Letter to C. Frankenstein, November 19, 1986.

14. *Saturday Evening Post*, July 27, 1968. In the same article, Bettelheim tempers the above statement by noting that: 'My own children study best with the door open and the record player going full blast, and in this radically different setting they learn as much and as well as I did.'

15. English translation: Before Daybreak.

16. In the essay entitled 'Essential Books of One's Life', p. 110.

17. Catalogue to the 1986 *Paris-Vienne* art exhibition, op cit.

18. Ibid.

19. The meeting of Gina and Wanda was to be the start of a friendship which was still going strong over sixty years later. Wanda, who like Gina had been born in Lemberg, was studying medicine, which greatly impressed her new friend. While Bruno and Hans were busy deciding how to change the world ('They were the serious types,' says Wanda) the two women were discovering the many things they had in common, notably an interest in psychoanalysis and a shared sense of humour, which led to many moments of helpless laughter.

20. Vol. 1 of Spengler's work appeared in 1919, and vol. 2 in 1923.

21. All the references and quotes relating to Bettelheim's reading given in this passage are drawn from his essay 'The Essential Books of One's Life', published in *Freud's Vienna and Other Essays*, p. 97 and *passim*. Bettelheim originally wrote the essay in 1987 for the Swiss magazine *Le Temps Stratégique*.

22. An expression which Bettelheim was later to make great use of, and which he borrowed from the American literary critic Edmund Wilson.

23. So much so that when the United States entered World War II, her name was on an FBI list of people considered a national security risk.

24. Sigmund Freud himself was to spend fifteen years teaching with the rank of *Privatdozent*, a kind of unpaid guest lecturer. It was only thanks to the intervention of one of his patients that he was finally to be awarded the fellowship that his standing merited. Cf Peter Gay, op cit, p. 138.

25. Letter to ER, September 10, 1954.

26. It has to be admitted that if Gina had not put me on the scent, I would not have thought of asking Wanda Willig about this.

27. Von Jauregg was famed for having discovered a treatment for the general paralysis that characterizes the final stage of syphilis. His method, which involved vaccination with malaria bacteria, won him a Nobel Prize.

28. R. Sterba, *Reminiscences of a Viennese Psychoanalyst*, Wayne State University Press, 1982.

29. Ibid, p. 34.

30. A few years later, Anna Freud would run what has since become known as the Jackson Nursery there.

31. In *Freud's Vienna and Other Essays*.

32. Ibid, p. 110.

33. Purchased with a loan from the *Autokredit Gesellschaft* company. It was to be confiscated by the Nazis in 1938. When Bettelheim was arrested, 1,100 Reichmarks of the debt were still outstanding.

34. Friedrich Torberg, *Die Tante Jolesch*, Ed. DTV, Munich, 1974.

35. Letter to ER, September 10, 1954.

36. In his essay devoted to the educationalist in *Freud's Vienna and Other Essays*, p. 197.

37. Letter to ER, September 1954.

38. In a small number of cases her statements were corroborated by Wanda Willig, and to some extent by Bettelheim's children Eric and Naomi.

39. In his letter to ER, September 10, 1954.

Chapter IV. Patsy

1. E. Buxbaum, unpublished memoirs.

2. The Sterbas were later to co-author a psychoanalytic study of Beethoven's relations with his nephew (*Beethoven and his Nephew*, 1954).

3. Gina does not remember the date, but Bruno Bettelheim mentions the autumn of 1932 in *The Empty Fortress*. That would be consistent with the documents I was able to find in Vienna, notably the police records on the whereabouts of Patsy's mother, Agnes Piel Crane.

4. Indeed, several times during our interviews, Gina confused the name of Patsy with that of her own daughter, born much later during her second marriage. She herself finally noticed the 'Freudian slip'.

5. Patsy was aged almost seventy when I interviewed her, in August 1991.

6. In his *Reminiscences of a Viennese Psychoanalyst* Richard Sterba tells how, shortly after the Anschluss, he had asked for help from a former American patient whose daughter was one of his wife's patients, and 'boarded with Bruno Bettelheim and his wife' in Vienna. In a laconic and exquisitely diplomatic comment, he adds: 'I believe that it was this experience with the girl that contributed to Bruno Bettelheim's interest in autistic children.'

7. Expression used by Bettelheim to describe autistic children in *The Empty Fortress*, p. 6.

8. Notably in the last television interview he granted to the French journalist Daniel Karlin on March 18, 1989, and during a conference in San Francisco four days later. Karlin included extracts from the interview in his film on Bettelheim (op cit).

9. *A Good Enough Parent*, p. 199.

10. Ibid, p. 200.

11. Ibid.

12. Interviewed by the author on August 5, 1991.

13. It would seem that she did not, however, take Patsy to see the great Swiss psychologist Jean Piaget, contrary to what Bettelheim was to state in some versions of the story. According to him Agnes Piel took her daughter to Piaget, who was by then famous in the United States for his work on the development of intelligence in children, before going on to Vienna. Piaget told her that he did not take patients, and referred her to Sigmund Freud, according to Bettelheim. But one wonders why Agnes, who spoke German as well as she spoke English and who being avidly interested in new ideas must have known about psychoanalysis, should not have found her own way to Vienna.

14. Patsy later readopted her original surname, i.e. the name of her officially recognized father.

15. His daughter Naomi recalls seeing one of them.

16. It is probably to this child that Bruno Bettelheim refers (as 'Johnny') in his essay 'How I Learned about Psychoanalysis', published in *Freud's Vienna and Other Essays*.

17. That was clear from the way in which some the people who had known her in Vienna asked me for news of her!

18. In *The Informed Heart*, ch. 1.

19. Letter to ER, September 10, 1954.

20. 'How I Learned about Psychoanalysis', published in *Freud's Vienna and Other Essays*, p. 28.

21. Ibid, p. 29.

22. Ibid, p. 28.

23. Gina was unaware that Trude had been a patient of Editha Sterba. But the two women did not know one another well.

24. Transference: 'the redirection of attitudes and emotions towards a substitute, such as towards the analyst during therapy' (*Collins English Dictionary*).

25. Letter to C. Frankenstein, December 14, 1986.

26. In *The World of Yesterday*, op cit.

27. Here again, what is important from the psychological point of view is not the literal truth, but the way Bettelheim interpreted it.

28. *Reminiscences of a Viennese Psychoanalyst*, op. cit.

29. Interview with Dr Maria Kramer, May 26, 1993.

30. *The Empty Fortress*, p. 79.

31. This expression is widely preferred to the word 'patient', which gives a too passive impression of the person in analysis.

32. None of this is at odds with what Bettelheim was trying to explain about psychotic children in the passage being quoted. For he wrote that when such children managed to create whole sentences to communicate with somebody else, in this case the therapist, that in itself was a sign of improvement, since it constituted an act directed towards the outside world. The formulation of complete sentences clearly represents an improvement in a child who up to then has been incapable of communicating with the outside world. But as Bettelheim refers here to the 'secret of psychoanalytic technique', we feel justified in broadening the field of application of his definition.

33. *Freud and Man's Soul*, ch. IV.

34. Made in a recording for his children.

35. *Freud's Vienna and Other Essays*, p. 27.

Chapter V. The Anschluss

1. *Mein Kampf*, Hutchinson, London, 1969, p. 114.

2. Renaissance painting in the first semester, and the art of Antiquity in the second.

3. This in particular explains the influence Mach exerted on thinkers like Freud and Musil.

4. Curiously, and for reasons which I was not able to elucidate, Gina's signature appears above Bruno's on the university registry.

5. In the first part of the dissertation, Bettelheim writes from a historical viewpoint to show how, with the development of urban culture and socialization, the natural world gradually became an object of aesthetic pleasure. He meanwhile deplores the fact that modern aesthetics either excludes nature altogether or views it as an inferior experience, far less important than art.

In part two, Bettelheim questions the distinction between beauty as applied to art and as applied to nature. He proposes to replace the dichotomy by a distinction between human creations, living creatures and landscapes. He attributes the fact that modern thinkers give precedence to art over nature both to historical factors (the history of art being an older discipline than aesthetics) and to system-related ones (the work of art, being an ordered object, is much more easily apprehended by the subject than nature, which leaves everything to his subjectivity).

Bettelheim goes on to discuss the two prevalent tendencies in modern aesthetics: idealism and formalism. Since idealism only pays attention to the ideational content of the work, it considers nature as a minor aesthetic object (as seen in Hegel or Vischer), in which the manifestation of the Idea is compromised or sullied by purely contingent elements. For the formalists, on the other hand, the only thing that counts is the form of the object (the relationship between its parts, the harmony of its colours, tones and rhythms, etc.). Their aim is to create a science of judgements of taste, based on an analysis of the elementary relations that go to make up any complex impression. Bettelheim sees a parallel between formalism and experimental psychology, criticizing the latter for only taking the simplest types of aesthetic expressions into account, and for being incapable of drawing up objective criteria for aesthetic values.

He then lists the various strains of formalism, noting that for most of them, the natural world can only attain the rank of an aesthetic object to the extent that the subject projects human feelings on to it, thereby bringing it to life or giving it a soul. This process occurs either directly or via the associations that the natural scene conjures up in the subject. In the case of the strictest type of formalism, the aesthetic effect is seen as springing from laws, such as unity in diversity, eurhythmy, the balance of proportions, harmony, etc. The aesthetics of nature is thus relegated to the sidelines.

In the next two parts of his dissertation Bettelheim seeks to show on the contrary that enjoyment of the natural world is a fully fledged aesthetic experience. He begins by stressing that aesthetic norms have almost always been deduced from the analysis of existing works of art, and that they cannot therefore lay claim to universal validity. He adds that in any case, the enjoyment of nature corresponds to the main criteria defined by various schools of thought: unity in diversity, specific human content, disinterested (i.e. non-utilitarian) stance of the subject, etc.

For Bettelheim, the reason that nature has been excluded from consideration as a valid aesthetic object has to do with the difficulty of clearly defining it. One's perception of a landscape is indeed dependent on many factors: one's vantage point, the way one frames the scene, the weather, season and time of day, and even the way one is feeling, both physically and psychologically. Furthermore, the experience involves not only vision but hearing, smell and other sensations, such as reactions to temperature.

In the case of an artwork, it is the artist himself who narrows the field of perceptions, a process which is indispensable if the impression is to have unity. But when the object is a natural scene, that narrowing has to be carried out by the observer alone. For Bettelheim, this proves that the enjoyment of nature is a more authentic aesthetic experience, as it is not mediated by a third party. It is also a more rounded one, since it involves all the senses, and not only sight. Lastly, it is closer to the origins of aesthetic experience, since its object has not yet been influenced by the work of an artist.

In the fifth part of his dissertation Bettelheim distances himself from both the idealist and formalist positions in an original way by transposing Reininger's psycho-physical theory of love on to the field of aesthetics. To give aesthetics its full meaning, he writes, one must put the accent on the experience itself, and not on either the subject (idealism) or the object (formalism) alone. The aesthetic experience constitutes an interactive relationship between the ego and the object, in which the object represents the outside world. In the instant when the experience occurs, the ego and the world merge, and it is precisely the transcendence of the ego/world duality that is the source of aesthetic pleasure.

What both idealists and formalists have failed to realize, writes Bettelheim in part six of his dissertation, is that such transcendence inhibits rational thought. As the forces that make up the ego (will-power and thought) dissolve in the aesthetic experience, there is no longer a clear opposition between the interior and the exterior, the subject and the object; the aesthetic experience takes place in a sphere from which the dualistic oppositions of rational thought (animate/inanimate, person/thing, spiritual/material, inside/outside) have been banished. The laws of aesthetics are thus at once objective and subjective; the object has to conform to certain aesthetic norms, and the subject must obey certain psychological laws.

What makes the natural world different from this standpoint is that, in the absence of an artist, the aesthetic object is entirely constructed by the subject. A person looking at a landscape enjoys the same freedom and spontaneity as an artist creating his work from impressions of the outside world. With one difference: here the object is not simply a representation of that outside world, it is itself part of it.

Bettelheim concludes by stressing that the aesthetic experience is an essential counterweight to the rationalist approach, particularly in a complex social structure in which any kind of unifying view has become more and more elusive. And nature can provide a purer and more complete aesthetic experience than art, because the latter is not freed from all the workings of reason. In the natural world, one does not think the world, one lives it, beyond the contradictions and questions that it raises. Aesthetic experience of nature is thus of fundamental importance for man, since it allows him to rise above his human condition.

6. Op cit, ch. I.

7. Cited by Alan Bullock in *Hitler, A Study in Tyranny*, Penguin Books, London 1962, p. 47.

8. *Last Waltz in Vienna, The Destruction of a Family 1842-1942*, Macmillan, London, 1981, part 4.

9. British Prime Minister Neville Chamberlain had refused to get involved in what he considered an inter-German affair. Czechoslovakia, like Italy, had been taken in by Hitler's promises. As for the French government, it had stepped down the previous day.

10. Quoted by William Shirer, *The Rise and Fall of the Third Reich*, London, 1960, p. 341.

11. Ibid.

12. Interview with M. Garner in May 1993.

13. Quoted in Clare, op cit, part 3. This treatment was meted out so widely in the weeks following the Anschluss that after the war, when the Vienna city authorities finally decided to erect a monument to the Jewish martyrs of Nazism, the sculpture that was adopted depicted a bowed, kneeling figure holding a scrubbing brush in its hands. It would be difficult to imagine an emblem more symbolic of Vienna's abiding ambivalence towards Jews!

14. Quoted by Anthony Read and David Fisher in *Kristallnacht – Unleashing the Holocaust*, Michael Joseph Ltd, London, 1989.

15. 'One people, one empire, one leader.'

16. A scene described by, among others, the American journalist William Shirer, op cit.

17. In 1938, $10,000 was equivalent to around six years' wages for a factory worker in the United States.

18. Quoted by Anthony Read and David Fisher in *Kristallnacht – Unleashing the Holocaust*, op cit.

19. *Reminiscences of a Viennese Psychoanalyst*, op cit.

20. *Last Waltz in Vienna*, op cit.

21. Quoted by Herbert Rosenkranz in *The Nazi Concentration Camps*, Proceedings of the 4th International Yad Vashem Historical Conference, published in Jerusalem in 1984.

22. *Nazi Conspiracy and Aggression*, US Government Printing Office, Washington, 1946, vol. VII (pp. 818-39).

23. In his *Reminiscences of a Viennese Psychoanalyst*, Richard Sterba states that he accompanied Peter Weinmann to the station on March 12, which would mean that Gina and Patsy left on that day, as they were on the same train. However Sterba himself gives erroneous dates for several other events, as for example when he states that Hitler arrived in Vienna on that same Saturday whereas in fact he came two days later. One can but reflect on the frailty of the human memory as regards traumatic events.

24. Once the 'Final Solution' was under way, this term would become synonymous with extermination. That was not yet the case in the Vienna of 1938, however. The term can be found in all the documents from that period.

25. At the time the Jewish population of Austria totalled some 192,000, of whom 95 per cent lived in the capital. The city was thus home to Europe's third-biggest Jewish community after Warsaw and Budapest. Already at the end of 1938, only 64,000 remained, and six years later, when the Red Army liberated Vienna, records indicate that there were only 200. As some Jews went uncounted because they had opted for conversion, however, the true figure can only be guessed at.

26. A striking example of this admiration is to be found in the minutes of the famous Berlin meeting that took place after the *Kristallnacht* pogrom in November 1938. Goering, presiding, heard reports from all the regional governors, with the

Vienna *Gauleiter* speaking last. When he had finished, Goering exhorted those present to follow the example set by the Austrians. They had done more in five months than the German Nazis had managed to do in five years, he added.

27. William Shirer, op cit, p. 350.

28. Richard Sterba, *Reminiscences of a Viennese Psychoanalyst*, op cit.

Chapter VI. Dachau: The Making of a Survivor

1. I would in particular like to thank Mrs Barbara Distel of the Dachau Memorial and Mr. Vidar Jakobson of the *Centre de Documentation Juive Contemporaine* in Paris for their invaluable help.

2. Paul Federn, whom Freud made the de facto head of the Vienna Psychoanalytic Society after 1923, when he was diagnosed as suffering from cancer.

3. Ernst Federn described his encounter with Bettelheim in *Witnessing Psychoanalysis*, a collection of essays published in London in 1990 by Karnac Books. I interviewed him in Vienna in October 1990 and June 1992.

4. Hans Bandler gave a brief account of his arrest and deportation in *Strauss to Matilda, 1938-1988*, a book on the Austrian community in Australia published in 1988 by the Wenkart Foundation, Sydney. I was able to meet him on October 9 and 11, 1991 in London.

5. In *Against All Hope* (Constable, 1994).

6. Indeed, when the other camps were built, former Dachau cadres were used to set an example of how things should be done. In addition to the notorious Auschwitz commander Rudolf Höss, and his successor Karl Baer, the heads of Flossenbürg, Ravensbrück, Bergen-Belsen, Mathausen, Lublin, Sachsenhausen, Natzweiler and other less well-known camps all got their initial training at Dachau.

7. As Olga Wormser-Migot writes, in *Le système concentrationnaire nazi* (Presses Universitaires de France, Paris, 1968, p. 73), 'For camps to be set up for the Jews, for the Nuremberg Laws to take on their full meaning, it was necessary for the war to be under way, and for the authorities to be able to deport the Jews outside the borders of the Reich, or to seek them out in the countries in which they had found refuge and deport them.' One is tempted to add, since Austria is such a special case in this context, '... and to eliminate them from the city in which Adolf Hitler had learned to hate them.'

8. *Surviving*.

9. Notably in 'Freedom from Ghetto Thinking', published in *Midstream* review in March 1962, and in 'Survival of the Jews', a review of Jean-François Steiner's book *Treblinka* which appeared in the magazine *New Republic* on July 1, 1967. Bettelheim was later to recast and merge those two texts to form the last chapter of his *Freud's Vienna and Other Essays*, which constitutes his last word on the subject. This also explains why he uses the concept of an 'Informed Heart'. See below, Chapter XIII, for more on that subject.

10. According to Bettelheim, the latter numbered no more than 500 for all of Germany at the beginning of 1938.

11. Seven years later, in his testimony before one of Judge Jackson's aides, Bettelheim mistakenly gave the date of his admission to Dachau as early May.

12. It is worth recalling that this annexation was at the time contested by practically nobody. Witness the fact that when Bettelheim arrived in New York eleven months later, the US immigration authorities recorded him as having been born in 'Vienna, Germany'.

13. Decree of February 20, 1933. Cf Olga Wormser-Migot, op cit.

14. In *The Other Kingdom*, Reynal & Hitchcock, New York, 1947

15. *Surviving*.

16. Himmler was at the time deputy police chief of the city of Munich.

17. The question of when exactly Freud left Vienna provides a good illustration of the dangers a biographer faces in interpreting his subject's acts long after the event. In his diary, Freud gave the time of his departure from the city as 3.25 p.m. on June 3. However his first biographer, Ernest Jones, said this was a mistake, and that the date was in fact June 4. A truly Freudian slip, which Peter Gay, in his *Freud, A Life for our Time*, attributes to the old man's ambivalence at leaving the city.

However Harald Leupold-Löwenthal, president of the Vienna Freud Society, who sifted through all the evidence with a fine-tooth comb (even establishing the precise minute at which Freud's train left, 3.14 p.m.), said it was Ernest Jones who had got the wrong day, because it was in fact he who felt ambivalent about Freud's arrival in London!

18. *Surviving*, p. 12.

19. According to the Dachau records the train was carrying 595 men on arrival. The average travel time from Vienna to the camp was 14 hours.

20. An account of a similar journey in the same period can be found in Victor Frankl's autobiographical book *Man's Search for Meaning*.

21. *Surviving*.

22. Ernst Federn, who had been taken to Dachau just over a week earlier, reported a similar experience. The ill-treatment lasted until the train arrived at Salzburg station. There a new team of guards took over, and the rest of the trip was relatively peaceful.

23. *Surviving*, p. 61.

24. Ibid, p. 63.

25. Ibid, p. 62.

26. At this stage, the Nazis' desire to appear respectable was not yet pure bluff: when Ernst Federn was freed from Buchenwald, eight years later, his personal effects were returned to him!

27. *Surviving*, pp. 12-13.

28. In *The Informed Heart*, p. 213.

29. A work team leader, chosen from among the prisoners.

30. A whole string of top Austrian civil servants were to die in that way in the quarries at Buchenwald.

31. *The Informed Heart*, ch. 4.

32. *Surviving*, p. 69.

33. Professor Leni Yahil of Haifa University commented that this was a good example of how, in the camps, the ideas and standards accepted by society in the outside world were stood on their heads. According to several witnesses, he said, professors and other intellectuals in Buchenwald worked in the latrines. They could be seen pushing their barrows along, engaged in philosophical discussion (*The Nazi Concentration Camps*, Proceedings of the 4th International Yad Vashem Historical Conference, published in Jerusalem in 1984).

34. *The Theory and Practice of Hell: The Concentration Camps and the System behind Them*, Farrar, Straus, New York, 1950. Originally published in German under the title *Der SS-Staat*, the work includes a report that Kogon drew up for the psychological warfare department of the US Army after the liberation of Buchenwald.

35. *Surviving*, p. 58.

36. *The Informed Heart*, ch. 1.

37. Ibid, ch. 4.

38. Ibid, ch. 4.

39. Cf *Surviving*, p. 51.

40. Ibid, p. 13.

41. Ibid, p. 52.

42. Ibid, p. 13.

43. In fact, he was ill informed: Norbert Bettelheim had filed the required statement on July 16. In addition to Bruno's car and his stake in his own company, the list mentioned two gold watches (estimated at 200 Reichmarks), a silver platter (RM80) and a picture (RM200). In a second inventory, filed in December, the lawyer referred to RM452 owed by Bettelheim as a result of an order made against him by a court in the district of Heitzing, where he lived. I was unfortunately unable to find out the reason for that. The only other debts Bettelheim had were the sums outstanding on his car (around RM1,500) and on his life insurance policy (RM189). At that time a Reichmark was worth two dollars and fifty cents.

44. It was not always to be thus. In 1942, War Minister Albert Speer ordered that Buchenwald be downgraded from the status of 'concentration camp' to that of simple 'labour camp'. Before that happened, all but 200 of the Jews in Buchenwald had been transferred to other camps, notably to Auschwitz. Those who remained behind were bricklayers, retained because of their skills. This is confirmed by Ernst Federn, who certainly owed his life to the fact that he chose early on to specialize in that much-needed craft.

Buchenwald's change in status also followed the departure of the appalling camp commander Karl Koch, at a time when the Nazi war effort demanded that the maximum use be made of the prisoners' labour power. At the same time, for reasons of efficiency, the SS put 'political' rather than 'common-law' prisoners in most key posts in the camp. (It was in the contiguous camp of Dora that the V-1 and V-2 flying bombs, which were to cause such havoc in England in the last months of the war, were built, in an underground factory.)

As for the living skeletons found by the US troops who entered Buchenwald at the war's end, and whose pictures shocked the world, they were in fact detainees from Auschwitz who had been moved to Buchenwald because of the advance of the Soviet forces in the east. As the ever-scrupulous Federn explains, a special camp had been built for the Auschwitz prisoners inside Buchenwald at the end of 1944.

45. *'Du neimand!'*

46. *Witnessing Psychoanalysis*, by Ernst Federn, Karnac Books, London, 1990, p. 4.

47. Cf *Medical Block, Buchenwald*, by Walter Poller, Souvenir Press, London, 1961. First published in German by Verlag das Segel, Offenbach am Main.

48. See *Against All Hope*, op. cit., by Hermann Langbein (first published as *Nicht Wie die Schafe sur Schlachtbank*, Fischer Taschenbuch Verlag, Frankfurt, 1980).

49. See Olga Wormser-Migot, op cit, p. 483 and *passim*.

50. And as Bruno Bettelheim and other writers have noted, the system fostered the delusion among many inmates, who had not had much direct contact with the SS, that some of the latter actually disapproved of the ill-treatment they were suffering.

51. A note dated May 16, 1945 in the unpublished diary kept by Ernest Thape at Buchenwald (Friedrich Ebert Foundation, Bonn), and quoted in Langbein, op cit. Later on the 'Reds' were put in charge of Buchenwald instead of the 'Greens', while at Dachau the opposite process occurred.

52. The slang expression *Karacho* can be translated as 'at full speed'.

53. From the start, the Nazi regime created a special status for those it deported. They were no longer described as *Gefangener* (prisoner), but as *Häftling*.

54. Walter Poller, *Medical Block, Buchenwald*, op cit, p. 30.

55. Poller gives the figure as 12,000, but the exact number was 9,845.

56. The figure is from the book *La nuit de cristal* by Rita Thalmann and Emmanuel Feinermann, Ed. Robert Laffont, Paris, 1972, p. 167. A total of 10,911 other Jews were to be sent to Dachau and some 9,000 to Sachsenhausen as a result of the pogrom.

57. *The Informed Heart*, ch. 4.

58. Koch was recognized even by the Nazis to be particularly venal, and was later sentenced for corruption.

59. Op cit, p. 234.

60. Penned for the *New Yorker*, which published it on August 2, 1976. It also figures in the book of the same name.

61. A large oak in the camp grounds was known among the detainees as 'Goethe's tree.' (The commentary of Alain Resnais' film *Nuit et Brouillard* (Night and Fog) read by Jean Cayrol, even says 'they built the camp around it, but they respected the tree.') Unfortunately, that pretty story has been demolished by the scholarship of Olga Wormser-Migot, who quotes Eckermann on a conversation during which Goethe refers to a beech tree (*Buche*) on which he and Schiller had carved their names. As for the famous oak, it was destroyed by bombing in 1944.

62. Op cit, p. 181.

63. Op cit, p. 62. In *The Informed Heart* (ch. 4), Bettelheim gives practically the same account, only this time in the first person.

Chapter VII. Buchenwald: The Price of Freedom

1. Eugen Kogon says that three prisoners tried to escape, but both Bettelheim and Hans Bandler mention only two.

2. This is the figure Bettelheim gives in *Surviving*, his last book on the subject. In *The Informed Heart*, however, the toll is reduced to around fifty. Eugen Kogon gives the figure as over seventy.

3. The song, '*Moorsoldaten*', or 'Marsh Soldiers', was officially attributed to the *Kapo* who worked in the camp post office, but in fact it had been written by two Austrian Jews. The words were by Löhner-Beda, who had written librettos for Franz Lehar, and the music was by the cabaret singer Leopolodi.

4. In 'The Dynamism of Anti-Semitism in Gentile and Jew', an article published in April 1947 by the *Journal of Abnormal and Social Psychology* (vol. 42, no. 2) and included in an edited version in *The Informed Heart*.

5. 'Gestapoman' was the expression Bettelheim initially used. However, when he edited the text for inclusion in *The Informed Heart*, he described the guard as an SS soldier. For his part, Ernst Federn remembers the infirmary guard being a prisoner.

6. 'The Dynamism of Anti-Semitism in Gentile and Jew', op cit.

7. See Chapter X.

8. Unless one is to believe that he remained without glasses from June to December 1938, when he finally got permission to ask for a new pair. Given that he required nine-diopter lenses, plus correction for his astigmatism, that seems highly unlikely.

9. *The Informed Heart*, ch. 4 (n).

10. 'The Ultimate Limit' in *Surviving*, part I (n).

11. Primo Levi, *I Sommersi e i Salvati*, published in English as *The Drowned and the Saved*, Michael Joseph Ltd., London, 1988, ch. 3.

12. In one of his letters he referred to it as the '*Presse*', but I was unable to ascertain whether it was the *Neue Freie Presse* or some other newspaper.

13. *The Informed Heart*, ch. 5.

14. Bettelheim makes no allusion to the question in his letters to his mother. It is however conceivable that he transposed on to the intellectual plane an incident linked to something else, for example his business affairs. He notably expressed great bitterness towards his partner Hans Schnitzer, who had not been arrested, but of course this is no more than a hypothesis.

15. See p. 109.

16. 'Individual and Mass Behavior in Extreme Situations', in *Surviving*, op cit.

17. *Witnessing Psychoanalysis*, by Ernst Federn, Karnac Books, London, 1990, p. xvii.

18. *Surviving*.

19. Letter to Federn, January 8, 1969.

20. *The Informed Heart*, ch. 4.

21. Quoted by Annette Wieviorka in *Deportation et Génocide*, op cit.

22. It was written for *Midway* review on the occasion of the publication of *Death in Life: Survivors of Hiroshima*, by Robert J. Lifton (Random House, New York, 1967).

23. This essay, considerably edited, forms the opening chapter of *Surviving*. Starting with his very first article on the camps, published in 1943, Bettelheim had used the expression to refer to the train ride to the camp, and the interminable roll-call of December 14, 1938, but he had not given a theoretical definition. Even seventeen years later, in *The Informed Heart*, he contented himself with rounding off a catalogue of ill-treatment suffered by inmates with the phrase 'All of which may explain why I speak of them as persons finding themselves in an "extreme" situation.' Readers would have to wait for *The Empty Fortress* in 1967 to find a first definition: 'This, psychologically, is what constitutes an extreme situation: when we ourselves respond to an external danger – real or imagined – with inner maneuvers that actually debilitate us further' (p. 77).

24. '*Mors ultima linea rerum est*', from *Epistles*, I.16,79.

25. He was to return to and further develop this idea a few years later in his introduction to *Surviving*. He used the first few pages of 'The Ultimate Limit' to open that work, although the opening was changed (see Chapter XIII). Quotes in the following paragraphs are taken from the original version of the article.

26. Written eighteen years earlier, and devoted to the patients of the Orthogenic School. Federn was in fact to criticize the title in his own book, *Witnessing Psychoanalysis*.

27. By way of an illustration, Bettelheim referred in his letter to the 'small child, who has as yet no conception of death, is unable to love, though very much in need of it', and for whom 'life is so taken for granted that it has no meaning'.

28. Bettelheim's relationship to Freudian thought is discussed in Chapter X.

29. This could be compared, in psychoanalytic parlance, to being dominated by the 'id', Freud's German term having being rendered in English by the Latin word meaning 'that'. See Chapter X.

30. *The Informed Heart*, ch. 1.

31. Ibid, ch. 4.

32. Published in Vienna in 1936. First published in English by The Hogarth Press, London, 1937.

33. Cf 'The Ignored Lesson of Anne Frank', in *Surviving*.

34. He had been issued with a new number, 9036, on arriving in Buchenwald.

35. Op cit, ch. 4.

36. Ibid.

37. Ibid, p. 165.

38. Quoted in *La Nuit de cristal*, by Rita Thalmann and Emmanuel Feinermann.

39. There was even a popular saying among non-Jews in Buchenwald, Bettelheim writes: 'There are only two ways to get out of here: feet first, or being a Jew.' Cf 'The Ultimate Limit', in *Surviving*.

40. Ibid.

41. In particular, the correspondence between Agnes Crane and the head of the State Department's visa section, which are still in the official archives.

42. At the Franklin D. Roosevelt Library in Hyde Park, New York State.

43. From various notes she sent, notably to the State Department, it emerges that in fact Mrs Roosevelt had not yet fully realized the extent of the persecution to which German and Austrian Jews were being subjected.

44. Archived in Columbia University, New York.

45. He arrived back in Vienna after that visit just in time for the birth of his last son, Ernst.

46. Aboard the SS *Pennland* from the Belgian port of Antwerp, with a US visa obtained in Vienna on August 24, 1939.

47. A man who was later to achieve fame for scaling Mount Everest.

Chapter VIII. A Short-Lived Reunion

1. The sum that figured next to his name on the ship's manifest.

2. From an address by Bettelheim to the San Jose Holocaust Conference, February 1977.

3. Information provided by Edith Buxbaum in 1978 during an interview with Dr Lawrence H. Schwartz, published by the Seattle Psychoanalytic Institute in 1990.

4. For instance, during his last interview with the French TV film-maker Daniel Karlin.

5. Interviews in December 1990 and May 1993.

Chapter IX. From Chicago to Rockford, and Back

1. Interviewed on July 25, 1991.

2. I was not able to ascertain, for instance, whether Bettelheim had any knowledge of a test carried out by Charlotte Bühler and her team on 'Children and Art', an account of which had been published by Amalie Koerperth-Tippel in 1935, a year before Bettelheim enrolled as a PhD student with Karl Bühler. The test, which was used on 200 children between three and fourteen, was aimed at finding out at what age art appreciation appears. Like the test designed by Bettelheim, it used a comparative method in order to prevent the results being influenced by the child's verbal skills. But unlike Bettelheim's test, it involved already made-up pairs of images, each one consisting of an art reproduction alongside a 'kitsch' representation of the same subject.

3. Interview with Lee Cronbach on July 18, 1991.

4. Bettelheim's own report on his test was published in *Appraising and Recording Student Progress*, edited by Eugene R. Smith and Ralph W. Tyler, Harper & Brother, New York, 1942, pp. 276-312. An appendix lists the pictures he selected.

5. In keeping with Bettelheim's philosophy and practice I have opted to use masculine singular pronouns and adjectives when referring to an unidentified child.

6. In an April 1975 letter to Candace Hilldrup, a former counsellor from the Orthogenic School who was in the process of settling in France. Subsequent quotes in this paragraph are from the same source.

7. See p. 29.

8. Surprising though it may seem, in the thirty years of his career at the University of Chicago, Bruno Bettelheim was never once asked to produce the slightest documentary evidence of his diplomas. I received proof of this during my first visit to Chicago, at a time when the most extravagant allegations were being made against him. Learning that I had started my research by going to Vienna the previous month, the university's legal counsel could not resist asking me: 'And did you see his dissertation?' My answer was clearly a great relief to him.

9. Interviews with Aimee Horton, Betty-Lou Pingree-Rellahan and Ronnie Dryovage, May-June 1993.

10. As stated in the introduction to the school almanac for 1943-44.

11. Published in 1947 in the *American Journal of Orthopsychiatry*.

12. The TAT was invented by C.D. Morgan and H.A. Murray in 1934.

13. Interview with Betty-Lou Pingree-Rellahan, May 1993.

14. The full test in fact consists of forty cards, from which the psychologist selects twenty depending on the sex and age of the subject.

15. Apraxia: 'a disorder of the central nervous system characterized by apparent loss of the memory of how to make certain purposeful muscular movements', (*Collins English Dictionary*, 1979).

16. In contrast, for example, with the material expressed in dreams, much harder to interpret. Cf Freud, 'The Poet and Daydreaming', *Collected Papers*, vol. IV, Hogarth Press, London, 1925.

17. Quote provided by Dr Erwin Angres, December 1990.

18. He turned down the request because he was giving a course on art in Chicago on that day, but he adjusted his regular teaching hours so that all students who wanted to could attend.

19. Interview, May 1993.

20. Interview, May 1993.

21. As shown by the letter of reference Cheek wrote for him in May 1944, when he applied for a job in a small Connecticut university. The tone was much more reserved that it had been in her letter to Tyler two years earlier.

22. The supervisor is an experienced analyst who guides a new practitioner's handling of his first patients by means of regular sessions. The latter of course take place in the absence of the patient or patients.

Chapter X. A New Man for the New World

1. When Trude applied for US citizenship, Ruth Eissler acted as one of her two witnesses.

2. It should be said that this was not technically a lie, since aesthetics is a branch of philosophy, and the faculty in which Bettelheim obtained his PhD was called the Department of Philosophy and Psychology!

3. A good example is provided by a series of interviews Bettelheim granted in autumn 1988 to the psychoanalyst David James Fisher, and which were published in the *Los Angeles Psychoanalytic Bulletin* in the spring of 1990. The interviewer, fascinated by the history of psychoanalysis, plied him with questions about the Vienna Society. Bettelheim was evasive: 'I don't really have any memories of this Society, but rather of those who attended it. Because, you see, I was not yet a member. I was very friendly with Wilhelm Reich, and ... Fenichel also became a good friend, and others. I got reports of what happened.' On his own analytical training, he also remained as close as he could to the truth without actually demolishing the legend, replying: 'I had just started the training analysis before the Nazis marched in,' to three separate questions. Then: 'I was interviewed, *as all candidates at the time were*, by Anna Freud and Paul Federn.' Finally he gave in to his interviewer's curiosity, telling him that on one occasion Sigmund Freud had entered the room where they had been working, and had said, 'A Bettelheim does not need any introduction to me,' and adding that one of his uncles had done his military service alongside Freud. While it is true that a certain Joseph Bettelheim was one of Freud's classmates (although it was not possible to ascertain whether he was any relation), the story appears fantastic for several reasons. Bettelheim's Uncle Jakob, the one who died in a duel, would have been four years younger than Freud, and he was the eldest of his uncles. And according to Ernst Federn, Bettelheim had not met his father before meeting him. Lastly, by well before 1938, the proceedings of the Psychoanalytic Society were no longer being held in the Freud household.

4. Cohler, a former student of the Orthogenic School, was in 1971 to take over from Bettelheim as its director for a year. See Chapter XVI.

5. In an interview on December 4, 1990.

6. In a tape cassette on which he recorded some recollections for his children.

7. In the French weekly *L'Evénement du Jeudi*, on October 28, 1993.

8. Interview with David Fisher, op cit. This is also confirmed by recent research, for example in the *International Handbook of Traumatic Stress Syndrome* (Plenum Press, New York, 1993), a collective work produced under the direction of J.P. Wilson and B. Raphael. An Israeli study published in this work reveals that eighty per cent of concentration-camp survivors suffer from 'repetitive nightmares'. The psychiatrist Marc-Antoine Crocq, who writes in the same work, told me: 'This post-traumatic symptom never completely disappears, and has a tendency to get worse at the time of retirement. The subject never gets used to it, and his average anxiety level remains considerably higher than that found in the population as a whole. For these subjects, everything in their daily life can generate anxiety or feelings of persecution. Which explains, for example, the rather paranoid attitude of someone like Solzhenitsyn towards the media.'

9. He probably did not get official confirmation of this immediately, but all the news he received from Vienna at the time pointed to it.

10. Letter to C. Hilldrup, February 19, 1975.

11. George Sheviakov, who was fascinated by psychoanalysis, outlines the problems he had with his Freudian friends on that issue when he was working on the 'Eight Year Study'. Recollections recorded on tapes for his children.

12. Cf Siegfried Bernfeld, 'On Psychoanalytic training' in *Psychoanalytic Quarterly*, 1962.

13. Revealing from this point of view is an exchange of letters between Franz Alexander and Karl Menninger, one of his former patients. (Menninger ran a

school for disturbed children in Topeka, Kansas, which for a long time was the only institution in the United States that could be compared with the Orthogenic School, even though it was run on different lines.) Cf *The Selected Correspondence of Karl A. Menninger*, Yale University Press, 1988.

14. There are twenty-four letters from Freud to Alexander. They are currently in the possession of Dr George Pollack, a former director of the Chicago Institute, who is writing Alexander's biography.

15. A story he tells in 'A Jury Trial of Psychoanalysis', *Journal of Abnormal and Social Psychology*, 1940.

16. *Freud, A Life for Our Time*, by Peter Gay.

17. During a symposium on lay analysis held as a prelude to the Innsbruck International Psychoanalytic Congress. The resulting texts were published in the same year, appearing simultaneously in German (in *Internationale Zeitschrift*) and in English (in the *International Journal of Psycho-Analysis*).

18. And also that between the patient and psychoanalysis itself.

19. *Freud et l'âme humaine*, Editions Robert Laffont, Paris, 1984.

20. *Analysis Terminable and Interminable*, 1937, Standard Edition, vol. XXIII, p. 229.

21. Daniel Karlin, 'Last interview with Bruno Bettelheim', recorded in June 1989.

22. Cf Chapter VIII.

23. Notably in his letter to Pastor Oskar Pfister, on November 25, 1928.

24. According to French historian and psychoanalyst Elisabeth Roudinesco (*Lacan and Others*, Chicago University Press, 1990), two basic conditions are required for psychoanalysis to take root in a country. These are democracy and the existence of a structured psychiatric (medical) system. She explains the medicalization of psychoanalysis in the United States by the non-fulfilment of the second condition when the first European analysts arrived in the country. As psychoanalysis offered psychiatry a model of the human psyche which it lacked, the latter discipline, she says, fell into a vacuum. In other countries, psychiatry had contented itself with integrating the model into its teaching. But in the United States it also in effect incorporated the practitioners. Which is why American psychoanalysts are often referred to as psychiatrists, and why up until 1993, those who were not also medical doctors had to be called psychologists. In that year the Supreme Court, in a ruling based on anti-monopoly principles, gave them the right to the title of psychoanalyst.

25. Letter to Theodor Reik, July 3, 1938, quoted in Gay, op cit, p. 633.

26. *Autobiographical Study*, Standard Edition, vol. XX, p. 52.

27. Paul Roazen, *Freud and his Followers*, New York University Press, New York, 1984, p. 5.

28. *Autobiographical Study*, op cit.

29. In particular, his contribution to *Das Psychanalytische Volksbuch* in 1926 and *The Ego Feeling in Dreams*, 1932.

30. The Hogarth Press, London, 1937.

31. Some foreign observers have tended to treat American psychoanalysis with considerable condescension. In France, in particular, the dismissive comments of Jacques Lacan seem to have left many of his followers with the impression that they could dispense with studying the question altogether.

32. The latter film came out only a few weeks before Bettelheim's death. One can only wonder if he saw it.

33. This was an attempt to bring together psychoanalysis and anthropology by questioning the universal nature of the Oedipus complex. Born from the interest shown in Freud's ideas by certain anthropologists (notably Malinowski, Ruth Benedict, Abram Kardiner and Margaret Mead), it was to attract a number of dissident Freudians, such as Erich Fromm and Karen Horney.

34. Notably in his book *Essays in Ego Psychology*, International Universities Press, New York, 1964.

35. *Freud and Man's Soul*, ch. 1.

36. Ibid.

37. Bettelheim notes that the French translations of Freud's key terms are much more faithful to the original. *Das Ich* is rendered as *le moi* (the me), *Das Es* by *le ça* (the it) and *Das Über-Ich* by *le surmoi* (the above-I).

38. I heard such replies in particular from members of the Chicago Psychoanalytic Institute, but also from a few Europeans.

39. On Freud's relations with the United States, see Peter Gay, *Freud, A Life for Our Time*, op cit, which includes a good bibliography on the question; Paul Roazen, *Freud and his Followers*, New York University Press, New York, 1971, and Elisabeth Roudinesco, *Lacan and Others*, op cit. For a French view of the debate over lay analysis, see Michael Schneider's commentary in *La question de l'analyse profane* (Gallimard, Paris, 1985), a collection of Freud's writings on the subject.

40. Letter to Arnold Zweig, March 5, 1939.

41. Letter to C. Frankenstein, August 10, 1981. His exact words were: 'I [have] finally finished my long essay on the translations of Freud into English in which I make him sound better than he deserves as a person. But what a mind! What insights into the foibles of man! and how unable, despite of it, to do something about the obvious limitations of his own personality and his inability to really deal respectfully with his followers, not to speak of his enemies. ... Well, I guess the limitations of a true genius, and one's mentor, are hard to accept.'

42. In Vienna, Bettelheim explained, patients ending their analyses were asked to wait around two years before applying to become analysts themselves, so as to be sure that their ambition was not simply an effect of the transference. (Interview with David James Fisher, op cit.)

43. This has recently been the subject of many symposiums, notably in Israel. Most psychoanalysts who were in the camps thought for a time that they could separate that experience from their professional activities. In France the German-born analyst Anne-Lise Stern, who was a patient of Jacques Lacan after her release from Auschwitz, was the first to show that this was impossible. But that was not before 1968 when, having worked with many drug addicts and otherwise troubled young people, she discovered how traces of the Holocaust remained present, and deadly, in the unconscious of patients who had not even been direct victims.

44. Letter to ER, July 1980.

45. The remark figures in all the different versions of his study on the camps, including his testimony to Judge Jackson.

46. In ch. 1.

47. See ch. 6.

48. In *Journal of Abnormal and Social Psychology*, Cambridge, Mass., October 1943.

49. *Ten Eventful Years*, Encyclopaedia Britannica, Chicago, 1947.

50. *Nazi Conspiracy and Aggression*, US Government Printing Office, Washington, 1946, vol. VII (p. 818-39).

51. As is noted by Paul Marcus and Alan Rosenberg in 'Reevaluating Bruno Bettelheim's Work on Nazi Concentration Camps: the Limits of his Psychoanalytic

Approach', in a special issue of the *Psychoanalytic Review* entitled 'Bruno Bettelheim's Contribution to Psychoanalysis', New York, autumn 1994.

52. See Chapter XIII.

53. See, for example, the remarkable *Mémoire et personne*, by Georges Gusdorf, Presses Universitaires de France, Paris, 1950.

54. 'Individual and Mass Behavior in Extreme Situations', in *Surviving*.

55. According to Bettelheim's editor Ruth Marquis, who saw the manuscript when the two of them were working on *The Informed Heart*.

56. *Surviving*, ch. 1 ('The Ultimate Limit').

57. *Mortal Storm* was not in fact banned, and although it was a failure its release in the US provided Hitler with an excuse to ban all MGM films from Germany.

58. *Surviving*, ch. 1 ('The Ultimate Limit').

59. Ibid.

60. This was the term he used in the early forties; in *Surviving* he would replace it by 'the SS.'

61. Ibid.

62. He states for example that he slept in a total of five blocks in the two camps, while it emerges from his letters that the number was in fact three. It was no doubt the same desire to reinforce his credibility that made him give an erroneous date for his arrival at Dachau in his testimony to Judge Jackson. He said he had been taken to the camp in early May 1938, which would have extended his incarceration by a month, taking it to only a few days short of a year.

63. Many of those observations are to be found in the descriptions of his camp experiences, in Chapters VI and VII of the present work.

64. Notably by the report on Buchenwald drawn up in April 1945 for the Psychological Warfare Division of the US Army by the Austrian journalist Eugen Kogon. This was later published in English as *The Theory and Practice of Hell: The Concentration Camps and the System behind Them*, Farrar, Straus, New York, 1950.

65. Readers who find this difficult to believe should bear in mind that up until the start of World War II, the Nazis were very careful to create a facade of legality to cover up their actions. As Bettelheim points out, they even tried to maintain this fiction inside the concentration camps. Although guards had the right to shoot prisoners, for example, they were officially forbidden to steal from them. In practice, they used blackmail to get the detainees to 'give' them whatever they coveted.

66. Kogon for example, writing six years after Bettelheim, describes three phases in the creation of the 'hardened' camp inmate: the shock of internment, the selection process of the initial months and the phase of adaptation. The last could stretch over years.

67. George Clare, *Last Waltz in Vienna, The Destruction of a Family 1842-1942*, Macmillan, London, 1981.

68. He made the confession to Alvin Rosenfeld, who quotes it in *The Art of the Obvious*, the book co-authored with Bettelheim.

69. *Surviving*, ch. 1.

70. As is shown by his correspondence, for example in a letter he wrote on February 19, 1975 to a friend in Paris. She had sent him a large number of press cuttings on the controversy sparked in France by the broadcasting of Daniel Karlin's films. He replied: 'All my life, since I began working, I have been accused of much worse things – when I spoke and wrote about the concentration camp at a time when nobody wanted to know about it, I was called psychotic, paranoiac, suffering from persecution neurosis ... I never defended myself, and five years later Eisenhower ordered all occupation officers to read the paper which had been declared a bunch of psychotic ravings. This was my first big lesson.'

71. A few days before the US Army's fourth armored division entered the main Buchenwald camp, on April 12, 1945, the troops stumbled almost by accident on one of its annexes, the small camp of Ohrdruf. There, the SS troops had shot all the detainees before fleeing. The first pictures of Buchenwald to reach the outside world thus showed piles of dead bodies. Cf Robert H. Abzug, *Inside the Vicious Heart*, Oxford University Press, New York, 1985.

72. As soon as he was freed, Federn also published an analysis of Buchenwald. This appeared first in Belgium, where Federn was then living, as 'Essai sur la psychologie de la terreur' in *Synthèses* (vols 7 & 8, Brussels, 1946). It was published in the United States as 'Terror as a System: The Concentration Camp' in *Psychiatric Supplement*, Utica, NY, 1948.

73. *A Home for the Heart*, p. 284.

74. Written in 1937 and published in vol. XXIII of the Standard Edition.

75. W.W. Norton & Co, New York 1942.

76. '*Penis envy*, the repressed wish of a female to possess a penis.' *Webster's Encyclopedic Unabridged Dictionary*, New York, 1989. Freud's theory of penis envy has been the focus of much feminist criticism of psychoanalysis.

77. *New York Times Book Review*, October 8, 1961.

Chapter XI. Orthogenic School: The Magical Years

1. In the preface he wrote for the published dialogues of Daniel Karlin's film, Bettelheim stated that 'No one at the school refers to the children as "patients".' He nevertheless does use the term from time to time in *A Home for the Heart*, his last book on the Orthogenic School, written after he had left it.

2. He says so in *The Art of the Obvious*.

3. Whenever I have had to use an alias for a child in the following chapters, this is indicated by quotation marks around the name.

4. 'On the whole, I have felt convinced of the validity of case histories and their authors' conclusions only where so many potentially verifiable data were presented that the individual came alive in my imagination as a three-dimensional person, moving in time and space. In these rare instances I felt that I knew much more than was actually stated,' he wrote in *Truants from Life*, The Free Press, New York, 1955, p. 4.

5. 'A Psychiatric School', from the *Quarterly Journal of Child Behavior*, January 1949. The text indeed made up part of *Love is Not Enough*.

6. *Love is Not Enough*, p. 35n.

7. A. Aichorn, *Wayward Youth*, Viking Press, New York, 1935.

8. 'Milieu Therapy – Indications and Illustrations', in the *Psychoanalytic Review*, January 1949.

9. Interview with the author, May 1993.

10. Several psychoanalysts, notably Paul Federn, had undertaken to cure psychotics, but the treatment had been individual and non-residential. As for the homes for children opened by Anna Freud in England during World War II, while they were of course based on psychoanalytic thinking, they recruited their pupils not on the basis of psychological problems, but because they had been separated from their parents by the war.

11. At a meeting dated August 11, 1944, the Department of Paediatrics had stressed that: 'The proper function of the OS is to provide resident facilities for adequate treatment of severe behavior problems in children of normal intelligence; and to afford opportunity for the instruction of medical students, social workers, interns, nurses, teachers and play therapists in the care and handling of such children.'

12. In 1986, on the occasion of a conference organized in Bruno Bettelheim's honour by the University of Chicago.

13. Interviewed by the author in May 1993.

14. A pathology identified in 1945 by René Spitz in children who had grown up in institutions, and had been deprived of any long-term emotional attachment.

15. Cf. Chapter X.

16. Bettelheim insisted on this last point. As he wrote in *Truants from Life*, 'What the children actually do and say, the very words and intonation they use, their facial and bodily expressions, are easily forgotten or distorted unless they are quickly written down .... Dictation that is separated by a week or longer from the observations reported, tends to be stale and of much less value in helping us understand the child's and our own behavior ... Instead of reflecting the impact of a symphony of feelings, interactions and experiences, played, so to speak, by full orchestra, a stale report recalls to mind only selected motifs played by but a few instruments.' Op cit, p. 475.

17. Cf B. Bettelheim and A. Rosenfeld, *The Art of the Obvious*.

18. A rumour which proved impossible to verify since by the time I started work on this book, Emmy Sylvester had already been diagnosed as having Alzheimer's Disease.

19. In the *American Journal of Orthopsychiatry:* 'Therapeutic Influence of the Group on the Individual' (Oct. 1947), 'A Therapeutic Milieu' (April 1948) and 'Notes on the Impact of Parental Occupations' (Oct. 1950). In *Psychoanalytic Study of the Child* (International Universities Press Inc.): 'Physical Symptoms in Emotionally Disturbed Children' (1949) and 'Delinquency and Morality' (1950). And, above all, the seminal text on their technique, 'Milieu Therapy – Indications and Illustrations', which was also published in 1949 in the *Psychoanalytic Review*.

20. As Patty Pickett points out, the testimony of Emmy Sylvester's former patients on this issue is less reliable than that of the former counsellors; for a young boy with problems it is much more frightening to feel one's inner anxieties or obsessions being probed and revealed by a woman than by a man.

21. He was to analyse 'Harry''s case in *Truants from Life*.

22. His was the first of the cases presented in *Truants from Life*.

23. Interview with the author in May 1993.

24. Interview with the author in May 1993.

25. By studying the families of several autistic children mentioned in *The Empty Fortress*.

26. 'Types of Institutional Structure', in *Psychiatry*, vol. 20, 1957.

27. Ibid.

28. Interview with the author in November 1990.

29. B. Bettelheim and B. Wright, 'Staff Development in a Treatment Institution', *American Journal of Orthopsychiatry*, October 1955.

30. Ibid.

31. See pp. 228-9.

32. Karen Zelan points out that, a few years later, Bettelheim's requirements had changed a little: 'The facts, he said, have to be sifted through a mind, and that's what's of interest to me.'

33. A highly regarded social worker with psychiatric training, who was a friend of Trude's and joined the Orthogenic School in the early days. Bettelheim was very dependent on her. She saw several children in therapy and, unlike the counsellors, had some contact with the students' patients.

34. As she was already married, Geneviève Jurgensen did not live at the Orthogenic School.

35. Candace Hilldrup, unpublished memoirs, Paris, 1975.

36. Interview with the author, May 1993.

37. Some are stored in the Bettelheim collection at the University of Chicago's Regenstein Library. Others are in the care of Dr Oliver Kerner.

38. Interestingly enough, Bettelheim's son Eric is in fact a lawyer.

39. Bruno Bettelheim and Alvin Rosenfeld, *The Art of the Obvious*.

40. *Dialogues with Mothers*, p. 4.

41. In his book, Daniel Karlin says that the sequence was actually shot on the morning of Bettelheim's last day with the children at the school, before leaving for California and retirement.

42. Interview with the author in May 1993.

43. See Chapter II.

44. Letter to C. Frankenstein, November 19, 1986.

45. Ibid.

46. *Dialogues with Mothers*, p. 201, from a chapter entitled 'Tyrannizing'.

47. *Dynamics of Prejudice: A Psychological and Sociological Study of Veterans*. See Chapter XII for more on this.

Chapter XII. Dr B the Enchanter

1. The trend was not confined to right-wing circles. Trotskyite groups in the US at this time took to referring to their pro-Soviet opponents not as 'Stalinists' but as 'Stalinoids', basing their jargon on the psychological terminology then in fashion.

2. Cf Russell Jacoby, *The Repression of Psychoanalysis: Otto Fenichel and the Political Freudians*, University of Chicago Press, Chicago, 1986.

3. Letter to Ernst Federn, September 9, 1945.

4. Interview with the author in July 1991.

5. In the fall of 1948, for example, the latter came to $4,533 per year. The university was also paying Bettelheim $1,967 for his teaching.

6. Indeed the Regensteins themselves, who financed the building of the library, were among the donors to the Orthogenic School.

7. See Chapter IX.

8. See Chapter XIV.

9. Macmillan, New York, 1981. Original title *L'Amour en plus*.

10. Issue dated December 16, 1981.

11. Letter to Madeleine Chapsal, January 19, 1982.

12. One can however question the judiciousness of an explanation which could easily be seen as encouraging racist attitudes. The reason the neighbourhood was changing was that black families were moving into it, and white ones leaving.

13. Bettelheim himself tells of such an incident in *Truants from Life*.

14. Jacquelyn Sanders, *Greenhouse for the Mind*, University of Chicago Press, 1989.

15. Interview with the author, May 1993. Once a child overcomes the problems that led to his deranged behaviour, it is normal for him to forget about them.

16. *Children who Hate*, by Fritz Redl and David Wineman, The Free Press, 1951, and, above all, *Controls from Within: Techniques for the Treatment of the Aggressive Child*, The Free Press, 1952.

17. Whence Bettelheim's comment on specialist case studies. See Chapter XI.

18. See Chapter XVII.

19. This is especially true of the books comprising case studies: *Truants from Life* and *The Empty Fortress*.

20. A journal founded by Gerard Piel, the nephew of Agnes (Piel) Crane.

21. The best-known result of which was to be *The Authoritarian Personality*, by David Riesman, a friend of Bettelheim's.

22. In their acknowledgements, the authors cite, in addition to Edward Shils, the philosopher and musicologist Theodor Adorno, one of Horkheimer's companions in the Frankfurt School, as having helped them draw up their research plan.

23. His best-known work is *The Professional Soldier*, published in 1960. In addition to numerous treatises, he also produced *Social Change and the Welfare State* (1976), *The Last Half-Century* (1978) and *The Reconstruction of Patriotism* (1983).

24. *Mobility, Subjective Deprivation and Ethnic Hostility*, by M. Janowitz, University of Chicago, 1948.

25. From an article by Karen Zelan, published in *Prospects*, Geneva, 1993, vol. 23 No. 1/2.

26. According to Maria Piers, who worked closely with Erikson, the latter never forgave Bettelheim for the way he had snubbed him in Vienna.

27. 'Harry, a Study in Rehabilitation', in the *American Journal of Abnormal and Social Psychology*, April 1949.

28. 'Oedipus complex: 1) The unresolved desire of a child for sexual gratification through the parent of the opposite sex ...' *Webster's Encyclopedic Unabridged Dictionary*, 1989.

29. *Chaga Childhood*, by O.F. Raum, Oxford University Press, London, 1940.

30. Bettelheim makes little mention in the main body of his text of circumcision practised at birth, simply noting that it probably has the same function as that carried out at puberty, since it is in general at the latter stage that boys truly become aware of it. He returns to the question in an appendix, to stress that Judaism, as the first monotheistic religion, was the most phallic, and the one in which the superego had most completely replaced the id. He concluded that Jewish circumcision, probably inherited from earlier, pagan, practices, reflected a greater level of symbolization of the initiation process, with a desire on the part of the men in the tribe to eliminate women from it altogether.

31. Op cit, chapter entitled 'Challenge to Theory'.

32. It is worth noting that Erik Erikson, as his biographer Paul Roazen points out, also took great care to link his own ideas to Freudian thinking, even when they were in fact far removed from the latter. Bettelheim and Erikson had several things in common, and the relationship between them, based on strong rivalry and a measure of mutual contempt, was abysmal.

33. Readers of the French version (*Les blessures symboliques*, Gallimard, Paris, 1971) did not have far to look for these opinions, since the editor of the series in which it appeared decided to include, at the end of Bettelheim's text, a discussion of it by the psychoanalyst André Green and the anthropologist Jean Pouillon. As is shown in his private correspondence, Bettelheim was furious at this move, which editor Jean-Bertrand Pontalis made without even informing him. He never raised the issue with the French publisher, however, being convinced that any complaint would have no effect (letter to C. Hilldrup, February 19, 1975).

34. Ruth Marquis, who had by then left Chicago, had not taken part in the final revisions of the first edition of *Symbolic Wounds*, with the result that its tone was much more academic than that of Bettelheim's other books. She resumed her activities as editor in time to supervise the second edition, however.

35. Op cit.

36. *Symbolic Wounds*, chapter entitled 'The Biological Antithesis'.

37. And, indeed, not all anorexics reach the state of near starvation that people usually associate with the condition. As a teacher at the Orthogenic School, Adrian was to display great intuition towards her anorexic students.

38. Interview with the author, May 1993.

39. Gayle Janowitz remembers, for example, one highly disturbed mother who sent her son pornographic photographs of herself, and accused Dr B of wanting to kidnap him, etc. In order to stop her from coming and disturbing the boy on Christmas Eve, the school's social worker had on several successive years spent the festival with her!

40. Several critics, and notably Gina Weinmann, have attacked Bettelheim for the catchy titles he used, considering that such a desire to attract casual readers was unworthy of a serious work.

Chapter XIII. The Ultimate Limit

1. Letter to ER, September 10, 1954.

2. Quote provided by Tom Lyons, among others.

3. In a letter to R. Marquis, dated March 1973.

4. Bettelheim's comments to this effect were reported by several people. Their testimony is backed up by his correspondence and interviews he gave at the end of his life.

5. As Ruth Bettelheim replied with total silence to all my requests for interviews, both written and passed on by other people, all the information I possess on her comes from third parties.

6. Naomi Bettelheim, who was of course much too young to remember the incident, later heard a different version of the story, which Bettelheim told to at least two people.

7. *Commentary*, September 1951.

8. See Chapter XV.

9. From an address delivered at North Shore Hospital on February 14, 1951.

10. 'A Home is to be Human', written in March 1974 and stored in the Bettelheim collection at the Regenstein Library.

11. Letter to R. Marquis, September 30, 1973.

12. Although I was only able to meet Naomi and Eric, I have little doubt that this is also true of Ruth.

13. See Chapter VII.

14. It should be noted that these visits, initially laid on for journalists and US politicians, soon became particularly unpleasant, in spite of the well-meaning ideas behind them. Cf *Déportation et Génocide*, by Annette Wieviorka (Plon, Paris 1992).

15. 'The Helpless and the Guilty', in *Common Sense*, July 14, 1945.

16. 'War Trials and German Re-education', in *Politics*, December 2, 1945.

17. Cf Chapter VII.

18. A vessel packed with Jewish war refugees from central Europe, some of them former concentration camp inmates, which in July 1947 tried to dock without permission in Palestine, then under British mandate. After much suffering among its passengers, the ship was eventually taken to France, from where the refugees were sent back to Germany.

19. 'Exodus, 1947', in *Politics*, Winter 1948 issue. The emphasis is Bettelheim's.

20. To quote from the opening remarks of his testimony to Judge Jackson, published in the US government record *Nazi Conspiracy and Aggression*, op cit, vol. VII, document L-73.

21. 'The Concentration Camp as a Class State', in *Modern Review*, October 1947.

22. 'Schizophrenia as a Reaction to Extreme Situations', in the *American Journal of Orthopsychiatry*, July 1956. Also included in both *The Informed Heart* and *Surviving*.

23. Better known as the members of the Frankfurt School.

24. 'German Schools Revisited', *Elementary School Journal*, November 1955.

25. 'Returning to Dachau', published in February 1956 in *Commentary*, and later included in *Freud's Vienna and Other Essays*.

26. Bettelheim had filed his first application on August 30, 1954, just ten days after the limit.

27. In spite of the existence of at least two letters from the bank testifying that the money paid by the Nazi buyer had been confiscated.

28. As noted by Paul Marcus and Alan Rosenberg in 'Reevaluating Bruno Bettelheim's Work on the Concentration Camps', *Psychoanalytic Review*, autumn 1994.

29. In his article, which is not aimed at a specialist public, Bettelheim defines the ego as 'the conscious, rational aspects of the personality ... which mediates between the demands of the instincts, the superego and reality', the superego being seen as the subject's conscience and ideals, and the id as his instincts (or drives, as Bettelheim would later call them).

30. 'Individual Autonomy and Mass Control', published in 1955 as part of a special edition of the Frankfurt Social Science Institute's review *Sociologica*, marking the sixtieth birthday of Max Horkheimer. Among the many signatures featuring alongside Bettelheim's were those of Theodor Adorno, Raymond Aron, Walter Benjamin, Franco Lombardi and Herbert Marcuse. The quotes in this and the following two paragraphs are all from the same source.

31. *Auschwitz, a Doctor's Eyewitness Account*, by Miklos Nyiszli, Frederick Fell, New York, 1960.

32. Quadrangle Books, Chicago, 1961.

33. *Harpers*, November 1960. Parts of the article were already in *The Informed Heart*, published the same year. The whole article was also to be included, with minor changes, in *Surviving*. Quotations in the following three paragraphs are from the same source.

34. Bettelheim was the first person to use the expression 'business as usual' in this context. It was subsequently to be widely employed in other works on the Holocaust.

35. *Midstream*, March 1962. Also figures, with minor alterations, in *Surviving*. Quotations in the following paragraphs are from the same source.

36. *Midstream*, September 1962.

37. Viking Press, New York, 1963.

38. 'Eichmann, the System, the Victims', in *New Republic*, June 15 1963. Reprinted in shortened form, with some changes, in *Surviving*. The quotations in the following paragraphs are all from this source.

39. *Jewish Resistance*, Waldon Press, 1964. The quotations in the following two paragraphs are all from this source.

40. Vilna is the Russian name of Vilnius, the Lithuanian capital.

41. Phone interview with Nell Pekarsky, May 1993.

42. See Chapter XV.

43. Op cit, ch. 4.

44. D. Karlin, 'Dernier entretien avec Bruno Bettelheim' (last interview with Bruno Bettelheim, broadcast in France after the latter's death).

45. J-F Steiner, *Treblinka*, Simon & Schuster, New York, 1967 (first published in French by Librairie Arthème Fayard, Paris, 1966). Reviewed by Bettelheim in *New Republic*, July 1, 1967 in an article entitled 'Survival of the Jews'. The quotations in the following paragraphs are all drawn from that source.

46. Writing in similar vein twelve years later, Bettelheim was to amend his article on 'ghetto thinking' for *Freud's Vienna and Other Essays* by including excerpts from this one.

47. *The Informed Heart*, ch. 1.

48. In particular, in *The Drowned and the Saved* (*I Sommersi e i Salvati*), Michael Joseph Ltd., London, 1988.

49. *Surviving*, ch. 2.

50. Originally published in *Encounter*, in December 1978.

51. 'The Ultimate Limit,' in *Midway* review, Fall of 1968.

52. *The Survivor*, by Terence Des Pres, Oxford University Press, New York, 1976.

53. A few months after the publication of *Surviving*, Des Pres hit back with a long article detailing Bettelheim's violations of accepted academic practices. Cf 'The Bettelheim Problem', in *Social Research*, Winter 1979.

54. First published in the *New Yorker* on August 2, 1976.

55. Notably Paul Marcus and Alan Rosenberg, in 'Reevaluating Bruno Bettelheim's Work on Nazi Concentration Camps: the Limits of his Psychoanalytic Approach', published in a special issue of the *Psychoanalytic Review*, 1994.

56. *'Il faut cultiver notre jardin.'*

57. Des Pres, op cit, p. 157.

58. Terence Des Pres died suddenly in 1987.

59. Several months after the publication of *Surviving* Des Pres was to strike back, with a long article listing all Bettelheim's violations of academic integrity (Terence Des Pres, 'The Bettelheim Problem', op cit).

60. Letter to C. Frankenstein, March 13, 1976.

61. Cf for example Paul Roazen, in 'The Rise and Fall of Bruno Bettelheim', *Psychohistory Review*, Spring 1992.

62. Letter to C. Frankenstein, November 20, 1978.

63. Op cit.

64. In his article on 'How to Arm our Children against Anti-Semitism', Bettelheim stresses the feeling of insecurity sparked in a child when some racist remark gives him the impression that his parents, even more than himself, are not 'good enough',

65. The Yiddish word for a Gentile, which by extension means 'he who understands nothing'.

66. *The Ultimate Limit*, op cit.

67. Letter to James Farrel, June 7, 1973.

68. From Paul Celan, *Speech Grille and Selected Poems*, E.P. Dutton, New York, 1971. Translated from the original German by Joachim Neugroschel; Bettelheim however specifies that the final two lines were retranslated by him.

69. *Freud's Vienna and Other Essays*, p. 213.

70. Op cit, ch. 2.

71. 'Owners of Their Faces', in *Surviving*.

72. Gallimard, Paris, 1980.

73. 'Children of the Holocaust', in *Freud's Vienna and Other Essays*.

74. Letter to M. Chapsal, October 12, 1979.

Chapter XIV. The Big Bad Wolf

1. 'Joey: a Mechanical Boy', in *Scientific American*, March 5, 1959.

2. Telephone conversation on August 7, 1994. I was calling from France.

3. In France, *The Empty Fortress* was the first of Bettelheim's books to be published, and has gone on selling ever since its appearance in 1969.

4. Which had five years earlier allocated him a grant to study childhood schizophrenia.

5. Bettelheim himself edited the film, shot by Charles Sharp, and used it to illustrate his method with autistic children. He showed it notably to Anna Freud, in London. In 1973, he allowed Daniel Karlin to use it in his documentary on the Orthogenic School.

6. Conversation quoted in *The Art of the Obvious*, p. 120.

7. See p. 271.

8. B. Bettelheim and D. Karlin, *Un autre regard sur la folie*, Stock, Paris, 1975.

9. These definitions still vary from country to country. For instance, the term 'schizophrenia' as used in the US refers to a much wider range of symptoms than it does in France.

10. Today, the clinical term 'schizophrenic' is no longer used before adolescence.

11. The term itself had been coined in 1911 by the Swiss psychiatrist Bleuler to describe adults – in *Dementia Praecox or the Group of Schizophrenias* (International University Press, New York, 1950). In a letter to Freud, dated December 6, 1906, Carl Jung, who worked under Bleuler, explained that the word was a contraction of 'auto-eroticism'. Kanner gave autism its modern definition in 'Autistic Disturbances of Affective Contact', *Nervous Child*, 1943.

12. Address given at the Amsterdam Congress in 1951, and published as 'On Child Psychosis and Schizophrenia: Autistic and Symbiotic Infantile Psychoses', *The Psychoanalytic Study of the Child*, 1952, vol. 7.

13. Having identified 'emotional growth and mental health' as key research themes, the Foundation decided in 1955 to provide 15 million dollars over five years to a Program of Support for Research in Mental Health covering fifteen projects centred on those issues. Three of the grants were assigned to research on 'Children's Disorders', and the applicants were both numerous and, in many cases, famous. In addition to Bettelheim, they included Anna Freud's and Dorothy Burlingham's Hampstead Child Guidance Clinic, in London, plus most of the Americans then working on childhood schizophrenia, notably Bender, Gardner, Rabinovitch, Rank, Loomis, the Menninger Clinic and even Dr Benjamin Spock.

14. Several authors have, for that very reason, paid homage to Bettelheim for the title of his book. 'What a good image that is, the *Empty Fortress*,' enthuses French psychoanalyst Denys Ribas. 'It warns us not to expect to find treasures hidden behind the autistic barrier! Only mutual exchanges are enriching.' From *Un cri obscur* (An obscure scream), Calmann Levy, Paris, 1992.

15. An expression he uses in *The Art of the Obvious*, p. 119.

16. Ibid.

17. Letter to C. Hilldrup, September 17, 1980.

18. Bettelheim was to use her case to illustrate his conviction that so-called 'feral children' were probably autistic children who had been abandoned or lost for a period by their parents. When they were discovered, people found their behaviour so disturbing that it was easier for them to believe that they had been brought up by animals. His article, published in March 1959 in the *American Journal of*

Psychology, elicited an enthusiastic reaction from the anthropologist Margaret Mead (July 1959).

19. *The Empty Fortress*, p. 7.

20. Ibid.

21. Ibid, p. 77.

22. Ibid, p. 73. Subsequent quotes in this paragraph are from the same source.

23. Which published the text of his address in July 1956, under the title 'Schizophrenia as a Reaction to Extreme Situations'.

24. Cf p. 272.

25. 'Punishment versus Discipline', *Atlantic Monthly*, November 1985.

26. 'Obsolete Youth', *Encounter*, September 3, 1969.

27. Op cit, p. 2.

28. On overhearing a new child say to another: 'Come, let's kill Johnny,' Bettelheim had laid down the school's ground-rules as follows: 'You're not here to kill Johnny or anybody else. Kids come here to be safe, not to be threatened. Nobody lays a hand on anybody in the school, except me.' Needless to say, the last sentence was backed up with a slap.

29. For example, in his study of the 'Rat Man'.

30. This was during our first interview, in the fall of 1990. Later, Tom Lyons was less categorical: 'There were I believe one or two times when I was not hit for over a year – certainly not the last two and a half years at the school,' he wrote to me in 1995.

31. For self-evident reasons, details of either the case histories or the pathologies of former Orthogenic School students cannot be revealed. The reader will therefore have to make do with a sketchy description of events.

32. Freud is very clear on that point. 'In our unconscious we are today still a band of murderers. In our silent thoughts, we eliminate all those who stand in our way, those who have insulted or harmed us, every day and at each moment. The "To the devil with him" that so often crosses the threshold of our lips like a weakened interjection, and which in reality means "To death with him", is for our unconscious something totally serious. It is really lucky that all of these ill wishes have no power whatsoever. Humanity would have disappeared long ago, the best and the wisest of men, the most beautiful and sweetest of women, would no longer exist.' (S. Freud, 'Death and Ourselves', a speech made to the Vienna branch of B'nai Brith on February 16, 1915.)

33. Op cit, p. 71.

34. Ibid, p. 69.

35. *The Pelican and After*, by Tom Wallace Lyons, Prescott, Durrell and Company, Richmond, Va, 1983.

36. Ibid, p. 24.

37. Each dormitory at the school had its own name, chosen by the children themselves.

38. The fax is dated September 14, 1994 and the phone conversation was a few weeks before that. My first interview with Tom Lyons was in New York in November 1990.

39. When this happened, between 1970 and 1972, Bettelheim's friend and first publisher, Jeremiah Kaplan, had become the head of Macmillan, after the big publishing group had bought out The Free Press. Tom Lyons's manuscript had been accepted and was in the hands of Robert Markel, editor-in-chief, when Kaplan learned of its existence. He demanded that the author obtain written permission from Bettelheim as a precondition to publishing it.

From what Jeremiah Kaplan himself told me in 1993, he had not read the novel when he gave that order, but he had been told that it slandered his friend. Whatever the case, a period of around three months elapsed between the time Bettelheim first heard of the book, and the time he actually got a copy of the manuscript. During that period, at Macmillan's request, Tom Lyons called him. 'I was eager to talk to BB. I actually believed the book would be a source of satisfaction to him.' But Bettelheim was not at all pleased. 'I don't appreciate that you want to libel me,' he said, adding that it was a 'very poor reward' for having rescued Tom. Following this conversation, Augusta Wallace Lyons, Tom's mother, who had always been on friendly terms with Bettelheim and was one of the school's donors, intervened on her son's behalf. In the course of a lengthy phone discussion, Bettelheim told her that he would sign the required authorization on condition that Tom dedicate the book to him and add an introduction making clear what state he was in when he entered the Orthogenic School. There followed a series of phone calls and letters, amid mounting tension, all before Bettelheim had even set eyes on the manuscript. During that period, a young teacher, Nina Helstein, happened to be in Bettelheim's office when he took a call, during which he said in an irritated voice: 'Publish it if you want. But remember that the author was a psychotic.'

As soon as he had actually read the novel, in April 1971, Bettelheim wrote directly to Tom Lyons and congratulated him. He repeated that he had no intention of opposing the book's publication, and once again raised the idea of a dedication and an introduction. On the same day he wrote to Mrs Lyons to say that, having realized to what extent his own relation with Tom was at the heart of the book (something he had not understood until then, he stressed), he preferred from then on to only discuss it with the young man himself. In passing, he remarked that he felt Tom's portrayal of both himself and the school was unfair. He seemed very irritated at the mounting suspicions about him, and stressed that Mrs Lyons was in possession of several letters in which he had promised not to oppose publication of Tom's book.

A week later, however, Tom Lyons was informed that Macmillan had rejected his manuscript, without any real explanation. In subsequent correspondence with both Tom and his mother, Bettelheim expressed regret, but refused to intervene: for personal reasons, he had decided to change publishers, he explained, but he had refrained from telling Kaplan this as long as Tom's manuscript was still under discussion.

In June 1971 he finally signed the required authorization after Tom Lyons showed him a (somewhat exaggerated) draft introduction in which he mentioned the initial diagnosis of childhood schizophrenia, paid homage to Bettelheim and stressed that the school portrayed in the novel was only loosely based on the one he had grown up in. A year later, having changed publishers, Bettelheim released Lyons from all the conditions he had initially laid down for his book's publication. The novel was finally published in 1983.

40. Interview published in the *Connecticut New Haven Register* on April 8, 1984.

41. At the time of its publication, at any rate. Apart from Fae Tyroler, only another one of Tom's counsellors, Diana Grossmann Kahn, told me straight off that she had liked his book. More recently, several of the people to whom I had mentioned the book, saying how much I enjoyed it, have since told me they had read or re-read it, finding it, with the benefit of hindsight, enjoyable. This sample is of course only partial, as I was not able to meet all the people who worked at the school.

42. Letter to T. Lyons, April 21, 1971.

43. This point is well illustrated in Tom Lyons's novel.

44. Her father was a prominent Chicago labour union leader, and her family belonged to the long-integrated liberal Jewish middle-class. Nina had also been a classmate of Ruth, Bettelheim's eldest daughter.

45. K. Carlson Zelan, *The Intellectual Development of an Autistic Girl*, University of Chicago, 1974.

46. As the study of autism is not the object of this book, I do not refer here to the results obtained by those whose work is aimed simply at changing a child's behaviour, but only to those who, like Bettelheim, have sought first of all to make him live at peace with himself.

47. I.e. after the training period of a few weeks during which a newcomer got into the spirit of the school by working alongside experienced counsellors. The length of time that took varied from person to person.

48. *On Learning to Read: The Child's Fascination with Meaning.*

49. Interview with the author, Paris, September 1993.

50. The grant had originally run to February 1961, but as Bettelheim had not spent all the funds by that date he had asked for, and obtained, a two-year extension.

Chapter XV. Israel: Understanding is Not Enough

1. Thanks to a grant from the Federal Delinquency Control Fund, obtained for him by Morris Janowitz.

2. In 1937, members of the kibbutz were to translate Freud's works into Hebrew, in exchange for psychoanalytic treatment that they could not otherwise have paid for.

3. See in particular Walter Laqueur, *A History of Zionism*, London, 1972. Laqueur also wrote *Young Germany, History of the German Youth Movement*, Routledge & Kegan Paul, London, 1962.

4. The following year, his cousin Edith Buxbaum was to work for a year at the Oranim kibbutz teacher training centre, apparently quite independently of Bettelheim, since at the time they were no longer in contact.

5. Of which the proceedings were published as *Children in Collectives*, ed. Peter B. Neubauer, Charles C. Thomas, Springfield, Ill, 1965.

6. *Sabra*: a person born in Israel. In this case I am stretching the definition to include Palestine.

7. Interview with the author at Ramat Yohanan, August 1992.

8. Harvard University Press, Cambridge, 1958. Bettelheim's review appeared under the title 'Nakhes Fun Kinder', in the *Reconstructionist*, April 1959.

9. 'Does Communal Education Work?' in *Commentary*, February 1962.

10. In the early 1930s the *Hashomer Hatzair* movement experienced deep divisions over their position towards the Soviet Union, so much so that there was an exchange of population between the two kibbutzes. The hard-core pro-Communists all settled in Bet Alpha while the moderates went to Ramat Yohanan, which became a kibbutz of the *Mapai*, or Labour Party. See W. Laqueur, op cit.

11. Letter of March 13, 1964.

12. Interview with the author, August 1992.

13. The New World Foundation, which had financed his trip.

14. Letters of March 24 and 26, 1964.

15. Letter of March 13, 1964.

16. March 13, 1964.

17. Letter to R. Marquis, March 24, 1964.

18. 'Personally I felt suffocated by the lack of privacy when I visited a kibbutz,' he wrote in the *Saturday Evening Post* of July 27, 1968 ('The Right to Privacy is a Myth').

19. Letter of March 13, 1964.

20. Sharp, whom Bettelheim had called in to film the progress of some very sick children at the Orthogenic School, notably 'Marcia', made two films during his stay in Israel. The first, *The Kibbutz*, won several prizes, including the top award at the 1966 International Film and Television Festival in New York. The second, *The Children of the Dream*, is a report on Bettelheim's research at the kibbutz.

21. Letter to R. Marquis, March 19, 1964.

22. Letter of March 24, 1964.

23. Letter of March 19, 1964.

24. Letter to R. Marquis, March 26, 1964.

25. 'Institutional Care of Problem Children', *Megamot* no. 2, Spring 1951, pp. 230-51.

26. On Bettelheim's youthful interest in Hans Vaihinger, see Chapter II.

27. Interview with the author, Jerusalem, August 1992.

28. Located in the Carpathian region, now divided between Romania and Ukraine.

29. *Last Waltz in Vienna, The Destruction of a Family 1842-1942*, Macmillan, London, 1981.

30. p. 33.

31. Interview with Haim Hadoumi's widow Leah Hadoumi, August 1992, London.

32. Letter of January 18, 1986.

33. Letter of April 30, 1987.

34. 'It was a religion that viewed women's very femininity as a curse, that condemned her to apartheid in its places of worship, that even forbade her to wear her own hair, and required her to shave it off at marriage.' (*The Children of the Dream*, p. 34.)

35. Ibid, pp. 39-40.

36. Ibid, p. 190.

37. Cf his comments on jealousy.

38. *The Children of the Dream*, p. 28.

Chapter XVI. The Bad Guy

1. This meeting, in which all children, counsellors and teachers participated, was created in the early sixties as a transition between classes and other activities. Bettelheim attended it when he was free.

2. According to the fifth edition of the *Directory for Exceptional Children*, dated 1965, annual fees at the Orthogenic School in that year were between 7,200 and 8,000 dollars. Although high in itself, this was relatively average if compared with other establishments of a similar type. In the same year, a place in the Menninger Foundation's hospital for children cost 21,900 dollars per annum.

3. G. Jurgensen, *La folie des autres*, Robert Laffont, Paris, 1973.

4. The file was found among documents turned over to the Regenstein Library by the Orthogenic School. It may well have been removed since, however, as the cards bore the real names of all children involved, and should therefore have remained confidential.

5. *The Empty Fortress*, p. 3.

6. Ibid, p. 74.

7. In the opening chapters of *The Empty Fortress*, Bettelheim indeed devotes himself to the development of the child's 'self' rather than that of its ego. He describes the self as including not just the ego, but the id and superego as well. This is an essentially post-Freudian concept, the contours of which vary from author to author. (Donald Winnicott, for example, speaks of the 'false self' that is developed by a child whose mother is not 'good enough'.) At the time when Bruno Bettelheim was writing, the self was just beginning a brilliant career in the United States. It was to appear as a kind of bridge between Ego Psychology and Freudian psychoanalysis. Its main theoretician, Heinz Kohut, was a friend of Bettelheim's. He was also a Viennese exile and an eminent member of the Chicago Institute.

8. From a footnote in Winnicott's essay 'The Use of an Object in the Context of *Moses and Monotheism*', dated January 16, 1969 and published in his *Psychoana-lytic Explorations* (Karnac Books, London, 1989). The passage is quoted by Elio Frattaroli, a psychoanalyst who worked at the Orthogenic School from 1970 to 1973, in his article 'Bruno Bettelheim's Unrecognized Contribution to Psychoana-lytic Thought', *Psychoanalytic Review*, New York, autumn 1994.

9. He believed that transference and counter-transference set in right from the first meeting, and that anything the therapist had previously read about his patient could only serve to obscure the intuitive knowledge he could draw from that encounter. For more on this point, see *The Art of the Obvious*.

10. France had until June 1967 been one of Israel's staunchest allies and its main supplier of arms with the United States. But President de Gaulle was adamant that Israel should not initiate war against Egypt in spite of the mounting threats from that country. Feeling that his message was not being heard in Tel Aviv, he imposed an embargo on the sales of arms to 'all countries in the region' just three days before Israel launched its air raid against the Egyptian fleet.

11. The decision not to renew her contract was apparently not due to her ideas, but to the fact that she had failed to fit into the team, and had not published very much. That is how the sociologists in the department at the time saw the affair. But Bernice Neugarten, who was in charge of the Department of Human Develop-ment, where the young woman also taught, disagrees. She accuses her colleagues of sexism. She also says that they failed to show a minimum of academic courtesy by not even informing her of their intention to let her contract lapse.

12. Comment reported by Mark Lubin, Kathy's husband.

13. *Chicago Sun-Times*, February 16, 1969. The quotes in this paragraph are all from that source.

14. The word printed in the newspaper is 'cares' and not 'chaos', but given the context and other statements by Bettelheim it seems likely that this was the result of a transcription error.

15. Notably in his article 'Obsolete Youth', published in *Encounter* on Septem-ber 3, 1969. Subsequent quotes in this paragraph are from that source.

16. February 16, 1969. The quotes in this paragraph are all from that source.

17. She had attended classes with Louis Falco and other dancers from the Martha Graham company, as well as with Charles Weidman, Doris Humphrey's partner.

18. Interview with the author, February 1991.

19. 'Don't talk to me about Candy: to this day, I can't think of her objectively,' one counsellor admitted frankly. She had been at the school for four years when Candy arrived, and had up until then been one of Bettelheim's inner circle, on whom he relied the most for support, and who were in therapy with him.

20. Interview with the author in Paris, July 1994.

21. Interview with Mrs Wallace Lyons, Paris, September 1992.

22. See Chapter XIV.

23. Letter to C. Hilldrup, January 29, 1971.

24. Letter to R. Marquis, September 1971.

25. Letter to R. Marquis, September 1971.

26. Letter to R. Marquis, September 1971.

27. Letter to R. Marquis, September 27, 1971.

28. See introductory quote to Chapter XIV.

29. Extract from the manuscript which Bettelheim gave as a gift to Candace Hilldrup. It is undated, and does not contain the final part of the book.

30. Letter to C. Hilldrup, August 7, 1971.

31. He had undergone an operation on his left leg. Letter to C. Hilldrup, January 19, 1972.

32. She was at the time known by her maiden name, Seevak.

33. Ugo Formigoni remembers to this day how she had him rewrite his first 'anecdotal' seven times, only to hear Bettelheim judge it not spontaneous enough! With the result that it was also to be his last one: Ugo refused ever to write another.

34. See Prologue, 'The Affair'.

35. 'A case study of a brilliant autistic boy with total reading disability; an investigation of the causes of this condition and the steps that led to his being able to overcome it', by Jacquelyn Seevak, University of Chicago Department of Education, September 1964.

36. See p. 288.

37. Letter to R. Marquis, January 1973.

38. Letter to R. Marquis, March 1973.

39. Letter to R. Marquis, January 1973.

40. Quote given by Karlin in his book *Un autre regard sur la folie*. (A different view of insanity). It comprises the soundtrack from Karlin's four TV programmes, an account of how they were made and a preface by Bettelheim.

41. Which was initially published as an afterword and then, in a subsequent printing, reinstated as the preface it was originally meant to be.

42. *Un autre regard sur la folie*, op cit. Quote translated from the French.

43. *'Le Roi se meurt'* is both a saying that was traditional at the French court and the title of a play by the post-surrealist Franco-Romanian playwright Eugène Ionesco.

44. Letter to C. Hilldrup, March 27, 1974.

45. Interview with the author in New York, August 3, 1991.

46. In *Réflexions sur la question juive* (Reflections on the Jewish Question), Gallimard, Paris, 1946.

47. This may be less true in the United States than elsewhere, but Bruno Bettelheim remained a European.

48. Hitler himself, in *Mein Kampf*, was quite explicit on that point.

49. The slogan was chanted in response to the decision of the government to expel from France one of the student leaders, Daniel Cohn-Bendit, who happened to be a German national. It is also worth noting that the link between the Final Solution and the events of the late sixties was made from the outset in Germany itself. During one of the first anti-Vietnam War protests, the Red Army Faction leader Ulrike Meinhoff said, referring to the Bonn government: 'How can we trust these people? They are the ones who created Auschwitz.'

50. Literally 'Under the cobblestones, the beach' – a popular slogan of the May 1968 revolt in France, where huge numbers of cobblestones were ripped up in Paris to make barricades and to be thrown at the police.

51. See the opening paragraph of prologue, 'The Affair'.

52. D. Karlin, *Un autre regard sur la folie*, op cit. Bettelheim's comment is translated from the French.

53. Letter to C. Hilldrup, June 29, 1973.

54. Letter to C. Hilldrup, March 20, 1976.

55. Interview with the author in May 1993.

56. Bettelheim is obviously referring to Ben Wright.

57. *Un autre regard sur la folie*, op cit, p. 225. Translated from the French.

58. J. Seevak Sanders, *A Greenhouse for the Mind*, University of Chicago Press, 1989. It is worthy of note that five years earlier, Bettelheim had published *Freud and Man's Soul*, in which he explained why the word 'mind' betrayed the essential tenets of psychoanalysis.

59. The letter was an attempt at reconciliation written in 1987, at the time when Jacquelyn Sanders was about to bring out her own book, and when, as she herself underlines, Bettelheim was likely to be called on to give his opinion of it.

60. In addition to Bert Cohler and Sanders herself, who spoke in their capacities as academics.

Epilogue: Chapter XVII. Trude and the Children

1. What he actually said in the letter is: 'I know how I trembled and still tremble for my children, how I always worried that something might happen to one of the children at the school ...' (June 30, 1980).

2. Published on May 16, 1988 in the French magazine *Elle*.

3. Letter to R. Marquis, September 30, 1973.

4. On September 30, 1973.

5. Letter to C. Frankenstein, January 13, 1975.

6. Letter to R. Marquis, September 30, 1973.

7. Letter to C. Frankenstein, January 13, 1975.

8. Particularly Alison Lurie, in a review of the book published in *Harpers* in June 1976, and Joan Blos, writing in the *Merrill-Palmer Quarterly* in 1978.

9. Although she refused to edit the final draft of *A Home for the Heart*, Ruth Marquis had in fact edited many of the texts that Bettelheim incorporated into it.

10. 'Bruno Bettelheim's Uses of Enchantment and Abuses of Scholarship', in the *Journal of American Folklore*.

11. J. Heuscher, *A Psychiatric Study of Fairy Tales*, Charles Thomas, New York, 1963.

Here are two examples. Referring to Snow White, Heuscher writes: 'Not wishing to deprive any one too much, she eats just a little from each of the seven plates and drinks just a drop from each glass (how different from Hansel and Gretel who, rather disrespectfully, start eating the gingerbread house),' while Bettelheim's version is 'Though very hungry, she eats just a little from each of the seven plates, and drinks just a drop from each of the seven glasses, so as to rob none of them too much. (How different from Hansel and Gretel, the orally fixated children, who disrespectfully and voraciously eat up the gingerbread house!)'

And discussing Hansel and Gretel's first return to their home: 'Hansel and his sister Gretel appear successful at first. But the frustrations at home continue. The mother seems to be more shrewd in her plans for rejecting her children ....' (Heuscher), and 'The children's successful return home does not solve anything .... The frustrations continue, and the mother becomes more shrewd in her plans for getting rid of the children.' (Bettelheim).

12. In *The Forgotten Language, an Introduction to the Understanding of Dreams, Fairy-Tales and Myths*, Rinehart & Winston, New York, 1951.

13. Letter to C. Frankenstein, January 13, 1975.

14. Letter to C. Hilldrup, February 19, 1975.

15. New York University Press, New York, 1971.

16. Letter to C. Frankenstein, August 16, 1975.

17. 'My trip to France worried me even more than the one to Germany, because the French intellectuals are all communists, of the most naïve type. Highly sensitive and intellectual, full of goodwill, they are convinced because they are French, once the communists take over, it will be all different from Russia and China. And since they know little about China, they are convinced that things there are ideal, or in Cuba. One could cry if it were not so ridiculous .... It seems people are only motivated by what they are against, and hardly by what they are for. They still fight de Gaulle so as not to have to realize that there was hardly any French resistance, and that ... the communists contributed greatly to the collapse of France.' Letter to C. Frankenstein, November 4, 1974.

18. Letter from C. Frankenstein, January 22, 1975.

19. The full quote is given at the start of this chapter.

20. Interview with Charles Walton, July 1991.

21. As was noted by the French psychoanalyst Thierry Braconnier, when he visited the United States in the early 1980s. His trip included a visit to the Orthogenic School.

22. Letter to C. Hilldrup, September 4, 1980.

23. Letter to C. Frankenstein, August 21, 1977.

24. Letter to C. Frankenstein, December 28, 1977.

25. Ibid.

26. Letter to GR, October 26, 1977. Translated from German.

27. Ibid.

28. Letter to C. Frankenstein, August 2, 1978.

29. Farrar, Straus & Giroux, New York, 1986.

30. Letter to C. Frankenstein, February 27, 1978.

31. Letter to M. Chapsal, October 12, 1979.

32. Letter to ER, September 1979. Translated from German.

33. Ibid.

34. From four schools in Berkeley and two in Massachusetts. Zelan was helped in this task by half a dozen researchers.

35. Of Karen Zelan, Bettelheim wrote to Ruth Marquis in January 1973: 'Her observations are excellent; only she can't criticize me.' He added: 'But who can, other than you?'

36. Dated January 15, 1979.

37. Letter to C. Frankenstein, May 24, 1978. The 'defeat' referred to was a US contract to supply fighter bombers to Saudi Arabia.

38. Letter to C. Frankenstein, March 1, 1979.

39. When Naomi Bettelheim visited her parents, she slept in a room that was next to her father's study. She often complained that the sound of his working late at night kept her from sleeping.

40. *Je ne lui ai pas dit au revoir*, Gallimard, Paris 1980. See p. 328.

41. Letter to R. Marquis, September 30, 1973.

42. Letter to R. Marquis, March 1973.

43. This slow-developing ailment had first surfaced many years earlier, with the appearance of a growth inside the throat. As it grew bigger, the diverticulum started pressing against his lungs, causing inflammation, secretions and a series of attacks of pneumonia. Bettelheim's doctors nevertheless advised against an operation; as the growth was just behind his vocal chords, he risked losing his voice.

44. Letter to C. Frankenstein, May 10, 1981.

45. Letter to C. Frankenstein, July 10, 1981.

46. Letter to C. Frankenstein, October 14, 1981.

47. Published in the US as *The Road into the Open*, University of California Press, Berkeley, 1992.

48. Letter to C. Hilldrup, March 2, 1982.

49. *New Yorker*, March 1982.

50. Letter to C. Frankenstein, January 28, 1982.

51. Letter to G. Janowitz, August 12, 1982.

52. Letter to R. Marquis, December 28, 1982.

53. Pantheon Books, New York, 1982.

54. Letter to R. Marquis, December 28, 1982.

55. Letter to C. Frankenstein, February 10, 1983.

56. 'Scandal in the Family', *New York Review of Books*, June 3, 1983.

57. Letter to C. Frankenstein, August 24, 1983.

58. A Viennese-style chocolate cake.

59. Letter to C. Frankenstein, October 4, 1983.

60. Interview with the author, November 1990.

61. Letter to ER, September 10, 1984. Translated from German.

62. Letter to C. Frankenstein, November 10, 1984.

63. Ibid.

64. Letter to C. Hilldrup, December 18, 1984.

65. Maria Kramer is a psychoanalyst who had been one of Richard Sterba's patients, before practising in Chicago and then moving to California. She is the widow of Dr. Paul Kramer, whom Bettelheim knew well and who was a consulting psychiatrist at the O.S.

66. Letter to C. Frankenstein, April 19, 1985.

67. Letter to ER, January 2, 1986. Translated from German.

68. Published – in French – by the Pompidou Arts Centre, in Paris, where the exhibition was first held. It was later to become the title piece of *Freud's Vienna and Other Essays*.

69. Letter to C. Frankenstein, November 20, 1985.

70. Poison themselves with drugs, of course. Letter to ER, June 1, 1985. Translated from German.

71. Saul Wasserman and Alvin Rosenfeld recounted their work in *Healing the Heart*, a booklet published by the Child Welfare League of America (Washington, 1990). It was Rosenfeld, who acted as a consultant for the unit, who had introduced Bettelheim to Wasserman.

72. Interview with the author in July 1991.

73. Letter to C. Hilldrup, June 3, 1985.

74. It is indeed perfectly normal that once a young patient has mastered the psychological mechanisms that cut him off from reality, he should forget how he saw things previously.

75. G. Bersihand, *Bettelheim*, Robert Jauze, Paris, 1977. It is a slim volume with no new information about Bettelheim but a reflection on his writings.

76. Letter to ER, January 6, 1990.

77. Letter to ER, December 4, 1984.

78. Ibid.

79. This assertion is based solely on statements by other sources and on photographs, as Ruth Bettelheim responded with complete silence to all my letters and requests for interviews.

80. Letter to ER, January 2, 1986.

81. Ibid.

82. Letter to ER, February 3, 1986.

83. Ibid.

84. Compassion.

85. Letter to C. Frankenstein, May 6, 1986.

86. Letter to C. Frankenstein, June 26, 1986.

87. Letter to C. Frankenstein, March 11, 1985.

88. Letter to ER, August 3, 1986. Translated from German.

89. A typically Viennese concept, which could be loosely translated as 'snug'.

90. Letter to ER, January 25, 1988.

91. 'Homage to Bettelheim', published in *Partisan Review* no. 4.

92. Letter to ER, September 1, 1986. Translated from German.

93. Letter to G. Janowitz, October 2, 1986.

94. Letter to ER, February 22, 1987. Translated from German.

95. Ibid.

96. Interview with the author in December 1990.

97. Letter to ER, March 9, 1987. Translated from German.

98. Letter to C. Hilldrup, March 18, 1987.

99. The tale is told in 'How I Learned about Psychoanalysis', in *Freud's Vienna and Other Essays*.

100. She devoted an essay to him, which attracted attention at the time (E. Sterba, *'Ein abnormes Kind'*, 1933, *Zeitschrift für psychoanalytische Pedagogie*, published in English in 1936 in the *Psychoanalytical Quarterly*). 'Johnny' attended Emmi Vischer's classes. But the precise historical facts are of little importance here.

101. *Freud's Vienna and Other Essays*, p. 32.

102. Letter to ER, December 8, 1987. Translated from German.

103. Letter to ER, January 28, 1988. Translated from German.

104. Letter to C. Frankenstein, March 6, 1988.

105. Letter to C. Hilldrup, June 16, 1988.

106. *Surviving*, p.4.

107. Interview with the author, July 1991.

108. The portrait had been commissioned for him by Eric years before.

109. A second cast was donated to the Orthogenic School.

110. See Chapter VII.

111. Letter to ER, January 25, 1987.

112. Interview published in *Society*, vol. 28, no. 3, March-April 1991.

113. Letter to ER, June 12, 1988. Translated from German.

114. Letter to ER, December 31, 1988. Translated from German.

115. See Chapter II.

116. Letter to C. Frankenstein, October 19, 1986.

117. Letter to ER, July 8, 1989. Translated from German.

118. Letter to ER, October 23, 1989.

119. Published in the *Los Angeles Times Magazine* under the title 'Love and Death' on January 27, 1991, almost a year after Bettelheim's death. All the quotes and other details concerning Celeste Fremon's discussions with him are from that source.

120. Letter to ER, December 3, 1989.

121. Letter to ER, January 6, 1990. Bettelheim was to receive the Lukas Prize posthumously, during a memorial ceremony for him on May 15, 1990.

122. Letter to ER, February 12, 1990.

123. Conversation reported in the *Washington Post* dated April 24, 1990.

124. In *Let Me Die before I Wake: Hemlock's Book of Self-Deliverance for the Dying*, Hemlock, Los Angeles, 1983.

125. Letter to G. Jurgensen, January 20, 1974.

126. Harper & Row, New York, 1980.

127. In the past, he had frequently denounced the abuse of such drugs.

128. In the meaning given by Donald Winnicot to this expression. As the reader will no doubt have understood, this is not intended as criticism of Paula Bettelheim who, from the little I know about her, always behaved in an exemplary manner to her son. And yet, Bettelheim devoted an entire book, which cost him much time and pain to write, to proving – maybe to himself first of all – that his parents had been 'good enough'.

Bruno Bettelheim's Works[*]

Books

Love is Not Enough, The Free Press, New York, 1950.
Symbolic Wounds, Thames & Hudson, 1955 (The Free Press, 1954).
Truants from Life, Collier-Macmillan, 1964 (The Free Press, 1955).
The Informed Heart, Thames & Hudson, 1961 (The Free Press, 1960).
Dialogues with Mothers, The Free Press, 1962.
The Empty Fortress, Collier-Macmillan, 1968 (The Free Press, 1967).
The Children of the Dream, Thames & Hudson, 1969 (The Free Press, 1969).
A Home for the Heart, Thames & Hudson, 1974 (Knopf, New York, 1974).
The Uses of Enchantment, Thames & Hudson, 1976 (Knopf, 1976).
Surviving and Other Essays, Thames & Hudson, 1979 (Knopf, 1979).
Freud and Man's Soul, Chatto & Windus, 1983 (Knopf, 1982).
A Good Enough Parent, Thames & Hudson, 1987 (Knopf, 1987).
Recollections and Reflections, Thames & Hudson, 1990 (*Freud's Vienna and Other Essays*, Knopf, 1990).

In collaboration:

With Morris Janowitz: *Dynamics of Prejudice: A Psychological and Sociological Study of Veterans*, Harper & Bros, New York, 1950. Re-published as a part of *Social Change and Prejudice,* The Free Press, 1964 and 1975.
With Daniel Karlin: *Un autre regard sur la folie*, Stock, Paris, 1975.
With Karen Zelan: *On Learning to Read,* Thames & Hudson, 1982 (Knopf, 1981).
With Alvin Rosenfeld: *The Art of the Obvious*, Thames & Hudson, 1993 (Knopf, 1993).

Chapters, prefaces and postscripts

'The Evaluation of the Appreciation of Art', *Appraising and Recording Student Progress*, vol. III, Harper & Bros, New York, 1942.
'Concentration Camps, German', *Ten Eventful Years*, vol. 2, Encyclopedia Britannica, Inc., Chicago, 1947.
'The Special School for Emotionally Disturbed Children', Yearbook of the National Society for the Study of Education, Part I, Chicago, 1948.

---

[*] I originally intended this to be the first comprehensive listing of all the published works of Bruno Bettelheim. However, he wrote so much and for such diverse publications that I had to curtail my ambition. Despite the efficient assistance of the American Library in Paris and a few others, it proved impractical to find some of the books or other publications to which he contributed. While not claiming to be exhaustive, this list can only hope to be 'good enough'.

'A Therapeutic Milieu', *Psychopathology, a Source Book*, ed. Reed, Alexander and Tomkins, Harvard University Press, 1958.

Preface, *Auschwitz – A Doctor's Eyewitness Account*, by Miklos Nyiszli, Fawcett Crest Book, Greenwich (Conn.), 1960.

'The Real Lesson of the Concentration Camp', *The Open Form: Essays for Our Time*, ed. A. Kazin, Harcourt, Brace & World, New York, 1961.

'Self-Realization for the Educated Woman', *The Role of the Educated Woman*, Rice University Symposium, 1963.

'The Commitment Required of a Woman Entering a Scientific Profession', *Women and the Scientific Professions*, MIT Press, 1965.

'How Much Can Man Change?', *Profile of the School Dropout*, ed. Daniel Schreiber, Random House, New York, 1967.

Postscript, *The Third Reich of Dreams*, by Charlotte Beradt, Quadrangle Books, Chicago, 1968.

'Alienation and Autonomy', *Changing Perspectives on Man*, ed. Ben Rothblatt, University of Chicago Press, 1968.

'Autonomy and Inner Freedom, Skills of Emotional Management', *Life Skills in School and Society*, ASCD 1969 Yearbook Committee, Washington, 1969.

'The Education of Emotionally and Culturally Deprived Children', *From Learning for Love to Love of Learning*, by R. Ekstein and R.L. Motto, Brunner/Mazel Inc., 1969

Preface, *Infantile Autism*, by Gerhard Bosch, Springer-Verlag, New York, 1970.

'Education and the Reality Principle', *Moral Education: Five Lectures*, Harvard University Press, 1970.

'About Summerhill', *Summerhill: For and Against,* Hart Publishing Co., 1970.

'Growing Up Female', *Starting Over, A College Reader*, Random House, New York, 1970.

'Infantile Autism', *The World Biennial of Psychiatry and Psychotherapy*, vol. 1, ed. Silvano Arieti, Basic Books, New York, 1970.

'The Change in Woman's Role in Home and Society', *What is Happening to American Women*, Southern Newspaper Publishers Association Foundation, Atlanta, 1970.

'About the Sexual Revolution', *Sexual Latitude: For and Against*, Hart Publishing Co., 1971.

'Mental Health in Slums', *The Social Impact of Urban Design*, University of Chicago Center for Policy Study, 1971.

'The Future of Residential Treatment in the Society of the Future', *Healing through Living*, Charles C. Thomas Co., Springfield (Ill.) 1971.

'The Anatomy of Academic Discontent', *In Defense of Academic Freedom*, ed. Sidney Hook, Pegasus, 1971.

Preface, *Faces of Authority*, by William T. Kulik, Scott, Foresman & Co., 1972.

'To Nurse and to Nurture', *The Psychodynamics of Patient Care,* by L. Schwartz, Prentice Hall, 1972.

'Regression as Progress', *Facts and Techniques in Psychoanalytic Therapy*, ed. P. Giovacchini, Science House, 1972.

'Middle-class Teacher and Lower-class Child', *Rethinking Urban Education*, ed. H.J. Walberg, Jossey-Bass Inc., San Francisco, 1972.

Preface, *La Folie des autres*, by G. Jurgensen, Robert Laffont, Paris, 1973.

Preface, *Les Mille et une nuits*, ed. T. Carlier, Seghers, Paris, 1978.

Postscript, *Je ne lui ai pas dit au revoir*, by Claudine Vegh and Louis Evrard, Gallimard, Paris, 1979.

'The Child's Perception of the City', *Literature and the Urban Experience: Essays* on the City and Literature, ed. Michael C. Jaye and Ann Chalmers Watts, Rutgers University Press, New Jersey, 1981.

Preface, *The Words to Say It,* by Marie Cardinal, Van Vector & Goodheart, Cambridge (Mass.), 1983.

Postscript, *The Third Reich of Dreams*, by Charlotte Bradt, Aquarian, Wellsborough, 1985.

'La Vienne de Freud', Catalogue de l'Exposition Paris-Vienne, Editions du Centre Pompidou, Paris, 1986.

'Lionel Trilling on Literature and Psychoanalysis', *Explorations: The Twentieth Century*, vol. 3, University of Southwestern Louisiana, 1989.

Articles and essays

1943 (October) 'Individual and Mass Behavior in Extreme Situations', *Journal of Abnormal and Social Psychology*.

1944 (August 1) 'Behavior in Extreme Situations', *Politics*.
(November 4) Review: *New Bearings in Aesthetics and Art Criticism,* by Bernard C. Heyl, *College Art Journal*.

1945 (January 2) Review: *Diagnosis of our Time*, by K. Mannheim, *Politics*.
(July 14) 'The Helpless and the Guilty', *Common sense*.
(December 2) 'War Trials and German Re-Education', *Politics*.

1946 (September) 'A Scientific Approach to the Problem of Prejudice', Public Relations Workshop Summary, American Council on Race Relations.

1947 'What Students Think about Art', General Education in the Humanities, American Council on Education.
'The Concentration Camp as a Class State', *Modern Review*, vol. 1.
(January) 'Self-Interpretation of Fantasy', *American Journal of Orthopsychiatry*.
(April) 'The Dynamism of Anti-Semitism in Gentile and Jew', *Journal of Abnormal and Social Psychology*, vol. 42.
(October) With E. Sylvester: 'The Therapeutic Influence of the Group on the Individual', *American Journal of Orthopsychiatry*, vol. XVII.

1948 (February 5) 'The Victim's Image of the Anti-Semite', *Commentary*.
(April) With E. Sylvester: 'A Therapeutic Milieu', *American Journal of Orthopsychiatry*, vol. XVIII, no. 2.
(June) 'Some Concomitants of Prejudice', *Intercultural Educational News*.
(July) 'Closed Institutions for Children?', *Bulletin of the Menninger Clinic*, vol. 12, no. 4.
(October) 'Somatic Symptoms in SuperEgo Formation', *American Journal of Orthopsychiatry*, vol. XVIII, no. 4.
(November) Review: *Myths of War*, by Marie Bonaparte, *American Journal of Sociology*.
(November) Review: *Essays on Anti-Semitism*, by K.L. Pinson, *American Journal of Sociology*.
(December) 'Exodus, 1947', *Politics*.
(December) 'The Social-Studies Teacher and the Emotional Needs of Adolescents', *School Review*, Chicago.

1949 With E. Sylvester: 'Physical Symptoms in Emotionally Disturbed Children', vols. III-IV, *Psychoanalytic Study of the Child*, International Universities Press, NY.
(January) With E. Sylvester: 'Milieu Therapy – Indications and Illustrations', *Psychoanalytic Review*, vol. 36, no. 1.

(January) 'A Psychiatric School', *Quarterly Journal of Child Behavior*, vol. 1, no. 1.

(April) 'Harry – A Study in Rehabilitation', *Journal of Abnormal and Social Psychology*, vol. 44.

(May) Review: *Resolving Social Conflicts: Selected Papers on Group Dynamics*, by Kurt Lewin, *American Journal of Sociology*.

(September) With M. Janowitz: 'Ethnic Tolerance: a Function of Social and Personal Control', *American Journal of Sociology*, vol. 55.

Review: *Doctors of Infamy – The Story of the Nazi Medical Crimes*, by Alexander Mitscherlich, *American Journal of Sociology*, vol. 55.

(December) 'On the Rehabilitation of the Offender', *Federal Probation*, vol. 13.

1950 With Emmy Sylvester: 'Delinquency and Morality', *Psychoanalytic Study of the Child*, vol. V.

With M. Janowitz: 'Dynamics of Prejudice', *Harpers*.

'Przypadek Harry's Ego', *Psychological Abstracts*, vol. 25.

Review: *Searchlights on Delinquency*, by K.R. Eissler, *American Journal of Sociology*.

(January) 'Love is not Enough', *University of Chicago Magazine*.

(Spring) With M. Janowitz: 'Reactions to Fascist Propaganda – a Pilot Study', *Public Opinion Quarterly*.

(June) 'The Relief of Understanding', *University of Chicago Magazine*, vol. 42.

(September) 'The Psychoanalysis of Anti-Semitism', Review: *Anti-Semitism and Emotional Disorder*, by N. Ackerman and M. Johoda, *Complex*, vol. 3.

(October) With M. Janowitz: 'Prejudice', *Scientific American*.

(October) With E. Sylvester: 'Notes on the Impact of Parental Occupations', *American Journal of Orthopsychiatry*, vol. 20.

(November) Review: *The Autobiography of Wilhelm Stekel*, by Emil A. Gutheil, *American Journal of Sociology*, vol. 56.

1951 Review: *Character Assassination*, by Jerome Davis, *University of Chicago Law Review*, vol. 18.

(February) Discussion: *Family Structure and Psychic Development*, by Jules Henry, *American Journal of Orthopsychiatry*, vol. 21.

(March) Review: *The Lonely Crowd*, by David Riesman, *University of Chicago Magazine*, vol. 43.

(April) 'Institutional Care of Problem Children', vol. 2, *Megamot* (Jerusalem).

(July) 'Love is not Enough', University of Chicago Round Table.

(September) 'How to Arm Our Children against Anti-Semitism', *Commentary*, vol. 12.

(October) 'Does Your Child Fight Sleep?', *Parents Magazine*, vol. 26.

(October) 'Helping Jewish Children to Face Prejudice', *Jewish Affairs*.

(November) Review: *Children in Conflict*, by Margaret L. Lambert, *Marriage and Family Living*.

(November) Review: *Personal Aggressiveness and War*, by E.F.M. Durbin and J. Bowlby, *American Journal of Sociology*, vol. 57.

(December) Review: *Personality and Psychotherapy*, by John Dollard and Neal Miller, *Elementary School Journal*, vol. 52.

'The Case of Michael', Institute for Juvenile Research.

1952 (January) 'Mental Health and Current Mores', *American Journal of Orthopsychiatry*, vol. 22.

(April) 'Schizophrenic Art: A Case Study', *Scientific American.*

(October) 'Mental Health and the Child', *The Elementary School Journal,* vol. 53.

(October) 'Remarks on the Psychological Appeal of Totalitarianism', *American Journal of Economics and Sociology.*

(December) Review: *Sex Education as Human Relations*, by Lester Kirkendall, *Federal Probation*, vol. 16.

1953 (January) 'Securing Our Children against Prejudice', *Jewish Center Worker*, vol. 14.

(June) Review: *An Autobiographical Study*, by S. Freud, *American Sociological Review*, vol. 18.

(December) Review: *Children in Play Therapy*, by C.E. Moustakas, *Elementary School Journal*, vol. 54.

1954 'Governor's Conference on Mental Health', *Elementary School Journal*, vol. 54.

(April) Review: *The Step-Child*, by W.C. Smith, *University of Chicago Magazine*, vol. 46.

1955 'Individual Autonomy and Mass Control', *Frankfurter Beiträge zur Soziologie.*

(January) Review: *Seduction of the Innocent*, by Frederic Wertham, *Library Quarterly*, vol. 25.

(March) 'Don't Deny Them Discipline', *National Parent Teachers*, vol. 49.

(June) 'Death Life's Purpose?' Review: *The Psychiatrist and the Dying Patient*, by K.R. Eissler, *Chicago Review*, vol. 9.

(September) 'Early Ego Development in a Mute Autistic Child', *Bulletin of the Philadelphia Association for Psychoanalysis*, vol. 15.

(October) With B. Wright: 'Staff Development in a Treatment Institution', *American Journal of Orthopsychiatry*, vol. 25.

(November) 'Educational News, German Schools Revisited', *Elementary School Journal.*

1956 (February) 'Returning to Dachau', *Commentary*, vol. 21.

(April) 'Discrimination and Science'. Review: *Prejudice and Your Child*, by Kenneth B. Clark, *Commentary*, vol. 21.

(July) 'Childhood Schizophrenia as a Reaction to Extreme Situations', *American Journal of Orthopsychiatry*, vol. XXVI, no. 3.

(October) 'Fathers shouldn't try to be Mothers', *Parents Magazine*, vol. 31.

1957 (January) Review: *The Life and Work of Sigmund Freud*, by Ernest Jones, *American Journal of Sociology*, vol. LXII, no. 4.

(March) Review: *Promise of Youth: Exploring Psychiatric Research in Juvenile Delinquence*, *Federal Probation.*

(March) With B. Wright: 'Professional Identity and Personal Rewards in Teaching', *Elementary School Journal.*

1958 'Psychiatric Consultation in Residential Treatment: The Doctor's View', *American Journal of Orthopsychiatry.*

(May 19) Review: 'Ernest Jones' Freud: A Dissenting Opinion', *New Leader*, vol. 19.

(Autumn) 'Segregation: New Style', *School Review.*

(October) 'Sputnik and Segregation', *Commentary*, vol. 26.

(November) 'Toward a New School', *Elementary School Journal*, vol. 59.

1959 Review: *Motility in Infants*, a film by B. Mittelman, *Contemporary Psychology*, vol. 4.

(March) 'Reading the Signs of Mental Health', *National Parent Teachers*, vol. 53.

(March 5) 'Joey: A Mechanical Boy', *Scientific American*.

(March) 'Feral and Autistic Children', *American Journal of Sociology*, vol. 64.

(April) 'Nakhes Fun Kinder', *Reconstructionist*, vol. XXV.

(May) Review: *Sigmund Freud's Mission*, by Erich Fromm, *New Leader*, vol. 42.

(August) 'A Note on the Concentration Camps'. Review: *From Death-Camp to Existentialism: A Psychiatrist's Path to a New Therapy*, by Viktor Frankl, *Chicago Review*.

(November) 'Help for our Troubled Children', *Think*, vol. 25.

1960 (May) 'Emotional Blocks to Learning: A Problem Learner', *Parents Magazine*, vol. 35.

(November) 'The Ignored Lesson of Anne Frank', *Harpers*.

1961 'The Decision to Fail', *School Review*, vol. 69.

(April) 'Delusions for Moderns', *University of Chicago Magazine*.

(April) 'Comment': Letter to the Editor responding to the review of *The Informed Heart*, *Midstream*, vol. 7.

1962 (Winter) 'The Problem of Generations', *Daedalus*.

(February) 'Does Communal Education Work? The Case of the Kibbutz', *Commentary*, vol. 33.

(Spring) 'Freedom from Ghetto Thinking', *Midstream*, vol. 8.

(March) 'Facing the Full-View Mirror', *WFMT Perspective*, vol. 11.

(May) 'Talks with Mothers', *Redbook*, vol. 119.

(October) 'Growing Up Female', *Harpers*.

1963 'A Noncontribution to Educational Research'. Review: *Educating Emotionally Disturbed Children*, by N.G. Haring and E. Lakin Phillips, *Harvard Educational Review*.

(January) 'Conversations with Parents', *University of Chicago Magazine*.

(February) 'How to Ask the Right Question about Your Child', *Parents Magazine*, vol. 38.

(March) 'Roadblocks to Learning', *NEA Journal*, vol. 52.

(May) 'Finding Identity in Mass Movements', *McCormick Quarterly Special Supplement*.

(June 15) 'Eichmann: the System, the Victims', *New Republic*.

(October 19) 'Class, Color and Prejudice', *Nation*.

(November) 'Parents versus Television', *Redbook*, vol. 122.

1964 'Art and Art Education: A Personal Vision', *Art*, New York.

(February 7) 'Why does a Man Become a Hater?', *Life*.

(April) 'The Class of '84', *Toronto Education Quarterly*, vol. 3.

(April 11) 'Speaking Out: Stop Pampering Gifted Children', *Saturday Evening Post*.

(May) 'Sex and Violence in Books, Magazines and Television', *Redbook*, vol. 123.

(May 9) Letter to the Editor on 'Segregating the Gifted', *New Republic*.

(July) 'What Children Learn from Play', *Parents Magazine*, vol. 39.

(September) 'How Much Can Man Change?' Review: *Stability and Change in Human Characteristics*, by Benjamin Bloom, *New York Review of Books*.

(November 7) 'Women: Emancipation is Still to Come', *New Republic* 50th Anniversary special issue.

1965 (March) 'Grouping the Gifted', *NEA Journal*, vol. 54.

(March) 'How Mothers-in-law Disrupt Marriages: An Old Problem in New Forms', *Redbook*, vol. 124. The article triggered a reply in the April issue: 'What Our Daughters-in-law Didn't Tell You', to which Bettelheim responded.

(June) Review: *Psychiatric Aspects of the Prevention of Nuclear War*, by the Committee on Social Issues, *Bulletin of the Atomic Scientists.*

(June) 'The Orthogenic School', *University of Chicago Magazine*, vol. 62.

(September) 'Teaching the Disadvantaged', *NEA Journal*, vol. 54.

(October) 'When Children Lie or Steal', *Redbook*, vol. 125.

(October) 'Young Children's Sex Behavior: Why Can't We Ignore It?', *Ladies' Home Journal.*

(November) 'Children's Jealousy: "We Got the Baby for You" ', *Ladies' Home Journal.*

1966 (January) 'Am I Ruining my Child for Life?', *Ladies' Home Journal.*

(March) 'Violence: A Neglected Mode of Behavior', *Annals of the American Academy*, vol. 364.

(March) 'Why Working Mothers Feel Guilty', *Redbook*, vol. 126.

(July) 'Training the Child-Care Worker in a Residential Center', *American Journal of Orthopsychiatry*, vol. XXXVI.

(September) 'The Danger of Teaching Your Baby to Read', *Ladies' Home Journal.*

(October 6) 'Children without Parents'. Review: *Children in Collectives – Rearing Aims and Practices in the Kibbutz*, ed. Peter B. Neubauer, *New York Review of Books.*

1967 (February) Review: *Microcosm: Structural, Psychological and Religious Evolution in Groups*, by Philip E. Slater, *American Sociological Review*, vol. 32.

(February 12) 'Parent and Child: Where Self Begins', *New York Times Magazine.*

(March 11) 'Speaking Out: Children Should Learn about Violence', *Saturday Evening Post.*

(July 2) 'Survival of the Jews', Review: *Treblinka*, by Jean-François Steiner, *New Republic.*

1968 A reply to Prof. Gary Merritt's review of *The Empty Fortress*, *American Journal of Orthopsychiatry*, vol. XXXVIII.

(July 27) 'Speaking Out: The Right to Privacy is a Myth', *Saturday Evening Post.*

(September) 'The High Calling of a University Student', *Rochester Review*, vol. 31.

(Autumn) 'The Ultimate Limit', *Midway.*

1969 Review: *Death in Life: Survivors of Hiroshima*, by Robert Jay Lifton, *Political Science Quarterly*, vol. 84.

'Personality Formation in the Kibbutz', *American Journal of Psychoanalysis*, vol. XXIX.

(January) 'The Anatomy of Courage', *Barat Review*, vol. 4.

(February) 'Where Do Nightmares Come From?', *Ladies' Home Journal.*

(March) Dialogue with Bruno Bettelheim: 'How Can Elementary Schools Help Boys', *Instructor.*

(April) Discussion of Dr. Flarsheim's Paper, *Bulletin of the Chicago Society for Adolescent Psychiatry*, vol. 2.

(April 7) 'Too Many Misfits in College': excerpts from a statement made to the House Special Subcommittee on Education, *US News & World Report*.

(April 13) 'Children Must Learn to Fear', *New York Times Magazine*.

(May) 'The Anatomy of Academic Discontent', *Change – In Higher Education*.

(May 4) 'On Campus Rebellion: a New and Potentially Dangerous Rite of Manhood', *Chicago Tribune Magazine*.

(June) 'Portnoy Psychoanalyzed', *Midstream*.

(June) 'Psychoanalysis and Education', *School Review*, vol. 77.

(September 3) 'Obsolete Youth – Towards a Psychograph of Adolescent Rebellion', *Encounter*, vol. XXXIII.

(October) 'Psychoanalysis and Education', *Education Digest*.

(December) 'Deviancy in Children', *Boston University Journal*, vol. XVII.

1970 'The Kibbutz: Dream and Reality', *Histradut Round Table Series*, no. 1.

(January) 'The Right and Wrong Way to Teach Sex', *Ladies' Home Journal*.

(February) 'Young People who Hate the Police', *Ladies' Home Journal*.

(February 8) 'Knitting: Its Role in the Life of Dr. Bruno Bettelheim': Letter to the Editor, *New York Times Magazine*.

(March) 'It Wasn't Me who Wet', *Ladies' Home Journal*.

(April) 'The Perils of Overexposing Youth to College', *Education Digest*, vol. 35.

(April) 'What Sleepwalking Means', *Ladies' Home Journal*.

(May) 'Oldest, Middle, Youngest Child – Which is Better Off?', *Ladies' Home Journal*.

(June) 'Why Working Mothers Have Happier Children', *Ladies' Home Journal*.

(July) 'Why Parents Should Take a Firm Stand', *Ladies' Home Journal*.

(August) 'How to Say No Without Guilt', *Ladies' Home Journal*.

(September) 'Meddling Grandmothers', *Ladies' Home Journal*.

(October) 'What Adoption Means to a Child', *Ladies' Home Journal*.

(November) 'Mothers and Daughters', *Ladies' Home Journal*.

(November) 'What Psychoanalysis Can do for Education', *Critic*.

(December) 'Redundant Youth', *Realities*.

1971 (January) 'What Does Independence Really Mean?', *Ladies' Home Journal*.

(February) 'Expressing Anger – The Right and Wrong Way to Discipline Children', *Ladies' Home Journal*.

(March) 'The Roots of Radicalism', *Playboy*.

(March) 'When Should Parents Push? – "I Can't Do It" ', *Ladies' Home Journal*.

(April) 'Learning Blocks', *Ladies' Home Journal*.

(May) 'What's Happening to the Family', *Ladies' Home Journal*.

(September) 'Why School Lunch Fails', *Family Health*.

(October) 'The Need for Roots', *Ladies' Home Journal*.

(November) 'The Meaning of Play', *Ladies' Home Journal*.

(November) 'Ten Who Don't Belong', *Critic*.

(December) 'Should Parents Encourage their Children to Believe in Santa Claus?', *Ladies' Home Journal*.

1972 'The Impatient Treatment of Psychotics', *Science and Psychoanalysis*, vol. XX.

'Psychotherapy and Psychopaedagogy', *Psychotherapy and Psychosomatics*, vol. 20.

(January) 'Our Children's Friends', *Ladies' Home Journal*.

(February) 'Divorce', *Ladies' Home Journal*.

(March) 'Teaching Your Child to Tell the Truth', *Ladies' Home Journal*.

(March) 'Why School Lunch Fails', *School Foodservice Journal*.

(April) 'Sibling Rivalry', *Ladies' Home Journal*.

(May) 'Bed-wetting', *Ladies' Home Journal*.

(July) 'When Should Parents Seek Professional Psychiatric Help for their Child?', *Ladies' Home Journal*.

(August) 'Some Unexpected Problems Between Mothers and Daughters in These Days of Women's Lib', *Ladies' Home Journal*.

(September) 'Helping the Handicapped Child', *Ladies' Home Journal*.

(October) 'Misplaced Anger and How to Deal with It', *Ladies' Home Journal*.

(November) 'Teaching Children How to Make Decisions', *Ladies' Home Journal*.

(November) 'Play and Education', *School Review*, vol. 81.

(December) 'Teaching Self-Control to a Screaming Two-Year-Old', *Ladies' Home Journal*.

1973 (January) 'Reading Problems and Dyslexia', *Ladies' Home Journal*.

(February) 'The Hyperactive Child', *Ladies' Home Journal*.

(March) 'Advice on Raising Children of Divorce', *Ladies' Home Journal*.

(April) 'A Look into Your Future: Child Raising', *Today's Health*, vol. 51.

(April) Review of books on the treatment of psychotic children, *Journal of Child Psychiatry*, vol. XII.

(April) 'Who's afraid of the Big Bad Wolf – And Why?', *Ladies' Home Journal*.

(May) 'Does your Child Throw Screaming Tantrums in Public?', *Ladies' Home Journal*.

(June) 'Teaching Children that Males and Females Should be Complementary, Not Competitive, Often Means that the Parents Have to Learn the Lesson First Themselves', *Ladies' Home Journal*.

(July) 'Teaching Children to Make Decisions: When Should You Let Them Choose?', *Ladies' Home Journal*.

(August) 'Child Identification at Age Four When Child's Parents are at Odds about Basic Beliefs', *Ladies' Home Journal*.

(September) 'Children Succeeding – Difference Between Encouraging and Pressuring a Child', *Ladies' Home Journal*.

(October) 'In Praise of Fairytales', *Ladies' Home Journal*.

(November) 'What Can such Fairytales as Hansel and Gretel and Little Red Riding Hood Teach Children about the Real World', *Ladies' Home Journal*.

1974 (November) 'Janet and Mark and the New Illiteracy – Reading and the Emotions', *Encounter*, vol. 43.

1975 (February) 'Some Further Thoughts on the Doll Corner', *School Review*, vol. 83.

(December 8) 'Reflections: The Uses of Enchantment', *New Yorker*.

1976 (August 2) 'Reflections: Surviving', *New Yorker*.

(September) 'Untying the Family', *Center Magazine*, vol. 9.

(October) 'Recreating Family Life: the Means are in Our Hands', *Parents Magazine*, vol. 51.
1977 (January 2) 'Where Psychoanalysis was Born'. Review: *Sigmund Freud's Home and Offices: the Photographs of Edmund Engelman*, *New York Times* Book Review.
1978 (April) 'Learning to Read: a Primer for Literacy', *Harpers*.
(December) 'The Holocaust, a Generation later', *Encounter*, vol. 51.
(December 23) 'Lessons for Life: the Uses of Enchantment', *Opera News*, vol. 43.
1980 (January 2) 'Children, Curiosity and Museums', *Child Today*, vol. 9.
(July 8) 'The Child's Perception of the City', *Humanities*.
1981 (October) 'The Art of Motion Pictures – Man, Superman and Myth', *Harpers*.
(November) With Karen Zelan: 'Why Children Don't Like to Read', *Education Digest*, vol. 47; and *Atlantic Monthly*, vol. 248.
1982 (March) 'Freud and Man's Soul', *New Yorker*.
(May 13) 'Scandal in the Family', *New York Review of Books*.
1983 (June 30) 'Scandal in the Family' (follow-up), *New York Review of Books*.
1985 (September 10) 'A Child's Garden of Fantasy', *Channels Commun*, vol. 5.
(October 28) 'TV Stereotypes "Devastating" to Young Minds', *US News & World Report*.
(November) 'Punishment versus Discipline; a Child Can be Expected to Behave Well Only if his Parents Live by the Value They Teach', *Atlantic Monthly*.
1986 'The Illustrated Fable', *Advocate*.
(October 5) 'Their Specialty was Murder', *New York Times* Book Review.
1987 (March) 'The Importance of Play', *Atlantic Monthly*.
(July 12) 'A Return to the Land of Fairy Tales', *New York Times*.
1988 (Winter and Spring issues) 'Les livres essentiels de Bruno Bettelheim', *Le Temps Stratégique* (Genève).
'The Holocaust in the Undermind of the West', *Dimension*, vol. 4.
1989 (Summer) 'Lionel Trilling on Literature and Psychoanalysis', *Explorations*, vol. 3.
1990 (Spring) 'The Birthplace of Psychoanalysis', *Wilson Quarterly*, vol. 14.

Index

Adler, Victor, 64
Adorno, Theodor, 302
Aichorn, August, 74, 84, 91, 202, 236
Alexander, Franz, 207, 208, 209, 229, 230, 236
Allen, Woody, 213, 433
Allport, Gordon, 220
Altstadt, Leopold, 61, 75
Altstadt, Max, 63
Altstadt, Mina, 63, 117, 133
Altstadt, Moritz, 63, 81
Andersen, Hans Christian, 45, 422
Angres, Ronald, 7-9, 12, 13, 388, 399
'Anna', 335, 342
Arendt, Hannah, 305, 308-9, 310-11
Aristotle, 103
Aron, Raymond, 382
Art of the Obvious, The, 263, 334
Austen, Jane, 279, 433

Bach, J.S., 138
Badinter, Elisabeth, 272
Bandler, Hans, 121, 123, 124, 125, 128, 129, 133, 138, 141-2, 145-6, 147, 148, 152, 162-3, 176-7, 225, 315, 452, 463
Beauvoir, Simone de, 314
Beethoven, Ludwig van, 30
Bettelheim, Anton, 23, 32, 34, 39, 43-4, 48-54, 56, 57, 64, 66, 70-1, 99-100, 128, 265, 303, 324, 443
Bettelheim, Eric, 292, 295, 298, 388-9, 429, 430, 432, 435, 439, 440, 442, 445, 446, 449, 452, 453, 454, 458
Bettelheim, Gina, *see* Weinmann, Regina
Bettelheim, Jakob Morris, 18-19, 22-3, 32, 37, 52, 99
Bettelheim, Kitty, 42
Bettelheim, Lewia, 18
Bettelheim, Marcus, 18

Bettelheim, Margarethe, 34, 42, 71, 117, 157, 159, 160-1, 196, 436-7, 442
Bettelheim, Morris, 23, 24
Bettelheim, Naomi, xiv, 61, 206, 293, 294, 295, 296, 298, 302, 305-6, 429-30, 431, 432, 433, 434, 436-7, 439, 441, 442, 444, 448, 452, 453, 454, 457, 458, 461
Bettelheim, Norbert, 122-3, 159, 303
Bettelheim, Paula, 22, 34-6, 39-42, 43, 44-5, 71, 117, 133, 142, 149-50, 157, 159, 160-1, 162, 163, 164, 169, 173-4, 196, 197, 266, 296, 299, 464
Bettelheim, Ruth, 61, 196, 292-4, 418-19, 429-30, 441-3, 444, 445-6, 449, 452-3, 455, 457
Bettelheim, Trude (Gertrude, née Weinfeld), 91-3, 94-5, 97, 98, 102, 106, 109, 113, 117, 147, 163, 174-8, 186-7, 189-90, 196- 7, 206, 222, 235, 239, 292-7, 302, 384, 393, 400, 419-20, 424, 425, 426-7, 430, 431-6, 440, 441-2, 443, 444, 449, 460, 463-4
Bibring, Grete Lehner, 73-4, 79
Blake, William, 290-1, 376-7
Blau, Bill, 5, 11, 254-6
Blitzsen, Lionel, 208
Bloom, Benjamin, 197-8
Blos, Joan, 422
Blos, Peter, 82
Boehm, Félix, 117
Bolgar, Heda, 447
Borzage, Frank, 221
Bowlby, John, 358
Brent, Stuart, 189, 270
Brieux, Eugène, 51
Brown, Jean, 274
Buber, Martin, 32-3, 55, 59, 139, 314

Bühler, Charlotte, 82, 103, 184, 200, 236
Bühler, Karl, 82, 103-5, 184, 202, 207
Burckhardt, Jacob, 69, 76
Burlingham, Dorothy, 82, 175
Buten, Howard, 352
Buxbaum, Edith, 42, 46, 47, 57, 59, 65-6, 67, 70, 71, 78, 80, 96, 106-7, 116, 170-3, 178, 437-8
Buxbaum, Jenny (née Seidler), 40, 41, 66, 116, 164, 165, 170, 179

Carey, Margaret, 358
Carné, Marcel, 191
Carotenuto, Aldo, 434
Carter, Jimmy, 428
Celan, Paul, 326, 327-8, 456
Centre for the Advanced Study of Behavioral Sciences (Palo Alto), 390-1, 394
Chagall, Marc, 314
Chamberlin, Neville, 133
Chaplin, Charlie, 221
Chapsal, Madeleine, 272, 328, 329, 395
Charles I, Emperor, 57
Cheek, Mary Ashby, 190, 191, 195, 196, 199
Chicago Child Care agency 295
Chicago Psychoanalytic Institute, 207-9, 230
Chicago Psychoanalytic Society, 206, 207-8, 215, 229-30
Children of the Dream, 295, 354, 358-9, 366, 367-70, 392, 400
Clare, George, 108, 110, 112, 225, 365
Cleaver, Leslie, 274, 288, 338, 349-50, 389, 399-400, 412-13
Cohler, Bert, 205, 245, 248, 253, 268, 286, 288, 290, 339-40, 347, 390-3, 396-7, 399, 401, 412
Conrad, Joseph, 292
Cowan, Mary-Ellen, 246-7
Crane, Agnes *see* Piel, Agnes
Crane, Percy Ed, 166
Cronbach, Lee, 184

Daladier, Edouard, 133
Des Pres, Terence, 319, 320-4, 424
Descartes, René, 27
Dialogues with Mothers, 263, 267, 290, 353, 362, 439
Dollfuss, Engelbert, 81, 107

Donat, Alexandre, 310, 311
Dostoevsky, Fyodor, 69
Dreyfus, Alfred, 24
Dryovage, Ronnie, 192, 239, 244, 267, 274
Duncan, Isadora, 74
Dundes, Alan, 422
Duras, Marguerite, 406
Dynamics of Prejudice, 279-80

Edelman, Nechama, 357-8, 359-62, 364-5, 369, 370
Eichmann, Adolf, 307, 308-9
Eight Year Study, 178, 183-4
Eisenhower, Dwight, 220
Eissler, Kurt, 9, 202, 207, 208, 404
Ekstein, Rudolf, 451-2, 455, 458
El Greco, 185
Empty Fortress, The, 10, 100, 120, 234, 250, 271, 273, 291, 330- 1, 334-6, 340-1, 342, 345, 367, 374-6, 392, 396, 401, 403, 417
ER, 181, 417
Erikson, Erik, 92, 280-1
'Erin', 347-8, 387, 392

Federn, Ernst, 121, 123, 134, 137, 145, 150-6, 160, 162, 218, 221, 225, 227-8, 269, 315, 336, 425
Federn, Paul, 134, 151, 161-2, 171, 213
Feinermann, Emmanuel, 138
Fellini, Federico, 319
Fenichel, Otto, 60-1, 70, 208, 268, 280, 448, 451
Ferenczi, Sandor, 156
Fermi, Enrico, 270
Feschback, Seymour, 446
Fischer, Alfred, 150, 225
Fisher, David James, 444, 451-3, 458
Flarsheim, Alfred, 288, 399-400, 447
Fleischmann, Inge, 353, 377
Ford Foundation , 271, 332-4, 353, 394
Formigoni, Maurie, 274, 288-9, 377, 378
Formigoni, Ugo, 261, 262, 274, 288-9, 346, 389
Fox, Seymour, 370, 400
Frank, Anne, xi, 31, 306-7, 308, 310, 316, 327
Frank, Otto, 306-7, 310, 327, 360
Frankenstein, Carl, 38, 48, 56, 59, 64, 98, 217, 231, 323, 325, 354, 363-4,

366, 370, 400-1, 415, 420, 421,
423-4, 426, 428, 436, 445, 449, 458
Frankl, Eleonor, 23
Franklin, Benjamin, 213
Franz-Joseph I, 18-19, 24, 30, 55, 57
Fratteroli, Elio, 274
Free Press, The, 277-8
Fremon, Celeste, 455-7
Freud, Anna, 9, 75, 81, 83, 84, 91, 124,
156, 175, 206, 213, 214, 216, 225,
280, 371-2, 434, 452
Freud, Sigmund, xi, xii, xv, 1, 9, 18,
25, 27, 28, 31, 32, 61, 63-4, 68, 72,
73, 74-5, 79, 81, 83, 94, 101-2, 104,
117, 120, 121, 124, 148, 150, 191,
195, 206-17, 229, 236, 237, 255,
269, 277, 281-3, 334, 338, 340, 341,
355, 367, 368, 371, 378, 404, 408,
409, 423, 431, 433, 434, 451
Freud and Man's Soul, 100, 101, 209,
210, 214-16, 279, 327, 423, 428,
434, 451
Freud's Vienna and Other Essays, 17,
32, 34, 60, 63-4, 65, 78, 139, 171,
454, 458
Friedell, Egon, 77
Fromm, Erich, 191, 208, 280, 422
Fuchs, Ernst, 388

Garner, Marylin, 275
Gaulle, Charles de, 314
Gay, Peter, 208
Giannini, Giancarlo, 319
Giese, Miep, 327
Gizidi, Adolf, 22
Goebbels, Joseph, 111, 428
Goering, Hermann, 109, 138
Goethe, Johann, 92, 138, 323, 461
Goldstein, Frieda, 142, 156, 158
Good Enough Parent, *A*, 35, 38, 43,
88-9, 382, 384, 395, 417, 418, 433,
438, 444
Gordon Myles, 'Paul', 246, 275, 347,
412
Grimm brothers 45, 421
Grinker, Roy, 208, 229
Groddeck, George, 208
Grossman, Diana *see* Kahn, Diana
Grossman
Grossman, Ron, 12

Habsbourg, François-Ferdinand de,
55, 129
Hadoumi, Haïm, 366, 367
Hadoumi, Leah, 366
Harper, Lou, 248-9, 274, 389-90
'Harry', 245, 247, 281
Hartmann, Heinz, 214, 280
Hashomer Hatzair, 355, 358, 368
Hatchek, Annie, 82, 83
Haus der Kinder (Montessori school),
74, 81, 91, 92, 117
Havighurst, Robert, 188, 198
Heidegger, Martin, 308
Helstein, Nina, 274, 347-8, 349
Hemlock Society, 433, 459
Henry, Jules, 251, 253-4, 256, 333
Hertzl, Theodor, 24, 25, 28, 29, 58, 314
Heuscher, Julius, 12-13, 422-3
Heydrich, Reinhard, 111
Hilberg, Raul, 305, 314
Hilldrup, Candace, 261, 274, 385-9,
393, 396, 397, 401, 409, 410, 423,
428-9, 440, 446, 450
Himmler, Heinrich, 111, 123, 162
Hitler, Adolf, xi, 79, 87, 103, 105, 107,
108, 110, 111, 122, 133, 157, 160,
166, 173, 268, 306, 307, 309,
317-18, 323, 324, 424, 431, 436
Hitschmann, Edward, 74
Hochschule für Welthandel (Vienna),
64-6
Hofmannsthal, Hugo von, 25
Hohenberg, Ernst and Max von, 129
Home for the Heart, *A*, 250, 256, 290,
396
Hoover Institution, 439, 441, 445
Horace, 153
Horkheimer, Max, 279-80, 302
Horney, Karen, 208, 229
Houston Chamberlain, Stewart, 27
Hudl, Paul, 115
Humphry, Derek, 433, 459
Husserl, Edmund, 308
Hutchins, Robert, 188-9, 200

Informed Heart, *The*, 100, 129, 137,
144, 150, 152-3, 158, 189, 214, 218,
219-20, 229, 290, 299, 304, 306,
311, 312, 353, 396, 438, 448

Jackson, Judge, prosecutor at
Nuremberg, 121, 219

Jakobson, Roman, 104
James, Henry, 87
Janowitz, Gayle (née Shulenberger), 239-41, 242, 243, 245-6, 247-8, 249, 253, 257, 258, 260, 267, 273, 274, 281, 285, 289, 290, 294, 299, 372, 444, 445
Janowitz, Morris, 267, 279, 280, 302, 372, 381, 394, 443-4
Jaspers, Karl, 308
Jatitch, Alida, 5, 13, 407
Jauregg, Wagner von, 73
Jewell, Marjorie, 238-9, 267
'Joey', 10, 329-30, 332, 343, 345, 351, 376
'Johnny', 448
Johnston, William, 25
Jones, Ernest, xv, 25, 31
Jung, Carl, 434
Jung Wandervogel, 47, 57, 60, 67-8, 80, 179, 202, 355, 367
Jurgensen, Geneviève, xii, 44, 253, 274, 330, 373, 380, 386, 390, 401, 412, 417-19, 460

Kafka, Franz, 64
Kahn, Diana Grossman, 273, 274, 285, 348, 353, 371, 372, 377, 379, 385
Kaiser, Cathy, 265, 337, 450
Kaiser, George, 274, 286-7, 389, 450
Kamschell, Mrs, 167
Kanner, Leo, 241, 332
Kant, Emmanuel, 30, 104, 443
Kaplan, Jeremiah, 267, 277-8
Karlin, Daniel, xii, 89, 206, 263, 312, 331, 401-3, 409, 410, 454
Kastein, Joseph, 112
Katzenstein, Connie, 49, 450, 453, 457
Kaufman, Jean-Paul, 205
Kautsky, Benedikt, 135, 301
Kennedy, John F., 311, 317
Kerem, Moshe, 368, 370
Key, Shelton, 274
King, Martin Luther, 309, 317, 374
Klein, Melanie, 208
Kliegerman, Charles, 230
Klimt, Gustav, 367
Koch, Karl, 137, 142
Kogon, Eugen, 129, 149, 301, 315, 322
Kohut, Heinz, 214, 371
Kollwitz, Käthe, 77

Korczak, Janusz, 52-3, 78, 426
Kramer, Maria, 437
Kraus, Karl, 25, 28, 70
Kris, Ernst, 18, 105
Krugh, Lilly, 67, 70, 92, 102
Kubie, Lawrence, 160
Kuypers, Adrian, 274, 284-5, 401, 443

Lacan, Jacques, 422
Lackner, Nikolaus, 114, 115
Lampl de Grot, Jeanne, 236
Langbein, Hermann, 121
Lange, Friedrich-Albert, 54, 70
'Laurie', 330, 376
Lawrence, David Herbert, 76
Lazarsfeld, Lisl, 60-1, 448
Lazarsfeld, Paul, 60
Lehmann, Herbert, 161-2
Leibniz, Gottfried Wilhelm, 104
Leopold and Loeb, 310
Lessing, Theodor, 28, 54, 70
Levi, Primo, 148, 316, 449, 456
Levy, Edward, 381
Lewis, Sandy, 392, 435, 440, 442, 451
Lewis, Sinclair, 70
Lifton, Robert J., 444
Little, Joan *see* Treeman, Joan Little
Love is not Enough, 120, 153-4, 234, 244, 250, 261, 268, 269, 271-2, 273, 277-8, 279, 284, 285, 291, 352, 357, 385, 394
Lubin, Kathy, 274, 348-9, 371, 377, 379, 385
Lubin, Mark, 404
Lueger, Karl, 24, 26, 31, 488
Lurie, Alison, 422
Lyons, Augusta Wallace, 391
Lyons, Tom Wallace, 329, 341-6, 391

Mach, Ernst, 27, 28, 103
Macmillan publishers, 272, 345
Mahler, Alma, 31
Mahler, Gustav, 25, 28, 31, 367
Mahler, Margaret, 332, 350
'Marcia', 10, 330-1, 350-1, 376
Marcuse, Herbert, 405
Marquis, Ruth (née Soffer), 276-9, 281-2, 283, 284, 290-1, 292, 294-5, 298, 331, 359, 360, 362, 368, 376, 389, 394-6, 400, 420, 422, 430, 439, 461-2
Marx, Karl, 28, 151, 269, 355, 375

Masson, Jeffrey M., 9-10
Matin de Paris, Le, 272
May, Karl, 86
Melville, Herman, 461
Mengele, Joseph, 305
Merritt-Singer, Isaac, 86
Messinger, Rahel, 360, 362, 369, 370
Messinger, Yehuda, 356-7, 359, 368
Middeldorf, Ulrich, 190, 199
Miklos, Wilhelm, 108
Montessori, Maria, 74-5, 91
Montessori school (*Haus der Kinder*)
    74, 81, 90-1, 92, 117
Montrelay, Michèle, 209-10
Morganthau, Hans, 311
Morris, Richard, 23
Murray, Henry, 450
Musil, Robert, 27, 29-30, 31, 189
Mussolini, Benito, 108

Nagai, Michio, 425
Nedelsky, Leo, 196
Nedelsky, Ruth, 196, 197, 372-3
Neugarten, Bernice, 198, 290
Neurath, Walter, 46, 47, 54, 66, 67,
    70, 80, 429
New World Foundation, 360
Newman, Julie, 274
'Nicky', 240-1
Nietzsche, Friedrich, 26, 103
Nixon, Richard, 383, 428
Nonnie, 379-81, 385
Nunberg, Herman, 70
Nyiszli, Miklos, 305, 306, 324

On Learning to Read, 45, 433
Oz, Amos, 461

Paxson, M., 190, 191
Pekow, Charles, 5, 6, 10-11, 373-4, 388
Pekow, Philip, 200, 269, 373
Pelican and After, The, 341-6
Perkins, George, 333, 443
'Pete', 259-60
Piaget, Jean, 434
Picasso, Pablo, 185
Pickett, Patty, 237, 242, 245, 248, 260,
    274
Piel, Agnes (later Crane), 84, 85-7, 89,
    90, 97, 109-10, 111, 116, 118, 160-1,
    162, 166-7, 175
Piel, Godfried, 86

Piel, Patricia, 'Patsy', 83-91, 93, 95,
    97, 109-10, 111-12, 113, 116, 118,
    166-7, 197, 203, 261
Piers, Gerhardt, 178
Piers, Maria, 178, 203
Pingree-Rellahan, Betty-Lou, 238-9,
    249, 267, 274, 289
Pink, Annie, 59, 66, 70
Plank, Emma, 'Nuci', 90-1, 117, 177
Polani, Ron, 359
Poliakov, Léon, 31
Poller, Walter, 135-6, 158, 315
Pouillon, Jean, 283

Rabin, Albert, 362
Radanowicz, Emmi (née Vischer),
    91-2, 107, 163, 175, 393, 424-5, 435
Radanowicz, Hubert, 'Bertel' von, 91,
    107, 166, 393, 424-5
Rado, Sandor, 170, 208
Raines, Theron, 440, 460-1
Ramat Yohanan, 354-6, 359-63, 364,
    365-6, 368-70, 400
Rank, Otto, 81
Rapaport, David, 355
Rath, Ernst vom, 136
Raum, O.F., 282
Reagan, Ronald, 383
Redl, Fritz, 81-3, 91, 107, 167, 168,
    171, 172, 179, 183, 184, 186, 188,
    196, 202, 235, 244, 271, 276, 292,
    311, 337, 356, 359, 394
Reese, Michael, 372
Reich, Wilhelm, xiii, 9, 66, 70, 74, 148,
    269, 455
Reininger, 103
Reiss Jr., Albert, 302
Renner, Karl, 58
Riesman, David, 302
Rimland, Bernard, 375
Roazen, Paul, 212, 423
Robert Bosch Foundation, 443
Rockefeller, John Davidson, 86
Rockefeller Foundation, 107, 183, 188,
    439
Rödl (SS commander), 142
Rommel, Manfred, 431
Roosevelt, Eleanor, 161, 203, 357, 391
Rosenfeld, Alvin, 262, 439, 440, 452,
    457, 459
Rothschild, Albert de, 23
Rothschild, Anselm von, 22-3

Rousset, David, 123

Sailer, Karl Hans, 108
Sanders, Jacquelyn, 5-6, 7, 275, 377,
   397-9, 401, 409-12, 421, 440, 443
Sartre, Jean-Paul, 404, 405
Schiele, Egon, 77, 367
Schiller, Friedrich von, 92, 138
Schindler, Emil, 31
Schlosser, Julius von, 65
Schneidman, Edwin, 450-1
Schnitzer, Hans, 57, 72, 87, 110, 115
Schnitzler, Arthur, 24-5, 25-6, 28, 29,
   339, 367, 431
Scholem, Gershom, 365
Schönberg, Arnold, 367
Schönerer, Georg von, 24
Schorske, Carl E., 25
Schuschnigg, Kurt von, 107-9, 110
Seidler, Adolf, 21-2, 34, 39-40, 41, 56,
   80, 86, 99, 164, 204, 265
Seidler, Alfred, 164
Seidler, Jenny, *see* Buxbaum, Jenny
Seidler, Pauline, *see* Bettelheim, Paula
Seidler, Rudolf, 40, 164
Seyss-Inquart, Arthur, 107, 109
Shankman, Sonia, 269
Sharp, Charles, 363
Sherman, Mandel, 179, 197, 198, 239,
   269
Sheviakov, George, 172, 178, 183, 188,
   196, 294
Shils, Edward, 280
Shirer, William, 117
Shulenberger, Gayle *see* Janowitz,
   Gayle
Singer, Isaac Bashevis, 314
Speer, Albert, 323
Spencer Foundation, 420
Spengler, Oswald, 69-70, 312-13
Spielrein, Sabrina, 434
Spiro, Melford, 358
Spock, Benjamin (Dr), 102, 265, 377,
   391
Stalin, Joseph, 268
Steinbach, Emil, 28
Steiner, George, 443
Steiner, Jean-François, 313-14, 315
Sterba, Editha, 81, 83, 88, 90-1, 92,
   94, 97, 175, 177, 200, 236, 248
Sterba, Richard, 32, 73, 74, 81, 86, 91,
   95-102, 111, 112, 117- 18, 120, 175,

177, 200, 217, 218, 236, 447, 448,
   463
Stroheim, Erich von, 262
Strzygowski, Joseph, 65
Surviving and Other Essays, 124, 139,
   159, 161, 162, 172, 219, 222-3, 292,
   299, 315-16, 318-28, 395, 426
Sylvester, Emmy, 200, 208, 235-6,
   242-5, 256, 332
Symbolic Wounds, 100, 214, 279, 280,
   282-4, 290

Thalmann, Rita, 138
Tillon, Germaine, 153
Torberg, Friedrich, 77
Treeman, Joan Little, 41-2, 274
Trollope, Anthony, 279, 433
Truants from Life, 241, 250, 271, 275,
   279, 281, 338, 394, 412
Tyler, Ralph W., 172, 179, 183, 184,
   185-6, 189, 190, 196, 197, 198, 199,
   200, 201, 269, 270, 394
Tyroler, Fae, 10, 274, 332, 344, 349,
   357

Ullman, Jane, 451
Uses of Enchantment, The, 12-13,
   44-5, 278-9, 291, 325, 409, 421- 3,
   425, 428

Vaihinger, Hans, 54, 70, 82
Vegh, Claudine, 430
Vischer, Emarina, *see* Radanowicz,
   Emmi
'Vivienne', 350-1, 378

Wagner, Richard, 26, 31, 65, 164
Waldheim, Kurt, 32, 443
Wanda (Polish carer), 453, 454, 460
Warren, A.M., 160-1, 162
Wasserman, Saul, 440
Weinfeld, Frederika, 186-7
Weinfeld, Gertrude, *see* Bettelheim,
   Trude
Weininger, Otto, 30-1, 367
Weinmann, Catherine, 292, 293
Weinmann, Joseph Peter, 94, 95, 107,
   110, 111, 166, 167-8, 196, 197, 427
Weinmann, Regina (née Altstadt), 60,
   61-3, 66-8, 72-9, 81-8, 90-1, 93-4,
   95, 96, 97, 98, 106, 109-10, 111-12,
   113, 116, 118- 19, 120, 124, 145,

156, 162, 163, 165-70, 174, 179, 189, 197, 211, 217, 292, 293, 385, 427, 442, 449, 463-4
Wertmüller, Lina, 138, 318-21, 424
White, Florence, 260, 333
Wiebold Foundation, 330
Wilde, Georg, 159
Wiley, George, 118
Willig, Hans, 46, 47, 70-1, 72, 75, 80, 93, 97, 171, 179, 437, 438, 454
Willig, Wanda, 47, 60, 67, 70-1, 72, 75, 78, 96, 167, 171, 174, 179, 229, 436, 437, 442, 453, 455, 462

Wingo, Josette (née Dermody), 259-60, 267, 274, 450
Winnicott, Donald, 376, 214
Wolf (SS captain), 138
Wright, Ben, 256, 270, 271-2, 274, 283, 294, 333, 389, 390, 397
Wundheiler, Luitgard, 274, 291, 302

Zelan, Karen, 10, 259, 274, 327, 331, 350-2, 353, 377, 378, 380, 381, 386, 387, 398, 427, 440
Zweig, Arnold, 217
Zweig, Stefan, 20-1, 35, 50, 51-2, 54, 99